The Letter Book of
James Abercromby
Colonial Agent

1751–1773

The Letter Book of
James Abercromby
Colonial Agent

1751–1773

Edited by

John C. Van Horne and George Reese

Richmond
Virginia State Library and Archives
1991

Library of Congress Cataloging-in-Publication Data

Abercromby, James, 1707–1775.
  The letter book of James Abercromby, colonial agent: 1751–1773
  edited by John C. Van Horne and George Reese.
  p.   cm.
  Includes bibliographical references and index.
  ISBN 0–88490–170–X : $40.00
  1. Virginia—History—Colonial period, ca. 1600–1775—Sources.
  2. Abercromby, James, 1707–1775—Correspondence. 3. Colonial
  agents—Virginia—Correspondence. I. Van Horne, John C.
  II. Reese, George Henkle. III. Title.
  F229.A24   1991
  975.5′02—dc20   91–8903

OCLC: 23382104

I aim at no more than Serving those
who Employ me to the Utmost of my Power.

—James Abercromby to Richard Corbin
1 January 1760

Write more plain for really
some of Your Letters I cannot well read.

—Robert Dinwiddie to James Abercromby
18 June 1754

Page 46, a typical page in James Abercromby's manuscript letter book, reveals why researchers have shied away for so long from this important historical source. The top of the page contains the last fourteen lines of Abercromby's 10 July 1757 letter to John Young, copied into the letter book in a clerk's precise hand. A routing instruction at the end of this document and the first half of an 11 July 1757 letter to the Council of Virginia are at the bottom of the page, written in Abercromby's virtually illegible scrawl.

Contents

The Letter Book

Foreword

Although historical and textual editing may well be, as Arthur S. Link has asserted, "the oldest scholarly discipline in the world," contemporary American historians sometimes take for granted the achievements represented by the modern documentary editions that have appeared on their library shelves since 1950. Such complacency cannot survive a confrontation with the original manuscript letter book of James Abercromby that for seventy years has resided in the Virginia State Library and Archives, physically accessible to scholars but its scrawled text virtually indecipherable. According to the presentation page bound into the volume, on 22 February 1919 the Virginia State Library and Archives accepted the James Abercromby letter book from the Virginia Daughters of the American Revolution, Alethea Serpel, regent, and Faith Thomas Parrott, historian. The letter book gives few hints of its provenance, except that a brief printed description apparently clipped from a dealer's catalog and pasted to a blank leaf near the front suggests that by the 1870s this manuscript and related books and papers were in the possession of a London dealer.

James Abercromby's pivotal role in imperial affairs during the quarter century from the eve of the Seven Years' War to his death on the eve of the American Revolution ensured that his letter book would contribute significantly to scholarship. As longtime agent for Virginia and other colonies, he was not far from the mark when he described himself as "more generally instructed as to the government, trade and strength of the colonies than any one else either in a public or private character who ever went to that part of the world." Abercromby, one of the few members of Parliament who had actually visited North America, knew as much about American imperial affairs as any of his British contemporaries. This fact alone—regardless of whether Abercromby was sensitive to the perspectives of American-born colonials—makes his letter book telling evidence about British policy making and the antecedents of the American Revolution. Fifty years ago Charles McLean Andrews also drew attention to the importance of Abercromby's views as expressed in two essays preserved in several manuscript copies prepared by clerks. By happy coincidence the American Philosophical Society has recently published these essays as *Magna Charta for America: James Abercromby's "An Examination of the Acts of Parliament Relative to the Trade and Government of our American Colonies" (1752) and " 'De Jure et Gubernatione Coloniarum,' or An Inquiry into the Nature, and the Rights of Colonies, Ancient, and Modern" (1774)* (Philadelphia, 1986), edited by Jack P. Greene, Charles F. Mullett, and Edward C. Papenfuse, Jr. Note should also be taken of the unpublished James Abercromby Letter Book, 1743–1750 (PC 1651), preserved in the collections of private manuscripts at the North Carolina State Archives, Raleigh. This letter book was found to contain no material related to Virginia's provincial affairs.

The edition you are now reading—with its clear pages of Caslon type transcribed from Abercromby's vexing manuscript and amply annotated—testifies to the historical erudition, editorial proficiency, and plain hard work of two talented scholars. John C. Van Horne is the director of the Library Company of Philadelphia. His published works include *The Correspondence of William Nelson as Acting Governor of Virginia, 1770–1771* (Charlottesville, 1975), *Religious Philanthropy and Colonial Slavery: The American Correspondence of the Associates of Dr. Bray, 1717–1777* (Urbana, Ill., 1985), and many splendid volumes of *The Papers of Benjamin Henry Latrobe*. George Reese retired from the faculty of the University of Virginia in 1983. His published editions range the centuries from the text of John Pory's *Proceedings of the General Assembly of Virginia, July 30–August 4, 1619* (Jamestown, 1969) through journals of Virginia's postrevolutionary Senate and Council of State to the *Proceedings of the Virginia State Convention of 1861*, 4 vols. (Richmond, 1965) and *Journals and Papers of the Virginia State Convention of 1861*, 4 vols. (Richmond, 1966). During the preparation of his comprehensive

Official Papers of Francis Fauquier, Lieutenant Governor of Virginia, 1758–1768, 3 vols. (Charlottesville, 1980–1983), George Reese grappled in earnest with some fifty letters from Abercromby to Fauquier in the Abercromby letter book at the Virginia State Library and Archives. In due time, that encounter led him to accept the challenge of transcribing more than three hundred additional letters for this edition and of preparing fresh and corrected transcriptions of the documents published in his *Papers of Francis Fauquier*. Working from Dr. Reese's literal renderings of these difficult texts, Dr. Van Horne refined the typescript for publication in accordance with the editorial method described on page xlix, prepared the annotation, wrote the Introduction, coordinated the proofreading, and oversaw Donald W. Gunter's compilation of the index.

Historians will discover rich insights about America and Great Britain in this important letter book, but as early as 1981 it was evident that an unstated personal quest bolstered the editors' intellectual commitment to this edition. Transcribing and editing *this* stubbornly unreadable document—daring to decipher its code, to triumph over Abercromby's scrawl, to scale this Matterhorn—posed a sheer challenge to the skills of these two talented scholars. Historians of Virginia, of the American colonies, and of eighteenth-century British imperial affairs will forever be the beneficiaries of their conquest. Skeptics, be there any, may travel to Richmond and confront James Abercromby's inscrutable penmanship for themselves.

The Historic New Orleans Collection JON KUKLA

Introduction

JAMES Abercromby was active in American affairs for almost half a century, but his early years give hardly a hint of what was to come. He was born in Scotland in 1707, the third son of Alexander and Mary (Duff) Abercromby, of Tullibody, Clackmannanshire. His father, an advocate, was member of Parliament for Clackmannanshire (in the Parliament of Scotland) from 1703 to 1707. (James would hold the same seat in the British Parliament from 1761 to 1768.) His father died in 1755 at the age of eighty-four. One of James Abercromby's brothers was George, who had four sons, of whom three later served as member of Parliament for Clackmannanshire. (In 1775, when James died unmarried, George and his son Burnet inherited James's estate, Brucefield, in Clackmannanshire.) Following the well-worn path that led south for ambitious Scots, James attended the Westminster School (1720) and later the University of Leyden on the Continent (1724–1725). Returning to England, Abercromby studied law at Lincoln's Inn, to which he was admitted in January 1726, and in 1728 he was admitted to the bar.

Abercromby obviously came from a well-established Scottish family that provided him with an education and with parliamentary, social, and military connections to ease his way into the world. And he must have made his own connections as well. Among the aspiring barristers at Lincoln's Inn at the time Abercromby studied there were Matthew Lamb, later counsel to the Board of Trade, and Dudley Ryder, later attorney general. Abercromby must have enjoyed the patronage of influential men, for in November 1730, still only twenty-three, Abercromby was appointed attorney general and advocate general of the Court of Vice-Admiralty for South Carolina, posts he apparently obtained with the help of Charles, ninth Baron Cathcart.[1]

Upon his arrival in South Carolina in 1731, Abercromby joined the Saint Andrew's Society, acquired land, and began to play a significant role in the life of the colony. He served in the spring of 1735 as one of the two South Carolina commissioners who met with counterparts from North Carolina to draw a boundary between the two colonies. Abercromby never found a place on the Council, but he did serve two terms in the colony's Commons House of Assembly, representing Prince Frederick Parish 1739–1742 and Prince George Winyah Parish for a few months in 1744. Of Abercromby's service it has recently been written: "Never one of the most conspicuous members of the Commons House, Abercromby was always among its second-rank leaders, serving on committees and drafting legislation covering a wide variety of subjects, including the encouragement of poor Protestant settlers, paper currency, the provincial judicial system, and Indian affairs."[2] This firsthand experience made Abercromby "one of the very few M.P.'s prior to the American Revolution to have served in a colonial legislature,"[3] although, as we shall see, it did nothing to reconcile him to the American cause.

---

1. Biographical information in this and the following paragraphs has been gleaned from several sources, principally Sir Lewis Namier and John Brooke, *The House of Commons, 1754–1790*, 3 vols. (New York, 1964), 2:2–3; Walter B. Edgar and N. Louise Bailey, eds., *Biographical Directory of the South Carolina House of Representatives, Volume II: The Commons House of Assembly, 1692–1775* (Columbia, S.C., 1977), 23–24; the introduction to Jack P. Greene, Charles F. Mullett, and Edward C. Papenfuse, Jr., eds., *Magna Charta for America: James Abercromby's "An Examination of the Acts of Parliament Relative To the Trade and the Government of our American Colonies" (1752) and " 'De Jure et Gubernatione Coloniarum,' or An Inquiry into the Nature, and the Rights of Colonies, Ancient, and Modern" (1774)* (Philadelphia, 1986); Michael G. Kammen, *A Rope of Sand: The Colonial Agents, British Politics, and the American Revolution* (Ithaca, N.Y., 1968); and *The Records of the Honorable Society of Lincoln's Inn . . . Admissions from A.D. 1420 to A.D. 1893. Vol. 1, Admissions, 1420–1799* (Lincoln's Inn, 1896).

2. Greene, Mullett, and Papenfuse, *Magna Charta for America*, 7.

3. Ibid.

Abercromby and James Glen, fellow Scots, had overlapping tenures in South Carolina; Abercromby did not embark for England for the last time until May 1744, and Glen had arrived in the colony as governor in December 1743. After Abercromby returned to England he undertook various commissions for Glen, although the exact nature of their relationship is obscure. The best hint of it is given in a letter from Abercromby to Virginia's lieutenant governor Robert Dinwiddie (which also reveals Abercromby's interest in the South Carolina agency):

> I thank you, for your overtures to Messrs Wragg & Cleland concerning the Agency of So Carolina. Messrs Pinkney & Crokat, stand in comp[et]ition for that Office, and to speak the truth, while Mr Glen heads that Province, I should not expect pleasure in the Service, and as little Justice, deserted by every body, he threw, himself into my hands, for taking charge of his public letters, he proposed for my trouble 50£ per an, three years without any manner of acknowledgment, at length I drew upon him by good luck I got my money & then dischargd myself from all correspondence with him.[4]

Besides this special agency for Glen, Abercromby retained his ties with South Carolina, entertaining visitors from the colony in London and attempting in 1749 to secure an exemption from a proposed act of Parliament abolishing paper money in America.[5] Although never appointed agent for the colony, he cooperated with South Carolina agents on matters of importance to the two colonies he later did represent—North Carolina and Virginia.

Two years after returning to England, Abercromby received a commission in August 1746 as "Judge Advocate of all the Forces employd in an Expedition to North America" under the command of Lieutenant General James St. Clair (or Sinclair). St. Clair had been appointed to the command of a force projected to be deployed against the French in Canada. However, when delays prevented the expedition from sailing that year, the force was used instead to attack the coast of Brittany. St. Clair led the force in a siege of Port L'Orient, the depot for the stores and ships of the French East India Company. The siege began on 24 September, but since the

---

4. JA to Dinwiddie, 16 Jan. 1755, pp. 132–135.

5. J. H. Easterby, ed., *The Journal of the Commons House of Assembly, March 28, 1749–March 19, 1750*, vol. 9 of *The Colonial Records of South Carolina: The Journals of the Commons House of Assembly* (Columbia, S.C., 1962), 348–349.

British were ill-prepared and ill-equipped, and since the French continuously reinforced the town, St. Clair raised the siege, quitting France on 17 October. Abercromby accompanied the expedition and served as judge advocate during two courts-martial. His distant kinsman James Abercromby, later major general and commander in chief of British forces in the American colonies, was also on the expedition, as was the philosopher and historian (and fellow Scot) David Hume, who was St. Clair's private secretary and who wrote a history of the expedition, generally known by the title "Descent on the Coast of Brittany." A curious fact about this expedition is that Hume is alleged to have been commissioned as judge advocate on 3 August 1746, the same day that Abercromby received his commission (which bears the notation at its foot, "By the Generals Command / David Hume Secretary"!) Hume's name does not appear (as does Abercromby's) in the proceedings of the two courts-martial.[6]

Abercromby's long-term relationship with North Carolina arose out of the so-called representation controversy that had disrupted

---

6. Abercromby's commission and six other documents concerning the courts-martial are found in the Abercromby Letter Book at the Virginia State Library and Archives, pages 1–24. For the expedition, see Arthur H. Buffinton, "The Canada Expedition of 1746: Its Relation to British Politics," *American Historical Review* 45 (1940): 552–580. Hume's history of the expedition is printed in John Hill Burton, *Life and Correspondence of David Hume*, 2 vols. (Edinburgh, 1846), 1:441–456. Hume's biographer J. Y. T. Greig gives the following account, in *David Hume* (London, 1931), 150–151, without documentation: "Besides acting as the General's Private Secretary, he had been commissioned as Judge-Advocate. And so, when the expedition ended, and his services were no longer required, he lodged a claim for half-pay. His claim was not admitted.

"Similar claims by four of the other officers, including Colonel Abercromby [JA's distant kinsman and later major general James Abercromby], were rejected at the same time. All five accordingly combined forces, petitioned the Secretary-at-War, and enlisted the support of M.P.'s and other influential friends. Within a year or two the other four gained their point. Hume alone failed.

". . . As late as 1763 he still hammers at the Treasury door. I think he must have got his money in the end. Nothing short of that would stop his hammering."

the colony for many years. The lower house of the colony's legislature enjoyed the right of creating electoral districts and apportioning representation by statute. While each of the precincts in the older Albemarle section in the northern part of the colony sent five representatives to the lower house, newer precincts were generally allowed only two. In November 1746 Governor Gabriel Johnston attempted to curb the power of the Albemarle precincts, whose delegates had thwarted his efforts to enact effective quitrent legislation, by convening the legislature in Wilmington, in the southern part of the colony. When the Albemarle members failed to attend, Johnston's rump legislature enacted a bill limiting to two the number of representatives from each county and another establishing the seat of government at New Bern, a town between the two sections.[7]

When the northern counties sent their usual five representatives to the next legislature in February 1747, the southern members declared the Albemarle elections null and void. The northern counties boycotted all sessions of the legislature for the next seven years and sent Henry McCulloh to London to secure disallowance of the two acts. For its part, the rump legislature of southern members passed a law in October 1748 appointing Abercromby North Carolina's permanent agent "to solicit and truly represent the Affairs of this Province at the several Boards in England."[8] The act provided for Abercromby to serve a term of two years, beginning 25 March 1749, at an annual salary of £50, and to answer to a committee of correspondence composed of two councillors and three representatives.[9] Abercromby had evidently already been serving the colony unofficially, for the act appointing him agent provided for £100 to compensate him for his efforts up

---

7. Walter Clark, ed., *The State Records of North Carolina*, vols. 11–26 (Winston and Goldsboro, N.C., 1895–1905), 23:251–267.

8. *NCSR*, 23:303–304; Jack P. Greene, *The Quest for Power: The Lower Houses of Assembly in the Southern Royal Colonies, 1689–1776* (Chapel Hill, 1963), 174–184; Lawrence F. London, "The Representation Controversy in Colonial North Carolina," *North Carolina Historical Review* 11 (1934): 255–270.

9. See JA to North Carolina Committee of Correspondence, 7 Oct. 1751, p. 8, n. 1.

to that time and until 25 March 1749, when the appointment took effect.

In 1751 Abercromby's appointment was renewed for a three-year term at an annual salary of £100, and again in 1754.[10] At the expiration of that term in 1757, however, the appointment was not renewed. (Although it has frequently been asserted that Abercromby's last term expired on 25 March 1757, in fact the act of 1754 stipulated that the appointment would be in effect until that date "and from thence to the End of the next Session of the General Assembly and no longer." The assembly session ended on 14 December 1757.) Governor Arthur Dobbs reported to Abercromby in December 1757 that he had spoken with Samuel Swann, the Speaker of the lower house, "to try whether the House would appoint you again but found them so crusty in granting any money for public services that I could expect little from them. They absolutely refused to appoint any at present alledging their heavy taxes and I find they would not even allow your extra expences so that I cant think to give you any trouble when you wont be paid for it, nor even pay you what you have earned." Abercromby did not receive Dobbs's letter until 10 April 1758, and three days later he notified the Board of Trade and the secretary of state that he was no longer agent for North Carolina.[11]

Abercromby did not rest, however, for he still hoped to collect the arrears of his salary and expenses.[12] The next few months saw him working for North Carolina's share of the parliamentary grant of 1775 to reimburse Virginia and the Carolinas for expenses incurred in their defense, forwarding the candidacy of Samuel Swann for the chief justiceship of the colony, and lobbying for the approval of a private act of the colonial legislature.[13] His zeal was soon rewarded, for in December 1758 he was unilaterally ap

---

10. *NCSR*, 23:362–363, 25:266–267.

11. Dobbs to JA, 28 Dec. 1757, in William L. Saunders, ed., *The Colonial Records of North Carolina*, 10 vols. (Raleigh, N.C., 1886–1890), 5:788–789; JA to secretary of the Board of Trade, 13 Apr. 1758, ibid., 5:928–929; JA to [James West], 19 Feb. 1760, Treasury 1/400, fols. 106–107, Public Record Office, London.

12. JA to Arthur Dobbs, 20 Apr. 1758, p. 256.

13. JA to Samuel Swann, 5 Oct. 1758, pp. 269–270.

pointed provincial agent by the lower house, again as the result of a bitter dispute. This time the lower house was pitted against Governor Dobbs in a battle for control of the colony's share of the £50,000 parliamentary appropriation.

Before receiving Dobbs's letter of dismissal in April 1758 Abercromby had already given much thought to the best use to which the funds could be put upon receipt from the Treasury. Abercromby's idea, which he related to several of his North Carolina correspondents, was that the money be allocated to sink the colony's highly depreciated paper currency.[14] He also recommended this course in the same letter to the Board of Trade in which he announced his dismissal from the agency.[15] Several leaders of the lower house, including John Starkey and Thomas Barker, the two public treasurers, and Speaker Samuel Swann, thought Abercromby's idea a good one, and in December 1758 they devised a means to accomplish that end. The lower house inserted into a military aid bill provisions for an agent to receive the funds in London and transmit them in specie to the colonial treasurers. Abercromby, the agent named in the bill, was to receive a grant for arrears owed him and an annual salary of £150 out of the parliamentary funds. The bill stipulated a two-year term and made Abercromby accountable to a committee of correspondence of five representatives but no councillors. Governor Dobbs opposed both the lower house's attempt to gain control over the funds and Abercromby's agency. He maneuvered the lower house into passing a bill for establishing the capital near New Bern (long a pet scheme) and then convinced the Council to enact the capital bill before rejecting the military aid and agent bill. This caused a great outcry from the lower house, which then acted extraconstitutionally to achieve its purpose. The lower house first obtained Dobbs's agreement to a resolution to pay Abercromby the arrears of salary owed him out of the parliamentary grant. Then, without consulting Dobbs and the Council, it appointed Abercromby "provincial agent," responsible only to the lower house, to procure the funds.

---

14. JA to Arthur Dobbs, 13 Mar. 1758, pp. 242–243; JA to Samuel Swann, 17 Mar. 1758 and 19 Apr. 1758, pp. 246–247 and 254–255; and JA to James Innes, 26 Mar. 1758, pp. 249–250.

15. JA to Samuel Swann, 19 Apr. 1758, p. 255, n. 3.

Dobbs and the Council responded in March 1759 by appointing Samuel Smith as their agent. (Smith, a London merchant, had long known Dobbs and had been involved with Dobbs's unsuccessful attempts to discover the Northwest Passage.) North Carolina was thus represented by both Abercromby and Smith, neither of whom had legal authority.[16]

The lower house again tried to appoint Abercromby in May 1759 by a rider to another military aid bill, but the Council refused to pass the bill, and Dobbs prorogued the assembly. Dobbs wrote to explain his actions to the Board of Trade on 18 May 1759, but the Board was not pleased.[17] In a letter that surely must have relieved Abercromby, the Board informed Dobbs that the lower house had the right to nominate the agent and the authority to appropriate the parliamentary funds. The Board also held that Dobbs might properly have assented to a separate agent act if the committee of correspondence had included Council members.[18]

In February 1760 Abercromby wrote to Treasury secretary James West, almost in desperation. He retailed the history of his attempts to receive the appropriation and of the protracted agency dispute, and then observed: "Thus this Money stands contested for two Years and must continue so, unless the Lords of the Treasury do interpose." He asked that, in any case, his arrears and salary be paid to him out of the money.[19] Finally in May 1760 Abercromby and Smith, co-agents, each received from the Treasury half of the £7,789 that was North Carolina's portion of the parliamentary grant, but since Abercromby had handled all of the negotiations he received the entire $2\frac{1}{2}$ percent commission on the transaction, amounting to £194.14. He also withheld from the grant funds to cover his back salary and expenses, and his salary of £150 per year until 1 March 1761.[20] (Smith, it turns out, never received any

16. *NCCR*, 5:1087, 6:1–5, 32–34, 40–41, 76–77, 92–93; Greene, *Quest for Power*, 99–100, 273–275. See also JA to [James West], 19 Feb. 1760, T 1/400, fols. 106–107.

17. *NCCR*, 6:32–34.

18. Board of Trade to Dobbs, 1 Aug. 1759, in *NCCR*, 6:54–55.

19. JA to West, 19 Feb. 1760, T 1/400, fols. 106–107.

20. JA to North Carolina Committee of Correspondence, 10 May 1760,

salary. The Council tried to pay him £1,000 sterling for five years' service in 1764 but the lower house held that he had never been appointed agent for the province.)[21] In May 1760 the lower house finally abandoned its attempt to appoint Abercromby agent against Dobbs's wishes and found another candidate.

The letter book provides ample documentation that, beyond his service as agent for North Carolina, Abercromby also served as the personal agent of Governor Gabriel Johnston. The two men evidently had an agreement whereby Johnston was to pay Abercromby £50 per year plus expenses to represent his interests.[22] Abercromby was particularly active in behalf of Johnston's efforts to collect the arrears of salary owed him and in defending Johnston in his protracted battle with London merchant Henry McCulloh. Johnston was a protégé of McCulloh and may have owed his governorship to McCulloh's influence. The two men were at one time partners in land speculation schemes in North Carolina but had had a serious falling-out. McCulloh believed he had been betrayed by the governor and undertook a campaign to have him removed from office. This dispute is easily confused with the simultaneous battle over the representation and seat-of-government acts, for the principals were essentially the same—McCulloh versus Johnston, with Abercromby representing Johnston's interests in London.

The month before Johnston's death in July 1752 Abercromby reported that McCulloh had received a warrant for £6,000 (actually it was for £6,200) for arrears of his salary as commissioner for inspecting the quitrents, payable from the South Carolina quitrent revenues. Abercromby characterized the amount as "far Short of his Demand" and gloated that McCulloh was on the verge of bankruptcy and arrest. "And when I reflect on the extraordinary trouble and Expence that the Man has put me to for Years by gone in the Exposition of him to those whom he has all along Deceived

---

enclosure, pp. 358–359. See *NCCR*, 7:622, 670, for the assembly's later attempts to recover from JA some of the funds he withheld.

21. *NCCR*, 6:1316–1317.

22. JA to Johnston, 7 Oct. 1751, enclosure, p. 20; and JA to Mr. Ormes, 10 Oct. 1752, pp. 51–52.

I cannot but congratulate you & myself that we are now so far got clear of him."[23]

But in the end it was in fact McCulloh who bested both Johnston and Abercromby. McCulloh's £6,200 may have been less than he had claimed, but Johnston had received nothing toward the more than £13,000 of his overdue salary by the time of his death. Abercromby, a creditor of Johnston for his own salary and expenses, thus became a creditor of Johnston's estate and probably never did collect what was owed him. And as for the representation controversy, the Crown in 1754 disallowed both the representation and the seat-of-government acts.

Abercromby's nearly quarter-century of service to Virginia began in 1752, when both the House of Burgesses and the Council appointed him in April a special agent to present two addresses—one of condolence on the deaths of members of the royal family and one on Virginia legislation—to the Crown. It was Virginia's lieutenant governor Robert Dinwiddie who recommended his fellow Scot for the assignment, for which Abercromby received £100 sterling.[24] Abercromby lost no time in immersing himself in Virginia affairs. Even before appearing at the Board of Trade on behalf of the two addresses in January 1753 he became involved in "Several Provincial & other Matters" recommended to his attention in Dinwiddie's letter of 20 July transmitting Abercromby's credentials and instructions.[25] Abercromby began at the outset, then, to operate in a gray area, working parallel to (and sometimes in conjunction with) Peter Leheup, the colony's longtime agent. Abercromby can in a sense be thought of as working on speculation, hoping to become the colony's agent at some time in the future. As Abercromby put it, he intended "that my Diligence may establish my Credit with your people."[26] Leheup, a Treasury clerk,

---

23. JA to Johnston, 5 June 1752, pp. 37–42.
24. JA to Dinwiddie, 17 Sept. 1752, pp. 45–46, n. 1.
25. JA to Dinwiddie, 17 Sept. 1752, pp. 44–45.
26. Ibid.

succeeded to a chief clerkship in October 1752 (the month after Abercromby received his appointment) and thereafter became less involved in Virginia affairs. Abercromby sensed an opportunity.

The most important and controversial matter that Abercromby undertook on behalf of Dinwiddie during this period concerned the pistole fee dispute, which arose over Dinwiddie's attempt to levy a fee of one pistole for sealing each patent of land. The House of Burgesses protested the fee, and after Dinwiddie refused to recede from his demand the House passed a series of resolutions in December 1753 declaring the governor's actions to be "illegal and arbitrary," tending "to subverting the Laws and Constitution of this Government," and stating that whoever paid the fee "shall be deemed a Betrayer of the Rights and Privileges of the People." The House also appointed Attorney General Peyton Randolph as special agent to carry its address to the Crown and "negotiate the Affairs of the Colony in Great-Britain."[27] Abercromby thus came very soon to represent the governor and Council against the House of Burgesses.

The results of the pistole fee dispute were mixed. Dinwiddie's actions were vindicated, but with several important qualifications. One result, however, was unequivocal—by zealously guarding the executive's prerogative Abercromby had earned the enmity of the House. When Leheup was dismissed from all his offices after the House of Commons in March 1754 found him to be implicated in a lottery scandal, Abercromby was able to secure appointment as agent at an annual salary of £200. Although he might be described as agent for Virginia, his appointment came only from the governor and Council, as was traditional in Virginia, and his salary was paid from the receipts of Crown revenues rather than from any legislative appropriation. For the next few years the House of Burgesses sought, unsuccessfully, to appoint an agent of its own choice but was always opposed by Dinwiddie, ever the champion of Abercromby.

One of the House of Burgesses's attempts grew out of its frustration with the delay in receipt of the parliamentary grant of

---

27. H. R. McIlwaine, ed., *Journals of the House of Burgesses of Virginia, 1752–1755, 1756–1758*, vol. 8 of *Journals of the House of Burgesses of Virginia, 1619–1776* (Richmond, 1909), 154–156, 167–169.

1755 reimbursing Virginia for expenses incurred in the colony's defense. On 3 August 1756 Abercromby notified the earl of Loudoun, governor of Virginia, that he had just received a representation to the king from the Council and assembly "complaining that they had no part of the Parliaments Bounty grant last Session" and praying for money and promotions for their officers. To give their remonstrance greater weight, Abercromby wrote, the House of Burgesses proposed to join another agent to him but was dissuaded by Dinwiddie.[28]

Upon Dinwiddie's resignation in January 1758, the House of Burgesses's prospects brightened somewhat. Speaker of the House John Robinson clearly expressed the House's frustration with the prevailing arrangement and skepticism that Abercromby truly represented its interests in a June 1758 letter to William Pitt, secretary of state for the Southern Department:

> It is true there is a Person residing in Great Brittain that bears the Character of Agent for this Colony, but when it is considered that his Appointment is from the Governor, or thro' his Influence, he can not be properly looked upon as the Agent for the Colony, but rather for the Governor, and as it is not uncommon for the Interest of the Colonies and that of their Governors to be very opposite, it will hardly be supposed that a Person so appointed will interest himself in the Affairs of the Colony committed to his Care, how much soever they may tend to his Majestys Service and the Wellfare of the Colony, if they happen to be disagreeable to the Governor or clash with his Interest.[29]

In April and October of that year the House passed agent acts, but they were rejected by the Council.[30] Abercromby lashed out against the second agent bill in a letter to Governor Francis Fauquier:

> Upon the Face of this Bill it carries with it its own Condemnation, for whatever Person should Act under the Authority of such a Bill must necessarily become An Agent for Faction in Place of Agent for Government, nor will the Liberality of the House of Burgesses by the Salary

---

28. Loudoun Papers 1410, Huntington Library, San Marino, California. See also JA to Dinwiddie, 27 May 1757, p. 192.

29. Robinson to Pitt, 11 June 1758, Chatham Papers, Gifts and Deposits, 30/8, vol. 96, Public Record Office, London, quoted in Greene, *Quest for Power*, 281.

30. JA to Fauquier, 28 Dec. 1758, p. 277, n. 5.

proposed for their Agent, establish the Rectitude of the arbitrary Principles of the Committees Authority, over such Agent.[31]

Abercromby's reaction was no more outraged than that of the Council itself, which, Richard Corbin reported to Abercromby, declared "that it was making an Alteration, and introducing a Power that was unknown to the Constitution, that it was striking at the Prerogative of the Crown, and taking from his Governor, who is his Representative, the Exclusive Power."[32]

In 1759 the House of Burgesses finally succeeded in appointing Edward Montagu as agent at a salary of £500 sterling per year, accomplishing for the first time in the colony's history such a legislative appointment. It was able to do so by finessing Governor Fauquier and the Council. As Fauquier related the incident to the Board of Trade, the House of Burgesses had agreed to a military appropriation bill,

> but to my great Surprize I found a Tack was made to the Bill, for the appointing an Agent, which had long been a Bone of Contention between the Council and Burgesses. I told some of the chief promoters of this Step, that I would not suffer the Tack, that I had an Instruction to the Contrary, and it should not pass. They answered that they imagined when it came to the point I would not refuse it, but not to give me uneasiness they would try the Council first by an Agents Bill, which they did and the Council pass'd it.[33]

According to Philip Ludwell (who alone among the Council opposed the act), Councillor Peter Randolph had assured the Council that Fauquier had promised to pass the act if the Council approved it.[34] Abercromby, fearing that at worst he would lose his job and at the least would suffer a dilution of his authority and a diminution of the commissions he earned on financial transactions, earnestly

---

31. JA to Fauquier, 28 Dec. 1758, pp. 275–276.

32. Corbin to JA, 21 Oct. 1758, Colonial Office 5/1329, fol. 163, Public Record Office, London.

33. Fauquier to the Board of Trade, 14 Apr. 1759, in George Reese, ed., *The Official Papers of Francis Fauquier, Lieutenant Governor of Virginia, 1758–1768*, 3 vols. (Charlottesville, 1980–1983), 1:208.

34. Ludwell to Robert Dinwiddie, 22 Mar. 1759, CO 5/1329, fol. 164.

set out to have the law disallowed.[35] Late in 1759 he solicited the
legal opinion of Attorney General Charles Pratt and submitted a
memorial to the Board of Trade.[36] Pratt held that the act did not
supersede Abercromby's appointment and that he was still empowered to transact business and entitled to the salary and perquisites
of office.

In his memorial to the Board of Trade, Abercromby represented
that the executive in Virginia was relatively independent of the
assembly and had always appointed the agent for the colony, who
was paid from the revenue of the two-shillings-per-hogshead
export tax on tobacco; that a new agent had been appointed by an
act assented to by the governor even though it had no suspending
clause, a violation of the governor's instructions; and that the
assembly had rejected his bill of £196.7.0 for services rendered,
including negotiations for Virginia's share of the money awarded
by Parliament. The memorial requested, finally, that the Board of
Trade should advise the king either to assume the direct appointment of an agent or to order the governor and Council to continue
Abercromby in his office, with an appropriate salary and expenses.
The Board read the memorial and its numerous enclosures and
ordered them to lie by, pending receipt of Sir Matthew Lamb's
report on the act. Lamb, the Board's counsel, was routinely asked
his opinion on all colonial legislation and had already received the
act the week before Abercromby submitted his memorial to the
Board.

In his opinion rendered on 15 May 1760, Lamb did not object to
the assembly's appointing an agent, "provided the same was
consistent with, and did preserve the Powers that belong to the
different Branches of the Legislature." Lamb did, however, object
to the fact that the act empowered the committee of correspondence (in which burgesses outnumbered councillors) to remove
and replace the agent. He opined that in assenting to the act,
Fauquier and the Council had "Departed . . . with that Share of the
Power and Controul which they ought to have, in the appointing of
a Province Agent," and he recommended that the act not be

---

35. JA to the earl of Loudoun, 29 Aug. [1759], Loudoun Papers 6138,
Huntington Library.

36. See JA to John Blair, 15 Dec. 1759, pp. 329–330, n. 4.

confirmed, but amended.[37] In transmitting this opinion to Fauquier on 13 June 1760, the Board agreed with Lamb and called the objectionable parts of the act "irregular and Improper." Rather than supporting disallowance, the Board instructed Fauquier to recommend that the Council and House of Burgesses prepare another bill not liable to the objections and warned that if this was not done the Board would be obliged to advise the king to repeal the present law. The assembly complied with "An Act to explain and amend the act, intituled, An Act for appointing an agent," passed on 20 October 1760.[38]

With Montagu now confirmed as agent, the scope of Abercromby's services contracted somewhat. Thereafter he concerned himself with "all business relative to royal revenues, land grants, military supplies, customs duties, administrative appointments, and other executive matters."[39] To reflect his new status, Abercromby was denominated "Agent for the Kings Affairs" or "Solicitor and Agent for His Majestys Revenue in Virginia" by his Virginia correspondents.

This is not to imply that Abercromby's involvement in the colony's affairs decreased. His responsibilities were still numerous, and he defined his obligations broadly. Montagu's performance of his duties was perfunctory and sometimes dilatory, and on those occasions when the two agents acted jointly it seemed to be the more experienced and energetic Abercromby who took the initiative. Montagu was dismissed from the agency in 1770, and when his term technically expired in March 1772, the House of Burgesses allowed the agency to lapse altogether.[40] (Colonel Richard Bland, in a letter to a friend in England, took some credit for displacing Montagu and continued, "I cannot recollect a single Instance in which he was serviceable to this Country and I think it

---

37. *Fauquier Papers*, 1:379–380.

38. Ibid., 1:376; William Waller Hening, ed., *The Statutes at Large; Being a Collection of all the Laws of Virginia, from the First Session of the Legislature, in the Year 1619 . . .*, 13 vols. (Richmond, Philadelphia, and New York, 1819–1823; Charlottesville, 1969), 7:375.

39. Greene, Mullett, and Papenfuse, *Magna Charta for America*, 10.

40. Kammen, *Rope of Sand*, 133–134; Greene, *Quest for Power*, 282–284.

useless & unjust to our selves, to continue him longer in office.")[41]
In the final years before the American Revolution, then, Abercromby was Virginia's sole agent in London, although affairs had
come to such a pass that the colonials had almost ceased any longer
to seek a hearing before the government councils.

The Virginia agency was particularly lucrative for Abercromby,
the more so given his great difficulty in collecting payment for
other services. From 1754 to 1774 he received £200 per year from
the revenues of the two-shillings-per-hogshead tobacco export tax,
and in 1762 he doubled his salary by successfully lobbying for a like
amount from the quitrent revenues. Abercromby began to agitate
for this supplement in 1758, when he wrote to John Blair of the
precedent he had discovered in the records of the auditor-general
of the plantations' office (where he had just the year before begun
serving as deputy auditor-general). Nathaniel Blakiston had received a royal warrant in 1716 for such an allowance in addition to
his regular salary of £100 per year. Abercromby believed that he,
too, was entitled to extraordinary compensation, for "the Government stand indebted to me, the Duty of Office vastly increased, in
matters of State, & other Business. . . . I find that many of the
Officers of your Government have additional Salarys from the
Quitrents, and why may not the Agent."[42] In June 1762 he
received a royal warrant authorizing the additional salary.[43]

Another agency that is documented at least superficially in this
letter book was that for the Bahama Islands. Abercromby seems to
have acted as unofficial agent for the Bahamas through the efforts
of Governor John Tinker. While in London on a leave of absence,
Tinker (former agent for the Royal African Company and the
South Sea Company in South America) pressed an application he
had made for ordnance and stores to fend off Spanish depredations on the islands. After Tinker's return to the Bahamas, Abercromby acted as Tinker's agent in the matter and also began to

---

41. Bland to Thomas Adams, 1 Aug. 1771, in *Virginia Magazine of History and
Biography* 6 (1898): 133–134.

42. JA to Blair, 8 Mar. 1758, pp. 236–237.

43. H. R. McIlwaine, Wilmer L. Hall, and Benjamin J. Hillman, eds., *Executive
Journals of the Council of Colonial Virginia, 1680–1775*, 6 vols. (Richmond,
1925–1966), 6:252–253.

perform other services typical of a regular agent, such as forwarding letters and documents from the Board of Trade and the secretary of state. His letter to Tinker of 13 June 1757 indicated that he expected to be paid for his services, and when he wrote again on 22 July 1757 Abercromby added, "good Words will not answer my Services and therefore to tell you the Truth I did expect of you payment for my past Services before I was called upon to take up New Solicitations. . . . In time to come . . . I do expect & shall accordingly charge to the account of Government the annual Salary of 100 per an Ster as their Agent."[44] No such official connection was ever established, for this is the last letter to Tinker in the letter book and Tinker died in 1758. The Bahamas did not establish a regular agency until Richard Cumberland was appointed following the arrival in 1759 of Tinker's successor, Governor William Shirley.[45]

Readers of this letter book will discover that a colonial agency could be a very amorphous thing. It can rarely be said with great certainty or accuracy that a particular person was the agent of a particular colony during a particular period. Abercromby provides an excellent case study of why this was so. It would be too facile, for instance, to describe Abercromby as "agent for Virginia, 1752–1775" when the reality is much more complex. There were occasions when he represented the General Assembly, the colony as a whole, and the governor and Council. There were times when he served as a joint agent with another man, when he was the colony's sole representative in London, and when he represented the executive while another man represented the House of Burgesses. And his title varied from agent to "Solicitor of the Virginia Affairs" to "Agent for the Kings Affairs" and finally to "Solicitor and Agent for His Majestys Revenue in Virginia" (to distinguish

---

44. JA to Tinker, 13 June 1757, pp. 195–196; and 22 July 1757, pp. 205–206.

45. Lillian M. Penson, *The Colonial Agents of the British West Indies: A Study in Colonial Administration, Mainly in the Eighteenth Century* (London, 1924), 104–107.

him from Edward Montagu, the "Provincial Agent in Legislative Matters").[46]

Compounding the confusion was the fact that Abercromby's legal standing was sometimes in doubt. Questions arose over whether he had been legally authorized to act in certain cases, or whether colonial legislation so authorizing him had expired.

A recurring theme throughout the letter book is Abercromby's dedicated service to his clients. Regardless of whether another man had been appointed to work with him or supersede him, or whether the acts appointing him agent had long since expired, or whether he had received any of the compensation due him for years, Abercromby continued to represent, as energetically and imaginatively as possible, the best interests of his employers.

An uncharitable view of Abercromby's assiduousness is that he hoped ultimately to collect the arrears owed him. Had he refused service he might have been refused what was owed him. Although this view is plausible, given Abercromby's somewhat mercenary nature, a more likely explanation derives from Abercromby's experience as a colonial legislator and agent. He understood that colonial agencies were frequently the objects of conflict between governors and assemblies, that appropriations for salaries and expenses were at times held hostage by being tied to unrelated matters, and that the slowness and uncertainty of the mails (especially during the long war with France) meant that his principals would not learn of his actions until some months after he had taken them. He therefore learned to act independently and sometimes without specific authorization, so as not to become responsive only to the fickle winds that blew east from America. Abercromby took the long view, knowing (or hoping) that whatever actions he took would eventually be vindicated and gratefully acknowledged.

And he did take actions. Abercromby worked tirelessly in behalf of his clients, appearing before (and submitting voluminous petitions and memorials to) the Board of Trade, the Privy Council, the Treasury, and the principal officers of state, waiting on the functionaries of those offices, testifying before parliamentary commit-

---

46. JA to Fauquier, 2 Sept. 1763, p. 418; and 26 May 1765, pp. 429–430; and JA to Corbin, 26 May 1765, pp. 428–429.

tees, paying gratuities, shepherding colonial officials' commissions through the requisite stages, and soliciting the royal approbation of colonial laws.

Abercromby's output of correspondence as agent was impressive, even prodigious. He wrote long and frequent letters in an effort to keep his clients apprised of the ever-shifting situation in London. He often repeated himself and sometimes even contradicted himself, but for this he had an explanation that speaks volumes about the difficulties of representing clients an ocean away. Defending himself against criticism by North Carolina governor Gabriel Johnston, Abercromby wrote:

> I could by giving my[self] less trouble than I have heretofore done, that is to Say by not writing till the Issue of Matters depending are finally Determind, by this means I could [avoid] Reproof of being Sometimes Contradictory in my Letters, & Unsteady in my Negociations. Whenever that happens the Fault is not mine, going thro So many Chanels in the Course of my Negociations I meet with Variety of Opinions, Men in Office & in high Office, changing Sentiments from Causes that I cannot Discover, I must therefore take things as they come to me, & by being too Earnest in my Correspondence I may on Some Occasion to you, for from the first Cause of such alteration in Sentiments appear as you say too volatile, however I have always thought it the most freindly way to write to you in the Strain that things appear in when I do write, & to write often as Occasions offer.[47]

It is tempting to conclude that Abercromby (indeed, any agent) was simply a hired pen who would represent any paying client regardless of the principles involved in any particular incident. Yet we know that Abercromby, perhaps more than other agents, held deep-seated views about the nature of empires and the proper role of colonies within them. He gave decades to the study that resulted in his two major treatises, "An Examination of the Acts of Parliament Relative to the Trade and the Government of Our American Colonies" (1752) and *"De Jure et Gubernatione Coloniarum*, or An Inquiry into the Nature, and the Rights of Colonies, Ancient, and Modern" (1774). Did Abercromby's service as agent conform to those views, or did he temporize in order to represent the interests

---

47. JA to Johnston, 18 Feb. 1752, p. 28.

of his clients even if such interests conflicted with those of the mother country?

Abercromby's long American experience and deep study caused him to recognize that the logical outcome of American political developments was independence, but to him this result would have turned the proper relationship between colony and mother country on its head. In order to forestall that unthinkable event and to bring the colonies back to their proper, subordinate position within the empire, Abercromby penned his two remarkable treatises for the benefit of Britain's policy makers.[48]

In the "Examination," Abercromby sought to rationalize imperial administration, to reduce the myriad means by which the American colonies were controlled—acts of Parliament, orders of the Privy Council, instructions to the governors, charters to proprietary governments—to a single act of Parliament, a so-called "Magna Charta for America." This was not, however, to be a charter of liberties or a guarantor of Americans' rights as the name implied, for Abercromby held that "the first principle . . . of Colony Government, whether amongst antient, or Modern Nations, has ever been, to make their Colonies, Subservient to the Interest of the Principal State."[49] All other principles espoused by Abercromby flowed from this one.

Abercromby's proposed act of Parliament would have accomplished this subordination through a systematic program that included extending the jurisdiction and strengthening the powers of the courts of vice-admiralty, ensuring that all naval officers and customs officials were appointed directly by the Crown, permitting the seizure of illegal goods anywhere in the empire, obliging every colony to obtain approval for its laws before putting them into effect, declaring null and void any colonial statute that contravened either the common law or any act of the British Parliament, and depriving colonial assemblies of an exclusive right to frame money bills. (Later he even recommended "the legal Conviction, and execution of One or more incendiarys, here and in America" to strike "terror in delinquents, and . . . to fortify and reinstate Law

---

48. The two treatises have been published in Greene, Mullett, and Papenfuse, *Magna Charta for America*.

49. Ibid., 45.

and universal Government in America.")[50] How Abercromby justified this draconian view of empire is laid out in the second treatise.

The "*De Jure et Gubernatione Coloniarum*, or An Inquiry into the Nature, and the Rights of Colonies, Ancient, and Modern," a survey of colonies from antiquity to Abercromby's own day, reflects the author's wide reading and deep thinking on the subject. It has been described, without exaggeration, as "the most learned disquisition on the relationship between metropolises and colonies written in English, and perhaps in any modern language, up to that time."[51] Abercromby's study of colonies in antiquity revealed two models, the Greek and the Roman. In the former, colonists from overcrowded Greek cities left their homes to establish separate, independent states that, according to Abercromby, were thus "equals with the Parent State, in Sovereignty."[52] In the Roman case, colonists were sent out by the metropolis to build settlements that would "add strength to the State, by extending its Dominion."[53] These colonists enjoyed no independence or equality with Rome, which retained its full sovereignty. Needless to say, Abercromby argued forcefully that Britain's American colonies conformed to the Roman model. Further, he contended that the colonies were subject to the jurisdiction of Parliament as well as the sovereignty of the Crown.

Abercromby acknowledged but refused to take into account the extraordinary degree of autonomy and self-government that prevailed in the colonies. In a sense he wanted to "restore" an "ideal" relationship between Britain and its American colonies that had never really existed. He wished to establish the kind of imperial administration and metropolitan control that, he believed, should have been instituted at the outset of colonization. For Abercromby, even 1774 was not too late to bring the colonies to heel.

But this seeming ideologue was also a pragmatist, one who could dissociate his personal views of colonies and empires from his responsibility to represent his clients' best interests. This was so

---

50. Ibid., 277.
51. Ibid., 23.
52. Ibid., 174.
53. Ibid., 203.

even though Abercromby was a member of the imperial establishment as deputy auditor-general of the plantations from 1757 to 1765, and a member of Parliament from 1761 to 1768. He wrote George Grenville in 1765 that his "conduct in Parliament, with regard to Plantation matters, which are now become so serious to this Kingdom as well as to the Colonies, may not correspond in many respects with the Sentiments of my Constituents in America,"[54] and he voted against the repeal of the Stamp Act in 1766. As a government official he thus voted his principles. Yet as an agent he put his clients first.

For instance, in his very first act as agent for Virginia, Abercromby presented to the Crown an address from the House of Burgesses and the Council that sought to gain what would have been a significant encroachment on the royal prerogative. The colony wanted permission to pass laws, without suspending clauses, to repeal, alter, or amend laws that had already been confirmed by the Crown. Abercromby appeared before the Board of Trade in support of the address, but the Board responded sharply, recommending to the Privy Council that the petition be denied because the result would be "to take away, or at least to render useless and ineffectual that Power which the Crown has so Wisely and properly reserved to itself of rejecting such Laws passed in the Colonys, as shall upon due Consideration be thought improper or liable to Objection and would destroy that Check, which was established not only to preserve the just and proper influence and Authority which the Crown ought to have in the Direction and Government of its Colonys in America, but also to secure to its Subjects their just Libertys and Privileges."[55] Abercromby could hardly have said it better himself.

His disinterestedness is also evident in the roles he played as agent for Virginia and North Carolina, as the documents in this letter book make clear. In Virginia Abercromby generally promoted the interest of the executive against the challenges of the popularly elected representatives (particularly in the case of the pistole fee dispute), while in North Carolina the opposite situation

---

54. Additional Manuscript 38204, fols. 9–10, British Library.
55. See JA to Dinwiddie, 17 Sept. 1752, pp. 45–46, n. 1.

usually obtained. Abercromby's own words, written to a Virginia friend near the end of his long career, provide the pithiest summary: "I aim at no more than Serving those who Employ me to the Utmost of my Power."[56]

James Abercromby died sometime before November 1775, just as the empire he studied so keenly and labored so long to serve began to crumble.

---

56. JA to Corbin, 1 Jan. 1760, pp. 334–335.

Acknowledgments

THE editors are principally indebted to the staff of the Publications Branch of the Virginia State Library and Archives, Richmond. Dr. Jon Kukla, formerly assistant director for publications, commissioned the editors to produce this book and offered encouragement and patience over the many years that it was in preparation. Sandra Gioia Treadway supervised the final stages of publication. Susan B. Sheppard and Brenda M. White keyed the transcriptions and notes into the NBI Oasys system. Emily J. Salmon provided invaluable research assistance and a careful copyediting. Daphne Gentry also provided research assistance, and Donald W. Gunter produced the index. We thank them all.

The Henry E. Huntington Library, San Marino, California, graciously gave permission for several manuscripts in its collections to be quoted in the notes to this edition, and the Virginia Historical Society, Richmond, likewise authorized some of the annotation of Abercromby's letters to Governor Francis Fauquier that appeared in George Reese's three-volume edition of Fauquier's *Papers* to appear herein in modified form.

John M. Hemphill, recently retired from the Colonial Williamsburg Foundation, provided a close reading of the text and made several important corrections and suggestions. Dorothy Twohig, associate editor of *The Papers of George Washington*, answered numerous queries concerning the Seven Years' War, and Malcolm Freiberg, editor of publications emeritus of the Massachusetts Historical Society, provided information concerning agent William Bollan.

Researching the background of Abercromby's letters concerning the two Carolinas and the Bahamas was facilitated by several archivists: Dr. Robert J. Cain, Historical Publications Section, Division of Archives and History, North Carolina Department of Cultural Resources; Ms. Wylma Wates, formerly of the South Carolina Department of Archives and History; and Dr. Gail Saunders, Department of Archives, Nassau, Bahamas.

Although an extensive search for a portrait of Abercromby proved futile, the editors are nonetheless grateful to those institutions that made the attempt: Westminster School; Lincoln's Inn Library; House of Lords Record Office; National Portrait Gallery, London; National Register of Archives (Scotland); Scottish National Portrait Gallery; and Scottish Record Office.

Finally, work on the book was slowed but made more enjoyable by the arrival of Alice C. Van Horne on 25 May 1988.

Editorial Method

THE James Abercromby letter book is a manuscript volume in the Virginia State Library and Archives, Richmond. In it are copies (or abstracts or memoranda) of about 360 letters written by Abercromby between 13 July 1751 and 1 March 1773. Since Abercromby's career during that period centered on his colonial agencies, the recipients are for the most part the governors, other officials, and merchants of Virginia, North Carolina, South Carolina, and the Bahamas. And since almost none of the recipients' copies of these letters has survived, the letter book is a document of prime historical importance. Most of the letters are published here for the first time.

Certain changes in the organization of the letter book have been made in preparing this edition. For instance, the letters have been placed in chronological order. (If two or more letters carry the same date, they are printed in the order in which they appear in the letter book.) Two or more versions of the same letter have not been printed in full; the version that seemed likely to be closest to the letter as sent was chosen as the text to be printed, and substantive differences between that text and any other in the letter book have been noted in numbered footnotes to the printed text.

Besides the letters dated 1751 to 1773, Abercromby's letter book contains seven documents on twenty-four pages concerning two courts-martial held in 1746 at which Abercromby served as judge advocate. The documents reveal nothing of Abercromby's role and do not at all concern American affairs; thus the editors decided not to print them in this volume.

James Abercromby's hand is as close to illegible as most scholars

are likely to encounter in a lifetime of reading historical manuscripts. The frontispiece of this volume, contrasting Abercromby's
scrawl with the polished hand of a clerk, should suggest to readers
of this book the great difficulty of producing a clean transcription
of Abercromby's letter book. Nevertheless the editors are confident
that their transcription is dependable. Readers who consult the
original manuscript letter book to resolve doubtful readings are
encouraged to submit any corrections to the editors or to the
Virginia State Library and Archives.

Abercromby was not scrupulous about capitalization, punctua-
tion, spelling, and abbreviation, probably because he knew that his
clerk would render his almost unreadable words into a fair copy
that would be intelligible to its recipient. Nonetheless the editors
have attempted to maintain the integrity of Abercromby's writing
to the greatest extent possible. We have not taken it upon ourselves
to act as Abercromby's latter-day clerks by producing fair copies of
his letters. We have, however, made several kinds of editorial
changes in producing the transcription published herein:

—All sentences begin with a capital letter.

—Periods are added at the ends of paragraphs.

—Tildes have been omitted and the letters represented by them
have been supplied.

—Superscript letters have been brought down to the line of type,
and the resulting abbreviations have been expanded silently only if
they could not be readily understood (e.g., "cury" is rendered
"currency").

—Abbreviations and contractions have been silently expanded
only if they could not be readily understood. If an abbreviation or
contraction is susceptible of more than one reading, the conjectural
expansion has been bracketed.

—Abercromby's marginal rubrics or precis at the head of some
letters have not been transcribed if they add nothing material;
otherwise they are quoted or mentioned in source notes or the
numbered footnotes.

—The name of the recipient sometimes written at the head or
foot of a letter has generally not been transcribed.

—The second (or close) parenthesis has been silently added if
inadvertently omitted.

—The tailed p has been rendered as "pre," "pro," or "per" depending on the context.

—The thorn symbol has been rendered as "th."

—Dashes at the ends of sentences have been rendered as periods.

—The complimentary close has been run into the end of the letter.

—The pound sign written above the sum is brought down to precede it.

Each entry is followed by an unnumbered source note that indicates the location of the text in the letter book. This note also provides pertinent information about the letter, such as address, enclosures, dating problems, other copies of the same letter, Abercromby's notations concerning mode of transmittal, and the like.

The numbered footnotes following each document are keyed to the text to explain editorial changes, identify persons whenever possible, translate foreign phrases, gloss obsolete terms, supply citations to documents or official papers mentioned, and provide explication of the matters mentioned by Abercromby in his letters.

Much of the Virginia material concerns Robert Dinwiddie, who served as lieutenant governor of the colony from 1751 until 1758. Dinwiddie's extremely valuable letter books, in the collections of the Virginia Historical Society, were published a century ago in Robert A. Brock, ed., *The Official Records of Robert Dinwiddie, Lieutenant-Governor of the Colony of Virginia, 1751–1758*, 2 vols. (Richmond, 1883–1884). Since Brock's transcriptions are frequently inaccurate, the editors have elected to transcribe directly from the manuscript letter books in cases where Dinwiddie's correspondence is quoted in the annotation in this volume. However, in instances where letters in Dinwiddie's letter books are only cited or mentioned rather than quoted, the editors have as a general rule cited the Brock edition.

Short Titles and Abbreviations

Adm.   Admiralty Papers, Public Record Office,
                          London.

APC   W. L. Grant and James Munro, eds., *Acts
                          of the Privy Council of England. Colonial Se-
                          ries*, 6 vols. (London, 1908–1912; reprint,
                          Nendeln, Liechtenstein, 1966).

Bio. Dir. S.C.   Walter B. Edgar and N. Louise Bailey,
House of Rep.   eds., *Biographical Directory of the South
                          Carolina House of Representatives, Volume II:
                          The Commons House of Assembly, 1692–1775*
                          (Columbia, S.C., 1977).

Bond, *Quit-Rent*   Beverley W. Bond, Jr., *The Quit-Rent Sys-
System*   tem in the American Colonies* (New Haven,
                          1919).

Brock, *Dinwiddie*   Robert A. Brock, ed., *The Official Records
Papers*   of Robert Dinwiddie, Lieutenant-Governor of
                          the Colony of Virginia, 1751–1758*, 2 vols.
                          (Richmond, 1883–1884).

CO   Colonial Office Papers, Public Record Of-
                          fice, London.

EJC	H. R. McIlwaine et al., eds., *Executive Journals of the Council of Colonial Virginia, 1680–1775*, 6 vols. (Richmond, 1925–1966).
Ekirch, *"Poor Carolina"*	A. Roger Ekirch, *"Poor Carolina": Politics and Society in Colonial North Carolina, 1729–1776* (Chapel Hill, 1981).
Fauquier Papers	George Reese, ed., *The Official Papers of Francis Fauquier, Lieutenant Governor of Virginia, 1758–1768*, 3 vols. (Charlottesville, 1980–1983).
Fulham Papers	Fulham Papers, Lambeth Palace Library, London; calendared in William Wilson Manross, comp., *The Fulham Papers in Lambeth Palace Library: American Colonial Section, Calendar and Indexes* (Oxford, Eng., 1965).
Gipson, *British Empire before the American Revolution*	Lawrence Henry Gipson, *The British Empire before the American Revolution*, 15 vols. (Caldwell, Idaho, and New York, 1936–1970).
Greene, *Quest for Power*	Jack P. Greene, *The Quest for Power: The Lower Houses of Assembly in the Southern Royal Colonies, 1689–1776* (Chapel Hill, 1963).
Hening, *Statutes*	William Waller Hening, ed., *The Statutes at Large: Being a Collection of All the Laws of Virginia, from the First Session of the Legislature, in the Year 1619* . . . , 13 vols. (Richmond, Philadelphia, and New York, 1809–1823; reprint, Charlottesville, 1969).

JBT	*Journal of the Commissioners for Trade and Plantations [Board of Trade], 1704–1782*, 14 vols. (London, 1920–1938; reprint, Nendeln, Liechtenstein, 1970).
JCHA	J. H. Easterby et al., eds., *The Colonial Records of South Carolina: The Journals of the Commons House of Assembly*, 13 vols. to date (Columbia, S.C., 1951–).
JHB	H. R. McIlwaine and John Pendleton Kennedy, eds., *Journals of the House of Burgesses of Virginia, 1619–1776*, 13 vols. (Richmond, 1905–1915).
JHC	*Journals of the House of Commons.*
Koontz, *Dinwiddie Papers*	Louis Knott Koontz, ed., *Robert Dinwiddie Correspondence Illustrative of His Career in American Colonial Government and Westward Expansion*, microfilm edition (Berkeley and Los Angeles, 1951).
Labaree, *Royal Government*	Leonard Woods Labaree, *Royal Government in America: A Case Study of the British Colonial System before 1783* (New York, 1930).
Labaree, *Royal Instructions*	Leonard Woods Labaree, ed., *Royal Instructions to British Colonial Governors, 1670–1776*, 2 vols. (New York, 1935; reprint, 1967).
Laurens Papers	Philip M. Hamer et al., eds., *The Papers of Henry Laurens*, 11 vols. to date (Columbia, S.C., 1968–).
LJC	H. R. McIlwaine, ed., *Legislative Journals of the Council of Colonial Virginia, 1680–1773*, 3 vols. (Richmond, 1918–1919).

Lonn, *Colonial Agents*	Ella Lonn, *The Colonial Agents of the Southern Colonies* (Chapel Hill, 1945).
Morton, *Colonial Virginia*	Richard L. Morton, *Colonial Virginia*, 2 vols. (Chapel Hill, 1960).
NCCR	William L. Saunders, ed., *The Colonial Records of North Carolina*, vols. 1–10 (Raleigh, N.C., 1886–1890).
NCSR	Walter Clark, ed., *The State Records of North Carolina*, vols. 11–26 (Winston and Goldsboro, N.C., 1895–1905).
Parliamentary History	*The Parliamentary History of England from the Earliest Period to the Year 1803*, 36 vols., (London, 1806–1820).
PC	Privy Council Office Registers, Public Record Office, London.
SCPR	*Records in the British Public Record Office Relating to South Carolina, 1663–1782*, 36 vols., microfilm edition (Columbia, S.C., 1973).
Sirmans, *Colonial South Carolina*	M. Eugene Sirmans, *Colonial South Carolina: A Political History, 1663–1763* (Chapel Hill, 1966).
T	Treasury Office Papers, Public Record Office, London.
VHS	Virginia Historical Society, Richmond.
VMHB	*Virginia Magazine of History and Biography.*
WMQ	*William and Mary Quarterly.*
WO	War Office Papers, Public Record Office, London.

The Letter Book of
James Abercromby
Colonial Agent

1751–1773

To Gabriel Johnston[1]

July 13th 1751 Edinburgh

Since my last have reced 2000 Dollars now in Mr Blands[2] hands of which paid Several of your Orders and My Disbursments on your Acct to July 1751 2000 More I expect by the Pegasus; the Money shall remain in Mr Blands hands Subject to your Orders to me which I fear by the D of Bedfords letter herewith Sent will be Restoration to the Spaniards, Am altogether in the dark as to that Affair, let me know the truth of this Matter that I may Speak to it properly.[3]

When Mr Bland gives me the Receipt for the Payments that he has made by My Order shall transmit them to you with the Particular Disbursments made by me on your Acct, I have had five Hearings before the Lords for Trade on Maccullochs Complt & not one 3d part gone thro, it is postpond on Mr Horace Walpoles Acct he not being able to Attend the day appointed, the Matter stands Suspended till Novr[4] I do not Fear Macculoch so Much as the Spanish Minister you may depend on all the Services in this or other Matters being Sir & ca

LB, p. 304. Sent "per a Ship from Leith."

1. Gabriel Johnston (1699–1752), a native of Scotland, was governor of North Carolina from 1734 until his death.

2. Presumably a British merchant.

3. JA alludes here to a dispute involving Johnston that arose the previous year. In Aug. 1750 the Spanish ship *Nuestra Segniora de Guadalupe*, Don Juan Manuel de Bonilla, commander and supercargo, was forced to put ashore at Ocracoke, N.C., by bad weather and damage. Johnston first sent James Innes (d. 1759), a member of the

Council, to offer assistance and warn Bonilla of the danger from the "Bankers," lawless inhabitants of the Outer Banks. Johnston then sent for HMS *Scorpion*, then in South Carolina, to protect the Spanish ship and its valuable cargo (money and cochineal) from seizure by customs agents. Bonilla and Johnston agreed to an arrangement whereby Johnston saw to the shipment of the valuable cargo to Europe, in return for which Bonilla pledged to pay the governor a commission on the effects and to pay the captain of the *Scorpion* the usual freight charges. Johnston reported to John Russell (1710–1771), fourth duke of Bedford, who was secretary of state for the Southern Department, that he would have been justified by the laws of trade and by existing treaties in seizing both the ship and its cargo for his own use, but that he had "studied How to act the just and Humane part as what I thought would be most acceptable to His Majesty." Bedford at first communicated to Johnston the king's approbation of his conduct, but then complaints were lodged by Richard Wall (1694–1778), a native Briton who was Spain's minister to Great Britain. Bedford submitted the matter to the Crown's legal officers, who on 4 June 1751 concluded that no commission was due to Johnston, who "ought not to demand any Duty or Gratification whatsoever to himself upon that Account." Bedford's letter to Johnston, which enclosed a copy of the law officers' report, was dated 13 June, and it is presumably the one JA enclosed in the present letter. Bedford told Johnston that the king's pleasure was that "full Restitution should be made to the Spaniards of whatsoever shall have been illegally exacted from them upon this occasion." In Feb. 1752 Thomas Child, then in London, appealed this decision, stating that Bonilla had himself calculated the amount of the commission paid to the governor, which sum "was so far from being secretly or by force taken as has been unfairly and untruely suggested." Child also stated that Johnston had retained only $5,500 "as a Gratification for those his generous, important, good Offices," and that the remainder of the commission had been spent on actual expenses incurred in preserving the ship and its effects (*NCCR*, 4:1300–1311).

4. JA refers to charges against Johnston brought by Henry McCulloh (1700?–1779), London merchant and speculator in North Carolina lands. Johnston had once been McCulloh's protégé and may have owed his appointment as governor to the influence of McCulloh and his friends. The two men had a serious falling-out over land claims, however, and McCulloh instituted charges against the governor, "accusing Johnston of sundry loose practices in granting lands, . . . and denouncing his arbitrary procedure in judicial matters, his assent to currency and quit rent laws in violation of his instructions, and other irregular actions." The hearings before the Board of Trade that JA mentions took place on 9 May, 12 June, 14 June, 18 June, and 19 June 1751. Horatio (or Horace) Walpole (1678–1757), brother of Robert Walpole, was auditor-general of the plantations from 1717 until his death. He did attend the meeting of the Board on 19 June, when after some discussion the Board agreed to "consider of this affair at another opportunity" (*JBT*, 9:194, 205–206, 207–209, 210; Charles G. Sellers, Jr., "Private Profits and British Colonial Policy: The Speculations of Henry McCulloh," *WMQ*, 3d ser., 8 [1951]: 535–551 [quote on 546–547]).

To Gabriel Johnston

[August 1751]

NB wrote to him in Augt by Mr Dinwiddie[1] & told him of the Receipt of 2000 Dollars Specie.

LB, p. 304. This note was appended to the preceding letter.

1. Robert Dinwiddie (1693–1770) was lieutenant governor of Virginia from 1751 to 1758. He was commissioned in July 1751 and arrived in Virginia on 20 Nov. 1751.

To [George Nicholas]

Sir[1]   Octr 4th 1751

By my last[2] I acquainted you that I had set the Aplication in behalf of the Inhabitants of Cape Fear a going, I am now further to acquaint you that I have procurd the Kings Orders to mr Keene to Solicit the Case of your Clients, with the Spanish Ministers, these Orders were transmitted to him by the Secry of State Some time last Month.[3]

I have expected Remittances from you to Answer the necessary Fees of Office. I must therefore desire that you will lose no time in Remitting me 50£ Ster for that Account, for my own trouble & what further Engagments I may find it necessary for me to enter into for Securing a Friend in Office in Case of Sucessful Services I shall leave to the Issue of this Negociation but at present you will take Care to have that Sum forthwith remitted to me I am always Sir Your

JA

LB, p. 301. Addressed to "Mr. Nichols." Sent "per Capt Taylor to Cape Fear."

1. George Nicholas, a lawyer, served as attorney general of North Carolina 1752–1756.

2. Letter not found.

3. In 1748, two Spanish privateers had sailed up the Cape Fear River "firing upon the Plantations, landing their Men, destroying houses Goods and taking away Negroes to a very great value." An account of the attack and an estimate of the damages had "been long since transmitted to the Spanish Court and is still [in Feb. 1752] depending for Reparation" (*NCCR*, 4:1301).

Sir Benjamin Keene (1697–1757) was British ambassador to Spain 1727–1739 and 1748–1757.

Robert D'Arcy (1718–1778), fourth earl of Holderness, succeeded Bedford as secretary of state for the Southern Department in June 1751 and held that post until 1761, except for a brief period in 1757.

To James Murray

[4 October 1751]
To Mr. Murray[1] the [*illegible*] by Mr Child[2] nothing Material to Say to him.

LB, p. 301. The date is inferred from the preceding letter, the only other entry on this page of the letter book. Brackets signify about four illegible words.

1. James Murray (1713–1781), a Scot who became a Wilmington, N.C., merchant, was a member of the North Carolina Council from 1754 until his suspension in 1757, and from his reinstatement in 1762 until he moved to Boston in 1765.

2. Thomas Child (fl. 1745–1767), a native of England, was attorney general of North Carolina 1746–1752 and 1759–1761, proprietary agent to Earl Granville 1749–1763, and a representative in the lower house of the assembly 1760–1761.

To the Committee of Correspondence of North Carolina

London Octr 7th 1751
I am favoured with yours of the 20th April[1] & with Duplicat thereof acknowledging my Letter of the 23d of Janry which inclosed Mr Attorney & Solictor Generals Report upon the two Acts of Assembly now under Consideration,[2] and from the Experience that you Gentlemen must have of the Fatal Consequence that will necessarily Attend a Repeal of those Acts of Assembly I do not at all Wonder at the Concern you shew least that shall be their Fate; I should deceive you was I to Insinuate any hopes of the Confirmation of these Acts in the Face of this Report, to the Contrary, And yet at the same time I have no Reason to apprehend their Repeal before Expedients are thought on here to prevent any

bad Consequence from the Repeal of that Act for Establishing an Equal Representation, for it is on this Act that the Contest rests principally & in what Manner to Separate the Case of this Act from that of the rest of the Acts concomitant thereon appears difficult to find out an Expedient, however Minutly this Matter has been considerd, not indeed in the Ordinary Course of Business, for every Member of the Board has given this Case a distinct & Separate Consideration & when this was done it appeard to the Whole a Matter of too great difficulty for them to Determine without the Oppinion of the Crown Lawiers,[3] for the Satisfaction of those Lawiers they had every Circumstance that could be thought on put together & added to the Governors Answer[4] with the Papers attending the Same besides this they Desird that Council might be Employd to Argue from the Facts Noted in the Report on Each side of the Question, & Never was any Cause better Argued than that on our Side; however after so full a Hearing you See Mr Attorney & Solicitor have left the Principal Point undetermind & the Lords for Trade find themselves Still at a Loss how to Form their Judgment thereon. Under Such difficulties I therefore Movd for a Hearing by Council before the Report which was Granted And had any thing Escapd our Notice before the Attorney & Solictor it was made up upon the Hearing before the Lords for Trade & I will Venture to Say that never was a Report Agitated with so much Freedom, or more cut to pieces[5] But after all Such is the Course of Business that after such a Negative put to the Propriety of the law, No Confirmation thereof is to be hopd for on good grounds But So far As I can Judge from the variety of Tempers which I have tryd on this Occasion I expect no Repeal of any of these Laws Reported against before Expedients are thought on here & I hope proposd to the present Assembly in your Province for what those Expedients may be I can not as yet Say however I will be very Attentive to every Circumstance that may occur in this Matter & give you notice Accordingly.[6]

As An Act of Parlt Continuing the Bounty on Naval Stores passd towards the Close of last Session and now Printed has made An Alteration with regard to the Bounty on Tar I send the Same to you for your Direction[7] And let me Conclude by acknowledging My Obligations to you Gentlemen for your promisd Recommendation of a proper Consideration of My Service & Augmentation of my Appointments,[8] I hope the Gentlemen of the Assembly will consider that Matters of so complicated a Nature are not to be Negociated in the ordinary method of Bussiness nor without extraordinary Labour and Diligence & tho I may not in the end have Success equal to my Expectations & Desire for the good of the Province Yet I flatter my Self with hopes that my Interposition may be a Means to prevent *all* the Evils that might Attend the Repeal of the Laws now under the Same Legislative Circumstances with that now immediatly the Object of Contest. I am Gentlemen Your &ca

JA

LB, pp. 298–299. Sent "per Capt Taylor to Cape Fear."

1. The North Carolina "Act to appoint an agent to solicit the affairs of this province at the several boards in England," passed on 15 Oct. 1748, established a committee of correspondence composed of Councillors Robert Halton and Eleazer Allen and Representatives Samuel Swann, John Swann, and John Starkey, who were to "advise, direct, and instruct [JA] in all such Matters relating to this Province, as may be moved or solicited, or that they may think proper, at any Time, to move or solicit before his Majesty in Council, or at any of the Boards in England" (*NCSR*, 23:303–304). The act was to take effect on 25 Mar. 1749 and remain in effect for two years, so that when the committee of correspondence wrote JA on 20 Apr. 1751 (not found), its authority (and JA's) had technically expired. This defect was remedied by the act to revive the 1748 act, passed on 12 Oct. 1751, which was to be in effect for three years from the previous 25 Mar. and which named to the committee of correspondence James Hasell and John Dawson in the rooms of Halton and Allen, deceased (*NCSR*, 23:362–363).

2. For the so-called representation controversy, see Introduction, pp. xxvi–xxviii, above.

JA's letter of 23 Jan. (not found) enclosed a copy of the report to the Board of Trade of 1 Dec. 1750 from Attorney General Dudley Ryder (1691–1756) and Solicitor General William Murray (1705–1793), afterwards first earl of Mansfield. The Crown's legal officers proposed the disallowance of both the act for limiting the number of representatives to two from each county and the act for establishing the seat of government at New Bern. They held that the acts had been "passed by Management Precipitation and Surprise when very few Members were present and are of such nature and Tendency and have such effect and Operation that the Governour by his Instructions ought not to have assented to them, tho' they had passed deliberately in a full Assembly" (*NCCR*, 4:1223–1224).

3. The Board of Trade was a body of eight regular commissioners who were charged with several duties, among which was the supervision of colonial affairs. The Board was also known as the Board of Trade and Plantations, Lords Commissioners of Trade and Plantations, and Lords of Trade. At the time of the present letter the

Board comprised the following members, appointed by a commission dated 21 Dec. 1749 (*JBT*, 9:1): George Montagu Dunk (1716–1771), second earl of Halifax, the president; Robert Sawyer Herbert (1695–1769); John Pitt (ca. 1706–1787), cousin of William Pitt; James Grenville (1715–1783); Thomas Hay (1710–1787), styled Viscount Dupplin; Francis Fane (ca. 1698–1757), who had been counsel to the Board 1725–1746; Charles Townshend (1725–1767), later famous as the author of the Townshend Duties; and Andrew Stone (1703–1773).

4. Johnston's "Answer" was his letter to the Board of Trade of 28 Dec. 1748 in response to a petition to the Crown of several inhabitants of the northern counties against the representation act (*NCCR*, 4:1158–1166).

5. The Board of Trade read the report of the attorney general and solicitor general on 11 Dec. 1750. On 13 Mar. 1751 JA petitioned the Board to be heard against the report, and hearings before the Board were held on 20 Mar. and 29 Mar. 1751 (*JBT*, 9:170–173, 176–179).

6. JA was correct in assuming both that confirmation of the laws was impossible and that repeal was unlikely until "Expedients are thought on" to resolve the dilemma. Despite the legal officers' report, the Board of Trade procrastinated, and the matter was not resolved until 1754. See JA to North Carolina Committee of Correspondence, 27 Feb. 1754, pp. 107–108, n. 1.

7. In June 1751 Parliament passed an act for encouraging the importation of naval stores from America. The act (24 George II, chap. 52) continued in force an act initially passed in 1729 (2 George II, chap. 35) and continued in 1740 (13 George II, chap. 28), with the proviso that no bounty would be paid on tar unless each barrel contained $31\frac{1}{2}$ gallons.

8. The 1751 act renewing JA's appointment as agent (for which see n. 1, above) raised JA's salary from £50 to £100 sterling per year and appropriated £111.9.2 sterling to reimburse JA "for extraordinary Expenses, Charges, and Trouble, in the Service of this Province."

To Samuel Swann

Dr Sir[1]   London Ocr 7th 1751

I am favour with yours June 29th[2] inclosing one from the Comee of Assembly which I have by this occasion ansd[3] & directed to your Care and I wish that I could add any thing by way of Answer to yours more Satisfactory than what I have been able to say to the Committee, the Arguments you have Advancd against the Attorney & Solicitors Report are very Just and these & many

More were Urgd against that Report upon the Hearing by Council before the Lords for Trade. The first Part of that Report as to Precipitation & Surprise is certainly not Supported in point of Fact; as was most fully set forth by our Council in his Argument from the Journals against this Report[4] As to the last Part Relative to the Governors Assent without a Suspending Clause it was also Argud by our Consull that the Bill in Question was not of Such a Nature as to bring it within his Instructions in Such Cases of Suspending Clauses[5] the Objection to the Bill for Establishing a more equal Representation having Repeald Other Acts by General words was taken from the Acts Regarding the Countys, of Tyrrell & Bertie which Said Acts ought to have been Repeald by Express words according to the Govrs Instructions;[6] As the Matter now stands it is to little purpose for us now to argue upon the Case of the Report as to the Propriety of these Laws Reported against, for I have too much Reason to believe that this Report Such as it is will prove a Bar to the Confirmation of these laws, But through out the whole Manner in which this Matter has been Agitated the Prudential way of Reasoning for Supporting the Essentials of these Laws has made the greatest Impression, And from hence I would fain flatter my Self that Expedients will be thought on & that till Such Expedients have been tryd in the Assembly that all these Acts will lye over in Suspence here it is where I now turn the Stress of my Solicitation; Mr Maculloh has thrown out one Expedient which will not take Effect over Separation of the Northern from the Southern Part of the Province & a Distinct Govert for the Northern District, Such a Scheme will make no Impression however liberal his Northern Freinds are in their offers for supporting a Seperat Govert,[7] I wish that I could have given you an agreeable Return to the first Favour that you have done me of a particular Letter, however I hope this will be no Bar to our Future Correspondence, And as I can at present add nothing to you but what you will See by My Letter to the Comee I shall conclude My Self Indebted to you for your Past Services to me in the Assembly & for the Continuance of them for the time to Come & believe me that I shall on all Occasions be glad of every hint that you can give me for promoting the Interest of the Province as I know no Person in it whose Judgement I shall more readily rely on being Dr Sir Your most Obedt Svt

PS   I beg my Complts to your Brother.[8]

LB, p. 300.

1. Samuel Swann (1704–1771), a surveyor by training, served in the lower house of the North Carolina Assembly 1725–1726, 1731–1735, and 1739–1762 (Speaker 1742–1754, 1756–1761).

2. Letter not found.

3. See preceding letter.

4. Alexander Hume-Campbell (1708–1760), JA's counsel, made this argument before the Board of Trade on 20 Mar. 1751. He held that "the Act was passed at an Assembly held at Wilmington, in November, 1746, in pursuance of a prorogation in the preceding June, whereby the time and place had been fixed four months before; that no certain space of time is pretended to be necessary by the constitution of the province for the meeting of the Assembly, and much less than four months is sufficient for the meeting of the Parliament; that the Assembly being duly prorogued and the place of meeting declared, it was not necessary to give special notice of any Act intended to be passed. For which reasons he [Campbell] apprehended this Act could not properly be said to have been passed by surprize" (*JBT*, 9:171).

5. Johnston's instructions enjoined him not to assent "to any law for repealing any other law passed in your government" without a clause suspending its operation until the Crown's pleasure is known (Labaree, *Royal Instructions*, 1:128).

The journals of the Board of Trade do not record that Campbell made such an argument about the governor's instructions. In fact, he twice tacitly acknowledged the impropriety of Johnston's having acceded to the acts. On 20 Mar. Campbell stated "that if a governor obtains an Act beneficial to his Majesty's interest, he might justly be blamed for not adhering strictly to his instructions, but such an Act ought not to be repealed," and on 29 Mar. Campbell stated that "the instructions to the Governor have not indeed been punctually obeyed, but as they were not intended to hinder him from doing a beneficial thing for his master, this should be no objection" (*JBT*, 9:172, 179).

6. The bill for equal representation implicitly repealed the 1722 law that created Bertie precinct with five representatives, and the 1729 law that created Tyrrell precinct with two representatives at first and the promise of more as the population grew (*NCSR*, 23:100, 25:212–213). Johnston's instructions stipulated "that no act whatever be suspended, altered, revived, confirmed, or repealed by general words, but that the title and date of such act so suspended, altered, revived, confirmed, or repealed be particularly mentioned or expressed" (Labaree, *Royal Instructions*, 1:126).

7. No evidence corroborating the existence of such a separatist "Scheme" has been found. See Ekirch, *"Poor Carolina,"* 104, 255 n. 50.

8. John Swann (d. 1761) served in the lower house of the North Carolina Assembly 1739–1751 and on the Council 1751–1761.

To James Glen

Sir[1]   London Octr 7th 1751

Altho I have none of yours to Answer, I write this to let you know that on My Arrival here from the North I calld at Mr Calverly[2] who I find has been in the Country for these 5 Weeks, but his Clerk Informs me that there has been one Argument upon the Case of the Dutch Ship viz on this Point only as to the Jurisdiction of the Court in South Carolina to Try this Offence committed in Jamaica, which to My very great Suprise he tells me was determind by Doctor Chapman Dr Henry Prices Delegate on this Ocassion, against the Jurisdiction of the Judge of South Carolina.[3]

However as this was a Nice Point and Colateral to Any other Matter Set forth in the Process & Papers, and the Council for the Decree not aware of it consequently not prepard, they Demur'd to the Decree & Prayd another Hearing which is granted for the first day of this Insuing Term viz the 23d Inst, this being the Case I cannot help thinking that this decree of Doctor Chapmans must be Revers'd, for if it is Confirmd & Suits on the Acts of Trade and particularly on that Act now in Question Decreed Local, there is an End of A Fair Trade with regard to this Nation whom it does not concern whether the Offence is done in one or tother of its Plantations, the Offence being Generaly National most certainly ought the Remedy to be General and not Local, & such I take it is the Intention of the Clause of the Act of King William I have given Directions to have Notice given me that I may Attend the 2d Argument.

I told you in some of My former that I heard you found fault with in the Secretarys Office for Interfering in the Case of the Spanish Effects in North Carolina, Since that amongst other Letters & Papers Sent me by Govr Johnston on that Affair I have yours to him recommending the Case of the Wrights & nothing can be Pend with more Caution than your Letter & carrys with it no More than Civilitys to those Gentlemen[4] As far as the Law will permit Such is your Expression in the Letter, you may be Sure that I shall take an opportunety to remove any prejudice that these groundless Reports have made.

I wonder that I have No Answer to Mine regarding my own Demands on the Assembly for My Services & Disbursements in the

Case of the Paper Currency You take No Notice of it neither have I one Word from the Speaker in Answer to the Letter on this head which was grounded upon a Letter to me by Directions of the House;[5] I am sure the Public of Carolina have no Right to expect Services from me as a Volunteer, this is out of the Case I was promisd to have Amends made to me for my services in the Case of the Currency I did Serve them most Effectually in the former as well as in the last Session of Parliament I beg therefore that you will let me know what I have to Expect from them.

I shall think My Self extreamly ill Rewarded if I am not allowd 100 Guineas out of which Mr Sharpe[6] has had 10 Guineas & a promise of a further Consideration to him according to My Consideration from the Public of Carolina.

I likewise Wonder that I have not a Word from you as to your concerns with Capt Wilson,[7] I gave you early Notice of the Reports agt him & afterwards a more full Account of your Affairs with him As it was from him that I had my Appointment of 50£ per An paid to me you will let me know to whom I am now to Apply, one Years Salary is due me the 18th of Next Month.

The Future Govert of Georgia is now under Consideration & the Lords for [Trade] have So far Reported in the Case that no Reunion ought to be with South Carolina the Report is now before the Council & probably will Shew itself next Session of Parlt in some Shape or other.[8]

I send you the Magazines for the four last Months, the Coffee house I find rings with a Contest that has been between you & the Assembly in which they Say that the Assembly got the Victory;[9] but It is of very little Moment the Judgment of that House, it is hereabouts where False Reports are to be Set to Rights & whenever any Such come to My knowledge I shall not fail to give you an opportunety of acquitting yourself being always Dr Sir Your Most Obedt Sert

Ja Aber

PS the Scheme of Creating & Uniting An Office of Secretary of State for the Plantations to the Plantation Office & in the Person of the first Comr of that Board is all over to the disapointment no

Doubt of particulars[10] let my Claim on the Assembly escape[11] your Attention on a proper Opportunety offering for that purpose.

LB, pp. 302–303.

1. James Glen (1701–1777), a native of Scotland, was appointed governor of South Carolina in 1738 but did not arrive in the colony until 1743. He served as governor until 1756. For JA's explanation of his relationship with Glen, see JA to Glen, 9 Nov. 1753 (first letter of that date), p. 96, and JA to Dinwiddie, 16 Jan. 1755, pp. 132–135.

2. This may have been Walter Calverley Blackett (or Calverley-Blackett) (1707–1777), of Calverley, near Leeds, Yorkshire, member of Parliament 1734–1777.

3. JA refers to the case of the *Vrouw Dorothea*, pending before the High Court of Admiralty. Under the Navigation Acts foreigners were prohibited from trading with British colonies, but inventive captains found ways to skirt the laws. The Dutch ship *Vrouw Dorothea* freely traded for a time between Jamaica and South Carolina, generally on the pretext that contrary winds prevented her from reaching Curaçao. In 1747 the owner of a Jamaica privateer seized the *Vrouw Dorothea* and carried her into Charleston, where in June 1748 she and her cargo were condemned and declared forfeited by James Graeme, judge of the South Carolina Vice-Admiralty Court, one-third going to the Crown, one-third to Governor Glen, and one-third to William Hopton, the naval officer in Charleston who brought the charges. The confusion over the jurisdiction of the colonial vice-admiralty courts arose from the ambiguous wording of the Navigation Act of 1696 (7–8 William III, chap. 22), which stated that penalties and forfeitures were "to be recovered in any of his Majesty's Courts at Westminster, or in the Kingdom of Ireland, or in the Court of Admiralty held in his Majesty's plantations respectively, where such offence shall be committed, . . . or in any other Plantation belonging to any Subject of England." Further confusing the issue was the question of appellate jurisdiction, for appeals were sometimes heard by the king in Council and sometimes by the High Court of Admiralty. Judge Graeme at first refused appeal of the *Vrouw Dorothea* case to the king in Council as contrary to his commission, but he then allowed appeal to the High Court of Admiralty, which eventually reversed Graeme's decision. Chapman and Price have not been further identified (Glen to the duke of Bedford, 10 Oct. 1748, CO 5/389, fols. 107–108; Joseph Henry Smith, *Appeals to the Privy Council from the American Plantations* [New York, 1950], 189–190; Thomas C. Barrow, *Trade and Empire: The British Customs Service in Colonial America, 1660–1775* [Cambridge, Mass., 1967], 146–147; *Laurens Papers*, 1:198n).

4. In a P.S. dated 20 Sept. to a letter of 18 Sept. 1750, Johnston told JA: "I have just now received advice that your old friend Tom Wright of Charlestown is among the Spaniards at Ocacock incognito That he is their great Oracle and that it is he who advises them not to take any notice of this Government But has advised them to carry their cargo on different Bottoms to Charlestown where I dont doubt you will hear of a fine scene" (*NCCR*, 4:1304). Glen's letter to Johnston (not found) may have

concerned this Tom Wright (and other members of his family) and his illicit activities in North Carolina.

5. On 14 Dec. 1749 the South Carolina Commons House of Assembly ordered the colony's committee of correspondence to transmit to agent James Crokatt a copy of the report of a joint committee of the assembly concerning the state of the paper currency in the colony. The committee of correspondence was also to instruct Crokatt "to use his utmost Endeavours to procure an Exemption of this Province out of any Bill that is now pending, or which may hereafter be brought into the Parliament, for the abolishing of Paper Currency in America." At the same time the Commons House agreed that its Speaker, Andrew Rutledge (d. 1755), be directed to send JA copies of the report of the joint committee "and acquaint him that this House desire that he will continue his Services to this Province on that Occasion, and in shewing the Reasonableness of an Exemption of this Province out of any Bill that may be brought into Parliament for the abolishing of Paper Currency in America." The Commons House also agreed to defray JA's expenses in this effort (*JCHA*, 9:348–349).

The resulting act of Parliament, the so-called Currency Act of 1751 (24 George II, chap. 53), was intended "to regulate and restrain paper bills of credit in his Majesty's colonies or plantations of Rhode Island and Providence Plantations, Connecticut, the Massachusetts Bay and New Hampshire in America; and to prevent the same being legal tenders in payments of money."

On 16 Apr. 1752 Rutledge presented to the Commons House a letter from JA (not found) to the committee of correspondence dated 20 Jan. 1751/52. JA's letter enclosed an account "for his Services and Disbursments in regard to a Bill which was pending in the Parliament of Great Britain concerning the Paper Bills of Credit in America," amounting to £107.19 sterling, which amount was allowed (*JCHA*, 11:190).

6. Probably Joshua Sharpe (ca. 1716–1786), a solicitor of Lincoln's Inn who frequently served as counsel for various American colonies before the Board of Trade and the Privy Council. Sharpe was a brother of Horatio Sharpe (later lieutenant governor of Maryland) and William Sharpe, a clerk to the Privy Council.

7. Not identified, but see JA to Glen, 25 Jan. 1752, pp. 26–27.

8. Although the government of Georgia by the Trustees under their charter was not to expire until 9 June 1753, the Trustees made it known that they wished to surrender their charter sooner, and as a result there was some talk of reuniting South Carolina and Georgia after control of the latter colony reverted to the Crown. The Georgia Trustees opposed the idea, telling the Board of Trade on 27 June 1751 that annexing Georgia "to South Carolina will soon reduce it to the same desolate condition, in which the southern parts of South Carolina were before the establishment of Georgia." The Trustees further held that such annexation "is absolutely repugnant to his Majesty's charter, which does expressly declare, that it shall be a separate and independent province, and that the inhabitants shall not be subject to the laws of South Carolina" (*JBT*, 9:213–214).

A year later Georgia agent Edmund Gray memorialized the Board that "Should Georgia be annexed to Carolina, it would damp her growing Prosperity; Involve the People in Disputes; Ruin her present Inhabitants, who have Settled there, on Faith of the King's Charter; wherein it is declared to be Seperate from, and Independant of South Carolina; Render her Suspected to, and despised by the Indians; her Situation remote and inconvenient to Charles Town, the Seat of Government, Deter non Planters from Settling, Prevent those who should not immediately be obliged to Abandon their Plantations from making the necessary improvements for raising, Silk, Wine, and Oil, so happily begun, by Planting more Trees since they nor their Posterity might never enjoy the Fruits, Endanger the loss of So hopefull a Province, the Indian Trade and Alliance; disturb the Quiet of the People of both Colonies; affect the most distant Colonys on the Continent & Even the Sugar Islands" (Allen D. Candler and Lucian L. Knight, eds., *The Colonial Records of the State of Georgia*, vol. 26 [Atlanta, 1916], 355).

South Carolinians were ambivalent about the idea. On 9 June 1750 the colony's committee of correspondence instructed agent James Crokatt to represent "the detriment it would be to this Province to have the Colony of Georgia annexed to it" (*JCHA*, 10:219). On 7 May 1752 a special committee of the Commons House reported that "the Interest Benefit and Advantage" of South Carolina would be promoted by such a move, but on 12 May 1752 the whole House resolved that annexing Georgia "would not conduce to the advantage" of South Carolina (*JCHA*, 11:294, 337). In the event, of course, Georgia became a royal colony independent of South Carolina.

9. This "Contest" was over Glen's veto of several bills in Apr. and May 1751 and the subsequent appointment of a joint committee of the General Assembly to consider the vetoes and "the present melancholly prospect of an Indian War." The Commons House resolved on 10 May to petition the Crown in protest against Glen's vetoes and his conduct of Indian affairs. Glen, who was in disfavor with the Board of Trade, quickly retreated. In a compromise, he signed the reintroduced bills after they had been altered slightly, and the Commons House shelved its plan to petition the Crown (*JCHA*, 10:13–16, 411, 424, 428–430; Sirmans, *Colonial South Carolina*, 290–291).

10. JA alludes to Halifax, the president of the Board of Trade, who sought to gain a cabinet post and increase the authority of the Board. For his later partial success in this endeavor, see JA to Glen, 6 Apr. 1752, pp. 32–33.

11. JA probably intended to write "not escape."

To Gabriel Johnston

Octr 7th 1751

Since my last have yours of the 24th April, the 4th of May, the 7th June, & 14th June,[1] those Inclosd are deliverd, that to Lord

Granville by my Self,[2] his Lordship as to the part relative to Politicks said he had nothing to do with to the last on Improvements pleasd him more, said he was your Freind & would So Continue till good Cause to the Contrary.

I have grounds to think him not so favourably Inclind to the Case of the Law Agt 5 Rep[r]esentatives, as at first, the first discovery I made of this was Soon after the Noise made by the discovery of his Letter to you,[3] probably his Agents for I find Mr Child is of Oppinion that this Matter is not altogether Indifferent with regard to his Lordships Interest in these Counties, this being thrown out Guess what Favour we are to Expect in the Face of the Att & Sol: Report against the Act.

But as the Apprehension of a Total Confusion must be the Consequence of Repealing the Acts Concomitant with the Act in Question has made Strong Impression, I am apt to think Expedients will be thought on & the Acts Suspended till these Expedients have been tryd by you with the Assembly which by no Means Disolve, as it will lay the Ministry under greater difficultys than before, with regard to the Tenor of the New Writts to be Issud thereupon, A Point much more agreeable to be Compromisd amongst yourselves, than by Great Men here who may differ in Opinion, Verbum Sapienti Sat est.[4]

These are no More than My own thoughts on this Matter, however I do expect that you will have Directions on this Head.

As to Maccullohs Case it lys over till the Lords Assemble probably Mr H Walpole can give his Attendance, I wish I could give you Hopes of seeing a Speedy Issue & happy Conclusion to this Affair Some Way or Other, I have often told you the Improbability of Success in the Qt Rents of South Carolina, in the face of the Atorney G's Report for Macculloh, this Report is now further Confirmd by Mr Fazakerleys Oppinion & likewise for the Legality of his Commission in contradiction to Mr H Campbells opinion, the Stir that I have Made agt Macculloh had inducd the Lords of the Treasury again to take the Oppinion of the Attorney Genal As to the Legality of the Commission & his Oppinion is for the Legality however ill Pend it is, In opposition to Repeated oppinions you See its in Vain to Contend where our Claim in[5] only *Favour* & his *Right*.[6]

I have thought upon this Application in the Most Seriouse Manner & can See no Prospect of Relief but in the Manner I have heretofore proposd from North Carolina & in this you agreed by your Letter of the 15th Feby[7] but your last Letter of 14 April is not so Clear I am therefore brought to the Necessity of wanting your positive directions in this Affair before I proceed, in Case Maccullohs to act posse for S. Carolina which I dare say will be the Case, And in Our Application for North Car: I can See Difficultys; Horace Walpole has already Declard agt you Lord Granville very Shy in the Case Says you have Convicted yourself by taking your Quitrents account to 1760, that its your own fault these Arrears have accrued by not calling for the Quitrents of the Vast Tracts held by Land Jobbers, Lord Anson I find is a Freind to you in point of Character, but will not intermedle with other Matters[8] Adair too Much employd in Business[9] & the Bishop out of Favour,[10] from those Circumstances little is to be Expected from Freindship of Great Men.

The Affair of the Spanish Money is also a very Serious Matter[11] & there is a Necessity for an Union with Child, whatever your Opinion of him is Whatever your Fate as to Restoration is he is determind to keep what he has got & so is Innes he tells me, Child is to prepare a Case of this Matter for the Secretary of State Copy whereof shall be sent you.

I send you the Magazines from March to this Month & an Abstract of your Acct & beg your Attention to My concerns with the Assembly you will observe I have been a Volunteer ever Since last March & this is a Service not be gone upon without good Encouragment which you Seem to promise me Septr Next when they meet.

I shall persevere in your Service however Perplexd your Affairs are in hopes of a Suitable Recompence when they take a better turn, & keep up your Spirits I am always Yours.

LB, pp. 304–306. At the foot of this letter JA wrote: "One Copy by Capt Taylor to Cape Fear. Another by Virginia much at the Same time."

1. JA's last letter to Johnston was probably that of Aug. 1751 (see page 5). Johnston's letters to JA have not been found.

2. John Carteret (1690–1763), Earl Granville, was president of the Privy Council from June 1751 until his death. Granville inherited a proprietor's share of Carolina upon the death of his father in 1695, and in 1729 he was the only proprietor to refuse to sell his rights to the Crown. To compensate him for his claims, the Crown established the Granville District in North Carolina. The district comprised the

northern half of the colony and fully two-thirds of its population. Granville retained all proprietarial rights in the district except government.

Johnston's letter to Granville may have been that of 1 May 1751 (Bath Papers, Longleat, Wiltshire), which principally concerned the production of silk and hemp in North Carolina.

3. Letter not found.

4. Translation: a word to the wise is sufficient.

5. JA probably intended to write "is."

6. This paragraph concerns efforts by both Johnston and Henry McCulloh to collect the arrears of salary due them. Johnston's salary of £1,000 sterling per year (and the salaries of several other North Carolina officials) was to have been paid from the colony's quitrent revenues, but since Johnston was never able to secure quitrent legislation satisfactory to both the lower house and the imperial authorities in London, quitrent collection was sporadic and never sufficient to cover the expenses of the civil establishment. (By the time of Johnston's death in July 1752 his salary was £13,462.7.2 in arrears.) Johnston evidently hoped that his arrears might be paid out of South Carolina's quitrent revenues, but JA here informs him that that fund would be used to pay the arrears due to McCulloh for his service as commissioner for inspecting the quitrents in North and South Carolina, a position he had held since 1739 at an annual salary of £600 sterling plus £200 sterling for a clerk. The "Attorney G's Report for Macculoh" was a favorable ruling of 28 Oct. 1749 by Dudley Ryder on McCulloh's claim to his arrears, which had initially been denied by the Treasury and by Horatio Walpole, the auditor-general (*NCCR*, 5:631). The "Oppinion of the Attorney Genal As to the Legality of the Commission" was Ryder's report to the Treasury of 17 July 1750 confirming the legality and validity of McCulloh's commission but noting that "it might have been less Exceptionably penn'd in some parts of it" (T 1/342, fol. 54). Neither "Mr. Fazakerleys Opinion" nor "Mr. H Campbells opinion" have been found. (H. Campbell was probably Alexander Hume-Campbell.) For the outcome of McCulloh's case, see JA to Glen, 29 May 1752, pp. 36–37. More than £11,000 of the arrears owed to Johnston (and later to his heirs and creditors) was eventually paid from the South Carolina quitrents, although the balance was not finally paid off until 1798 (Greene, *Quest for Power*, 142–145; Labaree, *Royal Government*, 333; Bond, *Quit-Rent System*, 418–419; Charles G. Sellers, Jr., "Private Profits and British Colonial Policy: The Speculations of Henry McCulloh," *WMQ*, 3d ser., 8 [1951]: 542–545; Alan D. Watson, "Henry McCulloh: Royal Commissioner in South Carolina," *South Carolina Historical Magazine* 75 [1974]: 33–48).

Nicholas Fazakerley (ca. 1685–1767), barrister, and member of Parliament 1732–1767, was an authority on constitutional law who was occasionally retained in state trials.

7. Letter not found.

8. George Anson (1697–1762), first Baron Anson of Soberton, had become First Lord of the Admiralty in June 1751.

9. William Adair was the absentee secretary of Virginia and an English army agent closely allied by patronage and interest to the second earl of Albemarle, Virginia's titular governor.

10. Perhaps a reference to the Rt. Rev. Isaac Maddox (1697–1759), bishop of Worcester 1743–1759. See JA to Rutherfurd, 29 Dec. 1757, pp. 218–220.

11. See JA to Johnston, 13 July 1751, p. 3.

Enclosure: Account

Copy of his Acct as transmitted over in the Above Letter.

Govr Johnston to James Abercromby Dr

	£	s	d
For disbursments prior to Novr 1748 in consequence of his Letters to me	9	19	0
1748 Salary from Novr 1748 to Do 1749 as per Agreement	50	0	0
1749 Salary from Novr 1749 to Do 1750	50	0	0
Disbursements from Novr 1748 to Octr 1751 being 2 Years & 11 Months at Sundry times & Sundry Accounts	39	12	0
July 5th 1751 paid Insurance pro 4000 Dollars at $2\frac{1}{2}$ per cent & Brokerage	24	0	0
	173	11	0

Govr Johnston with Jas Abercromby Cr

	£	s	d
By Cash from Mr Hall[1]	10	10	
Decr 4th 1749 by Cash from Do	20	0	0
Janry 2d 1749 by Bills from Watson & Cairns Virginia	30	0	0
June 1751 By Cash at Sundry from Mr Bland out of the Silver remitted by Capt Innes	113	0	0
	173	10	0

LB, p. 306. In the letter book the debit and credit entries are in parallel columns.

1. Probably Enoch Hall (d. 1754 or 1755), who had served as chief justice of North Carolina from 1745 until he departed for England in 1749.

To James Glen

[7 November 1751]
To Govr Glen with Magazine Novr 17th 1751 per the Reverd Mr Martyn[1] per Capt Rogers.

LB, p. 307.

1. Probably the Rev. Charles Martyn (b. 1725), who studied at Balliol College, Oxford (A.B. 1745), was ordained in 1748, and received the King's Bounty for South Carolina in Sept. 1751. Martyn served Saint Andrew's Parish, near Charleston, from Mar. 1752 to Apr. 1770, when he left South Carolina. Martyn later served the Octagon Chapel, Bath, Eng.

To Gabriel Johnston

London Decr 9th 1751/2
By Mr Watson[1] have yours July 4th one of 3d Septr & one of the 4th of Same Month,[2] thereby I find you had not then reced any Letter from me Since the Febry before I cannot account for the Obstruction attending My Letters in their Way those of May 18th Inclosing one to the Committee with my Accounts Directed by Winyaw to Mr Dry the Vessel having arrivd early in Augt ought also to have been reced.[3]

By yours of July 4th you desire me to Pay Mr Symons his Bond for 200 of an Old Date, provided it can not be aplyd for Services in Offices about your Arrears,[4] I wish I could with Truth give you hopes of Sucess in this application, I have heretofore told you that after nine Conferences with Mr West,[5] that he Seemd to be of Opinion that, as your Application was for a Transmutation of your Appointments from one to Another Fund, he therefore was inclind to think it properly belongd to the Council, but at the Same time told me not to take that for An Answer final from him While I was laboring this Matter Macculloh gave in a Complaint against you for having Obstructed him in the Regulation of the Revenue of Q Rents,[6] to get the better of this Complt, & of Mr H——— Walpoles Representation agt you at the Treasury I found no Method So likely to Obviate the Effect of such Complaints, as to Move that both Macullos & your Representation might lye over till My Lords for Trade had made Report upon their Memorial, by this Means he who was before hand with you in his Solicitation for Arrears came to a Stand & the laboring are put upon him to make good his Allegations agt you; JAs Memorl was under Consideration three different Days before the Lds for Trade, then their Lordships calld in Mr H——— Walpole, I knew what his Sentiments were with Regard to you however I waited on him to prepare him, thereupon he told me that whatever were his Sentiments as to Macculloh that as to you they were much Worse in Matters of the Revenue, and that Whenever his oppinion was askd that it should be against you, and that for his own Justification that he had complaind agt you to the Treasury It hapend I think luckely for you that he could not Attend the Board the Long Vacation thereupon Follow'd, and Since the Meeting of the Boards Ld H———x has been out of Order & till lately could not attend after the Holydays shall renew My application at that Board.

I do not think that by this Suspension your Cause has Sufferd, Mr S Hunt[7] is now dead & thereby Mac: may abate in Interest as well as in his Resentment to you, and in Case he does not press his Memorl before the Board of Trade by that means we may Escape mr Horace Walpoles who most certainly if calld upon will be against you & the Board will enter a Contest with him on yours especially in Matters of the Revenue within his own Office, his appearance therefore at the Board of Trade had therefore given your Solicitation for Arrears a Blow in no shape to be overcome in So far therefore this Delay has Favourd you & perhaps we may hear no More of the Complt before the Board of Trade. Thus far is present Situation of your Affairs, perhaps a few Weeks may give me more Light into this Matter after confering with Mr West which I shall endeavour to Do when Parlty Money Matters are Adjusted.

I have often told you the Difficultys that I had to get over from the Priority & Legality of S Car: Claim to the Q Rents to So. Car &

desird your Directions as to an Apli: for those of No: Car. Now Since *that time I have Some conferences with Ld. G*———*e*[8] *& as I cannot* from *thence* take *any great Incouragment to go to Council I am* Resolvd *in the first Place to See the Result of my Transactions with* Mr West at the Treasury & this I shall proceed in without Delay & shall be glad to have this Matter Settled in Some Shape or Other, and indeed in any Shape for you, was the Case my own I could not have it more at heart but besides the Difficultys that attends this matter from its own Circumstances I have others to Encounter; Capt Bonilla whom Mr Watson brought with him has already applyd to the Sp: Minister for Restitution from you. Mr Watson is your Freind in this Matter, yet as he is concernd for the Spaniards he can go no further to Serve you, than is Consistent with his Concerns with Bonilla, he tells me he has Represented your Case & that your Services to the S. Minister far Excceded your Reward of 5000 Dollars which Sum that Minister knows is all that came to your Share.[9]

Finding this Negociation going on I thought it fit to remind the Secrety of State Now Ld Holderness of your Letter whereby you Refer to Mr Child[10] & to acqt his Lordship that he was now in England & might be calld upon to Invalidate Mr Bonillas Memorial when it appears in publick; I do not find that Mr C——d bears you any ill will in this Matter, however the Hint you gave me is proper for I find Mr Watson has no good opinion of him & has engagd me not to let him know what passes between us, Child does not think proper to appear in this Matter till calld upon & in this he may Judge Right.

I am not able to Discover the turn that My Lords for Trade will give to their Report, but I am Sorry to find that Lord P——t[11] is alone for a Repeal & that too without any Expedient being previously Settled, this I acquaint you of in Confidence, as its not only Premature but improper from Such a Channel to be Communicated to the Committee.

Having done everything to Suport these Laws I must now agree in Opinion with you to lye by & Wait the Report from the Board of trade without pressing the Matter & the More because I am affraid Such Report will be against us in the End.[12]

I shall Solicit the Appointment of Messrs Dawson & Craven probably what you have Said to the Lords about Others having promisd to apply for Mandamus's & Such having been So good as their Word may Induce their Lordships to give Dawson & Craven the Rank of the rest, this Matter I shall Consider of because it may otherwise create Disturbance & Anemositys in your Comme which would not be for your Interest.[13]

As to Soliciting Leave I am advisd by Ld. G——e to Suspend that till I hear from you further, because Lord G——e told me that he knows of four Persons who would gladly Step into your Berth for these Considerations I hope I shall be Justefyd in Delaying this Application till I hear from you further upon it.[14]

Herewith comes magazines for Octr Novr & Decr[15] I am Yours &c.

LB, pp. 310–312. The date is properly 1751. Sent "Via Virginia." An earlier version of this letter, crossed out, is on pp. 307–308 of the letter book. Substantive differences between the two versions are accounted for in notes to the present letter.

1. The draft of this letter refers to Watson as "of Virginia."

2. Letters not found.

3. JA's letter of 18 May [1751] and its enclosure have not been found. The earlier version of this letter indicates that the letter of 18 May was "Directed to Mr Drys Care at Cape Fear by Winyaw in South Carolina."

Mr. Dry may have been William Dry (1720–1781), son of William Dry (d. 1740). The elder Dry was a former Speaker of the South Carolina Commons House of Assembly who moved to Cape Fear in the 1730s.

4. The draft of this letter reads "In yours of 4th July, you Mention the Payment of Mr. Symmons's Bond 200 Principal with Many years Interest, Unless that your Money can be more Advantageously Applyd for your Interest here you Did right to qualefy your Orders in this Manner considering the present State of your Affairs, for if that Payment were Made, there would not Remain wherewithall to Make a Genteel Offer for Services, According to the Turn that your Concerns may take." Symons (or Symmons) has not been identified.

5. James West (1704–1772) was secretary of the Treasury 1746–1752 and joint secretary 1752–1756 and 1757–1762.

6. JA may refer to Henry McCulloh's "reply to the Answer given by Governor Johnston to the several Articles of Complaint contained in Mr. McCulloh's Memorial," which was submitted to the Board of Trade and received on 12 June 1751 (*NCCR*, 4:1137–1152).

7. Not identified, but see JA to Glen, 25 Jan. 1752, pp. 26–27, n. 3.

8. Probably Earl Granville.

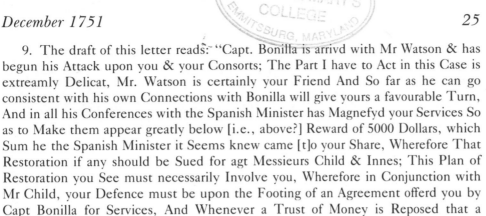

9. The draft of this letter reads: "Capt. Bonilla is arrivd with Mr Watson & has begun his Attack upon you & your Consorts; The Part I have to Act in this Case is extreamly Delicat, Mr. Watson is certainly your Friend And So far as he can go consistent with his own Connections with Bonilla will give yours a favourable Turn, And in all his Conferences with the Spanish Minister has Magnefyd your Services So as to Make them appear greatly below [i.e., above?] Reward of 5000 Dollars, which Sum he the Spanish Minister it Seems knew came [t]o your Share, Wherefore That Restoration if any should be Sued for agt Messieurs Child & Innes; This Plan of Restoration you See must necessarily Involve you, Wherefore in Conjunction with Mr Child, your Defence must be upon the Footing of an Agreement offerd you by Capt Bonilla for Services, And Whenever a Trust of Money is Reposed that a Consideration is due & the Question will then turn as to the Quantum, which we may Claim that the Law Do determine, in the Ordinary Courts, Or before the King in Council, In short I apprehend that Mr Child & you must Act conjunctly at first Seting out in this Affair, & in case I find that you are like to be treated with a high hand & in a high Strain, then & not till then it will be necessary for me to call particularly on Mr Child so when you have referrd this Matter by your Lre to the D of Bedford."

10. In his letter to Bedford of 2 May 1751, Johnston stated that "Mr. Child is now on His way to London, and will fully inform your Grace of the whole transaction" (*NCCR*, 4:1308–1309).

11. Earl Granville, the lord president of the Privy Council.

12. The draft of this letter reads: "As to the Laws, I have left nothing undone that could be Attempted to give this Matter a favourable Turn, and I have got an answer from My Lord P——t (viz) That when the Report comes from the Lords of Trade That it shall be Immediatly carried into Execution & that these Laws shall not Exist An Hour in Suspence, After this Peremptory Judgt I can do no More And this being the Ne plus Ultra I now must Leave it with the Board of Trade, I dare not write to the Committee in so Explicit a Manner, however you in your Discretion may Signefie to them what they are to Expect, finding that these Laws were not to Live an Hour, It was Natural to Ask what the Gover was to do, as the principal Matter of Debate was Still open, I was Ansd that you must Agree amongst yourselves there & whatever So Agreed might be hereafter approv'd of at home. But as to Saving of these Laws after the Officers of the Crown had Reported agt them, that it was not in the Nature of Bussiness to Do it by any Intermediate Expedient; But this I knew had been done in many Cases, & therefore I endeavourd to Enforce it in Our Case, what turn the Lords of Trade who thrô the whole of this Controversy have been Difficulted may in the End give to their Report against these Laws I cannot Say, however till their Report shews it Self I can Say no more on this head."

13. In a letter to the Board of Trade of 3 Sept. 1751, Johnston confessed that he was "at a loss where to find Members for an Upper House. There has been such a mortality among the Gentlemen of the Council for these three years past, that there remains only two of the original number [twelve]." Johnston went on to say that he had previously recommended several men to the Board, but that the men did not apply for writs of mandamus as they had promised. Johnston then recommended

John Dawson (ca. 1690–1761 or 1762), a member of the lower house intermittently 1734–1752, and James Craven (d. 1755), a member of the lower house 1740–1746, who he assured the Board would "immediately take out their Commissions" (*NCCR*, 4:1074–1075). The Board of Trade read Johnston's letter on 15 Apr. 1752, at which time it proposed to the regents that James Hasell, James Innes, John Rutherfurd, Francis Corbin, John Swann, John Dawson, James Craven, Lewis de Rosset, and John Rieusset be appointed to the Council (*JBT*, 9:297). Warrants appointing the nine men were issued on 28 May 1752 (*APC*, 4:793).

In the earlier version of this letter JA had written: "I shall solicit the Cases of Messieurs Dawson & Craven for the Council So Soon as I find that Orders are come for Payment of Fees on Dawsons Account, Mr Watson has Directions to Pay for Mr Cravens but after all the Enquiry that I have made I can find no Orders from Mr Dawson."

14. In the draft of this letter JA had written: "You are not Aware of the Danger that may Attend an Application to the King for Leave to Come home as Matters are now Circumstanced & therefore by the Advice of your Freinds I shall suspend it my application until I hear further from you especially as A Delay of this Application can be of no prejudice to you Since you say you are not to make use of Such your Leave when Allowed."

15. In the draft of this letter JA indicated that the magazines were sent "per Virginia to Watson & Cairnes Care."

To James Glen

Janry 25th 1751/2

Herewith comes Lre from Mr Sharpe[1] at the Same time News paper that Concerns you, very disagreeable Accts relating to the Indians from other Hands are daily put into the Papers but as you take no notice of them by you I hope they are false.[2]

Mr Caverly tells me that he is advisd to Appeal from the Sentence not only as to the Matter in issue but also as to the Costs of Suit, as you have acknowledged none of mine relating to Capt Wilson I fear they have Miscaryd, a Statute of Bankrupcy is now taken out agt him,[3] When you have appointed a Proper Person to receive your Salary you will give Such Person Directions to pay my Establishment 12 Months Whereof due last Novr.

Contest between Ld Halefax & Ld Holderness not determind as yet generaly beleivd that the first Comr of the Board for Trade will carry these Po[i]nts (viz) the Recomdation of all Govrs & Officers in the Plantations 2dly to take up Matters & Report thereon without any previous Reference, but not to have Access to the Interior Closet.[4]

Ld Granville Without leting me know this Intention has brought about a Coalition in the Agency between Mr Crokat & me,[5] I have enclosd Copy of My Acct to the Come of Correspondence amounting to 107.19. 1 on which I beg your Interposition.[6]

The Trustees of Georgia have Surrenderd their Charter & the Parlt have voted 4000 to the Trustees to pay off all Scores.[7] I am

JA

LB, p. 314. Sent "per Capt Mackenzie or Pearson."

1. Letter not found; probably Joshua Sharpe.

2. JA probably alludes to Glen's relations with the Choctaw Indians. In 1746 the Choctaw revolted against their French allies, but, largely through Glen's mismanagement in supplying the Choctaw with arms, ammunition, and trade goods, half the Choctaw towns had returned to French allegiance by the end of 1749, and by 1752 the entire nation had returned to the French interest.

3. In Dec. 1751 or Jan. 1752 one Alexander Wilson, a Westminster banker, went bankrupt (*Gentleman's Magazine* 22 [1752]: 45); it is not known whether this was the same man as "Capt Wilson."

4. See JA to Glen, 6 Apr. 1752, pp. 32–33.

5. James Crokatt (d. 1777) was a merchant in Charleston for many years before he left for England in 1737. "With his Carolina fortune he established himself as the foremost 'Carolina merchant' in London. On his arrival in London he was referred to as 'a Scotch Jew Lately come from So. Carolina.'" Crokatt served as South Carolina's agent in London from 1749 to 1756 (*Laurens Papers*, 1:2n).

The nature of JA's "Coalition in the Agency" with Crokatt has not been determined, but the agreement was canceled by 6 Apr. 1752. See JA to Glen, 9 Mar., p. 31, and 6 Apr. 1752, pp. 32–33.

6. Enclosure not found.

7. On 15 Jan. 1752 the House of Commons read a representation and petition from the Georgia Trustees stating that the Crown had "been graciously pleased to accept of the offer of the petitioners to surrender their trust," and praying that the House "enable them to defray the expences incurred by them since the last grant." On 21 Jan. the committee of the whole House resolved to appropriate £4,000 for this purpose (Leo Francis Stock, *Proceedings and Debates of the British Parliament Respecting North America*, 5 vols. [Washington, D.C., 1924–1941], 5:518, 519), and the appropriation became part of the supply bill of 26 Mar. 1752 (25 George II, chap. 25).

To Gabriel Johnston

Dr Sir   London Febry 18th 1752
I have reced yours of Septr 15th[1] wherein you blame me very
unjustly for being Unsteady not only in your Service but also in that
of the Province I wish to God you were here on the Spot yourself
to Witness the Difficultys that have from the first Setting out
attended these Matters, I impute a good deal of the Peevishness of
that Letter to your being out of order when it was Wrote; I could
by giving my[self] less trouble than I have heretofore done, that is
to Say by not writing till the Issue of Matters depending are finally
Determind, by this means I could [avoid] Reproof of being Sometimes Contradictory in my Letters, & Unsteady in my Negociations.
Whenever that happens the Fault is not mine, going thro So many
Chanels in the Course of my Negociations I meet with Variety of
Opinions, Men in Office & in high Office, changing Sentiments
from Causes that I cannot Discover, I must therefore take things as
they come to me, & by being too Earnest in my Correspondence I
may on Some Occasion to you, for from the first Cause of such
alteration in Sentiments appear as you say too volatile, however I
have always thought it the most freindly way to write to you in the
Strain that things appear in when I do write, & to write often as
Occasions offer.
    Mr West has given me for Answer that he will take Mr Pelhams
opinion So Soon as Parlty Affairs are further advanced, and
however little g[r]ound this is got yet its more than I have hetherto
been able to get.[2]
    Bonillas Papers being come over, the Spanish Minister has
applyd for Restoration, Mr Child has been calld upon, has had a
Conference & is to Commit to Writing the State of the Case in
which I am to Assist him.[3]
    The Laws Still lye over Owing I apprehend to the Difficulty of
their Reporting thereon, I cannot in point of Office press a Report
that I have no ground to Expect will be for me.[4]
    Whatever is the Issue of these Matters I have nothing to lay at my
Door having done every thing in my Power &c.

LB, pp. 312–313. Sent "Under Mr. Watsons Cover to Virginia."

1. Letter not found.

2. Henry Pelham (ca. 1695–1754), brother of the duke of Newcastle, was First Lord of the Treasury and Chancellor of the Exchequer from 1743 until his death.

The "Answer" JA received from Secretary of the Treasury James West concerned Johnston's arrears of salary.

3. See JA to Johnston, 13 July 1751, p. 3, n. 3.

4. For these two laws, see JA to North Carolina Committee of Correspondence, 7 Oct. 1751, p. 8, n. 2.

To James Glen

March 2nd [1752]

Send Magazines for Janry & Febry, tell him of the verdict that Capt Wilson is found a Bankrupt; that he will Pay 10s per Pound, Tell him that he will probably have letter from the Lords for Trade declaring their New Powers,[1] that Ld Adt often asks after him;[2] that I shall send him the Bill relating to the Forfeited Estates when it passes.[3]

LB, p. 314. Sent "per Capt Mackenzie."

1. See JA to Glen, 6 Apr. 1752, pp. 32–33.

2. JA may refer to the lord advocate, the principal law officer of the Crown in Scotland, answering to the attorney general in England.

3. "An Act for annexing certain forfeited estates in Scotland to the crown unalienably; and for making satisfaction to the lawful creditors thereupon; and to establish a method of managing the same; and applying the rents and profits thereof, for the better civilizing and improving the Highlands of Scotland; and preventing disorders there for the future" (25 George II, chap. 41).

To the Committee of Correspondence of North Carolina

March 2d 1752

Have none from you Since that of April 20th Last,[1] I am at a loss to know my Situation with the Public, however had any thing Material hapend in your Affairs had Informd you.

No Report as yet made by My Lords for Trade.

However disagreeable it is to me to have things long in Suspence yet when I consider how the Case Stands I must not press their Report, because it may be agt me, As the Laws Operate it is my Business to lay by, I have done every thing in my Power to prevent a Report without Concomitant Measures, Shall send the Bill when Enacted concerning the Probat of Wills Extended to the Planta-tions.[2] I am Always

LB, p. 315. At the foot of this letter JA wrote: "Original Went to Govr Johnston Via Virginia."

1. Letter not found.

2. See JA to North Carolina Committee of Correspondence, 29 May 1752, p. 36.

To Gabriel Johnston

March 2d [1752]

According to my last I now Inclose you the State of the Case as given by Mr Child to the Secretary of State[1] to which I have nothing to add on that head till I hear further I have reced yours of 13 Novr Inclosing letters that passd between you & Mr Child[2] & shall take no Notice of them Unless Mr Child alters his Conduct with regard to you, which I have No reason at present to find fault with; Considering the Uncertainty of success In Our Applications I would have you reconcile yourself to Disapointments, and en-deavour [to] Make yourself as easy as you can in the Enjoyment of the Govert as long as you can in the Situation that Affairs are now in; I am affraid it will require greater Interest than yours to Put matters on a better Footing as to the Instruments of Government; I have not the Smalest hopes to get any thing from British Funds, neither have any Hopes of Releif from South Carolina, and with regard to a Special warrant from the Treasury On the Funds of North Carolina I have got no Answer as yet: In Short to Speak honestly my own Sentiments I am affraid that your Interest is too Weak to Overcome Difficultys in Money Matters; However I shall carry on my solicitations till I have Mr Wests Final Answer; you will See my Sentiments on the Case of the Acts of Assembly; I can See no Reason why you should alter your former Sentiments for my laying by, as a Confirmation cannot be got Surely It is not proper that I should Press a Report that may produce a Repeal, by which we shall lose what we are now in Possession of; Its mor Macculochs Business than mine to Drive this Matter, the Attorney & Solicitors Report being more in his Favour than in ours; however I have Submitted my Self to the Legislature if they think it prudent for me to Press A final Report I shall Do it. I am

PS   Your Expectations are from another Quarter but Pray Consider that Money Matters are from the Treasury alone, the Matter of transposing your Establisht from one Fund to another vizt from North to S: Carolina may be a Matter of State as well as Money but as I have already told you this Seems reservd for your Successor whoever he is I cannot Say[3] Whatever may be the Event of this Solicitation for Arrears in the Mean while it will always give Ld G———[4] who wishes you very well an opportunity of Pleading Possession of the Govert at least till Arrears are paid off, I shall rest it at the Treasury, having begd Mr Wests help At the Council, but find that I must persist at the Treasury as the proper Board.

LB, pp. 315–316. At the foot of p. 315, after "I am" and before the catchword "PS," which is the first word on p. 316, JA wrote: "Magazines for Janry & Febry. I have no Line from the Comme for Many Months." This passage may be part of the PS, or it may be JA's note to himself. Sent "per Virginia enclosed Lre to the Committee," undoubtedly the preceding letter.

1. Not found.

2. Neither Johnston's letter to JA nor its enclosures have been found.

3. JA was correct; satisfactory arrangements for the salary of the governor of North Carolina were not worked out until Johnston's successor took office. See JA to Dinwiddie, 20 Oct. 1752, p. 56, n. 13.

4. Earl Granville.

To James Glen (not sent)

March 9th 1752

I am affraid my lettre desiring your Countenance to my Demand on the Public pro Disbursments in the Case of Paper Currency,[1] which I was desird to transmit came too late for this years Estimate, however I must desire yor Remem[b]rance of it.

I hope this Affair of Paper Currency is now over unless the

Obstinacy of the People of Rhode Island, who I am lately told have not reced the Act of Parlt, with that respect that is due, Should again revive the Contest & Extend it furth[er] than the views of the Act lately passd.[2]

Whatever turn this Matter may hereafter take there will be a Cooperation between Mr C——t & me in behalf of your Province, we are now come to a good understanding together & by Ld Granvilles recomdation An agreements concluded on the Same Plan as between Mr Fury & me,[3] And I hope that our Freind in Carolina will Act on the Same Principles of Agreement as we do here in what relates to the Public Affairs of your Govert.

It Concerns you to know that Capt Wilson &ca as before told him

LB, p. 316. At the foot of this letter are the following two "NB" notations, the first probably a memo from JA to himself, the second certainly so: "NB I Sent this Lre open to Mr. Crokat to be forwarded by him & also one to Dr Bull to the Same purpose per Capt Mackenzie. NB the above Letter did not go See that of April 6th 1752."

1. JA to Glen, 7 Oct. 1751, pp. 12–14.

2. See Elisha R. Potter and Sidney S. Rider, "Some Account of the Bills of Credit or Paper Money of Rhode Island, 1710 to 1786," *Rhode Island Historical Tracts*, No. 8 (Providence, R.I., 1880).

3. Peregrine Fury, of London, was South Carolina's agent from 1731 to 1749.

JA had served as a special agent assisting Fury in 1742–1743. During the War of Jenkins' Ear, the South Carolina Assembly drew up a petition to the king requesting that three companies be sent to the defense of the colony. JA (at that time attorney general of South Carolina), Capt. William Livingston, and Alexander Vander Dussen traveled to England to press the petition. Not until 1746 did Vander Dussen return to South Carolina with some troops. The agreement between JA and Fury has not been traced, but JA's letter to Glen of 6 Apr. 1752 (below) suggests that the agreement between JA and Crokatt called for JA to be compensated by Crokatt.

To James Glen

Dr Sir   April 6th 1752

At last comes the Declaration of the Powers of the Lords for Trade, And thereby you will See, that the grand Point Aimd at (vizt) Access to the King in all Matters relative to their Office is not containd in this Order of Council, on the contrary it is expressly Declar'd to be thro' the Secretarys of State.[1]

You have likewise the Magazine for last Month, And as acquainted you in one of my former Letters that Mr Crokat had come to an Agreement with me, in the Agency, Now this Agreement is Cancelld; & I have made him Pay me So long as this Agreement did Exist.

The King is now on the Sea for Holland and till news of his Arrival, the Ministers or rather the Regency are in the Country.[2]

Mr Atkins is lately come to Town & I find that he interests himself warmly in opposing a Reward to McNaire for his Services, But, as the Lords for Trade have reported in some Degree in favour of MacNaire, perhaps he may be considerd in some Small Matter of Money personally to himself; this I find, has been a strong Sort of Negociation between Mr C——t & him, And as they disagreed about the Distribution of the Reward when obtaind, McNaire has made No Secret to tell it.[3]

The point aimd at by Mr Atkins is to discover the Imposition put upon the Kings Ministers, by Solicitations taken up from Partial Journals of the Assembly only, And not as a House of Assembly but carryd on at the desire of a few Members of that House only, but likewise that the Agent had join'd his Provincial Authority to this Solicitation without Orders for so doing from the Governor or Council, this with an Insinuation that the Money to be granted was to come into the Agents Pocket for A Carolina Debt due by McNaires Partner bears no favourable appearance, how it will end in point of Reward to McNaire I cannot tell, but I am apt to think if Mr Atkins can Establish his Facts, that Neither the Agent nor McNaire have either Merit or Reward to Expect from hence.

LB, pp. 315A–315B (an unnumbered sheet, smaller than the letter-book pages, inserted between pp. 315 and 316).

1. The Order in Council of 11 Mar. 1752 represented a partial victory for Halifax in his campaign to be named to the cabinet and to augment the power and prestige of the Board of Trade. Although he failed to secure appointment as secretary of state, Halifax did make the proposals that formed the basis of the order, which directed the Board to "Apply themselves to a faithfull and vigorous Execution and Discharge of all the Trusts and Powers vested in them by their Commission under the Great Seal"; gave the Board control over patronage by granting it the right to nominate all colonial officials except those belonging to the Customs and Admiralty departments; authorized the Board to draft all commissions, warrants, and instructions for colonial officials; and, perhaps most important, named the Board as the "One Channel"

through which correspondence from the colonial governors was to pass (*APC*, 4:154–156). The last-mentioned decision was communicated to the colonial governors in an additional instruction of 14 Apr. 1752 (Labaree, *Royal Instructions*, 2:748–749).

2. On 30 Mar. 1752, the day before he left London, George II (1683–1760) appointed fourteen men to serve as "lords justices, for the administration of the government" (regents) during his absence. The list is printed in *Gentleman's Magazine* 22 (1752): 188.

3. Choctaw Indian trader Charles McNair claimed that in 1747 Glen had authorized him to give presents to the Indians and had assured him that he would be reimbursed by the government. McNair then distributed the goods, but, when he petitioned the assembly for reimbursement, Glen was called to account by the assembly for not having secured its prior approval of the expenditure. Glen then denied having given McNair any such direction. After the assembly rejected his petition, McNair traveled to England and petitioned the Crown for reimbursement of the expenses he had incurred in winning over the Choctaw to the British interest. Councillor Edmund Atkin (d. 1761), who had been in England since 1750, opposed McNair's claims, while agent James Crokatt supported McNair in hearings before the Board of Trade, allegedly because Crokatt was owed money by Charleston merchant Matthew Roche, McNair's former partner. The Board of Trade heard evidence on 26 and 27 Feb. and 18 Mar. 1752, and on 19 Mar. 1752 recommended to Holderness that McNair be allowed £1,000 as "a Reward due to his Services" (T 1/348, fol. 25; *JBT*, 9:280–282, 292–293, 295).

To Gabriel Johnston

April 15th 1752

Yesterday had yours of Febry 14th & one inclosd to the Earl of Holdernesse[1] it gives me great pleasure to hear of your recovery, from the Strain of your lettres for Some time by gone could discover your Spirits were low.

In Consequence of your last Lres I fixd my Solicitation for your arrears from No Carolina alone & Since the Parlt Prorogation,[2] have attended Mr West regularly twice a Week & altho he has promisd me from time to time to Consider with me in what Maner to State your Case to the Board I have not been able to do it hetherto, shall continue my Attendance, Have desird that the Arrears due to the Crown may be appropriated for payment of your Arrears, the Overplus if any hereafter there may be above payment of the Annual shall also go towards your Arrears And that a Warrant shall Issue for Ascertaining the Special sum due to you according to the State of Account now before the Board, the Same to be made payable to you & your Assigns; to this Mr West told me the Sum was too great for the Treasurys Disposal that the King must declare his Approbation thereon.

Till this Matter is determind shall do Nothing about the Quitrents & Recr Generals Demand of 5 per Cent over & above his now allowance;[3] Maculloh has now confind his Application to South Caro: Quitrents only; I shall endeavour to prevent any Reference to Mr H. Wal: One Circumstance might forward our Application (vizt) Maccullohs geting his Arrears from S Carolina, as a Precedent for Ours from N.C.

Mr. Hasels has Informd me that the Northern Counties now intend to apply for two Members only this was So Material Intelligence that I communicated the Same to the Lds for Trade, his Lettre of the 22d of Febry if this proves true it will Satisfie their Lordships that the Impeachment of the Laws was ill grounded.[4]

The Lords for Trade are now Adjusting the Council and to prevent those heretofore appointed by you from being postponed I have undertaken payment of Fees for them which will amount to a great Sum about 30 per each of them.[5]

Mr Hall is at New biggon[6] have heard nothing of him nor from him for Some Months, I send you Magazines for March & am always &c

JA

LB, pp. 316–317. Sent "per Virginia."

1. Johnston's letter to JA has not been found. His letter to Holderness, dated 14 Feb. 1752, is CO 5/13, fol. 309.

2. On 26 Mar. 1752.

3. The receiver general of North Carolina was John Rutherfurd (for whom see JA to North Carolina Committee of Correspondence, 13 Aug. 1752, pp. 43–44). His allowance was 10 percent of the receipts.

4. James Hasell's letter to JA has not been found, nor do the journals of the Board of Trade record the receipt of either the letter or a summary of its contents from JA.

Hasell (d. 1785), a native of England, had immigrated to the Cape Fear area by about 1734. He was a planter, chief justice of North Carolina for several years, a councillor 1749–1775, and acting governor for two months in 1771. Hasell was a loyalist whose estate was confiscated during the Revolution, but he was allowed to remain at home unmolested.

5. Johnston's instructions empowered him to fill any vacancies in the Council caused by the death or absence of members by making appointments "to the number of seven and no more" (Labaree, *Royal Instructions*, 1:52). Johnston had appointed James Hasell to the Council on 2 Oct. 1749, James Innes on 5 July 1750, and John Rutherfurd, Francis Corbin, and John Swann on 26 Dec. 1751 (*NCCR*, 4:961–962, 1041–1042, 1245). For the Board's "Adjusting" of the Council, see JA to Johnston, 9 Dec. 1751, pp. 25–26, n. 13.

6. Newbiggin is a town in Westmorland Co. (now in Cumbria), Eng.

To the Committee of Correspondence of North Carolina

Gentlemen of the Committee   May 29th 1752
  Our Affairs remaining with My Lords for Trade in Statu quo, nothing new presents for your Information, agreeable therefore to my last, I now Inclose two Acts of Parlt which were passed last Session (viz) one in relation to the Attestation of Wills,[1] the other for continuation of the Praemium on Naval Stores,[2] and I am very Sincerly Gentlemen Your Most Obedt Sert

                                                                        Ja Abercromby

LB, p. 323. Sent "per Mr. Watson."

1. "An Act for avoiding and putting an end to certain doubts and questions, relating to the attestation of wills and codicils, concerning real estates, in that part of Great Britain called England, and in his majesty's colonies and plantations in America" (25 George II, chap. 6).

2. See JA to North Carolina Committee of Correspondence, 7 Oct. 1751, p. 9, n. 7.

To James Glen

                                                                        May 29th 1752
  A Box from the Plantation Office, and 2 letters from Council Office comes with this,[1] likewise the Act relative to the Highlands,[2] give Joy of Miss Glens Marriage[3] tell him of MacCullohs Dismission,[4] tell him of Mcnaires Warrant for 1000£[5] & recom-

mend punctuality in Advices on Indian Affairs Send Magazine for April.

JA

LB, p. 323.

1. One of these enclosures may have been a circular letter of 28 Apr. 1752 from the Board of Trade to certain royal governors (CO 324/15, pp. 314–318) transmitting two additional instructions, one requiring them to correspond in future with the Board of Trade (see JA to Glen, 6 Apr. 1752, pp. 33–34, n. 1), and the other requiring them to produce a revised code of laws (Labaree, *Royal Instructions*, 1:167, 2:748–749).

2. See JA to Glen, 2 Mar. 1752, p. 29, n. 3.

3. Glen's sister, Margaret (d. 1772), had married South Carolinian John Drayton (1713?–1779) in Feb. 1752.

4. For the background of McCulloh's claim to arrears of salary, see JA to Johnston, 7 Oct. 1751, pp. 16–18. McCulloh's "dismission," as JA calls it, was in fact a Treasury warrant of 24 Mar. 1752 issued to George Saxby (d. 1786), receiver general of South Carolina, ordering him to pay McCulloh £6,200 sterling from the colony's quitrents "in Satisfaction and discharge of all his pretensions and Demands on account of" his appointment. The amount represented the arrears due McCulloh for service from 16 May 1739 to 16 May 1748 at £800 per year (£7,200), less £1,000 he had already received (*NCCR*, 5:615–616).

5. See JA to Glen, 6 Apr. 1752, pp. 32–33.

To Gabriel Johnston

June 5th 1752

In my last of the 6th April I acquainted you that I should persevere in my Solicitations at the Treasury till I had an Answer,[1] I am now to Inform you, that after many Interviews with Mr West before I could engage him to consider your Case Attentively, last Week was appointed for a Meeting and then the Inclosed State of your Case was considerd by him,[2] and thereon I have his Oppinion (vizt) That your best Way for Redress is by procuring Debentures from the Auditor, for that a New Warrant from the Lords of the Treasury can give you no More Aid than what you already have by the Kings former Warrant; and that it is to no Manner of Purpose for you to Expect Releif from any other Fund than from what is now appropriated to you by the Kings Establishment,[3] and that Debentures will best answer all the Purposes of this your Application & will not only Assertain your Demand but are also Assignable; This Opinion I communicated to a Person of long Experience in the Treasury & whose Services I had Engaged for Valuable Considerations, and he entirely agrees, that the Kings Warrant gives you all the Powers necessary to recover your Arrears provided there is where with all in the Fund, And that upon being refusd Debentures from the Deputy Auditor in N: Carolina[4] that you ought to Compell him by an Action at Law.

Had I desird a Reference of the Case to Mr Walpole I might have got it & indeed Mr West hinted that it should be referrd for Mr Walpoles oppinion I was too well acquaintedwith his Sentiments on this head to run the risk of a formal Reference to him in point of Office, I therefore parryd this Notion and thought it best to take Walpole in another way.

I waited upon him not as Complaining of himself but of his Deputy for refusing Debentures to the Officers in general,[5] after throwing out many Objections in the Usual Strain he referrd me to his Deputy, and tho by very prevailing Arguments I found means to engage his Deputy in my Way of thinking as to the Justice of the General Case of Debentures to the Officers, yet the Report made by the Deputy was rejected and in such a Manner as leaves me no room to hope for Success in Orders from him to his Deputy to Grant Debentures.

His principal Objections are that, the Recrs Accounts are not Ballanced 2d That Debentures are only to be granted after knowing what Money the Recr has in his hands, and 3d that Debentures are to be granted only pro rata to the Several Officers according to the Cash in hand; and denys that you have a right to have any Preference in payments; these Objections have Determind me now to take the Attorney Generals Opinion upon the Words of the Establishment as to the Preference due to you, & I have accordingly applyd to the Treasury for Copy of the Establishment;[6] And if I find the Attorney clear that you ought from the priority of your Commission according as I apprehend from the express Words of the Establishment of Salarys to be first *Fully* paid I shall on the Strength of this Oppinion make another

Attack upon him for Debentures; And in the mean time I would Advise you to try what you can do with his Deputy without taking any Notice of his Principals opinion; I am inform'd that he has no express Clause or Mode of Instruction to refuse Debentures, therefore by a Secret & proper Managment you may bring him to grant you Debentures for your *Arrears* which I am absolutly clear in opinion will Assertain your Debt and to you & your Assigns as much as any New Warrant from the Treasury can do; And it would Seem to me that as you have received from time to time Moneys and none of the other Officers have reced any, from hence it would appear that a Preference is allowd to you as to the Annual Payments & whereof may not the Same be done as to your Arrears And to Obviate the Objection made by Mr W——le that the Accounts are not Ballancd; wherefore in order to Discover what is due to the Crown, I think the Recr should Ballance the Account upon the Rent Roll as it now stands, No Matter whether the Rent Roll is or is not Exact, Let him ascertain the Arrears due by the Tenants as they Stand charged on the Roll, and according to Such Ballance apply for Debentures, by this means the Auditors grand Objection as you will see in the Case of Mr Childs Certificate now sent you,[7] and likewise Mr Walpolcs Objection as well as that made At the Treasury, that they can not tell how the Fund stands, will be remov'd, It does not concern the Crown whether the Arrears due by the Tenants are exactly Stated or not, Since you are to take those Arrears and Discharge the Crown, And in this Way I think you are most likely to Succeed, the Case being desperate, the only consideration now is how to make the Most of it, and by geting an Assignment of the Arrears due to the Crown which is to be done by Debentures, Some thing may be made by Way of compromising the Debt with the Tenants in Arrears, this Way of Negociating Arrears I am informd has answerd well in other Provinces particularly Pensilvania & Maryland and where Money is not to be got then their Bonds have been taken and may be taken in your Case in the Kings Name & assignd to you by the Recr, or they may be in your own Name which I should rather approve of, In Short you must exert your own Influence and Authority with the Officers of the Revenue as Macculloh is now out of your Way, And after having done your Utmost with them, let me know the Event, in the mean time according to the Attorneys opinion I shall proceed with Mr

Walpole Or at the Treasury; but so far as we have gone already with him may be best kept Secret.

By an Associated Interest Macullohs Creditors assisted by Lord Bathurst[8] (as I am told), A Warrant for 6000 from South Carolina Q Rents is granted to Macculloh, In Consideration whereof by Express Words of the Warrant he Surrenders his Office & all Claim whatever on the Crown to or Under the Said Office;[9] this Warrant comes far Short of his Demand, however they could make no more of it, this poor Wretch after all the Mischief & Confusion he has made in these Provinces is now reduced to the utmost distress, is obligd to have Lord Bathursts Protection from Arrests As his Menial Servant, but I am told he has brought himself into Such Difficultys by deceiving his Creditors in the application of this Warrant that they have Writts out against him in Most Places of Note particularly the Sea Ports all over Britain, and Intend an Application to that Lord to withdraw his Protection; from the Situation of his Affairs and of his health, I fancy you will be soon relieved from his future Negociations; And when I reflect on the extraordinary trouble and Expence that the Man has put me to for Years by gone in the Exposition of him to those whom he has all along Deceived I cannot but congratulate you & myself that we are now so far got clear of him, what will finally become of him God knows, thus his Warrant allowing the Whole Sum to be presently forthcoming from G S[10] only which is why the Case will not answer one half of his London Creditors, I am told he proposes becoming Bankrupt in Order to Extricate himself, and afterwards make the most of the Warant but this will not do.

As to public Affairs the Inclosed Paper will Shew you the Turn that I have given to the Controversy.[11] I could think of no other Expedient to prevent a Repeal and at the Same [time] & Saving the other Laws clear the way for their Lordships Judgment, what Stress they will lay upon it I can not Say however I have Reason to think it will before any other Measures are taken have their Consideration, unless Mr Hasels Information proves true, (vizt) that the Northern Countys Are to Do it of their own Accord;[12] I Submit it to you whether or no to communicate this Expedient to the Assembly I have not done it to the Committee, because I have not their Authority to propose Terms for them, So they are no more than hints from my Self upon my own Judgment of the Case as things appear to me here, besides I cannot Say that the Board of Trade will come into Such Measures, As the long Vacation now comes on and as I find Some Disposition to wait the Issue of Mr Hasels Information before they Report on the Law, I may have your Sentiments on this Plan of the Expedient that I have now sent you.

This with other Packets comes by Mr Watson & will take up some time to consider, And to Include all your Concerns in this Conveyance I conclude by acquainting you that Mr Child has been again calld upon and to give his Reply to Capt Bonillas Reply to his Narative, of the Proceedings in your Govert as to his Effects, he has delayd his Reply till Such time as Capt Bonilla was gone to Spain, now hes gone he is preparing Such Reply & so far as he has gone I approve thereof as being much to your purpose as well as his own, and on the Same Plan of Defence as what was containd in his Narative, Copy whereof I have heretofore Sent you; he has hinted to me his receiving a very provoking Letter from you, but I gave no Attention thereto rather Soothd Maters. As a Cooperation is absolutly necessary to Compleat a proper Defence against the Spanish Complaint, I have had confounded deal of trouble about the arangement of your Counsellors, the new regulat[i]ons amon[g]st the Offices have greatly increased the trouble & the expence of Bussiness, the Fees at the B of Trade are thereby double and thrise at the Council Office by these means I am greatly in Advance for some of them.

PS   You must transmit to me Such a Certificat from the Deputy Auditor in Case he refuses Debentures for your Arrears as that to Mr Child; but before you press it home to him I wish you would get the Recr to give in a rough Ballance of the Arrears due to the Crown from the Tenants; and let the Recr Certificate to be more Explicit as to what is due to you by Way of Arrears, to Save you trouble I transmit to you the former Certificat,[13] you will also observe how explicit the Deputy Auditor is in his Certificat to Mr Child & he must be equally So according to the Case of your Arrears, which at the Same time will fortefie the Recer's Certificat, I mention particularly these Matters to you because, we shall have Occasion to go to the Treasury against Mr Walpole or his Deputy in Case Debentures cannot otherwise be Obtaind; And therefore our Materials must be as Strong as possible; I do not See Why the Same Certificat may [not] be Signd by the Deputy Auditor & Recr General however you will consider this, with them and act accordingly by one or by two Certificates according to the Form of their Offices.

PS I see no Occasion for Insisting on preference with the Deputy Auditor yet your Debentures and the Law will determine that point to the Recer General by the Att G——— opinion which shall be transmitted to you.

JA

LB, pp. 318–322. At the top of p. 318 JA began a letter to Johnston on 20 May. He struck out those few lines and then began the present letter, which was initially dated 20 May. Sent "per Mr Watson."

1. No letter to Johnston of 6 Apr. 1752 has been found. JA's letter of 15 Apr. 1752, pp. 34–35, conveys this message.

2. Enclosure not found.

3. The "Kings Establishment" was the royal order of 25 Sept. 1733 directing that the governor's salary of £1,000 per year be paid out of the revenue of the colony's quitrents, and that other officers of government be paid out of the same fund (*NCCR*, 5:77).

4. Alexander McCulloh, nephew of Henry McCulloh, was deputy auditor-general of North Carolina, a post he owed to his uncle's influence. He was appointed to the Council in 1762, served until the Revolution, and was still living in 1797.

5. Robert Smith became Walpole's deputy auditor-general in 1746.

6. See following document.

7. Enclosure not found.

8. Henry Bathurst (1714–1794), afterwards second Earl Bathurst.

9. See preceding document, n. 4.

10. George Saxby. See preceding document, n. 4.

11. This paper about the act for equal representation has not been found.

12. Hasell had told JA that the northern counties would apply for two members each. See JA to Johnston, 15 Apr. 1752, pp. 34–35.

13. Enclosure not found.

To Gabriel Johnston

June 12th [1752]

Tell him the Attorney General refuses his opinion upon the Establisht unless referd to him in point of Office that I had laid it before Mr Fazakerly, to Send his Opin[i]on by Glasgow, going to Scotland for a few Weeks.

JA

LB, p. 323. Sent "per Mr Watson."

To Gabriel Johnston

Augt 2d [1752] from Tullebody

Inclosed Copy of Mr Fazakerlys Oppinion by the Way of Glasgow.[1]

LB, p. 323.

1. Fazakerley's opinion has not been found. JA was evidently not yet aware that Johnston had died on 17 July 1752.

To the Committee of Correspondence of North Carolina

Gentlemen of the Committee   Augt 13th 1752

Am favour'd with yours 30th May,[1] Mr Rutherford[2] has remitted Bill of Exchange for 100 and the Several pieces of Gold on payment of which Moneys the Accounte shall have Credit.

Am extreamly concernd you have Cause to Complain of receiving no Letters since last Octr, the fault not mine, Many have been Sent since that time,[3] however whatever Delays or Miscarriages happen be Assurd I loose no Opportunety of Writing.

With regard to Our Affairs more immediatly the Object of my Attention their Determination cannot be more anxiously Wishd for by you than by me & I am perswaded you will do me the Justice to believe that I have fought the Case thro every Channel it now rest[s] in Judgment with those of the Administration of Plantation Affairs And its no doubt owing to the Strength of Our Arguments in Support of the Principles of these Acts that we are Still in Possession of them Notwithstanding the Report agt them,[4] and from the Measures that have been taken I would fain hope, that these Laws will stand their ground till Such time as Others are Substituted in their room with a particular Salve for the Concomitant Acts as well as for the Acts passed by the present Assembly.

Thus Gentlemen Since I cannot Flatter my Self with the prospect of Obtaining the Kings Aprobation to these Acts I have endeavourd to prevent a Repeal ex parte the Dangerouse Consequence whereof I have so clearly Set forth that I cannot doubt of their Attention thereto.

LB, p. 330. On p. 323 of the letter book is a memorandum of this letter, which indicates that it was written at Menstrie (a village in JA's home county of Clackmannan) and sent via Glasgow.

1. Letter not found.

2. John Rutherfurd (1722–1782), who arrived in North Carolina about 1740, became receiver general of quitrents in 1750 and a councillor in 1751.

3. JA's letter book includes letters to the committee of 2 Mar. and 29 May 1752, pp. 30–31 and pp. 36–37.

4. For these acts, see JA to North Carolina Committee of Correspondence, 7 Oct. 1751, p. 8, n. 2.

To Robert Dinwiddie

Sept 17th 1752

On my arrival here two days ago, I had my Credentials & Instructions by your letter of the 20th of July, & the bill therein enclosed was immediatly accepted,[1] Mr Richardsons letter he being in the Country was transmitted[2] on his return which will be in 10 Days I shall enter upon the Affair of the Capture,[3] my present thoughts suggest, that you will find great difficulty in attaining payment in Europe, unless Precedents can be Pleaded, should this fail, Mr Richardson may think it advisable to Solicit an Order for Payment out of the Royal Coffers in America Such Orders I hear have been attended with Success, but shall be better Able to Judge when Mr Hume[4] returns to Charleston from the Havannah, whither he went to Execute Such orders for payment out of the Royal Coffers, by reason the Captors were insufficient.

I find that the Addresses to the King from the Legislature & from the Judges are come to the Plantation Office, & there I shall follow them, when the Board reasembles, which will be 15th of next Month unless further Adjournments happen.[5]

The 53 Acts the Confirmation whereof is recommended to Mr Leheup & me jointly are not as yet come to the Office, shall enquire for them at Mr Hanburys.[6]

As to the Several Provincial & other Matters recomended to my particular care you may depend upon my Attention thereto, that my Diligence may establish my Credit with your people and I am extreamly well plesed, that the Reasons transmitted in Support of the Address are so Strong and at the Same time so well Adapted to the Case, I have not met with any thing in the Way of Bussiness, more properly put together both as to the Maner & the Matter thereof, Mr Leheup having miscarryd heretofore in the Case of the Judges does not discourage me,[7] I think that their Address may be fortcfyd with Stronger Reasons than what the Address it Self sets forth, and such shall be made use of in due time.[8]

The Ministers at present are all dispersed they Steal out & into Town from time to time, but give no Attention to Bussiness till such time as his Majestys Arrival make it necessary for them to come together; by Chance I had a Short interview with Ld Hallefax who was in town for a few hours, he told me you had given him the first news of Gover Johnstons Death,[9] our Conversation was chiefly on the Affairs of that Province, however I opend my Credentials from Virginia to his Lordship who was pleasd to express his Satisfaction that these Matters came recommended to me, Mr Leheup being at Richmond I have had no Interview So am a Stranger to the Clergymans Appeal mentiond in yours of 5th June[10] having thus breifly taken Notice of your Announ[cemen]t I conclude with Complts to Mrs Din:[11] & Most Sincerly & Affectionatly

JA

LB, p. 326.

1. Dinwiddie's letter (not found) evidently informed JA that he had been appointed a special agent by the Virginia General Assembly to present two addresses to the king. One of the addresses was of condolence on the deaths of Frederick Louis

(1707–1751), prince of Wales; William IV (1711–1751), prince of Orange and son-in-law of George II; and Louisa (1724–1751), queen of Denmark and daughter of George II. In the other address, of 15 Apr. 1752, the Council and House of Burgesses requested that the General Assembly be empowered to reenact eight laws that had been disallowed in Oct. 1751, and that they be empowered to pass laws, without suspending clauses, to repeal, alter, or amend laws that had already been confirmed by the Crown (*LJC*, 2:1082–1087).

On 18 Apr. 1752 the House voted to appoint a special agent in London to present the addresses. After Dinwiddie recommended JA, the House and Council on 20 Apr. agreed to appoint him and pay him £100 sterling for his efforts (*JHB, 1752–1758*, 91–92, 96–97, 99, 103).

JA appeared before the Board of Trade in support of the address on legislation on 25 Jan. and 1 Feb. 1753 (*JBT*, 9:388, 391). On 14 Feb. 1753 the Board of Trade advised the Privy Council against permitting reenactment of six of the laws and in favor of permitting reenactment of two. The Board also recommended that the request regarding repeal, alteration, or amendment of laws already confirmed be denied because the result would be "to take away, or at least to render useless and ineffectual that Power which the Crown has so Wisely and properly reserved to itself of rejecting such Laws passed in the Colonys, as shall upon due Consideration be thought improper or liable to Objection and would destroy that Check, which was established not only to preserve the just and proper influence and Authority which the Crown ought to have in the Direction and Government of its Colonys in America, but also to secure to its Subjects their just Libertys and Privileges" (*APC*, 4:174). The Privy Council adopted all of the Board's recommendations on 7 Mar. 1753 (*APC*, 4:175). An additional instruction to Dinwiddie of 10 May 1753 authorized him to reenact the law concerning wooden chimneys and swine in Walkerton (Hening, *Statutes*, 6:214), and the act for the better support of the College of William and Mary (Hening, *Statutes*, 6:91–94), "excepting however that part of the first of the said laws by which a liberty is given to any person to kill swine which may be found running at large within the town of Walkerton, which clause appears to us to be highly unjust and improper" (Labaree, *Royal Instructions*, 1:163–164). The two laws were never reenacted.

2. This letter has not been found, nor has Richardson been identified.

3. On 28 Aug. 1748 the sloop *Patty*, owned by Dinwiddie and John Esten, of Bermuda, was seized by a Spanish privateer while on a voyage from Antigua to New York. Although hostilities between Britain and Spain were to have ceased on 9 Aug., the *Patty* was nonetheless taken to Puerto Rico and condemned as a prize. Dinwiddie and Esten secured a royal order to the British minister to Spain to obtain restitution for the seizure, and on 15 Aug. 1749 the Spanish government ordered the governor of Puerto Rico to make full restitution of the ship and its cargo, or the value thereof. Despite this order, Dinwiddie and his partner did not receive restitution, and on 31 Oct. 1752 they petitioned both the king and the earl of Holderness to assist them in obtaining the £1,608.13.5$\frac{1}{2}$ sterling at which they valued the ship and its cargo (CO 5/43, fols. 1–3, in Koontz, *Dinwiddie Papers*, 212–221). JA's letter to Dinwiddie of 4

May/20 May 1753, pp. 80–86, indicates that another Spanish order for restitution was received.

4. Charleston merchant John Hume was in partnership with Robert Stiell in the 1740s, and about 1751 Jeremy Wright and Charles Wright joined the firm.

5. The Virginia Council, whose members were also judges of the colony's General Court when sitting in their judicial capacity, petitioned the Crown on 23 Mar. 1752, asking that their salaries be raised from £600 to £1,200 per year (or £100 per judge) out of the revenues of the two-shillings-per-hogshead export tax on tobacco (CO 5/1327, fols. 240–241, in Koontz, *Dinwiddie Papers*, 190n; *EJC*, 5:380). Dinwiddie had enclosed the petition in his letter to the Board of Trade of 12 July 1752, in which he strongly supported the judges' case (CO 5/1327, fols. 213–214, in Koontz, *Dinwiddie Papers*, 188–192). In a report of 13 Feb. 1753 the Board of Trade recommended to the Privy Council that the judges' petition be granted (CO 5/1367, fols. 10–13), and the Privy Council so ordered the Treasury on 7 Mar. 1753 (T 1/351, fols. 169b–170; *APC*, 4:176).

6. On 9 Nov. 1752 the Board of Trade read Dinwiddie's letter of 20 July 1752 (CO 5/1327, fol. 216, in Koontz, *Dinwiddie Papers*, 193–194), which enclosed fifty-three acts passed on 20 Apr. 1752 (Hening, *Statutes*, 6:217–324). The Board referred the acts to its counsel, Matthew Lamb, for his opinion on them in point of law (*JBT*, 9:359–360).

Peter Leheup (d. 1774), at various times a clerk of the Privy Council and of the Treasury, was agent in London for Virginia 1723–1754. See JA to Dinwiddie, 30 Nov. 1753, pp. 98–99, and 29 Apr. 1755, pp. 146–147. John Hanbury (1700–1758) was a Quaker and a London merchant of the firm of J. Hanbury & Co., which carried on an extensive trade to Virginia.

7. Gov. William Gooch unsuccessfully sought an augmentation of the councillors' salary in a letter to the duke of Newcastle of 24 May 1748 (CO 5/1338, fol. 21). He told Newcastle that "Mr Leheup, our Agent, is instructed to give your Grace the fullest Satisfaction upon every Particular" contained in the Council's address to Gooch (*EJC*, 5:252).

8. On 22 Nov. 1752 the Board of Trade read an undated paper presented by JA entitled "Additional Reasons in Support of the Petition to his Majesty from the Judges of Virginia relative to the Enlargement of their Salaries" (CO 5/1327, fols. 223–223a; *JBT*, 9:367).

9. Dinwiddie's letter to the Board of Trade of 20 July 1752 (cited in note 6 above) reported Johnston's death on 17 July 1752.

10. Letter not found.

JA alludes here to the case of the Rev. William Kay (ca. 1721–1755), who became minister of Lunenburg Parish, Richmond Co., Va., in 1744. For reasons not known, he incurred the enmity of Landon Carter, a wealthy vestryman. As soon as Carter had the support of a majority of the vestry, Kay was discharged and his two churches locked up. For a year Kay conducted services in the churchyard. Then in Apr. 1747, on the advice of Gov. William Gooch and the Rev. William Dawson, commissary of the bishop of London, Kay brought suit before the General Court of Virginia for trespass against the three lay tenants who had rented Kay's glebe land from the vestry. The court being uncertain whether a minister who had not been formally inducted into a parish by the governor could enjoy security of tenure, it was not until two years later that the court finally awarded Kay £30 damages and costs. The three lay tenants, doubtless at the instigation of Carter, petitioned for permission for an appeal to be heard before the Privy Council, which petition the Privy Council granted on 31 Oct. 1751. On 15 May 1753 a committee of the Privy Council recommended dismissal of the appeal with £80 costs to be paid to Kay. The following Oct. the General Court awarded Kay an additional £200 for arrears of salary. Carter's actions gave rise to an important proviso in the revised "Act for the better support of the clergy," passed in Oct. 1748. By the amended law, clergymen were to enjoy security of tenure from the time they were received into a parish, whether they had been formally inducted by the governor or not. See JA to Dinwiddie, 4 May/20 May 1753, postscript, p. 86 (*APC*, 4:113–114; Hening, *Statutes*, 6: 88–90; Rhys Isaac, *The Transformation of Virginia, 1740–1790* [Chapel Hill, 1982], 143–144; Morton, *Colonial Virginia*, 2:759–762).

11. Dinwiddie had married Rebecca Auchinleck (d. 1793) by 1738.

To James Glen

Sir   Octr 2d 1752

I am favourd with yours July 29th[1] by Col Vander[2] and at Same time one for Capt Lovingstone,[3] which have transmitted to Ireland, having taken Copy thereof, shall call for his answer on his return if he has not Sent it from thence, Admitting the Case to be as you have Stated the Same Doubt not but that he will grant you the Declaration desird.[4]

You seem to have misaprehended my letter relative to Mottes Affair therein told you I desird to be excused from aplications to Mr Furye in behalf of any from Carolina finding it disagreeable to him, and as Such Solicitations did not come within our Agreement relating to Your Self, therefore declind any Such Aplication.[5]

May Assure yourself that as have hetherto very punctually complyd with the Agreement enterd into between Us & have even exceeded it in many other Services in the Way of Freindship to you[6] So now I have great Justice to call upon you for the performance of your New promise of paying me my Arrears, & more punctual payment for the future by Mr Calverly or any other person who receives your Salary.

You have with this the Magazines for the 5 last Monthes[7] I am always Your

JA

LB, p. 325. An earlier version of this letter, crossed through, is on p. 324 of the letter book. Substantive differences between the two versions are accounted for in notes to the present letter.

1. Letter not found.

2. Col. Alexander Vander Dussen (d. 1759), merchant and planter, was in South Carolina by 1731. An experienced soldier, Vander Dussen commanded a regiment of the South Carolina militia during the War of Jenkins' Ear. He served in the Commons House of Assembly 1739–1742 and 1746–1747 and on the Council from 1747 until Dec. 1755, when he was removed because he was "disordered in his senses and incapable of serving" (*APC*, 4:796–797).

3. Edward Lovingston.

4. The draft of this letter speaks more explicitly of Glen's connection with Lovingston. After "Copy thereof" it continues: "as I can recollect to have heard him say that he Stood Trustee for you for a large Tract of Land in S Carolina, I should be inclind to think, that he will not hesitate in giving you a Declaration of Trust, provided Such Trust is not by him transferred to Mr Hamilton, which I am affraid is the case for I have heard, but from whom I do not at present remember, that Mr Hamilton for the Consideration of an [allowance] of 20 per an to be paid by him to Mrs Loving[s]ton Wife of Capt Lovingston, had procurd a Surrender of Such Trust from C L & that Mr Ham: had transferred the Same to Mr Dacoste & other Jews on whose credit Mr Hamls undertakings in Car were carryd on, these matters may come to be cleard up on an Interview with Capt Lovingston."

5. Jacob Motte, Sr. (1700–1770) served in the South Carolina Commons House of Assembly 1739–1743 and as treasurer of the colony 1743–1770. The "Affair" JA mentions may have been Motte's financial difficulties. "Motte's public record was subject to severe criticism. He had no knowledge of double-entry bookkeeping, mixed public monies with his private funds, was chronically late with his reports, and allowed merchants to defer illegally payment of import duties. A hurricane in 1752 damaged his property and he could not pay his public or private debts. The House delayed investigating the treasurer's accounts for several months in hopes that Motte could get his financial affairs in order. He could not. The legislative investigation showed that he had misappropriated £90,000 from the provincial treasury. He was allowed to keep his position but had to turn over his estate to a trust. By 1759 the funds had been repaid and Motte regained control of his property" (*Bio. Dir. S.C. House of Rep.*, 2:479).

6. In the draft this phrase reads: "You may assure yourself that as I have hetherto been very punctual in calling from time to time at the Several Offices for their Commands to you and in transmitting to you what letters have been Sent to my

Lodgings from Offices or otherwise & doing other things for your Service in the Way of Freindship, So I shall continue to Do."

7. In place of this sentence, the draft ended with the following paragraph: "I never reced your Letter of the 8th of Octr last & I am yet to think that you have not sent it as you seem to hint."

To the Committee of Correspondence of North Carolina

Gentlemen   London Octr 8th 1752
Above you have the Substance of my former & last Letter Since that you favourd with yours 14th April[1] acquainting me with the Continuation of My Agency for which Gentlemen I beg you will make my Acknowledgments to your Several Houses of Assembly the Bill of Ex is paid After deducting 10 Sh for payment in London, the Gold is also paid according to Bill of Sales transmitted to Mr Rutherford amounting to 45.13 for which payments the Province have Credit accordingly.

You may depend on my Attention to the Affairs of the Province at all times but now more especially upon this Event of Gr J————s Death to whom no Successor is as yet named by Authority, tho of the Several Candidates to outward appearance Mr Lee High Bailiff of West is the most Sedulous[2] but as to his Success or that of any Others I cannot take upon me to Determine; As it is my Duty to Support the Measures of the Legislature I shall think it Incumbent on me, So Soon as His Majestys pleasure is known & De[c]lard as to the Person who is to head that Govert to make my Self known to him & the Relation that I Stand in with regard to the Legislature will Rather oblige me to call upon him to Cooperate with me in Supporting their Measures so essent[i]ally necessary for the good of the Province and a honor[a]ble Administration to himself; His Majesty is not expected before the 12th of next Month & till then I do not expect that our Affairs will be finally & Definatively Determind In the mean time from a thorough Conviction of the Rectitude of the Measures I shall add the part of a Freind to that of Agent & to you Gentlemen in particular I [*illegible*] Accept Thanks for the Book of Laws,[3] The Lds of Trade & Pt of the Council are to Expect Copys I am

LB, p. 330. This letter, which immediately follows JA's letter to the committee of 13 August 1752 in the letter book, is headed "To Do." The first sentence, which refers to the letter of 13 August "above," suggests that the present letter was appended to a copy of the earlier letter. The brackets near the end of the letter signify one or two illegible words. Sent "per South Carolina."

1. Letter not found.

2. Peter Leigh (1712–1759) had been high bailiff of Westminster since 1744. Though he sought the governorship of North Carolina, he instead accepted appointment as chief justice of South Carolina in Feb. 1753 (*JBT*, 9:382, 392).

3. *A Collection of All the Public Acts of Assembly, of the Province of North-Carolina; Now in Force and Use . . . Revised by Commissioners Appointed by an Act of the General Assembly of the Said Province, for That Purpose; And Examined with the Records, and Confirmed in Full Assembly* (New Bern, N.C., 1752).

To Mr. Ormes

Sir   Octr 10th 1752

Have yours 20th July[1] with disagreeable News of Governor Johnstons death, dead at the time when I had laid the Foundation for making the remainder of his Govert not only more agr[e]able but probably more profitable.

I most sincerely sympathize with Mrs Johnston[2] & am heartly disposed to Serve her & the family *by prosecuting the Measures already taken for recovering the Arrears* & likewise to continue my Endeavours to put an end & Extinguish the Spanish Ministers Claim made & Still carrying on by the Span Minister, so as not to come upon her & the Governors family for Restitution, these are the only 2 points that materially concerns the Govers Family the first to get some thing the 2d not to lose & from the Share that I have already had in these Matters no doubt I may be more able to help her out than any other person, But as neither you nor Mrs Johnston are Strangers to the immense trouble that Gover Johnstons public & privat Affairs have given for these Several years by gone in Justice to my Self, willing as I am to Continue my Freindship I must secure to my Self an Adequate recompence not only for what is passed but, likewise for my future Negociations of these Matters on her behalf; I have enclosed the Acct[3] between the Govr & myself by Agreement the Gover was [to] allow me 50 per an by Way of Salary for my personal Attendance, Extraordinary Services to be considered besides, & were these Articles for Extraordinary Services chargd by me according to my Expectations from his repeated acknowledgments of Services & Promises of Adequate Recompence they had been three times the Sums now charged, Mrs Johnston will Observe that I charge my Self with 109.6 & that upon the Credit thereof I have undertaken to proceed with my Solicitations in her favour & thereupon shall enter immediatly a Claim in her behalf for those Arrears & the first Step necessary for me to take is to use my Endeavours to prevent the appropriation of the Quitrents to any Succeeding Governor or other purpose till such time as by gone arrears are paid off.

And in order to Support the Claim it will be absolutely necessary to have Copy of the Govers Will properly Attested & that she get the Recers & Deputy Auditors Certificat upon Oath of what arrears of Salary is due by their Books to the Gover, my Lre to the Gover of the 5th of June[4] by Mr Watson is particular as to the Certificat necessary, let these things be transmitted to me with a Power of Attorney Ratefying all my Accounts & Transactions with the late Gover & Authorising me to appear in her behalf, let her Letter come by the first conveyance & more formal Powers may Follow.

I am not at liberty to mention the Names of those who are Candidates for the Govert but whoever he is be assured that I shall make mention of your Services to the late Gover & accordingly recommend you, its probable that the Contest I shall have on Mr Johnstons Account for preventing the Appropriation of the Quitrents to any New Gover may retard his Appointment.

You may acquaint Mrs Johnston that I have reason to believe the Govers Creditors & Debts are numerouse Many of his Creditors were turbulent, & I had trouble to Stop their Mouths.

You will carefully communicat this letter to Mrs Johnston & let me have her Answer or yours thereto nothing more to recommend to you but to take care that Letters passd between the Gover & mySelf during a long Correspondence do not come into bad hands, My Compts to Mrs Johnston I am Sir Yours

LB, pp. 328–329. At the foot of the letter are the following two notations: "NB it went enclosd to Messrs Watson & Cairns. NB See the Account Copy thereof in the Acct Book."

1. Ormes has not been identified, nor has his letter to JA been found.

2. Gabriel Johnston's second wife was Frances (Butler) Johnston (d. 1768), whom he married after the death of his first wife in 1741. After Johnston's death, his widow married John Rutherfurd.

3. Enclosure not found.

4. Printed on pp. 37–42.

To Robert Dinwiddie

Sir   Octr 20th 1752

My last was on Septr 17th.[1] Since that, the 53 Acts of your Province recommended to Mr Leheups Care & mine are come to the Plantation Office And there I have Cast my Eye over them, And I find that Eight of the 53 are lookd upon as Acts of a privat Nature (Vizt)

First The Act for Vesting the Right of two Acres of Land whereof Elizabeth Exum is Seized in Fee in the Justices of Southampton County &c.[2]

2d An Act to Dock the Intail of 250 Acres in the Parish of Westover the Property of Rebecca Wife of William Clinch And for Vesting the Same in certain Trustees in Fee Simple For &c.[3]

3d An Act to Vest certain Lands therein Mentioned in Reuben Skelton in Fee Simple &c and For Setling other Lands of greater Value &c.[4]

4th An Act to Confirm an Agreement made between John Drew & Benja Harison for the Settlement of their respective Rights to certain Lands &c A Suspending Clause to this Act.[5]

5th An Act To Dock the Intail of certain Lands whereof David Garland is seized And for Settling other Lands of greater Value to the Same Uses.[6]

6th An Act To Vest certain Intailed Lands therein mentioned in Henry Washington Gentleman in Fee Simple.[7]

7th An Act To Dock the Intail of certain Lands in the County of James City And Vesting the Same in Thomas Chamberlayn.[8]

8th An Act for Docking the Intail of certain Lands in the County of King William and Vesting the Same in William Dandridge and for Settling other Lands &c.[9]

These Acts being Acts of a Privat Nature in the Judgment of the Plantation Office, Certificates of their Notification before Passing ought to have been transmitted along with them, And as Certificates are wanting for Nos (1t) (2d) (8th) & (9th) of these Privat Acts, they must lay by till proper Certificates are transmitted;[10] accordingly with regard to the rest whether Public or Privat their first Progress is their being Referrd by the Lords for Trade to their Council Mr Lamb, and this I shall move for when that Board assemble which from a further Prorogation is Now fixd for the 7th of next Month[11] But you will please to take Notice that on all Privat Acts Mr Lamb expects to be Attended with a Fee of 5 Guineas for each Act And without Such Fee he will not look into any Privat Act, & besides this Fee his first Clerk has for each 5 shillings, this from Experience I know to be the Practise, and I believe you do not mean that in the Situation that I Stand in that I shoud go thro so expensive a Solicitation, besides other Disbursments at the Board of Trade and Council Office, While upon Examination of these Several Offices, I find in the whole will amount 22£11s Ster for the Kings final approbation or Confirmation of every Individual Privat Act, vizt at the Plantation Office 4.4.0 Council Office 12.16.6, Mr Lambs Office 5.10.6, this besides 10 Guineas to the Agent or Person who Solicits the Approbation or Confirmation of any Privat Act of Assembly where the Public is not immediatly concerned.

In Justification of my own Conduct I think it necessary to Mention these Particulars, that those concerned immediatly in having Such Acts Approved of or Confirmed where there are Suspending Clauses till Confirmed (which I find to be the Case of the Act Relative to John Drew & Benja Harison) May not Suffer from Delay or Expect what in Prudence cannot be performd by me or any other Agent without Particular Instructions and Credit to Support Such Applications.

Upon Perusing the Journals of both Houses I Observe that neither of them take the least Notice of the Act Intitled an Act Declaring the Process and Proceedings of the General Court between the Commencement and Repealing of the Act Intitled An Act for Establishing the General Court and for Regulating and Settling the Proceedings therein to be good & valid,[12] Nevertheless as 53 Acts in Number are mentioned in your Letter to the Board, this Seeming Defect of the Journals is got over And the Authenticity of the Act Admitted of, but it will be necessary that you Say something in your Letter to me on this Point that I may explain this

Circumstance to the Secretary of the Plantation Board who at first stated to me this Objection of this Act passd at the Same time its being so left out of the Journals, which in all other Respects seem Compleat, as to the Bussiness of that Session of the General Assembly.

I am told by Mr Sharpe that I must Present the original Address from the Province and that from the *Judges in the* first Instance thro the Council Office and for this Reason I must get at them from the Plantation Office to which you had transmitted them and very properly one might think according to the New Regulations for Plantation Bussiness, however I find that I am Still to proceed in the old Method of Offices (vizt) by Way of Reference in the first Instance from the Council to the Board of Trade, upon which Reference you know depends a Perquisit of Office in privat Cases.

Mr Richardson is expected in Town next week, Its probable that Mr Lee High Bailiff of Westr will be your Neighbouring Govr with more Solid Appointments than what his Predecessor Govr Johnston had, Mr Dobbs is a Candidate likewise but I am apt to think Mr Lee will have the Preference[13] You know that they owe him Favour on a former Occasion; Mr Leheup tells me that Mr Dawson is to have Place as one of your Council, that the Church may be taken care of[14] Adieu My Dr Sir with Complts to Mrs Dinwiddie and the Misses[15] and believe me always Most Affectionatly Yours

PS by Mr Bowens Death Mr Leheup Succeeds more to honour than Profit[16] which may not be So agreeable Because Mr West Succeeded to Mr Scroop has taken Some Branches of that Clerkship under his own Direction.[17]

26th PS tell him of Mr Smiths[18] Hint about his Allowance for 400 & of my Salary not being to be chargd as Agent.

LB, pp. 331–332. At the foot of the letter JA wrote: "to Mr Hanbury."

1. Printed on pp. 44–45.

2. Hening, *Statutes*, 6:283–284.

3. Ibid., 297–299.

4. Ibid., 300–302.

5. Ibid., 303–308. The first name appears as John New in the printed journals of the House of Burgesses and the printed act.

6. Ibid., 311–314. See JA to Dinwiddie, 7 Dec. 1753, p. 99.

7. Ibid., 314–316.

8. Ibid., 319–321.

9. Ibid., 321–324.

10. The instructions to the governor of Virginia ordered "that you do not give your assent to any private act until proof be made before you in council, and entered in the council books, that public notification was made of the party's intention to apply for such act in the several parish churches where the premises in question lie, for three Sundays at least successively, before any such act shall be brought into the assembly, and that a certificate under your hand be transmitted with and annexed to every such private act signifying that the same has passed through all the forms above mentioned" (Labaree, *Royal Instructions*, 1:140).

11. Matthew Lamb (1705–1768) was counsel to the Board of Trade 1746–1768 and a member of Parliament 1741–1768. The Board referred the acts to Lamb on 9 Nov. 1752 (*JBT*, 9:359–360).

12. Hening, *Statutes*, 6:229–230.

13. Arthur Dobbs (1689–1765), a native of Ireland, had long been involved in North Carolina land speculation. He was commissioned governor of North Carolina in Feb. 1753, but he did not arrive in the colony until Oct. 1754. Dobbs served as governor of the colony until his death.

JA's reference to "more Solid Appointments" concerned the governor's salary. Since the heirs of Governor Johnston were owed £13,000 for the arrears of his salary, Dobbs correctly concluded that the colony's quitrent revenues would be insufficient to liquidate that debt and pay the salaries of himself and certain other colonial officials. Therefore, early in 1754 he wisely petitioned that some other provision be made for the salaries. The Board of Trade supported his petition as far as it concerned the governor's salary in a representation to the Crown of 14 Mar. 1754 (CO 5/323, n.p.). That month the Privy Council, acting on the recommendation of the Board, ordered the Treasury "to consider of a proper fund" out of which to pay Dobbs £1,000 sterling per year. The Treasury decided to draw the salary on the revenues of the Barbados $4\frac{1}{2}$ percent export duty. For the remainder of the colonial period the governors of North Carolina thus enjoyed the security of this income, but other officers, still dependent on inadequate quitrent revenues, were rarely paid (*NCCR*, 5:20, 77–78, 114, 167–169; Labaree, *Royal Government*, 333; Greene, *Quest for Power*, 145–146).

14. The Rev. Thomas Dawson (1713–1760) was rector of Bruton Parish 1743–1759, commissary of the bishop of London 1752–1760, and president of the College of William and Mary 1755–1760. Dawson was appointed to the Council on 19 Jan. 1753 in the room of his deceased brother, the Rev. William Dawson, and was sworn in on 1 May 1753 (*EJC*, 5:423).

15. Dinwiddie's daughters were Elizabeth (1738–1773) and Rebecca (born ca. 1742).

16. Thomas Bowen, Esq., one of the chief clerks of the Treasury, died on 16 Oct. and was succeeded by Leheup (*Gentleman's Magazine* 22 [1752]: 478, 536).

17. James West and John Scrope (ca. 1662–1752) were joint secretaries to the Treasury until Scrope's death on 21 Apr. 1752 (he had served in that office since 1724). The following day Nicholas Hardinge became joint secretary with West.

18. Perhaps Robert Smith, Walpole's deputy auditor-general.

To James Glen

Decr 13th 1752

Acknowledge his of 25th Septr[1] tell him of Mr Leighs Acceptance of the Office of C Justice, That I shall Follow Mr Michies Recommendation pro Judge of the Admiralty,[2] that Mr Drayton stands recomended for the Council, but that Messrs Leigh, Wragg & Saxby Must be first Served[3] NB that he has been long in Arrear to me.

LB, p. 335. Sent "per Capt Carling in the Downs."

1. Letter not found.

2. James Michie (d. 1760), a Scots lawyer who was in South Carolina by 1737, served in the Commons House of Assembly 1742–1745 and 1752–1755 (Speaker 1752–1754), and on the Council from 1755. He was appointed judge of the South Carolina Vice-Admiralty Court in 1753 and held that post until his death. When Chief Justice Peter Leigh died in 1759, Michie temporarily filled that position as well.

3. Thomas Drayton (1700–1760) was not appointed to the Council until Oct. 1756 (*APC*, 4:797). In Dec. 1752 the Board of Trade recommended that William Wragg (1714?–1777) and George Saxby (d. 1786) be appointed to the Council (*JBT*, 9:379), which appointments were made in Jan. 1753 (*APC*, 4:796). Peter Leigh was never appointed to the Council.

To Robert Dinwiddie

Decr 20th 1752

My last of 7th Nov[1] conveyd to you The King of Spains Orders for Restitution,[2] And My Observations on the Acts of Assembly Since that the Publick Acts are Referrd to Mr Lambe, and those of a privat Nature remain still at the Board of Trade, till Instructions arive as to Payment of Fees, And till Such Time As Certificates of their being Published, before they were Passd, are Transmitted.

I must Observe to you That the Act to Confirm An Agreement between John Drew[3] & Benja Harrison contains a Suspending Clause, So that untill the Kings Pleasure is Declared thereon it is no Law Wherefore those concerned therein, Should give their Correspondents full & Proper Instructions as to the Expence thereanent.

Since My last I have [had] a Conference with Mr Horace Walpole who is extreamly your Freind & I have it in charge from him to tell you, and that he is Sorry that In point of Office he cannot agree to Passing the Article of Money Payd to you, without your having the Kings Warrant from the Treasury.

I have likewise had a Conference from Mr West and I am hopefull that He stands better Disposed to the Petition of the Judges than he was at first: This Matter and the Address relative to New Instructions are before the Council,[4] where nothing retards there again[st] Reference to My Lords for Trade, but the Common Delay of a Council which perhaps may be got over Wednesday next; from the late Regulations in Offices, Arises great Delay and Expence in Solicitations, for Instead of three References, there must be five. The Same Objections that I found by Mr Leheups oppinion I should meet with, as to the Judges Application I had from Mr Adair, (viz) That Additional Salarys would Increase Solicitations for being of the Council and render the Office venal, Such Objections are easily answerd; for certainly it is for the Interest of the Crown to have many Persons apply, that the best may be taken, With regard to Venality An Establishment of A Salary Adequate to the Office is the Most Effectual Means to prevent Venal Prectices, and So it has been thought in the Case of Judges in G.B. their are Some in the Administration Penetrating enough to See the Advantages of Granting Salarys upon the Footing of Councellors alone but this is a Point I would only touch upon as our Case is for the Judges and as such I have forfeited[5] their Petition by Additional Reasons annexd to the Petition.[6]

I have had within these few days a very long Conference of 3 Hours with Mr John Hanburry whom I find a very Sensible Man, amongst other things he told me of a Fee of a Pistol for the Great Seal to every Patent or Grant for Lands, Which some People

Objected to; I cannot help being of oppinion, that from the Practise of Other Provinces that you can Support Such a Fee, however, We have laid a Plan for geting the Same approvd of here, When the Lords for Trade take Under their Consideration What Matters you Recommended to them, before you left England, Which Matters I find that Mr Hanbury concerns himself in, and as amongst others an article relative to the Granting of Lands, in Which this Fee will Naturally come in.[7]

I find that he is extreamly well pleased with my being concerned with the Affairs of Virginia, Not only in so far as it will relieve himself from the Many Negociations amongst Offices which has fallen to his share by Mr Le Heups Engagments to Business in Office of more Value, So that his Attention to Virginia Matters has been as they came accidentaly in his way, more than from Any Immediate Concern therein; However he is not for Leaving Mr Leheup out of the Service alltogether, But is for taking Me in upon the Same Footing with him, Provided I would Act on Such Terms, to Which Proposal I made answer that I did not know what Plan you had cut for me, however that I should have No Objection to Serve on equal Terms in Salary with Mr Leheup But as Most of the Bussiness in all probability might be thrown upon me But am affraid we shall meet no Precedent of Fees being Settled And Established (in the first Instance) from hence; But when Fees are Settled by the Advice of Council in Matters where the Crown alone is concernd as in the Grants of Crown Lands, In such Cases you may be Assured that the Order of your Council on such Cases will Justefie your taking Such Fees So Settled, in Council, as was done In South Carolina when the Land Office was first Opened for Granting Lands under Grants from the Governor, and in Case of any Complaint agt you for taking this or another Fee I have not the least Doubt but that the Resolution of your Council will Establish the rectitude thereof as Such Fee does not Exceed what is a Reasonable Fee for the Great Seals being fixd to any Grant of Lands Whether Such Grant contains a Small or a Great quantity of Lands, My Complts to all with you.

LB, pp. 333–334. This letter was initally dated 9 December, then 13 December. It is in two parts. On p. 333 are the first four paragraphs; on p. 334 are the last two paragraphs, which have been entirely struck out. At the foot of each page is the notation: "per Mr Hanburys Ship."

1. Letter not found. At this point in the letter book JA added in parentheses: "NB see Bundle of Letters pro Copy."

2. See JA to Dinwiddie, 17 Sept. 1752, pp. 46–47, n. 3.

3. John New.

4. The "Address relative to New Instructions" was probably Dinwiddie's memorial of Aug. 1751 that he enclosed in a letter to Halifax of 10 Sept. 1751 shortly before sailing for Virginia (CO 5/1327, fols. 190, 191, in Koontz, *Dinwiddie Papers*, 104–106, 110–111). The memorial proposed some additions to be made to his instructions relating to presents to the Indians, the exemption of foreign Protestants from parochial regulations, and the establishment of a fee to the governor for grants of land. The Board of Trade read the memorial on 11 Mar. 1751/52, and the following day John Hanbury attended the Board about the memorial (*JBT*, 9:290).

5. JA probably intended to write "fortified."

6. See JA to Dinwiddie, 17 Sept. 1752, p. 47, n. 8.

7. The pistole fee controversy arose out of Dinwiddie's attempt to levy a fee of 1 pistole for sealing each patent of land. (The pistole was a Spanish coin worth something between 16 shillings, 6 pence and 18 shillings sterling.) In Aug. 1751, even before leaving England, Dinwiddie specifically asked the Board of Trade for permission to exact such a fee (see note 4 above). In Apr. 1752, shortly after arriving in Virginia, Dinwiddie sought the advice of the Council on the question. The Council agreed that requiring such a fee was reasonable, and the Council recommended that 1 pistole be the amount (*EJC*, 5:385). Dinwiddie again submitted the matter to the Board of Trade in a letter of 6 Oct. 1752 in order to remove any doubt about the legality of his actions (CO 5/1327, fols. 497–498, in Koontz, *Dinwiddie Papers*, 208–211). See Morton, *Colonial Virginia*, 2:chap. 18.

To the Committee of Correspondence of North Carolina

Decr 20th 1752

I think that its past all Doubt that Mr Dobbs will be Gover & Have assurances that the Provincial Affairs will be Settled by Proper Instructions to the New Gover; I shall think it Incumbent on me to give him such Hints as may Enable him to form a Right Judgt upon the Measures that have all along d[i]sturbed an Equal & consequently a Regular & Rational Administration of Govert.

The Settlement of a proper Establishment for a Govers Salary may take up some time & whatever Relief the Steps that I have taken may produce for the benefit of the Representatives to the late Gover I flatter myself that what I have done will prevent any New Appropriation of the Q Rents til the bygone Arrears are paid off And So Much I have thought proper to Do for the honour of Govert & Justice to the Succeeding Gover as Well as to the Officers of Govert, and altho this is a Matter not altogether relative to the Legislature I thought it my Duty to Interpose and as Such to Communicate My Proceedings to the Comee by the Way of Virginia I am

LB, p. 335. At the foot of p. 335 is the memorandum: "All the above per Virginia to Watson & Cairns, for Col Dawson, & all in Mr. Rices Packet," evidently in reference to this and the following three letters.

To James Hasell

[26 December 1752]
2d To Mr Hasell puting him in Mind to Remit his Fees to me Dated Dr 26.[1]

LB, p. 335.

1. The fees JA refers to are presumably those required in conjunction with Hasell's appointment to the Council. See JA to Johnston, 9 Dec. 1751, pp. 25–26, n. 13.

To Nathaniel Rice

[26 December 1752]
3d To Mr Rice[1] in Answer to his of Septr 1t[2] Ansr [omitted?] in his Letter Dated Decr 26th.

LB, p. 335

1. Nathaniel Rice (d. 1753), who had settled in North Carolina by 1730, served on the Council 1731–1753. He was acting governor for several months in 1734 and again from Johnston's death on 17 July 1752 to Rice's own death the following 29 Jan.

2. Letter not found.

To John Rutherfurd

[26 December 1752]

4th To Mr Rutherford of Same Date, tell him that Mr Walpole agrees to Interpose with the Treasury, for additional Allowance of 5 per Cent, provided for the future he exerts himself in Collecting more than his Predecessors had done,[1] tell him all the Contract for Victualing the Stationd Sloop & Capt Patersons Proposal,[2] Recommend to him Remittances on the Public Acct & to Remind Mr Hassell & J Swann, & to Present 5£ of Capt Patersons for payment of his Note to me.

LB, p. 335.

1. Rutherfurd sought an increase in his 10 percent commission on collections as receiver general of quitrents.

2. Not identified.

To Mrs. Gabriel Johnston

Decr 26th 1752

Tell her agreeable to my letter to Mr Ormes[1] should continue to prosecute the Matters recommended to me by G J——— in his life time, and should Enter a Claim for the Arrears to the Representatives viz his Widow & Children.

That the Lords of the Treasury had so far taken up her Case as to Refer the Petition to Mr H W with whom I should continue my Solicitations for a favourable Report;[2] That the early Measures taken by me had prevented any further Appropriations on the Quit Rents til our Claim was Determined and that I expected to hear from her upon the Several Matters mentiond in my Letter to Mr Ormes being Madam

LB, p. 336. Sent "by Virginia to Watson & Cairns."

1. JA to Ormes, 10 Oct. 1752, pp. 51–52.

2. On 2 Nov. 1752 the Treasury referred to Walpole Mrs. Johnston's memorial of 3 Oct. 1752 (T 1/350) that she have first claim on the colony's quitrents since Governor Johnston's salary (which was to have been paid from the quitrent receipts) was over £13,000 in arrears when he died. Walpole's report to the Treasury of 10 Apr.

1753 briefly recapitulated the troubled state of the colony's quitrent system. He stated that given the intermittent and irregular collecting and reporting of the quitrents, "it is impossible for me to ascertain the exact claim due to the Officers of the Crown." Regarding Mrs. Johnston's claim "that an appropriation of the Quit rents to any new purposes would deprive her from having relief from them," Walpole concluded that it "is (I apprehend) in the present state of the Quit rents but too true and that is the case of the rest of the Officers, who I must observe to your Lordships seem by the present Establishment equally entitled to their respective portion of their arrears out of the Quit rents due to the Crown as they are received, in the meantime if those arrears are to be pay'd in course and preferable to any new incumbrance I don't see how the salary of the Govr lately appointed can be charged upon them and payd, until the Quit rents by a new rent roll & a better management & collection of them shall be vastly increased" (*NCCR*, 5:21–23).

To Robert Dinwiddie

Craven Street Janry 1t 1753

Yesterday had yours Octr 6th & Duplicates inclosd, the Several Packets of Lres sent at Same time by Mr Handbury shall be Deliverd.[1]

Before the Holidays I obtaind a Reference to the Lds for T. of the Addresses,[2] their Report thereon I shall Solicit with the Utmost Diligence, The King of Spains Orders being with you before this will Convince you that I lose no time in the Execution of your Commands.[3]

Concerning the Pistol Fee &c This Matter Mr Hand——y had talkd over with me before the Receipt of yours, & with Lord Halefax the Result whereof was a Letter to you to Explain to them how the Matter Stood before your Arrival;[4] At present I can only give you my privat Oppinion Viz That this Fee relating to the Kings Lands only, not to Matters relative to the Administration of Govert in which the Subject of Right is concerned, that therefore as there is no Express Law giving & Assertaining any particular Fees for this Article, you are therefore Authorized without the Interposition of the Assembly, and Precedents in Point I have from South Carolina.

Mr Handbury tells me you have been Delicat in this point least it might in the Opinion of the Assembly, however I shall contrive to Serve you without being Seen in it and shall Conclude either to take the opinion of the Attorney General upon the Case Stated in a

Memorial or Shall give in a Memorial to the Lords for Tr: & let them do it, And with Complts of the Season I am always Dr Sir

LB, p. 336. Sent "per Mr Handburys Ship."

1. Dinwiddie's letter to JA of 6 Oct. 1752 has not been found, but it no doubt enclosed his letter of the same date to the Board of Trade (cited in JA to Dinwiddie, 20 Dec. 1752, p. 60, n. 7), in which he discussed, among other things, Indian affairs and reducing the number of justices of the peace. Dinwiddie also submitted the question of the pistole fee to the Board to remove all doubts about its legality.

2. JA probably refers to the address of the General Assembly on legislation and the address of the Council on judges' salaries (for which see JA to Dinwiddie, 17 Sept. 1752, pp. 45–46, n. 1; p. 47, n. 5). Both addresses were referred to the Board of Trade by the Privy Council on 21 Dec. 1752 (*APC*, 4:173, 176).

3. See JA to Dinwiddie, 17 Sept. 1752, pp. 46–47, n. 3.

4. Letter not found.

To James Glen

Janry 1t 1753

On Rect of yours of 27th Septr wrote you by Capt Carling then in the Downs,[1] the Lre not being returnd, I conclude it got on board.

I told you Mr Leigh had accepted the Office of C J, & I shall follow your Recommendation of Mr Michie at the Admiralty.

I have had two Conferences with Mr Lovingston who is to Answer yours to him but I am affraid not to your Satisfaction, as what you require he has already given to Mr Hamilton & his Reason for so doing will come from himself.

You have the 2 Magazines for Novr & Decr And in Consequence of your Letter of 29th July[2] I calld at Mr Calverly but found you had not performd your Promise as [to] the Payment of my Arrears & better payment hereafter, I am sorry I am obligd to be So Explicit on this Point but after 2 Years forgetfulness you cannot be Offended I should Remind you & now call upon you for more Punctual Payments hereafter.

Complts of the Season attend you & I am Yours

LB, p. 339. Sent "per Capt Leslie."

1. Glen's letter has not been found. For an abstract of JA's reply, see JA to Glen, 13 Dec. 1752, p. 57.

2. Letter not found.

To John Tinker

Janry 1t 1753

Tell him the Nature of the Report & the Difficulty in geting it at last, shall send Copy thereof when I receive it from the Office,[1] Pray Instructions on the Parlty Negociations as to the Balance.[2]

LB, p. 339. Sent "per Capt Leslie." At the foot of this letter JA wrote: "NB Wrote to him Octr 10th per Capt Ball."

1. John Tinker (d. 1758) was governor of the Bahamas from 1740 until his death. He was a son-in-law of Board of Trade member Martin Bladen and had served as agent for the Royal African Company and the South Sea Company in South America. Tinker had requested thirty cannons, with stores, for the use of Forts Nassau and Montague to fend off Spanish depredations on the islands. On 8 Feb. 1752 the Privy Council referred Tinker's request to the Ordnance Board (*APC*, 4:145). While in London on a leave of absence, Tinker wrote the Board of Trade in July 1752 in support of his application (*JBT*, 9:343). After Tinker's return to the Bahamas, JA seems to have acted as his agent in the matter. The report JA refers to here is probably that from the Ordnance Board to the Privy Council of 18 Jan. 1753, which for several reasons recommended against the application (*APC*, 4:145–147). The Board of Trade communicated the decision to Tinker in a letter of 7 June 1753 (*JBT*, 9:431, 437; "True Account of the rare proceedings of the Government of the Bahama Islands, under John Tinker, the present governor," n.d., Bruce of Arnot Collection, Estate Papers, Bundle 10, Scottish Record Office, H.M. General Register House, Edinburgh).

2. Not identified.

To Nathaniel Rice et al.

[16 January 1753]

Mr Rice Commee of Correspondence NB these are Duplicats both, NB tell the Commee, that I shall revive the Application to the King & Council on ordnance &c to Fortify It has been[1]

LB, p. 339. Sent "per Capt Paterson."

1. JA alludes to an application for ordnance and stores for the fort being erected on the Lower Cape Fear River near Brunswick (later Fort Johnston). Before Governor Dobbs sailed for North Carolina, he submitted a memorial to the Crown soliciting the ordnance and stores "for the safety of the Colony and shipping" (*NCCR*, 5:18–19). On 7 Mar. 1753 the Privy Council referred the memorial to its Plantation Committee, which in turn on 3 Apr. 1753 referred the matter to the Board of Trade, before whom Dobbs and JA appeared on 27 Feb. 1754. JA presented "several papers" in support of the memorial, but the Board did not believe it had sufficient information on which to base a report to the Privy Council, and so postponed further consideration of the matter until Dobbs could transmit "more particular information" (*JBT*, 10:13). After Dobbs had inspected the fort and reported to Halifax on 20 Nov. 1754 (*NCCR*, 5:157–160), the Board on 24 Apr. 1755 forwarded to the Privy Council Dobbs's plan of the fort and his account of its state and condition, recommending that such stores as were absolutely necessary be sent (CO 5/324, p. 176). On 7 May the Plantation Committee agreed with the Board's report and submitted the matter to the Ordnance Board for an estimate. Finally on 7 July 1756 two Orders in Council directed that a total of about £3,400 worth of cannons, ordnance, stores, gunpowder, balls, and flints be sent to the colony (*NCCR*, 5:592–594; *APC*, 4:204–206; *JBT*, 10:264).

To Robert Dinwiddie

[16 January 1753]

Virginia Janry 16th to Govr Dinwiddie about his Fee telling that the Lords of Trade had approvd thereof & should take the Attorney Gnals opinion & transmit the Same.[1]

LB, p. 339. Following this memorandum JA wrote: "NB this Lre Went to the Downs to Capt Robinson of the Osgood."

1. On 12 Jan. 1753 the Board of Trade read Dinwiddie's letter of 6 Oct. 1752 (for which see JA to Dinwiddie, 20 Dec. 1752, p. 60, n. 7) and ordered that a reply be drafted "signifying their lordships' approbation of his taking the said [pistole] fee" (*JBT*, 9:383). The Board's letter of 17 Jan. 1753 did not specifically mention the pistole fee, but stated only that the Board "commend your assiduity in establishing good order and government in the affairs of the colony" (CO 5/1367, pp. 5–7, in Koontz, *Dinwiddie Papers*, 260–261).

On 1 Feb. 1753 Attorney General Dudley Ryder rendered an opinion that upheld Dinwiddie's power to establish the fee by ordinance (CO 5/1328, fol. 83).

To John Tinker

[13 February 1753]

Govr Tinker of 13th Feby 1753 To the Madeira See Balance Bundle.[1]

LB, p. 339.

1. Here and elsewhere JA refers to what seems to have been a file of copies of his letters to various correspondents that has not been discovered; some of these copies were evidently full copies of letters of which only an abstract appears in the letter book, while others seem to have been copies of letters that are apparently complete in the letter book.

To Robert Dinwiddie

March 4th 1753

I am favourd with your Letter of 10th Decr & the Several Letters & Packetts Sent me therewith by Mr Hanburry I have personally Deliverd,[1] I have also Seen your Letter to My Lords for Trade, the Subject Matter of all which Lres relates to procuring A Warrant pro 1000 upon the Quitrents for Enabling Mr Hanbury to purchase Goods as Presents to the Indians according to the [Sketch?] transmitted.[2]

So far as I have procceded in this Negociation, I find the Sentiments of those in the Administration to be That the Presents are essentialy Necessary to those Indians, and that you have done a very acceptable Service to the Govert in So far Securing to the British Interest those People, and that you can do nothing that can so Effectually Establish your Reputation, as pursuing Right Measures in the Administration of Indian Affairs; But at the Same time I find that Such Measures Must be carried into Execution at the *Expence of the Colony* Those of the Ministry whom I have conferred with (viz) Lds Halifax, Duplin, Messrs Walpole West and the Several Members of the Board of Trade all Unanimously unite in oppinion that the Treasury will not be brought into a Charge upon the Quitrents for this Service & of this opinion I found Mr Leheup at first Setting out, Lord Presedt[3] is most heartily Disposed for the Service, because it coincides with his long Adopted Sentiments for making Freinds with all the Indians on the Continent, but at the Same time as the Ways & Means for doing of this does not so properly belong to his Office as to the Treasury, it cannot be expected that he will take the Lead in Directing the Fund: I have talkd the Matter over with Mr Hanbury now confind by the Gout told him the Difficultys that I had met with on the Point of the Q Rent Fund, and that the Ministry all agree in the Expediency of the Service, and in the Provision for the Same out of *the 2 sh*: per Hogshead; Lord Halefax having desird me to Examine for Precedents of Directions of this kind from the Quitrents, I have not been able to get any. But from Mr Hanbury however unwilling he is to Admit the Expediency of a Warrant from the Crown on the Application of the 2 Shill Fund, he tells me that he has heretofore had Orders, upon that Fund for Indian Presents, and from Mr Leheup I find that the Treasury is also poss[ess]ed of Precedents of this Kind from such Presents before and from the Necessity of the Service recommended by you, in which they all agree & from the unsurmountable Difficulty that we shall meet with in the Case of the Quitrents Or in Provision from any Home Fund: I Am apt to think that Provision will be Directed out of the 2 Shill per Hogshead, and how far Mr Hanbury will Imbark on the Credit of Such an order, I cannot Say, I shall Advise a Conference with him on this head.

I have Argued from the Service being a National Service to this Kingdom & the Colonies in General, that therefore the Expence thereof should not fall to the Share of Virginia Alone, the answer to this is that Other Provinces Do Occasionally Provide so far as they are able for Indian Services, and that the Principle upon which Indian Presents have been Granted from Home Funds were the Inability of Particular Provinces, & In Such Cases this Kingdom maid Provision; but without Precedent That the Kings Particular Revenue ever was appropriated for Such Services; In aid of Civil Establishments in America the Kings American Quitrents have been appropriated, because Such Appropriations go in Aid of his home Civil List Establishment, but the Reason does not hold for Extraordinary Services of Govert because Particular Provision is made in Such Cases per Parlt; Such is the Doctrine laid down in this & like Cases for American Services; I am Sensible that Provision has been made on particular Occasions to Georgia & Carolina for

Indian Presents, out of the overplus Money provided for the Military Service, And have Urged this by way of Precedent, yet I doubt of Success NB in the application for a Money grant 1755 on making out of the sum I had a Warrant pro 20000 out of the Military Savings in the Pay Office to be repaid by the Tobacco Duty which was never repaid by the Fund.

As to the former Matters particularly given in charge to me, they stand thus, the Lords for Trade in Conjunction with Mr H Walpole have made a very Favourable & Explicit Report for the Additional Allowance to the Judges;[4] And with Regard to the Address from Council & Assembly, Consisting of 2 Points, the First Praying an Instruction to the Gover for Leave to Re Enact So many of the Laws heretofore Repealed as to his Majesty shall seem Expedient On this Point My Lords for Trade have Reported in Favour of Reenacting 2 Laws (vizt) That to prevent the Building of Wooden Chimneys, and That for an Additional Duty to the Colledge of Williamsburgh, These are the only 2 Acts out of the eight Mentioned in the Reasons for Supporting the Address that has by My Lords for Trade been thought proper to Recommend to His Majesty in Consequence of the Address, And I flatter my Self that such their Report will meet with his Majestys Approbation; As to the Second Point Praying An Explanation of the Instruction that prevents the Gover Giving his Assent to any Law in Alteration or Amendment of a Law which said amendatory Law contains a Suspending Clause to which his Majesty had Assented, on this Head My Lords for Trade have Reported, That His Majestys Instructions to his Governors in the Cases Set forth in the Address from the Council & the Assembly are of Such a Nature as that the Same cannot be Dispensed with without breaking in Upon the Fundamental Maxims of Plantation Govert And therefore Most Explicitly Advise his Majesty to Adhere to the Same Generaly, Leaving the Examination of particular Cases of particular Laws to His Majestys Examination in consequence of the Suspending Clauses in Such Acts,[5] Such is the Substance of the Report for I write from my Memory as Deliverd to me at the Board, No Copys of Report being allowed without a Litigation thereof; from these Principles herein laid down you will be able to Perceive that their Lordships are Determind to Adhere Tenaciously to the Doctrine of Suspending Clauses in General, However I am apt to think that the

Objections that this Address has met with from the Generality of the Dispensation therein Prayd for, may be got over in particular Cases of A very Extraordinary Nature where the Measures will admit of no Delay in point of operation; And that the Arguments made Use of in the Address are of Such a Nature as must carry weight with them when Such particular Cases come under Consideration.

From the Progress that I have already made in these Solicitations thro the Offices, hence thro the Board of Trade & then for the 2d time before Council I find my Disbursments increase considerably, the Case of Additional Salary Must finaly take its Course thro the Treasury, But in both Cases, the Fees of Offices are paid by me, I must therefore have your Directions where or to Whom I am to apply for Reimbursement, as well on Account of what I advanced for the Judges, As for that of the Address from Council & Assembly Which Accounts I shall keep Seperately; As for my Disbursments on your particular Account Mr Hanbury I fancy will not hesitate to Pay me, But without particular Directions from the Council as Judges I cannot Ask it of him, Neither can I in the Case of the Address of the Council & Assembly, altho it may Produce a particular Instruction to you quasi Gover yet the Thing is for the Service of the Province and no doubt will be paid by them; In these Matters I shall Expect your Directions.

But in these Particulars I shall Expect Directions from you Whether I am to transmit my Accounts to you when these Matters are finished, or to have Credit here on Account of my Disbursments for the Public. In the mean time I shall continue the necessary Payments and am

PS   I am affraid that the Light House Act will be opposed by the Mary Land Agent as it in all [*illegible*] Imposes a Duty or Tax upon the Traders to that Province without their Agreemt this Matter may be easily Set to Rights with you, & till its well understood here the Confirmation of the Act will be Litigated And opposed by Mr Sharpe whose Brother the Capt is appointed as Governor of Mary Land.[6]

LB, pp. 340–342. The "NB" notation at the end of the third paragraph appears to have been interpolated after the fourth paragraph was begun. Material in the fifth and sixth paragraphs, beginning "As for my Disbursments" and ending "my Disburs-ments for the Public," was canceled.

1. Dinwiddie's letter to JA has not been found. The other letters that JA delivered were presumably some or all of the following letters from Dinwiddie, all dated 10 Dec. 1752: to the bishop of London (Fulham Papers, 13:99–100); to the Board of Trade (CO 5/1327, pp. 531–536); to the Admiralty (Adm. 1/bundle 3818); to the Treasury (T 1/348, fols. 232–234); to Peter Leheup (T 1/348, fols. 230–231); and to [Thomas] Hill, secretary to the Board of Trade (CO 5/1327, pp. 603, 614). All are in Koontz, *Dinwiddie Papers*, 235–257.

2. In his letter to the Board of 10 Dec. 1752 (preceding note), Dinwiddie proposed that £1,000 from the quitrent revenues be expended for presents to the Twightwee Indians (also known as the Miami) to secure them to the British interest. The Board read Dinwiddie's letter on 8 Mar. 1753 and approved giving the presents (*JBT*, 9:402). In its representation to the Crown of 16 Mar. 1753, however, the Board recommended that the funds be drawn from the revenues of the two-shillings-per-hogshead tobacco export tax rather than from the quitrents (CO 5/1367, pp. 24–26). After consulting with the Treasury and receiving a favorable report, the Privy Council approved the expenditure on 10 May 1753 (*APC*, 4:200–201).

3. JA probably refers to Halifax, the president of the Board of Trade, but he may refer to Earl Granville, the president of the Privy Council.

4. See JA to Dinwiddie, 17 Sept. 1752, p. 47, n. 5.

5. See ibid., pp. 45–46, n. 1.

6. JA refers to "An Act for erecting a Light-House at Cape-Henry," passed on 20 Apr. 1752 (Hening, *Statutes*, 6:227–229). The act provided for the erection, at the expense of the colony of Virginia, of a lighthouse at Cape Henry, on the south side of the entrance to Chesapeake Bay; and it provided further for a duty of 2 pence per ton on each vessel clearing out of the bay, to be applied to reimbursing the cost of building the lighthouse and to its maintenance. For the later history of the act, see JA to Fauquier, 28 Dec. 1758, pp. 275–276.

John Sharpe (ca. 1700–1756) was solicitor to the Treasury 1742–1756, member of Parliament 1754–1756, agent of many West Indian colonies, and occasionally solicitor of North American colonies.

Horatio Sharpe (1718–1790) was appointed lieutenant governor of Maryland on 7 Mar. 1753 (*APC*, 4:199). He served in that capacity until 1769.

To Robert Dinwiddie

March 8th 1753

My Letter of the 4th Inst[1] relates to Public Affairs, this to yours in particular herein you have the Attorney Generals opinion in Support of that of the Lords for Trade to the Pistol fee, to be made

Use of as you see occasion,[2] Col Heron is here but keeps close to Prevent an Arrest for Money Matters between one Davis & him, & to prevent which he is about filing a Bill in Chancery to Stop Proceedings at Common Law till Such time as the Accounts are Settled, this is not the only Scrape that attends him; for there is a Complaint of a very extraordinary Nature hanging over him before the King & Council, that of Supplying the Enemy during the War with Provisions for the Gar[i]son of St Augustine the Affair of the Swedish Ship is also before the King & Council as Part of the Complaint against him, all these Matters together with the many particular Demands on him here Shew him to be a Mad Man to have come home in pursuit of a Govert.[3]

I do not know where it is that he hid himself in a few Days after his arrival, but I have sent your Letter with one from me in the Way to come to him,[4] but I cannot promise you Success, I can make use of Some particular Arguments with him to Induce him to pay me this Debt & these shall not be Wanting So Soon as I can find my Way to him.

I observe what you Say about Mr Richardson & Shall make him a Present on your Account, for which & the Expenses of the Spanish Orders, and the Attorney Generals Opinion I shall call upon Mr Hanbury for Reimbursment.

As your last Letters to me has Imbarkd me farther into the Affairs of your Province, I shall be glad to know in what Situation I stand; I would not be thought to have a Design totaly to Eject Mr Leheup, And by what Mr Hanbury has said to me, I do not apprehend that it is Intended that he should be Set aside, But that the Stress of Provincial Matters is to come to My Share As Conjunct Agent; He askd me if I would go on in this Shape, to which I have told him, that I did not know upon what Establishment you had put me, however that I had no Sort of Objection to go on with Mr Leheup upon the Same Establishment with him, But that as he was Sencible that the greatest Share of Solicitations would go thro my hands & Consequently the Contingent Expences come to My Share, I should therefore Expect to be Reimbursed for all Such Contingent Charges, which according to a Computation thereof in Coach hire Postage of Letters, Gratuitys in Offices, & to Porters at Doors, &c, amount to about 30 per Annum & this Sum I have charged at a Medium & as Such is allowd me from North Carolina

As my Contingent Bill & Indeed without which the Personal Pay would be greatly under the Service of an Agent, I know that Mess[rs] Sharpe & Paris[5] take very great Latitudes in the formation of their Contingent Bills, however rather than take the trouble of keeping Accounts for Coach hire, half Crown & Shillings at Doors & New Years Gifts, I in Example of Mr Fury in the South Carolina Accounts charge these Articles to 30£ by which the Advantage is rather on the Side of the Colonie considering that the Disbursments of Agents are always in Advance for their Colonies, It is my real oppinion that Mr Leheup is so Situated that however Actively he was disposed in the Service, that it would not answer his purpose to break in upon his Treasury Service, by a Constant Attendance on other Offices & Attention to American Matters However as many of these Matters especialy where Money is in question of course comes before the Treasury, there his Service comes naturaly in his Way, Wherefore the Continuation of his Appointment becomes Necessary for his Services was it confind to this Part of Duty alone, But this is not all for with regard to my Self, I should not like to go on in Any Service where I should meet in the Course of Bussiness those who thought I had broke in upon them; But Whether it is that Mr Hanbury has closed up this Matter with Mr Leheup with regard to me, as he Said he had & that Mr Leheup understood it very well It is certain that Mr Leheup from first to last ever Since I had to Do with your Affairs is become remarkably Civil to me Indeed I am Indebted to Lord Halefax for one Circumstance that shewd Mr Leheup in What light they looked upon me at that Board, His Lordship at first Seting out addressed himself to me Alone tho Mr Leheup was the Senior Officer and after this I have found that Mr Leheup was not Summoned to Attend in these Cases more particularly recommended to me, However these Circumstances and Some others that Shew the oppinion of the Board of Trade to be, that they are to have my presence oftener than his has not So as I can perceive any wise created Umbrage or a Jealousy on his Part, all which makes me Conclude that provided his Salary is continued he will not take it amiss that We become Conjunct Agents, And the time of bringing this Matter on the Carpet with you may be when I come to Report finally the Success of these Negociations now properly in Agitation by me alone.

Foreign News we have none, Since the Alarm given by the King of Prussias Retention of the Silesia Loan,[6] the Case of which being extreamly New in its Doctrine, and remarkably well Answerd on our Part, I therefore Send you the Whole; To this Case Suceeded a Repetition of Cabinet Councils, no less I think than eleven Nocturnal Councils; the Subject of their Deliberations, Whether the Charge Exhibited by Lord Ravens——th, upon the Information of Mr Fossett Recorder of Newcastle, That Mr Stone & the Solicitor General Did In Company at the house of one Mr—— a Mercer in Ludgate hill Drink the Pretenders health on or about the Year 1732, Such say the Town was the Examination, which by all accounts produced nothing but a great Deal of trouble to those who Attended, and may hereafter be productive of Ill Will between the Persons Accused and their Accusers; that he might be at liberty & free from Office the Sol. General offerd his Resignation thereof to the King but was refused, and in the End he Made the finest Speech that ever was Spoke in the English Language Copy whereof the D of N[7] Demanded for his Majesty & to him only & the Duke of New: the Same was given; Whether the Duke of B——d will have all this Matter agitated de Novo in the House of Peers, or Whether Mr Stone who was principaly chargd will bring his Action against Mr Fossett by Way of Defamation, or whether it will finally End in Removing Mr Stone from the P of W—— the only meaning that Such acusations will have, time will discover.[8]

I just now hear that the Chicasaws have Repulsd the French & their Chactaw Indians with great loss to the french Army & but of 25 Chicasaws this Coincides with the Plan of operations pursued by the French with regard to your New Allies the Twightees viz their Intention seems to be to Demolish all Nations of Indians, more particularly Attached to Our Interest, An Object that deserves the greatest Attention of our Ministry.

LB, pp. 342–345. Sent "per Mr Hanburys Ship."

1. See preceding letter.

2. See JA to Dinwiddie, 16 Jan. 1753, p. 66, n. 1.

3. Lt. Col. Alexander Heron, who had served in Georgia and South Carolina, was the object of several charges that Capt. Caleb Davis had laid before the Privy Council. In June 1751 Davis appealed the Feb. 1749 verdict of a Savannah court of £1,600 sterling in favor of James Edward Powell, whose ship the *Murray* Davis had

taken as a prize for illegally carrying provisions to the Spanish at Saint Augustine. Davis alleged that Heron, "in Order to distress and ruin [him] by His Artfull Management and Officious Interposition," induced Powell to sue Davis. The Privy Council overturned the Georgia verdict and ordered that Davis be returned any money he had paid, with interest (*APC*, 4:128–130). In June 1752 Davis made other charges before the Privy Council, alleging that Heron had imprisoned him for demanding money he had left with Heron while on a cruise, imprisoned as pirates Davis and the captain and lieutenant of a privateer owned by Davis, taken from Davis a vessel Davis had captured as a prize and returned it to its former owner (probably the *Murray*), and committed other offenses. Heron returned his answers in writing to the Privy Council in Apr. 1753, at which time he entered into a bond of £500 not to leave the kingdom. In Mar. 1754 the Privy Council dismissed Davis's complaints (*APC*, 4:170–172). The "Affair of the Swedish Ship" is not mentioned in *APC*. Heron sought appointment, unsuccessfully, as the first royal governor of Georgia.

4. Neither Dinwiddie's nor JA's letter to Heron has been found.

5. Ferdinand John Paris, a London barrister, served at various times as agent for a number of clients: Maryland's lower house; the Pennsylvania and East Jersey proprietors; the freeholders of Halifax, Nova Scotia; the absentee landlords of Jamaica; and the clergy of Virginia.

6. Frederick II, king of Prussia, upset that Britain did not return Prussian ships carrying contraband that had been seized during the Second War of the Austrian Succession (1744–1748), impounded the last payment due to British creditors on the Silesian loan floated in 1753 by Charles VI. The payment was to have been £250,000.

7. Thomas Pelham-Holles (1693–1768), first duke of Newcastle.

8. To discredit Solicitor General William Murray and others influential with the Prince of Wales (later George III), Whigs circulated a story that originated with Christopher Fawcett, recorder of Newcastle. Fawcett, while dining with Henry Liddell (1708–1784), Baron Ravensworth, alleged that Murray, Andrew Stone (a member of the Board of Trade), and James Johnson, bishop of Gloucester, had toasted the Pretender in the house of a Jacobite mercer in Ludgate. Murray denied the charge. Fawcett was brought to London and examined before a cabinet council, and the charge was shown to be false. Murray's denial was accepted by the cabinet, but Bedford did move for papers on the subject in the House of Lords. After the whole affair was discussed again, Bedford's motion failed without a division.

To the Committee of Correspondence of North Carolina

Gentlemen of the Committee of North Carolina   March 8th 1753
I have little to add to my last by Capt Paterson[1] Parliamentary Matters having broke in upon the Lords for Trade their Lorships have not been able hetherto to Discuss the Affairs of No Carolina;

a few days More will put an End to the Matters now in hand & then they propose taking our Affairs into Consideration.[2]

The Governor talks of Seting out in May but I am rather Inclind to think that it will be later in the year, as the Provincial Affairs & those more immediatly relating to him quasi Gover, seem to go hand in hand It will be for his Interest not to Depart from hence till Matters are brought to Such an Issue as to lay the foundation of an honourable & Peaceable Administration of the Interior Government & Such as may hereafter help him out in the pursuit of what farther Schemes he may have in view for the good of the Colonie.[3]

I shall lose no time or opportunety in acquainting you, how our Affairs now at an Issue go on & am Gentlemen

LB, p. 345. At the foot of the letter JA wrote: "March 6th per Capt Pearson," and "Inclosd in a few Lines to Mr Rice," likely the letter to Rice of 14 March 1753, below.

1. See JA to Rice et al., 16 Jan. 1753, p. 65.

2. The journals of the Board of Trade do not suggest what these parliamentary matters might have been.

3. For the "Provincial Affairs" that delayed Governor Dobbs's departure for North Carolina, see JA to Dinwiddie, 20 Oct. 1752, p. 56, n. 13.

To James Glen

March 8th 1753

I am Surprized that I have not heard from you by these Several Ships cannot acct for such forgetfulness.

My Lds for Trade may with Reason complain of your Remissness when Acct came of Remarkable Events as that of Attacks on the Chicasaws & no notice thereof from you.[1]

It would not be prudent in me to write with that freedom as I could wish to Do, but if you have any particular freind in Power its time to put him on his Guard lest Clamour make Impressions that in the End may burst and Did Mr Shirly whose freinds say and not I from my own knowledge Act with the Same Delicacy as Mr Tinker did you need fear no harm.[2]

PS We have Many Reports of our Country Mens breaking Graeme is gone & more Said will Soon Follow.[3]

PS Let Not these Bills come repeated in any Shape from you.

JA

LB, p. 346. Sent per "Capt Leslie."

1. This is the first hint in JA's letter book that imperial authorities were displeased with Glen. The Board of Trade, which had begun to reprimand Glen in 1748, criticized him for failing to adhere to his instructions and failing to uphold the royal prerogative. See "The Decline of Governor Glen, 1750–1753," chap. 12 in Sirmans, *Colonial South Carolina*.

For the attacks on the Chickasaw, see JA to Dinwiddie, 8 Mar. 1753, pp. 71–74.

2. William Shirley (1694–1771) was governor of Massachusetts 1741–1756.

3. JA may allude here to the declining influence of native Scots in South Carolina affairs. James Graeme, a Scottish attorney who was an ally of Glen, had died on 29 Aug. 1752. Graeme was chief justice of the colony and a councillor at the time of his death.

To Nathaniel Rice

March 14th 1753

Acknowledge his of Decr 13th[1] Inclose therein One to the Committee.[2]

LB, p. 346. Sent "per Pearson." At the head of this memorandum JA wrote: "for [*or* See?] the Carolina letters."

1. Letter not found.

2. See following entry.

To the Committee of Correspondence of North Carolina

[15 March 1753]

March 15th 1753 acknowledge their Bill for 30£ on Mr Wilkins & when paid to give Credit See Original in Bundle of Letters.

LB, p. 346.

To Robert Dinwiddie

March 20th 1753

Tell him the Representation from the Lords for Trade to Council recomding the 1000 to be pd out of the 2 Shlls, That the King being very Jealouse of his Q rents their Lordships cautiously Guarded against giving any bad Impression of him on Acct of his Desiring the Money from the Q Rents.[1] The King had agreed to the Report of the Committee, on the Judges Salary out of the 2 shills per Hogshead & Instruction to Reenact the 2 Laws heretofore mentiond.[2]

LB, p. 346. Sent "per Capt Randolph."

  1. See JA to Dinwiddie, 4 Mar. 1753, p. 71, n. 2.

  2. See JA to Dinwiddie, 17 Sept. 1752, pp. 45–46, n. 1; p. 47, n. 5.

To James Glen

[23 March 1753]

March 23d 1753 Desire a more punctual performance of his Ingagments & Promises.

LB, p. 346. Sent "per Pearson with a Box from the Lords for Trade &c."

To Robert Dinwiddie

April 9th 1753

About a finesse in Office on Affair of the Judges Salary See Copy of Letter in the Bundle NB finesse to set the Precedent of a Kings warrant on the Revenue 2 shlls per hogshead.[1]

LB, p. 346.

  1. See JA to Dinwiddie, 4 Mar. 1753, p. 71, n. 2. The "finesse in Office" refers to gaining the assent of the Treasury to the proposal. See JA to Dinwiddie, 3 May 1753, pp. 79–80.

To John Tinker

May 1st 1753

Vide Bundle of Letters pro Balance.

LB, p. 346. Sent "per Capt Cheesman."

To Robert Dinwiddie

Sir   May 3rd 1753

I am now to congratulate you on the successful Issue of our
Negociations for an Augmentation of the Salary to the Judges of
your Province of 50 per an from the Tobacco Duty; The Kings
Warrant for this purpose now inclosed to you,[1] no doubt will be
very acceptable to these Gentlemen, however meritorious their case
may be thought, that alone I doubt had not carryd their point, for
it is to the weight of your recommendation, properly applyd, that
this negociation, which had hetherto miscarryd standing on the
same principles has at length succeeded, and this success is the
more agreeable, since the difficultys which at my first seting out in
this solicitation, were represented to me as unsurmountable with
the Treasury, have been overcome or rather artfully evaded, by
steering another course, but it is from the matter as much as from
the manner of this negociation, that proper acknowledgments may
be expected from those who reap the Succeeding benefit.

The fees and gratuitys in Office, disbursed by me are particularly
Stated in the account now inclosed;[2] my personal Services &
expences through this Solicitation, I must leave to your good
Offices with the Several Gentlemen concerned, but on this head
permit me to Suggest to your consideration, a proposition which I
think may be reasonably agreed to, and as such I had it in my view
by contending for a retrospective allowance to the Judges, (vizt)
That as the Warrant for additional Salarys carrys with it a retrospective payment of Six Months all but a few days (vizt) from the
25th of October, preceding the 25th of April which is the usual
period or term of payment of the Judges Salarys, that such
retrospective additional Salarys go towards payment of the Solicitation, which according to this proposition & proportion will be no

more than 25 Ster to each of the Judges for the whole expense of this Solicitation including Fees of Office,[3] which Same if reduced into the Articles of a Solicitors Bill would for Attendance alone to every of the Judges concerned ammount to three times that Sum; and as this Case stands by managment in the Solicitation thereof from the retrospective allowance of Six months additional Salary the Success goes farther than the original Address, for neither the Address, nor my Instructions thereon point out any Solicitation for a retrospective allowance; So that in fact by such allowance going towards the Solicitation they carry their Address according to the letter thereoff, without any expence at all; this proposition I have thought proper to furnish you with and referring to other Letters herewith sent[4] I am always Dr Sir Most Obedly Yours

LB, p. 348. Sent "per Mr Hanburys Ship." At the head of the letter, following the dateline, JA wrote: "as to Additional Salarys pro Judges." A canceled draft of this letter is on p. 347 of the letter book. Substantive differences between the two versions are accounted for in notes to the present letter.

1. See JA to Dinwiddie, 17 Sept. 1752, p. 47, n. 5.

2. Enclosure not found.

3. At this point in the canceled draft JA wrote: "this proposition I had in view, by contending for a Retrospective Clause which with a good deal of Pains & managment I at length carryd for Six Months as you will See by the Words of the Warrant."

4. For the other letters sent, see the following letter, source note.

To Robert Dinwiddie

Sir   May 4th 1753

Inclosed you have his Majestys Instruction Authorizing you to give your assent to Acts for reenacting two of the ten Acts heretofore repealed by his Majesty, which Instruction you will observe is subject to some particular Exceptions;[1] it does not come within my Duty to Animadvert on his Majestys Judgment with regard to this Instruction so qualified; and it was more through favour, than of right, that I had any Intimation of the Objections that had laid the foundation for the repeal of these ten Laws; some of which Laws (I could not but observe in my Arguments before my Lords for Trade in support of the Address,) were of such a Nature and so very well precedented throughout the American Colonies as scarce to deserve his Majestys attention much less to draw his Resentment against them, however I have just grounds to be Satisfyd that not one of these Laws so repealed but was objected to in the strongest manner by the Governor who had given his assent thereto; the inconsistency of such Conduct I am at a loss how to account for.

The 2d part of the Address, praying his Majesty to dispense with that Instruction which injoins Governors not to assent to any Act proposed for altering or amending any Acts that have been confirmed or Assented to by his Majesty, is totally rejected, in consequence no doubt of My Lords for Trade having given judgment against it and from the disagreeable reception that this part of the Address has met with I have cause to think that their displeasure on this point may come repeated to you by letter[2] However tho we have not met with Success in obtaining a general explanatory Instruction on this point, yet in the course of my Negociations & arguments in support of the principles of the Address, I think that I am warranted to conclude that particular Cases coming within the Inconveniencys pointed at in the Address will be favourd according to the circumstances attending such Cases, and however tenacious & attentive those in the Administration of Plantation Govert are to the Doctrine of Suspending clauses in Acts, nevertheless that the rectitude of such Measures will Still be determind according to the urgency of the particular Motives productive of Such Acts; In short that it is from the latitude of this part of the Address, that it has not been granted in the general manner prayd for; and from the penetration of My Lords for Trade I am led to think that they will stedfastly adhere to their opinion, against breaking in upon this Instruction (which they deem a fundamental one) from sugestions of Eventual Inconveniencys I have disbursd the Fees in Offices upon the Ad: of Council & Assembly preparatory to this Instruction amounting to 15.3.0 which you will take care to see reimbursed to me & you will observe that I have been chargd with no Fee for the Instruction itself in none of the Offices, as it does not fully answer the purpose of the Address.

NBB *You have also inclosed* Copy of His Majestys order of Council for 1000£, for Indian Presents out of 2 shil per hogshead,[3] which

Order comes out in the Shape, that from the beginning I thought it would, the Original Order I have left in the Treasury, and as his Majesty in Council has thus approvd of the Services & directed the Money Mr Hanbury seems to think that I had better suspend the farther Application for A Warrant from the Treasury & rest the [*illegible*] on the Order of Council, & in this oppinion Mr Leheup joins, whereupon since Mr Handbury is the person mostly concernd in this Matter by advancing the Money I shall acquiesse in resting the Matter where it now stands till I have your farther Directions therein the Fees advanced by me for this affair I shall get from Mr Handbury & for My own trouble [*illegible*] in Solicitation thereof I have chargd nothing to the Province tho it comes not within my original Instructions.

These Several Matters recommended to my particular care being thus finished I shall now long to hear from you what farther disposition is made of me in the Service of the Colony; I would [not] willingly be thought to act out of Character officiously, nor on the other hand would I be thought neglectfull of any Service that you had so much as hinted to me, I am therefore now under some difficulty with regard to following the Provinces Affairs now in agitation, more particularly the Laws on which I have heretofore corresponded & the Cannon for the Ohio settlements[4] however I think it best to go on & continue my Solicitations in the character of Agent especially Since Mr Leheup & Mr Hanbury play it into my hands and with pleasure without any kind of Jealousy while Mr Leheup receives his usual Salary, Act or not Act, but as I said before, his Acting in Treasury Matters will make amends for the Continuation of his Salary.

The reception that I have met with from Lord Halifax & the Lords for Trade during these my Negociations for Virginia and indeed from all the Offices leaves me no room to Doubt of their Countenance to me in this Service and as Lord Halifax in particular has expressd himself in so kind a manner I have grounds to believe my Continuing in the Colony service will be very acceptable to him I woud not wish however to be looked upon as [an Intruder or Interloper amongst them,][5] these Motives together [with] what Mr Charles agent for New York[6] our acquaintance very genteely opened to me within these few days makes me a little more attentive to the Service of the Colony, he told me that a freind of his had acquainted him that your Assembly had under their consideration the want of a proper Agent as a Provincial Agent their former Agent by whom Mr Leheup apparently was meant not being Such,[7] & from this matter having been talkd of in the Assembly in Virginia that his freind had mentiond his name, but, recollecting that I was concernd in Some shape or other for the Province, he had not pursued this Intelligence without aprising me, thereof, from what quarter his Intelligence came, I cannot tell, nor did I ask him, perhaps all this may have arisen from the Operation & repetition of your Measures with regard to me, I fairly told him the Connexion of a very long Standing that had Subsisted between you & me; and that considering the Singular Service that you had just now done for your Council in procuring what former Governors could not an Augmentation of Salary Solicited thrô me that Such Services could not but give you the most Solid Pretensions of the recomendation of An Agent, and from Such recommendation, I could not doubt of Success, was Mr Leheup to be removed, but that thinking Mr Leheup may be of Service in Treasury Matters that I had therefore recommended the continuation of him as Dead gain in the Agency, & was willing to go on with the Business as Conjunct Agent with him, but that, at present, I acted alone only on special Affairs, and conjunctly with Mr Leheup on other Provincial Matters; and should continue to do So, from these Motives therefore I am induced to go on & to follow the Several Other matters relative to your Govert, till I hear from you; and this leads me to Repeat to you the opposition taken up to the light house Act by Mr Sharp Solicitor on behalf of Mary Land, he has not gone so far as to Move for the Repeal thereof, but far enough to leave no room to expect a Confirmation or approbation thereof;[8] to Obviat this Difficulty if it is a favourite Act with your Province, you had better try to Compromize the Matter with Mr Horatio Sharp who sets out in a few days Gover of Mary Land, to whom I have made mention of this Matter; and While the Objections heretofore communicated to you with regard to the privat Acts now at the Board of Trade, vizt the Want of Certificats of their having been previously published in the Several Parishes, before passing thereof till Such Certificates come[9] they must lay by this I have heretofore taken Notice of as well as to Public Acts I think it is for the Service of the Colony not to press too Speedily his

Majestys approbation thereof unless they do contain Suspending Clauses that prevent their operation in the meantime, that I do not find to be the Case of any of these public Acts [*illegible*] as of the Fees to be paid on the privat Acts, nothing further remains to be taken Notice of but the 30, 3 pounders mentiond in your last letter, for the Ohio Settlements; this Matter was properly Represented to the King in Council by the Lords for Trade, and by the Council Referred to the board of Ordnance & according to the Custom of that Board Reported against, there being no Forts in that part of the World within the Department of the Office.

The Report of the Board of Ordnance having been considered in Council was Referred to the Consideration of the Lords for Trade, and their Lordships have taken it to pieces, and represented to his Majesty that the Services Intended by Such Cannon is not for regular fortifications but for Redoubts or Wooden Forts against Indians in order to cover & protect your out Settlements and in Short they stren[u]ously recommend the Same to his Majesty on State principles as well as for the safty of the out Settlements, & I have no Doubt but that Lord President[10] will enter into & Support the Report of the Board of Trade in opposition to that of the Board of Ordnance, who have led me a Dance for these 12 Months past for Ordnance for Mr Tinker of Providence,[11] and in order to get the better of them I am at last obligd to get the Board of Trade to Interpose.

May 20th
Here begins a new Lre I conclude this my letter on Business with remarking that on the whole we have no Reason to complain of our Winters Campaign with regard to the Affairs of Virginia; the Order for Restitution from the Spaniards for your Sloop, (of which I am surprizd you take no Notice of its arrival) was obtaind in the most expeditious as well as what was Judged to be the most effectual Manner;[12] that of the Judges Salary went on with greater Alacrity than Solicitations for Money generaly do, and this is the more remarkable considering that the Same Application had miscarryd heretofore; The Address from Council & Assembly tho not alltogether Successfull, yet brought to an Issue carrying with it Some degree of favour, Notwithstanding the general Disaprobation the later part thereof had at first Sight met with, Carr[y]ing

with it Such Doctrine in the oppinion of those of the Administration by coming from So Loyal a Colony as that of Virginia as could not but Alarm his Majesty; and here let me give a privat hint never to Countenance any Address in general terms, that has a general Tendency to defeat any one of your Instructions; In particular Cases, particular Remonstrances will always have their weight with the Lords for Trade; I found the Resentment so warm, to the general latitude prayd for by the later part of the Address, that I had recourse to Establish the Doctrine thereof from the mischief Arising from a particular Act that had reced his Majestys approbation, & which Act could not be altered without the Liberty prayd for however detrimental Such Law was discoverd to be in its operation I mean the Act that affects Remiting on protested Bills of Exchange[13] & for this I was obligd to Colonel Beverlys letter to Mr Athaws,[14] this hint engagd their Lordships Attention to this particular Law & they immediatly thereupon gave Mr Pownal Orders to Follow the Same for a Report thereof[15] & tho the Objections to this Law after the King has assented thereto came from the Merchants I do not find that they bestir themselves in it; and its not my business to do it To remove their public or Official Resentment to you as representative of the Crown for having countenanced an Address of so general & of so intensive a Tendency I argued with them, in public & afterwards privat, that you had taken no other share therein than by transmitting the Same to his Majesty which your Duty most certainly obligd you to do & had you taken upon you to have stopt the chanel of Addressing his Majesty you had justly drawn upon you his Majestys & their Lordships Resentment as well as that of the Legislature of the Province, in short upon the whole we are well off that the Kings Instruction now Sent you passes that part of the Address Sub Silentio & on this Point we are obligd to Our Freinds in Office Pownal & Will Sharpe[16] that the Instruction goes not So far as the Several Reports upon which the Same is grounded, I have no occasion to make use of Arguments with you In favour of my own Address in the Managment of these Matters but I assure you that there is a certain degree of confidence & knowledge necessary to be attained by a Person who acts as Agent that in all Cases will give him Singular Advantages in the Service of his Constituents and occasionally very interesting to his particular friends, beyond what others have whose Reputation in business is not so well establishd, and whether I am or am not to continue on the Colony Service you may be assurd my Dr. Freind that I shall always Interest mySelf in what personally concerns you (from this principle I took part in the Pistol Fee so soon as Mr Hanbury broke the Same to me), & now with Compts to Mrs Dinwiddie & the young Ladies I am Most Affectionatly My Dr Sir Yours

PS   I had almost forgott to tell you that I attended the hearing on tuesday last at the Cockpit[17] on the appeal against Parson Kay whose case you recommended to me, & then the Matter was Determind in favour of the Parson against the Church Wardens with this Singular favourable circumstance of 80£ Sterling Costs to be paid to the Parson, the Solicitors tell me that they never remember to have had above 60 pound for Costs, however from the hardship of the Parsons case they gave him 80£.[18]

LB, pp. 350–354. The letter was initially dated 3 May. At the head of the letter, following the dateline, JA wrote: "with the Kings Instruction of the Address from Council and Assembly." At the foot of the letter he wrote: "NB the 3 preceding letters went out by the ship of Mr Hanbury, vizt the Dinwiddie"; it is unclear exactly which letters this refers to. An undated, canceled draft of about the first two paragraphs is on p. 349 of the letter book.

1. See JA to Dinwiddie, 17 Sept. 1752, pp. 45–46, n. 1.

2. No such letter from the Board of Trade has been found.

3. See JA to Dinwiddie, 4 Mar. 1753, p. 71, n. 2.

4. In a letter to the Board of Trade of 10 Dec. 1752 (CO 5/1327, pp. 531–536), Dinwiddie recommended that forts be built on the Ohio River to protect Virginians and Indians in alliance with the British, and he proposed that twenty or thirty three-pound cannons be provided for such forts. The Board read Dinwiddie's letter on 8 Mar. 1753 (*JBT*, 9:401–402), and on 16 Mar. signed a representation to the Crown in support of Dinwiddie's recommendations (CO 5/1367, p. 23.) The Privy Council on 3 Apr. referred the matter to the Ordnance Board, which objected to the application as premature since no forts had yet been built (WO 47/41, pp. 396–397). On 19 Apr. the Privy Council referred the report of the Ordnance Board to the Board of Trade, which considered the matter again on 1 May 1753 (*JBT*, 9:416–417). In a representation of 10 May (CO 5/1367, pp. 31–34), the Board of Trade held that the small size and number of cannons Dinwiddie had requested indicated that he was not proposing that "Forts of Strength" be built, but rather "small Wooden Block-houses such as are usually erected in His Majesty's Colonys in America for the Security of the Indians and the Defence of His Majesty's Subjects, transient Traders amongst

them." The Privy Council on 15 May ordered the Ordnance Board to prepare an estimate of thirty three-pounders with stores. The Ordnance Board replied that there were no three-pounders available, but that it could provide thirty four-pounders with stores for about £1,200. An Order in Council of 10 Aug. 1753 approved the sending of these cannons and stores (CO 324/28, pp. 362–367; *APC*, 4:201–203).

5. JA struck out this phrase. It has been retrieved to complete the sense of the sentence.

6. Robert Charles (1706?–1770), who had served as private secretary to Pennsylvania governor Patrick Gordon from 1726 to 1736, served as New York's agent from 1748 to 1770 and as joint agent for Pennsylvania from 1754 to 1761.

7. According to Landon Carter, the House of Burgesses criticized Leheup on 16 Apr. 1752 as it considered appointing an agent to present an address to the Crown (Jack P. Greene, ed., *The Diary of Landon Carter of Sabine Hall, 1752–1778*, 2d ed. [Richmond, 1987], 1:104; JA to Dinwiddie, 17 Sept. 1752, pp. 45–46, n. 1).

8. See JA to Dinwiddie, 4 Mar. 1753, p. 71, n. 6.

9. See JA to Dinwiddie, 20 Oct. 1752, p. 56, n. 10.

10. Earl Granville.

11. See JA to Tinker, 1 Jan. 1753, p. 65, n. 1.

12. See JA to Dinwiddie, 17 Sept. 1752, pp. 46–47, n. 3.

13. On 10 May 1749 Gov. William Gooch assented to "An Act for ascertaining the damage upon protested bills of exchange, and for the better recovery of debts due on promissory notes; and for the assignment of bonds, obligations, and notes" (*JHB, 1742–1749*, 401, printed in Hening, *Statutes*, 6:85–87). Early in Dinwiddie's administration the House of Burgesses directed its Committee of Propositions and Grievances to prepare a bill to amend this act, but after several rounds of debate and amendment the House on 11 Apr. 1752 "passed in the Negative" its engrossed bill for that purpose (*JHB, 1752–1758*, 14, 49, 69, 71, 76, 84). The political context of this legislation is summarized by Gwenda Morgan, " 'The Privilege of Making Laws': The Board of Trade, the Virginia Assembly and Legislative Review, 1748–1754," *Journal of American Studies* 10 (1976): 1–15.

14. Letter not found. Edward Athawes was one of the most prominent London merchants trading to Virginia. Colonel Beverly may have been William Beverley (d. 1756), a councillor 1752–1756.

15. John Pownall (1720–1795) was solicitor and clerk of reports for the Board of Trade from 1 May 1745 until 6 June 1753, when he became joint secretary to the Board with Thomas Hill. He served as sole secretary from 25 Oct. 1758 to 23 Jan. 1776 (*JBT*, 8:163, 9:430–431, 10:416, 14:2). In 1768 Pownall became undersecretary of state for the colonies as well. The journals of the Board of Trade do not record the order to Pownall to which JA refers.

16. William Sharpe (d. 1767) was clerk of the Privy Council in extraordinary 1722–1730 and in ordinary 1730–1767. He was a brother of Maryland governor Horatio Sharpe and agent Joshua Sharpe.

17. The Privy Council chamber in a building erected opposite Whitehall on the site of a cockpit.

18. See JA to Dinwiddie, 17 Sept. 1752, pp. 47–48, n. 10.

To James Glen

May 8th [1753]

Tell him of Mr Pinkneys arrival in town,[1] that Mr Leigh will have an opportunety of Serving him; whose privat affairs retard his Motions, I have heard it often mentiond that he aims at the Govert, but have no reason to apprehend danger from that Quarter, what may be your fate agt next general Election cannot say, by Vacating their Seats for the Ad: they must be provided for, the Case of Sir Danvers Osborn for New Yorke.[2]

I am sorry for your being incommoded by the Case of Dutch Ship,[3] but I cannot think that an Excuse for preventing your punctuality with me, am [*illegible*] to have mentiond this Affair so often but there is nothing so likely to lessen you in the opinion of your Freinds as that of trifling with your promises I send you the last Magazines & am

LB, p. 346. Sent "per Cheesman."

1. Charles Pinckney (ca. 1699–1758), South Carolina planter, lawyer, member of the Commons House of Assembly 1729, 1731–1741 (Speaker 1736–1740), and councillor 1741–1758, had removed to England.

2. Sir Danvers Osborn (1715–1753), third baronet, was married to Lady Mary Montagu, a sister of Halifax. He was a member of Parliament from 1747 until the prorogation of 7 June 1753. Having vacated his seat, he was recommended on 30 May 1753 by the Board of Trade to the Crown for the governorship of New York in the room of George Clinton, who had asked permission to return to England (*JBT*, 9:428, 430). Osborn was appointed governor in July and arrived in New York on 10 Oct. 1753. Two days later he committed suicide, apparently in despair over the recent death of his wife.

3. See JA to Glen, 7 Oct. 1751, p. 14, n. 3.

To James Glen

[12 May 1753]

Governor Glen May 12th 1753 about the Report of Mr Pitts being Governor[1] See Bundle Letters per Cheesman.[2]

LB, p. 349. Sent "per Cheesman."

1. Thomas Pitt (1705–1761), an older brother of William Pitt, controlled three rotten boroughs. In exchange for his interest in the boroughs, Henry Pelham and Halifax offered him the governorship of South Carolina, proposing to raise the salary from £1,900 to £2,500 per annum. Instead Pitt accepted a pension of £1,000 per annum. The new governor appointed in 1755, William Henry Lyttelton, was a brother-in-law of the Pitts.

2. George Chisman (*Laurens Papers*, 2:27).

To Samuel Swann

June 7th 1753

Inclosd you have Mr Quinnes[1] Bill pro 123.7.6 with the Protest the Bill I have Sent by reason the Notary tells me that its necessary as I told you before that I have chargd the Public with [provincial?] Interest on the Bill from the day on which payment should have been made you will take care that Mr Quinne makes the Same good from the 4th Inst to the Public I am always

LB, p. 354. Sent "per the Baltimore." At the foot of the letter JA wrote: "NB this Letter & Bill was recalld & [sent?] per Mr Lane."

1. Not identified.

To Robert Dinwiddie

[8 June 1753]

To Mr Dinwiddie June 8th 1753 per the Same Ship[1] See the Copy of Lre in the bundle of Lres about the Agency & Cannon.

LB, p. 354.

1. It is unclear what ship JA refers to, for this memorandum follows the letter to Dinwiddie of 4 May/20 May 1753 in the letter book.

To James Glen et al.

[29 June 1753]

Governor Glen June 29th See Bundle of Letters, Do Michie with Commission for Judge of Admiralty[1] & Bull & Jas Wright[2] Magazines for May per Capt Brown Do to Michie 3d July Manegault & Cleland about the Agency.[3]

LB, p. 355.

1. See JA to Glen, 13 Dec. 1752, p. 57, n. 2.

2. Bull was likely either William Bull I (1683–1755), a councillor from 1720 until his death, or William Bull II (1710–1791), a councillor from 1749 until the Revolution.

James Wright (1716–1785) was attorney general of South Carolina 1742–1760 (succeeding JA), agent of the colony in London 1757–1760, lieutenant governor of Georgia 1760–1761, and governor of Georgia 1761–1782.

3. JA evidently wrote to Assemblyman Gabriel Manigault (1704–1781) and Councillor John Cleland (d. 1760) about the South Carolina agency after learning that James Crokatt intended to resign. Crokatt wrote to the committee of correspondence of the Commons House of Assembly on 6 July 1753 stating that he would at all times be ready to assist anyone appointed to replace him except JA, "whose treatment will not admit of my having any Connexions with him on any account whatsoever" (*JCHA*, 12:312n).

To Robert Dinwiddie

[29 June 1753]

Governor Dinwiddie June 29th 1753 per Dinwiddie See Letter Bundle saild the [*illegible*] 22d the Downs.

LB, p. 355.

To James Hasell

[29 June 1753]

North Carolina June 29th per Capt McDonnel in the Baltimore to Mr James Hasell with protest of Bill of 35 on Mr James Hamilton of Hull, & draw upon him pro 39.12. in favour of Capt Mcdonnel, per his Bill payable here.[1]

LB. p. 355.

1. Hasell's bill of exchange was presumably to cover the fees required for his appointment to the Council of North Carolina. See JA to Johnston, 9 Dec. 1751, pp. 25–26, n. 13, and JA to Hasell, 26 Dec. 1752, p. 61.

To James Innes et al.

[29 June 1753]

To Col Innis Mr Murray Mr Rutherford inclosing Mrs Johnstons, Mrs Allen[1] NB Mrs Johnstons see Copy bundle Letters.

LB, p. 355. The heading of the preceding entry (through "Baltimore") probably refers to this entry also.

1. Sarah (Rhett) Allen, eldest daughter of William Rhett, of South Carolina, was the widow of Eleazer Allen (1692–1750). Allen served in the Commons House of the South Carolina Assembly 1725–1728 and on the North Carolina Council 1734–1750. He was appointed receiver general of quitrents by Gov. Gabriel Johnston and the Council in 1735 and received a royal commission confirming him in that office in 1741. Allen and JA served together on the 1735 boundary commission to run a line between the two Carolinas. JA's letter to Mrs. Allen may have concerned the state of her late husband's accounts as receiver general. See JA to Swann, 4 June 1758, pp. 259–260.

To John Tinker

[29 June 1753]

To Govr Tinker June 29th 1753 see bundle of Letters about the Letter from Board of Trade relating to his Memorial.[1]

LB, p. 355.

1. See JA to Tinker, 1 Jan. 1753, p. 65, n. 1.

To [Gabriel] Manigault and [John] Cleland

[3 July 1753]
{For this letter, see JA to Glen et al., 29 June 1753, above.}

To John Swann et al.

[10 July 1753]
North Carolina per Capt Mcdonnel July 10th 1753 to Mr John Swann to Mr Saml Swann, to Mrs Allen, Mr Job How[1] See Bundle of Lettres.

LB, p. 355.

1. Job How has not been positively identified, but a Robert Howe (d. 1724?), who had been born in South Carolina and served in that colony's Commons House of Assembly 1713–1717, had a son named Job.

To John Tinker

[20 July 1753]
July 20th to Do with one from the B of Trade by the Govrs Sloop.[1]

LB, p. 355. This memorandum was appended to the memorandum of JA's letter to Tinker of 29 June 1753, above.

1. The journals of the Board of Trade do not record that any letters were sent to Tinker between 7 June and 5 Dec. 1753.

To the Committee of Correspondence of North Carolina

[12 September 1753]
Committee of North Carolina Septr 12th from Scotland via S Carolina See Bundle of the Letters.

LB, p. 355. A virtually identical entry, which JA canceled, appears on p. 354 of the letter book.

To John Tinker

[10 October 1753]

Govr Tinker Octr 10th 1753 Tell him Domestick News, mention Capt Bob Haldan to Mr Scott desire Mr Scotts Lres to go through me;[1] Send him 4 Pamphlets concerning the Jew Bill[2] to Col Austins[3] care.

LB, p. 359. The month was originally written as "Nov." Sent "per Capt Cheesman." At the foot of this memorandum JA wrote: "saild this the 15th of Novr a fair wind & continud so."

1. Haldan has not been identified. Scott may have been James Scott, who was appointed to the Bahamas Council in July 1752.

2. "An Act to permit persons professing the Jewish religion to be naturalized by Parliament, and for other purposes therein mentioned," the so-called Jew Bill, received the royal assent in June 1753 (26 George II, chap. 26). A historian of the bill has written: "The measure was a modest one, technical in nature and merely permissive in its effect. It actually naturalized no one; all it did was to modify the statutory requirements for naturalization so that Parliament *in future cases* could, if it wished, naturalize professing Jews, a thing impossible under existing law. Any foreign Jew wishing to be naturalized would still have to obtain passage of a private Act of Parliament. Since this was an expensive proceeding, there were certain to be few applicants; and of course future Parliaments were in no way bound to accept all or even any of these." Nonetheless, a great clamor arose over the bill's passage, chiefly among London merchants and Tories throughout the country. During the summer and fall of 1753 opposition to the bill (actually an act) grew, and when Parliament convened in Nov. 1753, one of the first orders of business was the repeal of the Jew Bill. The act of repeal is 27 George II, chap. 1 (Thomas W. Perry, *Public Opinion, Propaganda, and Politics in Eighteenth-Century England: A Study of the Jew Bill of 1753* [Cambridge, Mass., 1962], quote on p. 1).

The four pamphlets JA sent to Tinker cannot be identified, for a multitude of pamphlets issued forth from London presses during the controversy. A nearly complete list of such pamphlets is printed in Cecil Roth, ed., *Magna Bibliotheca Anglo-Judaica: A Bibliographical Guide to Anglo-Jewish History* (London, 1937).

3. Not identified.

To the Committee of Correspondence of North Carolina

Octr 25th 1753

The death of Lady Halefax at his Lordships house in the Country[1] has protracted his Lordships Stay from Town, so that

Plantation Board have not as yet met,[2] I expect his Lordships return to business in ten days hence & then I shall press their deliberations on our Provincial Affairs & by that time Mr Dobbs informs me he shall be ready to leave Dublin where he now is & cooperate with me for dispatch.

Inclosd I send my Account with the Public to the 25th of March 1753[3] to which I beg your Attention and as Capt Mcdonnel has been so kind as to promise me his Bills from time to time & I hope by that means to facilitate my remittances from the Province. I am with great Attachment Gentlemen

LB, p. 355. Sent "per the Aloi." At the foot of this letter JA wrote: "NB the Account is Lre annexed ——— & Copy of my letter from Scotland inclosd in this to Committee. NB all inclosd to Mr Rowan of this date."

1. In 1741 Halifax (then George Montagu) married Anne Richards Dunk, who brought her husband a fortune of £110,000. (Montagu also assumed her name.) She died on 13 Oct. 1753, at the age of twenty-seven, at Horton, Northants.

2. The Board of Trade did not meet again until 14 Nov., and Halifax did not attend until 27 Nov. 1753 (*JBT*, 9:454, 459).

3. Enclosure not found.

To John Rutherfurd and Samuel Swann

[25 October 1753]

Mr Rutherford & Mr Saml Swann Octr 25th 1753 per the Aloi. See bundle of Letters.

LB, p. 355.

To Robert Dinwiddie

Octr 25th 1753

I am favour with yours July 2d[1] have nothing now to add to my former of May[2] but that shall continue good correspondence with Leheup in Pro Matters & in correspondence with you shall distinguish your privat from public Affairs.

The only Stir in town is about the insuing Elections the clamor agt the Jew Bill having occasiond that every body Still in country Lady Halefaxs death keeps his Lordship no business going on in Offices.

In our Affairs with France talk big I hope the Same Spirit may extend itself to the Continent particularly to Virginia where I see they are making encroachments.[3]

tell him the Tragicial end of Harry Lasceles.[4]

I see the Assembly do not meet before the Spring when my bygone proceedings will be laid before them by you.[5]

& Conclude by telling Colonel Herons relief from a spunging house[6] Complts affectionatly to you & Family.

PS the Attorney Generals opinion on the Pistol Fee[7] operates so far in your Favour as to Warrant their Lordships Judgt that the King can Establish Fees in the Plantations without acts of Assembly.

JA

LB, p. 357.

1. Letter not found.

2. Since his letter to Dinwiddie of 4 May/20 May 1753, pp. 80–86, JA had written to Dinwiddie on 8 June, p. 89, and 29 June 1753, p. 90.

3. French "encroachments" in the Ohio Valley, which was claimed by both France and Britain, began in earnest after the arrival in Canada in 1752 of the new governor, Ange de Menneville, marquis de Duquesne. Early in 1753 Duquesne sent Pierre Paul de La Malgue, sicur de Marin, and 2,000 men to the area to establish a chain of forts, thereby effecting French occupation of the disputed territory. It was in response to this new and threatening French presence that the British in 1754 dispatched a force to dislodge the French, touching off the French and Indian War.

4. Henry Lascelles (1690–1753), collector of customs at Barbados 1715–1730, director of the East India Company 1737–1745, and member of Parliament 1745–1752, had died on 16 Oct. 1753, leaving an estate of £284,000. This news would have been of interest to Dinwiddie, for during his tenure as surveyor general of the customs for the southern part of America 1738–1745, Dinwiddie had exposed fraud on the part of many customs officials in Barbados, among them Henry Lascelles and his brother Edward. Dinwiddie's investigation showed that Henry Lascelles had systematically defrauded the government by pocketing about one-third of the revenues of Barbados's $4\frac{1}{2}$ percent export duty on sugar. As a result, the customs commissioners filed a bill against Lascelles in the Court of Exchequer, although the Treasury later halted the action against him.

5. In fact the Virginia General Assembly convened, after several prorogations, on 1 Nov. 1753 (*JHB, 1752–1758*, 103).

6. A sponging house was a house kept by a bailiff's or sheriff's officer, formerly in regular use as a place of preliminary confinement for debtors.

7. See JA to Dinwiddie, 16 Jan. 1753, p. 66, n. 1.

To James Glen

Novr 9th 1753

Having for these 3 years bygone expected your promised Remittances, but more particularly since your letter of 23d April[1] wherein you excuse yourself to me for non punctuality in your bygone payments, and then tell me in these Words (vizt): That I may depend upon never having cause to complain of this for the future; you cannot now take it amiss that I draw upon you for 3 Years Arrears of Salary due vizt from 18th Novr 1750 that being the last payment to Do 1753, at 50 per annum amounting 150 and this my draft payable to Mr John Hume Mercht in Charlestown at 30 Days sight I doubt not will be duly honourd by you on account of Sir Your Most Obedt Sert

JA

PS for public concerns I refer you to my letter of the same date with this.[2]

LB, p. 357. Sent "per Capt Cheesman." This letter was apparently enclosed in the following letter.

1. Letter not found.

2. See JA to Glen, 9 Nov. 1753, pp. 97–98.

To John Hume

Novr 9th 1753

According to my former & your Advise[1] to me have drawn upon my Friend Governor Glen for 150£ letter of Advise peruse & Seal & deliver with Your Bill,[2] & I beg you make no stir in this Matter but keep the thing absolutely secret that he may have no grounds to complain of any affront being put upon him by you or by me.

I do not apprehend that he will slight my Bill as he must pay me in the long run the only thing that prudence should direct him in this case, is to make me an Apology for being so long in my arrears whatever his Inclination may be I am sure its not for his Interest to add more to the Number of his Enemys. I am

LB, p. 358. Sent "per Capt Chisman."

1. Neither letter has been found.

2. See preceding letter.

To James Glen

Do Novr 9th 1753

Of this date have drawn for Arrears of Salary upon you also Lre of Advise therof[1] altho I have no Letters from you in ansr to mine to you of 12th May[2] per Cheesman find by those thro Mr P.[3] that you are alarmd in Pitt perhaps your fears exceed your danger, since former Lres, no one circumstance here that need to alarm you, as I have formerly told you he may have the Govert but its as certain he will not take it on your terms, here therfore is a difficulty in his Way, point therefore is if his Political situation is such by having 4 Members will bring the Ministry to his terms for the Govert.

I have heard a conversation that you held with a quaker lately returnd to C[4] by which I find you think the Complt from one of your Council has hurt you I think there is no foundation for this conceit, I may venture to assure you that there are no formal Complaints agt you in writing there or elsewhere by any person, what private people may say in Conversation with My Lords for Trade I cannot answer for, nobody without Enemys, am sorry you in particular have So many but withall am apt to think youll maintain your ground till superior Interest of others supersede you.

Next Session of Parlt will determine Mr Pitts Views at all events it will be later end of next year before his appt take place prudential reasons may require his Reelection, nobody has a better opportunity of proving his American Inclinations & shall not fail to let you know from time to time that you may conduct your

Province Matters accordingly, herewith send you magazines to Novr[5] & 2 New Pamphlets upon the Jew Bill & am

[PS] the Plantation Board broke up the 1t of Augt So there has been a Stagnation of Plantation Affairs ever since.[6]

LB, p. 358. Sent "per C: Cheesman." A memorandum of this letter appears on p. 357 of the letter book.

1. JA to Glen, 9 Nov. 1753, p. 96.

2. Printed on p. 89.

3. Charles Pinckney.

4. Possibly Sophia (Wigington) Hume (1702–1774). After the death of her husband, Robert Hume, in 1737, she lived in London, returning occasionally to Charleston. During a visit there in 1747 she wrote *An Exhortation to the Inhabitants of the Province of South-Carolina to Bring Their Deeds to the Light of Christ, in Their Own Consciences* (Bristol, 1751; London, 1752).

5. In a memorandum of this letter on p. 357 of the letter book, JA noted that he sent "Magazines from June to Novr viz 5."

6. In fact, the Board of Trade met on 9 Aug., 16 Aug., 28 Aug., 18 Sept., and 11 Oct. 1753 before beginning to meet more regularly on 14 Nov. 1753 (*JBT*, 9:451–454).

To John Hume

[18 November 1753]
NB a Second letter by his Brother[1] & 2d Bill 18th Novr 1753.

LB, p. 358. This memorandum was appended to JA's letter to Hume of 9 November 1753, pp. 96–97.

1. Not identified.

To Robert Dinwiddie

[30 November 1753]
Govr Dinwiddie Novr 30th 1753 per Mr Handburys Ship tell him Leheup & Fanes agreable,[1] Send him Epitaph on Lasceles of the Jew Bill; that the only Revenue matter in my view the Acts of Assembly before Mr Lamb, that the Lds for Trade would not in a

hury dispatch these Laws but consider thereon,[2] hope through Mr Furye to get Col Herons Money as many of his depend in the Pay Office.

LB, p. 359.

1. This passage suggests that there may have been an agreement by Leheup and Board of Trade member Francis Fane for JA to take over the duties of the Virginia agency because of Leheup's legal difficulties. Leheup had been one of the commissioners in charge of a lottery to raise £300,000 for the purchase by the government of the museum of Sir Hans Sloane and the Harleian manuscripts (which then became the nucleus of the British Museum). The House of Commons began an inquiry into his conduct in Dec. 1753, and on 14 Mar. 1754 the Commons resolved to condemn him, upon which Newcastle suspended him from all his offices. The attorney general then prosecuted Leheup before the Court of King's Bench, which on 19 Apr. 1755 found him guilty of malfeasance. On 9 May 1755 he was fined £1,000, which he paid immediately (*Parliamentary History*, 15:192–249).

2. Fifty-three acts passed on 20 Apr. 1752 were transmitted by Dinwiddie to the Board of Trade on 20 July 1752 and referred by the Board to Matthew Lamb on 9 Nov. 1752. He did not begin reporting on them until Mar. 1754 (*JBT*, 9.359–360, 10:18).

To Robert Dinwiddie

[7 December 1753]

Governor Dinwiddie Decr 7th 1753 Mr Walpoles Complt, about Cypress Poles about Leheup, & the privat Act of Assembly under Mr Hanburys Care, that I was a[s]kd about at the B of Trade.[1]

LB, p. 359. The date was initially written as "3d."

1. JA may be referring to "An Act to dock the entail of certain lands whereof David Garland is seised, and for settling other lands and slaves of greater value to the same uses," passed 20 Apr. 1752 (Hening, *Statutes*, 6:311–314). The Board of Trade read the act on 9 Nov. 1752 and referred it to Matthew Lamb. On 11 July 1753 the Board read Lamb's favorable report and recommended confirmation to the Crown. On 16 Nov. 1753 the Board read an Order in Council of 10 Aug. 1753 approving the Board's recommendation (*JBT*, 9:359, 360, 446, 456). The journals of the Board do not record that JA was asked about this or any other private act about this time.

To James Glen (not sent)

Decr 13th 1753

Tho have very great Reason to resent the Usage I have had from you, yet still shall befreind you so far as to let you know to prepare your Self for whatever turn your Situation may take, have no longer any Doubt of Mr Pitts Intentions to Solicit your Gover, & will not flatter you with hopes that he will not Succeed, but for particular Reasons his Commission will be Suspended,[1] Send you the last Months Magazine & am Sir Yours

LB, p. 359. Although this letter has the notation "per Capt Coales" by the date, it has been canceled, and JA wrote "NB Did not go" at the foot.

1. See JA to Glen, 12 May 1753, p. 89, n. 1.

To James Glen

[15 December 1753]

Governor Glen Decr 15th 1753 per the Friendship Capt Coales in the Downs to tell him of Sir Danvers Osborns death that might perhaps prove a Reprieve.[1]

LB, p. 359.

1. See JA to Glen, 8 May 1753, p. 88, n. 2. JA seems to suggest that Osborn's death, which created a vacancy in the governorship of New York, would result in the postponement of the appointment of a successor to Glen.

To James Glen

[21 December 1753]

Governor Glen Decr 21t 1753 per Capt Peacock with Magazine pro Novr & tell him that I have nothing to add.

LB, p. 359.

To John Tinker

[24 December 1753]

Governor Tinker Decr 24th 1753 per Capt Peacock per So Ca to Mr Humes care See the Bundle of Letters (Bahamas) tell him of Box Sent to me for him from the B of Trade,[1] of Mr Leheups Inquiry, of Sir Danvers Osborns death of Mr Pitts views to So Carolina Govert.

LB, p. 360.

1. The box from the Board of Trade likely contained the Board's letter to Tinker of 5 Dec. 1753 and royal warrants of 11 Dec. 1753 appointing Robert Stewart and Nehemiah Duncombe councillors (*JBT*, 9:460; *APC*, 4:783).

To John Tinker

[28 December 1753]

Governor Tinker Decr 28th 1753 Send him a Packet from Ld Holdernesses Office[1] acknowledge the rece[i]pt of his 11th of Augt[2] See the Bundle his Letter & ansr annexd, per Do Capt Peacock as above.

LB, p. 360.

1. Enclosures not found.

2. Letter not found.

To James Glen

[28 December 1753]

Governor Glen Decr 28th 1753 Send him a Packet from Lord Holdernesses Office[1] did not write him per Capt Peacock as above.

LB, p. 360.

1. Enclosures not found.

To John Tinker

[29 January 1754]

Governor Tinker 29th Jany 1754 vide letter.

LB, p. 360.

To Robert Dinwiddie

[29 January 1754]

Governor Dinwiddie Janry 29th per Liverpoole See Bundle of Virginia Letters as to the Pistole Fee.

LB, p. 360.

To James Glen

January 30th 1754

With this comes Magazine for Decr, what I formerly told you is now past all doubt, Mr Pitt his succeeding you in the Govert,[1] as you have taken no Notice of my former Information I conclude that you have put another Construction than what was Intended. Mr Pinckney has no doubt told you what passd betwixt Mr Pitt & him concerning P———ys house & Mr Calverly tells me he has fully informd you anent the Dutch Ship[2] I am Sir Your Most Obedt Sert

LB, p. 360. Sent "per Capt Hunt."
1. See JA to Glen, 12 May 1753, p. 89, n. 1.
2. See JA to Glen, 7 Oct. 1751, p. 14, n. 3.

To Robert Dinwiddie

February 11th 1754

Sir about ten days ago I wrote you per Liverpoole[1] & then told you that having Sounded every Channel, I found all clear in your

Favour that I had no doubt of your coming off with flying colours & that the Attor & Solicitor General, were retaind with Mr H Campbell that he may speak in case the Attorney does not attend which is very often the case; before repeating my Visits to a Noble in Arlington Street I had the privat hint given me not to wait for the Attack, but to take it up immediatly, accordingly I did instruct Mr Jos Sharpe and your Petition was on friday last by him presented to My Lords for Trade praying their Lordships to give directions for preventing Neglects of taking out the Patents of Lands that have lain in the Office & Non payment of the Quitrents in Arrear thereon And that the Fee of one Pistole to be taken by the Gover of the Said Colony for the time being for the afixing the Seal of the Said Colony to the Grants for Lands there may be Establishd by the Authority of the Crown a Copy of which Petition drawn upon the plan as hinted to me in Arlington Street, you have now inclosd.[2]

Having thus taken up your ground all is ready in case of an Attack; perhaps the case may appear upon the face of the Petition So interesting to the Crown in regard to the Province that their Lordships may give Your Petition no delay, in presenting the Same to the King in Council But as it was necessary for me in privat to lay the whole case with all its circumstances open to those at the head of the respective boards, from thence they are aprizd of an Application intended to be made here against this Fee So that I must for some time now let the Case so rest with their Lordships in their own discretion whether to proceed thereon or to Suspend their consideration thereof till the Arrival of the Complaint in order that I may not be thought to hurry or Surprize their Judgment in the Affair.[3]

Whatever turn it takes you are prepared, & should their Lordships of Trade or of the Council desire to hear Council thereon I am Satisfyd that whatever this method of proceeding may take out of your Pocket by way of expences it will add to your Reputation at home & So Signal a Victory as you have good grounds to expect in the face of your Adversarys will no doubt discourage them from future Attacks upon you.

As the Case of the Pistole Fee cannot be blended with those Other Fees of 10 sh for probat of Wills & 10 sh for Lres of Administration I must Suspend the Case of these Fees till I am

Instructed by you, 1t whether Such Fees were taken by your Predecessors, 2d Whether these Fees have been approvd of by your Council & 3d Whether they are meant in Sterling or in Proclamation Money; If approvd of by the Council transmit me the Same.[4]

I am glad that my Conduct has been approvd of by the Gentlemen of your Council, had they been acquainted with the Secret Springs of business the Article of Gratuitys had not alarmd them, In business of my own I ever found My account by Such Disbursments, & in the case of others I never shall let difficultys Stand in my Way when they are to be got over upon reasonable terms; I observe that you take no Notice of an Article in my Account (vizt) £15.3.0 Fees paid by me at the Board for Trade & Council Office for the Kings Instruction in relation to the Address of the Assembly concerning the Laws,[5] and from your Silence I conclude that the Assembly Are not to Repay me the Same, & indeed I had rather be out of pocket than occasion any contest with them on this head.[6]

I shall not fail to give you particular Advice from time to time whenever I can do it by proper channels, & am Sorry to hear that every channel is not So, that of opening of letters it would Seem to me was a Distemper incident to the American Climat, and to escape the Curiosity that may be predominant on the present occasion I sent my last to Col Hunter[7] & this I send to Mr H———y & I am always

PS Mr Hanburys have just now Sent me your Letters to Mr West & the Secry of the Treasury which shall be deliverd on Monday[8] at the same time they informed me the Attorney General[9] is arrivd at Bristol & no doubt his arrival has occasiond the Inclosd Article in the Newspaper as from Dublin, Such Puffs will not avail The Complaint, M[ess]rs Hanburys dayly expect another Ship to Inquire after Mr Pamers Nephew relieve him from Goal & pay 30 Ster.[10]

LB, pp. 361–362. Sent "per Capt Randolph to Messrs Hanbury."

1. See JA to Dinwiddie, 29 Jan. 1754, p. 102.

2. The journals of the Board of Trade do not record the receipt of such a petition from Dinwiddie through Joshua Sharpe. However, on 31 Jan. 1754 the Privy Council

read and referred to its Plantation Committee a petition from Dinwiddie that accords with JA's summary here (*APC*, 4:232–233).

3. The "Application . . . against this Fee" came from the House of Burgesses. After Dinwiddie failed to satisfy the House of the legality of his taking the pistole fee, the House members appealed directly to the Crown for redress. In Dec. 1753 they prepared an address and appointed Peyton Randolph (1721–1775), the attorney general of the colony and one of the burgesses who had drawn up the address, as their agent to carry the address to London and "negotiate the affairs of this Colony in Great Britain" (*JHB, 1752–1758*, 154, 156, 167, 168, 169).

4. In his reply of 26 Apr. 1754 Dinwiddie wrote JA: "As for Probates of Wills, & Letters of Administr. I desire to give up, therefore take no Steps in regard to them" (Dinwiddie Letter Books, 3:43–45, VHS).

5. See JA to Dinwiddie, 17 Sept. 1752, pp. 45–46, n. 1.

6. In his reply of 26 Apr. 1754 Dinwiddie wrote JA: "As to the Complt. of Gratuities on the Council's Affairs, it met with no great Oppositn. but I think You shd. have wrote me a Letter of Yr. being satisfied with what they gave You, that I cd. have shewn it to them. The 15£ due from the Ho of Burgesses, I believe was a Neglect, but [I] shall at a proper Time remind them thereof" (Dinwiddie Letter Books, 3:43–45, VHS).

7. Probably John Hunter, of Elizabeth City Co., Va., who was agent for Thomlinson & Hanbury, the London firm through which the British government supplied funds for its military forces in North America. Hunter sold his considerable land and business interests in Virginia in 1766 and removed to England.

8. Dinwiddie's letter to the Treasury of 29 Dec. 1753 defending his actions in the pistole fee dispute is T 1/353, fols. 240–241 (Koontz, *Dinwiddie Papers*, 429–434). His letter to Mr. West (probably James West, secretary to the Treasury), perhaps a letter covering that to the Treasury, has not been found.

9. Peyton Randolph.

10. In his reply of 26 Apr. 1754 Dinwiddie wrote JA: "I shall endeavour to find out Mr. Palmer if in this Colony & notice Yr. Directs. therein," and on 23 Sept. 1754 Dinwiddie added: "I can hear nothing of Mr. Palmer tho' I took true Pains to enquire after him" (Dinwiddie Letter Books, 3:43–45, 101–103, VHS).

To Robert Dinwiddie

[23 February 1754]

Governor Dinwiddie 23d Febry per Capt Randolph vide Bundle of Letters.[1]

LB, p. 362.

1. From Dinwiddie's reply of 26 Apr. 1754, it can be inferred that JA's letter (not found) concerned the pistole fee case, Leheup's predicament (Dinwiddie agreed with JA that "it is right that he does not appear in the Affair"), and Halifax's chagrin with Dinwiddie, evidently either because of the fee or because Dinwiddie did not write frequently enough (Dinwiddie Letter Books, 3:43–45, VHS).

To John Tinker

[26 February 1754]

Mr Tinker Febry 26th per Capt Haldan.

LB, p. 362.

To John Rutherfurd

[26 February 1754]

To Mr Rutherford per Do[1] & inclose Miss Isabellas Halls power of Attorney tell him that he is to draw 6 per cent on all ready payments & Commission besides as Attorney & of my 100£ pro negociating her Arrears Feby 26th 1754.[2]

LB, p. 363.

1. This letter presumably went by a Mr. Pearson, for in the letter book it follows the two succeeding letters, below.

2. Isabella Hall, who has not been identified with certainty, may have been a daughter and the executrix of the late Enoch Hall. The arrears may have been owed to Hall's estate for his salary as chief justice of North Carolina.

To the Committee of Correspondence of North Carolina

Feby 27th 1754

The repeated delays that have from time to time prevented the consideration of the Affairs relative to your Province during these three Months last past afording me no more Matter of Intelligence I was therefore Silent; now for this forthnight past these Affairs have been under deliberation, and as yesterday the Measures and Matters for the Governors Instructions upon the Several points that have been so long the Subject of Debate in the Province & some other related Matters relative to the Province were finally agreed to by the Board of Trade & their Report is preparing accordingly in order to be laid before the King in Council, What these Measures are, its not within my Province to come to the knowledge of;[1] While these Matters were under consideration Seconded by Governor Dobbs I revived My Application for Ordnance & Stores for the Provincial Forts & my answer thereto was that from the Uncertainty of the present Condition of the Forts & particularly that on Cape Fear River they could not Advise his Majesty to Send over any Ordnance without having reced a more particular Account, & therefore that their Lordships should Instruct the Gover upon his Arrival to make his Report to them concerning the Same;[2] The Representation in Favour of the Governors Salary being likewise agreed to by the B of Trade[3] will accompany their Report in relation to the Public Measures & having no Reason to apprehend any extraordinary Delay hereafter, very probably the Governor may be in readiness to Imbark in the Mermaid Man of War in May to be landed in N Caro: from that Ship on her way to New England where she is Stationd[4] In the mean time this comes by Capt Sinkler Sucesor to Capt McDonald & be assurd that I am with great truth Gentlemen

LB, p. 363. Sent "per Pearson." Enclosed in the following letter.

1. While preparing instructions for Gov. Arthur Dobbs, the Board of Trade had to address the representation controversy, which had gone unresolved for several years (see Introduction, pp. xxvi–xxviii). The Board considered the matter on 14 Nov. 1753, 31 Jan., 7 Feb., 22 Feb., and 25 Feb. 1754 (*JBT*, 9:455; 10:7, 10, 11). In the resulting representation to the Crown of 14 Mar. 1754 the Board of Trade recommended the disallowance of the 1746 representation act and twelve other North Carolina laws that created electoral districts. The Board also recommended that Dobbs be "directed to confirm the rights of the several Towns Precincts or Counties by Charters of incorporation." Each of the northern counties would thereby regain its five representatives. But to alleviate the overrepresentation of the northern counties, the Board recommended that Dobbs be instructed that, as the colony's population grew, he erect towns and counties within the southern parts with the privilege of sending representatives to the assembly so that "each different district or division [has] a reasonable and just proportion" (*NCCR*, 5:81–108). The Privy Council put the Board's proposals into effect, disallowing the offending statutes in Apr. 1754 and incorporating the other suggestions into Dobbs's instructions of 17 June 1754. One of the more significant articles of his instructions forbade the

governor to assent to any law altering the number of representatives in the lower house, thereby removing from the legislature the power to create constituencies and establish representation, an instruction made general for all royal colonies in 1767 (Labaree, *Royal Instructions*, 1:103–104, 108–111; *APC*, 4:187–188; *NCCR*, 5:116–118).

2. See JA to Rice, 16 Jan. 1753, p. 66, n. 1.

3. See JA to Dinwiddie, 20 Oct. 1752, p. 56, n. 13.

4. In fact Dobbs sailed in July aboard the man-of-war *Garland* and landed in Virginia on 6 Oct. 1754.

To Matthew Rowan

[27 February 1754]
To Mr Rowan[1] per the Same & the above inclosd therein.[2]

LB, p. 363.

1. Matthew Rowan (d. 1760), a native of Ireland and a prominent North Carolina planter, served on the Council 1734–1760. JA writes him here in his capacity as acting governor, a position he occupied from the death of Nathaniel Rice in Jan. 1753 until the arrival of Dobbs in Oct. 1754.

2. See preceding letter.

To James Glen

[28 February 1754]
Governor Glen Febry 28th 1754 per Capt Haldan with Magazine & nothing remarkable more congratulate his safe return to C Town.[1]

LB, p. 362.

1. In order to protect and retain the allegiance to Britain of the Cherokee from the lower and middle towns (and to counteract the influence of the nativist faction centered in the overhill town of Chota), Glen decided to build a fort in the lower towns. In Oct. 1753 Glen led an expedition into the lower towns, and near the town of Keowee he erected a fort of earth and wood named Fort Prince George. Glen completed the fort in Dec. 1753 and stationed a small garrison there before returning to Charleston (Sirmans, *Colonial South Carolina*, 288–289; David H. Corkran, *The Cherokee Frontier: Conflict and Survival, 1740–1762* [Norman, Okla., 1962], 38–49).

To James Glen

[3 March 1754]

Govr Glen March 3rd 1754 Nothing material but that to consider if the Institution of a Suit in West Hall may not remove the Danger of after prosecution of Hopton, in the case of the Dutch Ship,[1] of Mr Pitts departure in Septr[2] Send Magazines pro Decr & Janry per C Haldan.

LB, p. 364.

1. See JA to Glen, 7 Oct. 1751, p. 14, n. 3.

2. JA may allude to rumors of Thomas Pitt's being appointed governor of South Carolina. See JA to Glen, 12 May 1753, p. 89, n. 1.

To Robert Dinwiddie

March 25th 1754

Having spraind my writing hand I am scarce able to let you know that the Situation in which Mr Leheup is brought to by the Resolves of the Ho of Coms,[1] & in consequence thereof a formal Suspension from all his Offices, by order of the D of New: now at the head of the Treasury Since Mr Pels death[2] has induced him to resign the Agency of your Govert and in consequence thereof has transferd to my care the Sole direction of Affairs now in agitation relative to You & His Majestys Council; I could have wishd that Mr Leheup had been able to have maintaind his Station with reputation till the present controversy had been decided, not that I apprehend any defection on your Part or on the part of the Council as to the merits of the present Contest, (which I am extreamly concernd to find so greatly inflamd beyond what the Nature of the Case required) but more from the Defect in my not having in the present case Such Authority as the Agent for your Govert has properly hetherto acted under I mean that of the Governor & Council without whose Authority no person in whatever cause engagd can properly assume to Represent your or any other Government formed according to the British Constitution without breaking in upon the Executive Powers of Govert lodged in the head thereof which

never has nor ever will be permitted by those now in the administration & more than ever attentive to preserve the propriety of
Plantation Govert but in spite of all difficultys I have not the least
doubt of maintaining the present Cause with all the Success due to
the Justice thereof and upon Mr Leheups Resignation let my past
conduct in the Service of your Govert recommend me to the
continuance thereof as Sucesor to Mr Leheup upon Such terms as
you & the Council shall think consistent with the dignity of the
Province & the Duty incident to the Office I am

LB, p. 364. At the head of this letter JA wrote: "upon Leheups Resignation."

1. See JA to Dinwiddie, 30 Nov. 1753, p. 99, n. 1.

2. Henry Pelham died on 6 Mar. 1754. His brother Thomas Pelham-Holles
(1693–1768), first duke of Newcastle, gave up his post of secretary of state for the
Northern Department to succeed him as first commissioner of the Treasury.

To the Council of Virginia

25th of March 1754

By His Honour the Leut Gover you will be made acquainted with
the Resignation of Mr Leheup and on this Occasion let the Zeal
that I have hetherto occasionally shewn for your Service now
recommend me to the continuance thereof as his Sucessor, and
whatever Terms the Leut Gover & you shall think proper [to]
prescribe to me in Your Service I shall acquiesse in.

I should not do Justice to you was I to conceal from you the
agreeable reception that your Address to his Majesty[1] & the whole
of your Public Conduct during this disagreeable Provincial controversy has hetherto met with and Such must be the reception where
Business is conducted with a due Consistency & with Candor
temper & Moderation, And taking Example from the Disposition
that you have shewn for accomodating Matters I should have
thought myself most singularly happy had there been the smalest
opportunety left open for attempting to adjust the Controversy on
this Side of the Water in a privat Manner, but after having given it,
in all its circumstances a most attentive deliberation I can see no
resource but in his Majestys Judgment thereupon, and that we shall
now soon have, you will I hope Gentlemen forgive this my general

Address to you, being from an Accident to my right hand disabled from writing in a more particular manner without great pain I beg leave therefore to Conclude Gentlemen with thanks for your acknowledgment of my former Services.[2]

LB, p. 365. At the foot of this letter JA wrote: "NB these 2 letters & a 3d see Bundle more privat to Governor Dinwiddie per Mr Hanburys conveyance to Col Hunter." It is not known which letters are referred to. A fair copy of this letter is in the Virginia State Library and Archives.

1. On 15 Dec. 1753 the Council "Ordered That an humble Address be made to his Majesty representing the unblameable Conduct of his Honour [Dinwiddie] in demanding the said Fee agreeably to the Advice of his Council and the Approbation of the Lords of Trade." William Fairfax, John Blair, Richard Corbin, Philip Ludwell Lee, and Thomas Dawson were asked to prepare it. On 19 Dec. William Fairfax signed the address on behalf of the Council (*EJC*, 5:455, 457). The address is CO 5/1328, pp. 75, 85–87 (Koontz, *Dinwiddie Papers*, 420n–421n).

2. Dinwiddie laid this letter before the Council on 20 June 1754, at which time the Council unanimously approved JA to be agent (*EJC*, 6:1).

To James Glen

[9 April 1754]

Governor Glen April 9th 1754 Send him Letter from Secretarys Office Sir T Robinson,[1] also Magazine for Feby & March, tell him Mr Pitt takes his Seat in the New Parlt,[2] Introduce Mr Murray to him as a freind of the Lt Governors.[3]

LB, p. 366. Sent "per Capt Elms."

1. Holderness vacated the office of secretary of state for the Southern Department when he succeeded Newcastle as secretary of state for the Northern Department. At that time, Thomas Robinson (1695–1770), second baronet, afterwards Baron Grantham, reluctantly accepted the office vacated by Holderness. Robinson had served on the Board of Trade 1748–1749 and was a privy councillor from 1750. He was a member of Parliament 1727–1734 and 1748–1761. He served as secretary of state for the Southern Department until Nov. 1755.

Robinson's letter to Glen has not been found.

2. Thomas Pitt represented Old Sarum, one of the three rotten boroughs he controlled, in the Eleventh Parliament, the first session of which convened on 31 May 1754.

3. There was no lieutenant governor of South Carolina at this time. JA may be alluding to William Bull I, who was president of the Council and had served as lieutenant governor 1738–1743. Murray has not been identified.

To Robert Dinwiddie

[13 April 1754]

Governor Dinwiddie April 13th 1754 per Capt Merry See bundle of Letters.

LB, p. 366.

To Robert Dinwiddie

[25 April 1754]

Governor Dinwiddie April 25th to Mr Hanbury See Bundle.

LB, p. 366.

To Robert Dinwiddie

[23 June 1754]

Governor Dinwiddie June 23d on the hearing of the Pistole Fee[1] per the Tryton to Maryland.

LB, p. 366.

1. The Privy Council heard the case of the pistole fee on 18 June 1754. Dinwiddie was represented by William Murray and Alexander Hume-Campbell, while Alexander Forrester and Robert Henley, afterwards first earl of Northington, appeared for the House of Burgesses. Although the Privy Council upheld Dinwiddie's right to exact such a fee, it forbade his taking the fee for land patents that were in the governor's office before 22 Apr. 1752 (when the Virginia Council approved the fee), that were for less than one hundred acres, or that were west of the Allegheny Mountains. The Privy Council also recommended that Dinwiddie reinstate Peyton Randolph, whom Dinwiddie had dismissed as attorney general after the House appointed Randolph to present its case in London. The Board of Trade's letter to Dinwiddie of 3 July 1754 (CO 5/1367, fols. 94–100, in Koontz, *Dinwiddie Papers*, 562–565) conveyed the decisions of the Privy Council (Jack P. Greene, "The Case of

the Pistole Fee: The Report of a Hearing on the Pistole Fee Dispute Before the Privy Council, June 18, 1754," *VMHB* 66 [1958]: 399–422; "The Pistole Fee Controversy," vol. 2, chap. 18 in Morton, *Colonial Virginia*; Greene, *Quest for Power*, 159–165).

To the Committee of Correspondence of North Carolina

June 25th 1754

I am favour'd with yours of the 17th of last March[1] notifying to me your Commands for Supporting the Act Intitled An Act for Directing the Disposal of Goods taken upon Executions &ca,[2] previous to the Receipt of your letter I had found that this & several other Acts containing Matters Interesting to the Kings Royal Prerogative & Revenue were under the consideration of the Lords for Trade;[3] And to this Act in particular their Lordships Attention I believe was directed, by the repeated complaints that had been exhibited by the Auditor General of His Majestys American Revenues[4] in consequence of Remonstrances that had been made to him by the Officers of the Revenue upon the difficultys they lay under in the Execution of their Office,[5] by means of this Act so far as the Same relates to the disposal of Goods taken by Distress, and more particularly the last part of the first Clause thereof Directing the property of the Goods so Appraized to be to and in the party for whom taken; To this Clause I find the first Objections are pointed out by the late Recer General Mr Allen in his Office Letters to Mr Walpole as Auditor General aforesaid And by him set in so strong a light to Mr W——— as being the principal cause of Such large Arrears, And under this Act it is, that Mr Allen in a great Measure does justify himself for the non recovery of these Arrears,[6] No Wonder then that this Act on a general review of our Provincial Laws became an Object of Resentment to My Lords for Trade and more particularly So to My Lords of the Treasury.

To these Objections on the part of the Crown I have heard others alledged in behalf of the Fair Trader, vizt that from the operation of this Act the Creditor in payment of his just Debts became obliged to take in Fence Rails & other commoditys of no Sort of intrinsick Value, and of Such Abuses Several Instances are alledged to have happened; Had the stress of the case rested on privat Inconveniencys arising from this Act[7] I might perhaps have been able to have Suspended the Repeal thereof, till authentick Proof had been produced of Such Abuses & the motive of such abuses fully tryd & examined, But Arguments comming from Officers of the Revenue such as that of not being able to do their Duty by Reason of this Act, because the Goods taken by Distress being thrown into the Recers hands he thereby became lyable to the Party ad Valorem of the appraizment it was therefore at his peril & risk that Distress was made, consequently his Duty became dangerouse to him by means of this Act, to which prevalent Arguments urged against me on the part of the Crown, Uninstructed it became impossible for me to combat. However on the receipt of your letter I lost no time to Inforce the Arguments in support of the Act contained therein, & in this I was seconded by Gover Dobbs But all that we have been able to do could not prevail so as to save the Act; The Repeal thereof was a fixed & determined point, and no other Remedy can now obviate the Difficultys that must attend the Repeal thereof in the light that you have represented the same, But to Reenact the Law with amendments leaving out Such Part thereof as affects the Crown and public Credit, and to such Law with a Saving Clause the Governor by his Instructions may give his Assent,[8] Such is the Answer that I have got to my Remonstrances on this Act & such no doubt will be the general answer upon all those other Acts likewise adjudged to be Repealed, Many of which may also be Reenacted with amendments, so as to gain His Majestys approbation.

I have moved for a Copy of his Majestys Instruction in relation to these Laws that I may transmit the Same to my Constituents, but whether I shall be Indulged herein, or the Matter reservd for the Governor after his arrival I cannot as yet say be that as it will the Governor probably may be with you as Soon as this letter and by him you will be informd in a more particular Manner as to the Nature of the Objection on the part of the Crown against these Acts, this being the next conveyance that offers I lay hold of it to acknowledge your last Favour and to express my gratitude for the Honour done me by the Legislature in continuing of me to be their Agent,[9] & the continuance of my Zeal for the Service of the Province they may rely on for what I have hetherto thought my Duty by long Service is now become my Inclination & indeed in some degree my affection, and tho I have not profited in the Service so much as Agents for other Governments have done, it is nevertheless to me a real Satisfaction that none can boast of more repeated Testimonys approving his conduct, In this the Legislature have Done me ample Justice, and their sentiments, have been from time to time communicated to me in the Most polite Manner by you Gentlemen of the Committee thro whom permit me now to beg continuation of their favour & to let them know to return my thanks to both Houses of Assembly, the early Assistance sent to Virginia from their Province I have reason to believe appears in a very Favourable light to his Majesty & his Ministers[10] & I am in hopes that the Colonys Spirit will have great Weight in obviating the Objection taken to Paper Currency Acts in ordinary Cases.

PS doubt not of your care in making me Remittances when opportunity offers.

LB, pp. 367–368. An earlier version of this letter, dated 24 June and crossed through, is on pp. 366–367 of the letter book. Substantive differences between the two versions are accounted for in notes to the present letter.

1. Letter not found.

2. See following note.

3. In a representation to the Crown of 14 Mar. 1754, the Board of Trade recommended the repeal of eighteen acts passed in North Carolina between 1715 and 1749 (among them the act mentioned here by JA) (CO 5/323, end of vol., unpaged). The Privy Council issued an Order in Council to that effect on 8 Apr. 1754 (*NCCR*, 5:116–118).

4. Horatio Walpole.

5. In the earlier version of this letter JA had written: "from the difficultys that had attended the Recovery of the Kings Quitrents."

6. In the earlier version JA had written: "and under this clause it is that with regard to Arrears Mr Allen Justifys in a great Measure the non Execution of his Office because the Goods appraised being thrown into the Recrs hands he thereby became lyable to the Party ad Valorem of the appraisment."

7. In the earlier version JA had written: "had the Salvation of this Act depended on the prooff of Such Particular Instances."

8. Since 1730, instructions to the governors of North Carolina enjoined them not to assent to any bill "of unusual or extraordinary nature and importance wherein our prerogative or the property of our subjects may be prejudiced or the trade or shipping

of this kingdom any ways affected" without a clause suspending its operation until the Crown's pleasure was known (Labaree, *Royal Instructions*, 1:144–145).

9. JA was reappointed agent by an act of 9 Mar. 1754 that was to be in effect from 25 Mar. 1754 until 25 Mar. 1757 "and from thence to the End of the next Session of the General Assembly and no longer" (*NCSR*, 25:266–267).

10. North Carolina raised some 400 men to join George Washington in a projected expedition against the French at the Forks of the Ohio, but the troops did not reach Washington before the surrender of Fort Necessity on 3 July 1754.

To Robert Dinwiddie

June 30th 1754

By a Maryland Ship the 23d inst I told you, that the Pistole Case had been argued the friday In Committee of Council,[1] that the Petition from the House of Burgesses had been rejected, the Attorney General Mr Randolph dismissed from his Office,[2] And that you was to have an Instruction for your Direction in the Pistole Fee, which Instruction you now have by this conveyance[3] & thereby you will observe that there is an Exemption of Fees to all Lands where the King has thought fit to grant an Exemption of Quitrents &ca, Which exemption of Quitrents & Rights, being grounded on the Exemption of Provincial Taxes by your Acts of Assembly in Such Cases to all Lands on the Waters of the Mississippe, your Instruction altho it mentions Lands beyond *the Mountains* I take it is to be construed so as to carry an Exemption of your Fee, according to the Lands intended by Acts of Assembly to be exempted from Taxes of all kinds, I mention this as the foundation upon which your Instruction I apprehend was Intended & I shall endeavour to get it so explaind which will make it appear more reasonable & correspondent with the Kings Measures.

This Case being now over and favourably for you let me tell you, that altho I from time to time gave it an agreeable turn in my letters to you, it remaind long extreamly cloudy in a quarter where I did expect to have met with the greatest sunshine & clearness; In this Situation, I determind to put the Favour of the Lords for Trade to Tryal by presenting a Memorial to them[4] for supporting the Measure that they had givcn a Position to heretofore, They could not reject the Memorial, without an Impeachment of their former

Judgment, at the Same time I knew that their privat language was that you had Surprized them into this Fee, that be the Fee reasonable or not that you was greatly to blame to have inflamd the Country for paultry Perquisites to yourself more than with a view of advantage to the Province and this way of reasoning gaind ground more and more upon the Alarm from the French, and, in short that by your Means they were brought into a Scrape with the King and the Ministry for giving their approbation, for they openly declard that it was no order of theirs to a Measure that was like to make so great noise, In this temper they were when I presented the Memorial, and in doing thereof my chief View was to bring them to an open Explanation of the part they were to take therein, And this operated accordingly for by privat managment with them I found they wishd that I would fight the Battle & withdraw my Memorial before another Board, and deal tenderly with their approbation of the Fee & indeed it was a very tender point with me after withdrawing my Memorial how to keep them in Such temper so as to carry their approbation along with us and without laying the whole Stress of the Cause upon it, And to Do this I thought it was best for me secure of Ld Granvilles Judgment to Shew Spirit in the case. I therefore gave out amongst them that having the Attorney Generals oppinion on your Side in point of Law, I did therefore hope that they would do nothing to invalidate what they had already done.

In this ticklish situation with the Lords for Trade, came & very a propos the Journals of the Ho: of Burgesses, & from thence I was enabled to give quite another turn to the Battle, Govert & the Property of the Crown to Crown Lands being Attacked by the Resolves of the H. of B. the Public Money applyd by the Sole Authority of one Branch of the Legislature contrary to Provincial Acts of the Genl Assembly & contrary to the Constitution of this Kingdom, an Agent & the Kings Servant sent home to Represent generally the Affairs of Govert with no other Authority than that of the Burgesses,[5] from the Manner more than from the Matter of the Contest the Lords for Trade at length found themselves calld upon to Support your Measures for the sake of Govert But after all it was to Lord Granvilles taking the case up with Spirit, in some Measure directing My Proceedings that Lord Halefax at length Engagd & being engagd I must do him the Justice that at the hearing &

indeed before it he shewd me great Warmth on your Side of the question, & the second day after the hearing at a full Board dismissd Mr Attorney General from his Office.[6] *Thy Friends* behaved with great address during the whole of the Affair and its to the Confidence that Subsists between them & to your [meeting?] [*illegible*] [often] with those great Men that we have all along acted consistently & have been able to carry into execution the Posterior part of the Plan, & there personal Freindship for you & me the same time their Interest in keeping well with your Adversarys however tenacious to your side of the question made me readily concur & agree to any proposition of theirs that consistent with your honour would tend to restore Peace after the Battle had been decided, and I must do them the Justice to say that they had my Interest in View at the Same time by making me a Party to the Plan of Peace as an Introduction to the Provincial Agency pointed out to you in the Letter from hence Impowering you to Restore the Attorney General if you think proper Lord Granville askd me how I should like this turn to be given to Mr Randolph, I told him that I could answer for you that it would be acceptable to you, as by it you would have the pledge of Peace in your own hands for yourself & your Friends, but you have still a Stronger game to Play which I must point out to you. Col Beverley undertook to speak to Some point the night of the Tryal I think that it was to explain how the Treasurer came to apply the 2500, & most unlukily & injudiciously he discoverd what I had from the beginning endeavourd to hide, and was accordingly not mentiond by my Council (vizt) that the Speaker of the House of B: for the time being by an Act of Assembly appointed Treasurer he was therefore obligd to comply with the Order of the House,[7] you may be Sure that such a Law could not but alarm Lord H——x & Lord Granville who have for some time past been endeavouring to Strengthen the hands of Government amongst other Measures [for] that purpose Repealing all Laws whereby Treasurers were appointed by the Authority of a Law Independent of the Crown; & I know that this case of Virginia has now furnishd them with the most Solid Argument to Support these Measures in so doing, And there is no doubt but that this Law will become an Object of their Resentment tho perhaps not at present, While the Province is in a State of Forcign War, but I have reason to believe that it stands as a Mark, and finding this to be the case I have laid the Foundation for your having the Speaker at all events under a Commission from the Crown by your recommendation of him thro my Solicitation,[8] & hereby you will have a Sub[t]le game to play in support of your Administration & at the Same time to throw some merit into my hands with the Speaker in case if a Provicial Agency is thought on.

Thus My Dr Sir I have brought this Matter to an Issue with no Small trouble and anxiety of mind on your Account as being amongst the first Acts of your Administration deemed by some an Act of Venality, & mercenary Views under the speciouse pretext of promoting the Kings Revenue, however it has taken now a more favourable turn, and tho you have got the Victory I know you will shew no Resentment to Such of your Adversarys as are willing to Sue for Peace by acknowledgeing their Error meet them half way and I believe I may venture to assure you that some of them never will be led again out of their way as accessairys to complaints against you in doubtfull cases, & much less in Cases that are aimd agt Govert & the Right of the Crown; I have Study'd Oeconomy in my conduct as much as possible, Finding that all Interviews between thy Friends & me became dangerouse to them after Notice given them from Virginia of the Intended Address I therefore at first Setting out calld upon them in your Name for 100 Ster & when the tryal was over I calld for another 100 of which I advanced at the beginning to Mr Jos Sharpe 30£ to retain & pay the Council their usual Arguing Fees[9] To which I myself added extra Fees for Additional Briefs to our Council *10.10.0* in consultation with Our Friends when the hearing was over altho I had nothing to boast of by Mr Pownals Services or good Offices to you on the contrary from the beginning to the end dark & mysterious & then thinks you have had good luck to get out of this Scrape Ive thought adviseable to make him your Freind at least to take no Notice of his Coolness for that purpose by way of extraordinary trouble I gave him in your name 10. Guineas to Gildebrand & Rogers[10] who have all along been ready with all their Books & Papers to give me Matter for the Briefs to them & the Clerks who attended the tryal with the Books of Office amongst them *five* Guineas more; At the most moderate computation for Coach hire from Grovenors Square to the Tower Repeatedly During this Negociation I must allow *25.0.0.* for occasional pocket Expences including Money paid to House Porters & footmen I must likewise allow *25* all which Articles as above making *105.15*[11] reduces the Ballance of the above 200 had of Mr Hanbury to 94.15.0[12] out of which I have still to Pay the Office Account of the Plantation [Office] due for Copys of Papers of which we have had numbers relative to the constitution & Govert of Virginia into which expence we were led by Mr Paris who was our Adverse Solicitor and likewise the Ordinary Fees of the Council Office for Copys of Papers & for the Instruction relative to the Pistole Fee what these may come to I cannot now tell you but whatever the ballance may be after all is paid shall stand for your use, I have orderd Mr Sharpe to give me his Lawers Bills & whatever that may come to I may venture to assure you that it will come very considerably under that of Mr Parrisses and with regard to my own demands as your Agent in this case I shall make none however as my Adversary Agent must be paid & as he cannot be paid without the Consent & concurrence of you & the Council whose cause this is as well as yours, before that is had I dare say that both you & they will think it incumbent before that is had to make Terms for your Agent, your Adversarys Petition being rejected they have lost their cause consequently lyable to pay costs & this no doubt may be brought to a compromise So as that you may be reimbursed the Expenses on your part.

The hope that this matter had occasiond made me give notice to all your Freinds in this end of the Town & in the City to attend the hearing & I never saw a Cause so well attended by hearers or Lords of Council for no less than   sat in Council, thank God its now over & I most heartily give you & Mrs Dinwiddie Joy, & refer you to another letter concerning your Spanish Claim.[13]

PS   It weakend your cause extreamly that their was no Limitation in the Order of Council with regard to Small Grants or Patents, and that the Order made no Exception to Grants that had lain in the Office & not taken out before your Arrival, because the delay was not the Fault of the Grantee but in the Secretarys Office for not having recorded those Grants & from thence arises the Limitations prescribd in the Kings Instruction to you on the Fee. NB Added a paragraph concerning the Agency from the Authority of the Governor & Council with Salary of 200£.[14]

LB, pp. 370–373. Sent "per Governor Dobbs in the Garland."

1. See JA to Dinwiddie, 23 June 1754, pp. 112–113, n. 1. In fact, the Privy Council hearing was on Tuesday, 18 June, and the resulting Order in Council was drawn up on Friday, 21 June. See Jack P. Greene, "The Case of the Pistole Fee: The Report of a Hearing on the Pistole Fee Dispute Before the Privy Council, June 18, 1754," *VMHB* 66 (1958): 399–422.

2. Randolph appeared before the Board of Trade on 20 June, at which time Halifax "acquainted him that his Majesty having been informed that he had come over here from Virginia without the Governor's leave, contrary to the tenor of his patent, by which he was appointed Attorney General only during his residence in that colony, and being apprehensive that such a precedent might be attended with very bad consequences to his service, had thought proper to direct that it be signified to him, that his Majesty does consider his office as vacated by such proceeding; whereupon Mr. Randolph said he hoped that if the nature of his case would admit of it, his conduct since he has been here would recommend him to his Majesty's favour, and then he withdrew" (*JBT*, 10:50).

In its letter of 3 July 1754, the Board of Trade informed Dinwiddie that Randolph had been dismissed but gave Dinwiddie permission to reinstate him if he behaved in a proper manner. The Board continued: "This Measure We think will tend to quiet the Minds of the People, and to stop the unjust Clamour that has been raised; and We recommend it rather, if from Circumstances you shall be of Opinion it can be done with Propriety, as it appears to Us to be at this time particularly necessary for His Majesty's Service, that Harmony and Mutual Confidence should be established between the Governors & the People in all His Majesty's Colonies" (CO 5/1367, fols. 94–100). See JA to Dinwiddie, 30 Mar. 1755, pp. 138–142.

3. The "Instruction" was the Board of Trade's letter of 3 July 1754.

4. JA's memorial has not been found.

5. After Dinwiddie failed to recede from his position on the pistole fee, the House of Burgesses on 4 Dec. 1753 passed a series of resolutions declaring the governor's actions to be "illegal and arbitrary," and tending "to subverting the Laws and Constitution of this Government"; providing for an appeal to be made to the Crown for relief; and stating that whoever paid the fee "shall be deemed a Betrayer of the Rights and Privileges of the People." On 15 Dec. 1753 the House appointed Peyton Randolph to present the address in England and granted him £2,500 Virginia currency to undertake the mission. The House also promised him £300 sterling a year for life if he lost the attorney generalship because of his role in the dispute (*JHB, 1752–1758*, 154–155, 167, 168–169; Dinwiddie to JA, 9 Feb. 1754, in Brock, *Dinwiddie Papers*, 1:72).

6. See note 2 above.

7. From 1699 to 1710 the office of treasurer of Virginia was held by former or current Speakers of the House of Burgesses, and from 1710 to 1766 (except for the period 1715–1723) the two offices were combined by acts of the General Assembly.

The act in force at the time JA wrote this letter was "An Act for appointing a treasurer," passed on 20 Apr. 1752 (Hening, *Statutes*, 6:248–250). See Greene, *Quest for Power*, 243–244.

8. Jack P. Greene has written of the power to appoint speakers of colonial legislatures: "The English House of Commons had won complete authority over its speaker in 1679 when it refused to accept Charles II's nominee. Following the Commons' example, all American lower houses assumed the power to nominate and control their speakers. The Crown insisted upon retaining for its governors the privilege of rejecting the lower houses' choice for the speakership, but no governor in the southern royal colonies attempted to exercise that privilege in the years before 1763" (*Quest for Power*, 206–207).

9. At this point the following passage was crossed through: "I have likewise occasionally disbursed in various Articles some of whom were not proper to be taken into a Lawers or Solicitors Bill, and on various occasions Exclusive of Coach hire & to Servants about 18.0.0 So that upon the whole Allowing for Coach hire & gratuitys to Servants 20 making in all £68.0.0 the Ballance in my hands applicable to your use will be 32.0.0 out of which I must deduct some small charges attending the case of the Spanish Capture which shall be the Subject of another letter herewith sent by Governor Dobbs who probably will have an Interview with you, to conclude whatever Mr Sharpes Bill may be I am Satisfyd that it will come far short of Mr Parriss, and with regard to my own Demands as your Agent I make none, however as the adversary Agent must be paid & as he cannot be paid without the concurrence of you & of the Council before that is had I dare say you will think it incumbent upon you to make Terms for your Agent their Petition being absolutely rejected they have lost their cause consequently lyable to pay Costs & this no doubt may be brought to a compromise so as that you reimburse yourself the expences of this case."

10. Samuel Gellibrand (d. 1758) was deputy secretary and Richard Rogers was clerk to the Board of Trade.

11. JA's addition is in error here; the total should be £106.5.0.

12. Again, JA's calculation is in error; £200 less £105.15 equals £94.5.0.

13. See following entry.

14. In his reply of 25 Oct. 1754, Dinwiddie reported that he had "called the Council & prevailed with them to augmt. Yr. Salary to 200 per Ann." (Dinwiddie Letter Books, 3:112–114, VHS).

To Robert Dinwiddie

[ca. 30 June 1754]

Governor Dinwiddie at same time an Ansr to his concerning the Spanish Capture[1] see Lre June 30th 1754.

LB, p. 373.

1. Dinwiddie's letter has not been found.

To James Glen

July 1t 1754

My last per Mr Murray,[1] I expected to have Sent you Letters from the Plantation Office but they are adjou[r]nd,[2] perhaps Governor Reynolds first dispatches may draw them together,[3] Mr Pitts privat affairs prevent his pressing his Nomination at Same [time] its too far gone for any other person.

Motions of the French may be productive of Erecting a Fort amongst the upper cherokees, long since pointed out by S Car: Govert first by Col Vander & now judiciously by Mr Pinckney,[4] Presents to the Indians may be concommitant of some other general Measures that may appear with Governor Reynolds.

Governor Sharpe has got the Command on the Ohio by Governor Din[wid]dys recommendation,[5] have reced 100£ of your Bill & gave you credit for Same.

LB, p. 373. At the foot of this letter JA wrote: "per Mcleland for Port Royal. Magazines for April, May & June."

1. See JA to Glen, 9 Apr. 1754, p. 111.

2. In fact, the Board of Trade had met on 27 June and again on 2 July 1754 (*JBT*, 10:54).

3. JA evidently knew that John Reynolds (1713?–1788) would be appointed the first royal governor of Georgia. He was appointed in Aug. 1754 but did not arrive in the colony until late Oct. 1754.

4. Charles Pinckney had written to Board of Trade secretary Pownall on 11 Sept. 1753 concerning the necessity of building a fort among the Cherokee (*SCPR*, 25:344–346), although the Board did not read the letter until 5 Apr. 1754 (*JBT*, 10:34). He also submitted a memorial on 1 June 1754 "relating to the designs of the French to build a fort in the upper Cherokee nation, which if not timely prevented will prove of the most fatal consequences to the peace and safety of [South Carolina] and the neighbouring Provinces" (*SCPR*, 25:40–43; *JBT*, 10:46). The Board of Trade took the memorial into consideration on 14 June, when Pinckney appeared before it on the subject, and on 20 June the Board signed a letter to Secretary of State Thomas

Robinson asking him to lay the matter before the king (*SCPR*, 26:52–55; *JBT*, 10:47–48, 49, 50).

5. Maryland lieutenant governor Horatio Sharpe was appointed lieutenant colonel and commander in chief of all the British forces opposing the French in the Ohio Valley on 5 July 1754.

To the Executors of Nathaniel Rice

[ca. 5 July 1754]

To the Executors of Mr Rice with an Order for 100 to be given by them on Mr Rutherford.[1]

LB, p. 373. Sent "per Govr Dobbs."

1. Nathaniel Rice had died on 29 Jan. 1753. It is not known why his executors owed JA £100.

To John Rutherfurd

[ca. 5 July 1754]

To Mr Rutherford with an Order inclosd & Account of 500£ to Mrs Frances Johnston for payt of the same 500.

LB, p. 373. Sent "per Govr Dobbs."

To [James] Murray et al.

[ca. 5 July 1754]

To Mr Murray, Mr Swann, Samuel, Committee of Correspondence see Letter in bundle of Letters, John Swann, Col Innes, Mrs Allen.

LB, p. 373. Sent "per Govr Dobbs."

To Robert Dinwiddie

[5 July 1754]

Per Gover Dobbs to Virginia Govr Dinwiddie July 5th relative to Mr Randolph see Lettre in bundle Letters.

LB, p. 373.

To Robert Dinwiddie and James Innes

[12 July 1754]

Per Do[1] to Governor Dinwiddie & Col Innis about Governor Sharpes command to Regiment[2] July 12th.

LB, p. 373.
1. Governor Dobbs.
2. See JA to Glen, 1 July 1754, p. 124, n. 5.

To Robert Dinwiddie

[23 July 1754]

To Virginia per Capt Pearson July 23d Governor Dinwiddie about the Kings Warrant for replacing the 20000 Sent to Virginia from the Pay Office[1] Col Innis on the Ohio.[2]

LB, p. 374. At the foot of this memorandum JA wrote: "NB these Lres [i.e., this and the following letter] were returnd from the Downs & went by Mr Hanburys ship see Bundle 18th Augt 1753 [i.e., 1754]."

1. On 5 July 1754 Secretary of State Thomas Robinson sent £10,000 in specie to Virginia and credit for an additional £10,000, as well as 2,000 stands of arms for the defense of the colony. The king's warrant, dated 3 July 1754 (CO 5/211, pp. 77–79; Koontz, *Dinwiddie Papers*, 560–561), stipulated that the £20,000 was to be reimbursed from the revenues of the two-shillings-per-hogshead tobacco export tax. In his letter to Robinson of 25 Oct. 1754 acknowledging receipt of the specie (Brock, *Dinwiddie Papers*, 1:352–355), Dinwiddie stated that the tobacco revenues had to support the salaries of the governor, the Council, the agent in London (JA), the judges of the court of oyer and terminer, the adjutants, the attorney general, as well as other incidental expenses, and that the tobacco revenue was therefore "greatly loaded."

He further explained that the tobacco revenue was the only source of emergency funds, and he therefore asked Robinson to use his influence with the king to suspend the reimbursement.

As John R. Alden has written about this ostensibly generous act of the Crown, "The British ministry proposed, in effect, to spend Virginia tax money for military purposes." Dinwiddie at first kept the warrant secret from the House of Burgesses, but "the home government denied his plea that the £20,000 sent him not be reimbursed out of the tobacco export tax. He and his Council were embarrassed and irritated. He was forced to send Virginia money to London. That the money was going across the ocean could not long be concealed from the House, who were the more exasperated because Dinwiddie could spend the royal grant of Virginia money as he wished" (*Robert Dinwiddie: Servant of the Crown* [Williamsburg, 1973], 33–36).

2. James Innes led the North Carolina regiment raised for the expedition to the Ohio.

To John Rutherfurd

[23 July 1754]

North Carolina by Capt Pearson also of July 23rd 1754 to Mr Rutherford about the Six per cent on the Arrears[1] See the letter of this date, & his letter in the Account book.

LB, p. 374. See the source note to the preceding entry.

1. JA evidently expected to receive 6 percent of the arrears of salary owed to the estate of the late governor Gabriel Johnston. See JA to Rutherfurd, 16 Oct. 1754, p. 127.

To Robert Dinwiddie

[18 August 1754]

To Governor Dinwiddie 18th Augt containing Remarks on Warrant for the 20000 See Letter.

LB, p. 374.

To Robert Dinwiddie et al.

[14, 15 October 1754]

Virginia Octr 14 & 15th 1754 per Mr Randolph Govr Dinwiddie 2 letters, Rd Corbin, Mr Pride[1] vede Lres Bundle Virginia NB pro Additional Salary to me[2] another concerning Repayment to Mr Dinwide his Military Disbursments[3] See Bundle.

LB, p. 374.

1. Richard Corbin (1708–1790) served on the Virginia Council from 1750 to 1775 and as deputy receiver general from 1762 until the Revolution. Possibly James Pride, who was naval officer for the York River district 1763–1764 (*Fauquier Papers*, 2:1021; 3:1183, 1469n).

2. See JA to Dinwiddie, 30 June 1754, p. 122, n. 14.

3. Dinwiddie had advanced more than £1,000 sterling for the support of the three independent companies under his command, and he had been seeking reimbursement from Secretary at War Henry Fox since Aug. (Dinwiddie to Fox, 15 Aug. 1754, in Brock, *Dinwiddie Papers*, 1:280; see also 284, 285, 325, 328–329, 337, 340–341).

To John Rutherfurd

[16 October 1754]

North Carolina Octr 16th 1754 To John Rutherford via Virginia per Mr Randolph about the Provisions for the Troops, & desire that Mrs Rutherford[1] may Sign a joint letter for the payment of 6 per cent or give me a Sum constant per Bond[2] See Rutherfords Answer without date amongst his letters.[3]

LB, p. 374.

1. Formerly Mrs. Gabriel Johnston.

2. See JA to Rutherfurd, 23 July 1754, p. 126.

3. Letter not found.

To Arthur Dobbs et al.

[26 October 1754]

North Carolina per Capt Heron Octr 26th 1754 To the Gover, & To the Committee, about an Additional Salary inclosd in the

Govers Letter See Letter to the Committee in Bundle to Samuel Swann.

LB, p. 374.

To James Glen

Octr 30th 1754

I send you the last Magazine, and as your Brother[1] is now on the Spot, I must desire of you to look upon me Releasd from the continuation of your Agreement with me as the Channel of your letters, I have therefore drawn upon you for the last years Salary payable to Mr Cleland for my Use, As to my Disbursments on your Account from the date of your Agreement they are not of consequence enough to make a particular Acct, on payment therefore of the salary now due I discharge you from all further Demands on acct of the Agent or otherwise and am, Sir

LB, p. 374. Sent "per Mr Rutledge."

1. Dr. Thomas Glen (d. 1786), younger brother of James Glen, served in the Commons House of Assembly 1749–1751 and 1752–1754. After returning to England he married, in Sept. 1755, Isabella Wright, daughter of Robert Wright and widow of James Graeme.

To John Cleland

[30 October 1754]

To Mr Cleland with Bill inclosd pro 50£ Ster on Governor Glen See Lre in Bundle with an Account of his Debt with Capt Frankland[1] NB the Bill is dated Novr 8th 1754 that being the day of the Commenct of my agreement with Governor Glen.

LB, p. 374.

1. Not identified.

To James Michie et al.

[30 October 1754]
To Mr Michie at Same time, Mr Manegault & Mr Chas Wright.

LB, p. 374. This memorandum was appended to the preceding entry.

To Robert Dinwiddie

[28, 30 November 1754]
Gover Dinwiddie Novr 28: & 30th 1754 See Bundle of Letters for the most material Letter, Copyd per Mr Shirleys Sectry to Genal Braddock,[1] as Ansr to the Govers by Capt Dalrimple,[2] concerning the Supply Bill pro 20000 Pro:.[3]

LB, p. 375.

1. William Shirley, Jr. (1721–1755), eldest son of Massachusetts governor William Shirley, had been in England since 1745. He was named secretary to Braddock without rank in the fall of 1754 and sailed for Virginia in Dec. 1754. Shirley was killed at the battle of the Monongahela on 9 July 1755. Major General Edward Braddock (ca. 1695–1755) had just assumed the North American command.

2. Dinwiddie's letter of 15 Aug. 1754 (Dinwiddie Letter Books, 3:85–86, VHS) was carried by Lt. John Dalrymple, who "comes home in order to procure a Como. to succeed Lieut. [Peter] Mercier in Ct. [James] Mackay's Compy." Dalrymple was appointed captain lieutenant in Jan. 1755 and returned to America, where he was placed in command of Johnson's Fort in North Carolina.

Dinwiddie's letter expressed the opinion that "without a sufficient Aid from Home we shall not be able to drive the French from the Ohio"; informed JA of the congress at Albany and the resulting Albany Plan of Union ("there are some Articles in it of an extraordinary nature, the Presidt. of the Grand Council is to be invested with large Powers & indeed very near to that of a Viceroy"); asked JA to find out why Dinwiddie had not heard from Halifax in so long; asked JA to inquire of the secretary at war whether he would be reimbursed for the money he had advanced for the three independent companies (more than £1,000 sterling); communicated the latest news from the frontier; and complained of the inadequate assistance of North Carolina, Maryland, and Pennsylvania to the projected expedition against the French.

3. In a letter to JA of 1 Sept. 1754 (Dinwiddie Letter Books, 3:87, VHS), Dinwiddie explained that on 29 Aug. the House of House of Burgesses had passed a bill for raising £20,000, but that on 31 Aug. the House tacked on, as a rider, a provision for paying £2,500 to Peyton Randolph for representing the House in the

pistole fee dispute. Because of this rider, the Council rejected the bill, and on 5 Sept. Dinwiddie prorogued the assembly until 17 Oct. (*JHB, 1752–1758*, 196, 199, 205). For the final passage of the supply bill, see the following entry.

To Robert Dinwiddie

[6 December 1754]

Gover Dinwiddie Decr 6th 1754 per Genal Braddock concerning my Negociation with Mr Randolph to quiet the minds of the Ministry about the Supply Bill per Do to acknowledge the Governors of Octr 25th with the Advice of the Supply Bill being passd & to answer his Lre more particularly by another opportunity in the mean time thank him for the Addition to my Salary.[1]

LB, p. 375.

1. In his letter to JA of 25 Oct. 1754 (Dinwiddie Letter Books, 3:112–114, VHS), Dinwiddie informed JA that "After long Disputes & Argumts., and pushing all my Intt. I at last have prevailed with our Ho. of B: to vote 20,000 towards conducting the Expeditn., which gives me much Satisfactn." The "Act for raising the sum of twenty thousand pounds for the protection of his majesty's subjects against the insults and encroachments of the French" was passed on 2 Nov. 1754 (Hening, *Statutes*, 6:435–438). In exchange for the supply bill, Dinwiddie agreed to a compromise whereby he and the Council passed Treasurer John Robinson's accounts, which included the disputed payment of £2,500 to Peyton Randolph (Greene, *Quest for Power*, 102–103).

Dinwiddie also expressed dismay over the Board of Trade's letter to him of 3 July 1754 on the pistole fee dispute (see JA to Dinwiddie, 30 June 1754, above). He complained that the Board was "not explicit enough" in its regulations for his future conduct. (He wrote in a similar vein to the Board on 25 Oct. 1754 [Brock, *Dinwiddie Papers*, 1:362–365].)

For JA's salary, see JA to Dinwiddie, 30 June 1754, pp. 116–120.

To John Tinker

[23 December 1754]

Gover Tinker Decr 23d 1754 to Virginia care of the Post Master per Mr Mcculloh Acquaint him that we are likely to Suceed in our Ordnance Affair,[1] of Mr Littletons appointment for Carolina,[2] of the Domestic News.

LB, p. 375.

1. After receiving word that his first request for ordnance for the Bahamas had been denied (see JA to Tinker, 1 Jan. 1753, p. 65), Tinker wrote to the Board of Trade on 24 Jan. 1754 renewing his appeal. On 24 May 1754 the Board submitted to the Privy Council a report on the matter, enclosing an extract of the letter (*JBT*, 10:36–37, 41–42). The Privy Council on 18 July in turn referred the matter to the Ordnance Board. JA must have learned that the Ordnance Board was looking favorably on Tinker's request, and in May 1755 the Privy Council, acting on the Ordnance Board's report, ordered that the stores be sent (*APC*, 4:147–148).

2. William Henry Lyttelton (1724–1808) was appointed governor of South Carolina in Jan. 1755, although he did not arrive in the colony until June 1756. Lyttelton was governor of South Carolina until 1762.

To Arthur Dobbs

[23 December 1754]
Gover Dobbs Decr 23d 1754 to Virginia from Bristol per Mr Mcculloh, tell him the News, Send him the Regulations as to Rank amongst the Officers,[1] & clause of the Mutiny Bill.[2]

LB, p. 375.

1. The regulations concerning rank and command in the American campaign, promulgated by the king's order under sign manual of 12 Nov. 1754, stipulated that colonial officers were to be subordinate to regular officers of similar rank (*Archives of the State of New Jersey*, 1st ser., vol. 8, pt. 2 [Newark, 1885], 29–30).

2. "An Act for punishing mutiny and desertion, and for the better payment of the army and their quarters," approved 19 Dec. 1754 (28 George II, chap. 4), contained a clause providing that all officers and soldiers of any troops in America who had been raised by the authority of colonial governors or governments "shall, at all times and in all places, when they happen to join, or act in conjunction with, his majesty's British forces, be liable to martial law and discipline, as the British forces are; and shall be subject to the same trial, penalties, and punishments."

To Robert Dinwiddie

[25 December 1754]
Gover Dinwiddie by Mr Mcculloh via Bristol 25th of Decr 1754 Send him the Regulation about Rank, & clause of the Mutiny Bill.

LB, p. 375.

To Robert Dinwiddie

[30 December 1754]
Governor Dinwiddie Dr 30th per Capt Dalrymple See Lre.

LB, p. 375.

To Arthur Dobbs

[30 December 1754]
Governor Dobbs Decr 30th 1754 per Capt Dalrymple with clause of the Mutiny Act.

LB, p. 375.

To Robert Dinwiddie

Sir   Craven Street Janry 16th 1755
Last night I had the pleasure of yours of the 16th of November with the several papers therein inclosed;[1] in answer to which, let me in the first place return you thanks, for the Bill of 100£ which Messrs Hanburys have paid on sight,[2] and at the same time I thank you, for your overtures to Messrs Wragg & Cleland concerning the Agency of So Carolina.[3] Messrs Pinkney & Crokat, stand in comp[et]ition for that Office, and to speak the truth, while Mr Glen heads that Province, I should not expect pleasure in the Service, and as little Justice, deserted by every body, he threw, himself into my hands, for taking charge of his public letters, he proposed for my trouble 50£ per an, three years without any manner of acknowledgment, at length I drew upon him by good luck I got my money & then dischargd myself from all correspondence with him.
The restoration of peace between you, & the Assembly gives great pleasure, every Article of your letter relative to Military Affairs will be answerd by General Braddocks arrival & the powers

he brings with him and so far as I can learn, they are determind to take no step here, that may in the least, break in upon him, & his Command in the military way, whatever therefore relates to the military operations, he alone must stand accountable.

The Address, from his Majestys Council, will of course, be presented to the King, by the Secretary of State, & with regard to the publication, thereof in the Gazette Mr Amyand is to take the pleasure of his Principal thereon.[4] I thought to have found the Bishop of London at his house in the Temple, but to my disappointment this morning, I was there informd, that his constant residence is at Fulham, and there I shall attend him, with your packet; the Address to you from the Clergy is really a good performance, I shewd it this morning to Lord H–l—x & to Lord G————le and they both declard their approbation thereof, your reply is also much to the purpose, both these, I shall take upon me to have inserted in the News papers, which shall, according to your desire, be transmitted to you.[5]

The Lords for Trade have the matter of the Arrears of Quitrents under their, deliberation & the result thereof you will be Instructed in, without loss of time, Lord Halefax told me that it should be determind this day, if so, the next ship will bring your Instructions thereon.[6]

In a former letter, I told you, of the answer, I had received concerning, the suspending the Warrant for replacing the money remitted from hence which I again repeat to you, (vizt) that the Warrant was gone, and that you knew your duty in regard thereto.

I cannot tell what stress is laid, on the execution of this Warrant, in the Orders that you have from the Secretary of State, I hope that they are, for your sake extreamly explicit, for in the light that the case appears to me, it seems to be a determind Measure of Government here, to adhere to the Warrant, I intreat you therefore to attend to the spirit of your orders on this head, without making yourself a volunteer in opposition thereto, as our Freind Hanbury did, your case and his do differ greatly; If remonstrances are made to you on your side of the water, by the Officer of the Revenue to whom your Warrant shall be directed it may become your duty to transmit such remonstrances, for your further Directions thereon, I cannot help as ty'd, through friendship to you, dwelling on the delicacy of your conduct in this respect this

Warrant has made great noise in the Ca—net, as I have heard, and I am sensible that it has done so out of doors. I most heartily wish, that our friend Hanbury had not stopt it, because from thence, sprung the alarm, of a design and, a premeditate design, to withstand the operation thereof, whatever Arguments are now urged, since that are invalidated on that account, and are turn'd in some measure against those who make use of them, as being in some shape or other personally interested, in making an opposition thereto, from hence, it is, that I dispair that your arguments now urged with the Secretary of State produce A dismission of [the w]arrant the resentment that was shewn on account of its being stopt here, adds great strength to the measures for the execution thereof now that it is sent, to which may be added another disagreable circumstance, (viz) that I am affraid in the course of the agitation of this Warrant, some thing has dropt as if the right of the Crown to apply this Money to this purpose of Government might be calld in question by the Governor & Council of Virginia, on the whole I sincerely wish that both you & the Council may not be embarased by means of the Warrant; you will perhaps be better able to judge from the Secretary of States answer to you on this head how to conduct yourself,[7] what I have said thereon proceeds from a Supposition, that he gives you no explicit directions thereon, In which case I submit to your consideration, the Issuing your Warrant [to] the proper Officer [in] the general Terms of the Kings Warrant to you, that thereupon the Officer do so far comply with your Warrant in point of payment as the circumstances of his case will admit of, this will obviat & remove the Jealousy of any Impeachment of the Kings right to grant this Warrant, and perhaps the further application of the remaining Ballance now acknowledged by the Receiver towards the Exigencys of Government may have reduced that ballance, for I conceive that the Kings Warrant goes no further than to the excressence of the Fund beyond the ordinary occasions & the Extraordinary Purposes & exigencys of your Government, if this construction of the Warrant then is just which I take it to be, because otherwise it might not only distress you in the ordinary annual purposes but also in the occasional & unforeseen Extraordinary services of Govert what reservation therefore may be necessary to make on that account out of the present Great ballance which has been pointed out to the

Ministers of Govert by Mr Horace Walpole or, out of any Subsequent annual ballance becomes with you & with the Council a Matter of prudential consideration absolutly necessary for the Kings Service in so far as that the application of the whole of the annual ballance of this Fund after payment of the ordinary Establishment, would leave the necessary & the unforseen Extraordinary Services absolutly unprovided for, which cannot be the Kings Intention.

LB, unpaginated, but falls between pp. 24 and 25. In the margin at the head of the letter JA wrote: "To Governor Dinwiddie relative to the Warrant pro 20000£."

1. Dinwiddie's letter of 16 Nov. 1754 is in Dinwiddie Letter Books, 3:123–124, VHS.

2. After gaining the Council's assent to raising JA's salary to £200 per year, Dinwiddie "further prevailed [with them] to pay You one half Year's Salary to end the 25th Octr.," for which he enclosed a bill of exchange on John and Capel Hanbury.

3. After the South Carolina Assembly learned in early 1754 that Crokatt wished to resign, the colony's agency became an object of dispute between the Council and the Commons House. The Council wished to replace Crokatt, while the Commons House hoped to retain him in office. In Sept. 1754 the Commons House learned that Crokatt had agreed to continue as agent, but by that time Glen and the Council had already procured the services of Charles Pinckney. When South Carolinians William Wragg and John Cleland were in Williamsburg in Nov. 1754, Dinwiddie recommended JA to be agent of that colony, but "they only objected it wd. be disagreeable to the People while you was Agent for No. Carolina." Dinwiddie then "told them I believed You wd. resign that if You was sure of being appointed for So. Car. I sd. what I thot. proper. You may write on the Head to Mr. Glen, Cleland or any other of Yr. Friends." (For JA's earlier overture to Wragg and Cleland, see JA to Glen et al., 29 June 1753, n. 3, above.) Finally, in a compromise in Jan. 1756, the assembly appointed William Middleton (1710–1785), like Pinckney a native of South Carolina resident in London (Sirmans, *Colonial South Carolina*, 301–304; Greene, *Quest for Power*, 268–271).

4. The Council's address to the Crown sought further protection from the attacks of the French (CO 5/15, fol. 24). Dinwiddie enclosed it in his letter to Robinson of 16 Nov. 1754 (Brock, *Dinwiddie Papers*, 1:403–405).

Claudius Amyand (1718–1774), member of Parliament 1747–1756, was undersecretary of state 1750–1756 and commissioner of customs 1756–1765.

5. At a convention of Virginia clergymen held in Williamsburg on 30–31 Oct. 1754, the clergy took exception to an order of the Virginia Council of 2 Nov. 1752 that prohibited ministers from serving as county justices of the peace. The Council held

"that every Clergyman has enough to do, to discharge his Duty as a Minister without engaging himself in Civil Affairs" (*EJC*, 5:409). The clergy petitioned Dinwiddie to influence the Council to reverse its order, which was done. The clergymen's addresses to the king and to Thomas Sherlock (1678–1761), bishop of London 1748–1761, and their address to Dinwiddie and his reply, are Fulham Papers, 13:132–161, printed in William Stevens Perry, *Historical Collections Relating to the American Colonial Church*, 5 vols. in 4 (Hartford, Conn., 1870–1878), 1:411–427.

6. The Board of Trade had under consideration Dinwiddie's letter of 25 Oct. 1754 (CO 5/1328, fols. 124–126), which sought clarification of several points concerning land grant procedures in light of the Crown's decision on the pistole fee. One of the stipulations of that decision was that no fee should be charged for patents for which preliminary steps had been taken before 22 Apr. 1752. Dinwiddie explained that he "asked no Fee for these Lands, but as they [landholders] had possessed and occupied them for many Years, in Order to defraud His Majesty of His Quit Rents; I thought it my Duty, as one of the Stewards of that Revenue, to demand the Arrears of Quit Rents before I Sealed and Signed their Patents; On this head, your Lordships are Silent, & I defer granting the Patents till I have Your Determination thereon." On 15 Jan. 1755, the day before JA wrote the present letter, the Board agreed on a reply to Dinwiddie, but the letter was not signed until 18 Apr. 1755 (*JBT*, 10:97, 100, 101, 136). The Board told Dinwiddie that it was not advisable to assess quitrents prior to the date of patents, and if any prejudice to Crown revenues arises, "it must happen either from the Neglect of the proper Officer in making out the Patent immediately upon the return of the Survey, or a defect in the Surveyor's not returning the Survey to the Secretary's Office within a limited time." The Board admonished Dinwiddie to ensure that officers of the Crown did their duty (CO 5/1367, fols. 66–68).

7. From this point on, the remainder of the letter is crossed through.

To Arthur Dobbs

[28 January 1755]
Gover Dobbs Janry 28th 1755 In Ansr to his of 26th of Novr 1754[1] See the Bundle of Lres per Mr Hanburys Ship Betsy Capt Castleton.

LB, p. 376.

1. Letter not found.

To the Committee of Correspondence of North Carolina

Jany 28th 1755

As the Bounty of Indico expires in March 1756 Some favorable circumstances now offering have induced me in conjunction with Mr Pinkney to apply to Parlt for the further continuation of the B: towards these Provinces, & I have the Satisfaction to let you know that hetherto we have met with no opposition in a public or in a privat way.[1]

This ap: might have come in time for the insuing Session but then some Motives now urging might have been lost this early solicitation I hope will therefore have your approbation I am alway with great regard

LB, p. 376. Endorsed as enclosed in the preceding letter.

1. "An Act for continuing an Act, intituled, 'An Act for encouraging the making of indico in the British plantations in America,'" approved on 25 Apr. 1755 (28 George II, chap. 25), extended the earlier act for a term of seven years from 25 Mar. 1756 and from then to the end of the next session of Parliament. A bounty of 6 pence per pound of weight was allowed on all indigo of a certain standard produced in America and imported into Great Britain.

The journals of the House of Commons do not record what role JA and Pinckney played in the passage of the act.

To Robert Dinwiddie

[28 January 1755]

Gover Dinwiddie 28th Jany 1755 Tell him of the delivery of his Lres to the Bishop of London of the Reports about Braddocks being Gover, not being true, tell him the State of the Case per the Bettsy Hanburys Ship.[1]

LB, p. 376.

1. Virginia's royal governor, William Anne Keppel (1702–1754), second earl of Albemarle, had died on 22 Dec. 1754. Almost immediately rumors evidently circulated that Braddock would be appointed to succeed him. Upon learning the news, Dinwiddie wrote JA on 17 Mar. 1755: "The Death of Ld. Albemarle gave me very great Concern, & if H Majesty shd. think proper to keep it open a few Years the Salary [generally split between the royal governor and his lieutenant governor] wd.

reimburse a very great Expence I have been at in the Publick Service these last two Years, & if properly considered will be no very great Favo. But I must submit to my Fate on that Head" (Dinwiddie Letter Books, 3:153–154, VHS). On 6 June Dinwiddie further reported to JA: "Genl. B———k's Friends write him he is likely to get it if so he desires my Continuance as Lieut. Govr. however that is too premature" (Dinwiddie Letter Books, 3:165–166, VHS). Dinwiddie was fortunate, for not until Mar. 1756 was John Campbell (1705–1782), fourth earl of Loudoun, appointed to succeed Albemarle.

To Robert Dinwiddie

[21 February 1755]

Gover Dinwiddie Febry 21t 1755 in answer to his of the 20th Decr 1754[1] (See Bundle) about Governor Glen & the Quitrents upon the Subseqt Grants.

LB, p. 376.

1. In his letter to JA of 20 Dec. 1754 (Dinwiddie Letter Books, 3:126, VHS), Dinwiddie enclosed copies of two letters "in a very odd Style" he had received from Governor Glen, as well as a copy of his reply. Dinwiddie also said that he hoped to have raised 1,000 recruits by the middle of Feb., that he had heard reports that two regiments from Ireland were being sent to America, and that he was appointing two commissaries to purchase provisions and store them in a magazine at Winchester.

To Robert Dinwiddie

Sir   March 30th 1755

I have yours of the 10th & of the 24th of Febry[1] by Capt Sprag in the Gybralter who made his passage in 17 days the Box containing the Laws & Journals are deliverd to the Plantation Office;[2] I greatly approve of the *Measures* as well as of the Method *you have taken* in regard to the Warrant for payment of the *Ballance of the Tobacco Duty* & having Signifyd the Same to Some of the Administration who have their Eye more particularly to this Matter I do not find that the Suspension of your Warrant till the ordinary Accounts are made up by the Recer General has occasiond any Suspicion of your Zeal in the execution thereof in April next.[3]

By Mr Amyand I understand that the Secry of State is to lay your letter on this head before the Treasury, & from the usual slow progression of Business thro that Office probably no Notice may be taken thereof till you have brought it to an Issue with the Recers next Accounts to be transmitted by you all that Mr Pownal can do all that I can do cannot prevail with the Secretarys of the Treasury to answer the case of the Virginia Q Rents, as laid before them by the Lords for Trade; they are taken up, with other Matters.

You have acted very Judiciously in your manner of Restoring Mr Randolph to his Office,[4] & herein you have the approbation of the Earls Granville & Halifax, and that I might [not] lose time in the confirmation of your Measures the very next Morning after the Receipt of your Letter and of Mr Randolphs[5] I was with Lord Halifax & his Lordship then assurd me that Mr Randolphs Commission shall be with the first Commissions that are laid before the King & Mr Pownal has therefore promisd me to forward the Same, I am obligd to you for the hint you give me of acting gratis in this Case and shall be obligd to you on all future occasions for throwing such opportunetys in my way of obliging particular Persons who may either strengthen your hands, Or my Interest with your Folks & whenever I have the hint given me by you, I shall pointedly comply therewith without Fee or reward for so doing; I am extreamly Indebted to you for the Stand that you have made for the continuation of My Agency in opposition to two Competitors,[6] you have now brought that Service into A greater Degree of Reputation than ever, My Interest and My Inclination are now united therein & the Countenance that I meet with from those of the Administration adds greatly to the Satisfaction I have in the Service, And their is another consideration that comes very near to me (vizt) that as Agent I am thereby intimatly connected in Interest as well as in Affection with my Freind Mr Dinwiddie thereby, and I look upon myself in a great measure posted as a Watch Man over his Interest; All these considerations put together, with the loss of appointment of 200 per an so punctually paid, had been extreamly Mortifying to me conscious to my self of having as much zeal in the Service with as great prospect of Sucess in my Negociations as any of those who may have attempted to break in upon me, I have heretofore returnd my thanks to the Gentlemen of the Council for their appointment of me I shall now repeat the Same adding thereto my obligations to them for an Addition to my Salary and shall take care to make no charge of Coach hire, nor of any other Contingent Charges except where the same do bona fide arise from the Service.[7]

Mr James Buchannan with whom I dined tother day in company with a very pretty lad a Son of Mr Corbins, had recommended to my care Mr Eyre's Act,[8] the Act is now come into the Office & I shall Follow the Same with as much Expedition & dispatch as the Standing Rules of Office will admit of, All privat & Public Acts lay over Six Months after the Council for the Board has made his Report thereon, in order that no advantage may be taken by a too speedy Confirmation thereof, this rule is Seldom departed from; I most heartily rejoice with you that by Genal Braddocks arrival you will in a great Measure be relieved from part at least of Military operations. I have great pleasure in hearing from Lord Halefax & from some others, that he found Things upon his arrival in much better order than he expected on setting out. I suppose these Accounts come from the General whose Harmony with you will carry you far in the King's favor as well as in the Dukes.[9] The repeated Remarks that you have made on the Conduct of the Collonys are very striking; had you not given the Alarm, on the first appearance of danger God knows what might have been the consequence to this Nation & her Colonies, had the Administration here treated your Alarm with as much Indifference as your Neighbours in America have done, or had it been possible for the Kings Servants here to have acted so treacherously as Some of his Servants not far from you have done, or for the Parlt of Great Britain to have Stood Still & lookd on with indifference as American Assemblys have so long done to the Views of France, this Kingdom now the Metropolitan State had soon become a Province; But thanks to you for the Alarm from the Ohio to those in the Administration for the credit given to your Judgment thereof & the Measures taken by you to withstand the danger, & above all to the Magnanimity of the King & the Magnanimity & the Unanimity of the Parliament declaring the Sence of the Nation by the Grant of a Million towards Supporting His Majesty & his Dominions without one Negative in either house;[10] & the Speeches of both houses if possible more animating than the Money, 25 Sail of the finest Ships in the World now at Spithead ready to put to Sea justly Said to be under Volunteer Comdrs Officers & privat Men, & 20 More geting

ready besides 50s, 40s, 20, & Sloops, the Repeated Proclamations
for Bounty Money given not only by the Public but by many
Corporated Towns thro the Nation, for Seamen & land men to
entry,[11] a Levy of 5000 Marines to be a permanent Body altogether
under the Admiralty without Colonels, only 3 Leut Colonels & 3
Majors, over the whole an Additional of 20000 Men to our Land
Forces in G B. are Such Measures as leave no room to doubt of
the truth of what was thrown out a few days ago in the House of
C———s by Mr Tho—s R———n (viz) That the Matter in
question between Us & France "was not to be left to the Determination of Commissarys nor to Conventions with France in whom
we could not confide" But that an Evacuation of all their Encroachments meaning from Nova Scotia to the Newtral Islands was our
preliminary & the ultimate Object of any Treaty to be made, &
such Treaty should [be] carryd into Execution under the Armaments now making, in short, Such dignety in Negociating, and
Spirit in Public Measures has not been paraleld Since Olivers[12]
time, what Pity it is, that the Colonys cannot be mov'd and activated
by the Same glorious Spirit to Strike home at once to the root from
whence all this Mischief proceeds & thereby put an End to all bad
Neighborhood by a general Ejectment of their Enemy, but before
this can be done I am affraid their must be a reformation in the
Government of some of our Colonys and Government must be
taken out of the hands of Traytors as well as of Quakers, had Mr
G—n in fact been what he seems to have Affected to be thought
from the beginning to the end of this Affair a French Governor he
had lost his Head with his Govert for betraying his Trust, he has I
am told once more hinderd the Catawbas from going to Virginia,
when this comes to be made known for the Accounts are but just
come from Carolina I do expect that he will be immediatly
dismissed & the Reins of Govert given to the Leut Gover till Mr
Littletons arrival his Demand on you for 7000 is lookd upon in the
light that in all probability it deserves, to put one half of the Sum
into his own pocket[13] by the Pamphlet herewith Sent you will find
the Quaker Administration severly handled,[14] this pamphlet having been put into the hands of all the Members of both Houses has
greatly alarmed the Friends on this Side the Water, I wish that the
Friends in Pensilvania had the Same Rational as well as Religious
Principles as Some of their Friends with us; their is no doubt but

that the Parlt will on a proper occasion take Measures to put the Govert of that Province into the hands of those who are [at] liberty to Exercise the Same; Inclosed I send you Duplicate of Mr Jos Sharpes Bill in the Case of the Pistole Fee and the Same is paid by Messrs Hanbury as I did apprehend as it comes out much under that of Mr Parisses As Costs are to be by the Public to your Adversary I hope you will take care at the Same time of your own, that Matter is now totally Subsided with us, and I hear that your Speaker is become one of the greatest Courtiers in Virginia.

Our Friend in Tower Street has been laid up almost the whole Winter, with the Gout, I have heard the cause, to Arise frome good claret he met with in Arlington Street at Ld G—n—ls, good claret & good company are not soon to be parted from, when Virginia is as the Subject of discourse Adieu My Dr Friend I have nothing more at present to Say than that you have my heart in your Service, May God grant you Sucess in your undertakings & with Complts to Mrs Dinwiddie who with her Family was very kindly mentiond at a large Meeting of her Friends in Mr Buchannans a few days bygone I remain always Your &c

LB, pp. 376–380.

1. Dinwiddie's letter of 10 Feb. 1755 is in Dinwiddie Letter Books, 3:143–144, VHS. His letter of 24 Feb. has not been found.

2. The journals were those of the House of Burgesses from 17 Oct. to 2 Nov. 1754 (*JHB, 1752–1758*, 209–227), and the laws were seven acts passed on 2 Nov. 1754 (Hening, *Statutes*, 6:435–452; *JBT*, 10:127).

3. In his letter to Secretary of State Robinson of 12 Feb. 1755 (CO 5/15, fols. 154–155), Dinwiddie claimed that the £20,000 advance from the Crown could not be repaid immediately from the revenue of the two-shillings-per-hogshead tobacco export tax. Dinwiddie stated that Receiver General Philip Grymes would be able to do so in Apr. 1755, when the next semiannual account would be prepared. Dinwiddie expressed the hope that "the Delay of two Months will not be charged to me, as I shall at all Times be ready in complying with such Orders as I may receive from Time to Time, that can possibly be put in Execution."

4. Dinwiddie explained to JA in his letter of 10 Feb.: "As to Mr. Randolph, from the many Lets. he brot. me, & his acknowledgmt. under hand of his havg. acted inconsistt. with his Duty, & clearg. himself from the unjust Reflects. agst. me in the News Papers at Home & his sincere Promise to conduct himself more regularly for the Future & with more Regard to H Majesty's Service & proper Respect to me I have reinstated him in his office of Atty. Genl. & have agreeable thereto wrote to the

Lds of Trade & I believe he writes you to get his Commission pass the Seals, for yr. trouble herein I advise You to charge Nothing."

In a representation to the Crown of 22 Apr. 1755, the Board of Trade proposed that Peyton Randolph be appointed to the vacant attorney generalship of Virginia (CO 5/1367, p. 145), and on 13 May 1755 the Lords Justices issued a warrant to Dinwiddie authorizing and requiring him to make the appointment (CO 324/51, p. 63).

5. Letter not found.

6. Dinwiddie had written on 10 Feb: "There are two Persons with You [i.e., in London?] that have made Intt. to be agent for this Domn. but I think You may remn. easy durg. the Time I preside & I fancy I have secur'd Yr. Intt. with the Council, & am perswaded none can be appointed witht. my Approbatn. I think a Letr. of Thanks from You to the Board for yr. Appointmt. & Augmentatn. of yr. Salary will be very proper."

7. Dinwiddie had told JA on 10 Feb. that with the increase of his salary, "You must now be tender in Yr. extra Charges & no Coach hire, which I promised to write You on that Subject."

8. "An Act for vesting seven hundred acres of land, with the appurtenances, lying on Cherristone's creek, in the parish of Hungar's, and county of Northampton, in Littleton Eyre, gent. in fee-simple" was passed 2 Nov. 1754 (Hening, *Statutes*, 6:443–446). Dinwiddie had asked JA to use his influence to gain the royal assent to the act, and he referred JA to London merchant James Buchanan "to supply You with Money to pay the necessary Exps. thereof." The act was read by the Board of Trade on 2 Apr. 1755, at which time the Board referred it and the six other acts passed at the same time to Matthew Lamb for his legal opinion (*JBT*, 10:127). On 24 June 1755 the Board read Lamb's report of 17 June (CO 5/1328, fols. 156b–157a) and agreed to recommend confirmation of the act to the Lords Justices (*JBT*, 10:159). The Board's representation was dated 3 July 1755 (CO 5/1367, pp. 147–148), and on 12 Aug. the Lords Justices approved the Board's representation (*JBT*, 10:178).

Gawin Corbin (ca. 1740–1779), eldest son of Richard and Elizabeth (Tayloe) Corbin, went to school at Grinsted, Essex, under a Mr. Harris, and was admitted pensioner to Christ's College, Cambridge, in 1756. He remained at the university until Mar. 1759, when he was admitted to the Middle Temple, and he was called to the bar in 1761. Corbin returned to Virginia in Aug. 1761 (Jeffrey L. Scheib, "The Richard Corbin Letterbook, 1758–1760" [Master's thesis, College of William and Mary, 1982], 19, 148).

9. William Augustus (1721–1765), duke of Cumberland, son of George III.

10. In Nov. 1754 Parliament had voted £1,000,000 to strengthen the army and navy and an additional £50,000 for raising two new regiments in America and paying Braddock's officers.

11. A boarding of ships.

12. I.e., Oliver Cromwell.

13. In a letter to Dinwiddie of 5 January 1755, Glen asked for £7,000 (out of the £10,000 advanced to Dinwiddie by the Crown) to build a fort in the upper Cherokee country, stating that he had received orders to do so from London. In his reply of 8 Feb. (Dinwiddie Letter Books, 3:137, VHS), Dinwiddie disputed Glen's claim by quoting a letter he had received from Secretary of State Robinson; he called Glen's interpretation of Robinson's orders "monstrous."

14. [William Smith], *A Brief State of the Province of Pennsylvania in which the Conduct of Their Assemblies for Several Years Past Is Impartially Examined* (London and Dublin, 1755).

To the Council of Virginia

April 2d 1755

I have heretofore paid my acknowledgments to you for the honour done me in appointing of me your Agent, I am now to repeat the same and to add thereto my further Obligations to you for the Addition to My Salary, from this new Instance of your favour My gratitude is thereby added to my Duty in your Servce, And as my Situation is now entirely agreeable to me, I shall use my utmost endeavours to maintain the continuance of your Favour and whether in my public or in privat capacity neither Zeal nor Assiduity shall be wanting in the Execution of My Duty, which will become more and more agreeable to me if I shall be but happy enough, in the course of my public Negociations to gain the confidence & Freindship of Individuals.

From this Addition to My Salary and the punctual payment thereof I shall find my self enabled to forego a very considerable Article of expence incident to & usualy charged by Agents whatever their Appointments are, (vizt) Coach hire; and with regard to other Expences attending the Service you may rely upon me these shall be none but such as are consistent with the Reputation of your Government, become annually unavoidably necessary to Agents of American Colonys in the ordinary course of public Business thro public Offices, and the propriety or Impropriety of throwing of Articles upon the Agent or upon the Province I shall Submit entirely to your Judgment, & I am with great regard Honoble Gentlemen

LB, pp. 380–381. Sent "per Capt Teague."

To Peyton Randolph

Sir   April 2d 1755

It gives me very great pleasure to have the account of your being reinstated, by your letter of the 14th of Febry,[1] I never knew a person more disposed to Acts of friendship than Mr Dinwiddie & I never did any thing more agreeable to my self than the Solicitation of the Kings confirmation of what Mr Dinwiddie has done, and that no time might be lost I immediatly waited on the Earl of H—f–x to beg his Lordships good Offices therein, and his Lordship then told me that Gover Dinwiddie had desird his Interposition on your behalf, and he assurd me that he was very well pleased with what Mr Dinwiddie had done and that your Commission should be amongst the first laid before his Majesty and Mr Pownall has promisd me his Attention thereto, according to your Directions I shall call on Mr Hanbury for the Fees of the Commission, and as to any other charges You will do me the Justice to believe me when I tell you that the pleasure I take in Serving of you on this or on any other occasion does far exceed my trouble therein.

I cannot conceive thro what channel Mr Pride has reced so bad an Edition of the Reasons which did so long obstruct the Kings consent to this Act of Assembly[2] had the Case stood upon a misunderstanding between Sir Mathew Lamb & me as has been represented to Mr Pride, I should not have been able to have overcome the Objections made to the Act upon the strength of a Single Objectn made by a 3d Person the truth is that from my punctuality in business with Sir Mathew Lamb he has complaind to me of others who let acts lay before them for years without so much as calling for them or paying the Fee for his Report, however Considering the difficulty which I find by your letter must have attended geting the better of the objections in Virginia I am very glad that they are overcome here tho attended with some extra charges.

Our preparations for War are extreamly Vigorous, and from the National Unanimity & Magnanimity there still arises some hopes, that France will come into our Terms for accomodating Matters, I hope that Mrs Randolph[3] has got the better of the fatigue of her voyage please make my Complts to her & let me repeat, that on all occasions I am with pleasure Sir

LB, pp. 381–382. Sent "per Do [i.e., Capt. Teague]."

1. Letter not found.

2. The act has not been identified.

3. Elizabeth (Harrison) Randolph, whom Randolph had married in Mar. 1746.

To Robert Dinwiddie

[17 April 1755]
Governor Dinwiddie April 17th 1755 Sent him inclosd 2 Instructions one relative to the Execution Law,[1] another relative to the Exemption of the Quitrents on Frontier Lands,[2] and the Paper relative to the Drawback on Linnen.[3]

LB, p. 382. Sent "per Do Teague."

1. Virginia's "Act for declaring the law concerning executions and for the relief of insolvent debtors" had passed on 10 May 1749 and received royal confirmation (Hening, *Statutes*, 5:526–540). British merchants objected to a clause in the act that stipulated that writs of execution sued out upon any judgment, decree, or recovery for sterling money should be levied in current money at the rate of 25 percent advance upon sterling. They petitioned that the act not be approved, but since it had already been confirmed, an additional instruction to Dinwiddie of 27 Aug. 1754 directed that he should "earnestly recommend it to the assembly of [Virginia] to pass another act of the like nature . . . taking care that no clause be inserted in such act for regulating the rate of exchange to the prejudice of the merchants" (Labaree, *Royal Instructions*, 1:236).

2. An additional instruction to Dinwiddie of 27 Aug. 1754 authorized and required him to grant lands west of the Allegheny Mountains "to such persons as shall be desirous of settling there free from the payment of any quit-rent" for ten years from the date of the grant. Dinwiddie was also to restrict grants west of the mountains to no more than one thousand acres per person (Labaree, *Royal Instructions*, 2:647–648).

3. In his reply of 23 June 1755 (Dinwiddie Letter Books, 3:171, VHS), Dinwiddie wrote: "As to the Drawback on GermanLinen I shall leave to the Legislature not knowg. how the Ministry incline therein."

To Robert Dinwiddie

April 29th 1755
Herewith I send Letter from the Plantation Office,[1] My Account for Contingences amounting to 18.2.6, wherein nothing is charged

towards Coach hire, on these Articles I have this to remark, that my publick Negociations in Calling me frequently to Newcastle House occasiond that first Article of two Guineas which is the only Article out of the ordinary course of Demands made at Christmas upon American Agents who Act up to their Character, and with regard to the last Article of 5 which is properly the only Article relative to my Self I hope the Gentlemen of the Council will deem it to be reasonable,[2] My Constituents of No Carolina poor as they are allow the Christmas Gratuitys to Offices and besides that to the Agent for Coach hire and other Disbursments 25 Sterling its true their Salary is but 100 per an & that not regularly paid The Tryal of My Predecessor Mr Leheup was one day last Week & lasted till 2 in the Morning when the Jury found all the Facts laid in the Information fully proven, on the last day of Term Judgment will be given against him, No penalty being declared by the Act of Parlt, it lays with the Court to Declare the Fine which perhaps may be inconsiderable, Since the Intention of the Prosecution is answered by his being found Guilty of the Breach of Public Trust which renders him Uncapable of any public Employment his own Witnesses helpd to convict him.[3]

I send you the Kings Speech of Friday last[4] this Morning his Majesty set out for Harwich, its generally allowd that the Regency will keep to the full Spirit of the Measures necessary from the present posture of Affairs & the more So Since the Duke of Cumberland is at the head thereof.[5] I cannot learn for a certainty however variously reported that the Armament from Brest is Saild, its Said to consist of 4000 Men with 8 Sail of the Line all for Canada[6] Mr Bascawen is Saild from Spithead with 12 Sail of the Line to take on board Col Yorkes Regiment at Plymouth & probably Some More Ships with 8 Months Provision on board which makes it conjectured that he is destind for North America to observe the French Fleet, and probably on his Orders depends the Definitive Issue of Peace or of a General War[7] in the mean time our Levys for Sea & Land Service go on with wonderful Sucess all over the three Kingdoms, but more especially in Scotland where the Spirit of Resentment Against France has Shewn itself in a very distinguishing Manner Mr Glens recent Conduct has anticipated Mr Lyttletons departure to S Ca by 4 Months the enclosd paper[8] will shew you how consistently Inconsistent with his Duty he has acted in regard to the French Encroachments Adieu My Dr Sir.

LB, p. 383. Sent "to Mr Hanbury."

1. See JA to Dinwiddie, 16 Jan. 1755, p. 136, n. 6.

2. In his letter to JA of 23 July 1755 (Dinwiddie Letter Books, 3:177, VHS), Dinwiddie commented on JA's account: "Yr. Acct. against the Govt. for Yr. incidt. Expences came too late for this Year as did that also in regd. to the Pistole Fee it must lie over till next Settlemt. but I know the Council do not expect You shd. charge any Incidents however I shall at a proper Time push it."

3. See JA to Dinwiddie, 30 Nov. 1753, pp. 98–99.

4. On 25 Apr., the last day of the session, the king attended Parliament. He assented to several bills, addressed the Parliament, and prorogued it to 27 May, although it did not meet again until 13 Nov. 1755. His short speech expressed appreciation for the £1,000,000 "extraordinary supply" granted for the augmentation of the king's forces "by sea and land" (*Parliamentary History*, 15:523–526).

5. The king left London on 28 Apr. on one of his frequent visits to Hanover, and he did not return until 16 Sept. During his absence the regency was headed by the duke of Cumberland, his only surviving son. The regent was Augusta, princess dowager of Wales (d. 1772), widow of the king's eldest son and mother of the heir to the throne, Prince George (1738–1820), later King George III. The princess could not act during the king's absence without the consent of the group headed by Cumberland.

6. In order to reinforce its position in Canada, France had decided to send 3,000 regular troops, under the command of the baron de Dieskau. The expedition was to have sailed from Brest on 15 Apr., but adverse winds delayed its departure until 3 May. The French squadron consisted of fourteen ships of the line and four frigates.

7. In response to the French preparations, the British cabinet resolved to send a squadron to North America with instructions to oppose any French force and seize any French ships with troops or warlike stores aboard. Vice Adm. Edward Boscawen (1711–1761) was appointed to this command and sailed from Portsmouth on 21 Apr. Four days later he moored in Plymouth Sound to take on a detachment of Col. Joseph Yorke's regiment, and on 27 Apr. sailed for North America with eleven ships of the line and two frigates.

8. Not found.

To Robert Dinwiddie

[29 May 1755]
Gover Dinwiddie May 29th 1755 via Maryland See Bundle for the Lre.

LB, p. 384.

To [Robert Dinwiddie] (not sent)

[ca. May 1755]

I cannot learn that the Government of Virginia is Settled,[1] people reason variously thereon, some are against Sine cure Governors, their enjoying the benefit of Provincial Establishments without Provincial Service, the dignity of the State by that means not properly supported, and a bad example for accomplishing the grand object of the present Administration (vizt) Permanent & certain Establishments for Governors and Government from the respective Provinces. Again that the present situation of Affairs requires a Military Capacity to reside there, this last Argument may be more easily obviated by General Braddocks presence who I hear may be hereafter intended for New Yorks Govert as the most proper Military Station in North America, the Consistency of the first way of arguing backd by the Emoluments of the Government of Virginia in favour of some Person of high rank I cannot help seeing however much I may Feel for you & for myself on such an Event, be that it will I have the Satisfaction to be convinc'd that you will be taken care of either at home or abroad & that no other consideration can remove you from a station where your services are fully known & understood except general Measures of Government coinciding with the Views of great Favorites, to which Individuals of course each at all times must give Way, there is no such thing as having a Freehold in the Government of Colonys, it must [be] matter therefore of great Satisfaction to your self & to your Friends that your Conduct Is such & so much approvd of as to carry reputation all along with you if the King shall think fit to shift you from one Station to another, should this be the case I hope you will come nearer home to us, however all this is merely speculative, yet I could not help giving you at the same time the Satisfaction to know, that while such Arguments are talk'd of, that at the Same time I have all the reason in the world to believe, & I am satisfyd that care will be taken of you, should this way of Argument determine & influence the Kings Measures, which however at present I have no other foundation to apprehend than from general conversation out of doors, which perhaps may in some degree arise from Lord Delaware not having immediatly got the Government upon his having askd for the same,[2] my privat

Judgment of the Matter is that there will be no appointment for that Government till towards the close of the Sessions or the Kings going abroad & perhaps not then, in the mean time I am hopeful that the Salary will come in your way from Lord Albemarles death whose Widdow has got a Pension of 1200 per annum from the King the Same Establishment which by Lord Granthams death became vacant.[3]

My Complts to Mrs Dinwiddie & the young Ladys concludes me always Most Affectionatly

PS   I was in hopes to have sent you Mr Sharpes Account but he has disapointed me, next Ship shall bring it.

LB, unpaginated sheet that falls between pp. 24 and 25. In the margin at the head of this letter JA wrote: "NB not sent."

1. See JA to Dinwiddie, 28 Jan. 1755, pp. 137–138, n. 1.

2. John West (1693–1766), seventh Lord Delawarr and afterwards first earl of Delawarr, was governor of Guernsey 1752–1766.

3. Henry D'Auverquerque (ca. 1672–1754), baron of Alford, viscount of Boston, and earl of Grantham, died on 5 Dec. 1754.

To the Committee of Correspondence of North Carolina

Gentlemen   July 9th 1755
I did not receive your letter of the 13th of Febry[1] before last week, nor do I know what Ship brought it, the Repeal of so many of your Laws, some whereof having no relation to the Legislature whose Authority was then calld in Question, was a Matter of very great Surprise to me,[2] but Other Provinces and other Agents then and Since have met with the Same Fate, and from thence it may be concluded that Provincial Agents as Such are not Consulted on Govert Measures relative to the Plantations when Such Measures are thought as in the Case of these Laws fit for the Kings Ministers only, and that Measures by them absolutely Agreed on, may likewise in the Way of Office be carryd into Execution thro Instructions to Governors, without the previous knowledge of the most penetrating Agent, what became me as Agent I did so soon as I came to the knowledge of the Repeal of these Laws, by Remonstrating the

Expediency of an Additional Instruction to the Governor authorising him to Suspend the Publication of the Repeal of the Acts til
Such time as provision was made by New Laws not lyable to the
exceptions taken to the former Laws, in this Particular Emergency
Gover Dobbs will do me Justice I am glad to find during the Session
to Remedy the Inconveniency that might arise from the Repeal of
former Laws. Amongst Others you take Notice of a Quitrent Law
with a Suspending clause, this Bill containing Matters relative to
the Kings Revenue was in the first place taken under deliberation
& hereupon I found it necessary to move My Lords for Trade for
an Office copy of this Bill, & it being referred by their Lordships to
Sir Mathew Lamb, who is Council to the Board, I attended him
thereon & offered Such Arguments as occurd to me in order to
procure his favourable Report thereon & within these few days I
had a Summons to attend the Board of Trade in consequence of
their Lordships having taken this Report into consideration at the
same time, Mr Child on behalf of the Earl of Granville was
Summoned & did attend, their Lordships having been pleased to
grant me a Copy of Sir M Lambs Report I inclose the Same to you
and am now preparing by their Lordships orders to Reply thereto.[3]

But how is it possible for me to Suggest the Reasons which
induced the Legislature, in the present Bill to depart so far [from]
the Principles of all former Quitrent Bills so as to reduce the
Penalty for not registring Deeds,[4] Such a Deviation in the capital
Scope of the Bill, however ill grounded from thence occasion has
been taken to call the Integrity of the Legislature in Question, it
therefore becomes a more difficult task to defend their Proceedings, and so much the more Reason have I in behalf of the
Legislature to regret the lack of Instructions from them on the
Laws particularly Mentioned in your letter Most particularly that of
the Q Rent, to which My Lords for Trade are more immediatly
attentive, I hope the Reasons that I shall Offer in Support of the
Bill will go so far as to prevent the absolute opperation of Sir
Mathew Lambs Report and the Arguments offerd by Mr Child on
the part of the Earl of Granville for Rejecting the Bill, & generaly
that their Lordships may Judge it more expedient to propose to the
Legislature proper Amendments to the Bill and so wait the Issue of
Such Amendments, before the Fate of the Present Bill is finaly
resolvd on, and should my arguments prove ineffectual as to

Supporting the confirmation of the Bill as it now stands which I can scarce hope for considering from what quarter an opposition comes Not from your Side the Water as you seem to apprehend nevertheless they may So avail as to Support the Proposition for Amending the Bill, it is on this & on no other bottom can I suggest or form any Plan for Saving this Bill, and my arguments in this case shall be transmitted to you if time permits me by this opportunety or by the next.

As to the Act for Establishing Supreme Courts &ca So far as I can form a Judgment from a cursory perusal thereof in the Office it seems also to Stand upon New & unprecedented Principles & I have Some Suspicion that Objections will be thrown out against it when it comes under the deliberation of My Lords for Trade, which probably may not be for Some Months to come as the Long Vacation in Offices will now take place, & from the early Alarm given you, you will be enabled to fortify me with Reasons in Support thereof that objection in particular I have already heard thrown out vizt that thereby a number of Supreme Courts of Justice are Established in place of one, & probably there may be other objections arise from the Same quarter but you will be prepared to observe that what I have Said upon this Act must not be construed as the Sence of Office, & only as prudential hints from me arising from what I have occasionally heard upon the Subject Matter of this Act for Establishing the Courts of Justice.[5]

His Exellys Attention to the payment of my Arrears is the more agreeable to me, when I consider that the Favour of my constituents Stands on so precarious a foundation as that of Sucess in my Negociations; I should deceive my Constituents was I [to] Solicit their Favours on Such Terms, I am under no Influence of Inclination nor am I byased by any collateral conexions or Interest to make me betray or neglect my Duty to my Constituents & am not conscious to my Self that the province has hetherto Suffered thro me, and while I have the honour to continue in their Service my Endeavours shall not be wanting to do all in my Power & consistent with my Duty to advance their Service, this, & no more can I in justice to my own Reputation undertake to promise, but on the present and on all future occasions permit me to observe to you how much it would Strengthen the hands of an Agent in Supporting favorite Laws, to furnish him with the Reasons that may have induced the Legislature to Pass Such Laws.

The additional Grant from your Province for his Majestys Service has appeared in a very favorable light[6] & with this let me conclude my answer to your letter & remain Gentlemen Your Most

PS   My Solicitation for Warlike Stores for Fort Johnston is in a fair Way for Sucess[7] and on this Account I shall be considerably in Advance for Fees to the Several Offices the particulars whereof shall be laid before you when the Service is done.

LB, pp. 386–389. Sent "per Gover Littleton Inclosd to Governor Dobbs." An earlier version of about the first third of the first paragraph, crossed through, appears on p. 384 of the letter book.

1. Letter not found.

2. See JA to North Carolina Committee of Correspondence, 25 June 1754, p. 115, n. 3.

3. On 9 Apr. 1755 the Board of Trade referred to Matthew Lamb twelve acts passed in North Carolina in Jan. 1755, one of which was "An Act for ascertaining and securing the payment of quit rents due to his Majesty and Earl Granville, for quieting freeholders in the possession of their lands and for other purposes" (*NCSR*, 25:304–309; *JBT*, 10:130). The Board read Lamb's report of 17 June 1755 (T 1/361, fols. 182–184; *NCCR*, 5:448–449) on 25 June, resolved to consider it the following week, and ordered the secretary to notify JA and Child (*JBT*, 10:159). On 2 July JA and Child appeared before the Board, at which time JA asked for a copy of Lamb's report "and that he might be at liberty to give in his answer to the objections made to it in writing." The Board acceded to JA's request, gave Child a copy also, and agreed to suspend consideration of the act (*JBT*, 10:161).

The Board again took up consideration of the act in Nov. 1755. On 12 Nov. it read JA's undated "Reasons humbly offered to the [Board of Trade] in support of the Quit Rent Bill of North Carolina, in answer to the Objections taken to [it by Matthew Lamb]" (*NCCR*, 5:449–456) and Child's objections to it (T 1/361, fols. 159–168) and referred those two papers, the act itself, and Lamb's report to the Treasury for an opinion (*JBT*, 10:187). In Feb. 1759 the Treasury still had the act under consideration (*APC*, 4:402).

4. The 1755 act failed to fix forfeiture as the penalty for not registering patents.

5. In Jan. 1755, Governor Dobbs assented to "An Act for establishing the supreme courts of Justice, oyer and terminer, and general gaol delivery of North Carolina" (*NCSR*, 25:274–287), even though he had been instructed to establish courts by executive action rather than by statute (Labaree, *Royal Instructions*, 1:299). The act was not questioned in London until early in 1759, when the Board of Trade

submitted the act not only to its counsel, Matthew Lamb, but to two North Carolina officials who were in London at the time—Chief Justice Charles Berry and Attorney General Thomas Child. Berry and Child raised numerous charges against the act in a letter to the Board of 24 Feb. 1759, the Board recommended disallowance to the Crown on 12 Apr. 1759, and the Privy Council issued an Order in Council disallowing the law on 14 Apr. 1759 (*NCCR*, 6:13–15, 25–29).

6. On 14 Jan. 1755 Governor Dobbs approved "An Act for granting an aid to His Majesty and for other purposes," which contained a provision giving the governor discretion "either to raise recruits with the five thousand pounds in the Bill mentioned for that purpose to be sent to Ohio, or remit the same in Provision for accommodating his Majestys Troops Already ordered to serve there as shall seem most Convenient for his Majestys service" (*NCCR*, 5:268, 279).

7. See JA to Rice, 16 Jan. 1753, p. 66, n. 1.

To the Council of Virginia

Gentlemen   7th August 1755

I am this day favoured with your letter of the 11th of June Inclosing an Address to the King in relation to the ballance of the Revenue of 2 Shills per Hogshead,[1] the receipt of this Important Address by the first opportunety which offers by a Ship to Sail as to Morrow I think it my Duty to Notifie to you, at the Same time to acquaint you of the Adjournment of the Several Boards interested in the Revenue, that of the Treasury & the Bd of Trade which circumstance with the Absence of the Duke of Newcastle & of the Earl of Halefax will probably for Some Weeks protract the Consideration of this Address in the Way of Office, but to Shew my Zeal and Attention to this Service I shall forthwith present the same to the Secretary of State,[2] and by remaining in Town Attentive to this Business only I shall lay hold of every opportunety that may forward or favour this Address. Mr Fairfax's[3] good Intentions to promote the Service of Virginia on this or on any other Emergency, I have no room to doubt, & when he is in town which is but Seldom I shall desire his good Offices, & be assured that there shall be nothing Wanting in the Way of Solicitation to Attain Success & the progress of this Negociation I shall from time to time communicate to you I am Gentlemen

To the Honoble Wm Fairfax Esqr President of His Majestys Council of Virginia.

LB, p. 392. Sent "per the Mountgomery Capt Peterson." A draft of this letter appears on p. 390 of the letter book. At the foot of this letter JA wrote: "NB Inclosd to Governor Dinwiddie."

1. The Council's letter to JA (not found) enclosed an address to the king of 11 June 1755 (T 1/361, fols. 119–120), in which the Council asked that the royal warrant of 3 July 1755 sent to Dinwiddie requiring him to repay the £20,000 advanced to the colony out of the balance of the two-shillings-per-hogshead tobacco export tax be revoked. The Council claimed that the tobacco revenue was to be used "for the better Support of Government" in Virginia "and for no other use whatsoever." The Council's concern was that Virginia's revenues would be used to reimburse the Crown for expenses incurred in other colonies. The Privy Council on 26 Aug. 1755 referred the address to its Plantation Committee (*APC*, 4:312; *EJC* 6:3).

2. See following letter.

3. William Fairfax (1691–1757) had been a councillor since 1744.

To the Committee of the Council of Virginia

Augt 28th 1755

By Commodore Keppel[1] I have reced Duplicate of *your Address to the King on the Tobacco Duty* the Original Whereof I had presented to Sir Thomas Robinson together with a Memorial in Support thereof Copy whereof I send you inclosed[2] & thereby you will See how much I have labord the Case with the Ministry to every one of whom at the head of Offices I have presented Copys of the Address with the Memorial, previous to my presenting the Address I had opend the Nature thereof to the Ministers Seperatly And according to their different tempers & Sentiments on the Address I prepard My Memorial So as to obviate the objections most likely to arise thereon; As this Matter has not been taken up as yet by the Regency I cannot pretend to Anticipate their Measures. So far as I can judge, we are not likely to Succeed in Terminis[3] of the Address for a total Revocation of the Warrant on the 2 Shills per Hogshd.

You may rely on my attention to every circumstance that may Serve the Cause, and I have accordingly from the fatal Miscarriage of our Military operations Urgd the necessity of the free application of the Tobacco Revenue by the Governor & Council for Provincial Services only.

The precipitate Retreat of the Forces under the Command of Col Dunbar was very alarming and the more so as their was ground to apprehend a total Dereliction of our Frontiers from his Marching towards Philadelphia, the Regency from such apprehensions have given immediate & Express orders for that Gentlemen to cover the Frontiers of Virginia;[4] Mr Shirley is now appointed Commander in Chief in North America,[5] I most heartily wish him Success in his operations and to gratify your Curiosity I send you the Gazette Edition of his Predecessor Mr Braddock;[6] the Yauchts are gone for his Majesty & by the 20th of Next Month his Arrival is expected here I am with great regard

LB, p. 393. Sent "per Express to America. See Letter to Mr Fairfax Septr 3d [i.e., 5th] 1755 postea in this Book."

1. Royal Navy Commodore Augustus Keppel (1725–1786) was a son of Virginia's late royal governor, Albemarle.

2. JA's undated memorial to Newcastle in support of the Council's address is T 1/361, fols. 117b–118c (printed in *VMHB* 17 [1909]: 273–278).

3. *In terminis terminantibus* translates as "in express or determinate terms" or "exactly in point."

4. On 9 July 1755 the French, with their Canadian and Indian allies, ambushed and routed British and colonial forces under Braddock on the Monongahela River, near Fort Duquesne. A few hours before Braddock's death on 13 July, Col. Thomas Dunbar (d. 1767), of the 48th Regiment of Foot, took command of the defeated forces. Over the strong objections of Dinwiddie and others, Dunbar ordered a hasty withdrawal to winter quarters at Philadelphia, leaving the Virginia frontier without adequate protection.

5. William Shirley (1694–1771), governor of Massachusetts 1741–1756 and formerly second-in-command to Braddock for the North American theater, was commander in chief of British forces in North America from Aug. 1755 to June 1756.

6. Enclosure not found.

To Robert Dinwiddie

Dr Sir   Augt 28th 1755
    I am favourd with yours of July 23d[1] & by mine to the Corresponding Committee of the Council[2] left under a flying Seal,

you will See what Steps I have taken on their Address, I was obligd
to labor the Propriety of the Council of Virginia taking cognizance
of this Matter, finding Some of the Ministry Warm in their
Resentment that your Council of State should propose to call in
Question what the Council of State of this Kingdom had done &
accordingly Ratifyd by the King; writing to the Committee I cannot
properly point out to them the difficultys that I am laid under from
the manifest Inconsistency of the Measures attending their Address, the Committee desire Me to take the Assistance of Mr
Hanbury in this case when at the Same time Mr Hanbury will not
come to it but as the Merchant & very properly not having Money
of the Receiver Generals in his hands on Account of this Duty
absolutly refuses to Comply with Mr Grymes's[3] Order in Consequence of your Warrant this revives in the Mind of the Ministry Mr
Hanburys former opposition in the case of Indian Presents to the
Warrant upon the Principles that the Crown had nothing to do
with this Duty; *The Council* in their Address *are far from taking* up
this Matter on this Principle, they with great propriety Remonstrate against the application of the Money *to extra Provincial*
Services, & construe the 1000£ to So Carolina to be Such, tho the
Ministry Must agree, that the Council are in so far Right that the
Money is applicable to Provincial purposes *only* yet they construe
the 1000 for Services done by Forts in the Indian Country to be
tending to the Security of Virginia, & therefore as such might have
been overlookd by the Council of Virginia at a time when this
Country was so liberal to the American Colonys. However tho the
Ministry may be brought to Remit the 1000 as to So Carolina rather
than Strain the Law of the Province of Virginia it from thence
Follows, that they will thereby remain more tenacious of the
Execution of the Warrant quo ad the application of the occasional
Ballance for Services actually Provincial, and indeed I have had it
thrown at me, that they see the drift of all this, is to keep the Money
in the Recers hands as an Emolument, and by a finessing between
him & his Freinds in the Council & with Mr Hanbury the Crown is
to be deceivd thereby, and some of them actually have gone so far
as to tell me that they know how to cut this Matter short, by
Sending another Receiver who will do his Duty, all this I have told
to Mr Hanbury as having a very great regard for Mr Grymes & so
have [I] but my Duty to you & to the Council will not allow me to

countenance any Proceedings that can admit of an Insinuation of Connivance to Deceive or frustrate the Measures of Government here or in Virginia, you have Executed the Warrant so far as it can go & you are accordingly approvd of, the Council have concurrd therein & on this Principle they now Pray for the Revokation thereof in future; On this footing I shall Stand to the Address let privat Persons act as they think proper, Mr Fairfax is in the Country his letter I have sent to him,[4] I do not expect that he will take this Matter directly or Indirectly upon him It is [*illegible*] of too much Delicacy to be enterd upon by those who are not well acquainted with the Nature of the case.

As to my Bill for Incidental Expences I did not conceive that any hesitation could have Arisen by the Council Since I forgo the Article of Coach hire & confine my Self to Disbursments only however I submit the Same to you without contending with the Council.

My Letter on Fraziers Character must either have miscarryd or been over lookd by you, I gave Col Forresters Character of him in whose Company he was, I also Sent you My Brother Johns letter Characterising of him who is of the Same Regiment, all confirmd by Col Abercromby & all did agree that he is a very bad Man, a bad Subject & a bad Soldier, & by no means to be trusted, he was by some means or other transported in Consequence of a Court Martial for his Transgressions.[5]

As to the Quitrents whatever Orders are given thereon whether they are Remitted or not and whatever Terms the Patents are Granted you nor I are neither of us to blame; if the Crown Suffers by the Treasury's not attending to your Report on that Matter it lies with the Treasury it was there business to attend thereto as after being [described?] by me & by the B of Trade as they did not the Lords for Trade in some measure at my Instance have done it of their own Accord.

I think that you have done from first to last great Matters with your Assembly, whether it comes from the Joint Agents for Pensilvania Freind Partridge & Robt Charles, or from the Quakers I cannot Say but that Province has for some time by gone in the News Papers Extold the Generosity of their Govert or rather their Assembly & at the Same time abusd their Gover and all those Neighbours, &c to Governts Contracts for the army & for so doing have by way of Authority made use of Braddocks approbation of there Conduct who in his Letters said that without their Assistance he could not have taken the Field, I wish in God he never had;[6] So Much Fatigue to your Person, So great anxiety of Mind, So great Expence of Money & Blood to Virginia So Much of the Honour & Reputation of this Nation thrown away, in the hands of one that by So precipitate a Retreat by the next to him Col Dunbar who thereby has turnd a Bush fight into a Battle, & by his Retreat into a Defeat, & Victory to those who never thought of one these are Points that really are like to bring to Tears from me, our People in and out of Power are full of Resentment, Expostulating yesterday with the Duke of Newcastle on the Situation of our Affairs he told me that Orders are made out to go with the Utmost Dispatch for Mr Dunbar to cover our Frontiers & to put himself under Mr Shirleys Command, who now to Command for the present Succeeds Mr Braddock but in case of more Extensive Operations in America a Leut General may be Sent from hence; your Attention to your Militia on this occasion is greatly approvd of; keep up your Spirits for you have done your Duty whatever others may have fell short of theirs you will see by the Gazette our Edition of this Affair Mr Dunbars Account of Philadelphia is thereby expected by the next Ships, I can not tell what Stratagems those American Quakers make use of to captivate our Military Gentry, good eating & no fighting are Principles adopted by Quakers, however probably his R Highness the D: by no means will think Quakers good Company for his Majestys Troops, nor does he think the Climate in Virginia So Severe as to oblige Col Dunbar to take up his Winters amongst those So early as July; His Majesty is expected with great Impatience, and the Yauchts being gone, by the 20th of next Month we shall have him here; Lord Halefax being the only person of the Administration whom I have not had access to on this Occasion I intend making of him a Visit next week at his Seat at Northampton & then I shall labor the Address of the Council tho I have no great room to hope his assistance therein: before I conclude I must not forget to give you my oppinion of keeping in your own hands in Virginia the full amount of the Salary for the Governor, this I think you may venture to do according to the letter of the Law while you are Comdr in Chief & Subject to no Restraint in Powers thro' a Superior Governor to you, whether the Council & you will take upon you to apply the Salary of 2000 in totidem Verbis[7] to you, without Special Warrant from hence depends on the Form heretofore used, but if their is no Precedent against you as Leut Governor the Law I should think will Support you & the Council in the application thereof to you as Comdr in Chief while there is no other Governor appointed by the Crown I conclude with Complts to Mrs Dinwiddie & the Family I am always

LB, pp. 393–396. Sent "by an Express to No Carolina."

1. In his letter to JA of 23 July 1755 (Dinwiddie Letter Books, 3:177, VHS), Dinwiddie enclosed a letter to JA and an address to the king from the Council (see JA to Virginia Council, 7 Aug. 1755, p. 155, n. 1), and a letter to William Fairfax (not found), evidently from the Council, asking him to assist JA in the matter of the address to the Crown. Dinwiddie also remarked on JA's account (see JA to Dinwiddie, 29 Apr. 1755, pp. 146–147); criticized the Board of Trade's letter to him on land patents (see JA to Dinwiddie, 29 Apr. 1755, pp. 146–147); remarked on the recent General Assembly's defense measures and noted that Maryland and Pennsylvania "continue obstinate & refractory"; and reported on the early word he had received of Braddock's defeat, hoping that another express would bring a letter to "contradict the former or at least soften the News."

2. See preceding letter.

3. Philip Grymes (d. 1761) was receiver general of Virginia 1748–1761 and a member of the Council 1749–1761.

4. See note 1 above.

5. Simon Fraser (or Frazier) was adjutant for the companies of Virginia rangers and artificers with Braddock's army. He is probably the man of that name who advertised in the Williamsburg *Virginia Gazette* on 10 July 1752 to teach "Military Discipline, according to the new Way of Generals *Bland* and *Bleekny*" (W. W. Abbot, ed., *The Papers of George Washington: Colonial Series*, vol. 3 [Charlottesville, 1984], 229n).

Second Lt. Col. William Forster and Lt. John Abercromby served in the 1st Regiment of Foot (*List of the Officers in the Several Regiments . . . to May 1756* [London, (1756)], 121). The earlier letters of JA to Dinwiddie and of John Abercromby to JA have not been found.

6. The feud in Pennsylvania between the assembly and Gov. Robert Hunter Morris (ca. 1700–1764) centered on the governor's instructions from proprietor Thomas Penn not to assent to any excise bills or bills to emit paper money on loan without a provision for a veto power over the expenditures of the money they produced. The assembly petitioned the Crown on 7 Jan. 1755 against the instructions, "charging them with preventing Morris from passing a £20,000 excise bill, with sabotaging the British interest in North America, and with violating the charter of

1681." The assembly's petition was presented in Apr. 1755 by its joint agents, Richard Partridge (1681–1759), London merchant, Quaker, and agent of several colonies, and Robert Charles. The Privy Council referred the matter to the Board of Trade, which dismissed the petition in May 1755 (*APC*, 4:288; *JBT*, 10:138, 140, 143, 144, 149, 152; James H. Hutson, *Pennsylvania Politics, 1746–1770: The Movement for Royal Government and Its Consequences* [Princeton, 1972], 6–17 [quote on 16]).

7. Translation: in just so many words.

To Robert Dinwiddie

Septr 3d 1755

I have a letter from Mr Fairfax[1] on the address for revoking the warrant on the 2 shills per hogshead, my answer thereto[2] I Send for your perusal I can assure you that neither jointly nor separately the Ministers are no ways flexible in the alteration of their Measures tho perhaps they may not declare thear Judgment on the Warrant for Some time, unless Mr Hanburys refusing the Govs order bring it about & not favourabley Mr Hanbury will not concern himself in the Address. tell him the News & that none of the Ministers will now father the Ohio Exedition So that it must fall on John Hanburys Shoulders.

LB, p. 400. Sent "per Capt Baker."

1. Letter not found.
2. See following letter.

To William Fairfax

Sir, Craven Street Sptr. 5th 1755

I have receiv'd your obliging letter of the 26th of June, in the name of His Majestys Council, and theirin their Judgment with regard to German Lennen, if this matter, with that of Lisbon Salt shall come before Parliament my Attention thereto shall not be wanting.[1]

My Letter, by a man of War, going Express to America, a few Days Since, with the Memorial therein inclosed, will shew you, how much I have at heart, the Success of your Address to the King on the Case of the Warrant on 2 shills Hhd as well as, the particular interest of those, viz the Revenue Officers from whence it comes.[2]

The Council of Virginia, not being the first who had taken up an Opposition, to this Measure of Government, it has been heretofore fully agitated, and Accordingly there is not one person in the Administration here, whom I did not find engaged, in support of what has been done viz granting the Warrant it became therefore necessary for me, in the first place to remove the particular resentment to the Council of Virginia, for prezuming as a Council of State in Virginia to Call in question what had been fully deliberated, and resolved on by the Kings Council here, And approved of Accordingly by the King. Another very unfavourable circumstance Attending the Address met me likewise at first Seting out, (Viz) that, this Address is lookd on, as a Sort of Contrivance to favour particular persons in Office, more than the good of Government, and this Insinuation has been carryd so far, that I have been told, that they know very well, how to cut this matter Short by Sending over another Receiver who knows his Duty, and I have Reason to believe, that Governour Dinwiddies early zeal, in remonstrating against this Warrant met with a cool reception here, and Mr. Hanburys opposition thereto with a very Severe reprimand, I shall not take upon me to State to you, the principles, on which Mr Hanbury Grounded his Opposition and Objections to the Kings Warrant, but from the language, that I have met with, Since this matter has Come into my hands, I am apt to believe, that he must have called in question, the Right of the Crown to Apply the Tobacco Duty in any Instance whatever, a Doctrine no doubt extreamly alarming to the Crown & by no means tenable, by *the Law*, nor from practise, Witness the *Address* from the Council to the Crown, for Additional Salarys from this Fund,[3] from this arises a Tenaciousness in the Ministry, to parry and defeat every measure, that points like an Attack upon the Right of the Crown, in this case, bearing some Sort of resemblance To the case of Public money in Ireland, which is now become very embarassing to the Councils of this Kingdom.

Intangled with such prejudi[c]es and Diffecultys, I found it was best for me, to labor the case upon the abstracted points of the Law, and of Policy of State (Viz) that the Thousand pounds paid to So. Carolinia was straining the Law of Virginia, but to this it has been said, that securing the Peace & Friendship of the Indians, does manefistly tend, to the Security of Virginia and Accordingly on this principle, the King thought fit to Apply the one thousand pounds to this Service, thro' the hands of the Governour of South Carolina, it has been also said, that it is extreamly unbecoming, And ill timed in the Government of Virginia to sound the alarm, on so trifling an occasion as that of 1000 pounds for Indian Services, at a time when, this Nation is expending Millions for the Colonys, it being my Duty to adhere to your Address, I have Accordingly done it, and by the manner in which I have pressd your Argument as to *the illegal[i]ty of the Application of the 1000 pound*, I am satisfyd that the Ministry are thereby brought under difficultys; but on the other hand, I am apprehensive, that by laying fast hold of this Flaw (in point of Law) in the Warrant, and the Secretary of States letter thereon, that our Arguments, from Prudence and Policy tho urged with their utmost Strength for *Revoking the Warrant,* will lose Ground; for to speak the truth as one in my Station ought, I find the Temper and the disposition of the Ministry, extreamly Averse to any Alteration of their Measures, And how much more will they be irritated, when they come to enter into this Affair, and find this Address, pleading the Kings favour, upon the avowed Suggestion, that in Obedi[e]nce to his Order, the Warrant has been so far executed when the Fact comes out to be, that not one farthing has been paid thereon, nor likely to be paid in pursuance of the Receivers order from the Governor because Mr. Hanbury does refuse the order as he has none of that money in his hands will not the Ministry hereupon infer: as has been insinuated already, a conuivance, to impose upon the Crown and on the Government of Virginia, and thereby Evade the Order, and may not the Kings Ministers, from thence take Occasion, to urge and press (rather than Revoke) the Execution of the Warrant; Judge then, from this state of the case, with what dexterity I must Steer my course for the honour and for the Interest of Government in Virginia, and what difficultys are to be met with in this negotiation, when Public, & Privat interest interfers, difficultys I Suspect, of such a nature, might be increasd rather than removed by the interposition of the *Virginia Merchants.*

After the most mature consideration of this matter I can devise no Shape more proper, or more favourable to turn it into than what is already done, by the Address, and by the Memorial Attending the same, both of which are built upon the Foundation, of the Warrant being carryd into execution pro tanto.[4]

That no circumstance might be overlookd, I have from the fatal miscarriage of our military operations under General Braddock, Again Urged, to the ministry, the further necessity of the full and free Application of this Revenue being left with the Governour & the Council of Virginia and to conclude, I have left nothing undone, in my Public as well as privat capacity, to remove prejudices, and Give this matter a favourable int[r]oduction to the Regency before whom it now lies, and from the freedom in which I have circumstantially laid this case opon to you, I hope I shall offend nobody, for on this, and every Occasion I think it my duty to act with great circumspection here Attention, and Sincerity to you, and to the rest of my Constituents in Virginia where Government is Concern'd, least otherwise (thro: me) the Cause of the Publice might Suffer, while I am with Great regard Sir Your most Obedt Servant

James Abercromby

To the Honoble. Mr Fairfax P of Council in Virginia

LB, pp. 397–400. In a clerk's hand, except for a few interlineations in JA's hand. Sent "per Capt Baker Charming Ann." A fair copy of this letter is in the Virginia State Library and Archives.

1. Fairfax's letter has not been found, nor do the surviving journals of the Council discuss German linen or Lisbon salt.

2. See JA to the Committee of the Council of Virginia, 28 Aug. 1755, pp. 155–156.

3. See JA to Dinwiddie, 17 Sept. 1752, p. 47, n. 5.

4. Translation: for so much.

To the Council of Virginia

Septr 23d 1755

Since my last letter to you of the 28th of August[1] the Lords of the Regency have been pleased to refer the Address from the Council of Virginia concerning the Warrant for Repaying the 20,000£ to the Council and in consequence of this Reference, I have attended My Lord President of the Council[2] thereon; Whatever may be the oppinion of the Lords of the Council in relation to this Address, it could not have reced a more favourable turn in point of Office, than a Reference to the Council, but considering the Multeplicity of National Matters now under deliberation, Upon his Majestys Arrival this Matter may rest for some time, the final Result thereon, shall be communicated to you.

Public Matters remain undetermind as to Peace or War Some circumstances Seem to denote a Tendency towards accomodation, whatever material Event may occasionaly arise during the Controversy between Us & France shall be communicated to you by me who am with great regard Gentlemen Your Most Obedt Sert

LB, pp. 400–401. Sent "per the Boy from Coffee House."

1. Printed on pp. 155–156.

2. Earl Granville.

To Robert Dinwiddie

Septr 23d 1755

Nothing remarkable has happend Since my last of the 3d Inst,[1] the Kings arrival has not hetherto cleard up the Doubt as to Peace or War, the Order for Restoring the Blandford Man of War having on board Gover Lyttleton for So Carolina, taken the 13th of last Month by Monsr De Guys Squadron Seems to denote a Tendency on the part of France for Accomodating Matters, Gover Lyttleton after cruising thro contrary Winds Some Weeks on Board the French Admiral at length got safe into Brest with the French Fleet who were lucky enough to escape Ad: Hawke, the Governor was landed and by the Admiral orderd to Rennes in Britany upon his Parole there to remain but on the road thether had an Express from Paris relcasing him of his Parole & thereby left at large, by the Said Express he was Inform'd that the King of France had also given Orders to Release the Blandford, Mr Lyttleton however thought fit to proceed to Paris and arrivd here as Saturday last, having missd of him on my Visit I cannot give you from himself his adventure; as the Blandford has not as yet cast up, some people conclude from thence that Counter Orders may have been sent for her Retention it Seems strang[e] that this Ship shall be released, and So many of theirs retaind by Us.[2]

NBB You will See by My Letter to the Committee[3] the Situation of the Councils Address, I have no great hopes from what I had Said to me by L—— G————[4] that we shall Suceed in the Revokation of this Warrant, it had a very narrow Escape of being Rejected & Condemned by the Regency, I am in hopes however that his Lordship will Soften in some shape or other, the Sentence upon this Address I can do no More for it than I have done, and Some share of his Lordships favour has Enabled me to Say more to him on this Account than I could have Said to any other of the Kings Ministers with Complts to Mrs D & the Ladys I am Dr Sir

LB, p. 401. At the foot of this letter JA wrote: "NB per a Ship from the Coffee house in October."

1. Printed on page 161.

2. At a meeting of the Board of Trade on 9 Oct. 1755, Lyttelton related that HMS *Blandford* "fell in with and was taken by a squadron of French ships of war under the command of Monsieur de Guay, and that he thought it adviseable upon this occasion to throw overboard his instructions and other papers which he had received from this office." The Board ordered a new set of instructions prepared immediately and advised Lyttelton that as "his speedy departure for his government would in the present situation of affairs be of very great consequence to his Majesty's service," he should "repair thither as soon as possible." Lyttelton agreed, but he did not in fact arrive in Charleston until 1 June 1756 (*JBT*, 10:176–177).

3. See preceding letter.

4. Earl Granville.

To Robert Dinwiddie

[10 October 1755]

Governor Dinwiddie Octr 10th 1755 See Bundle to Mr Hanburys care per Convoy of a Man of War.

LB, p. 402.

To Arthur Dobbs

[10 October 1755]

Gover Dobbs Octr 10th 1755 per Virginia convoy to Col Hunters care See Bundle pro letter NB Pamphlet inclosd relative to Mr Hanbury.[1]

LB, p. 402.

1. This pamphlet has not been traced.

To the Committee of Correspondence of North Carolina

[ca. 10 October 1755]

Committee of No Carolina per the above Opportunity inclosd in the Governors See Bundle.

LB, p. 402.

To Robert Dinwiddie

[2 November 1755]

Governor Dinwiddie Novr 2d 1755 Acknowledge his of Septr 8th[1] had attended Sir T Robinson on arms & Amunition, 6000 heretofore orderd 4000 More Since, Sent to Boston under the direction of the Genal in No: America for the time being, with Officers from the Ordnance Office here,[2] for Blank Commissions I am referrd to the War Office; Col Dunbar greatly blamed great opposition to Subsidys, A Packet Established to hear Monthly from me by that conveyance hear of Johnsons Success towards Crown Point[3] NB at Same time to Mr Washington his Secretary[4] per A Passenger by Convoy from Spithead.

LB, p. 402.

1. Dinwiddie's letter of 6 (not 8) Sept. 1755 (Dinwiddie Letter Books, 3:196–197, VHS) asked JA to attend to the twenty-two acts of the General Assembly that Dinwiddie had sent to the Board of Trade; informed JA that the assembly had adjourned after having granted £40,000, which would allow Dinwiddie to augment

Virginia's forces by 1,000 men; asked JA to inquire about Dinwiddie's request to the secretary of state for blank commissions for officers; and reported on the state of the war and Dunbar's irresponsible conduct.

2. Dinwiddie had told JA in his letter of 6 Sept. that he had written "for all sorts of military Stores our Magazine is exhausted."

3. In fact, Gen. William Johnson (1715–1774) did not reach Crown Point, N.Y., on Lake Champlain during his summer and fall campaign. The success JA refers to was Johnson's defeat of the French and their Indian allies under the baron de Dieskau at the battle of Lake George on 8 Sept. 1755, after which he built Fort William Henry at the lower end of the lake. Thus while Johnson fell short of reaching and taking Crown Point, his expedition was not a failure.

4. JA seems to have confused the names of two parties to a dispute over land. Dinwiddie's secretary was William Withers (1731–1802), who came to Virginia from England in 1745 as heir of a Stafford Co. estate. The daughter of the testator, however, had sold the estate to Augustine Washington, who in turn devised it to his son Samuel (1734–1781) (George Washington's younger brother). Withers contested Washington's title, and the matter was settled by an act of assembly confirming a transaction in which Withers received £600 in consideration of his claim (Hening, *Statutes*, 6:513–516). In his letter to JA of 6 Sept., Dinwiddie had asked JA to do what was necessary to have the private act confirmed, and he enclosed a letter to JA from Withers (not found) as well as a bill of exchange for £30 for expenses.

To Arthur Dobbs

Novr 20th 1755

Have yours of the 22d Augt,[1] Quitrent Bill referrd to the Treasury where it will probably lay for Some time considering the present State of Foreign & domestic Affairs;[2] Boundary Line must rest till Report comes from you & G Lyttleton[3] to leave this some time next Month Lds for Trade have Reported in Favour of Warlike Stores,[4] but having applyd to the Ld President[5] I find him backward thereon as he is on all Such Matters till the Parlt has made Provision; opposition to the new Ministry hinders business going on regularly,[6] tell him the Premises of great Men, that Ld Halefax from principle & not Resentment had opposed the Subsidys; Affairs in Ireland are made up, Send him the Speech & the Address,[7] tell him that more Arms go to Boston & an Office of Ordnance there to be fixd & all Provincial applications for Arms to be made to the General in North America hereafter,[8] haveing nothing to Say to the Committee, as the Season for Remittances draws near hope to have them & beg his good Offices therein with the Committee to Virginia.

LB, p. 402.

1. Letter not found.

2. See JA to North Carolina Committee of Correspondence, 9 July 1755, p. 153, n. 3.

3. The North Carolina–South Carolina border had been virtually nonexistent except for the hundred miles nearest the coast that had been surveyed in the 1730s. (In fact, in the spring of 1735 JA had served as one of South Carolina's two commissioners to draw the boundary.) In the early 1750s the Board of Trade attempted to fix the boundary more firmly, but Governor Glen refused to cooperate with Dobbs and the settlement was not effected. See Marvin L. Skaggs, *North Carolina Boundary Disputes Involving Her Southern Line* (Chapel Hill, 1941), 30–72.

4. The journals of the Board of Trade do not shed light on this report.

5. Earl Granville.

6. See JA to Dinwiddie, 23 Nov. 1755, pp. 170–171.

7. The king's speech of 13 Nov. 1755, which opened the third session of the Eleventh Parliament, and the addresses of the Lords and Commons to the king in reply, are printed in *Parliamentary History*, 15:527–542.

8. See preceding entry.

To John Rutherfurd

Novr 20th 1755

I have yours of no date or place,[1] the Q Rent Bill is with the Treasury & there according to Custom it will rest[2] I have Said thereon what became me in Duty of my Office; it is now full time I had the fruits of my labor & the Season draws near that I may hope for Remittances, unless my Services are forgot.

I am very well Satisfyd with yours & Mrs R——furds joint letter by way of Security but the Expence of London Residence constantly while the American Storm remains exceeds my home Finances & obliges me to call upon my friends for Remittances, small or great will always help me out.

Whatever change may happen in the Ministry I shall always attend to your affairs with Complts to Mrs Rutherfurd I am

LB, p. 403. Sent "per Virginia to Col Hunter by the Packett from Falmouth."

1. Letter not found.

2. See JA to North Carolina Committee of Correspondence, 9 July 1755, p. 153, n. 3.

To Robert Dinwiddie

Novr 23d 1755

In my last of the 2d Inst[1] I acquainted you that 10000 Arms were orderd for NA, that A General Magazine with a kind of Office of Ordnance was to be there Establishd, that all applications for Warlike Stores were to be made, to the Comdr in Chief for the time being in NA, that Sir T R had referrd me to the Secretary at War in relation to Blank Commissions, in consequence thereof I attended Mr Fox before he left the War Office, his answer was that tho they could not be granted nor could the Examples of the Commissions to Sir Wm P:[2] & Shirley, be urged in the Case of V: whose operations did not stand in So favourable a light as in the more Northerly Provinces, I from this took occasion to plead the Galantry of the Virginians on the Mohongela, to which he replyd that it was not the Galantry or personal Courage of these people in Virginia that was found fault with Not explaining himself on this head, I have some Suspicion that Messrs Braddock or Dunbar may have set some of the Virginia Measures in a Light by no means favourable, the former I have heard had exclaimd outragiously against Some of the Virginia Contractors, If the latter the Virginians have their amends as [he] is dismissd from his Regt, & by the Intercession of the D of C[3] is appointed Leut Gover of Gibralter but not to go there.[4] It had indeed appeard ridiculous to trust a person with Gibralter who could not defend Fort Cumberland, however by this appointment, he draws by way of Pension 20 Shils per day others say 40 Sh on consideration of his having bought his Leut Cols Commission; I send you the K Speech & the Commons Address, to which a very warm opposition was made in the H: of commons.

In this opposition which shewd it self the first day of the Sessions are the Chancellor of the Excheqr Mr Legg, Mr Pitt Pay Master Genal, Mr G Grenville Treasurer of the Navy, Col George

Townsend & his Brother Charles Townsend of the Admiralty, Sir George Lee of the Princess of Wales's Family and many more of the Commons the best Speakers in the House,[5] Lord Halefax & Temple in the H of Lds Ld Halefax I am satisfyd out of principle & not personal Resentment the consequence of the opposition which is now fixd by Most of the opposers against every Measure of the New Ministry formed by the Duke of Newcastle & Mr Fox now Secretary of State[6] United together in their Plan of Measures will be an Obstruction to all Business in Public Offices & altho the Suplys are carryd by a great Majority I am affraid Such an opposition may injure our Public Measures with regard to France, for altho Mr Legg Chan of the Exqr is removd & replaced by Mr G Lyttleton,[7] and Mr Pitt by Ld Egmont[8] & G Grenville by Mr Dodington as Treasurer of the Navy[9] their Mouthes will Still be open to oppose, Many more changes & Removes are talkd of, but amongst others I have not heard of Ld Halefax nor of Mr Oswald from the B of Trade, tho James Grenville & Jack Pitt of that B: are said to go out,[10] a Distinction may for some time be carryd on between those who oppose from principle & from personal peak & Resentment, however ere long probably all those distinctions may work up & center in a Strong & determind opposition; In this Present Situation of affairs it is in vain to hope for the Ministerial Attention to Civil American Matters Subject to any Sort of difficulty and Such is the case of the Address in regard to the Tobacco Duty now before the Council, I have tryd Lord President[11] on this head & Mr West on the point of your application concerning the Virg Q Rents but to no purpose, pressing therefore such affairs at present can answer no other purpose than puting those in office out of business, which rather hurt than serve the Cause.

All outward appearances & preparations on our part denote a General War, France remains still A Spectator to all the Sea Captures, nor can the most penetrating people account for their present Conduct, in any other Manner than by their not having been able to engage other Powers, nor of themselves as yet ready for War, they will not expose their honour by declaring War till their Fleets are in greater readiness for Sea, it is in the mean time clear that they are preparing for some great Stroke Adieu My Dr Sir with Compts to all with you.

LB, pp. 403–404. Sent "per the Packett from Falmouth."

1. JA to Dinwiddie, 2 Nov. 1755, p. 167.

2. Sir William Pepperell (1696–1759), baronet, of Massachusetts, was appointed major general in 1755.

3. Duke of Cumberland.

4. Thomas Dunbar became lieutenant governor of Gibraltar on 22 Nov. 1755.

5. These members of the opposition not previously identified are Henry Bilson-Legge (1708–1764), member of Parliament 1740–1764; William Pitt (1708–1778), paymaster general and member of Parliament 1735–1766; George Grenville (1712–1770), treasurer of the navy and member of Parliament 1741–1770; George Townshend (1724–1807), member of Parliament 1747–1764; and Sir George Lee (1700–1758), member of Parliament 1733–1758.

6. Henry Fox (1705–1774) succeeded Thomas Robinson as secretary of state for the Southern Department on 22 Nov. 1755.

7. Sir George Lyttelton (1709–1773), baronet, succeeded Henry Bilson-Legge as Chancellor of the Exchequer on 22 Nov. 1755.

8. Viscount Dupplin and Henry Vane (ca. 1705–1758), first earl of Darlington, were appointed joint paymasters general on 16 Dec. 1755 in place of William Pitt. Egmont was John Perceval (1711–1770), second earl of Egmont in the Irish peerage.

9. George Bubb Dodington (1691–1762) succeeded George Grenville as treasurer of the navy on 22 Dec. 1755.

10. A shake-up in the Board of Trade occurred with the issuing of a new commission under the Great Seal on 29 Dec. 1755. New members were John Talbot (d. 1756), Soame Jenyns (1704–1787), and Richard Rigby (ca. 1722–1788), who replaced John Pitt (ca. 1706–1787), James Grenville, and Richard Edgcumbe (1680–1758) (*JBT*, 10:34, 197). Oswald was James Oswald (1715–1769), who served on the Board of Trade 1751–1759.

11. Earl Granville.

To the Committee of the Council of Virginia

Novr 23d 1755

I told you in last[1] of Reference to the Council of your Address relative to the 20,000, I have repeated Solicitations to Ld G:[2] thereon but to no purpose, nor have grounds to hope for Ministerial Attention to cases of this nature but in time of more Serenity at home & abroad, however I shall in conjunction with Mr Fairfax now attending Parlt have a watchfull Eye to every opportunity that may offer to serve you, Notwithstanding an opposition of Some consequence is taken up to the Administration, our Measures are Vig[o]rous but not explicit as to Peace or War I am always with great regard

LB, p. 405. Sent "inclosd to the Governor [i.e., in the preceding letter] by the Packett to Falmouth."

1. JA to Virginia Council, 23 Sept. 1755, pp. 164–165.

2. Earl Granville.

To Robert Dinwiddie

[8 January 1756]

Governor Dinwiddie Janry 8th Vide letter in Bundle per Capt. Johnson.

LB, p. 405.

To [Robert Dinwiddie?]

[18 January 1756]

Governor D———y[1] Jany 18th See letter in bundle per a Ship in Downs.

LB, p. 405.

1. This letter (as well as the one following) was probably to Dinwiddie, but it may have been to James De Lancey (1703–1760), lieutenant governor of New York 1753–1755 and 1757–1760, for JA does not generally use "D———y" when referring to Dinwiddie.

To [Robert Dinwiddie?]

[18 January 1756]

Governor D———y by the lad from the Virginia Coffee house 18th Jany.

LB, p. 405.

To the Council of Virginia

[18 January 1756]

To the Council of Virginia 18th Jany by Sd Lad[1] See Letter in Bundle.

LB, p. 405.

1. I.e., "the lad from the Virginia Coffee house" mentioned in the preceding entry.

To Arthur Dobbs et al.

[20 January 1756]

To No Carolina, vizt Governor Dobbs Messrs Murray Rutherford & Innis See Lres Bundle of 20th Jany 1756 per Quines Ship to Cape Fear.

LB, p. 405.

To Robert Dinwiddie

[22 January 1756]

To Governor Dinwiddie Jany 22d under cover of Mrs Stone at Deal for Capt Crookshanks to Notify Ld Loudons & Col Abercrombys Nomination.[1]

LB, p. 405.

1. At a meeting on 20 Jan. in the duke of Newcastle's apartments, Cumberland urged that John Campbell, earl of Loudoun, be appointed to succeed Shirley as commander in chief of British forces in North America, a recommendation that was accepted by the other ministers present. Loudoun's commission did not pass the seals until Mar., and he did not arrive in America until July 1756.

Loudoun was preceded to America by Maj. Gen. James Abercromby (1706–1781), who served as temporary commander in chief for a month.

JA has often been referred to as a cousin or relative of the general, but the editors have unearthed no evidence to substantiate such a claim, and the letter book provides negative, though circumstantial, evidence. A letter to the general bears the salutation

"Dear Sir," and on three occasions the agent refers to the general in letters to others as a "friend" (to Young, 10 July 1757, pp. 201–202; to Swann, 4 Mar. 1758, pp. 227–228; and to Dobbs, 4 Mar. 1758, pp. 229–231). A letter from the general to the agent is also addressed "Dr. Sir" (19 Aug. 1758, T 1/380, fol. 54). While they may have been very distant relations, their connection was obviously so tenuous that it precluded any familiarity. The agent was alert enough to any possibility of influence that he would surely have capitalized on such a connection were there the least grounds for doing so.

To John Tinker

[23 January 1756]

Governor Tinker 23d Jany See Lre Bundle per Virginia to Plymouth.

LB, p. 405.

To William Fairfax et al.

[28 January 1756]

To Mr Fairfax & Committee of Council of Virgin[i]a 1756 28th of Jany to Plymouth inclosd to Governor Dinwiddie, with Ld Granvills Ansr to the Address pro Warrant of 20,000 final answer thereon[1] See Lre annex'd to this A.

LB, p. 405.

1. Granville's "final answer" has not been found, although his decision was that the warrant had to be paid (and was).

To Robert Dinwiddie

[12 February 1756]

Governor Dinwiddie Feby 12th 1756 vide Bundle per Mr Mountgomerys Ship.

LB, p. 405.

To the Committee of Correspondence of North Carolina et al.

[13 February 1756]

Committee of North Carolina Feby 13th 1756 See Bundle Mr Hasell, Rutherford, Saml Swann, Jas Murray inclosd to Mr Lewis per Plymouth.

LB, p. 406.

To Samuel Swann

[15 March 1756]

To Mr Sam Swann inclosing my Public Accounts per Major Rutherford March 15th 1756 See Lre Bundle NB letters per Major Rutherford arrivd in Augt thereafter NB turn to other end of this Book for continuation of Correspondence.[1]

LB, p. 406.

1. There is a hiatus of more than a year between this memorandum and the following letter. After recording this memorandum JA continued his letter book by turning it over and beginning with what was the last page.

To Robert Dinwiddie

Sir   May 13th 1757

I have none from you later than Janry 4th[1] which I answerd by the Packet 10th of March,[2] and afterwards by the Virginia Convoy, one of which of Forty Guns remains as I am informed for the protection of the Colony in consequence of yours & the Merchants Application;[3] My former letters told you of the Resignation or rather Dismission of Mr Pitt,[4] ever since that there has been by all accounts strong Contests concerning an Arangment for a Ministry and now from all appearances, the Administration will be formed thro a Coalition of the Duke of Newcastle with Mr Pitt, and their friends, and those lately remov'd will in consequence thereof resume their former Stations,[5] and from hence we may expect the execution of such Measures as we had reason to hope for from Parliament in Favor of the Southward Colonys; I have heretofore told you, that Mr Pitt had procured the Kings orders for Marching one and if necessary two thousand of Lord Loudons Forces towards the Frontiers of Virginia to be at hand to protect that & the Southward Colonys, and that a grant of Money from Parliament had been agreed to in the Cabinet Council, and accordingly Mr Legg when Chancellor of the Excquer had opened in Parliament an Intention of granting 50,000 towards the Southward Colonys, besides those Measures by Mr Pitts application Col Montgomerys New raisd Regt of Highlanders, were destind directly for So Carolina,[6] thus stood the plan for the Southward Colonys when Mr Pitt was dismissed, his Restoration with Mr Leggs will I hope not only restore but bring to full Maturity such Measures of which you shall be informd ere long the period for this Session of Parlt being fixed for the 29 instant.[7]

As to Foreign News the King of Prussia having enterd Bohemia from different quarters carrys all before him hetherto,[8] the Army of Observation under the D of Cumberland is forceing to oppose the French already in Westphalia[9] our American Fleets under Holborn supposd to have sailed as the 3 Inst from Corke of which you will hear soon,[10] I am glad to hear by a Vessel to Whithaven a short passage of your return from the Congress, where I hope Matters went to your Satisfaction,[11] Complts to Mrs Dinwiddie concludes me always

JA

PS   please to acquaint the Council that the Bill for importing Bar Iron into all the Ports of Great Britain, in which I took part for Virginia is carryd into a Law now passed notwithstanding great oposition thereto.[12]

LB, pp. 25–26. Sent "by the April Packet to New York."

1. In his letter to JA of 4 Jan. 1757 (Brock, *Dinwiddie Papers*, 2:579–580), Dinwiddie discussed Indian affairs, commented on Loudoun's secrecy concerning his plans for the next campaign, informed JA that he had requested additional ships for the colony's defense (see note 3 below) and asked JA to pursue the application, enclosed a letter from the Council (not found) concerning South Carolina's reported attempts to prevent Virginians from growing indigo and instructed JA to work to

defeat any such attempts, informed JA that the revenue from the two-shillings-per-hogshead tobacco export tax was exhausted and that Dinwiddie had asked British authorities for a warrant allowing him to draw on the quitrent revenues to prosecute the war, and stated that he was in ill health and had applied to Loudoun for permission to return to England.

2. Letter not found.

3. In letters of 4 Jan. 1757 to the Treasury, the Board of Trade, Paymaster General Henry Fox, and Halifax (Brock, *Dinwiddie Papers*, 2:575–579), Dinwiddie had requested naval protection in addition to the one twenty-gun ship then defending the colony. Merchants of London and Bristol trading to Virginia and Maryland had submitted petitions to the Crown requesting additional support for the colonies' defense. The London petition, received 1 Jan. 1757, is CO 5/18, fols. 1–2; the Bristol petition, undated, is CO 5/18, fols. 7–9.

4. William Pitt served as principal secretary of state from 4 Dec. 1756 until the king demanded his resignation on 5 Apr. 1757.

5. Pitt was given the seals on 29 June 1757. Among those restored to office were Newcastle as First Lord of the Treasury, Anson as First Lord of the Admiralty, Holderness as secretary of state for the Northern Department, Richard Grenville-Temple (1711–1779), Earl Temple, as Lord Privy Seal, and Bilson-Legge as Chancellor of the Exchequer.

6. Pitt had ordered the 1st Highland Battalion, under Lt. Col. Archibald Montgomery, from Ireland to South Carolina to defend the southern frontier.

7. The fourth session of the Eleventh Parliament did not close until 4 July 1757.

8. Three of Frederick's armies moved toward Prague, defeating, but not destroying, the Austrians under Prince Charles of Lorraine (1712–1780), brother-in-law of Maria Theresa, in a bloody battle near that city on 6 May 1757. The subsequent siege of Prague, to which the Austrians had retreated, did not hold, however. Frederick suffered heavy losses in mid-June attacking an Austrian army under Field Marshal Count Leopold von Daun at Kolín, east of Prague, and was forced to lift the siege and retreat from Bohemia.

9. The duke of Cumberland commanded an army of 45,000, composed of Hanoverians and mercenaries from other German states. George II had ordered it to maintain a defensive posture toward the French.

10. Francis Holburne (1704–1771), vice admiral of the Blue, commanded the fleet that sailed from Cork on 8 May 1757, intended for the reduction of Louisburg.

11. Dinwiddie had traveled to Philadelphia to attend a meeting Loudoun had called with the governors of the southern colonies for the purpose of planning the defense of those colonies. Governors Lyttelton, of South Carolina, and Ellis, of Georgia, did not attend, but Dinwiddie, Dobbs, William Denny, of Pennsylvania, and Horatio Sharpe, of Maryland, attended, along with George Washington. The meeting took place during the last two weeks of Mar. 1757.

12. "An Act to extend the liberty granted by an Act of the twenty-third year of the reign of his present majesty, of importing bar iron from his majesty's colonies in America, into the port of London, to the other ports of Great Britain; and for repealing certain clauses in the said act" received the royal assent on 6 May 1757 (30 George II, chap. 16). The "great opposition" to the bill came from the owners of woodlands in the West Riding of Yorkshire (*JHC*, 27:848–849).

To Arthur Dobbs

Sir   May 13th 1757

My last by the Store ship told you the resignation or Dismission of Messrs Pitt & his friends from the repeated refusal of others to accept of the Vacant Offices, they have remaind so from the present aspect of Affairs, a Coalition between the D of New——le seems to be at hand, as the basis of a New Administration, Should Mr Pitt be restored I flatter myself that the Measures projected by him may still be carryd into Execution, I have in my former letters told you that in consequence of Addresses from the Southward Colonies in which I took the lead in behalf of your Province[1] that by Mr Pitts interposition orders were sent to Ld Loudon to detail one & if necessary two thousand to the Frontiers of Virginia to be at hand for the Better protection of the Southern Frontiers, he also procured the Kings orders for Colonel Montgomerys New raised Regiment of Highlanders to proceed directly to Charlestown[2] there to be disposed of according to Emergencys a Grant of Money for the use of the Southward Colonys applicable by Lord Loudon was also agreed to in the Cabinet Council & accordingly Mr Legge before he went out of Office, opened to the House an Intention of Granting 50000 Ster, thus stood the Plan of Measures projected by Mr Pitt, whom we have reason to see restored to Power in hopes of being benefited thereby thro the execution of those Measures so projected by him.

Upon receipt of Letters by Capt Heron put into my hands as public letters directed to the Lords of the Admiralty[3] I attended their Lordships thereon tho the Contents thereof neither communicated to me by you nor by the Committee of Correspondence but from Mr Heron finding they contain an Address from the Governor & Council I took them upon me & accordingly Solicited the renewal of the Cape Fear Station by a Sloop of War.[4] Lord Winchelsea[5] now at the board gave me to understand that the Merlin Sloop part of the South & North Carolina Convoy was orderd to Cape Fear to relieve the Baltimore, but as advice that very day was come of her being taken by the Enemy, orders should be sent to Admiral Holborn to send a Sloop Stationd for your Province as the most speedy way to assist you & that proper orders should go for that purpose.

The Multiplicity of Captors from So & No Carolina has greatly alarmd the Merchants and in all probability will be productive hereafter of regular Convoys out & home, I would in this Event suggest to you the necessity of throwing your Trade under Such Convoy as may be concerted by your merchants & those of South Carolina or Virginia whichever may best suit your trade, and whatever Measures you may propose shall be laid before the Admiralty for their orders accordingly.

Our News from Bohemia is very favorable, the King of Prussia having forced his way into Bohemia by different passes, he carrys all before him, & a few days Since the Prince of Bevern gained a most compleat Victory over Count Koningseck,[6] thereby the Prussians being united the King at the head of the combined Armys is in full March to attack Count Brown, who must fight or fly under cover of Prague.[7]

The D of Cumberland by this time is at the head of the Army of observation to oppose the progress making in Westphalia by the French who have just now formed the siege of Guelder;[8] a neutrality has been proposed for Hanover as well as for Hesse Cassel but rejected by both with Spirit every Mail will bring some thing new from that quarter, Wishing you success in your Field of Action I remain always very truly Dr Sir your Excelcys Most Obedt Servt

PS My Remittance of Indigo is gone to France who have got almost the full crop of both Carolinas, scarce a Ship has escapd the Enemy from these Provinces, 10 out of 12 from South are taken by the Enemy & but one of 7 from North (that is Mr Herons) having escaped, the underwriters are much down in the mouth hereupon, & have now at last given over Insuring Carolina Ships without Convoy.

LB, pp. 26–28. Sent "by the April Packet to New Yorke." At the foot of this letter JA late wrote: "See Governor Dobbs Answer to this of Decr 20th 1757 he tells me the Assembly will not pay my arrears &ta."

1. In the margin at about this point JA wrote: "NB My first application for Supplys of Men to Mr. Pitt."

2. In the margin at about this point JA wrote: "sent [send?] to Governor Dinwiddie."

3. In the margin at about this point JA wrote: "apply to the admiralty for a sloop of war."

4. The address from the governor and Council to the Admiralty, dated 3 Mar. 1757, complained that the sloop appointed to Cape Fear was frequently absent, leaving the North Carolina coast in an "unguarded and defenceless Situation." They recommended to the Admiralty that Lt. Benjamin Heron of the Royal Navy be appointed to the Cape Fear Station "as a reward for his good behaviour some few Months since, in driving from this Coast an Enemys Privateer . . . as also from his great Knowledge of this Coast, and the danger of the Sands that surround this Bar," and because of his North Carolina connections (Adm. 1/3818). Shortly before the address was written, the Admiralty had ordered a twenty-gun ship and sloop to North Carolina to protect the province and annoy the enemy (John Clevland to John Pownall, 28 Feb. 1757, Adm. 2/519, pp. 406–407).

5. Daniel Finch (1689–1769), eighth earl of Winchilsea and third earl of Nottingham, was First Lord of the Admiralty 1741–1744 and 1757.

6. August Wilhelm, duke of Bevern-Brunswick, defeated the Austrians under Count Koningsneck at Reichenberg in Bohemia on 21 Apr. 1757.

7. Count Maximilian Ulysses von Browne (1705–1757), an Austrian field marshal, was wounded while leading a bayonet charge in the battle of Prague and died on 26 June.

8. Guelders capitulated to the French on 23 Aug. 1757.

To John Rutherfurd

May 13th 1757

I have a few lines from Capt Heron, and by the preceeding letter from you of 14th Jany[1] which came safe I did expect a very particular Account from you, on the Subject of my Remittances in that of January you take Notice that the agreement proposed by you for taking Indigo with you, to be paid for ad Valorem here, was broke thro by those with whom you did so agree, That Mr Saml Swann would not accept of money from you in order to remit the same to me; That thereupon you could fall on no other Method than to purchase the best Indigo & for me to take the chance of the Market here.

Now I do agree to your taking this Method to make me Remittances hereafter, in Indigo, but at the Same time You must give me due Notice of Shiping the same by the New Yorke Packet that may sail before the Indigo shiped, & by other opportunitys to Out Ports rather than London and at no rate to ship any for me unless, under Convoy or a probable chance of Convoy thro South Carolina or Virginia, for I must observe to you that the loss from the Carolinas & Virginia has been so great that scarce one Carolina Ship having escaped the Enemy that the Insurers tendre refusing to Insure without Convoy, this will in all probability be productive of Standing Convoys out & home to & from So Carolina & Virginia, and as to your Trade your S[t]ationd Sloop of War or perhaps any other vessel of Force may be Imployd to carry your Ships to the Place of Rendevous, I have given my thoughts on this to the Governor & Mr Swann;[2] Lord Walpole being dead Mr Cholmondely Suceeds him as Auditor General,[3] I am not sure but that by Lord Walpoles death you may stand longer as Receiver General, however I am possitive that you must not only be more exact in the Manner of your Accounts & Following the Rules laid down by Govr Dobbs as near as possible which I find Mr Walpole did greatly approve of, & was resolvd to have moved the Treasury for Suspending of you, by reason of the lumping Method of your Accounts, as well as for your short Receipts, probably Mr Walpoles letters to you told you all this, the Treasury I find too are very angry with you, & from this Cause refused you leave to come home & ever will, till you have improved the Receipt & the manner of accounting for the Receipt, consult with the Governor & D Auditor on these Matters You will take notice that Yours & Your Wifes agreement with me is, that I am to be paid out of the first Money comming in as Arrears, my Orders, upon, & accepted by you from the rest of the Officers on Arrears are to the same purpose[4] I observe by your Accounts transmitted home that you have made payments to the Heirs & Executors of the late Governor[5] as part of his Arrears; but I observe none made to other Officers or their Executors as Arrears; I therefore beg to be informed of you what money you have now in hand for my use arrising from the payment of Arrears, that an open Account Current may be opend between us hereupon. Mr Cholmondely as Auditor General having made proposals to me to be his Deputy Auditor General in Great Britain,[6] if we do agree my acquaintance with the Revenues of Your Province will thereby become greater than it now is.

P.S. Let me have your answer to this by the New York Packet.

LB, pp. 29–30. The postscript is in a clerk's hand. Sent "per the April Packet to N.Y."

1. Letters not found.

2. See preceding and following letters.

3. The Rev. Robert Cholmondeley (1727–1804) was a son of George Cholmondeley (1703–1770), third earl of Cholmondeley, and Mary (Walpole) Cholmondeley, a daughter of Robert Walpole, first earl of Orford, and a niece of the late auditor-general. Cholmondeley was therefore a grandson of Robert Walpole and a great-nephew of Horatio Walpole, who had died on 5 Feb. 1757 and whom Cholmondeley succeeded as auditor-general.

4. In the margin at about this point JA wrote: "see copy of his last Accounts with his Ltr to me in Book of Accounts [fol.?] (2)."

5. Gabriel Johnston.

6. JA served as Cholmondeley's deputy auditor-general from 1757 to 1765.

To Samuel Swann

Sir   May 13th 1757

The Packet being the most certain & ready way to acquaint you of your son's safe arrival,[1] I send this under the Governor's Cover for this Purpose, Mr Heron may have had an opportunity from Portsmouth unknown to me, I have seen Mr Heron as yesterday he tells me, he is informed from his friends at Portsmouth, that your son goes on well, since his arrival & proposes to keep him for 12 months in the Isle of Wight whereof I approve; by which he will be better prepared for Acton, he gives the most promising accounts of his person & Capacity, I wish he was nearer to me, I shall give him the recommendation of a very worthy man there, Capt. George Makenzie at Cowes, you did well in sending him over while young, and are so far very lucky as to have escaped the Enemy who have taken, 10 out of 12 Ships from South Carolina, and Capt Heron is the only one out of seven got safe from No. Carolina as I am informed, amongst others the John & George Dean Master with my Indigo is carried into France, by good Luck the Copy of Bills of Loading and Invoice are come by Mr Heron, therby the Insurance will be recovered, but I am affraid Mr Barclay[2] made short Insurance as to the Value; from such repeated Losses, the Insurers are resolved, to Insure no more Carolina Ships without Convoy, this may probably be productive of regular Convoys from South Carolina & Virginia, out and home, I *have hereupon suggested to* Governor Dobbs the Expediency of concerting measures in your Province, that your Trade may be thrown under such Convoys,[3] and whatever Plan you shall propose, I shall lay before the Admiralty for their orders; In the mean time, Captain Heron, having put into my hands Letters to the Admiralty, the Contents thereof, not mentioned to me by the Governor, nor by the Committee, however understanding from Mr Heron the purport thereof, I did take them upon me, and presented them to the Lords of the Admiralty, thereupon Lord Winchelsea told me, that the Merlin Sloop which made part of the Carolina Convoy, had orders to relieve the Baltimore on your Station, but as they had that very Day received Advice of her being taken by the Enemy, they should send Orders to Admiral Holborn to dispatch one of his sloops for your Service, with proper orders, relative to her station thus the effect of the Address may have served the Province, I wish it had served Mr Heron at the same time.

Mr Byng so far as his Life could, made attonment for his Cowardice,[4] the Grand Inquiry before Parliament in relation to the loss of Minorca is now finished, and without any Criminality or neglect, laid to The charge of the then Administration,[5] this being over, most people did then expect the Settlement of a Ministry, however we are still in Suspence, tho' a Coalition between the Duke of Newcastle and Mr Pitt is expected, so as to exclude Mr Fox from any share thereof, by Mr Pitts restoration, we hope to see the measures projected by him while in Office, brought to execution, I have heretofore informed you, that the moment he came to be Secretary of State, that I gained Ground in my Solicitations, that by his means orders were sent to Lord Loudon, to march one & if necessary two thousand men towards Virginia So as to be at hand to advance to protect the Southward Colonies, that a Grant of mony for the Southward Colonies had been agreed to in the Cabinet Council, and thereupon Mr Legge while in Office as Chancellor of the Exchequer did open to the house of Commons an Intention of Granting 50,000 ster: applicable by Lord Loudon for the Service of the Southward Colonies, and moreover two days before Mr Pitts Dismission he notified to me that he had procured the Kings approbation for sending 1100 men being Colonel Montgomry's new raised Regiment of Highlanders directly to Charles Town, to be destined as Emergencys might require on the Southern Frontiers, such was Mr Pitts plan of Measures while in, it concerns us therefore, that he becomes restored, for the execution of such measures, and I hope to have the satisfaction by my next letters to acquaint you thereof.

The King of Prussia threatned from all the greatest Powers of Europe combined together is clearing his way gloriously, having forced his way into Bohemia, from four different passages, one of his Armys under Prince Bevern having gaind a compleat Victory over Count Kenningsegge tho' strongly posted and Intrenched with a superior Army the Prussian Army now united under their King are in full march to attack Count Brown, who must fight or fly to Prague there to be starved, the Prussians being Masters of the Country & greatest part of the Austrian Magazines. The Duke of Cumberland by this time is at the head of the Army of Observation to stop the French now in Westphalia laying siege to Guilders; Our King as well as the Prince of Hesse Cassel have with Spirit, rejected the proposed Neuterality, tho the French are on their Borders, all these opperations do engage our attention, but to your part of the World, we must above all cast our Eyes, and hard winds for near three months that prevent your Succors going.

In the present situation of affairs you may easily conclude that Individuals cannot succeed in private application, but your friend Mr Jones is not foregot, I shall not fail to Stir in his affair, so soon as I find an opening so to do,[6] this will serve as my duty to the Committee, of Correspondence, haveing nothing to say to the Public in particular, I hope the Levant Store ship got safe, farewel with Compts. to your Brother I am always most sincerely.

LB, pp. 30–34. In a clerk's hand, except for the memorandum on routing in JA's hand, which reads: "by the April Packet to New Yorke."

1. Not identified.

2. David Barclay.

3. See JA to Dobbs, 13 May 1757, pp. 179–180.

4. In Apr. 1756 John Byng (1704–1757), admiral of the Blue, sailed with a squadron to relieve the Mediterranean island of Minorca, which was under threat of a French attack. In an encounter with a French fleet on 20 May 1756, Byng failed to break through the French line and reach the island, and he retired to Gibraltar with his squadron. Throughout the fall of 1756 Byng's court-martial was held. The naval officers who composed the court found Byng guilty of negligence, but they also unanimously recommended a royal reprieve from the death sentence. The reprieve never came, and Byng was executed on 14 Mar. 1757.

5. The resolutions of the House of Commons of 3 May 1757 that came out of its investigation into the loss of Minorca are printed in *Parliamentary History*, 15:822–827.

6. Probably Robert Jones, who was eventually appointed to the North Carolina Council.

To Samuel Swann

Sir   May 26th 1757

The above is coppy of my last by the New Yorke Packet to which I have to add that the Bill for 30£ Ster on Bourdeaux is paid by Messrs Loubier & Co: in London, My letter inclosd to the Committee of Correspondence[1] under your cover thro the hands of Govr Dobbs will shew you the agreeable Issue of My Provincial Solicitations. I have been greatly obliged to Mr Pitt & his Administration for Success His Zeal for the prosperity of the Colonys makes me desire his restoration to Office, its thought a few days will determine the Arrangment of Ministers I wish I could say that Mr Pitt was certainly to be replaced, but his objections both to *Men* and to *some* particular Measures may be too strong to take place.

On the 6th Instant the King of Prussia in Person gaind a most memorable Victory over the Combind Armys of the Empress under Count Brown, every day produces new circumstances Attending this Victory, the consequence whereof is that Prince Charles of Lorain & Count Brown are with the broken remains of the Right Wing of their dismayd Army shut up in Prague & the King of Prussia disposition is such as makes it impracticable to Supply that Place with Provisions to hold out; the rest of the Imperial Army are totally dispersed; the D of Cumberland & the French must soon come to Blows in Westphalia if the French stand their ground where they now are[2] I am ever My Dr Sir

LB, p. 34. Sent "per Ship from Plymouth from Mr Lewis."

1. See following letter.

2. JA's account of the European military situation was much too optimistic. See JA to Dinwiddie, 13 May 1757, p. 178, n. 8.

As for Cumberland and the Army of Observation, it was they rather than the French who failed to stand their ground. The French under Marshal d'Estrées crossed the Rhine and poured over Westphalia in northern Germany, approaching the Weser. Cumberland, who was guarding the strategic river, wanted to make a stand, but the electoral council of Hanover ordered him to retreat across the river. Cumberland continued to retreat east and north until, on 8 Sept. 1757, he surrendered at Kloster-Zeven.

To the Committee of Correspondence of North Carolina

Gentlemen   May 26th 1757

I am not inclind to give you the trouble of letters without having something material to lay before you, My last of 15th March[1] by the Levant Store Ship under Convoy to Virginia acquainted you with the result of a very long & troublesome Solicitation for Such Stores as the ——— carryd to North Carolina; all which I hope are come safe; This Letter inclosing the Proceedings of the House of Commons will inform you of the agreeable Issue of another Solicitation, according to what I just hinted to you in my last;[2] In the course of this Negociation I think my self obliged to declare to you how much I have been Indebted to Mr Pitt and his Administration for Success, His zeal for the welfare of the Colonies shewd it self very remarkably during his too short Administration.

As the Money granted by Parliament agreeable to the Kings Message and the Commons Resolves thereon will probably be transmitted to Lord Loudon applicable by him in proportion to the services of the Several Provinces interested therein, your Government therefore cannot be too early in giving in your Claim to his Lordship; and perhaps Nothing farther may remain for my negociations hereupon on this Side; I must on this occasion remind you of what I took the liberty by my last letter to desire your Attention to, & Interposition with the General Assembly, upon the extra Articles in my last years Accounts for Extraordinary Services, these Articles as charged by me are very far short of being adequate to the nature of the Service. A Repetition of such Negociations will therefore lay me under the neceessity of Inlarging my Expectations from the Province, either by way of an Addition to my Salary, or by a greater latitude in my Annual Accounts for Extraordinary Services, and on this proposition I shall be glad to have the sense of your Government for my future Conduct in the mean time be Pleased to do me the Justice of having endeavoured to Serve the Province thro a long tract of years with great Inclination and desire of Success, & whenever that has faild, I have nothing to reproach my Self with in point of Neglect.

The Bill of 30£ remitted me by Mr Swann is duly paid and the Indigo in Capt Dean being taken by the Enemy The Insurance thereupon, when paid, shall be carryd to the Credit of the Public.

From The immense losses sustaind by the Captors of so many Ships from the three Southern Provinces within the space of three or four Months last past those of the Admiralty Administration are greatly Alarm'd & this may be productive of not only strengthening your Stationd Ships of War but likewise of Establishing Regular Convoys hereafter out & Home to So Carolina & Virginia I have hereupon taken the liberty to Suggest to His Excelcy Govr Dobbs the expediency of throwing your Trade under Such Convoys,[3] & when the Plan for so doing is fixed upon so far as the Interposition of Admiralty orders in Execution thereof becomes necessary I doubt not of having [it] I am with great regard Gentlemen

LB, pp. 35–36. In the margin at the head of this letter JA wrote, in part: "NB to Mr Lewis from Plimouth NB one by the same convoy same to Rutherford show expences then to the end 23d Decr NB see Bundle Letters anno 1756 My Agency expird by the agency Law 3 months previous to this Letter."

1. Letter not found.

2. JA refers to the recent appropriation by Parliament of £50,000 for colonial defense. On 16 May 1757 the House of Commons received this message: "His

Majesty, being desirous that his faithful Subjects in the Provinces of North and South Carolina and Virginia, in America, should receive a proper Recompence for such Services, as, with the Approbation of the Commander in Chief of his Forces in America, they respectively shall have performed, or shall perform, either by putting the said Provinces in a State of Defence, or by acting with Vigour against the Enemy, recommends it to this House to take the same into their Consideration, and to enable his Majesty to give them a proper Recompence for such Services." On 19 May the Commons resolved "That a Sum, not exceeding Fifty thousand Pounds, be granted to his Majesty, upon Account, to be paid to such Persons, and in such Manner, and by such Proportions, as his Majesty, shall direct, for the Use and Relief of his Majesty's Subjects in his several Provinces of North and South Carolina and Virginia, in America" (*JHC*, 27:894, 901). The appropriation was ultimately divided as follows: Virginia, £32,268.19.0$\frac{1}{4}$; South Carolina, £9,941.19.10; and North Carolina, £7,789.1.1$\frac{1}{4}$.

3. See JA to Dobbs, 13 May 1757, pp. 179–180.

To John Rutherfurd

Sir   May 26th [1757]

I have nothing to add to my last[1] copy anexd except but to acquaint you considering the extraordinary prices of Naval Stores at home I shall be glad you make me for once Remittances therein giving me Notice for Insuring for Plymouth for these to Mr Lewis let mine be consignd, but if you have the chance of Convoy you may ship for London, but without Convoy you may Ship for Plymouth that I may try the chance of the Market for Naval Stores, provided you get them cheap with you Turpentine I hear is the best for home Market[2] I again recommend to you great diligence & attention in execution of your Office otherwise I shall not be able to Support you against the Complaints lodged against you I am always Yours

JA

LB, p. 38. In the margin at the head of this letter JA wrote, in part: "Mr Lewis had this to Del[ive]r by his Ship—Duplicat by Mr Blair per Boston Convoy."

1. JA to Rutherfurd, 13 May 1757, pp. 181–183.

2. JA was evidently willing to take some of his arrears of salary in the form of naval stores to be sold in Britain.

To Arthur Dobbs

Sir   26th May [1757]
   The inclosed to the Committtee[1] will shew you the Success of my
Negociations to which I have nothing to add, the Extraordinary
Gazette gives an Account of a Memorable Battle fought the 6th
inst, Major Grant Aid de Champ to the K of Prussia is since arrivd
& gives many more circumstances of this Matter P Charles & Count
Brown are with the shaterd remains of the Left Wing of the
Austrians shut up in Prague & so environd by the Prussians no
possebility of Supplys. We expect dayly an Account of Blows
between the D of Cumberland & the French in Westphalia, during
this Universal Storm who will believe me, We have no Ministry
please to forward the enclosd as directed & believe me always
   Your Exellys

   LB, p. 39. Sent "to Mr Lewis from Plimouth."

   1. See JA to North Carolina Committee of Correspondence, 26 May 1757,
pp. 187–188.

To the Council of Virginia

Gentlemen   London May 27th 1757
   I am not willing to give you the trouble of my Letters, without
having something material to communicate therein. My last therefore of the 10th of March last[1] by the then New York Packet &
Duplicat thereof by the Virginia Convoy, acquainted you of the
receipt of your Letter in relation to the apprehended application to
Parliament on the Part of So Carolina against Indigo in Virginia,[2]
whereupon I then was, and still am of oppinion that your apprehensions on this head are groundless, at the same time I told you
of my taking part (in consequence of an application to me from the
Merchants of Bristol for that purpose) in their Petition to Parliament for Extending the Free Importation of Bar Iron into all Ports
of this Kingdom;[3] I farther acquainted you that I was likely to meet
with Success in my Solicitations with the Ministry as well [in] regard
to Succours of Men as of Money.
   I have the Satisfaction hereby to inform you that all these

Matters and Negociations are now brought to an Issue, and with Success, a Law is passed for the General Free Importation of Bar Iron to all Ports of Great Britain, what the King of himself could do, As to Succours, some time since has been done, by repeated orders to Lord Loudon to March one thousand if necessary two thousand towards your Frontiers, Since that, the Parliament as you will See by their Proceedings herewith sent, have enabled His Majesty to comply with a Pecuniary Aid, and a Sum is accordingly granted for that purpose,[4] applicable in the manner in which I just hinted might be the case by my last letter viz according to the Earl of Loudons approbation, in proportion to the Services of the Several Provinces interested therein, this being the Case your Government cannot be too early in laying in your Claim with His Lordship.

Nothing farther remaining for my Negociations hereupon on this side, I think myself obliged in justice to Mr Secretary Pitt to let you know, how much I have been indebted to his good offices for Success in my Negociations, his Zeal for the welfare of the Colonies, shewd itself very remarkably, during his too short Administration and Acknowledgment of Thanks from thence, becomes due to him as well as to Mr Legge the then Chancellor of the Exchequer.[5]

With regard to myself it will give me great pleasure to have the approbation of the Council and House of Burgesses, in whose behalf I have Acted and An acknowledgment for the extraordinary trouble and Expence attending these Negociations I submit to their consideration and Discretion, and I am on all Occasions with great regard Gentlemen

LB, pp. 36–37. In the margin at the head of this letter JA wrote, in part: "from London to Virginia Coffee house Duplicat by Capt Paterson June 28th."

1. Letter not found.

2. See JA to Dinwiddie, 13 May 1757, pp. 177–178, n. 1.

3. See JA to Dinwiddie, 13 May 1757, p. 179, n. 12.

4. See JA to North Carolina Committee of Correspondence, 26 May 1757, pp. 188–189, n. 2.

5. JA's advice was heeded by the Virginians. On 12 Nov. 1757 Dinwiddie proposed to the Council "that a Committee be appointed to prepare a Letter of

Thanks from this Board, to Mr. Secretary Pitt, and Mr. Legge, Chancellor of the Exchequer, for the Zeal with which they have exerted themselves in serving the American Colonies in general, and Virginia in particular." John Blair, Philip Ludwell, and the Rev. Thomas Dawson were appointed the committee (*EJC*, 6:74). On 22 Dec. the letters (not found) were produced, read, and approved (*EJC*, 6:76).

To Robert Dinwiddie

May 27th 1757

To this is annexed copy of my last,[1] the inclosed to the Council[2] will shew you the result of my Negociations and thereupon I hope to have the approbation of your respective Branches of Government with some acknowledgment for my Services from the House of Burgesses in so far as that they have interested themselves in this Measure & it gives me the greater pleasure to have stood alone in this Negociation, with Success since without it your having opposed a Coadjutor to me on the part of the Assembly might have been censured from your partiality to me, and as it has so happend that by Mr Jennings's death I have stood alone, may I not from thence ground my expectations of some consideration in his stead.[3]

The inclosed Extraordinary Gazette will shew you, how gloriously the King of Prussia clears his way thro his Enemys, every day produces new advantages on his side, to all which your Acquaintance Mr Andrew Mitchell our Minister is an eye Witness;[4] I wish we could bring these Operations home to British Measures against the French, but it is from America and from thence alone that the Fate of Britain must depend & for my own part I can discover nothing on our side that denotes Success equal to that of the King of Prussia in Bohemia; We are in dayly expectation of a blow between the Duke of Cumberland, at the head of the Army of observation & the French in Westphalia; in the midst of this universal Storm will you believe me, that we have no Administration as yet fixed, those who wish well to the Colonies, must desire the restoration of Mr [Pitt].

I long much to hear from you since your return from the Congress,[5] it is probable that I have lost some of your letters by the captures of so many of our Virginia Ships, My complts to Mrs Dinwiddie & the Young Ladies concludes me always

LB, pp. 37–38. In the margin at the head of this letter JA wrote, in part: "to Virginia Coffee house."

1. JA to Dinwiddie, 13 May 1757, pp. 176–177.

2. See preceding letter.

3. Edmund Jenings (d. 1756) had been a member of the Council of Maryland. On 24 May 1756 Dinwiddie had written JA (Dinwiddie Letter Books, 3:260, VHS): "The Ho. of Burgesss. endeavd. to appt. Edmd. Jennings Esqr. a Gentleman with You [i.e., in London] formerly Secretary of Myld to be Agent for 'em, but I by no means wd. pass their Act for that purpose, Mr. Jennings is a worthy good sensible Gent. & one I have great Friendship for, however I told 'em I thot. the Affs. under yr. managemt. were properly conducted & I had a Majority of the Council with me." As JA reported to Loudoun on 3 Aug. 1756, the Virginia Council and assembly were "complaining that they had no part of the Parliaments Bounty granted last Session," and that to give their remonstrance to the Crown greater weight the House proposed to join another agent to JA but that Dinwiddie told them their cause was in good hands and prevailed (Loudoun Papers 1410, Huntington Library, San Marino, Calif.). See also *JHB, 1752–1758*, 389–393, for the passage on 3 May 1756 of "An Act for appointing an agent" by the House, which bill died in Council.

4. Andrew Mitchell (1708–1781), barrister, was British envoy 1756–1765 and 1765–1771 to Frederick II, king of Prussia.

5. See JA to Dinwiddie, 13 May 1757, p. 178, n. 11.

To John Cleland

Dr Sir   June 12th 1757

In my last of 28th March[1] I told you that after all the pains taken for an ad: Salary I got for Answer that the Commissioners had ordered Mr Wood[2] to advise you to transmit your Account of the Charges on the Georgia Service, & for the future to take no more trouble on that Service without their orders I also told you that I had made these payments to Mr Corben

1755	23d	Septr	70.2.6	
1756	19	April	20.2.6	£217.5.0
1757	4	Janry	60.0.0	
Do	11	Janry	67.0.0	

I have accepted your Bill for 75.0.0 presented to me in favour of Mr John Watson which shall be paid tho it exceeds the half yearly Salary, which is no more than neat Money to you 70.3.0.

The half years Salary payable to you is after deductions for Taxes (thereon for the Service of Government) no more than 73.2.6 out of which are paid the customary Fees to Clerks in the Custom House £1.3.0 and for receiving & paying the same by me 1.16.6 So that the ballance of 73.2.[6] due to you is no more than 70.3.0.

Our News from the King of Prussia his Success against the Empress of Germany is great Victory after Victory on his side, nothing material has happend between the D: of Cumberland & the French in Westphalia as yet.

Great difficulty attends the arrangment of a New Ministry since Messrs Pitt & Legge their Dismission, the well wishers to the Colonys desire their restoration; Governor Reynolds & his Mistress being carryd into France occasiond the rumour of Governor Glen & his Lady being taken;[3] the Nabob an Usurper in Bengal has totally destroyd all our Settlements in that part of India, a Force is gone from other parts of India to retake these Settlements & probably may have Success but the Goods & Effects are lost to us[4] Adieu my Dr Sir I am always Yours pray complts to Governor Lyttleton if near you.

LB, pp. 39–40. Sent "per Coffee house."

1. Letter not found.

2. JA probably refers to the Customs Commissioners and William Wood, Customs secretary.

3. Lt. Gov. Henry Ellis arrived in Georgia to relieve John Reynolds in Feb. 1757. En route home Reynolds was captured by the French, but he seems to have reached London on 7 July 1757 (William W. Abbot, *The Royal Governors of Georgia, 1754–1775* [Chapel Hill, 1959], 54 and n).

4. In the spring of 1756 the Nabob Áli Vardi Khan (ca. 1674–1756) died and was succeeded by his grandson Siraj-ud-daula (ca. 1734–1757). The new nabob sought to destroy the British in Bengal, ostensibly because they had abused privileges accorded to the United East India Company and because they had taken steps to repair the decaying fortifications of Fort William in Calcutta. In mid-June 1756 the nabob, at the head of an army numbering 30,000 to 50,000 men, attacked Fort William, defended by about 440 soldiers and militia, and the British surrendered within a few days. (The surrender was followed by the infamous episode of the Black Hole, during which most of the approximately 150 people placed in the guardhouse died overnight.) Col. Robert Clive (1725–1774) led the expedition to recapture Calcutta. With a force of about 600 European and 1,200 sepoy troops, he left Madras on 16 Oct.

but did not reach the vicinity of Calcutta until mid-Dec. After a short bombardment, the defenders fled Calcutta, and Clive took possession of the city on 2 Jan. 1757.

To John Tinker

Dr Sir   London June 13th 1757

It is long since I had a letter from you the last is of 1t June[1] was 12 Months, perhaps later letters may have had the Fate of the Carolina Ships, the greatest part of which have fell into the Enemys hands be that as it will, as my letter of 25th Septr last in ansr to yours 3 of June[2] Signefyd to you my Intention of Soliciting the Case of Your Carriages[3] and also My Expectations of being paid by Your Order *here* for my past Services the Ballance of my Account (vizt) 75.0.0 to which I should add the Interest of 5 years from June 1755. In some of your letters you gave me to understand that I must have patience till your Treasury was in Cash, I thereupon told you that I should depend on you alone for payment as it was thro' your Intervention that I undertook the Service, I again repeat the Same in order to prevent my own loss as well as yours so far as the Public may be called upon by you to reimburse you.

Altho I have often put Mr Wood the Deputy Secretary of State[4] in mind of your application for the charges of Carriages I find that no orders are as yet gone to the Board of Ordnance on this Matter I am not indeed surprized at it considering the short duration of Mr Pitts Administration however attentive he was to the Affairs of the Colonys his Power lasted no longer than bringing to Maturity an Expedition of which you may have heard beforehand.[5]

Since Mr Pitts dismission various Negociations have been carryd on to Accomodate an Administration between the D of N. & Mr Pitt, but within these few days all these Negociations are at an end, by Mr Foxes Nomination to the Office of Chancellor of the Exeqr, Lord Waldegrave to the first Lord Commissioner of the Treasury Lord Egremont Secretary of State for Mr Pitts Department,[6] how long this Ministerial Plan may hold is uncertain, Since hereupon in disapprobation thereof Lord Holdernesse the other Secretary has resignd, also resigned the Dukes of Rutland & Leeds, their Offices of Lord Steward, & Cofferer Marquess of Rockingham Earls Leicester & Coventry theirs of Lords of the Bed Chamber, many other Resignations are expected, so that the general dislike to this Ministerial projection may overset it before it is well erected,[7] Discord at home & Success abroad greatly agitate the Minds of all ranks, the Populous since Byngs Execution have been pretty quiet, however they were inclind to take part in opposition to this New Administration.

The King of P goes on victoriously against the Empress, nothing material has happened between the D of C[8] & the French in Westphalia, if Prague falls soon as is expected unto the King of Prussia thear is an end of the Bohemian War nothing then to Stop his Way to Vienna Peace must ensue, and then pray God that all hands may join against the French & take their revenge.

Your friend Capt Gambier has paid dear for his Love of Mrs Knowles Saturday last in Guildhall he was cast in dammages, & hereupon will be grounded a Divorce on the part of Ad: Knowles[9] Adieu I am always

PS Have you any body to recommend to Mr Cholmondely for Casual Recr of the Kings Fines & Forfeitures, &c or for being his Deputy Auditor in Your Government, send Your recommendation to me & they shall take place, Mr Cholmondely succeeds Lord Walpole & is now about extending the Execution of his Office to all the Plantations in America, the Office of Auditor General of all the Kings Revenues in America is very comprehensive he allows his Deputys half of all perquisites viz 1 half of 5 per cent the Credit of all accounts of Prizes taken before the War & adjudged to the King is considerable in Some of the Provinces, *perhaps may be same* with you.

LB, pp. 40–41. Sent "per Charlestown So Carolina per Drayton & Convoy."

1. Letter not found.

2. Letters not found.

3. Gun carriages.

4. Robert Wood (1714–1771) served as undersecretary of state 1756–1763 and 1768–1770.

5. JA probably refers to the expedition against Quebec or Louisburg that Pitt ordered Loudoun to undertake.

6. These men were Henry Fox (1705–1774); James Waldegrave (1715–1763),

second Earl Waldegrave; and Charles Wyndham (1710–1763), second earl of Egremont.

7. JA's prognostication was correct, for on 29 June a new Pitt-Newcastle ministry was finally put in place, with Newcastle at the Treasury; Henry Legge as Chancellor of the Exchequer; Pitt as secretary of state for the Southern Department; Holderness as secretary of state for the Northern Department; Earl Temple as Lord Privy Seal; Halifax at the Board of Trade; Earl Granville as lord president of the Privy Council; William Cavendish, fourth duke of Devonshire, as lord chamberlain; Fox as paymaster general; and George Anson, Baron Anson, as First Lord of the Admiralty.

8. Duke of Cumberland.

9. The *Gentleman's Magazine* reported the trial before the Court of King's Bench of John Gambier, a member of the Council of the Bahamas under Tinker, against whom charges had been brought by Adm. Charles Knowles (d. 1777), governor of Jamaica 1752–1756. The third party in the affair was Knowles's wife Maria Magdalena Theresa, daughter of the comte de Bouget, whom Knowles had married in 1750. After the fact of criminal conversation between Gambier and Mrs. Knowles had been "fully proved," the jury on 11 June awarded Knowles £1,000 damages (*Gentleman's Magazine* 27 [1757]: 286).

To Robert Dinwiddie

Sir   June 28th 1757

Your letter from Philadelphia of 22d March and that from Williamsburgh 16th May came to hand together on the 21th June,[1] and by the date of the Kings Warrant for leave you will see that I lost no time,[2] I wish that the letters sent before these had come to hand, thereby your departure had been sooner adapted to the state of your health, but I still hope that the thoughts of Bath may now keep up your Spirits, there you have found relief, & there I hope you will again find it, I long much to have you here, and hereupon let me return my thanks for your attention to my Interest with the Council, who hereafter shall have all extraordinary News Papers as they desire as for letters on business I have never faild to write according to the circumstances arising thereon, my last to them,[3] & Duplicates thereof contain the Result of my Negociations for last year of which they can have no reason to complain.

I do not find that Lord Loudons recommendation of Colonel Young is arrivd[4] at least I have heard nothing of it in any of the Offices You will still be surprized to hear that our Administration is not as yet settled, this keeps the Parliament sitting by repeated Adjournments, without Secretary of State for the Southern District, & without Board of Trade I was obligd to go out of the ordinary Tract of Business in your behalf; you will be sorry to know that Lord Halefax has resignd in resentment to the slight put upon him by the D of Newcastle who in the arrangment of Offices did not so much as attend to what concernd Lord Halifax therein upon the various Ministerial Schemes that have been agitated of late Ld H——x was offered Promotion, but declind every offer but that of being a 3d Secretary viz for the Plantations, to which the King did agree nevertheless the D. of N—— in the arrangment with Mr Pitt made this no part of his Plan[5] Mr Oswald has likewise resignd tho I may be (as well as others) again mistaken in my account of the Administration,[6] I shall once more tell you that Mr Pitt resumes the Seals the D: of Newcastle the Treasury, Mr Legge the Chancellor of Excheqr, Lord Anson the Admiralty, & Mr Fox to the Pay Office but neither of the Privy nor of the Cabinet Council in short circumscribd as to all or any share of the Administration, Lord Dupplin to head the Board of Trade, Lord Temple to be Privy seal, Ld Gower Master of the Horse, in the Room of the D of Dorset late Groom of the Stole such are the Capitals of the new projected administration which may perhaps still be shaken from the difficulty of accomadating every Individual necessary to support the whole, and in my privat oppinion such is the composition of Hetrogenial humours, that ere long they will ferment & burst, tho for some time they may have a seeming agreement.[7]

As to Foreign News the Bombardment of Prague goes on with vigor, & ere long must be in ashes.

LB, pp. 42–43. Sent "per Capt Paterson by the New England Convoy & Duplicat by Mr Blair by sd Convoy."

1. When Dinwiddie wrote to JA on 22 Mar. 1757 (Brock, *Dinwiddie Papers*, 2:601–602), he was in Philadelphia at Loudoun's request to consult with Loudoun and other governors on the defense of the southern colonies. Dinwiddie related that he undertook the journey with difficulty because of his poor health, that he had applied to Loudoun and received permission to request leave to return to England, that he had written to Pitt and Halifax the same day asking for leave (Brock, *Dinwiddie Papers*, 2:599–601), and that Loudoun had recommended Lt. Col. John Young of the Royal Americans to succeed him as lieutenant governor. Dinwiddie also

asked JA to press his application for leave and to apply to the Admiralty for passage home in a navy vessel.

In his letter to JA of 16 May 1757 (Brock, *Dinwiddie Papers*, 2:627–628), Dinwiddie recapitulated his letter of 22 Mar., enclosed copies of his speech to the assembly that convened on 14 Apr. and the addresses to him from the Council and House of Burgesses (Brock, *Dinwiddie Papers*, 2:610–612, 613–616), discussed the current military situation, and enclosed a bill of exchange for £100 for a half year's salary. Dinwiddie told JA that the Council complained of the agent's tardiness in writing and admonished him to "send 'em a few of the latest News Papers."

Concerning Dinwiddie's request for permission to return to England, the Board read on 23 June 1757 his letter of 16 May 1757 to Halifax (Brock, *Dinwiddie Papers*, 2:625–626) and an undated memorial from JA on behalf of Dinwiddie (CO 5/1329, fol. 34). The Board wrote Holderness in support of Dinwiddie's request and prepared a royal warrant (*JBT*, 10:326–327).

2. The king's warrant granting Dinwiddie permission to return to England was dated 23 June 1757 (CO 324/51, p. 103, in Koontz, *Dinwiddie Papers*, 1299).

3. JA to the Council of Virginia, 27 May 1757, pp. 190–191.

4. Letter not found. See note 1 above.

5. Halifax did not attend any meetings of the Board of Trade between 15 June and 5 Nov. 1757.

6. James Oswald did not attend any meetings of the Board of Trade between 15 June and 3 Nov. 1757.

7. Those not previously identified are Granville Leveson-Gower (1721–1803), second Earl Gower, and Lionel Sackville (1688–1765), first duke of Dorset.

To the Council of Virginia

June 28th 1757

Gentlemen, the above is copy of my last of 27th May[1] to which I have only to add the public news containd in the Chronicle which paper I shall occasionally send you, as the best collection of News, and as my letters to the Leut Governor contains his Majestys Warrant for leaving his Government as leave, on this occasion I cannot omit to beg the continuance of your favor on the departure of my Friend Mr Dinwiddie, and you may rely on my Inclination: to serve you, on public and privat occasions to the utmost of my power. I have not heard of any steps as yet taken publickly in the way of Office towards the nomination of a Leut Governor in the room of Mr Dinwiddie due perhaps to unsettled state of the Administration more particularly that of the Board of Trade by the resignation of the Earl of Halefax for some time may prevent the nomination of a Leut Governor for Virginia but so soon as this is done you shall be made acquainted therewith in the mean time I am always with great regard Gentlemen

LB, p. 43. Sent "per Capt Paterson under Convoy so far."

1. Printed on pp. 190–191.

To John Rutherfurd

June 28 [1757]

I have nothing to add to that of the Duplicat of 27 of May[1] but to notifie my Agreement with Mr Cholmondely as Deputy Auditor,[2] that I may have the Quitrent Revenue more under my Inspection for advancement thereof let me have a particular State of the Money paid into your hands on my acct as by orders given you for that purpose by the New York packet let me have your Answer to this Lre.

LB, p. 44. Sent "by Mr Blair to Virginia."

1. JA's last letter to Rutherfurd was dated 26 May [1757], p. 189.

2. See JA to Rutherfurd, 13 May 1757, p. 183, n. 6.

To James Michie

[30 June 1757]

To Mr Michie June 30th 1757 see Bundle for copy thereof.

LB, p. 44.

To Robert Dinwiddie

[10 July 1757]

Gover Dinwiddie July 10th Send Duplicat of Kings Warrant for leave per the New York Packet, tell him of having lre from Col Young & thank him for his recommendation of me.[1]

LB, p. 44.

1. Young's letter to JA of 27 Apr. 1757 (not found) asked JA to press his appointment as governor. JA mentioned the letter, and thanked Loudoun for recommending him to Young, in a letter to Loudoun of 13 July 1757 (Loudoun Papers 3934, Huntington Library, San Marino, Calif.).

To John Young

Sir.   Craven street London 10th July 1757

By the New York Mail arrived on the 7th. instant, I have the favor of your Letter, of the 27th Aprile,[1] and am obliged to you, for your Trust and Confidence, you are so kindly pleased, to put in me, and to my good friends in America, for laying so good a foundation, for an ensuing Correspondence and Connexion; For the present, no further Powers from you become necessary but as matters of Public and Privat nature, come within the Negociations of Agents, for the Colonies and the Constitutions of Agents are occasionally called for, by the Board of Trade, in order to be laid before Parliament, I submit to your Consideration, how far, it may be hereupon necessary, to have the original Order of Governor and Council renewid in my favor, thro' your recommendation of me, when you come to the Government, according to the usage and Custom of that Government.[2]

I do only hint this, to you, as the Case is my own, I am the more tender on your part, to avoid noveltys, So far as concerns, my Negociations here, with the Kings Ministers, and Public Offices, by having the Authority of your Letter, added to the former Resolution of Governor and Council, Copie whereof is inclosed. I am under no pains of having my Credentials called in Question, by any of the Boards, or, by Parliament; as the Case then now Stands, I can go on with the Public service and with yours in Particular, And

I have the Satisfaction to acquaint you, that from the Progress that I have already made, thro' the Ministers, I have no room to doubt of your Success, from the Recommendation of the Earl of Loudon, I cannot omit telling you, how much the Duke of Argyle is your friend on this occasion,[3] and the Earl of Halifax is no more, at the head of Plantation Affairs, he has nevertheless given Lord Loudouns application, a favorable turn in Office, into the hands of Mr Pownall, where we shall make the most of it, for your service.[4]

Your O[r]ders relative to a post Charriot shall be executed, and as it may give Mrs Young, very great Satisfaction, to hear the progress that I make, I shall not fail to give her notice.[5] I am now called upon to return my Compts and thanks to my good friend Lord Loudon, and my friend Genl Abercromby,[6] and be assured that I am very Sincerely Sir Yours &c

P.S.   Your Friend Lord Hume has been gone some time for his Govert of Gibralter.[7]

LB, pp. 45–46. In a clerk's hand except for the routing memorandum in JA's hand, which reads: "per New Yorke Packet July 10th." A draft of this letter, in JA's hand and crossed through, is on pp. 44–44A of the letter book. Substantive differences between the two versions are accounted for in notes to the present letter.

1. Letter not found.

2. At this point in the draft JA added: "which was pointed out to me by my Predecessor Mr. Leheup and by Mr. Dinwiddie approved of."

3. Archibald Campbell (1682–1761), third duke of Argyll, was a vastly influential Scot.

4. At this point in the draft JA added: "Nothing shall be wanting on my part and while notwithstanding by the Vacancy of the B of Trade I am not without hopes of doing your Business thro the same channel wherein I have got the Kings Warrant for Mr. Dinwiddies return to England which I have transmitted to him by this & by another opportunity."

5. Young was so confident of his appointment that he had evidently ordered a post chaise be sent to Virginia so that he could ride in appropriate fashion.

6. At this point in the draft JA wrote: "and be so good as acquaint Capt McAdams of his Lordships Family that his Brother the sailor is arrivd well in the Edgcotte from the East Indies and the Ship by this time at Gravesend, they were attacked in the East Indies but cleard themselves of four of the Enemy with little damage to themselves." This was Lt. Gilbert McAdam, an aide-de-camp to Loudoun.

7. On 16 Apr. 1757, the king appointed William Home (d. 1761), eighth earl of Home, governor of Gibraltar.

To the Council of Virginia

Gentlemen   July 11th 1757

My last 28 June[1] told you of procuring the Kings Warrant for Governor Dinwiddies leaving your Government which Event presuming on the sincerity of my Inclinations to Serve I took occasion to desire the continuance of your Favour on the departure of my worthy Friend I hope reception here will be very favourable, I have since that on the 7th June reced a Letter from Colonel John Young dated at New York 27th April In very obliging Terms acquainting me, That the Earl of Loudon General Abercromby and some others having recommended me to him, from thence he took occasion to desire my Services in his behalf and to Solicit Lord Loudons recommendation of him to Succeed Mr Dinwiddie in consequence thereof Mr. Dinwiddie having leave to return home I am Soliciting Lord Loudons recommendation of Mr Young & from the progress that I have made therein I have no reason to doubt of his Lordships recommendation taking place in favour of a Person so universally Esteemed as Colonel Young is and from his general good Character there is reason to expect a Harmony in Government the Event of this Solicitation you shall be acquainted of.

This comes by Mr Blair[2] a Gentleman whose Sobriety and attention to his Studys on the Law has gaind him friends here, by him I send the latest News Papers with the Kings Speech[3] Public Affairs abroad stand without any material variation from their appearance in these Papers and with regard to the Administration at home an arrangment of Offices is at last settled, every where but at the B of Trade from which Board the Earl of Halefax to the great concern of every Body has withdrawn. Negociations are in agitation to induce his Lordship to resume his Office but I am affraid this will not take place I cannot omit congratulating you on Mr Secretary Pitt Being reinstated his Services to the Colonys to Virginia in particular are too recent to be forgot by me who felt the benefit thereof in my Negociations for your Government I hope to have your acknowlegment of thanks to make him which I shall do with great pleasure as Gentlemen

LB, pp. 46–47. Sent "per Mr Blair."

1. Printed on pp. 199–200.

2. John Blair, Jr. (1732–1800), after studying at the College of William and Mary, entered the Middle Temple, London, in 1755. After returning to Virginia, Blair went on to become a burgess for the college 1766–1770, clerk of the Council 1770–1775, a delegate to the Philadelphia Convention of 1787, and a justice of the U.S. Supreme Court 1789–1796.

3. The king's speech of 4 July 1757, at the close of the fourth session of the Eleventh Parliament, is printed in *Parliamentary History*, 15:828.

To the Committee of Correspondence of North Carolina

Gentlemen   July 12th 1757

My last of 26 May[1] acquainted you with the Success of my Negociations upon the Several Addresses from the Province According to the Votes of Parlt then and now sent you, at the same time I told you, that as the Earl of Loudon as Comdr in Chief of His Majestys Forces in America might have the Superintendancy of the Money so granted by Parlt that you could not be too early in giving in your Claim to his Lordship according to the Merit of your pretensions, as you will See by Copy of my letter hereto annexed, And to the Contents thereof so far as relates to myself, I again take the liberty to beg your attention & Interposition with the Genal Assembly;[2] Nothing having happend relative to Provincial Matters since my last, except the payment made to me, by Mr David Barclay of the Proceeds of the Indigo remitted to me on account of the Province which having been taken by the Enemy the Money recovered on the Insurance and paid to me by Mr Barclay is £101.10.0 according to Mr Barclays Account herein inclosd. The Public Affairs of Europe have had no material alteration of late except in Bohemia where the King of Prussia by attacking Count Daun who was vastly Superior to him in Numbers and more advantagiously Situated was beat, the consequence whereof has been his being thereby obligd to raise the Blockade of Prague, and as both Armys are recruiting, another Battle is expected whereby the Fate of the German Cesar will be decided. If the King of Prussia proves victorious, he will be able to reinforce the D of Cumberland now much Inferior to the French in Westphalia, but by great Military Skill and address in shifting from Camp to Camp has hetherto keept them at Bay on the opposite side the Weser I hope that our American Affairs may be attended with Success and on this Occasion I cannot omit congratulating of you on Mr Secretary Pitts being reinstated in Office his late Services while in Office are too recent to be forgot by me who felt the good Effect of them in my Solicitations for your Province & it will give me pleasure to have your directions to acknowledge the Same to him with Thanks for His Services to the Province I am always with great regard Gentlemen

LB, pp. 47–48. Sent "per Convoy to S Carolina per Drayton."

1. Printed on pp. 187–188.

2. In the margin at about this point in the letter JA wrote, evidently later: "by this it appears that according to former letters Governor Dobbs had given in his claim to Lord Loudon for the Money by my advice to the Committee."

To Peyton Randolph

[15 July 1757]

Payton Randolph Attorney General of Virginia. July 15th 1757 per Mr Blair desire his assistance in the House of Burgesses payment of allowance on account of the Addresses to King & Parlt.[1]

LB, p. 48.

1. The journals of the House of Burgesses do not record that Randolph ever laid JA's request before it.

To John Tinker

Sir   London July 22d 1757

Since my letter of the 13th of last month[1] I have reced yours of the 29 of Feby[2] which came to hand the 18th inst by Tulleridge[3] whom I have not as yet seen personally, good Words will not answer my Services and therefore to tell you the Truth I did expect of you payment for my past Services before I was called upon to take up New Solicitations, if you are not long since reimbursed Your Money in consequence of my solicitations of the Kings order to the Board of Ordnance its not my Fault,[4] I could do no Service in that case than to get the Kings orders to Pay, thus I did after infinite trouble, I at the same time told you of the Demur made at the Board of Ordnance from the insufficiency of your Power of Attorney to Mr Baker[5] so that if your Attorneys here have not given you notice of this difficulty or if after notice you have not cleard up this point the delay is with Yourself as with them & not with me, But as I like to deal openly with you in the way of Business, I do again tell you that I expect to have your order on your Agent here for the ballance of my last account, and in time to come that is to say from the 20th Inst July I do expect & shall accordingly charge to the account of Government the annual Salary of 100 per an Ster as their Agent together with an allowance for my Disbursments and I desire that you do communicat these my stipulations and *Terms* to your Council & Assembly for their approbation or Disaprobation thereof that I may govern myself accordingly in the meantime I shall go with the Affairs of your Governt as their Agent, I have not seen Mr Baker these 12 Months whether he retird from Business or not I cannot tell, I mention this to you to let you see that I Shall have no dependances on his assistance or Interposition in what comes recommended to me of public Affairs, your Company matters I shall not concern myself with in any shape, this being a Letter pointedly to Business I shall confine it solely to that & conclude that I do expect your answer thereto by the first opportunity in the mean time I am very sincerly

PS   You will probably soon have a letter from the Board of Trade asking to have from you a State of the Islands as by a Plan of Defence then will be the time to suggest being put under the Board of Ordnance or for an annual Establishment for support of the fortifications.[6]

LB, p. 49–50. Sent "per Mr Drayton with Convoy."

    1. Printed on pp. 195–196.

2. Letter not found.

3. Not identified.

4. See JA to Tinker, 23 Dec. 1754, p. 131, n. 1.

5. Not identified.

6. On 23 June 1757 the Board of Trade read Tinker's letter of 12 Apr. 1757 "setting forth the expediency of making proper provision for the defence of those Islands, and referring to his letters to the Board during the last war for his opinion as to what may be proper to be done." The Board ordered that "a state be made from Governor Tinker's correspondence with the Board during the last war of what is therein represented as necessary to be done for putting the Islands under his government into a proper posture of defence, and that the said state be laid before the Board at their next meeting" (*JBT*, 10:327). At the Board's meeting of 1 July 1757, the secretary reported that in Tinker's correspondence "he found frequent representations of the expediency of augmenting the military establishment there, stationing two sloops to cruize amongst the Islands, and erecting a redoubt at Phenny's Hill and a small battery upon the point of Hog Island" *(JBT,* 10:329). The Board's resulting representation to the Crown of 12 July held that Tinker's previous correspondence was not a proper foundation on which to ground an opinion of what should be done, and the Board therefore "thought proper to direct [Tinker] to transmit a full and particular Account of the present actual State of defence of the [Bahamas], to the end that they may be enabled to form a Judgment of what is really necessary for their Security, and propose such measures to His Majesty" (*APC*, 4:148).

To John Young

Augt 3d 1757

Since my last[1] copy whereof is annexd I have repeated my Solicitations in your behalf at the Board of Trade for their Representation to the King in Council that you may be by his Majesty appointed to Succeed Mr Dinwiddy as Lieut Gover of Virginia Such is the Channel of Office in this and the like Cases, and such is the Right of Office incident to the Board of Trade, and accordingly My Lord President of the Council[2] & Mr Secretary Pitt (through which offices your appointment must also pass) have assurd me that you shall meet with no delay on their Part when the

Case comes before them, but til then they cannot take it up in the Way of Office; This being the Case no further progress can be made in your Affair until the Ministerial Negociations with Lord Halefax for inducing of him to resume his Office at the B of Trade are over one way or the other, and to say the truth His Lordship who wishes you extreamly well has given me the hint to suspend my Solicitation for some time lest it become necessary for your Interest and Service being in a Military Station, that his Royal Highness be made acquainted with this Matter, this Case therefore under such circumstances must be conducted with great prudence & Caution not only with regard to Lord Halifax himself but likewise with regard to the D of Cumberland provided his Lordship shall think himself obligd to communicate this matter to his Royal Highness previous to the Representation of the Board of Trade to the King in Council, But in whatever manner this Matter shall operate I have no reason to doubt of Success in the end, in the meantime I thought it right to let you know how it stands, and I have done the same to Your Friends here amongst others to Mr Adair to whom I see you have wrote on this Subject, as Lord Halefax is now & for some time past has been in the Country & from his situation arises a kind of Stagnation to all Business out of the ordinary Course I do not therefore under such circumstances expect that I shall be able to accomplish your Appointment before this October when the respective Boards resume their Activity preparatory for Parliamentary Business.[3]

European Affairs of late have taken no material turn, Battles in Westphalia, Bohemia, and in Pomerania are expected, our Secret Expedition goes on time will shew its destination[4] in the mean time France has taken the alarm towards their Coast, No News hetherto of Lord Loudons Arrival at Halefax nor of Admiral Holborns & from hence arises great anxiety.

LB, pp. 51–52. Sent "per Mr Harrison in the Mermaid."

1. JA to Young, 10 July 1757, pp. 201–202.

2. Earl Granville.

3. In fact, the Board of Trade did not reconvene until 3 Nov. (*JBT*, 10:333).

4. See JA to Swann, 4 June 1758, p. 260, n. 1.

To Robert Dinwiddie

Augt 9th 1757

I wrote you by 3 opportunitys of late by the Packet, Mr Blair & Capt Paterson,[1] with your Leave of absence from the Adjournment of the B of Trade til 20th Octr, both the Vacancy at that Board, by Lord Halefaxes not having come to a Resolution to resume by the Notification of the recommendation of Col Young to the D of C,[2] these are circumstances that will retard Col Youngs appointment, how far to objections I cannot say. I intend to apply to Parlt, for the free Importation of *Salt* desire the Instructions of Council & Assembly if they approve for my Support herein also credit here for the Expences attending it[3] My last years Services are under their Consideration, to a bill the Merchants object to the late Paper Currency Bill because it carrys no Interest as former Bills did, if 5 per cent which did Support the credit of the Currency and for that Reason they did not apply to have the Bill for 40000 in 1755 repeald, I am affraid of its Repeal if the Bill is, as they say it is[4]

LB, p. 52. Sent "per Mr Harrison in the Mermaid."

1. JA to Dinwiddie, 28 June, pp. 197–198, and 10 July 1757, p. 201.

2. Duke of Cumberland.

3. Dinwiddie laid this letter before the Council on 2 Jan. 1758 (*EJC*, 6:78). For the Council's instructions to JA on this matter, see JA to Blair, 31 Mar. 1758, pp. 250–252.

4. See JA to Dinwiddie, 3 Nov. 1757, pp. 211–212.

To John Young

October 20th. 1757

For three months past, by the resignation of the Earl of Hallifax, no matterial Business has been carried on by the Board of Trade, but through the Interposition of Mr Secretary Pitt, his Lordship has, within these few Days, been induced to reasume his office, and for that purpose comes to Town next week to go on with Business.[1] My former Letters acquainted you, how the Case of the Govert of Virginia Stood, so it has remained ever since, I am again at Liberty to prosecute this matter with Lord Hallifax, and by what Mr

Pownall tells me I apprehend a Difficulty may meet us, with regard to holding this Government together with your Military Employment, this has been thrown out by Lord Hallifax, tho', not in such a manner, as to imply a fix'd measure in bar of your Success, I therefore only make mention of it, to prepare you, by giving you time to consider of the Alternative, in Case it should come to rest there, whatever General Rules in Office, may have been laid down with regard to Goverts. in other Cases many reasons do naturally occur, and may be urged, from the nature and Locallity of your Millitary Service, for an exception in this Case. More of this after an Interview with Lord Hallifax.

I am extreamly glad you are got out of the Scrape of Fort Wm. Henry so well, you have lost some Blood but no honour;[2] least you had not an early opportunity of writing to Mrs Young, in order to prevent any impression from the false report of your being returned to the Secretary at War in Genl. Webbs List amongst the Dead,[3] for this was told me as from Lord Barrington,[4] however by exam[in]ing the List I immediatly found the mistake to have arisen from not having attended to the manner of arrangment of Names in this List, and from other hands, I heard that your Wounds were not dangerous, all which I notified to Mrs Young for her satisfaction; her being in the Country during my short Stay in Scotland prevented my seeing her there.

Now you are at large, may you not become your own Negociator at home, however this shall not prevent my Solicitations in your absence. Compts. to our friends with you concludes me always, very sincerely

LB, pp. 52–53. In a clerk's hand except for the routing memoranda in JA's hand. At the head of this letter JA wrote: "per Major Smith 9th Novr per Packet," and at the foot of this letter he wrote: "per the Packet to N Yorke."

1. Halifax was admitted to the cabinet (though not as a third secretary of state) and resumed his position as president of the Board of Trade.

2. Young was severely wounded when Fort William Henry, on Lake George, N.Y., fell to the French in Aug. 1757 (Brock, *Dinwiddie Papers*, 2:602n).

3. Brig. Gen. Daniel Webb had been left by Loudoun temporarily in supreme command of the British land forces, and his egregious military blunders were responsible for the loss of Fort William Henry. Webb was relieved of his office and called home: "It is therefore almost inexplicable that he continued to enjoy the

favour of men of high influence in the government and received, after leaving America, more than one promotion" (Gipson, *British Empire before the American Revolution*, 7:88).

4. William Wildman Barrington (1717–1793), second Viscount Barrington in the Irish peerage, was secretary at war 1755–1761 and 1765–1778.

To Robert Dinwiddie

Dr. Sr.   Nover. 3rd. 1757

Having none of your's to answer, I wish that my former Letters, with your Warrant for quiting the Govert. got safe. For three months past by Lord Hallifax's resignation, and by the usual adjournment of the Board of Trade this season of the year, nothing matterial has been done; his Lordship having reasumed his office, with the Cabinet annexed thereto, came to Town last week to go on with business, but is hetherto confined by the Gout, and sees no body.

I am likely to meet some Difficulty in Col. Young's Case; his holding the Govert. together with his military Employment, this Difficulty has been taken notice of by Lord Hallifax, tho' it is not carried so far, as to have become a fix'd poin[t], in bar of the Govt. if it does it must rest with Col. Young alone, to clear it up, as to which of the Employments he declines, this however need not hinder you, leaving a place, where your health is in danger.

In my last I informed you that the merchants had made mention to me of a Law lately passed in Virginia for Paper money making the same a Legal Tender, and that they were resolved to apply to have the same repealed, their objection principally rests on its being made Legal Tender, I have no instructions on this Law, nor do I find it at the Plantation Office, it will require very strong arguments to support it, if it is, as Mr Buchannan and others have stated it to me quo ad the Legality of the Clause of Legal Tender, for here lays the Stress of the Parliamentary, as well as that of the Mercantile objection to Paper money.[1]

The situation of our public affairs is so very disagreeable that I cannot dwell upon them with any Satisfaction, I refer you to the News papers.

The King and his Ministry having in the most solemn manner

disavowed the Convention made by the Duke of Cumberland for the Army of observation under his Commd. abroad, he no sooner came home, than he resigned his Empts. and retired to Windsor, Three Genls. The Duke of Marlbrough, Lord G. Sackville and Genl. Waldgrave are nominated to enquire into the Conduct of Genl Mordaunt, who commanded the late memorable Expedition to Rochfort, how far an Enquiry by such people may stifle the national Cry for a Parliamentary enquiry, to me is doubtful.[2]

Col Haldane has got the Govt of Jamaica,[3] your friend Col Heron lately arrived in Holland from the Danish Settlements in the East Indies, said to have brought home great Treasure, the spoils of a plundered Indian Town in our Alliance, Which banished him the service and Settlements of our East Indie Compy. is just now dead insolvent, as Mrs Heron who has been over in Holland gives out, so that her dependance is now on Mr Wright, just arrived as Agent for So. Carolina I long to see you, till then farewell with Compts to Mrs Dinwiddy and the Ladys, I am always most affectionatly Yours &c.

P.S. I hope young Mr Blair is arrived, I have reason to think that his Father will reap Some Benefit from my recommendation of him to the Auditor General.

LB, pp. 54–55. In a clerk's hand.

1. Merchants of London and Bristol opposed the legal tender clauses of "An Act declaring the law concerning executions; and for relief of insolvent debtors," passed in Oct. 1748, and "An Act for granting an aid to his majesty for the better protection of this colony, and for other purposes therein mentioned," passed in Apr. 1757 (Hening, *Statutes*, 5:526–540, 7:69–87). In a memorial to the Board of Trade, the London merchants objected to the provision of the second act that declared that the £80,000 (actually £180,000) in paper notes authorized to be issued and rated at proclamation money would be legal tender for all debts except the payment of quitrents. The merchants asked that an additional instruction be issued to the governor ordering him to urge the assembly to pass an amending act stipulating, among other things, "that all debts due & owing before the passing the said Acts shall remain & stand payable in Sterling money only" (*Fauquier Papers*, 1:38–41). (The memorial of the Bristol merchants, to the same effect, is CO 5/1329, fol. 57.)

The Board of Trade read both memorials on 21 June 1758. It agreed to consider the memorials and the act on 5 July and ordered the secretary to notify the merchants, former governor Dinwiddie, and "the agent." On 5 July the Board heard from all the interested parties and decided in favor of the merchants, presenting its recommendations to the Privy Council in a representation of 12 July 1758 (*JBT*, 10:410, 411–412; *APC*, 4:389–393). The result was an additional instruction to newly appointed Governor Francis Fauquier of 9 Feb. 1759 ordering him to act as the merchants had requested (*Fauquier Papers*, 1:172–173; Labaree, *Royal Instructions*, 1:237–238).

Fauquier communicated this instruction to the Council on 3 Sept. 1759, when the Council advised him that the requirements of the instruction had already been provided for and that it was therefore not necessary for him to call the assembly, although the Council advised him to lay the instruction before the assembly when it did meet (*EJC*, 6:145–146). On 1 Nov. 1759, in his opening address to the General Assembly, Fauquier reported that he had received the instruction and recommended that the assembly should consider the interests of British merchants in recovering their sterling debts and, if the merchants' interests were not already fully secured, provide full and ample security for them. The House quickly resolved that British property was secured in *"the fullest and amplest Manner"* by an act passed in 1755, for which see JA to Blair, 21 Mar. 1759, pp. 284–285, n. 2 (*JHB, 1758–1761*, 134, 141). The most lucid treatment of this complex problem is Joseph Albert Ernst, "Genesis of the Currency Act of 1764: Virginia Paper Money and the Protection of British Investments," *WMQ*, 3d ser., 22 (1965): 33–74.

2. Gen. Sir John Mordaunt (1697–1780) had commanded the land forces in the unsuccessful expedition of Sept. 1757 against the French naval base at Rochefort on the Charente, which flows into the Bay of Biscay. Pitt had conceived the expedition as a means of forcing the French to remove their troops from Germany and of striking a blow against French naval power. The expedition achieved the surrender of the island of Aix in the bay, but an attack on the mainland was called off as too hazardous. Mordaunt was censured by a military court of inquiry consisting of Charles Spencer (1706–1758), third duke of Marlborough; Lord George Sackville (1716–1785), later Germain; and John Waldegrave (1718–1784), afterwards third Earl Waldegrave, but a court-martial subsequently acquitted him.

3. The governorship of Jamaica had been vacant since the resignation of Adm. Charles Knowles early in 1756. (Henry Moore had been appointed lieutenant governor in Feb. 1756.) The Board of Trade recommended George Haldane on 26 Jan. 1758, and on the following day the Privy Council approved his commission (*JBT*, 10:211, 365, 370; *APC*, 4:273, 274, 369).

To Robert Dinwiddie

Novr 9th. 1757

Humanity added to my Connexions with Virginia having called upon me to assist the Bearer hereof Major John Smith, with my Solicitations, Mr Secretary Pitt being made acquainted with his Case, procured for him, from the Treasury, by way of free Gift

£100 to which Mr Pitt added as a mark of his approbation of the behaviour of this old Warior £20, with an order to the first Pacquet for New York to convey him to America, free of any Expence; and that no time might be lost, in an interview with Lord Loudoun, I have Mr Pitt's orders to send him to fallmouth directly, so that fitting off the poor old man out, leaves me no more time to tell you, that I have wrote fully by the Fleet now ready to sail for North America I am always Dr Sir Yours &c.

P.S. From Discoverys made by Mr Smith during his Captivity, I think good use may be made of him at the head of a Party, he is a brave old Warrior as Mr Pitts stiles him, I have no Letters as yet, by the Garland arrived some Days since.[1]

LB, p. 56. In a clerk's hand except for the routing memorandum in JA's hand, which reads: "per the Packett NB wrote of the 19th Novr by Mr Bailley."

1. Maj. John Smith, of the Augusta Co., Va., militia, had been captured at the fall of the fortified house of Ephraim Vause near the headwaters of the Roanoke River on 25 June 1756. Smith was the leader of about twenty-five defenders when a party of more than a hundred Indians and about twenty-five French Canadians attacked. Smith was eventually taken to Canada, where he was exhanged for French prisoners, and sent to England in 1757.

Before returning to Virginia in early 1758, Smith conceived a scheme (supposedly approved by Pitt) whereby a party of only 800 men "might, if properly conducted, easily destroy those [Shawnee Indian] Towns and perhaps some of the *French* Forts" (this from Smith's memorial, read by the House of Burgesses on 3 Apr. 1758). George Washington, Loudoun, Gen. John Stanwix, and Gen. John Forbes all thought Smith's scheme almost ludicrous (*JHB, 1752–1758*, 499; W. W. Abbot, ed., *The Papers of George Washington: Colonial Series*, vol. 5 [Charlottesville, 1988]). See also Charles F. Mullett, "Military Intelligence on Forts and Indians in the Ohio Valley, 1756–1757," *WMQ*, 3d ser., 3 (1946): 398–410.

To John Young

Sir.   Cravenstreet London Decer 9th 1757
My last of the 20th Octr.,[1] from conversation with Mr Pownall, did suggest to you some difficulty that might attend your appointment, as Lieut. Governor of Virginia, Since that, I find that however favorable is the opinion of Lord Halifax from a personal

acquaintance with you, yet, Such is the System, laid down in relation to American Goverts, together with some particular Circumstances arising from your Military Connexion, that from thence I am convinced, that such difficultys are not to be overcome, in the ordinary Course of Solicitation, how far an interposition of further & Stronger Solicitations added to your presence here on the spot, might get the better of such objections, I cannot take upon me to say.

But to do you and myself Justice, I cannot help leting you know, that from what has come in my way of Solicitation, I am sorry to say, that I have little hopes of success.

You will therefore be pleased to take it into Consideration, what is further to be done, and whether the pursuit of this Object ought to lead you out of your way. If this Case which is still open shall hereafter take a more favorable turn, you may be assured, that I shall to the utmost of my power improve it for your service I am &c.

LB, pp. 57–58. In a clerk's hand except for a marginal note in JA's hand, which reads: "Do 29 per the Express to Gblr [i.e., Gibraltar] tell him of Ld Loudons recall." A draft of this letter, in JA's hand and crossed through, is on pp. 56–57 of the letter book.

1. Printed on pp. 209–210.

To the Committee of Correspondence of North Carolina

[Gentlemen of the Committee]   Decr 15th 1757
It is now above 9 Months since I had the honour of hearing from you, my Several letters of the 26th of May last and the 12th of July[1] have not been acknowledged, the first to Mr Lewis's care from Plymouth, Copy by Mr Drayton I therefore transmit Duplicates by this opportunity of the Zephire Sloop of War which My Lords of the Admiralty on my Representation have been pleased to Station in No Car it is to be hoped that your Trade may avail itself of the Convoy from So Carolina or Virginia which tho not so regularly established as were to be wished for according to repeated Assurances given thereof never the less as they do occasionaly offer I

thought it my Duty heretofore to point out this expedient to Governor Dobbs for your Trade.[2]

Lord Halefax having resumed his Seat at the Board of Trade how soon he is able to go to the Office Plantation Affairs will go on as usual.[3]

It has no doubt occurrd to you that my Legal Authority as Agent for the Province ceased by the expiration of the Law on the 25th of March last and that my Solicitations Parliamentary & Ministerial in consequence of the Provincial Addresses have taken place since that.[4] Whatever may be the pleasure of your Government with regard to the Agency I must in a particular manner beg your assistance in the Case of my Arrears and if the Government does me the honour to continue me in their Service I must remind you of what I have heretofore said that I do expect an augmentation of my Salary to 200 per an that I may stand in the same degree with Agents for other Colonys in the meantime I shall do my endeavours to Serve the Province to the utmost of my Power I am with great regard Genlmn[5]

LB, p. 64. Sent "per the Zephire Sloop to Cape Fear." A draft of the first portion of the letter, crossed through, is on p. 58 of the letter book; another earlier version, almost twice as long as the letter as sent, is on pp. 59–60 of the letter book. The salutation is supplied from the second version, and substantive differences between the drafts and the letter as sent are accounted for in notes to the present letter. The position of this letter in the letter book suggests that it may have been written about 30 December, although JA retained the date of the earlier versions.

1. Printed on pp. 187–188 and pp. 204–205.

2. The draft on p. 58 includes the following passage: "In the first [26 May] I informd of the successful Issue of my Solicitations for Money £50000 was given by Parliament applicable by Lord Loudon in proportion to the Services of the Provinces of Virginia No Carolina & So Carolina, as my Solicitation in behalf of your province led the way for the rest, the greatest share I may add the whole of this Negociation fell upon me, and in my former letters I told how greatly I had been obliged to Mr. Secretary Pitt for his Services and from thence did suggest to you that the Thanks of the Province became due to him on this occasion."

The draft on pp. 59–60 stated that the present letter and copies of the two earlier letters were being sent "by this Opportunity of the Zephire Sloop of War which the Lords of the Admiralty on my representation that Ad: Holborn had not complyd with their Lordships directions heretofore given for sending a Sloop from his Squadron have been pleased to Station for No Carolina and by means of this Sloop it is to be hoped that your Trade may avail it self of the Convoys from So Carolina or Virginia, which tho not so regularly Established as were to be wished for, according to repeated assurances given thereof never the less as they do occasionaly offer I thought it my Duty heretofore to point out this expedient to his Exy Governor Dobbs for your Trade."

3. The draft on pp. 59–60 reads: "Lord Halifax having resumed his Seat at the Board of Trade, how soon he is recovered well enough to go to the Office Plantation Affairs will go on as before, Several Matters relative to your Province Laws and the Boundary Line are before them, Gover Lyttleton on the case of the Line has made his Report to their Lordships but the contents thereof are not as yet become publick."

4. The draft on pp. 59–60 reads: "It has no doubt occurred to you that my Legal Authority as Agent for the Province by the expiration of the Act of Assembly ceased on the 25th of last March 1756 [i.e., 1757] My several public Solicitations Parliamentary & others which have taken place since that having been undertaken while I had Authority so to do I ran no risk to my own character in pursuing the same but the case is now become more difficult where public Negociations of a new Nature are to be carryd on under the Character of an Agent, more especially in cases which become litigated of which two do at present occurr, That of the Boundary Line, in what manner the Lords for Trade may discuss this Matter I cannot at present say, if by way of Argument before them, my right of appearing as Agent may be called in question as I knew it done in the case of the agent for Pensilvania where the Law was new expird, another matter may arise in Parliament, I am informed that the agent for So Carolina is instructed to apply to Parliament for the Free Importation of Salt to So Carolina if this is the case I cannot by way of agent for N C Petition for the same liberty for No Carolina, in this Situation then I can only speak as a privat Person to my particular Friends to extend the Act & for that purpose I shall give the Agent for So Carolina what assistance I can."

In fact, JA's authority as agent did not end on 25 Mar. 1757. See JA to Dobbs, 13 Mar. 1758, p. 243, n. 3.

5. The draft on pp. 59–60 reads: "in the mean time having no notification that their Affairs are in other hands I shall do my Endeavours to serve the Province as far as in me lys & in particular I am with great regard Gentlemen."

To Robert Dinwiddie

Sir   London Decer 16 1757

I lay hold of a Ship masters taking his Letters away to inform you, that such difficultys have arisen in Col Youngs Case, as appear to me unsurmountable, a Military Person, Governor and a Military Lieut. Governor, are deemed Characters not properly adapted to the civil administration of Govrt. A Commander in Chief nominated in Cases, where the right of recommending is not admitted as absolute, is a Language, not at all understood, nor is a negociation of a matter of this nature by a Military Agent Mr Cal-c——t[1] through an indirect Channel, as I am told some months before, this matter came to me any wise approved of.

Under Such Circumstances, you will not be surprised, that my solicitation has proved abortive, at the same time, those with whom such matters do rest, have to me expressd the highest regard for Col Young from a personal acquaintance, in short Lord Loudouns Interest has not proved effectual, to carry this point in favour of his friend.

What turn it may take hereafter I cannot pretend to say, but in Justice to myself and to Col Young by last packet,[2] I have informed how the Case appears to me. Our friend Mr John Hanbury has had a Severe Stroke of the Palsy, by the Doctors account he has no Ground to hope for an absolute and entire Cure however he is greatly better. I beg your Care of the inclosed for North Carolina,[3] as it concerns me much that it go safe, My Compliments to you all, in hopes of seeing you soon, As Mr Fairfax tells me your Leave was come to hand, I am, &c

LB, p. 61. In a clerk's hand except for the routing memorandum in JA's hand, which reads: "per Ship from Mr Hanbury NB one inclosd for Robt Jones Esqr of No Carolina."

1. John Calcraft.

2. See JA to Young, 9 Dec. 1757, pp. 214–215.

3. See source note for this letter.

To John Rutherfurd

Decr 29 1757

I wrote you of the 13th May last by the New York Packet, of the 26th of same month by Mr Blair to Virginia;[1] In the first I told you that as Mr Swann did not incline to take money from you on my account to remit the same to me again in Indigo, That thereupon I did agree to your own proposition of having Indigo remitted to me of the best sort giving me Notice to Insure the same; I also told you that your agreement with me confirmed by Mrs Rutherford was that I should be paid out of the first Money comming in from Arrears, that notwithstanding of such agreement that by your last accounts transmitted home to the Auditor General I did observe that you had paid to the Heirs of the late Governor Johnston on the 15th of January 1755 the sum of 96 Ster which sum ought to come to me according to our agreement confirmd by your Several letters to me and more particularly by that of the 13th of May 1754 obliging yourself & Mrs Rutherford to pay me out of the first & readiest of the arrears the Sum of 807.6.6 Ster and charging the Estate of Govr Johnston accordingly, at the same time I desired to be informed by you what payments had been made to you by the Executors of the rest of the Officers upon whom you have orders for paying of me more particularly that of the Executrix of Mr Chief Justice Hall & of Mr Secretary Rice,[2] That tho as Deputy Auditor General these payments may come before me never the less I desired to have an exact account from you of all Payments that had been made of Arrears & how much thereof is now in your hands on my account besides what I do observe from your similar Accounts transmitted to the Auditor General & here let me observe to you that Mr Cholmondely is greatly surprisd that no Accounts are come home since that of 30th April 1755 Duplicates at all times seem to be sent home, and to prevent complaints against you what you may expect it will be for your Interest with the Auditor General that I have Duplicates sent to me lest his Deputy neglect transmitting your Accounts I in my former letters told you that the Governor had opposed your comming home while the Affairs of the Quitrents are so far in arrear, & nothing will get over this, but Sickness making your leaving the Province absolutly necessary Pray what you have done as to the Governors Arrears, I have very lately discovered a Secret Negociation going on for Salarys to the Council of No Carolina payable out of the Quitrents of the Province,[3] had you known of this affair you could not but have seen how much it must affect the Property of the Creditors of the late officers of the Revenue who have no other Remedy but from the Arrears, however advisable it may be for the Crown to grant Salarys to the Council but where privat property is at stake, you may be assurd that Mr Adair the Bishop of Worcester[4] & Several others will oppose this Negociation I am astonished, that you have been Silent on this head, the thing has been a Secret to me till lately, and I desire that your knowledge thereof may not come as from me, but take your own Measures, by way of Petition to the King, or to the Secretary praying that no other appropriation may be made till the arrears are paid off, because your Property will be thereby affected, unles that the payment of arrears are first provided for before such Salarys take place.

You may assure yourself that for my own sake who am so large a Creditor I shall attend to this affair, when I am paid off I think that the rest of the Creditors may be brought to an easy composition for their Debts this I hinted to you before, Lord Walpole[5] has given me a hint of this as to his fathers arrears, propose a bargain & I shall fix it here with his Lordship Complets to Mrs Rutherford

29th PS Since the above letter I have yours that is a Copy according to custom without any date, which I reced the 23d instant by Capt Pilkington, the original not come to hand, thereby I am to have as you tell me a more particular letter of Public & privat concerns by Col Innes by the New York Packet as the Indigo is so bad in the Market I shall expect none from you, but how are Naval Stores, it is very mortifying that I am able to get no Remittances from you no not one penny since you came to the Administration of Gover Johnstons Estate neither on his nor on any other Persons account does the Money that you have in your hands on my account lay dead or does any Interest accrue to me thereupon, You say you shall do the best for my Interest, but what is the best I hope you will let me know by your next letter.

It concerns yourself as well as it does me that you make the most of the Quitrents & while you do your Duty as an Officer of Government and as an honest Man to the Publick & those you have to deal with I think you need not be affraid of Gover Dobbs's resentment, if your health shall require your absence for 12 Months let the state of your health be certifyd, & I shall not doubt of geting 12 Months leave for you, I shall lay your last letter to me setting forth the pains you are taking about the Quitrents before my Principal[6] & do not doubt of being able to give him a favorable impression of your attention to the Revenue, What becomes of Mr Dobbs's Quitrents for his thousands of Acres, I see none upon your last Receipt of Rents perhaps his Excely may be more attentive to the Case of others than his own, it is long since I had the honour of any of his letters or of the Committees Adieu.

LB, pp. 62–63. Sent "per two Ships under soone Convoy of the Zephire."

1. Printed on pp. 181–183 and p. 189.

2. See JA to Rutherfurd, 26 Feb. 1754, p. 106, and JA to Executors of Nathaniel Rice, [ca. 5 July 1754], p. 124.

3. See JA to Rutherfurd, 10 Feb. 1758, pp. 222–223.

4. The Rt. Rev. Isaac Maddox (1697–1759) was bishop of Worcester 1743–1759.

5. Horatio Walpole (1723–1809), eldest son and heir of the late auditor-general and afterwards first earl of Orford (of the second creation).

6. Cholmondeley.

To the Committee of Correspondence of North Carolina

Janry 1t 1758

I tell them since my last[1] that by some conversation at the Board of Trade that I am apprehensive that the Law for Quieting Possession being part of the Quitrent Law & of the same purpose ought not to have been assented to by the Governor while the Q Rent Law was depending it is contrary to his Instructions to pass Such Laws[2] nothing further having occurd since my last I am Gentlemen

LB, p. 65. In the margin at the head of this letter JA wrote: "NB by the same convoy arrivd," probably a reference to the *Zephire*, which carried other letters from JA to North Carolina. This letter was enclosed in a letter to Governor Dobbs of 17 January 1758 (see following entry). The addition of part of a complimentary close to his summary of a letter written (or to be written) is unusual for JA.

1. JA to North Carolina Committee of Correspondence, 15 Dec. 1757, pp. 215–216.

2. The North Carolina assembly passed "An Act to quiet freeholders in the possession of their lands, and other purposes" on 15 Oct. 1755 (*NCSR*, 23:432–434), while the Jan. 1755 quitrent act (for which see JA to North Carolina Committee of Correspondence, 9 July 1755, above) was still under consideration. The new act was passed without a suspending clause, which constituted a violation of the governor's instructions not to "assent to any bill or bills . . . of unusual or extraordinary nature and importance wherein our prerogative or the property of our subjects may be prejudiced" without such a clause (Labaree, *Royal Instructions*, 1:144). Because the new act had several provisions "being in Substance the same as those contained for the like purposes" in the earlier act, and because the earlier act was still under consideration, the Privy Council disallowed the new act on 2 Feb. 1759 (*APC*, 4:402).

To Arthur Dobbs

[17 January 1758]

To Governor Dobbs inclosing the Commees Lre[1] 17th Janry 1758 desire him to lay same before the Committee.

LB, p. 65.

1. See preceding entry.

To Samuel Swann

[17 January 1758]

To Mr Swann per Do Convoy see Lre in Bundle for No. Carolina Janry 17th 1758.

LB, p. 65.

To John Rutherfurd

Sir   Feby 10th 1758

Since my last to you,[1] I have been informed that Governor Dobbs has made Application for Salarys of £50 Sterling pr Annum to the Members of the Council for the time being, and that his application is grounded, on a Supposition and Declaration, that the Quitrent Fund is fully able to pay Arrears, the present Annual Salarys and at the same time the Salarys now proposed for the Council (600£. st) this by no means appears to be the Case by your Accompts returned to the Auditor General.

I shall be sorry to obstruct any measure that has a tendency to serve the Gentlemen of the Council or Government, but Justice to myself as well as to the rest of the Creditors of the Late Governor Johnston (and of other Officers of that Government also dead) who have no prospect of relief, but from the arrears of Quitrents due to such Officers, will oblige me to use my Endeavours to prevent such or any appointments out of the Quitrents, upon the same Grounds and reasons which prevented Govor Dobbs's Salary taking place upon that Fund, til such time as the Arrears are in some Degree paid off at least till there appears a better prospect of the Quitrents producing a Sinking Fund over and above the Annual Salarys to the Officers of Government already on the Establishment, and who first of all must be paid. Till this is done creating new Establishments will injure the present Offic[e]rs of Government, the Creditors of those who are dead, & at the same time be of no real service to the Gentlemen of the Council, but on the Contrary deprive them of the Salarys which they now have by Law from the Province.[2]

On this occasion the Auditor General will expect, and I am authorised by him to call upon you for your report on the State of the Quitrents that he may thereby be able in virtue of his Office to lay the same before the Lords Commrs. of the Treasury more fully than can be done by the Accounts of Quitrents, now in the Auditor Generals Office and as Cases of this nature do in the Course of Office come referred to the Auditor General of the Plantation Revenues, you will lose no time to Inform him thereof, in the meantime I cannot help being surprised that an Application of this nature, should be made in behalf of the Council of which you are a Member, and no notice taken thereof by you when the nature of such Application has so near a Relation to your office of Receiver of the Quitrents &c which it is your Duty to inform the Auditor General off I am

PS   do not forget to remark to the Aud Genal on the Remission of large Arrears or Debts & the Collectors Lands to the Dimi[nishm]ent of the Revenue.

LB, pp. 65–66. In a clerk's hand except for the dateline, complimentary close, and postscript in JA's hand. JA also wrote at the foot of this letter: "per Convoy of the Zephire & Mr Bridgen" and "NB I laid this letter before Mr West."

1. JA to Rutherfurd, 29 Dec. 1757, pp. 218–220.

2. Councillors in royal colonies were not remunerated for their services in an executive capacity. In some colonies, such as Virginia, they were compensated for their service as judges of the General Court or other colonial courts. In North Carolina they were allowed a stipend of 7 shillings and 6 pence proclamation money per day during their attendance at the General Assembly, in their legislative capacity as the upper house of the assembly (Labaree, *Royal Government*, 163–164).

In a letter to the Board of Trade of 30 May 1757 (*NCCR*, 5:761–764) Dobbs enclosed a petition of 28 May to the king from the North Carolina councillors (*NCCR*,

5:760–761) asking for an allowance out of the quitrent revenues in consideration of "not only great Fatigue and Trouble but a very great expence" in fulfilling their responsibilities in the Council and in the several courts in which they sat as judges. The petition was referred by the Privy Council's Plantation Committee to the Board of Trade, which on 22 Dec. 1757 reported that Dobbs had informed the members that the quitrents "are daily improving, and will, if properly collected, soon be able to discharge all the Arrears now due from them, as well as to pay the whole establishment of the Province." The Board therefore recommended that the request be granted, and stated that "as six hundred pounds was the yearly Sum originally allowed to the Judges of the General Court of the Colony of Virginia," the same amount to each member of the North Carolina Council "may be a proper allowance on the present Occasion" (*NCCR*, 5:788). On 16 Jan. 1758 the Plantation Committee referred to the Treasury the petition and the Board's favorable report of 22 Dec. 1757 (*APC*, 4:361), but the Treasury evidently balked at the proposal, for the Council and later governors of the colony made similar applications for remuneration for the Council in 1768, 1770, and 1773 (*NCCR*, 7:698–699, 799–800; 8:211; 9:375–376, 646–647).

To John Rutherfurd

Dr Sir.   February 20th 1758

Since my last to you of the 10th inst.[1] I have represented to the Secretary of the Treasury, also to the Secretary to the Board of Trade, the Case of the Arrears of Quitrents, and have laid before them, Copie of my letter to you hereupon, this will probably hinder Govr. Dobbs's Application for New Salarys taking place, till your State of the Quitrents comes to the Auditor General, who has interposed in this matter, in Virtue of his Office.

In Consequence of what I have done, I shall be called upon to Authenticate my Right on the Quitrents, for payment of the Debt due to me by the late Govr. for which Mrs Rutherfurd[2] and yourself stand bound; I do therefore desire, that by the first safe Conveyance by the New York Packet, if none offers from Virginia under Convoy, that Mrs Rutherfurd & yourself as Executors to the Late Governor Johnston, do send me a formal Assignment of the first, and the readiest of the Arrears, due by way of Salary, out of the Quitrents, as a further Security for the payment of the said money, as it now stands charged by you to the Estate of the said Governor Johnston, this will enable me to support the Application, that I have made, and at the same time I advise you & Mrs

Rutherfurd to write a joint Letter to the Auditor General, open for my perusal and delivery, seting forth, that by the Will of the Late Governor Johnston, the Arrears of Salary out of the Quitrents, are devised for payment of his Creditors, and in fact, are the only means whereby his Creditors, as well as the Creditors of the other Officers deceased, can expect relief, by this means the Auditor General will be enabled, to set forth the same to the Lords of the Treasury, I am affraid that a Vessel to Mr Lewis with Turpentine got safe into Jersey comming from thence is taken or lost, I hope I have no concerns therein, She has been long missing my Compliments to Mrs Rutherfurd, I am &c[3]

LB, pp. 66–67. In a clerk's hand.

1. See preceding letter.

2. Formerly Mrs. Gabriel Johnston.

3. This is the last communication to Rutherfurd in the letter book, except for the memo of a letter written about 28 Mar. 1762. Rutherfurd finally received a royal warrant on 5 Feb. 1761 (T 52/51, p. 437) for the payment from the South Carolina quitrents of the arrears due to Johnston's estate. Mrs. Rutherfurd died in 1768; by the time of Rutherfurd's death in 1782, he had received from the South Carolina quitrents all but £2,018 of the more than £13,000 of arrears, but the remainder of the claims of Johnston's heirs were not settled until 1798. It seems unlikely that JA ever received the money Johnston had owed him ([Janet Schaw], *Journal of a Lady of Quality; Being the Narrative of a Journey from Scotland to the West Indies, North Carolina, and Portugal, in the Years 1774 to 1776*, ed. Evangeline W. Andrews and Charles M. Andrews [New Haven, 1921], 294–295, 308, 310–312).

During Mr Fauquieres Govert Commencing Jany 1758[1]

To John Blair

Sir   London March 3rd 1758

In answer to my Letters March 10th. May 27th. June 28th July 12th.[2] am favored with yours, in behalf of the Council, bearing date 23rd Decer.[3] by Mr Dinwiddy, and thereby I have the satisfaction, to learn that my Conduct in the service of the Colony is approved of.

By Mr Secretary Pitts confinment by the Gout, Governor Dinwiddy, has not hitherto been able, to present your Address of thanks for his services, but will lay hold of the first opportunity of doing it.[4]

I am obliged to you, and to the rest of the Gentlemen of the Council for your attention, to what my former Letters suggested to you, with regard to extraordinary trouble and Expences, and for the Assurance you give me, that you shall recommend the same accordingly to the next Assembly; but wish I had done as Mr Leheup used to do, by giving in my Accompt of my Expences incurred, and also at the same time refer the Consideration of a Gratuity for extra trouble, this shall be observed in time to come, and with regard to past services, I beg Leave to lay before the Council the Accounts inclosed as seperately charged to the Council, and to the Assembly, whereupon you will observe the Articles of money actually paid by me, for Fees of Office are distinguished, from my personal Expences,[5] such as relate to the Assembly, you will be pleased to recommend accordingly, & what concerns the Governor and Council will come immediately under their consideration, and on this occasion permit me to remark, that there are two Standing and Capital Articles of Expence attending the Agent (viz) Coach and Chair hire & Gratuitys at Christmas to Public Offices, and to servants of the Ministers of State; Coach or Chair hire at a moderate Computation, from the variety of Business going through my hands in the City & Court end of the Town amounting at least to 40£ pr An: that of Gratuitys to Servants &c 25 Guineas, these Articles alone, if not made good to me, adding thereto postage, and other incidental personal Expences, naturally arising from the Service, will reduce the Establishment for my Labour and trouble to a very narrow Sum, scarcely adequate to the Business of State and Government, for the Govr. and the Council alone, exclusive of Assembly Business. I must therefore submit the Case to your Consideration, both with regard to the Council as well as the Assembly.

Colonel Youngs Military Situation & Connexions, have stood in his way of being Lieutenant Governor of Virginia, Mr Dinwiddy is Succeeded by Mr Fauquier a Gentleman of whose Capacity and Abilitys the King and his Ministers (and none more so than the Earl of Hallifax) have very high regard, and from the Late intercourse that my connexions with your Government have given me with

Governor Fauquier, I can take it upon me to Assure you, and the Gentlemen of the Council that no Governor ever went abroad better disposed to make a people happy.

He does me the honor to take Charge of this Letter, and wishing you a good and harmonious Administration, I conclude with my hearty thanks to the Gentlemen of the Council, and to yourself, for the regard you are pleased to express for my past services, which encourages me to continue therein. You will be pleased to pay my respects to them, and believe me on all occasions very Sincerely Yours &c.

LB, pp. 68–70. In a clerk's hand except for the heading above the letter in JA's hand.

1. Francis Fauquier (1703–1768) was lieutenant governor of Virginia from 1758 until his death. His appointment was announced in Jan. 1758, his commission was issued the following month, and he arrived in Virginia in June.

2. JA's letter to Blair of 10 Mar. 1757 has not been found. His letters to the Virginia Council of 27 May, 28 June, and 11 (not 12) July 1757 are printed on pp. 190–191, 199–200, and 203–204.

3. Letter not found. For its contents, see JA to Blair, 5 Mar. 1758, below.

4. See JA to Virginia Council, 27 May 1757, pp. 191–192, n. 5.

5. The enclosed accounts have not been found, but they were likely similar to, or copies of, the accounts JA enclosed in his letter to Blair of 8 Mar. 1758, pp. 236–238.

To Samuel Swann

Cravenstreet March 4th. 1758

Last nigh[t] Mr Rutherfurd arrivd in Town, but brought me no Letters, there being company with me when he called upon me, I only learnd that he was under Suspension from the Council, and from his Office of Receiver General, in neither of which Cases he seems sanguine for restoration, but more disposed, to mind his private affairs.[1] As these matters lie between the Governor and him; I am resolved to take no share in the Contest as provincial Agent, which by him, I find still rests with me, notwithstanding Mr Bridgens and others information to the Contrary, which seem'd by no means impossible, considering I have had no letters from your Govt. for many months past,[2] from the little Conversation that I have had with Mr Rutherfurd, the situation of Affairs in your Province denote Contests in Government, which must in such event, hurt the public as well as priviet Int. I am here up[on] led to be more urgent in what I have heretofore suggested to you, as the most likely way to Discharge my Demands on your Government, and from whence my own services intitle me to payment (viz), out of the money granted last session of Parliament to Lord Loudoun, for behalf of North Carolina, as this money must either still remain in Lord Loudons hands, or come remitted to Governor Dobbs for the use & benifit of the public; if not remitted to the Province. It of Course will come into my friend Genl Abercromby[s] hands for the same purposes, upon application therefore to him, for his Bill in my favour, as so much of the money appropriated by Parliament towards the service of North Carolina, he will not hesitate to grant the same, and for this purpose I shall advise him thereof and in this matter I beg the favour that you will concurr according as you find the money is, or not remitted to the Governor.

I cannot conclude my Letter without telling you, as I find that you and your brother are Securitys to the Crown for Mr Rutherfurd as Receiver General, that I do no[t] find in the Auditor General's office, that at any time during Mr Rutherfurd's being in Office, any fraude or Imbezzlement of the Revenues is laid to his Charge it may be for your satisfaction to know this, but as to the reasons for his being Suspended, I am as yet ignorant of, however So soon, as they are laid before the Treasury, of Course they will be communicated to the Auditor General, and from thence to me, and so far as may concern you or your Brother, as his Security to know, shall be notified to you. I am &c.

LB, pp. 75–76. In a clerk's hand.

1. Soon after his arrival in North Carolina, Dobbs encountered difficulties with John Rutherford, receiver general of quitrents, whose inefficient practices Dobbs attempted to improve. After several irregularities had been discovered, Dobbs, with the approval of the Council, in Dec. 1757 suspended Rutherfurd from his positions as councillor and receiver general. Rutherfurd had traveled to England to plead his case directly. In 1759 he was restored as receiver general, and in 1761 he was restored to the Council.

2. Edward Bridgen (d. 1787) was a London merchant who had extensive landholdings in North Carolina. Bridgen was at various times an alderman of London,

a fellow of the Royal Society, a member of the Royal Society of Arts, and treasurer of the Society of Antiquaries. In 1765 Bridgen himself had designs on the North Carolina agency, and in that year and the next he lobbied for the repeal of the Stamp Act.

To Arthur Dobbs

Sir.   Cravenstreet March 4th 1758
   Last night Mr Rutherfurd arrived here, I find under Suspension from Council and Office of Receiver General of the Quitrents, there being Company with me, amongs[t] others Governor Dinwiddy I had very littl[e] Conversation with him on Carolina matters, however I observe, that he is by no means Sanguine, in the Case of his Suspension, on the Contrary, is resolved to have no more to do in Government affairs. I find by him that the Report currently affirmed here, by some people connected with your Province, that your affairs were in the hands of another Agent is groundless, I should have taken it unkind in my friends, to have delt so abruptly by me, without notice of such Event likely to take place, and without provision for my Arrears, and hereupon I must earnestly desire your kind Interposition and Assistance, that provision may be made for all deficiencys of Salary &c. And as Remetances are so very difficult to be made, and when made have hitherto turned out to the disadvantage of the Public, and my Disappointment in the sale of Commoditys remitted home, I must therefore desire to have remittances made me by Bills of Exchange, or other ways from the mony comming to your Government from Parliament, Granted by my Solicitation, Justice and my services, do entitle me to your Consideration hereon, and on this particular occasion, allow me to say, that I have not been treated as I might have expected from your Government, My Letters on this service, have not so much as been acknowledged, nor have any acknowledgments been made in behalf of the Province to the King's Ministers, as desired by my letters for their good Offices, I did them justice in my advice thereof to the Province, I did the same for Virginia, they attended thereto and in a very handsom manner, returned their address of thanks to the Secretary of State and Chanceller of Exchequer,[1] I wish your Government had done the

same, because the Interposition of the Secretary of State and
Treasury is still absolutely necessary, to bring this Grant of mony
home to you. For upon Examination I find that this mony so
granted by Parliament, remains still in the Treasury, not to be
issued from thence to the Commander in Chief of the Kings Forces
in America according to the Destination of Parliament, till such
time, as he shall have fixed the respective Proportions due to each
of these Provinces, Virginia No Carolina and So Carolina. I gave
your Government early notice to give in their Claim to Lord
Loudoun as Commander in Chief.[2] But not one word has been said
to me of any Step taken therein, so that I cannot tell how to
proceed If my interposition with my friend Genll Abercromby
Successor to Lord Loudon, be of any Service to your Govert as the
money must now pass through his hands in Consequence of
Instructions to be given from the Treasury or Secretary of State, it
shall not be wanting so soon as I know how the Case stands,
between your Govert and him, with regard to your Proportion
fixed by him Virginia have given in their claim to Lord Loudoun
upon the footing of the several Aids of money raised by their Genll
Assembly for Military services during the war, previous to the
Grant of Parliament,[3] this indeed seems to be the best and only rule
Whereby to apportion this parliamentary Grant. In my private
opinion your proportion should be made in Specie Gold and Silver,
so as to sink your paper Currency, at lea[s]t the kind of it, that is by
all accounts in so detrimental a State both as to the Public and
private Credit,[4] I advise you to lose no time, in your application to
General Abercromby as Commander in Chief, in the Case of this
money, and get your proportion fixed, if it is not done soon, I shall
not be surprized, to find the money appropriated to other and
more pressing purposes of Govert in America. I shall not concern
myself directly nor indirectly in the Case of your Suspension of Mr
Rutherfurd from Council, but the large Demand I have from
Governor Johnston's Estate, payable from the Arrears due to that
Estate, and from the personal regard, that I have for my good
friends Messrs Samuel and John Swanns, who stand Securitys to
the Crown for Mr Rutherfurd, as receiver General of the Quitrents
will give me great Concern, in Case Fraude or Embezzlement of the
Revenue shall have occasioned his Suspension from Office, from
any thing that has occurred to me from the Auditor Generals

office, I have no foundation to charge him with misdemeanors of this nature whereby his Securitys must have been affected, I beg that you will take the first opportunity by the New York Packet to inform me, what is done as to the Payments of my Arrears now as by Account transmitted to the Committee of Assembly ammounting to £586.19. Sterling I am

LB, pp. 77–78A. In a clerk's hand.

1. See JA to Virginia Council, 27 May 1757, pp. 191–192, n. 5.

2. See JA to North Carolina Committee of Correspondence, 26 May 1757, pp. 187–188.

3. On 5 Nov. 1757 Dinwiddie proposed to the Virginia Council that a committee be appointed to write a representation to Loudoun "setting forth the many large Supplies raised by this Government since the Commencement of the War with France towards promoting His Majesty's Service, whereby his Lordship may be better enabled to judge what Part of the said Aid this Government is justly intitled to." On 12 Nov. the Council read and approved the letter drafted by William Nelson, Richard Corbin, and Philip Ludwell Lee, and on 14 Nov. the letter was signed by the Council (*EJC*, 6:72–73, 74). The letter (not found) evidently itemized the £207,600 raised by Virginia for defense. Loudoun replied on 17 Jan. 1758 that he "had not received any Account from the King's Ministers, either of the granting of that Money, or his being to have any Share in the disposing of it, and assuring that if the Division of that Money is intrusted to him, he shall make the Rule of Equity his Guide in it" (*EJC*, 6:81). For the renewal of this application to Loudoun's successor, see JA to Fauquier, 15 Mar. 1758, pp. 244–245.

4. For JA's recommendation that North Carolina use its portion of the £50,000 appropriation to sink its paper currency, see JA to Swann, 19 Apr. 1758, pp. 254–255.

To John Blair

Sir   London March 5th 1758

On the 3d instant I had the honour to answer yours on behalf of the Council, of the 23rd of last Decer. relative to two Applications on the part of your Province;[1] The first an aid from the Kings Quitrents, to make good the Deficienceys of the Tobacco Revenue, which now properly concerns the Governor and Council.[2] The last being for Relief from Parlt. from an Act lately passed against the Exportation of Grain &c. which Case you observe may be taken up by the General Assembly, with regard to the insuing Crop, the last not being worth Exportation, and consequently I presum not within the mischief of the Act.[3] By way of instructions on carrying on these applications, you direct me to consult with Governor Dinwiddy, and act by his advice and herein your orders shall be punctually complyd with, and I shall have the pleasure to acquaint you, that from the Ceremonial Progress that he has made upon his arrival amongst the Kings Ministers of all Ranks, I never was witness to a more kind and favorable Reception.

To thankfull acknowledgments for a wise prudent and national[4] Administration, has been added a very great Concern that his health did not permit him to continue longer therein, from such tockens of Approbation, and regard, I have reason to conclude that Mr Dinwiddy's interposition on this, or any other occasion will add weight to my Negociations, which in these particulars, Matters shall be taken up, so soon as Mr Dinwiddy is settled.

Mr. Cholmondeley being in the Country for a few days, your Letters has been transmitted to him;[5] on his return, I shall have them together, with the State of the Tobacco Revenue under my Consideration, I am &c.

LB, pp. 70–71. In a clerk's hand.

1. JA to Blair, 3 Mar. 1758, pp. 225–227.

2. The Virginia Council sought from the Crown permission to replenish the revenue usually derived from the two-shillings-per-hogshead tobacco export tax with revenues from the quitrents. A memorial to the Treasury submitted by JA about 15 Mar. on behalf of Fauquier and the Council (*Fauquier Papers*, 1:7–8) explained that the production of tobacco for several years had been greatly diminished "from the Extraordinary Exigencys of Government, and from many of the Inhabitants being obliged to quit their Settlements, and from various other Causes and Calamitys of War," and stated that as of 25 Oct. 1757 the two shillings account showed a deficit of almost £500. The memorial further stated that from Oct. 1744 to June 1756 more than £3,000 from the two shillings account had been applied "in Aid of Quitrents, and by way of Contingent Charges, for Deficiencys in the Quitrent mony, and for other special Services of Government, usually provided for, out of the Quitrents" and asked that the £3,000 be replaced to the two shillings account.

3. "An Act to prohibit for a limited time, the exportation of corn, meal, malt, flour, bread, biscuit, starch, beef, pork, bacon and other victual . . . from his Majesty's colonies and plantations in America, unless to Great Britain or Ireland, or to some of the said colonies and plantations" (30 George II, chap. 9). The "Application" has not been traced, nor do the journals of the Council shed light on it.

4. JA's clerk may have mistranscribed the word *rational* here.

5. Letters not found.

To Richard Corbin

Sir.   Cravenstreet March 6th. 1758

I am favoured with your obliging Letter of 24th Decer by Governor Dinwiddy.[1] It gives me very great Satisfaction, that my Zeal in the service of the Province meets with the approbation of his Majestys Council, so far as think me deserving of an adequate reward for my past services, which have been branched out into a variety of negociations, more particularly set forth in the account of Contingent Expences, now transmitted by me to the President Mr Blair to be laid before the Council for their Consideration.[2]

In my Letter to the President, it escaped me to observe, the great pains I have taken with the merchants trading to Virginia, to reconcile them to the Paper Currency, lately issued by Act of Assembly, and to prevent an application on their part for having the Act repealed.[3]

I find some of them extreamly sanguine in this case from an apprehension, that their sterling Debts as they term them, must be depreciated by payment in Paper money, while this matter is agitated, it happens well, that from Governor Dinwiddy's representation of the State of the Case, upon the Absolute necessity of such measure, arising from the New Circumstances of the Province, I shall be able to maintain the Act, and from this Negociation with the Merchants, I may at the same time hope, to engage the approbation of the Assembly, and the rather, by my having declined, a proposition made me, some months since on the part of the merchants for becomming their Solicitor in mercantile Concerns, with an Annual Sallary for so doing, but this I could not accept of least it might occasionally (as in the present Case) have interferd with my Duty to the Province, how far this may avail me in my Plea with the Council, for being allowed my Contingent Expences as Stated in my Letter to the President, or by way of an Addition to my Salary from the Assembly for their Business which Mr Dinwiddy tells me has been talked of, I must leave to your Consideration.

Another Mercantile matter has been proposed to me, by the Agent for South Carolina in Consequence of his Instructions, Viz, an application to Parliament for the liberty of importing Baysalt into the Southern Provinces, as done to the Northren Provinces, the like application a few years since, on the part of these Provinces did miscarry, nevertheless we are resolved to attempt it once more, in this or the next Session of Parliament as we shall be advised, in the mean time it may be proper to give me particular Instructions on this head to Justify my application to Parliament in behalf of Virginia.[4]

In the Interim, the two Cases recommended to me by Mr Blair,[5] shall be taken up so soon as Govr Dinwiddy (by whose advice I am instructed in these Cases to conduct myself) is properly settled; as to any assistance from Mr Hanbury I am sorry to tell you, that I can expect none, a late Stroke of the Palsy having disabled him in public as well as in private affairs.

Your good opinion of your Late Governor is fully confirmed by the kind reception, he has met with from the Ministry upon his arrival, His Successor Mr Fauquiere promises very fair for a happy & harmonious Administration in Government, and this I most sincerely wish you I am &c

LB, pp. 79–79A. In a clerk's hand.

1. Letter not found.

2. See JA to Blair, 8 Mar. 1758 and enclosure, pp. 236–238. John Blair (1687–1771) served on the Virginia Council from 1745 until his death (and as acting governor on four occasions) and was deputy auditor of Virginia from 1728 until his death.

3. See JA to Dinwiddie, 3 Nov. 1757, p. 212, n. 1.

4. The New England and middle colonies were allowed to import salt directly from Europe, but the southern colonies could not bring salt from Europe unless it had been landed in England and a duty paid before transshipment. In 1749 South Carolina agent James Crokatt unsuccessfully memorialized the Board of Trade for the right to bring salt directly from Europe. Agents for Virginia and South Carolina petitioned again in 1763 and 1765, and agents for Virginia and North Carolina petitioned in 1771, all unsuccessfully. See JA to Fauquier, 6 Feb. 1764, p. 419 (*NCCR*, 9:208–209; Lonn, *Colonial Agents*, 168–169).

JA and James Wright, agent for South Carolina, do not seem to have petitioned Parliament on this matter.

5. See preceding letter.

To John Blair

Cravenstreet March 7th. 1758

Your public Letters to me as Agent, being already answered, I am now to acknowledge yours of the 16th Decer. as Deputy Auditor,[1] So soon as Mr Cholmondeley became fully informed of the Nature of your Duty, his own Consideration and Generosity induced him to depart from all thought of reducing your Establishment under him, & whatever might have been suggested in his first Letters to you, tending to the reduction of your Allowance, I am satisfied, arose from insinuations, that your Duty and trouble became more easy, at the same time that your Emoluments were advanced, afterwards finding that this was not the Case, no hesitation was made to continue you in Office, under the same terms, as his Predecessor did,[2] and I have not the smallest Grounds, to doubt of his being extreamly well disposed towards you, and you may be assured, that nothing shall be wanting on my part, to maintain his good opinion of you, and of carrying of it on, in Succession to your Son whom it may not be amiss, to instruct in the nature of your Duty while your health admits thereof,[3] his good Conduct, sober and dis[c]reet behaviour while in the Temple, tho' surrounded with temptations of every kind warms my Inclinations to serve him, and to his own personal merit, I am satisfied, the long and faithful Services of the Father will have great Weight with a Gentleman of Mr Cholmdys. Temper of mind, tho' you are to correspond directly with him as Auditor General, in matters Relative to the Revenue Nevertheless if difficultys at any time should arise, you need be under no restraint of communicating the same to me, which for the good of the Kings service, for the Interest of my Principal and friend I shall give due attention to, and believe me to be on every occasion &c.

LB, pp. 71–72. In a clerk's hand.

1. Letter not found.

2. The deputy auditor in Virginia received commissions of 5 percent of the receipts of the two-shillings-per-hogshead tobacco export tax and of the quitrents. These commissions were divided evenly between the deputy auditor and his principal in England. In addition, the auditor-general received a salary of £100 per

year from the tobacco revenue and a salary of £150 per year from the quitrent revenues.

3. Blair served as deputy auditor from 1728 until his death in 1771. On 14 May 1772 his son, John Blair, Jr., produced to the Virginia Council a commission from Cholmondeley appointing him deputy auditor, and he was sworn in (*EJC*, 6:464).

To John Blair

Craven street March 8th 1758

Added to the trouble already given you, permit me to ask your attention to the enclosed Accounts more particularly to the Articles therein of Coach hire and Christmass Gratuitys; As these Articles are actually standing Taxes upon the Agent, unless he carrys on the Service as a Smugler in Office, more than as the Representative of your Government, he cannot forgo such Expence.

What Degree of Reputation my Predecessors carryd with them in the service I cannot say for my own part, I desire nothing more, than to be enabled to carry along with me, a Consistency between my public and private Character in Life without detriment or reproach to either.

When the proposition for allowing of £50 Ster pr Annum, by way of Contingent Expences, comes to be considered, as regarding me, it may have some weight with the Governor and Council, from their occasional Applications and Solicitations, going through my hand for Aid, to your Tobacco Revenue, in Cases of Deficienceys therein My services shall not be wanting.

This leads me to lay before you, an Establishment, to a former Agent, which I have met with, in the Auditor General's Office,[1] from this Example Mr Leheup tells me, he applyd, Sir Robert Walpole's[2] answer was that as he already stood overloaded with favours from the Treasury, he could ask nothing more for him; This is not my Case, on the Contrary, the Government stand indebted to me, the Duty of Office vastly increased, in matters of State, & other Business, and hereupon, by adding my personal Interest to a Representation from the Governor & Council in favor of such an Establishment from the Quitrents, it might be brought about. I find that many of the Officers of your Government have additional Salarys from the Quitrents,[3] and why may not the Agent, which Allowance may with parity of reason, may be urged in behalf of the Agent for Govert. I mean Governor and Council as such, this matter I submit to your Consideration in a public or private manner, as you think proper[4] I am with truth

LB, pp. 72–73. In a clerk's hand. In the margin at the head of this letter JA wrote: "with the Acct to Council & to the Assembly A. 81," a reference to the enclosures, below.

1. JA's salary of £200 per year was paid from the two-shillings-per-hogshead tobacco export tax receipts. The "Establishment" he refers to here was a royal warrant, dated 23 Aug. 1716, ordering the governor of Virginia to pay agent Nathaniel Blakiston £200 per year out of the quitrents "as addition to his Salary of 100 per annum in consideration of the Extraordinary Services by him performed to his Majesty" (*Fauquier Papers*, 1:10). Blakiston, who was governor of Maryland 1698–1701 and then agent for that colony, was agent for Virginia from 1705 until 1721 or 1722.

2. Robert Walpole (1676–1745), first earl of Orford.

3. Officials who received a salary from the Virginia quitrents in addition to one from the colony's two-shillings-per-hoghead tobacco export tax revenues were the auditor-general of the plantations and the colony's attorney general.

4. JA later submitted to the Board of Trade an undated memorial and several attachments (including a copy of the warrant to Blakiston), which the Board read on 21 Nov. 1759 (CO 5/1329, fols. 152–155; *JBT*, 11:66–67). In the memorial, JA asked to be confirmed in his appointment as agent for Virginia and to receive either an addition to his salary or whatever salary the Board considered him entitled to, with a further allowance for his expenses. On 21 June 1762 JA received a royal warrant allowing him an additional salary of £200 per year from the quitrents (*EJC*, 6:252–253).

Enclosure: Account with the Governor and Council of Virginia

[8 March 1758]

The Governor and Council of Virginia their Acct. for Contingent Expences from Janry. 1753 to Do. 1758

March the 8th 1758.

Paid in the Address of Council for revoking the Kings Warrant on the Revenue of 2/. pr Hhd; for Copies of Papers from Offices £3.3.—

This Solicitation was attended with great trouble and with difficulty got the better of, thereupon many petty Expences arose, not taken down by me.

The Expence of Coach and Chair hire, and Christmas Gratuitys to Offices, and to the Servants of the Kings Ministers together with that of Postage, and many other incidental Expences attending the Service for these five years, I submit to the Consideration of the Governor and Council.

But in so far as, that the Articles of Coach hire and Christmas Gratuitys, are expences Absolutly necessary for carrying on the Service; for these and all other incidents I hope the Governor and Council will give me leave hereafter and without Account, by way of Contingent Expences in the Service of the Governor and Council £50 Sterling per Annum, which is by no means beyond the nature of the Expence incident to the Service, and however small in itself, is too great to be thrown upon me, out of my Salary, which if duely considered, is no more than adequate for my personal trouble and Fatigue in the service all which is submitted to the Consideration of the Governor and Council.

LB, p. 74. In a clerk's hand.

Enclosure: Account with the Assembly of Virginia

The Assembly of Virginia Dr to James Abercromby Esquire for money disbursed on their Account and for Business done As Agent from Janry 1753. to Do 1758

In the Case of their Address to re enact Laws that had been theretofore Repealed, and for an explanatory Instruction in relation to the passing of Laws

Paid by me in this Case to Mr. Leheup Clerk of the Council for References and orders of Council at different times.	£7.16.—
Paid by me in said Case at the Board of Trade for Representations to the King in Council.	4. 4
Paid at the Board for Trade for their Report on Reference from the Council	2. 2
Paid at said Board for an order relative to the Instructions for the Laws to be re enacted	3. 3
Postage of Letters	0. 7.6
Expences and trouble attending this Solicitation, and submitted to the Consideration of the Assembly at	10.10

2d. In the Case of the Light House Bill

For Several attendings thereon at the Board of Trade, and on Mr John Sharp concerned for Maryland, in opposition to said Bill for my Trouble & Incidental Expences	5. 5

3rd. In Case of the Solicitation for Protection of the Province.

NB. as this matter previously to the Address, was first taken up by me in Mr Fox's Administration, and solicited in his time afterwards, while Sir Thomas Robinson was Secretary of State, and finally and with Success with Mr. Secretary Pitt, from the Commencment of this Negociation, trusting to the Generosity of the Assembly upon the Success thereof, I kept no Account, it is therefore submitted to the House by way of Gratuity for my services   100.—.—

4th In the Case of the free application to Parliament for importing of Iron

> Negociating this matter amongs the Merchants of London, and Bristol, for C[o]ach hire Incidental Expences, and for my trouble in Attending Parliament in all   42.—.—

5 In the Case of the Paper Curcy. Bills

> Various attendings on the Merchants in the City to recon[c]ile them to the last Act, and prevent their application for a Repeal therof trouble and Expences attending this Negociation and former Negociations with the merchants on former Paper mony, Bills or Treasury orders is submitted to the Assembly at   21.—.—

> £196. 7.6[1]

LB, pp. 81–82. In a clerk's hand.

1. On 29 Sept. 1758 Fauquier sent to the House of Burgesses a letter and an account from JA. Neither the letter nor the account was identified, but the account was said to enclose an account of money spent by JA and of services rendered by JA as agent for Virginia. The account was likely the present enclosure, for in his memorial to the Board of Trade read on 21 Nov. 1759 (cited in covering letter, n. 4, above), JA referred to an outstanding account for extraordinary charges of £196.7.0. The House disallowed the account on 2 Oct. 1758, resolving that JA had not "been appointed by the Assembly to solicit the Affairs of this Colony, except in a particular Instance for which he has received Satisfaction, and therefore this House is under no Engagement to pay the same" (*JHB, 1758–1761*, 30, 34).

To Samuel Swann

Cravenstreet March 8th 1758

I forgot in my last[1] that Mr Rutherfurd delivered your Message to me, that you had some money of the Public for my use, in your hands, but not enough to make good the deficiencys, that therefore by Mr Jones's assistance, application should be made to the Assembly for further Supplys on the next meeting. I her[e]upon send you my Account up to the 25 of March, and at the same time, my Letter to Govr. Dobbs[2] for your perusal, and afterwards transmitting to him, from them you will be able to inform me whether the proposition of paying me out of the Govt money is agreed to.

March 25th. 1757 Ballance due	£557. 3.1
By Proceeds for Indigo. by Mr Barclay	101.10.—
due	455.13.1
From March 25 1757 to Do 1758. } £100 Contingencys £31.6 }	131. 6
Due March 25th 1758	£586.19.1

LB, p. 76. In a clerk's hand. The account appears to be appended to JA's letter to Swann of 4 March 1758 (the preceding entry in the letter book), for a line is drawn between the account and the beginning of the present letter. But the account clearly belongs with the letter to Swann of 8 March.

1. JA to Swann, 4 Mar. 1758, pp. 227–228.

2. JA to Dobbs, 4 Mar. 1758, pp. 229–231.

To Major General James Abercromby

Sir.   Cravenstreet March 12th 1758

This will come to you forewarded by Governor Dobbs in behalf of North Carolina, to let you know, that upon Enquiry I do find that the £50,000 which was granted by Parliament last Session, to the Provinces of North, South Carolina and Virginia, remains still in the Treasury and there is to remain, until such time, as you as Commander in Chief of the Kings Forces in America, have asertaind the respective Provincial Proportions due, and have notified the same to the Lords of the Treasury.

And in order to enable you so to do it becomes necessary for these provinces herein concerned, to lay before you, if not already done (to the Earl of Loudon) their respective Claims, from the several Aids granted by their General Assemblys for Military Services, if this Shall be thought the Rule to follow, in the Distribution of the mony, but this must be finally left to the Orders of Government here, after that you have reported your oppinion thereon to my Lords Commissioners of the Treasury, and to the Secretary of State, for as the Case appears to me in the Channel of Office, I do not apprehend that you can draw for, or apply, this money, till the proportions are fix'd, and finally approvd at home; and the sooner this is done, the better with regard to the Provinces concerned therein, and this I have signified to the Governments for whom I am Concerned.

LB, p. 80. This letter was enclosed in JA's letter to Fauquier of 15 March 1758, pp. 244–245.

To Arthur Dobbs

Cravenstreet March 13th 1758

This by Governor Fauquier Successor to Governor Dinwiddy, with my Letter to General Abercromby[1] will inform you, as to the state of the money granted last Session of Parliament, hereby you will observe, that this affair, must still become the Subject of various negociations of Office before it comes to you.

It seems to me that the manner of bringing home this money to your Province requires Consideration if by Remittances in Gold and silver, you may avail yourselves, of thereby sinking in Proportion your Paper Currency, may not directions from home become necessary for this purpose.

To remind you of the Sense of Parliament on his Majestys Message to the house of Commons, and how this Matter stands, I have inclosed to you Copie of the Votes hereon, which you will please lay before the Council & your Assembly if necessary.[2]

I must hereupon repeat to you, that I think myself in Duty bound to attend to your Provincial Affairs notwithstanding the expiration of the Law,[3] til such time as I am in form discharged from this Trust, and let me assure you, that Duty to the Province more than any other motive, leads me still to interest myself, that their Interest may not suffer so far as I can prevent, But I desire to be informed what I have to expect from the Province; the Committee of Correspondence, I must conclude from their Silence to me, do not think themselves authorized to correspond with me any longer, it therefore rests with you, to give me an explicit Answer on this head, In the meantime, in Conjunction with Mr Wright Agent for South Carolina, I have under Consideration the Petition of Governor Morris, Copie whereof inclosed to you, and hereupon I have desired the sense of the Carolina, as well as the Virginia Merchants, and from thence shall be better able to oppose this Petition taking place, at least prevail for putting of the Consideration thereof till your Province is apprised of the Contents thereof.[4] Mr Bacon who is a Trader to North Carolina, has informed me that he is now engag'd in, or about Salt Works, and will be greatly affected by this Petition of Mr Morriss's Monopoly,[5] there may be others with you interested, it will therefore become necessary, for you to take notice of this matter, in a public manner, as from me who am still attentive to the service of the Province and to &c

LB, pp. 83–84. In a clerk's hand except for two minor corrections in JA's hand.

1. See preceding letter.

2. See JA to North Carolina Committee of Correspondence, 26 May 1757, pp. 188 189, n. 2.

3. JA served as agent by virtue of an act of 9 Mar. 1754 that was to be in effect from 25 Mar. 1754 to 25 Mar. 1757 "and from thence to the End of the next Session of the General Assembly and no longer" (*NCSR*, 25:266–267). The assembly was prorogued on 30 May 1757 and met again on 21 Nov. 1757, which session ended on 14 Dec 1757 (*NCCR*, 5:843, 868, 925).

4. South Carolina agent James Wright and JA joined forces to oppose a petition presented to Parliament by Robert Hunter Morris (ca. 1700–1764), who had been governor of Pennsylvania 1754–1756. In his petition of ca. 11 Feb. 1758 (*Fauquier Papers*, 1:9), Morris offered to undertake at his own risk and expense the production of salt in the colonies, "provided he can be secured in the Enjoyment of the Profits which may arise therefrom (in Case it succeeds), for such a Term of Years as may seem to the House [of Commons] a proper and adequate Compensation for so great an Undertaking." On 2 Mar. 1758 the petition was referred to a committee of Commons. JA and Wright appeared before the Board of Trade on 22 Mar. to oppose the application (*JBT*, 10:390). For the outcome, see JA to Dobbs, 20 Apr. 1758, p. 256.

5. Anthony Bacon (ca. 1717–1786) is not known to have been engaged in salt works, but in 1758 he did contract with the government to victual British troops garrisoning Senegal, in West Africa, an undertaking that would have required a great deal of salt for the preservation of food. See Lewis Namier, "Anthony Bacon, M.P., an Eighteenth-Century Merchant," *Journal of Economic and Business History* 2 (1929–1930): 20–70, esp. 25–30.

To Francis Fauquier

Sir   March 15th 1758

Inclosed you have the following papers for perusal, First my Letter to General Abercromby relative to the money granted last Session of Parliament,[1] what I have said thereon to him as Commander in Chief of his Majestys Forces, will lead you into the necessary Correspondence on this Subject.[2]

2nd Copie   My Memorial to the Lords of the Treasury in the Case of the application for an aid out of the Quitrents, to the Tobacco Revenue which comes recommended to me from the President & Council of Virginia, to which I shall give my utmost attention in Concurrence with Governor Dinwiddy as directed so to do.[3]

3rd Copie.   Of Governor Morriss's Petition to Parlt. for an exclusive Right to make Salt in No America, which Petition the Agent for So Carolina, and myself for Virginia, together with the Merchants of these Provinces have under Consideration, in order to form an opposition thereto, at least to have put it off 'til the Provinces are apprised of the Nature of the Application, and are heard thereon.[4]

4th Copie.   Of the Establishment granted to Mathew Blackiston heretofore Agent for Virginia,[5] whereby the Council of Virginia, will see the Encouragment some former Agents have had on the Service of that Government, and should the Governor and Council of Virginia, think proper to remonstrate to My Lords for Trade, the great Increase and Multiplicity of Affairs relative to Government, attending the Duty of the Agent, by throwing in some personal Weight into the Scale, I should hope to succeed, at a proper time, for pressing the matter, and the rather, since where the nomination of Agents is with their Lordships as in Georgia, and Nova Scotia, they allow £300 per An: as Salarys, besides Extras for Contingencys.[6] But in the Interim, I have submitted it to the Consideration of the Gentlemen of the Council, that as the Articles for Coach hire, and for Christmas Gratuitys, to Offices, and to the Servants of the Ministers of State, are very heavy, and Standing Annual Charges upon the Agent, And as all other American Agents, and Solicitors of every nature are allowed for their Contingent Expences, I have therefore desired the permission of the Council to make an Annual Charge, Including Coach or Chair hire, Christmas Gratuitys Postage Pen Ink and Paper, and all other Petty Disbursments £50. per An: which I hope will be thought reasonable, by you and the Gentlemen of the Council, which shall be remitted, whenever the Establishment on the Quitrents takes place.[7]

I have these five years past carryd through a very great variety of Bussiness for the Assembly of Virginia, recommended to me by the Governor and Council and without the least allowance from the Assembly, for so doing, the success whereof has amply testified my Zeal in their service, Added to my trouble, I have been greatly out of Pocket, the Gentlemen of the Council sensible of Success have thereupon undertaken to recommend me to the Assembly,[8] and herein let me beg your Concurrence, I have stated my Account to the Assembly to the President Mr Blair for what is passd,[9] and in time to come, It will be equally agreeable to me if so to the Assembly, to make me an Annual & certain allowance for their Service, otherwise to charge them occasionally for Business done for them, to either propositions I shall acquiesse as they shall think fit, wishing you and your Family a very good Voyage,[10] and happy arrival I am &c.

LB, pp. 84–86. Fauquier communicated this letter to the Council on 15 June 1758 (*EJC*, 6:102–103).

1. JA to Abercromby, 12 Mar. 1758, pp. 241–242.

2. On 5 June 1758 Fauquier laid JA's letter to General Abercromby before the Council, upon which the Council agreed to write to General Abercromby "informing him of the several Sums of Money raised by this Colony since the Encroachments of the French, that he may be enabled to judge, what Proportion of the said Grant this Province is intitled to." The letter was on 15 June "produced, read, and approved of, and order'd to be fairly transcribed," and on 19 June was signed by President Blair in behalf of the Council (*EJC*, 6:100–101, 105, 106). The Council wrote that it had applied to Loudoun on 14 Dec. 1757 for a share of the £50,000 granted by Parliament (see JA to Dobbs, 4 Mar. 1758, pp. 229–231) and had submitted a memorandum on the total of £207,600 raised by Virginia for defense; it now renewed its application and laid before the general "An Account of the Money rais'd for His Majesty's Service in the Colony of Virginia reciting the respective Acts of Assembly," probably a copy of its memorandum previously sent to Loudoun. The Council also pointed out that to the £207,600 ought to be added at least £2,500 for the 400,000 pounds of tobacco paid to the militia. The Council's letter to the general and the memorandum are Abercromby Papers 975 and 344, Huntington Library, San Marino, Calif.

3. See JA to Blair, 5 Mar. 1758, pp. 231–232.

4. See preceding letter.

5. For Nathaniel (not Mathew) Blakiston, see JA to Blair, 8 Mar. 1758, p. 237, n. 1.

6. The civil establishments of both Georgia and Nova Scotia were supported by parliamentary grants, and their agents were appointed by the Crown. See Lillian M. Penson, "The Origin of the Crown Agency Office," *English Historical Review* 40 (1925): 196–206.

Benjamin Martyn (1699–1763), formerly secretary of the Georgia Trustees from Oct. 1732 until their surrender of the charter to the Crown in June 1752, was agent for Georgia from Feb. 1753 to 1763. He was at once both Georgia's agent in London and the Crown's agent for Georgia affairs. Martyn held a royal commission and was paid £350 per year by the Crown.

The agent for Nova Scotia was Christopher Kilby (1705–1771), Boston merchant, government contractor, and agent for Massachusetts.

7. See JA to Blair, 8 Mar. 1758 and enclosure, pp. 236–238.

8. JA's letter to Blair of 3 Mar. 1758, pp. 225–227, suggests that the Council's approval and support were conveyed in a letter from Blair of 23 Dec. 1757 (not found).

9. JA's accounts with the assembly and with the governor and Council were enclosed in his letter to Blair of 8 Mar. 1758, pp. 236–238.

10. Fauquier's wife was Catherine (Dalston) Fauquier (1710?–1781), daughter of Sir Charles Dalston, Bart. They had two children: Francis, Jr. (ca. 1731–ca. 1805), who accompanied them to Virginia; and William (ca. 1733–1805), who came to Virginia in 1763 or 1764 and remained until Apr. 1765.

To Samuel Swann

Sir   London March 17th 1758
Herewith you have my power of Attorney whereof I beg your Acceptance, Mr Rutherfurd by the inclosed to Mrs Rutherfurd[1] has desired her to sign the Assignment and to pay over to you for my use the sum of £333.6.8. Pro: money,[2] which money with what may be hereafter received by you for me, you will be pleased to lay hold of the most advantageous manner of remitting to me, or otherwise dispose thereof most to my Advantage, I am sensible that remittances in time of War is difficult and precarious, however I am not against trying Indigo on good Terms, but this and every method I submitt to your prudence and judgment I have hereto-

fore hinted to you the prospect I have of payment from the money granted by Parliament whether this money comes home to you in Specie or Bills of Exchange through General Abercromby; The first I should think most eligible for the Province in order to sink your Currency. Pray therefore let me have the Instructions of your Government on this Case, which I think so matterial, that the like may not happen again in whatever depends on the Interposition of my friend General Abercromby you may Command. I have sent my Letter to Genl Aber: open to Govr Dobbs that he may thereby see how the Case stands as to this Money.[3] If Provisions were wanted from your Province by the Contractor Mr Kilby, I could by my Acquaintance there get Bills for my Currency all which you will please to consider on. Mr Rutherfurd having told me that the Estate of Governor Johnston was liable to be sued for a Debt due to the Public of your Province rather than hurt Messr[4] Johnston I have agreed to the Proposition, Copie whereof follows. viz

Sir,   London March 15th 1758
    I do hereby agree that whatever money may be in the hands of your Receiver General of the Quitrents of North Carolina on my Account be applyd towards the relief of Governor Johnstons Estate in Case the Estate shall be sued at the Suit of the Public of the said Province, the said Estate being Made accountable to me for payment with Lawful Interest for the same that shall be so paid. Directed to John Rutherfurd.
                                         Jas Abercromby

    By the above you will see the nature of this matter I am &c

LB, pp. 88–90. In a clerk's hand except for the routing memorandum in JA's hand, which reads: "per Govr Fauquier." In the margin at the foot of this letter JA also wrote: "NB this letter is receivd by Mr Swann as by his letter thereof Septr 15th 1756, wherein he tells me that Mr Rutherford had executed the Assignment of the Arrears."

    1. Enclosure not found.

    2. Proclamation money, that is, foreign coins at the rates established by a proclamation of Queen Anne on 18 June 1704.

3. JA to Dobbs, 13 Mar. 1758, pp. 242–243.

4. The clerk should no doubt have written "Mrs." here.

Enclosure: Power of Attorney to Samuel Swann

[17 March 1758]

Know all Men by these presents that I James Abercromby of London Esquire Have made ordained Constituted and appointed, and by these prests. Do make constitute and appoint Samuel Swann of No Carolina Esquire my true and Lawful Attorney for me the said Constituent and on my behalf and in my Name or otherwise To ask Demand & receive of and from the Receiver General of his Majestys Quitrents in North Carolina for the time being or whom else it may Concern all Moneys due and to grow due by Quitrents as Arrears of Salary due to the late deceased Governor Gabriel Johnston Also for me the said Constituent and on my behalf and in my Name or otherwise To ask Demand and receive of and from all and every other Person and Persons whom it doth or may Concern All moneys and Effects due owing and belonging or grow due and oweing to me the said Constituent for or upon what Account soever nothing excepted or reserved Upon Receipts to give one or more Acquittance or Acquittances or other sufficient Discharges in due form of Law But in Case of a Refusal or Delay by the Receiver Genl. of his Majesty's Quitrents in No Carolina for the time being or by any other person or persons whom it doth or may Concern to make and render just and true Account Payment and Satisfaction in the premises him them and every of them thereunto. To Compel by all Lawful ways and means whatsoever And Generally in the premisses to do perform Tran[s]act and Accomplish all and whatever shall be requisite and necessary as fully and effectually to all Intents and purposes as I the said Constituent might or could do being personally present with power to my said Attorney to substitute one or more Person or Persons to act under him and the same at pleasure to revoke And I the said Constituent do hereby promise to ratifie Confirm and hold for good and Valid all and whatever my said Attorney or his Substitutes shall Lawfully do or cause to be done in the Premises by Virtue of these Presents In Witness whereof I the said James Abercromby have hereunto sett my Hand and Seal this seventeenth Day of March One Thousand seven hundred and fifty Eight.

    Sealed and delivered (being first
    duely stamped) in the presence of

LB, pp. 87–88. In a clerk's hand.

To James Innes

Dr Sr,   Cravenstreet March 26. 1758
    I have your short Epistle[1] by Governor Dinwiddy now at Bath, rather better than worse, since his arrival in England, being at rest, he may get the better of his Complaint in some Degree, tho' it is partly the Effect of old Age; I am glad to find, no want of health on your part; I have seen Mr Rutherfurd who recovers his health, the Cause of his and Mr Murray's Suspension, rests still on your side of the water, till we have it transmitted by Governor Dobbs.[2] Mr Rutherfurd does not seem sanguine for restoration to either of his Offices, but in justice to his Character, and to those Gentlemen who are his Securitys, he must exculpate himself of the Governors Charge; I find, he has been with Lord Walpole, who insists that the Currency of your Province received by him as Receiver General, shall be made good as real Proclamation money by Act of Parliament, this probably may be productive of a Law Suit here, on his Lordships part against Mr Rutherfurd, if so, I am affraid it may take money out of Mr Rutherfurds Pocket, for at present I know of no Law of the Province confirmed by the King authorising the Receiver General to take Currency in payment of the King's Quitrents at or under the real Value of Sterling, or Proclamation in Silver or Gold, much less to take Paper Currency under the real Value of Proclamation money, which it seems that your Paper Currency in Fact is.[3]
    Since no relief for the Province from the Depriciation of your Currency, unless the mony granted by Parliament, shall be applyd, towards calling in the Paper Curency, this I have Suggested to the Govr. and to Mr. Swann, and ought to engage the attention of every honest man in your Province; If the Currency is so perniciously depriciated as Mr. Rutherfurd alledges, the Receiver Gen-

eral whoever he is, ought to have particular Instructions for his Justification, how Mr Rutherfurd will be able to justifie I cannot tell, this matter wants to be cleared up to the Treasury, and to the Officers concerned in the Kings Revenue, perhaps Mr Rutherfurd or Mr Dobbs may be able so to do, when called upon.

As I do not like the appearance that offers to my view of matters relative to your Province, I wish I could bring myself home, as to the Arrears, before this Discord takes place amongst you, I recommend to your share in Government that of Reconciliation of Partys if Practicable so to do. Governor Dobbs is a good natured man if not misled by others, is not inclind to take violent measures, however I Am an absolute Stranger to the Cause of Discord amongst you, I can say nothing more than that I wish a Reconciliation, was brought about here and with you, which did it depend on me, should be attempted, for the good of Govert. in General, and for the sake of Individuals whose private Interest must suffer from Friction and Party in Govert. I am

LB, pp. 90–92. In a clerk's hand.

1. Letter not found.

2. Murray was suspended from the Council by Dobbs in Dec. 1757, at the same time as Rutherfurd. Dobbs believed that Rutherfurd, as receiver general, had allowed Murray to pay his quitrents with the promissory notes that had been issued in lieu of Murray's salary as secretary and clerk of the Council. Murray was restored to the Council in June 1762 (*APC*, 4:386; Bond, *Quit-Rent System*, 305–306).

3. In fact, two North Carolina acts, of 1748 and 1754, declared that bills of credit issued under the acts were legal tender in all cases whatsoever as proclamation money or as sterling at the usual difference between proclamation money and sterling (*NCSR*, 23:392–398). An additional instruction to Dobbs of 2 June 1759 required him to insert in all such legislation a clause "declaring that the paper bills of credit already issued or thereby to be issued shall not be a lawful tender in payment of our quit-rents or of any debt of what nature soever due or to become due" to the Crown (Labaree, *Royal Instructions*, 1:229–231).

To John Blair

Sir.   Cravenstreet March 31st 1758

I have your favour of the 2nd of February[1] by the Norwich man of War in answer to mine of the 9th of August,[2] concerning an intended Application to Parliament for the free Importation of Salt into Virginia,[3] whereupon I am authorised by your Letter to apply to Parliament, when I shall find a favourable opportunity for so doing, and to advance the necessary Expence thereof to be repaid me, which was Virginia alone to take up the Application for an Act of Parliament in this Case, if procured, would cost near £200 sterling, however, whenever this matter shall be taken up, it shall be so contrived by me, as to act in conjunction with the Agents for other Colonies, under the like Circumstances, by that means share the Expence with them.

In the meantime Mr Morrisses Petition for an Exclusive Right to make Salt in America is very warmly pressed And by many Members of the Committee before whom it is now, and as warmly opposed by the Merchants and Agents for Virginia and South Carolina, and from the present appearance I am affraid we shall not be able to get the better of it, in the Commee. which will lay us under the necessity of applying to the House to be heard by the Council, in the mean time we are making Without Doors all possible Interest against it, and such proportion of the Expence attending the Case, as shall by the agreement of the Partys concerned be allowed for your Government I shall advance.[4] But for my Justification in all Cases where I may think it for the Interest & Benefit of the Province, to take up or join in any application or opposition before Parliament or elsewhere, I think it necessary for me to have a General Instruction from the Governour and Council authorising me so to do, by looking into the Credentials given me as Agent bearing date June 20th 1754 you will see that my Negociations would thereby seem confined to the Board of Trade, I am the more cautious from what was like to have been the Fate of the Agent for the Massachussets Bay not long since, having interposed by way of Petition as Agent for that Colony, in some matters depending in Parliament, Having no General nor particular Instruction from his Government in such Case, he had been Committed, had it not been for the Interposition of Friends,[5] from such Instances in Parliament And in Public offices I am the more tender from bringing myself into a Scrape.

In case the Merchants shall persist in their objections to the money Bill, against which Bill some of them are very sanguine, in its support, I shall urge the reasons offered in your Letter, amongst many others that occur to me thereon, at all Events Time certainly will be allowed to guard against the Mischiefs that must insue a sudden repeal thereof.[6]

Governour Dinwiddy is at Bath for his health the time too short to have produced the Benefit expected from the Waters[7] I am

LB, pp. 92–94. In a clerks's hand except for the complimentary close and perhaps one correction in JA's hand.

1. Letter not found.

2. Letter not found.

3. See JA to Dinwiddie, 9 Aug. 1757, p. 209.

4. See JA to Dobbs, 13 Mar. 1758, p. 243, n. 4.

5. In 1750 William Bollan (ca. 1710–1782), who was agent for Massachusetts 1745–1762 and for the Massachusetts Council 1768–1775, opposed the bill that became the Iron Act of 1750. He drew up a petition against the bill but had to lay it aside because his power of attorney from the colony did not authorize him to act in the case (Malcolm Freiberg, "William Bollan: Agent for Massachusetts," in *More Books: The Bulletin of the Boston Public Library* 23 [1948]: 136).

6. See JA to Dinwiddie, 3 Nov. 1757, p. 212, n. 1.

7. Bath, a resort in Somerset (now Avon), was the most fashionable spa in England from the early part of the century. The warm springs were valued for their curative properties.

To Samuel Swann

Mr Speaker,   Cravenstreet London April 13th. 1758
In consequence of a Letter from his Excellcy Governor Dobbs,[1] which I received the 10th. instant, Copie whereof becomes necessary for me to lay before you, and thereupon, to acquaint the honourable house of Assembly, that I look upon the Governor's Letter, as a Dismission, from the service of the Province, be pleased therefore, to notifie the same to the House, and at the same time to recommend to their Consideration, the Arrears due to me, in their service.

The Continuation of my Services for last year, before Parliament, and elsewhere, notwithstanding the Expiration of the Agency Law, I hope will Intitle me, to the usual Salary and Allowance, and to the Extra Articles of Expences charged, at the most moderate rate, in my Accounts, now, and heretofore transmitted.[2]

Trusting to the justice and Candor of Government, I did not think myself warranted to relinquish this service, til I had notice given me, by Authority, of its being no more wanted these Considerations I do not doubt, will have their due weight in my favour, who now takes Leave of their service, with his most hearty thanks, for the honour, for so many years conferr'd on him, as Agent for the Province, and with the Grateful acknowledgment thereof, I am with great regard &c

LB, pp. 94–95. In a clerk's hand except for the routing memorandum in JA's hand, which reads: "per Liverpool Copy per Bristol to Virginia."

1. Dobbs's letter to JA of 28 Dec. 1757 (*NCCR*, 5:788–789) notified JA that his appointment "expired last month." Dobbs wrote that he had spoken with the Speaker of the assembly (Swann) "to try whether the House would appoint you again but found them so crusty in granting any money for public services that I could expect little from them. They absolutely refused to appoint any at present alledging their heavy taxes and I find they would not even allow your extra expences so that I cant think to give you any trouble when you wont be paid for it, nor even pay you what you have earned."

2. At a meeting on 25 Nov. 1758 of a joint committee of the North Carolina General Assembly "to examine state and settle the Public Accounts" of the colony, Swann produced the accounts of the committee of correspondence, which showed that the committee had received from the Treasury £1,786.14.8, of which it had remitted £1,474.5 to JA. Swann's commissions amounted to £68.18.10, and there remained in Swann's hand £243.10.10 The joint committee opined that the balance "ought to be applied towards the Contingent charge of Government" if JA was otherwise paid.

Swann also produced JA's accounts, in which he charged £263.11 "for yearly Gifts to Office Keepers Door Keepers and Messengers, Coach hire Postage of Public Packets and Letters Money paid to Servants and Ministers and many other incidental charges and his extra Services for which your Committee [the joint committee] is of Opinion he ought to be allowed" £190.18. The committee recommended disallowance of JA's claims of £51.4.11 for interest and £83.6.8 for salary to 25 Mar. 1758. There then remained a balance due to JA of £332.9.7 sterling (£190.18 plus an earlier balance due of £141.11.7). On 20 Dec. 1758 the lower house resolved to pay JA the £332.9.7 out of North Carolina's share of the £50,000 parliamentary grant to Virginia and the Carolinas, and on 23 Dec. the Council concurred (*NCCR*, 5:969–970, 1035, 1039).

To Samuel Swann

Dr. Sr.   Cravenstreet April 19th 1758

My Letter to you of the 13th. as Speaker of the Assembly,[1] with Copie of Governor Dobbs's Letter, I thought it incumbent on me to write, in order to justifie my having declined the service of the Province.

I could have wished my Dismission from the service had been done in better terms, and with regard to my Arrears more consistent with justice due to an old Servant, however I do not dispair of having another and better Edition of my fate.

I am realy at a loss what Construction to put upon the Governor's Letter, it seems as if he was out of humour with the Assembly in the Case of a Storekeeper,[2] but this Case has no relation to mine, and tho the Assembly do not incline to have any Agent in time to come, it does not follow that my Arrears shall not be paid, nor is it to be expected that while I have friends in the House of Assembly, and while Gentlemen sit there, under whose unjust Authority I have served, that I shall rest the Case of my Arrears of Salary & Disbursements on so laconick a Decision as that of the Governors Letter, which I should have wished to have been concealed from the Assembly, and which if you think may be productive of Discord, you are at Liberty still to do, if by any means I am to come at my Arrears, without calling the Governors name in Question.

My last year's services, tho' the Agency Law was then Expired, speak for themselves in the Case of the Mony granted by Parliament, and it is the fault of your Govert. if the right use is not made of my service in that Case of Passing an Act of Assembly for applying this money towards paying off your paper Currency, which will restore the Public Credit, put the Creditors of the Public as to the Paper Currency on a Par; otherwise if due Care is not taken of the manner of remitting and applying this money, the Person or Persons into whose hands such money shall come, will have it in his power to pocket one half thereof, by b[u]ying up the Paper money at its depriciated value, and to Reissue the same again at its nominal value as a Tender in Law in Discharge of the Public Creditors, it is obvious that a Traffick of this kind is open unless guarded against by Law, but to whatever purposes of Government this money shall be applied, I may reasonably plead payment of my

Arrears amongst the first services, as the fruits of my Labour in obtaining the same, through the Interposition of those now at the head of the Administration.[3]

I am not certain but that in my Accounts heretofore sent for last year, the Article of 30£ sterling by Bill on Bourdeaux was omitted on the side of the Credit due the Province, it is now therefore corrected, I shall long to hear from you, in answer to these Letters, in the mean time I am always

LB, pp. 95–96. In a clerk's hand except for the routing memorandum in JA's hand, which reads: "per Liverpool Copy per Virginia to Bristol by Mr Bird." At the foot of this letter JA also wrote: "NB I told Mr Swann of my proceedings in the Salt affair as enterd in the Govers Letter."

1. See preceding letter.

2. Two Orders in Council of 7 July 1756 provided for the supply of £3,400 worth of cannons, ordnance, stores, gunpowder, and balls for Fort Johnston (see JA to Rice, 16 Jan. 1753, p. 65). A third Order in Council of that date directed Dobbs to appoint a storekeeper "with a proper salary" and to "recommend it to the Assembly to provide for the payment thereof" (*NCCR*, 5:592–594). Dobbs appointed a store-keeper at £80 per year North Carolina currency and sought an appropriation from the assembly, but the legislators refused because, according to Dobbs, "They had not the Nomination" (*NCCR*, 5:949). Later, the assembly allowed a mere £12 per year (*NCCR*, 6:199).

3. JA had obviously given much thought to the best method of disposing of North Carolina's share of the £50,000 parliamentary grant. In a letter to the secretary of the Board of Trade of 13 Apr. 1758 (*NCCR*, 5:928–929), in which he enclosed a copy of Dobbs's letter of 28 Dec. 1757 and notified the Board that he was no longer agent for North Carolina, JA nonetheless wrote: "as I take my leave of these affairs I cannot help recommending to their Lordships consideration a measure which by my letters to Governor Dobbs and to the committee of correspondence I have heretofore earnestly urged (vizt) That the Province should avail themselves of the Money granted last Session of Parliament in order to sink their paper currency which is become greatly depreciated and dayly becomming more and more so and for that purpose pass an Act of Assembly calling in so much of their paper money as may be paid off by the money so granted by Parliament. . . .

"Great attention is to be had to the manner of remitting and applying this money otherwise the person or persons into whose hands such money shall come may pocket one half of the whole by purchasing the paper money at its depreciated value and so reissue the same as a Tender in Law in discharge of the public Creditors according to its nominal value by Law to the manifest prejudice of Public and private credit.

"To prevent which and to put all creditors of all sorts on a Par with regard to the paper money I humbly apprehend the most eligible method (if approved of by their

Lordships) is to instruct the Governour to recommend it to the Assembly to pass an Act to call in so much of the paper money to be paid off by the money granted by Parliament and till this shall be done the money to remain in the Treasury."

To Arthur Dobbs

Cravenstreet Aprile 20th 1758

I have your Letter of 28 Decer., and in Consequence thereof have notified to the Secretary of State, and the Lords for Trade that I am no longer Agent for the Province of North Carolina,[1] I cannot allow myself to think, that you are in earnest in giving up the Case of my Arrears I must therefore beg your Interposition with the Assembly that they may be paid the Account whereof amounting to £557.9.1 as by particulars heretofore transmitted, you need no other Argument than common Equity in my favour, however to that you may add my Services last year before Parliament, and should no other Provision be made for my Arrears from the Plea of heavy Taxes, this may be obviated, by paying me from the money granted by Parliament, and this you will please to urge with the Assembly, in case you shall find it necessary.

In my former letter by Governor Fauquier I transmitted to you copy of Mr Morrisses Petition to Parliament for the sole priviledge to make Salt whereupon I desird the oppinion of your Province,[2] after a very warm Strugle before the Commee of the House, the Merchants of Virginia & the Carolinas in conjunction with me as Agent then acting for North Carolina and for Virginia and with Mr Wright agent for So Carolina have prevaild in our opposition to this Petition and the same was on friday last accordingly after five different hearings of the agents dismisd and the Case of North Carolina as being at this very time engaged in Salt Works by Mr Bacons Evidence was in point and was the most prevalent Evidence as urged by me in this Case and herein I hope you will do me justice with the Assembly in notifying the Share I have had in this Service of the Province and urge the same to their consideration for payment of my Arrears for this last service I add nothing of Expence to their account.

LB, pp. 96–97. The first paragraph is in a clerk's hand; at the end of it, "I am" is deleted and the second paragraph, in JA's hand, is added. Sent "per Liverpool Copy per Virginia to Mr Bird."

1. In his letter to the secretary of the Board of Trade of 13 Apr. 1758, JA enclosed a copy of Dobbs's letter of 28 Dec. 1757 (*NCCR*, 5:928–929, 788–789). The Board read both letters on 2 May 1758 (*JBT*, 10:400). Dobbs's letter of the same purport to Holderness has not been found.

2. JA to Dobbs, 13 Mar. 1758, pp. 242–243.

To Francis Fauquier

Cravenstreet April 26 1758

I lay hold of this opportunity from Bristol to inform you, that after a very hard strugle before the Committee of the house of Commons, who had under their Consideration the Petition of Hunter Morriss Esqr for the sole priviledge of making Salt in North America, the Merchants for Virginia and Maryland in conjunction with the Agents for Virginia and the Carolinas, have prevailed in their opposition to this Petition, & the Petition is accordingly dismissed, after five hearings thereon, we have been the more strenuous in our opposition before the Committee, from the Extraordinary trouble and Expence, that must have attended an Opposition in the house, had Mr Morriss gained his point for bringing in a Bill for the purposes set forth in his Petition.

The Petition before the Treasury for an Aid to the Tobacco Revenue out of the Quitrents has not as yet been taken into Consideration, the hurry of Business in money matters depending before Parliament for Home, as well as Foreign Subsidys, allows no time for other matters, but from this Delay, I shall avail myself of Mr Dinwiddy's assistance on his return from Bath, which place he purposes to leave as next week, having found some benefit from the Waters.

The public Newspapers collected together for your use, being too bulky by Post to Bristol, I shall hereby take notice of the most matterial Events; a Convention between England and Prussia to act conjunctly against France, and make no seperate peace, in Consideration whereof, we give 2 Millions to the King of Prussia, payable by equal proportions in the space of three years, if the War shall so long continue, and this Exclusive of paying the Army of Hanoverians &c. now under the King of Prussias direction.[1]

The Capture of the Foudrouyant of 84 Guns and the Orpheus of 64 going under the Command of Monsr. Dequesne (now in England at Northampton), to reinforce Monsr Declue at Carthagona, this proves a very great Disappointment to the French who are still block'd up at Carthagona,[2] Add to this Sir Edd. Hawkes having about 15 Days ago drove on shore five Ships of the Line near Rochfort with many Transports having 3000 men ready to embark therein for America, the mud was soft where those Ships run ashore, however having thrown their Guns & Stores overboard, their intended Expedition becomes frustrated, whether they do or do not get off;[3] Upon the whole our affairs in Europe, as well as in America by Genl Abercrombys Letters of the 17th March have a better Aspect than heretofore.[4] I wish you Success on your Frontiers & with Compts. I hope you and your Lady find the Country agreeable after the fatigue of your Voyage. I am &c

LB, pp. 97–99. In a clerk's hand except for the routing memorandum in JA's hand, which reads: "by Bristol."

1. The convention between the king of England and the king of Prussia, signed 11 Apr. 1758, in fact provided that the parties should not conclude any treaty of peace unless both agreed to it and that England should pay Prussia a subsidy of approximately £670,000. The text of the convention is in *JHC*, 28:188.

2. Six French warships under the command of Admiral Duquesne were ordered to the relief of Admiral de la Clue, whose division, bound for North America and the West Indies, had been driven into the Spanish port of Cartagena and blockaded there. On 28 Feb. 1758 Adm. Henry Osborn intercepted the French force and captured the *Foudroyant*, Duquesne's flagship, and the *Orphée*. Duquesne was taken prisoner and brought to England; the *Annual Register* reported that he arrived in London on 8 May, and the *Gentleman's Magazine* (28 [1758]: 501) reported that he set out from Northampton on 21 Oct. on his way to France on parole, "perhaps to facilitate a peace."

3. On 5 Apr. 1758 Adm. Sir Edward Hawke (1710–1781) intercepted off the French port of Rochefort a large French convoy bound for America, five men-of-war, six or seven frigates, and about forty merchantmen with 3,000 troops aboard; most of the French vessels were driven ashore. The French salvaged some of the ships but lost a quantity of guns and gear they had jettisoned, and their dispatch of supplies to America was thwarted.

4. Although General Abercromby wrote on 17 Mar. 1758 to Secretary at War William Wildman Barrington acknowledging receipt of the notification that he had been appointed commander in chief (Abercromby Papers 51, Huntington Library, San Marino, Calif.), his letter to William Pitt of 16 (not 17) Mar. is a much more detailed report of the state of affairs in America and the steps Abercromby had taken to prepare for the coming campaigns (Abercromby Papers 47, Huntington Library).

To Samuel Swann

Dr Sr.   June 4th 1758

I beg the favour of you convey the inclosed Letter from the Auditor General to his Deputy Mr McCulloch, and as the purport thereof has reference to the payment of Sterling Salarys out of the Quitrents, it will be your Guide in receiving the late Governor Johnstons on the Assignment thereof by his Representatives to me, heretofore transmitted to you, as to the Dispute between Lord Walpole, and Mr Rutherfurd, I am in hopes that his Lordship will depart from his Intention of suing Mr. Rutherfurd for sterling money in place of Paper Proclamation, with which he charges himself as Receiver General.

The Case may very easily be compromised, by charging the Crown with the defi[ci]ency due to Lord Walpole's Sterling Salary; Sterling money is due by the Establishment from the Kings Revenue, the Revenue therefore ought to make it good, not the Receiver General out of his own pocket, and this you find to be the principle laid down by the Auditor General which is extreamly just and equitable in itself.

Our Grand Expedition has been gone for four days, but no body but the Cabinet knows where,[1] the Suspension of Messrs Murray and Rutherfurd so far as the Lords for Trade can carry it is confirmed by their Lordships Reference to the King in Council, I hear no cause alledg'd, at least They give none, to those concerned, nor to the Public for their Confirmation of the Suspension, the reasons are of a Secret nature,[2] my Compliments to your Brother and all friends.

When you see Mrs Allen, be so kind as make my Compliments to her, and let her know that Mr Rutherfurd has stated Mr Allen's

Account with the Revenue, in such a Light, as may prevent any after call upon her on that account, on the King's Part, at least it appears in this Light to me after perusing Mr Rutherford's accounts given to the Auditor General; But how the Account stands between Mr Allen and Lord Walpole I cannot say, as it does not come within Mr Rutherfurds accounts. I am &c.

LB, pp. 101–102. In a clerk's hand.

1. On 1 June 1758 two British squadrons sailed out of Portsmouth with the intention of taking the French port of Saint-Malo, on the English Channel. The operation, involving 34,000 men and almost two hundred ships of all descriptions, was one of the largest naval assaults on France before the twentieth century. The troops were landed on a bay east of Saint-Malo on 2 and 3 June, and on 7 June British light-horse cavalry raided two smaller French ports, burning many ships and destroying naval stores. But the British could not move their siege artillery close enough to Saint-Malo, and rumors began to spread of a gathering of 10,000 French troops. Therefore, the British reembarked on 12 June.

2. On 10 May 1758 the Board of Trade read a letter from Dobbs of 27 Dec. 1757 (*NCCR*, 5:945–950) giving his account of the suspensions of Rutherfurd and Murray and enclosing numerous supporting documents. The Board then took into consideration Dobbs's letter and enclosures as well as Rutherfurd's and Murray's memorials in their own defense (*NCCR*, 5:956), "spent some time therein," and agreed to submit the relevant papers to the king (*JBT*, 9:389, 403–404). The Board's representation to the king of 12 May 1758 (*NCCR*, 5:957–958) recommended confirmation of the suspensions. On 2 June the Privy Council referred the matter to its Plantation Committee, and on 15 June the committee referred to the Board a letter from Rutherfurd to Earl Granville of 22 May 1758 (*NCCR*, 5:958–959) and directed the Board "to hear Rutherford in his own defense" (*APC*, 4:386). In its reply to the Plantation Committee of 28 July 1758 (*NCCR*, 5:959–960), the Board presented its reasons for not hearing Rutherfurd and concluded that "the Case does not admit of the indulgence which he desires" and "that his taking upon [himself] to arraign in so extraordinary a manner the Justice of this Board is in our opinion such a proceeding as deserves censure."

Enclosure: Robert Cholmondeley to Alexander McCulloh

Sir.[1]   London May 30th. 175[8][2]

A Dispute has arisen between Lord Walpole son and Heir to my Predecessor in Office & Mr Rutherfurd late Receiver General of the Quitrents in North Carolina, concerning the payment of the Auditor General's Salary. Lord Walpole insisting according to the words and Tenor of the Kings Establisht., that his Fathers Salary is to be paid in Sterling money, but if paid in Paper money, that payment shall be made ad valorem of Sterling money according to the known and notorious rate of Exchange or difference between Sterling & Paper money where payment is made.

I find from the Accounts in my Office from other Colonys that this is the Rule and Practice of Payment where Sterling Salarys are paid in the Colonys in Paper money.

You will therefore on receiving my Salary take Care, that the same be accounted for at the real rate of Sterling according to the Establishment thereof, and if payment is made in Paper money the same to be according to the difference between Paper money and Sterling, for whatever denomination may be given to the Paper money, the nature of the Debt is not thereby altered from sterling to Proclamation Paper money; and I can see no reason, why the Officers on the Establishment in No Carolina, shall not have equal justice, with Officers in Other Colonys under the like Circumstances, and this you will signify to the Receiver General for the time being of the Quitrents.[3]

As Mr Drayton who had my Deputation and Instructions to you under his Care, has been gone some months to South Carolina, I shall expect ere long, to hear from you thereupon.[4]

I wrote to you in my last, that with relation to the Salary and Fees, the Officers in Actual service were to be preferrd, and that Lord Walpole's great Arrears were to be no obstruction, to the regular payment of my Salary &c. which you will please to observe I am &c

LB, pp. 99–101. In a clerk's hand.

1. Alexander McCulloh was deputy auditor-general of North Carolina.

2. The letter is clearly dated 1757, but it was enclosed in JA's letter to Samuel Swann of 4 June 1758, pp. 259–260.

3. With Rutherfurd in England, "the important office of receiver-general was left for four years without a properly authorized incumbent" (Bond, *Quit-Rent System*, 307–308).

4. Perhaps Thomas Drayton (1700–1760), who was in England when he received an appointment to the South Carolina Council in Oct. 1756 (*APC*, 4:797).

To Francis Fauquier

Sir, London June 23rd. 1758

Inclosed, I lay before you, Copie of the Memorial presented by the Merchants of London relative to the Paper Money Bill, another of the same nature, is presented to the Lords for Trade by the Merchants of Bristol, and one is expected from Liverpool, to that presented by the London Merchts. no other answer is given as yet, than, that their Lordships, shall take it under Consideration when the affairs of Virginia come in Course before them.[1]

The Memorial some time since, presented to the Lords of the Treasury for Aid, out of the Quitrents to make good the Deficiencys of the Tobacco Revenue, lays still in Suspence, and no reference made thereof to the Auditor General of the Plantations, by Examination of the Books in the Auditor Genl's Office, I have found Precedents, in our favour, which Shall be pointed out to the Auditor General, when the Case comes before him.

No Provincial matters requiring my Animadversion, for Public Events, since you left us, I refer you to the Newspapers now transmitted that of the 21t inst. will shew you, our proceedings in France, and at Senegal, with both of which Events the City of London are vastly pleased, whether our Troops are now gone to Granville, or elsewhere is a Secret.[2]

You will be pleased to communicate so much of this, as concerns the Gentlemen of the Council to be informed of, I remain on all occasions, Sir yours &c

LB, pp. 102–103. In a clerk's hand.

1. For the memorials from the London and Bristol merchants, see JA to Dinwiddie, 3 Nov. 1757, pp. 211–212. There is no evidence that the memorial expected from Liverpool was ever submitted.

2. The proceedings in France are described in JA to Swann, 4 June 1758, p. 260, n. 1. The proceedings in Senegal were an attack on French settlements in West Africa: a squadron arrived at the mouth of the Senegal River in late Apr., and at the beginning of May captured Fort Louis and various stations farther up the river, thus cutting off the supply of slaves to the French West Indies.

To Francis Fauquier

July 20th 1758.

Tell him of the hearing of the Merchants on the Paper Money, that the Lords for Trade seem disposd to grant their Petition on the Paper Money Act.[1] That notwithstanding Mr Dinwiddies Representations & mine on the Aid out of the Quit Rents nothing done therein before the Adjournment of the Treasury that the Lords of Treasury had referd Messrs Randolphs & Byrds case to the B: of Trade who probably was to refer the same to the A Genal but it must rest til their meeting in Octr.[2]

Tell him the News with News Papers.

LB, p. 104. At the foot of this letter JA wrote: "by Mr Hanburys Ship."

1. See JA to Dinwiddie, 3 Nov. 1757, pp. 211–212.

2. On 4 July 1758 Samuel Martin, secretary to the Treasury, sent to the Board of Trade a memorial from William Byrd III (1728–1777) and Peter Randolph (1713?–1767) upon which the Treasury desired the opinion of the Board (CO 5/1329, fols. 58–66). The undated memorial from Byrd and Randolph to the Treasury represented that by Dinwiddie's commission of 23 Dec. 1755 they had been appointed commissioners to negotiate a treaty with the Catawba and Cherokee and that the governor and Council had approved their statement of expenses and ordered that an application be made to the Treasury for their reimbursement. The memorialists cited a royal warrant of 1744 for £1,620.2.11 to pay the expenses of a treaty with the Six Nations and repeated their request for reimbursement, as they had had no allowance, and they appended a number of extracts from the journal of the Council concerning their mission and the earlier mission to the Six Nations. On 6 July the Board considered the memorial from Byrd and Randolph, but concluded that as it had "no knowledge of any of the facts stated in the memorial, nor of the precedent, upon which the demand is grounded, they are not enabled to give any opinion upon it" (*JBT*, 10:413). The Treasury did not refer the matter to the auditor-general until July 1759. See JA to Randolph and [Byrd], 28 July 1759, pp. 320–322.

To Francis Fauquier

London September 12th 1758

I have your favour of the 26th June,[1] & rejoice on your safe arrival after so agreeable a Voyage.

I hope you may find an Administration and every other Circumstance of Life to your's & Mrs Fauquier's best wishes.

I do not doubt of General Abercromby's disposition to serve your Province, so far as lies in his Power, and the Council have done well to lay their Claim before him.[2]

I shall repeat my Application for an Aid out of the Quitrents to the Tobacco Revenue with the Alteration of the Deficiencys being now become greater, and the liklyhood of their becoming more and more so, during the War, & this I took Care to suggest to the Treasury in my Original Memorial on this head.[3]

Since my last Govr Dinwiddy & myself have had a long Conference, with the Secretary of the Treasury Mr Martin,[4] who has this matter before him, the chief purport of our Application to him was, to get the Memorial refer'd to the Auditor General, because through this Channel, I shall be better able, to give it a favourable turn, from the Precedents I have with some difficulty met with by searching the Books in the Auditors Office, you may assure the Council that nothing shall be wanting on my part to procure Redress.

I am sorry that the Council have other Ideas of the Tendency of Mr Morrisses application for a Temporary Monopoly of Salt, than what I, and every other Agent for the American Colonys, and the Trading Interest of this Kingdom conceived,[5] could I have foreseen this, I had saved myself an immense trouble and some Expence, however it shall be a Caution to me for the future to act by particular instructions only, and the rather since from what is insinuated by you that, the Council do not seem inclined to give me Credit for Extraordinary trouble and Expence, and as little to be hoped for from the House of Burgesses.

The Lords for Trade being under their long adjournment,[6] since the Merchants appeared before them, on their Memorial against the Paper Currency Law, their Lordships have hetherto come to no final Official Measures in this Case.

Public affairs abroad have for the present a tollerable good appearance, and should they continue so, I should not be surprised to see overtures of Peace from France, the Victory obtained by the King of Prussia over the Russians, was of the most obstinate kind therein was added Rage and Resentment to Valour on both sides.[7] My Compliments to your Lady concludes me with thanks for the tender of your good offices in what concerns me, which shall on my part at all times be acknowledg'd by Sir &c

LB, pp. 104–106. In a clerk's hand except for several interlineations in JA's hand and several deletions presumably by JA.

1. Letter not found.

2. See JA to Fauquier, 15 Mar. 1758, pp. 244–245.

3. JA's renewed application was perhaps a representation presented about 23 July 1759 (T 1/389, fols. 107–111). His original memorial was presumably that of about 15 Mar. 1758, for which see JA to Blair, 5 Mar. 1758, pp. 231–232.

4. Samuel Martin was a secretary to the Treasury from Nov. 1756 to Apr. 1757 and from May 1758 to Apr. 1763.

5. There is no record of the Council's opinion about Governor Morris's petition.

6. The Board of Trade did not meet between 3 Aug. and 11 Oct., according to the journal.

7. On 25 Aug., Frederick the Great had attacked the Russians under Count William of Fermor at Zorndorf in Brandenburg (now Sarbinowo in Poland). There is some question as to how complete Frederick's victory was, but the battle was the bloodiest of the war; the Prussians suffered 13,500 casualties and the Russians 42,000 (of whom 21,000 were killed).

To John Blair

Sir   London September 12th. 1758

By the purport of a Letter of June 24th 1758.[1] by the Ludlow Castle, tho' the same is not signed, I know it comes from Mr Blair, but it brings a more disagreeable mistake, refering me to Bills therein sent of £50 each for Salary to 25th April last, which you say the Embargo prevented coming sooner, but these Bills are not in the Letter, nor have I any other Letter or Set of Bills.

By a Letter from Governor Fauquier of 26 June[2] I find his safe arrival, and that he had laid my Letters before the Council, and that some steps were taken in Consequence thereof, relative to the Parliamentary Grant.[3] I could have wished that what regarded myself had been more promising from the Council, & the House of Burgesses however from what you say I shall suspend judgment on my demands from the House of Burgesses who must pay if they expect my services.

My Application to the Treasury for an Aid to the Tobacco Revenue out of the Quitrents meets with difficultys and delay That to the Lords for Trade by the Merchts. against the Paper Currency

Law; As their Lordships are under adjournment, nothing is done therein, but at all Events the Law as it now stands I apprehend will not be repealed.

Governor Dinwiddy and Family have for some weeks been in Scotland, but are soon to return hether, I hope your Son and Family are well Mr Cholmondly being in the Country, I have not seen nor heard from him for a Month Past, I am with Compliments to your son and Family. &c.

LB, pp. 106–107. In a clerk's hand except for several interlineations in JA's hand.

1. Letter not found.

2. Letter not found.

3. See JA to Fauquier, 15 Mar. 1758, p. 245, n. 2.

To Francis Fauquier

Sir   London Octr 5th 1758

Since my letter of Septr. 12 nothing material has happend in the way of Office, and while Mr Martin of the Treasury, who has before him my Several Memorials relative to the Quitrents going in Aid of the Deficiencys of the Tobacco Duty, and for Reward to Messrs Byrd & Randolphs Services, while Mr Martin is in the Country all these Matters rest, in the mean time I have met with more Precedents in our favour from the Books in the Auditors Office, so that when these Memorials come referrd to the Auditor General I shall be able to form a very favourable Report to the Treasury in both Cases and[1]

Hereupon let me observe that by thus Acting in a double capacity in the service of your Government I have the greater reason to expect their proper Encouragment, but as Mr President Blairs letter to me[2] tells me, that my chief hopes must rest on the Governors & Councils Assistance in obtaining for me a Warrant on the Quitrents for 200 per an: as Mr Blakiston heretofore Agent for Virginia had; this being the Case I must rely on your recommendation of this matter to the Council (A)[3] I have taken the liberty to point out to Mr Blair,[4] the manner of taking this Matter up in Council vizt by Representing the great increase of public Business,

Acknowledging, above my Diligence and Zeal in the Public Service, and thereupon to recommend me to the Lords of the Treasury to Mr Secretary Pitt as Secretary of State for the Colonys, and to the Lords for Trade for the like Establishment of 200 per annum out of the Quitrents as Mr Blakiston had this being done, what may be further wanted rests with my personal Interest, & Solicitation in which by Mr Pitts means I do not doubt of Success at the Treasury where the Stress of the Case lays, but as these are the three Channels of my Business as Agent, it must come recommended to all of them, In this and in no other way do I see any hopes of my making up for Contingencys that ought to be allowed and I do believe in every other Colony Agency are allowd for the Service beyond the Salary.

The news papers now sent, will inform you of the public Situation of affairs Two Expeditions are preparing, their Destination not known, to Affrica, America, or Italy time will shew,[5] General Abercromby takes his leave of America, and I can from very good Authority tell you, that he comes home in a Situation entirely to the satisfaction of himself & his friends[6] my best Compliments to Mrs. Fauquiere concludes me always very Sincerly Sir Your Most Obedt Sert

LB, pp. 108–109.

1. JA evidently neglected to finish this sentence.

2. This must have been Blair's letter of 24 June 1758 (not found), to which JA replied on 12 Sept. 1758, pp. 265–266.

3. For the meaning of this parenthetical insertion, see the notation at the head of the following letter.

4. See following letter.

5. One of the two expeditions was probably a fresh attack on French possessions in West Africa; Commodore Augustus Keppel commanded an expedition that, after some delay, sailed on 11 Nov. 1758 from Cork and on 29 Dec. captured the fortified island of Gorée, a center of the slave trade off Dakar. The other expedition may have been that against Quebec under Vice Adm. Charles Saunders and Maj. Gen. James Wolfe.

6. On 8 July 1758 General Abercromby attacked Fort Carillon (which the British called Ticonderoga), built in 1755 by the French to command the route between Lake Champlain and Lake George. Although Abercromby had a force of more than 15,000 men, he suffered a crushing defeat by Montcalm, who had only 3,600 men.

Upon learning of the disaster, Pitt replaced Abercromby with Jeffery Amherst. Nevertheless, Abercromby was promoted to the rank of lieutenant general on 31 Mar. 1759, and it would appear that the defeat at Ticonderoga was not a permanent disability for him.

To John Blair

London Octr 5th 1758

NB the same as to Mr Fouquiere[1] til Letter (A) then follows (viz)

In my letter of this date to the Lieut Governor I have acquainted him, of my application to you as President of the Council and taking the Liberty of pointing out to you at the same time the most proper Manner of taking this Case up in Council (viz) by a Resolution of the Board Representing the great Increase of Public Business, Acknowledging my Diligence and Zeal in the Service, and thereupon recommending me as Agent for your Government to the Lords of the Treasury, to the Secretary of State Mr Pitt, and the Lords for Trade for the like Establishment as Mr Blakiston had from the Quitrents, as these are the three principal Offices for my Negociations it becomes proper and necessary to engage their Interposition in the Case, and indeed through Mr Pitt is my chief hopes of Success with the Treasury, I need not repeat to you the assurance I hope for of your taking the proper part with the Council and of the Lieut Governors concurring with you herein which shall not fail of a proper return on my part I shall say no more on this Subject, Please to make my Compliments to Messrs Byrd & Randolph, and let them know, that I have their application much at heart, and that altho the Lords for Trade have not reported so favourably to the Treasury as might have been wished,[2] I never the less hope to bring it about through the Treasury for an Allowance for their Indian Services, Mr Dinwiddie is much their friend and he concurs with me in their Service, and as one good turn deserves a return so I do not therefore doubt of their Seconding your Services to me, on the occasion which now offers, my best Complts to your Son and his Family & believe me always most ready to serve you & your Family being very truly Sir

PS   In the Resolution of the Council Board please to desire the Governor to transmit the Resolution of the Council to the several Offices above mentiond, & to write to them accordingly, as by the Desire of the Council, for the Public Service of Government.

LB, pp. 110–111.

1. See preceding letter.
2. See JA to Fauquier, 20 July 1758, p. 263, n. 2.

To Samuel Swann

Octr 5th 1758

Your favour of last May[1] I reced in Scotland, and that no time might be lost, I transmitted Mr Dobbs's letter in your favour to Mr Pownall saying what I think you deserve as a Candidate for the Office of Chief Justice;[2] I was calld to London immediately after my letter, and then repeated my Solicitations to Mr Pownal on Lord Halefaxes absence in Northampton Shire, and hereupon I found that the Earl of Granville had on the first Notice of the Vacancy engagd Lord Halefax in favour of one Mr Berry, a Gentleman whom I know nothing at all of and I believe I may venture to add that he knows as little of the office to be given him,[3] I most heartily wish it had taken another turn for the good of the Province, and for your Satisfaction, you may be assurd from me that no personal objection has been made to you on this occasion, but the Recommendation of the Earl of Granville carrys with it too much weight for Gover Dobbs's Influence or mine to overcome; By a letter from Mr Heneage Jones I am Soliciting the confirmation of an Act of Assembly as it comes recommended by you my good offices shall not be wanting and herein I do not forsee any difficulty that can arise from an opposition thereto, but from the Rules of office all privat Acts lay in the office for some Months to give time to Partys who may be Interested[4] Much about the same time I have a letter from Mr Robt Jones, who is warm in his Wishes for your Success, from the same quarter I find my endeavours to serve him are frustrated, at the same time Mr Child is no way benefited from the office of attorney General,[5] Mr Jones promises me his assistance joind to yours in my Demands on the Public, he indeed seems to carry his Views further, and for the Renewal of the Agency Act, but in this piece of Service I will excuse my friends my Views go no further than Satisfaction for my past Service, and while the Assembly demur to this I cannot expect that they will render the Service more Inviting than it has hitherto been, my late Parliamentary Services I did hope might have duly pleaded for the punctuality of my Pay without any sort of Difficulty on the part of that Northern Faction, which has and I am affraid ever will obstruct public & privat Justice in your Province and whose Influence in some degree reaches this.

Mr Rutherfurd advises the Remitting to me Naval Stores provided you get fr[e]ight on Moderat Terms this I must leave to your Judgment, and if no Remittance can be made I should advise your puting my Money to Interest in good hands till Peace give a turn to your Trade, taking particular care that the Bonds specefy Sterling Money or Currency at the real value of Sterling according to the Exchange when paid, Copy of Such Bonds please to transmit to me If Commoditys are sent please consign them to Mr Lewis at Plymouth, to Portsmouth to Mr Heron if to London to myself.

I cannot omit telling you that Mr Barclay refusd acceptance of your Bill, but this circumstance should not have stood in your way could Money have bought Success it had not been wanting for your Use & Service My Complts to your Brother concludes me always very Sincerly

LB, pp. 112–113.

1. Letter not found.

2. At a meeting of the North Carolina Council on 28 Apr. 1758, Dobbs informed the Council of the death of Chief Justice Peter Henley and proposed James Hasell to succeed him, which recommendation was unanimously agreed to (*NCCR*, 5:991). A commission was issued to Hasell that same day (*NCCR*, 5:962). The journals of the Board of Trade do not record the receipt of any letter from Dobbs recommending that Samuel Swann be appointed chief justice by the Crown, nor has such a letter been found.

3. On 25 Oct. 1758 the Board of Trade recommended to the Crown that Charles Berry be appointed chief justice in the room of Henley (*JBT*, 10:416), and on 27 Nov. 1758 a royal warrant was issued ordering Dobbs to appoint Berry (*NCCR*, 5:963–964). Berry (d. 1765), of London, arrived in the colony in Dec. 1759, was appointed a councillor in June 1762, and died by shooting himself in the head (*APC*, 4:794).

4. Heneage Jones's letter to JA has not been found. The private act mentioned may have been "An Act to dock the intail of certain lands now in possession of Harding Jones, under a devise in the will of Frederick Jones, Esq., his grandfather, deceased, by whom the same were intailed," passed in Dec. 1757 (*NCSR*, 23:481–482). On 18 July 1759 the Board of Trade took the act into consideration, along with Matthew Lamb's report on it, and recommended that it be confirmed (*JBT*, 11:49, 50).

5. Robert Jones's letter to JA has not been found. Evidently, JA and Jones planned to pay Thomas Child to resign the attorney generalship so that Jones could be appointed to the post (see following letter). Child did select Jones as his successor, resigning the attorney generalship in Jones's favor early in 1761. The Privy Council commissioned Jones as attorney general in Apr. 1761 (*APC*, 4:484).

To Robert Jones

Octr 5th 1758

Tell him of receiving his letters from Mr Mills that so soon as I am at leisure shall consult with Mr Mills about the Proposition to be made Mr Child as Money alone can bring about a Resignation,[1] tell him of Mr Swanns disapointment thro Lord Granvills recommendation of Mr Berry, desire his concurrence with Mr Swann for the arrears due me, & tell him that I do not expect the Assembly will make their Service worth while to accept by an Augmentation of Salary.

LB, p. 114. Sent "per Capt Rutherfurd from Plymouth Octr 5th."

1. Mills has not been identified. See preceding letter, note 5.

To Francis Fauquier

Sir   London 17th Novr. 1758

Since my last,[1] notwithstanding the repeated and pressing applications made to the Treasury by Mr. Dinwiddie & myself, I have not been able hitherto to bring the Case of the Tobacco Revenue to a Hearing by the Lords of the Treasury, and from such Answers as we get from the Secretaries, it is hard to form any Judgment what may be the Event of our Sollicitation.

I now inclose for your Consideration Copy of a Letter I have lately received from General Abercrom[b]y relative to the Money granted by Parliament for the three Colonies:[2] from the fluctuating State of the Commanders in Chief of his Majesty's Forces, I am led to conclude that the most ready way to bring about a Distribution of this Money will be to submit the Matter to the Lords of the Treasury; if you are of this Opinion, it will be necessary to send me proper Instructions on this head, with proper Documents to establish your Right to a large Proportion of the Sum so granted by Parliament: from the Steps already taken by your Government with Genl. Abercromby, your Instructions may be more pointed. I shall only observe that as the Case may require a further Explanation by the House of Commons, the sooner my Instructions come, the better for your Service, and by the several Agents concerned concurring together in an Application to the Treasury for a Distribution, the matter may be the sooner accommodated.

The Parcel of News Papers herewith sent will tell you the Publick Events, Altho' Peace has been for some Days the City Talk, I have no reason to believe it has any Foundation: for According to the present System, Peace must come from the American Continent, come what will of Other Continents, My best Wishes for yourself and Family concludes me always Sir Yours &ca

LB, pp. 114–115. In a clerk's hand. Fauquier communicated this letter to the Council on 6 Apil 1759; it is mentioned simply as enclosing a letter from General Abercromby (*EJC*, 6:678).

1. JA to Fauquier, 5 Oct. 1758, pp. 266–267.

2. General Abercromby's letter has not been found. It was presumably written about two months before the date of this letter, and thus before the general had notice of his recall.

To John Blair

Dr. Sir   London 18th Novr. 1758

I have your Favours of Septr. 18th[1] inclosing two Bills £50 Each, that on Messrs. Hanburys was no sooner presented than paid, the other on Mr. James Russell[2] accepted; and when due will be paid; I long much to hear from you concerning my Demands on the House of Burgesses, I do not at all doubt of the Recommendation ask'd of the Governor & Council to have me put on the like Establishment with Mr Blackiston, and accordingly I hope in due time to bring it about with the Treasury.

Mr. Dinwiddie and myself are pressing the Case of Relief to the Tobbacco Revenue from the Quitrents, but none but them who have experienced the Delays at the Treasury can judge of the Difficultys attending Negociations there: The chief Point now urged is a Reference to the Auditor Genl. was this got over, I should so far have the Field before me, We shall persevere, & the Result thereof you shall know. I do not as yet despair of further Advantages over the Enemy, before our Troops take Winter Quarters: The Fate of the Party under Major Grant before Fort du Quesne is not very favourable;[3] We do conclude that Brigr. Forbes must die before the Affair is finished, as by all Accounts he is in a very dangerous State of Health.[4] Compliments to your Son & Family concludes me Dr. Sir yours &ca.

LB, pp. 115–116. In a clerk's hand.

1. Letters not found.

2. James Russell was one of the London merchants who memorialized the Board of Trade against the Virginia act that declared paper money emissions legal tender in payment of any debt except quitrents (*Fauquier Papers*, 1:38–41).

3. On 13 Sept. 1758 Maj. James Grant, of the Highland Regiment, arrived at Fort Duquesne with 800 men. The objects of the operation were to make a reconnaissance of the fort and, if circumstances were favorable, to make a night attack on the Indians thought to be camped around the fort. On 14 Sept., however, the French and Indians attacked from the fort, and in the ensuing engagement the British suffered heavy losses and retreated. Grant was captured.

4. Brig. Gen. John Forbes (1710–1759), who orchestrated the successful campaign against the French at the forks of the Ohio in the late autumn of 1758, had long been in bad health. About 27 Nov., two days after taking the remnants of Fort Duquesne, he suffered an acute attack of illness, and he died in Philadelphia on 11 Mar. 1759.

To John Blair

Sir. London 30th Novr. 1758

I have by this Opportunity transmitted to Govr. Fouquier Copy of a Letter from Genl. Abercromby to me concerning the Money granted by Parliament for the three Southern Colonies together with Copy of the Resolves of Parliament in that Case,[1] and from the fluctuating state of those who have the Command of His Majests. Forces in North America, and the Perplexity of Military Concerns more immediately engaging their Attention, it may be presumed that the Merit of the Services of these Colonies concerned in this Grant may at last come to be discuss'd by His Majesty in England. Should this be the Case, of which however I shall be the more able to judge, after having had Genl. Abercromby's Thoughts thereon, whose Arrival, by his last Letters, I may expect to be about Christmass, In the mean time, in order to forward the Service of your Province, I have desired particular Instructions, with Regard to this Money to warrant my Application, through whatever Channel I may find it necessary so to do, and from the share that my Sollicitations have had in this Matter, I am inclined to think that the Merits of the Case will turn on these Points, First, as to the Money that has from time to time been granted to His Majesty during the War, Secondly, the Number of Forts built for the Defence of the Province, their Situation, Strength, and the particular Purposes to be answered with Regard to the French or Indians by such Forts, Thirdly, the Number of Forces (exclusive of the Militia from time to time on Service) that has been raised and paid during the War and previous thereto on the first Invasion of the Frontiers, when Virginia stood alone, Fourthly, the Services on which Such Forces have been employed whether offensively or defensively.

It may not be amiss in your Instructions to me also to take Notice how much the Tobacco Revenue is exhausted by Extraordinary Services: this I throw out to You that the Governor and Council may avail themselves of this Money, so as to refund & replace the Deficiencies of the Tobacco Revenue, in Case our Application to the Treasury shall miscarry on the Quitrents: At all Events it becomes prudent for the Governor & Council to turn their Thoughts to the Money granted by Parliament as the final Expedient for Replacing to themselves the Deficiencies of the Tobacco Revenue in Case the Quitrents shall not take Place. In the mean time I shall not take one Step towards the Distribution of the Parliamentary Money, least it might suggest this Expedient to the Treasury, so as to give a Negative to our Claim on the Quitrents, and tho I have been strongly sollicited by the Agent of South Carolina to concurr with him in an Application to the Treasury for a Distribution of the Money granted by Parliament, I have not only declined it, but have prevailed with him to suspend his Application 'till I have proper Instructions from Virginia.

I should not do Justice to your worthy Friend Mr. Dinwiddie, was I not to tell you How ready he is to Cooperate with me in all my Measures for the Service of your Province. You will be pleased to lay these my Sentiments before His Majesty's Council with my Sincere good Wishes for their Service,[2] and believe me to be always with true Regard, Sir &ca

LB, pp. 116–118. In a clerk's hand.

1. See JA to Fauquier, 17 Nov. 1758, pp. 271–272. For the resolves of Parliament, see JA to North Carolina Committee of Correspondence, 26 May 1757, pp. 188–189, n. 2.

2. There is no record in the journals of the Council that Blair ever laid JA's "sentiments" before it.

To Francis Fauquier

Sir   London Decr 28th. 1758

I had the Honour to write you very lately & probably Mr. Gibson may bring this with my former Letters;[1] Since my last the Lords for Trade have had under their Consideration the Act passd in 1752. with a suspending Clause for erecting a Light House on Cape Henry, their Lordships thereupon desired my Attendance, and at the same Time that of the Agent for Maryland.[2]

However well disposed their Lordships appear to support the Measures proposed by this Act nevertheless from the Impropriety thereof by Carrying its Operation beyond the territorial Jurisdiction of Virginia (vizt) into Mary land, their Lordships cannot therefore advise His Majesty to assent thereto, inforce, or extend the Act to another Province.

Their Lordships have therefore been pleased to direct the Agents for these Governments to take the Opinion of the Merchants and Traders to Virginia and Maryland upon the Utility of a Light House so proposed, and if the Trading and Provincial Interests do concur together, their Lordships on the Principles of a general Utility are inclined to take it up as a Measure of Government in Parliament, in which Case 'tis to be supposed that the diferrent Provinces as Parties concerned with the Trading Interest will mutually contribute to the necessary Expence.[3]

However much I am out of Pocket in Publick Services, more particularly so in my Parliamentary Solicitations, Witness the Cases of the Supply from Parliament and the Salt Bill, and on other occasions, in Business more immediately relative to the Assembly, and for all which I have not received the smallest Allowance from the House of Burgesses since the Commencement of my Agency, & for which my Bill of Expences are now before them:[4] that this Service may not suffer I shall nevertheless advance the Proportion of the Expence on Account of Virginia, if the Lords for Trade with the Approbation of the Merchants and the Agent for Maryland, think fit to take the Matter up in Parliament before I can Know the Pleasure of your Government hereon. I cannot conclude this without acquainting you that I have seen Copy of a Bill projected in the House of Burgesses (but rejected by the Council) for appointing Mr. Paris Agent for Virginia: Upon the Face of this Bill it carries with it its own Condemnation, for whatever Person should Act under the Authority of such a Bill must necessarily become An Agent for Faction in Place of Agent for Governnment, nor will the Liberality of the House of Burgesses by the Salary proposed for their Agent, establish the Rectitude of the arbitrary Principles of the Committees Authority, over such Agent. This Bill being rejected by the Council I shall take it for granted that I am at Liberty to correspond with the Governor without incurring Censure for so Doing.[5] Complements of the Season attend You & Yours from me, who am on all Occasions with truth Sir Your most Obdt &ca.

LB, pp. 119–121. In a clerk's hand. At the foot of this letter JA wrote: "NB by Mr Greeme," probably the Rev. Richard Graham, who was returning to Virginia to resume his professorship at the College of William and Mary.

1. There is no record of any letter from JA to Fauquier between this one and that of 17 Nov. 1758, above. Gibson has not been identified.

2. For the lighthouse act, see JA to Dinwiddie, 4 Mar. 1753, above. On 24 Nov. 1757 the Board of Trade took the act into consideration and concluded that it might affect the interests of the proprietor of Maryland and the inhabitants of that colony;

it therefore ordered a copy of the act to be sent to the proprietor's agent and invited his comments upon it (*JBT*, 10:350). On 14 Dec. 1758 the Board discussed the act with Robert Dinwiddie and afterwards agreed to call in the agents for Virginia and Maryland for further discussion of the act on 19 Dec. On that day the Board heard what was said about the act by a Mr. Hamersley, in behalf of Lord Baltimore, the proprietor, and Caecilius Calvert and JA as agents for Maryland and Virginia; there was agreement that a lighthouse at the entrance to the Chesapeake would be of great value to the trade and shipping of both colonies, and the agents were asked to ascertain what British merchants trading to those colonies thought of the idea. However, as soon as the agents had withdrawn, the Board ordered the preparation of a representation to the king, recommending repeal of the act (*JBT*, 10:436–437).

3. The essential objection to the act was that Maryland shipping would be taxed by Virginia, and thus Maryland would be made liable to the authority of Virginia. The act was repealed by an Order in Council of 2 Feb. 1759 (*APC*, 4:401–402). JA had informed the Board on 9 Jan. 1759 that the merchants approved of the idea of a lighthouse at Cape Henry but objected to a tax on shipping and would not contribute in any way to the cost of the lighthouse (CO 5/1329, fols. 90–93; *JBT*, 11:1).

4. See JA to Blair, 8 Mar. 1758, enclosure, pp. 237–238.

5. The bill was passed by the House of Burgesses as "An Act for appointing an agent," on 2 Oct. 1758; on the following day it was referred to the Council, which ordered amendments to it on 7 Oct. and then rejected it on 9 Oct. (*JHB, 1758–1761*, 21, 25, 31, 34; *LJC*, 3:1193, 1195, 1196). The text of the bill has not been found. Paris was presumably Ferdinand John Paris, a solicitor who often acted as agent for the colonial governments, and presumably the same Mr. Paris who was appointed agent in a bill passed by the House in Apr. 1758 and likewise rejected by the Council (Richard Corbin to JA, 26 Apr. 1758, Corbin Letter Book, Colonial Williamsburg Foundation). Corbin told JA that the House opposed his appointment in Apr. 1758 because of his failure to defend the colony's emission of paper money.

To the Council of Virginia

Honoble Gentlemen   Jany 9th 1759
The Lords for Trade having under their consideration the Bill for Erecting a Light House on Cape Henry desird of me as Agent for Virginia to take the opinion of the Virginia Merchants upon the Utility of a Light House as proposed by the said Bill, I did accordingly lay the Bill before the Merchants of Virginia and their oppinion thereupon as contained in their Secretary Mr Collets letter to me copy whereof is enclosd,[1] I have Reported to the Lords Commissioners for Trade & Plantations with these observations thereon for further explanation thereof, That I do find from some

of the principal Merchants that they have objections to the Taxation of shiping only as the said Bill directs, which they think too partial in so far as that the Cargos ought to bear their share nor are they disposed to be at any part of the Expence that must necessarily attend An application to Parliament in this Case for an Act to carry its operation to Maryland, which can not be done by the Bill now under consideration, and hence I am led to believe that the Bill as it now stands will not have His Majestys Assent.

Were the several Provinces and the Merchants all to be Benefited thereby to agree together upon the Principles of a Law for Erecting a Light House on Cape Henry I have no doubt of the concurrence of the Lords for Trade therein, but as the Case stands at present, I see no appearance of such agreement, without which it cannot be supposed that the Lords of Trade will Interest themselves in a Point that may meet with opposition in Parliament from the Partys themselves.

Of late several Prisoners belonging to the Different Provincial Troops are landed from Cartel ships from Canada and Old France, & amongst others is one belonging to Virginia by name Robert Walpole who says he was an Indian Trader before Inlisting under Col Washington, as a Ranger and as such was made Prisoner, Money having been granted for the Use of the New York Provincials who make the greatest number, I have got this man to be Subsisted out of the Money, by the Agent to whom the same was issued and the person is to be conveyd according[ly] to America with the Rest of the Provincials.[2]

Great Matters are in agitation for the North of America, and however far the season is advanced we nevertheless hope to View Sun shine except for Fort Dequesne, which by the accounts from France, the French have of themselves abandoned[3] I am

---

LB, pp. 121–122. Sent "to Portsmouth per the fle[e]t under Convoy." In the margin at the head of this letter JA wrote: "to Portsmouth under the Governors Cover, by the Fleet & Convoy."

1. Letter not found. Collet has not been further identified.

2. Walpole has not been further identified.

3. The French abandoned Fort Duquesne in Nov. 1758.

To Francis Fauquier

Janry 31t 1759

In a conference which Mr Secretary Pitt honourd me with, on thursday last on the Affairs of Virginia I was from thence encouraged to apply to His Majesty for an Aid to Virginia in the manner set forth in the Inclosed Memorial[1] and that the Money which may thereupon be Granted May not rest in the Treasury as the former Grant still does by Reason that the application thereof is circumscribed to the express Approbation of the Comdr in Chief of His Majestys Forces in No America I have taken the liberty to lay before Mr Pitt an Amendment proposed to the Resolves of Parliament in that Case and in any future Grant of Money[2] (Vizt) That the Services shall be attested by the Comdr in Chief of the Forces *on the Spot* and such Attestation to be certifyd to the Secretary of State by the Governor of the Province under the Provincial Seal, and where no Comdr in Chief shall be present, the Attestation to come from the Governor, how far this amendment may take place I can not say but what I have done herein you will please communicate to His Majestys Council from Sir

LB, p. 124. Sent "per Passengers at Portsmouth."

1. The memorial has not been found.

2. For the resolution of Parliament, see JA to North Carolina Committee of Correspondence, 26 May 1757, pp. 187–188. No amendment to the resolution has been traced in the journal of the House of Commons, nor has any such amendment proposed by JA to Pitt been found.

To John Blair

Febry 10th 1759

From a conference which Mr. Secretary Pitt honourd me with a few days since I was encouraged to Address the King for an Aid of Money to the Province of Virginia, as you will see by the inclosed Memorial[1] and as the Money heretofore Granted by Parliament still rest in the Treasury by Reason that the application thereof from the Votes of Parliament is circumscribd to the approbation of the Comdr in Chief in North America, I have proposed An

Amendment to Mr Pitts Consideration which may facilitate the Distribution of that Money and of what may now be granted Viz That the Services, by Forces raised, Forts Erected, Money & Supplys granted by the Province for Military Purposes, within the Meaning of the Parliamentary Grant be Attested by the Comdr in Chief of the Forces on the spot or by the Governor in his Absence and so certifyd to the Secretary of State for the Kings Order thereon.

I have now likewise depending before the Treasury a Memorial for Indian Presents to our new Allies the Ohio & Western Indians the Result of all which shall be communicated to you,[2] in the mean time be pleased to lay these my Proceedings before His Majestys Council and assure them that I have not forgot the Case of an Aid to the Tobacco Duty from the Q Rents nor that of the Indian Commrs which Cases have long been before the Treasury and are likely there to continue unattended to amidst the Multeplicity of other Business that engages their Lordships Attention.

LB, p. 126. Sent "per Mr Hanburys Ships." In the margin JA wrote: "NB Inclosd to Governor Fauquier with a few Lines to the same purpose."

1. This memorial has not been found.

2. JA's memorial, dated 20 Jan. 1759 (CO 5/1329, fols. 95–98), was addressed to Pitt. It represented that the fall of Fort Duquesne had reopened communications with the Ohio and the Indians to the westward of it, that a supply of presents to those Indians would engage them in the British interest, and that a grant of £3,500 for these presents (such as the king had lately made for presents to Indians living to the southward of Virginia) would further the progress of His Majesty's forces in North America. Robert Wood, undersecretary of state, referred JA's memorial to the Treasury on 22 Jan. 1759.

To Francis Fauquier

Sir   March 21t 1759
I wrote you about 3 weeks since that from some Motions relative to Tobacco made in Parliament I apprehended an Additional Duty might insue, and that thereupon I had applyd to the Merchants with a view to oppose the same,[1] Deputys from the Merchants of Bristol being sent up as was imagined in opposition, but by my information at their first Audience with the Ministers the Bri[s]tol

Deputys being askd their Sentiments declard they had authority to admit of an additional Duty of a penny per pound this being admitted the London Merchants in vain found their opposition, hereupon I attempted an opposition on the part of the Province upon the Reasons copy whereof I lay before you,[2] but after a good deal of trouble to little purpose for a general Duty of 5 per cent on Dry goods amongst the rest Tobacco took place, and this on Tobacco is about a penny per pound, the Bristol Deputys I am informd alledge they had reasons to apprehend that a partial Taxation of Tobacco of 2 pence per pound was intended and of two Evils they adopted the least.[3]

In a former letter I told you that Mr Secretary Pitt having recommended to the Treasury my Memorial for Indian Presents I did expect Success therein[4] The Memorial being referrd to the Board of Trade that Board Reported to the Treasury thereupon, That as they did not know how far the Measure of Indian Presents might have been taken up by General Forbes with the Government of Virginia, or with the Comdr in Chief of the Kings Forces in America, who had upon the application of the Indian Commissioners of the Northern and Southward District Authority to make provision for Indian Measures, their Lordships could not give their oppinion on the Case of my Memorial so that it stops at the Treasury upon circumstances not in my Power to remove in time so as to answer Mr Secretary Pitts Views to the Service of the Western Indians.[5]

In the Midst of Parliamentary Business relative to Supplys and other Matters, it is not in my Power tho I have in conjunction with Mr Dinwiddie labord the thing as much as possible to give Motion to my Memorials relative to the Aid from the Quitrents. My Case in behalf of Virginia is not singular others with as much reason complain of Delays which in the end prove a Denial.

I am greatly Surprisd to find by General Abercromby that no correspondence had been taken up between your Government & him relative to the Money granted by Parliament I expected to have been informd by him how this Matter stood and from thence to have taken it up with the Treasury.

I must therefore once more repeat my application to you for Instructions on this head, containing Certificates of the Forces raisd & Maintaind by your Province the Service wherein they were imployd, the Forts built at the Expence of the Province and the Service and Purposes proposed by such Forts, and whatever Military Services you may think within the meaning of the Kings Message to Parliament copys whereof I have heretofore sent you, In the mean time when I movd for another Aid to Virginia at some time I proposed to the Secretary of State an Amendment to the Resolves of Parliament in that case so as to leave the application of the Money to the Lords of the Treasury without the Intervention of the Comdr in Chief upon the proper Certificates being laid before their Lordships of the Services perform'd within the meaning of Parliament, All these Matters I have more than once laid before you for Instruction thereon, to which I have no Answer hetherto.

You will please however to take notice that by desiring Certificates to be sent to me of your Military Services and Provincial Aids of Money granted that I do not mean to divert you from pursuing your Correspondence with General Amhurst as the Resolves of Parliament direct in this case my meaning is no more than that I may be prepard to apply to the Treasury in case the Votes of Parliament shall be alterd so as to leave the Apportionment of this Money to the Direction of the Treasury without the Intervention of the Comdr in Chief who probably has no Instructions from home no more than his Predecessors had I am

LB, pp. 128–131. Sent by "Mr Withers."

1. No letter from JA to Fauquier of about 1 Mar. 1759 has been found. No information has been found on JA's application to the merchants, but the journal of the House of Commons throws some light on the "Motions relative to Tobacco made in Parliament": on 15 Feb. 1759 the Commons ordered accounts to be made of tobacco imported into England, with specific reference to imports, exports, duties, allowances, fines and forfeitures, and discounts, and on 19 Feb. another account was ordered to be made of tobacco imports and exports for Scotland. These accounts were submitted on 2 Mar. and considered on 7 and 9 Mar. On 10 Mar. the committee responsible reported that a duty of 12 pence in the pound sterling be laid on tobacco and other items imported into the kingdom, in order to raise a supply of money for the king (*JHC*, 28:431, 433, 455–456, 465, 468–469, 469).

2. Enclosure not found.

3. The general duty of 5 percent was levied by "An Act for granting to His Majesty a subsidy of poundage upon certain goods and merchandizes to be imported into this kingdom; and an additional inland duty on coffee and chocolate; and for

raising the sum of six millions six hundred thousand pounds, by way of annuities and a lottery, to be charged on the said subsidy and additional inland duty" (32 George II, chap. 10). The first article of the act authorized an additional duty of 12 pence in the pound sterling (which is 5 percent) on the value of tobacco and other named articles imported into Great Britain to be levied from and after 5 Apr. 1759. JA notes that for tobacco this meant a tax of about 1-penny-per-pound avoirdupois weight; and he seems to say that the spokesmen for Bristol were inclined to agree to the tax of 12 pence in the pound sterling so as to avoid the imposition of a specific tax on tobacco of 2-pence-per-pound avoirdupois.

4. No letter to Fauquier with this information has been found, although JA's letter to Blair of 10 Feb. 1759, pp. 279–280, indicated that his memorial about presents for the Indians had been submitted to the Treasury.

5. JA's memorial, with the letter from Pitt's secretary that referred it to the Treasury, was transmitted to the Board of Trade by Samuel Martin, secretary to the Treasury, in a letter of 20 Feb. 1759. On 1 Mar. the Board of Trade replied that since the king had entrusted the management of Indian affairs to his commander in chief in North America, with two agents to act as his subordinates, it appeared to the Board that the proper method of offering such a proposal as JA's would have been an application through one of the agents to the commander in chief; since the Board of Trade had no information on what steps the agents might have taken to negotiate with the Indians on the Ohio or to procure a supply of presents for them, the Board could not form any judgment on JA's proposal; and, finally, the Board considered that if a distribution of presents to the Indians was thought to be expedient, and if no steps had been taken by the commander in chief, or General Forbes, or the government of Virginia, or that of Pennsylvania, to provide such presents, it would no doubt be necessary to send the presents from England. The letter from Martin to the Board of Trade has not been traced; the Board's reply is CO 5/1367, fols. 181–183.

To John Blair

Sir   March 21t 1759

Inclosd you have copy of my Letter to the Governour with the papers relative thereto thereby you see the situation of Provincial Affairs, to which I have to add copy of the King's Instruction upon the Merchants application,[1] the original Instruction no doubt will be transmitted by the Merchants themselves.

Upon this occasion it is Incumbent on me to take off the reproaches I find have been thrown upon me for not having opposd the Merchants application, by representing to them that the Execution Law complaind of was by a Subsequent Law amended and the Evil thereby removed[2] I cannot say how far the

Merchants are satisfyd with the Amending Law since they have it under consideration And it is within these few days, that this Law has been discovered, for according to the Rules of the Plantation Office all Laws are directly sent to the Counsel of that Board Sir Mathew Lamb and before him with other Virginia Laws it lay above 12 Monthes on the return thereof to the Office it lay by til the consideration of the Virginia Laws came in their turn and this did not happen til monthes after the Merchants application, and so very little was it known to the Board on the hearing on the Merchants Petition, that tho it was alledged to be the practise of the General Court to Regulate the Exchange[3] and this fact came out from Interrogatorys to some of the Merchants lately from Virginia yet it was not understood that such practise was supported by Express Law on the contrary it was inferrd that the Practise being so, that accordingly it ought to be supported by a Law and thereby the Merchants Plea was strengthend, This being the Case I hope to be acquitted for not urging it against their Petition since without Instruction from Journals Letters or any Information directly or Indirectly it became impossible for me to know of such Law, Mr Fauquiere will do me Justice how much I labord the pres[e]rvation of the Paper Curren[c]y Act before he left England by preventing a direct application for its Repeal the fatal consequence whereof I did not neglect to urge to the Merchants previous to their Petition to the Lords for Trade for an Amendment or Explanation thereof in place of the Repeal with my humble Respects to the Gentlemen of the Council I am always

LB, pp. 132–134.

1. JA presumably enclosed a copy of the additional instruction to Fauquier of 9 Feb. 1759 (for which see JA to Dinwiddie, 3 Nov. 1757, pp. 211–212).

2. The subsequent law was "An Act to amend an act, intituled, An Act declaring the laws concerning executions, and for the relief of insolvent debtors; and for other purposes therein mentioned," passed on 9 July 1755. This act stipulated "That in any action which hath been or shall be commenced, and is or shall be depending, for the recovery of any sterling money, in any court of record in this dominion, wherein the plaintiff or plaintiffs shall recover, such court shall have power, and are hereby directed by rule to be entered, at the foot of their judgment, in such action to order judgment to be discharged or levied in current money, at such a difference of exchange as they shall think just; any law, usage, or custom, to the contrary thereof,

in any wise notwithstanding" (Hening, *Statutes*, 6:478–483 [quote on 479]; *JHB, 1752–1758*, 293).

3. In a letter to the Board of Trade of 5 Jan. 1759 Governor Fauquier stated that "Sterling Debts are by Law to be paid according to the Rate of Exchange at the Time of payment or Judgment obtained; which is always fluctuating, and is settled twice a Year by the general Court" (*Fauquier Papers*, 1:145–146).

To John Blair

March 30th 1759

Since mine to you of the 21t Inst[1] I have reced your Favour of 20th Decr inclosing Several Bills of Exchange in favour of Lord Loudoun, the Auditor General & myself all which are deliverd accordingly[2] General Abercromby being calld upon by the Treasury to let their Lordships know the Number of Men raisd & Cloathd in the Several Colonies for 1758 ther[e]upon I have had several Conferences with General Abercromby & Major Halket[3] so far as relates to Virginia, I have some ground, to immagine that the More Northern Colonys more particularly Massachusets Bay New Hampshire Connecticut & Rhode Island in order to agrandize the proportion coming to their share, have or will given in very large Pretensions, But all that the Parliament I apprehend can do at present is to Make a General Provision, which afterwards comes to be proportiond by the Treasury according to the respective claims from the Several Colonies, and the best Principles for supporting your Claims will be to State the annual Supplys of money granted for Military Services, from the commencement of the War, the Number of Men in Pay, the Time of their Service, Forts Built, and the nature of such Forts and all other Military Services for the Kings Troops or the Provincial Troops all which to be properly Certifyd by Commissarys of Musters and the Commissioners for Military Accounts if any have been appointed during the whole Service of the War, if none have been appointed In that case the Persons who had the Direction of Such Services must certify the same. Major Halket can help us out as to the Number of Men for 1758 from the Muster Returns made to General Forbes, and considering that upon the proportioning of this Money I shall require every circumstance properly certifyd that can strengthen our Claim for Virginia at the Treasury you will think it necessary that I am well Instructed as to the above particulars Not that we are to expect Payment by way of Debtor & Creditor but in order to recover a Proportionable recompence with other Colonies, And as your Province may have reced Aid in Men and in Money from other Colonies which they will no doubt carry to their Credit in the way of Supplys you must therefore specify the nature of Such aid, and I must observe to you, that by the rules of the Excheqr a particular Power of Attorney becomes necessary to receive Money, & Such is the Case of the Agents for Payments whoever therefore your Government shall think fit to receive the Money must have Special Authority from your Government for so doing and if you think proper as some of the Agents have allready reced thereby on such Occasions for former Donations, I should desire that Messrs Hanburys to be joind with me in any such Power that may be sent to me as Agent I am Sir

LB, pp. 134–136. At the foot of this letter JA wrote: "all the above letters with this per Mr Withers who saild the 26th of April from Spithead."

1. Printed on pp. 283–284.

2. Blair's letter of 20 Dec. 1758 has not been found. The bill of exchange for Lord Loudoun was presumably that for £180.19.2 (Loudoun Papers 5962, Huntington Library, San Marino, Calif.), which represents one-half of the salary and perquisites due to the governor of Virginia (divided evenly between the royal governor and the resident lieutenant governor or president of the Council serving as acting governor) for the period 25 Apr. to 5 June 1758, during which Blair served as acting governor (*Fauquier Papers*, 1:109–112).

The bill of exchange for Auditor-General Cholmondeley was presumably for £430.10.5$\frac{1}{2}$, which comprised £50 for half a year's salary out of the revenues of the two-shillings-per-hogshead tobacco export duty for the period 25 Apr. to 25 Oct. 1758; £113.1.6$\frac{1}{2}$ out of the same fund (one-half of £226.3.1, the allowance of 5 percent of the receipts divided evenly between Cholmondeley and his deputy in Virginia, John Blair); £150 for one year's allowance out of the revenue of quitrents for 1757; and £167.8.11 out of the same fund (one-half of £334.17.2, the allowance of 5 percent of the receipts divided evenly between Cholmondeley and Blair).

The bill of exchange for JA was presumably for £100 for half a year's salary as agent, out of the revenue of the two-shillings-per-hogshead tobacco export duty. These accounts are printed in *Fauquier Papers*, 1:295–302.

3. Maj. Francis Halkett had served in America as brigade major of Braddock's army and as aide-de-camp to General Forbes.

On the same date as the present letter JA submitted a return of the number of men raised by Virginia and the other colonies in 1758 (T 1/388, fols. 83–85).

To John Blair

Sir.   May 3rd 1759

Altho' time will not, by this opportunity of a Ship ready to sail from Bristol (perhaps before this gets there) Allow me to answer your public Letter in behalf of the Council dated the 11th of Novr. tho' received only this day,[1] I doubt not by the next opportunity to be able to remove the severe Censure thrown upon me by the Gentlemen of the Council of Neglect of Duty in the Case of the Merchants petition against paper Money Acts.

The Lords for Trade having ordered Copy of the Act of Assembly passed Anno 28 of his present Majesty, whereby the Act for paying Sterling Debts at 25 per Cent is repeald to be laid before the Merchants, for their Opinion, how far the Evil complained of from the Paper money Acts is thereby removed,[2] on this Occasion I have had many conferences with the Chief Traders to Virginia, tho' the Case has been long with them, no Report is made to their Lordships, all I can say at present, is that I find their way of reasoning is by no means unanimus, with regard to the Operation of paper money payments, whatever their opinion m[a]y be you may rely on my utmost Endeavours to support the Paper Money Acts, and if necessary to be heard by Council thereon, of all which be pleased to acquaint the Board. I am on all occasions with Great regard Sir,

LB, p. 146. In a clerk's hand.

1. Letter not found.

2. For the act, see JA to Blair, 21 Mar. 1759, pp. 284–285, n. 2. The journal of the Board of Trade of 23 May 1759 states that the act was communicated to the merchants "in January last" (*JBT*, 11:39).

To John Blair

Sir   May 11th. 1759.

I hereby acquaint you that on the 30th. of last Month the Parliament in Consequence of the Kings Message by Mr. Secretary Pitt were pleased to grant £200000. for the Benefit of the respective Provinces in North America[1] and I have the Satisfaction to think that my early Application to Mr. Secretary Pitt on the Part of Virginia by Memorial Copy whereof in my Letters to Govr. Fouquier and to you of 31st Janry. and in March thereafter was transmitted,[2] and my ardent Solicitation thereof contributed in some Degree to this Measure, And while I applyd for the further Supply, at the same time I represented the Difficulty attending the Apportionment of the £50000. heretofore granted, from the appropriating Clause of the Act of Parliament, which prescribes the Manner of Proportioning this Money by and with the Approbation of the Commander in Chief of His Majesty's Forces in North America, and proposed an Amendment thereof, all which was fully set forth in my Letters to the Lieut. Governor & to you, and no doubt have accordingly been laid before the Council, thereby my Attention to the Concern of the Province will Appear.

The Parliament have not thought fit to deviate from the Method prescribed as to the £50000. but in the Case of the £200000. have left it more at large, as by the inclosed Resolves you will see.[3]

I must now in Conjunction with the Agent for South Carolina think of some Method to have the £50000. issued to the Several Provinces concerned therein, and indeed I had done it sooner, but the Gentlemen about the Treasury advised me to rest 'till the further Sum was granted. This Matter requires great Attention, for the Parliament being once up, extraordinary Demands, & unforeseen Occasions for Money coming from all Quarters, from thence the Treasury may plead other Services more necessary & preferable to that of ours, & accordingly avail themselves of this Money, from such Circumstances I am advised to lose no time in geting this Money issued; but how to have it apportioned agreeable to the Act of Parliament is the Difficulty; hereupon I shall advise with Lord Loudon & General Abercromby on the point of their Approbation of Services, and if it can be brought about so as to get their Approbation of Services according to our Supplies granted, I shall perhaps be able to bring this about with the Treasury; In the mean time you may assure the Gentlemen of the Council that I shall do my utmost to serve the Province in this and in all other Respects, I am with great Regard Sir their & your most humble Servt

LB, pp. 148–149. In a clerk's hand.

1. By "An Act for enabling His Majesty to raise the sum of one million for the uses and purposes therein mentioned; and for further appropriating certain supplies granted in this session of Parliament" (33 George II, chap. 18), Parliament voted £200,000 "to enable his Majesty to give a proper Compensation to the respective Provinces in North America, for the Expences incurred by them in the Levying, Cloathing and Pay of the Troops raised by the same, according as the active Vigour and strenuous Efforts of the respective Provinces shall be thought by his Majesty to merit." On 30 Mar. 1759 JA submitted to the Treasury a return of troops raised in the North American colonies for 1758, and on 19 June following he submitted a claim for Virginia's share of the £200,000 for expenses incurred in levying, clothing, and paying troops raised for 1758; the total claimed was £52,000 Virginia currency, or £41,600 sterling (T 1/388, pp. 83–85, 172).

2. JA to Fauquier, 31 Jan. and 21 Mar. 1759, p. 279 and pp. 280–282; JA to Blair, 21 Mar. and 30 Mar. 1759, pp. 283–284 and pp. 285–286.

3. The resolution, passed on 30 Apr. 1759, does not specify the method of distributing the £200,000 (*JHC*, 28:564).

To John Blair (not sent)

Sir,   19th May 1759.

I have but this Moment received your private Letter of 15th Janry. inclosing the 2d Bills for £50, each, being Salary to 25 Octr. last, and at the same time your publick Letter on the Part of the Council,[1] this last will require a more particular Answer than Time now permits by Major Christy in the Packet for New York, who is just gone from me, and sets out this Evening. In the mean time bythis be pleas'd to assure the Gentlemen of the Council, that no Doubt rests with me of my being able to acquit myself of the Imputation of Innatention to the Interest of the Province in the Case of Paper-Currency, when this Matter is explained to them. At present I have no more Time than to transmit to you Copy of my Memorial relative to the Distribution of the £50000. granted 1757 to the three Southern Colonies, and the £200000 granted a few days ago to the general Use of the Colonies; As to the 50000; Since the Session of Parliament draws near to a Conclusion, and as the Interposition of Parliament, in case of any Difficulty, might become necessary, a joint Application, on the Part of the Agents for these Provinces, was advised and agreed to, rather than be tyed up till another Session, & having accordingly stated our respective Claims from the best Vouchers to be met with in publick Journals & Governmt. Letters, On the Part of Virginia, I had no Vouchers to direct me, since the Grant of the 80000 anno 1757,[2] none appearing in the Plantation Office, however as the other Provinces were under the same Difficulty for Want of Journals, we have thereupon mutually reserved, that whatever further Sums may hereafter appear to have been granted by our respective Provinces, that the same shall be accordingly apportioned out of the 200000.; Upon these Principles, the Treasury desired that we would agree amongst ourselves, as to our respective Proportions, which being done, the due Proportion of the 50.000, according to the Claim entered for Virginia comes to £30,047. Sterling. For So. Carolina £12,183.9.0. North Carolina £7,769.11.0. and we have accordingly prayed that the same be forthwith issued to us for the use of our respective Provinces, but whether the Treasury will issue the same to the Provincial Agents, or to the Contractors for Payment of the Kings Forces in America rests with the Treasury, in the mean time we thought it became our Duty as Agents for these Colonies to claim the Same, and before the £200000, just now granted to the Colonies in general, comes to be taken up at the Treasury, I hope to have particular Instructions long since desired in the case of the 50000, and to find Journals in the Office for what further Supplies you may have granted, that the same may be given in by way of Balance, due on the former Claim.

If I have come short in stating your Claim on the 50000 I am not to be blamed; for I have spared no Pains to come at proper Vouchers, so far as the same were attainable from publick or private Documents. I am with great Regard for the Gentlemen of the Council and for you in particular Sir Your most Obedt Servt

LB, pp. 136–138. In a clerk's hand. At the foot of this letter JA wrote: "NB not sent, but instead thereof was sent that of the 3d postea."

1. Blair's public letter to JA has not been found. JA submitted an extract of Blair's

private letter of 15 Jan. 1759 to the Board of Trade in Nov. 1759 (*JBT*, 11:66). In this letter Blair told JA that the House of Burgesses not only had rejected JA's account, "but sent up a Bill to appoint one Mr. Paris to be our Solicitor. This we [the Council] rejected as thinking the Governor would not pass it, but I am afraid Some thing of that Sort will be done, when they meet the 22d Febry" (CO 5/1329, fol. 165).

2. By "An Act for granting an aid to his majesty for the better protection of this colony," passed in Apr. 1757 (Hening, *Statutes*, 7:69–87), the Virginia General Assembly authorized the treasurer to issue £180,000 in new paper money bills and £99,962 to be exchanged for all paper bills then circulating.

To Francis Fauquier *(not sent)*

Sir, May 19th 1759

Having none of yours to answer, I must refer you to the inclosed,[1] from whence you will see what is immediately in Agitation before the Treasury, when it may Please His Grace the Duke of Newcastle to give a Hearing to our other Matters depending I cannot take upon me to say, in the mean time there are others, who have equal Reason with myself to complain of Delay of Business at the Treasury, but Complaints do not avail. I am always Sir Your most obedt Servt &ca

LB, p. 138. In a clerk's hand. At the foot of this letter JA wrote: "NB not sent vide 3d as above [i.e., JA's letter to Blair of 3 May 1759]."

1. Enclosure not found.

To John Blair

Sir May 20th 1759

Finding a packet just going from the Plantation Office, I am indulgd sending a few Lines therein to acquaint you that notice is given me that the Revd Mr Camm, has by his Solic[i]tor Mr Parris exhibited a Remonstrance to the Board for Trade against an Act of Assembly passed last October, Entitled an Act to enable the Inhabitants to discharge their public dues, Officers fees and other Tobacco Dutys in money for the ensuing year.[1]

I have thereupon moved their Lordships for a Copie of the Act, and of the Remonstrance against it, which Remonstrance shall be transmitted to you for your Instructions thereon, in the meantime the Act with the Objections thereto are laid before the Bishop of London for his Consideration,[2] I find the Act is but for one year, but as it may be continued, the Principles thereof will come in question upon the present Act.

LB, p. 147. In a clerk's hand. At the foot of this letter JA wrote: "NB per New Yorke Packet with Copy of last therein from the Board of Trade this went."

1. JA refers to the second of Virginia's so-called Two Penny Acts, which aroused bitter opposition from some of the clergy. The act, passed on 12 Oct. 1758, stipulated that tobacco debts could be paid in money at the rate of 2 pence per pound (Hening, *Statutes*, 7:240–241). Since a clergyman's annual compensation was set at 16,000 pounds of tobacco, the act forced the clergy to accept payment in money instead, even if the market value of tobacco was considerably higher than 2 pence per pound. A convention of about thirty-five clergymen (half of the clergy in Virginia) chose the Rev. John Camm (ca. 1718–1779) to go to England to contest the act. Camm was minister of Yorkhampton Parish, York County, and had been professor of divinity at the College of William and Mary until he was dismissed in 1757 for refusing to submit to the authority of the visitors of the college. He was reinstated in 1764 and became president of the college in 1771, commissary of the bishop of London in 1772, and a councillor in 1773.

Camm submitted to the Board of Trade, as agent of the convention of the clergy, "The Humble Representation of the Clergy of the Church of England in his Majestys Colony and Dominion of Virginia" (CO 5/1329, fols. 119–120).

2. On 23 May 1759 the Board ordered that copies of the "Humble Representation," of an undated petition to the Crown on the same subject submitted by Camm and referred by the Privy Council to the Board (CO 5/1329, fols. 116–118), and of the act in question be transmitted to the bishop of London for his consideration (*JBT*, 11:39; Fulham Papers, 13:248–249). Bishop Sherlock replied on 14 June 1759, recommending disallowance of the act (Fulham Papers, 13:250–251; CO 5/1329, fols. 131–133). The act was disallowed by an Order in Council of 10 Aug. 1759 (*Fauquier Papers*, 1:232–233).

To John Blair

Sir   May 20th 1759

Since mine of the 11th Inst.[1] agreeable to what I then had the Honour to inform you therein, the Agents for the three Provinces concerned in the £50000 have petitioned the Treasury seting forth their respective Claims thereto, and praying the same to be apportioned and issued for the Use of these Provinces: from Acts & Journals, so far as my Instruction from such to be met with in the Plantation Office, were able to carry me, I have formed the Claim as *set forth in the Memorial Copy whereof is now laid before you*:[2] if I am short I cannot be blamed. I had repeatedly desired Instructions from your Governor on this head, but none coming, I had Recourse to the only Means in my Power, that of Journals and Acts of Assembly in the Plantation Office, to which I ventured to add private Information, as in the Case of your Letter to Mr. Dinwiddie.[3] The Agent for South Carolina upon the same Principles at 500264 Currency equal to 71466 Sterlg. has given in his Claim; and that Virginia and South Carolina might not suffer on Account of the Claim not being made for North Carolina, as late Agent for that Province, & having as such solicited the Parliamentary Grant, with the Approbation of the Agent for South Carolina, I formed the Claim of North Carolina, which, in proportion to their Supplies granted amounts to 60700 Proclamation at $33\frac{1}{3}$ equal to £45575. Sterling: how far these several Claims as exhibited on the Part of the Agents will be admitted by the Treasury, I cannot as yet say, but no pains shall be spared to establish that for Virginia, and if admitted off, the Proportion for Virginia will amount to £30815.10.7d Sterl.

In the Formation of this Claim I had two Difficulties to encounter, so as to fix the Demand of my Proportion at the Currency Value at 25 per Cent, and 2dly not to give Credit for the 20,000 Sterlg. granted at the Commencement of the War;[4] but from the perfect good Understanding that subsists between the Agent for South Carolina & me, Preliminaries were so settled, & at the same time stipulated; that, in what our respective Claims might come short from Want of Instructions as to the 50000. that the Deficiencies should be carried over to the £200000.: My further Proceedings in this Case shall be communicated to you by next Opportunity, in the meantime do me the Justice with the Council to assure them that I always am &ca[5]

LB, pp. 150–151. In a clerk's hand except for several interlineations in JA's hand. Sent "By Mr Eyres to N Carolina."

1. Printed on pp. 288–289.

2. JA probably enclosed a copy of the undated memorial to the Treasury signed

by JA and James Wright, the agent for South Carolina, that suggested the apportioning of the £50,000 appropriated in 1757 for Virginia and the Carolinas. Virginia's share was set at £30,815.10.7, South Carolina's at £11,714.3.3, and North Carolina's at £7,470.6.1 (T 1/372, fols. 132–135). In the event, the distribution was as follows: Virginia, £32,268.19.0$\frac{1}{4}$; South Carolina, £9,941.19.10; and North Carolina, £7,789.1.1$\frac{3}{4}$.

3. Letter not found.

4. JA presumably refers to the £20,000 that the ministry granted to Virginia and that was to be repaid from the royal revenues in the colony.

5. Blair laid this letter before the Council on 12 Dec. 1759 (*EJC*, 6:151). See JA to Blair, 3 Aug. 1759, p. 327, n. 6.

To the Committee of Correspondence of North Carolina

Gentlemen of the Committee   London Cravenstreet June 1st 1759

It is but three days since I received your favour of 24th Decer. with the papers attending the same, all which I have now under my Consideration in order to apply them with propriety in the most effectual manner, to answer the purpose proposed by the Committee.[1]

Before I received your Letter the Lords Commrs of the Treasury had taken up the Apportionment of the £50,000 heretofore granted by Parliament to Virginia North and South Carolina, and on this occasion, the Agent for North Carolina being called for, I thereupon thought it incumbent on me to appear in your Behalf, and accordingly from the best documents to be met with Vizt Journals at the Plantation Office so far as they do go, Correspondence between Governor Dobbs and the Earl of Loudon, from Genl. Abercrombies Report to the Lords of the Treasury, upon his being called upon to lay before them a State of the Provincials in Actual Service in the field 1758 which he did for your Province from the returns made to him by Major Halket now here, and who had acted as Brigade Major to Brigadeer Forbes, by this return the Effective Provincials of No Carolina were no more than 127 men under Genl Forbes nevertheless I brought your Claim up to £60700 pro: money equal to £45575 Ster. and accordingly your due proportion of the £50,000. from this Claim comes to be £7470 Sterling if the claim as so stated is admitted of by the Treasury.

You will observe that the Claim exhibited by me comes to £7006 pro: short of that transmitted by you, but from thence no Injury will arise because it was previously stipulated between the Agent for South Carolina and me on behalf of Virginia and North Carolina, that whatever our several Claims should fall short from want of proper Instructions from our respective Provinces, that the respective Deficiencys in our Claims on the £50,000. should be carry'd over, and stand charged on the further sum of £200,000 just now granted for the General use of all the Colonys, and the Deficiency of your Claim shall accordingly be carry'd to that Account.

Lord Loudon having furnished me with Governor Dobbs's Letter to his Lordship of the 28th Decer. 1757,[2] wherein the Governor states the Claim of No Carolina then to be £50000. Pro: Money and accordingly claimd an Allowance out of the 50000 Ster in proportion to the Claim so made; from this foundation I made my Claim, but least the Governor might not have inserted in his Account the money granted by the Province in 1754 for Forts and Arms, I prevail'd with the Agent for So. Carolina to admit the Articles of £6000. so granted in 1754,[3] and likewise the sum of £4700. which by the Information of Gentlemen of your Province I found had been granted in 1758[4] by this means the Claim given in by me exceeded that made by the Governor on Lord Loudon by £10700 Pro:

From this State of the Case you will be able to satisfy the Assembly that my attention to the Interest of the Province *still remained notwithstanding* the discouragement I had *to expect* from Governor Dobbs's letter to me of the 28th of Decer. 1757 which I received in April thereafter 1758 and when I consider the great trouble and Expence that attended my Solicitation of the Parliaments Bounty, which was after the expiration of the Agency Law, and the pains taken in forming the Claim for the due proportion thereof[5] I cannot help feeling the ungenerous treatment on the part of your Government for not allowing my Sallary from 25 March 1757 to Do 1758 as charged in my account Duty called me to continue in the Service 'til I had notice to the Contrary and it was not before the 15th of April 1758 that I had such notice from the Governour, by going on in the Service (upon the Faith of Government) I deemed myself entitled to the usual allowance and I cannot help thinking that on a reconsideration of the Case, that the justice of the Assembly so far as depends on them will make provision accordingly.

I have received a letter from Mr Johnson late Paymaster to the King's Forces in No. America[6] Signifying to me a Demand he has on the money granted by Parliament to No. Carolina to replace £500. Ster. advanced by him by Genl. Shirley's Warrant for the use of your Provincials also £500. Ster. advanced by him by Lord Loudon's Warrant which his Lordship does expect to be replaced to Mr Johnson according to Govr Dobbs's engagt. to his Lordship[7] These Demands with that of Brigadeer Forbes's[8] go deep in your proportion, and it is to be presumed that Govr Dobbs may have signified to the Assembly such Engagts. on the part of your Province, whether he has or has not, I think it my Duty to lay the same before you, and you may rely on hearing from me more fully by the next opportunity, this serves to notify to you, the receipt of your several letters and papers attending the same, and believe me to be with great Regard Gentlemen Your's &c

LB, pp. 139–143. In a clerk's hand, but JA added the last twelve words of the first paragraph, the phrase "Pro: Money . . . 50000 Ster in" before the semicolon in the second paragraph, and several minor interlineations.

1. The committee's letter (not found) no doubt informed JA that on 20 Dec. the lower house had appointed him agent for the province for a two-year term beginning 1 Mar. 1759. His salary of £150 per year was to be paid out of the proceeds of the £50,000 parliamentary grant, and he was to be directed by a committee of correspondence comprising Samuel Swann, Thomas Barker, John Starkey, George Moore, and John Ashe (*NCCR*, 5:1087).

The committee's letter may also have communicated the action taken with regard to JA's accounts (for which see JA to Swann, 13 Apr. 1758, p. 253, n. 2).

2. Dobbs's letter to Loudoun of 24 (not 28) Dec. 1757 (Loudoun Papers 5083, Huntington Library, San Marino, Calif.) expressed the "hope your Excellency will allow us a proportional Share of the £50,000 granted by his Majesty for the Southern Provinces. We have already issued £50,000 this Currency for the use of this and the other Provinces, so that we are entitled to a good Share of the Dividend which is left to you to proportion among the Colonies."

3. JA may be referring to the £5,000 appropriation that was debated in the assembly late in 1754 and approved by Governor Dobbs in Jan. 1755. See JA to North Carolina Committee of Correspondence, 9 July 1755, p. 154, n. 6.

4. There were evidently two North Carolina military appropriations in 1758,

though neither of them was for £4,700. In Apr. £7,000 was appropriated for the assistance of General Forbes, and in Nov. £4,000 was appropriated for two companies at Forts Granville and Johnston (*NCCR*, 8:214).

5. JA wrote "NBB" in the margin opposite this paragraph up to this point.

6. This letter from William Johnston, deputy paymaster general, to JA has not been found.

7. Loudoun's warrant for the advance of the £500 was dated 17 Aug. 1756 (Loudoun Papers 534, Huntington Library, San Marino, Calif.).

8. Gen. James Abercromby reported to the Treasury on 30 Mar. 1759 that North Carolina had raised 157 troops for service in 1758 and had paid the men "untill they joined Brigadier Forbes, who thereafter was obliged to advance them a Sum of Money, to subsist, & carry them home" (T 1/388, fol. 90).

To Samuel Swann

Dr Sr.,   Cravenstreet June 1st 1759

My Letter to the Committee of this date[1] will give you a small Sketch of Provincial affairs, this acknowledges your private letters of the 28th Decer. and 2nd. January,[2] I am much obliged to you, and to the Messrs. Jones Barker and Starkee of the Assembly,[3] and to your Brother of the Council for your services, I am satisfied that you could do no more considering the opposition on the part of the Governor and his Party, My friend Mr Dobbs has contrived matters so, as to give himself full Employment abroad, and his friends, may have their share at home, to support his measures abroad.

While he makes the measures of Government subservient to his personal attachments & national connexions, it is almost impossible that an Administration on such falacious and narrow principles can be attended with harmony so as to promote the public good.

From such partial military promotions of Officers, I understand proceeds the dispecable appearance of your Provincials in the field, and from the same principles, the most advantageous & Constituti[o]nal Offices of Government become prostituted in the hands of Weak and wicked men and Boys and Such I see you have in Offices by Mr Dobbs's nomination, I wish I had influence enough to Correct such abuses, by having all such removed but it becomes impracticable for one in my Situation to attempt it 'till such time, as a proper breach is made in the Influence and favour which attends all Governors, believe me I do not want full Inclination to serve my friends in North Carolina, and the time may come, when I shall be more able so to do.[4]

This comes by the Chief Justice Mr Berry I have no personal acquaintance with him, Our appointments for a meeting having miscarryd, but from his Character I hope you will find in him a good Auxiliary in publick and private Justice, with him Mr Child once more takes the field of Office perhaps more attentive to Lord Granvilles Concerns than those of the Crown, whatever part he may act on your side the Water, I can assure you that here he is no Partizan of the Governors, His abode in North Carolina I hear is not intended to be long, Some New Regulations being proposed in the Administration of Lord Granville's affairs becomes the Object of this his Voyage, I wish it may answer his purpose, by a better Establishment on his return to England, I hope in such Case that Mr Jones and he may come to an understanding about the Office, and such as may put it out of the Power of Governor Dobbs to finesse it into other hands as he did in the Case of the Chief Justice.

If I see any probability of success for the Office of Chief Barron for Mr Barker, you may Assure yourself and him that I shall attempt it, at present I must Expect opposition, on the part of Mr Berrys friends.[5] I beg you will make my Compliments to all my friends, and in particular your Brother, and believe me always, and on all occasions Dr Sr Your's &c

LB, pp. 144–145. In a clerk's hand.

1. See preceding document.

2. Letters not found.

3. Robert Jones, Jr., Thomas Barker (1713–1787), and John Starkey (d. 1765).

4. A. Roger Ekirch has written of Dobbs's military and civil appointments: "Although highly prized plums of patronage, most of the commands Dobbs granted were to intimates related either by blood or nationality who carried slight weight in the province. Hugh Waddell, who received command of a backcountry fort in early 1755, was originally a poor immigrant whose father had known Dobbs in Ireland. The following year, Dobbs commissioned Waddell as a major of three provincial companies ordered to join the British general John Forbes and other provincials in an attack on Fort Duquesne. Others who benefited included Dobbs's son, Edward, a former British officer who was given command of four Carolina companies sent to New York in 1756; and the governor's nephew, Richard Spaight, who was appointed as paymaster for all the forces assembled in North Carolina. . . .

"The governor's civil appointments betrayed an equal lack of political finesse. Samuel Swann, in particular, made no secret of his desire to join his brother, John, on the council. But Dobbs ignored this and other valuable opportunities by which he might have cemented the loyalties of leading assemblymen to his administration. Past inefficiency on the part of provincial officials might partially explain his reluctance. Soon after his arrival in North Carolina, Dobbs complained about the appointment of 'improper persons who know nothing of the Business, and therefore neglect it, and leave it all to their Deputies or Clerks, who only work for themselves, and not for the Publick.'

"But Dobbs did little to remedy such problems. When council vacancies appeared, he simply appointed his son and nephew. If it was possible to compound this error, he did so when he used his London connections to have his nephew appointed secretary of the colony in 1756. Two years later, he succeeded in obtaining the post of chief naval officer for his son. Still worse, Dobbs rewarded the relatives of Henry McCulloh, his longtime associate. In 1755 McCulloh's cousin Henry received a seat on the council. Not long afterward, when McCulloh's nephew, Alexander, lost his office as deputy auditor, Dobbs made sure that he was reinstated. In the meantime, McCulloh himself—no doubt with the governor's approval—had been doing his best to obtain lucrative offices for himself and his relatives. Already, his cousin had held the twin posts of secretary and vice-admiralty judge up until his death in 1755; McCulloh had also been instrumental in helping his nephew initially procure the deputy auditorship" (Ekirch, *"Poor Carolina,"* 117–119).

5. The office of chief baron of the Exchequer of North Carolina had been established by an Order in Council of 18 Sept. 1733 with a salary of £40 sterling per year, even though no business was ever done by such a court (*NCCR*, 7: 483, 498–499). In a letter to the Board of Trade of 27 Dec. 1757, Dobbs explained that establishing a court of Exchequer "might throw the Province into a flame as there is none fixed in the neighbouring Colonies so dare not venture to do it without express Orders from his Majesty" (*NCCR*, 5:949).

James Hasell, who became chief baron of the Exchequer in 1753, resigned on 28 Apr. 1758 at the time Dobbs appointed him chief justice of the colony (see JA to Swann, 5 Oct. 1758, pp. 269–270). At the same time Dobbs proposed that Councillor John Rieusett be appointed chief baron of the Exchequer, to which the Council unanimously agreed (*NCCR*, 5:35, 930, 991). Dobbs again appointed Hasell chief baron upon Rieusett's resignation in 1760 (*NCCR*, 6:620–621).

To John Blair

Sir. June 25th 1759
Herewith come Copys of my Letter of 20th May[1] and Memorial thereto referred; the Agents for Virginia, North & South Carolina, being called upon to attend the Treasury in Consequence of their

respective Memorials relative to the Distribution of the £50000, their Lordships were pleas'd to signify to them that their Claims upon the 50000 must be confined to Services performed previous to the Year 1758, & at the same time directed that we should apply to Lord Loudon as the then Commander in Chief of his Majesty's Forces for his Approbation of our respective Services, & accordingly, we are now regulating the same with his Lordship.[2] And for the Services of the Year 1758 I have given in my Claim on the £200,000. as the same is now laid before you from Documents in the Plantation Office.[3] The Agents for all the American Colonies were heard on their respective Claims,[4] & much Squabling arose thereupon, as to the Proportions of the 200000., some of them arguing that they should have Credit for what was given by them to Virginia, particularly by New York: however I am inclined to think that the Rule laid down by the Lords of the Treasury for proportioning the 200000. is according to the Number of men actually employed, that is, cloathed & paid by the respective Provinces, according to Genl. Abercrombys Report to the Treasury,[5] Copy whereof I inclose, which goes no further than for the Year 1758., and so far as depends upon him, he has, by his additional Remarks added to Major Halket's Return to him of the Effectives from Virginia, done us Justice. So soon as we have obtained Lord Loudon's Approbation of our Claims on the £50,000. we shall move the Treasury to have the same issued to us, the Remitters by Contract with the Treasury having given up their Claim for having this Money issued to them, in favour of us as Agents for these three Colonies.

The Apportionment of the £200,000 becomes much more difficult through the Multiplicity of Claims standing on different Principles, all which must be discussed by the Treasury, whereas the Settlement of the 50,000 rested in a great Measure between Mr. Wright for South Carolina & myself for Virginia & North Carolina. These Matters you will please to lay before the Council,[6] from Sir &a

LB, pp. 161–162. In a clerk's hand.

1. Printed on pp. 292–293.

2. The minutes of the Treasury indicate that on 12 June 1759 it considered the

memorial (for which see JA to Blair, 20 May 1759, p. 292, n. 2) of JA and James Wright regarding the services of the southern colonies in the war, and that on 19 June JA, Wright, and Samuel Smith (described as the agent for Governor Dobbs and joint agent with JA for North Carolina) informed the Treasury that they had applied to Loudoun for the required certificates of performance and that Loudoun promised he would lose no time in providing them (T 29/33, pp. 190, 192).

3. JA's claim for Virginia's portion of the £200,000, addressed to the Treasury and dated 19 June 1759, is T 1/388, fols. 172–173.

4. The colonial agents appeared before the Treasury on 19 June 1759 (T 29/33, pp. 193–197). The Treasury minutes do not record any "Squabling," nor do they record that Robert Charles, the agent for New York, raised the question of that colony's payment to Virginia. However, the Treasury papers contain an estimate, dated 1759, of New York's extraordinary war expenses from 1754 to the end of the 1758 campaign that makes reference to a £5,000 loan to Virginia (T 1/388, fols. 100–101).

5. Gen. James Abercromby's report, dated 30 Mar. 1759, is T 1/388, fols. 89–90.

6. Blair laid this letter before the Council on 12 Dec. 1759 (*EJC*, 6:151). See JA to Blair, 3 Aug. 1759, p. 327, n. 6.

To Richard Corbin

Dear Sir   June 29th 1759.

By a private Letter to our Friend Mr Dinwiddie I was informed that the Agency-Bill was revived, & the successful Reception it met with in Council, from the Assurance therein given that the Governor was to give his Assent thereto,[1] soon after I find he has passed the Bill, it being (as he says) upon the same Principles and Plan, with the Agency-Act of South Carolina, Copy whereof I now send you;[2] compare it with that of the Virginia Act, you will at once see (if the Virginia Act agrees with their former Bill, Copy whereof you was so kind as send me)[3] that the Governor has been deceived, or, of his own Accord has given up the Agency to the Assembly: for this is effectually done by the Proviso added to the Virginia Act.

Whatever Impropriety the Governor & Council may have been guilty of, by thus deviating from the ancient & customary Manner of nominating the Agent for Virginia and thereby giving up the Right of succeeding Governors & Council, tho' this Measure, from Examples in other Colonies (if such can with Propriety be urged as Law for Virginia) might be justified in so far that the three

legislative Powers do unite in the Constituting of a Provincial
Agent, at the same time Instances there are where Assemblys have
their Agents as well as the Governor & Council theirs, yet there is
not an Instance to be met with, where the three Powers do concur
as in the present Case to give the Sole Power to the Assembly, that
is to the Majority of the Committee of Correspondence, being of
the Assembly, to direct, place & displace the Agent and to become
accountable to the Assembly alone for so doing: so stands the
Virginia Act, if I am rightly informed upon the Plan of the former
Bill, and if so, there can be no Ambiguity in the Meaning &
Intention thereof as to the Assembly: for this very Assembly
declared their Sense and Intention of this Point in the famous Case
of Mr Randolphs Agency,[4] likewise in their Arbitrary Resolve of
Octr. 2d 1758. disallowing my Account (not from any Merit or
Demerit of the Articles) but "because I was not appointed by the
Assembly to solicit the Affairs of the Colony" their Language is too
strong to be misunderstood:[5] had they not intended to exclude the
Governor and Council, why did they not provide, as the Carolina
Act does, that two of the Council should at all times be necessary to
make up a Committee?[6] why do they by the Proviso to the Act,
assume to themselves being the Majority of the Committee of
Correspondence, the sole Right of displacing the Agent of the
Legislature and appointing another without the Authority or
Approbation of the General Assembly, that is of the Governor
Council & Assembly. If the Concurrence of the Governor &
Council became necessary to authorize the Assembly to nominate
an Agent for their Service, which Authority on no other Principle
was necessary than in raising Money for Paying such Agent, why
did not the Act reserve to the Governor & Council their ancient
Right of nominating the Agent for Government? no Money being
raised by the Assembly for his Payment, the Plea for maintaining
their Right, by a Saving Clause in the Act, was very strong, and had
the Govr. & Council left me any Ground to stand upon, I should
have maintained my Establishment under their Authority, it being
evident from the Act now in Question, that the Agent thereby
constituted, the Moment the Act Commences becomes the Agent
of the Assembly only, if their Committee shall think proper to
exercise their Authority for so doing. Was I tenacious of my
Authority, there is a fine Field for Argument, on the side of the

Government, here, as well as with you, and I find that the Crown, has occasionally interposed, by Way of Instruction to the Govr., in case of a Controversy about the Powers for Constituting an Agent, as was done in Jamaica, whereby it appears that the Agent had been theretofore appointed by Act of Assembly 1693, that, on the Expiration of the said Act, the Assembly prepared a Bill for the same purpose, wherein the Council were entirely excluded from any Share in the Management of Affairs with the Agent, the Govr. thereupon is instructed to give his Assent to a new Act for raising Money to pay an Agent, provided the Council are thereby allowed to exercise the several Powers given them by the former Act.[7] From this Doctrine may be formed a strong Plea for repealing the Act now in question, because it not only deprives the Governor & Council of their ancient & customary Right, but, at the same time, in a Case, where no money becomes necessary to be raised by the Assembly, it puts the Exercise of the Powers relative to the Agent solely in the Assembly, whenever they shall think proper to avail themselves thereof.

But it is no longer my Duty nor my Inclination to fight for those who have given themselves up, the only Point I have now to contend for becomes personal and more Matter of Right than of Favour, the Perquisite of the Agency, on the Money granted by Parliament. As other Agents have done, so do I claim, as my Right as Agent for Virginia, and the Remitters of Money to America, by Contract with the Government have accordingly given it up to the Agents, and have signified the same to the Treasury.

The whole Solicitation of the 50000. came to my share as Agent for Virginia, my Interposition in a Publick and private Capacity with Mr. Pitt, Solicitations in and out of Parliament, and after the Money was obtained, my Negociations with Lord Loudon and General Abercrom[b]y as Commanders in Chief, into whose hands the Apportionment of the Money, by my Application to the Treasury was put, and with whom I have used my utmost Endeavours to serve Virginia most effectually: These are Circumstances too much in my Favour to give up the Fruits of my Labour & Service to others Strangers to, and having no Part in this Negociation.

The Perquisites of Agency, in common with other Agents, if rated at $2\frac{1}{2}$ Per Cent, will come to about 600, for my Share, & this is the only Recourse now left me for extraordinary Labour & Expences during six Years Service; let the projected Encouragement to my Successor in Office, who probably may have more Ability but less Trouble than I have had, be compared with mine, this additional Perquisite will not make up an Equivalent to me, however as this Matter arises from common Justice with other Agents, as such do I claim it. Whether the Point will come to be decided with you or here I cannot say, if with you, I must beg the Favour of your Interposition with the Council to support my Pretensions,[8] and by giving you this early Hint you may prepare the Council (before the Matter comes before the Assembly) by Resolving that the Right of Agency of this Money belongs to me as coming within my Service.

However disagreeable to me to act on so depreciated an Establishment from that of my Successor to be I must nevertheless continue in the Service: for there are so many Things brought on the Anvil since the Breaking up of Parliament[9] which I could not give Motion to sooner, I cannot withdraw my Service now they are under Consideration, before the long Adjournments of the Boards. So

When the Act comes over, whether it will or will not stand it's Ground does not concern me much, at all Events it will put an End to my Service for 200. when another is thought worthy of 500. Per Ann: after all, some Doubt, and not with me alone, still rests, how far this Act repeals my Nomination by the Govr. and Council, as it takes no Notice of such Nomination as Agent for the Govr. & Counl., under which as such, no way connected with the Assembly, I have several Matters now in Agitation, the Case of Aid to the Tobacco Revenue from the Quitrents, the Case of the Memorial of Messrs. Randolph & Bird, which has already cost me much Trouble & some Expence. I shall take the Liberty to inform those Gentlemen of the Revenue, who are in Council, that if they do expect equal Service from me, where their particular Interests are concern'd therein, as if I was their Agent, they will find themselves mistaken, some of them have already experienced my Friendship, others may want it, I had much greater Reason to expect to be informed from others than from you, of what was in Agitation, however Matters are not as yet ripe enough to draw Consequences that will determine my Conduct to them from theirs to me, but in

every Situation, I shall remember the good Offices of my Friends &
of yours in particular, & I am &ca

LB, pp. 152–157. In a clerk's hand except for a few interlineations in JA's hand.
Sent "By Mr Lucas."

1. "An Act for appointing an agent" (Hening, *Statutes*, 7:276–277) was signed by
Fauquier on 5 Apr. 1759 (*JHB, 1758–1761*, 118). JA evidently learned of it from a
letter to Dinwiddie of 22 Mar. 1759 from Philip Ludwell (CO 5/1329, fol. 164), which
begins, "You need not be surprised that the Governor [Fauquier] has dispensed with
his Instructions, if you knew the great Services that are expected from the
Subserviency of that Gentleman and all his Connections," and goes on to say that
Ludwell alone (of all the Council, presumably) had opposed the act, but in vain, for
Peter Randolph had assured the House of Burgesses that Fauquier had promised to
pass the act if the Council approved it.

2. South Carolina's "Act appointing James Wright, Esquire, agent to solicit the
affairs of the inhabitants of this province in Great Britain" was passed on 19 Nov.
1756. The act stipulated that eight members of the Council, the Speaker of the
Commons House of Assembly, "and such other members of the said House as shall
be by them appointed for that purpose, and they, or any five of them, two of which
to be of the Council, are hereby appointed a committee to correspond with . . .
Wright, and to give him such orders and instructions as they shall judge will be for the
service of the said inhabitants" (Thomas Cooper and David McCord, eds., *The
Statutes at Large of South Carolina*, 10 vols. [Columbia, S.C., 1836–1841], 4:34–35).

3. For the "former Bill," see JA to Fauquier, 28 Dec. 1758, p. 277, n. 5. Corbin
had sent JA a copy of the bill in his letter of 21 Oct. 1758 (CO 5/1329, fol. 163).

4. JA probably alludes to the House of Burgesses' appointment of Peyton
Randolph as its agent in the pistole fee dispute in 1753.

5. See JA to Blair, 8 Mar. 1758, second enclosure, pp. 238–240.

6. JA appears to believe that the South Carolina agency act (quoted in note 2
above) prevented the Commons House of Assembly from exercising sole control of
the agent by the stipulation that two councillors had to be among the five members
of the committee of correspondence to constitute a quorum. In fact, the eight
councillors named to the committee of correspondence were easily outnumbered by
the twelve representatives appointed by the Commons House, and the South
Carolina Commons House thus gained effective control of the agent (Greene, *Quest
for Power*, 271–272).

7. An instruction to the governors of Jamaica in force from 1718 until the
Revolution empowered them to "consent to a new law for raising money to solicit the
affairs of [Jamaica] in England, provided that such levy do not exceed three hundred
pounds sterling yearly, and that two of our council in conjunction with five of the
assembly to be named by their respective bodies be thereby authorized to exercise
the several powers given them by the former act passed in 1693 ['An Act for raising

money to solicit in England the affairs of this their majesty's island']'' (Labaree, *Royal Instructions*, 1:386–387).

8. Corbin was present at the meeting of the Council of 12 Dec. 1759 at which JA's rights as agent were upheld. See JA to Blair, 3 Aug. 1759, p. 327, n. 6.

9. The sixth session of the Eleventh Parliament had closed on 2 June.

To John Blair

Sir   June 30th 1759

In my former Letter of May, I informed you that I had Notice from the Lords for Trade of an Application on the Part of the Revd. Mr. Camm against the Act of Assembly pass'd in Virginia last Octr. to enable the Inhabitants to discharge their publick Dues, and other Tobacco Duty's in Money for the ensuing Year, that thereupon I had moved their Lordships for Copy of the said Act, and the Remonstrance exhibited against the same, by Mr. Camm & his Solicitor Mr. Paris, which being granted I now enclose them to the Council.[1]

A few days since, their Lordships, on hearing this Case, desired my Attendance in behalf of the Legislature;[2] And, in Support of the Act, I advanced Precedents of former Acts that had passd on the Deficiency of Tobacco, also Precedents, where the Genl Assembly had, on their part in 1753, increased the Clergy Allowance, where the Price of Tobacco was low, as in Fredrick & Augusta Parishes also in Hampshire Bedford & Halifax Parishes[3] that in the present Case, the Legislature had not deviated from the Rules & Principles of reciprocal Justice, nor had this Act any partial Tendency to the Prejudice of the Clergy alone, that it was a General Remedy against a general Calamity of which the Clergy as such, from Principles of Christianity ought to be first to acquiesce under, that the Fact of a Deficiency of Tobacco must be allowed, & that being granted, the Remedy was adequate from the Equivalent in Money, and no Instance could be given where any greater Allowance for the Value of Tobacco had been given as an Alternative in Payment of Dues.

You will please to observe that the Prayer of Mr. Camm's Petition is that the Act shall be declared ab initio Void, meaning thereby, a Retribution, this was much laboured by Mr. Paris, to this I argued that there was no Repugnancy in this Act to any Act of Parliament whereby to bring it within the Statute of 7 & 8 of Wm. Cap: 22 [sec.] 9.[4] but that if it had carried with it such Repugnancy, that it did not ly within their Lordships Jurisdiction to declare it ab initio void, all that they could do was, if they saw good Cause, to represent it to his Majesty voidable, nor could the King, from the manner in which Mr. Camm had pursued his Remedy, go further than to repeal the Law, which Repeal cannot carry along with it any Retribution, against those who had acted in consequence of the Act, whether in their publick or private Capacity.

Upon the whole, tho my Arguments have not prevaild so far as to save the Act, Mr. Camm has lost the grand Point aimed at, of Retribution, which, in my humble Opinion, he can never attain through the Rules of Office, nor even through the ordinary Course of Law, by means of an Appeal to the King in Council, because, as I have already observed, this Act does not come within the Statute of King William, so as to make it ab initio Void.

Their Lordships have reported against the Act,[5] & there's no Doubt of its being repealed upon Principles which relates more to the Impropriety of the Lt. Governor for having assented thereto than to the Merits of the Act itself. And all collateral Circumstances, such as Payments in Paper Theory, &ca. tho' by Mr. Camm thrown into the Case, had no share in their Lordships Judgment.

All which you will be pleased to communicate to the Council[6] from &ca

LB, pp. 162–164. In a clerk's hand.

1. See JA to Blair, 20 May 1759, pp. 292–293.

2. Camm, Paris, and JA all appeared before the Board of Trade on 27 June (*JBT*, 11:46).

3. JA alludes to "An Act for paying the ministers of the parishes of Frederick, in the county of Frederick, and of Augusta in the county of Augusta, and Hampshire, in the county of Hampshire, one hundred pounds annually, instead of the salaries now allowed," and "An Act for allowing the inhabitants of the counties of Halifax, Hampshire, and Bedford, to discharge their public dues and officers fees in money instead of tobacco," both passed on 19 Dec. 1753 (Hening, *Statutes*, 6:369–370, 372; *JHB, 1752–1758*, 170).

4. This was "An Act for preventing frauds, and regulating abuses in the plantation trade," the Navigation Act of 1696. The ninth paragraph stipulated that

"all Laws, Bylaws, Usages or Customs, at this time, or which hereafter shall be in Practice, or endeavoured or pretended to be in Force or Practice, in any of the said Plantations, which are in any wise repugnant to the before mentioned Laws [relating to plantations] . . . or . . . to this present Act . . . are illegal, null and void, to all intents and Purposes whatsoever."

5. The Board of Trade recommended disallowance of the Two Penny Act of 1758 and three earlier Virginia acts (the first one mentioned in n. 3, above; the first Two Penny Act of 1755 [Hening, *Statutes*, 6:568–569]; and another act passed in May 1755 [Hening, *Statutes*, 6:502]) in a representation to the Crown of 4 July 1759 (CO 5/1367, pp. 373–381). The Privy Council disallowed the acts by an Order in Council of 10 Aug. 1759 (*Fauquier Papers*, 1:232–233).

6. Blair laid this letter before the Council on 12 Dec. 1759 (*EJC*, 6:151–152). See JA to Blair, 3 Aug. 1759, p. 327, n. 6.

To John Blair

Dr. Sir (Private)   July 6th 1759

I find by Mr. Fouquier's Letter to Mr Pownal that he has assented to the Agency-Bill, which he says is agreeable to that of So. Carolina,[1] 'till the Act makes it's Appearance I must continue to act, and cannot judge thereof: if it is such as the former Bill that was rejected, by the Council,[2] it will be found to differ very matterially from that of So. Carolina, and probably meet with Opposition, but whether it does or does not stand its Ground, or whither the Right of the Govr. & Council may not be held to remain as it was with Respect to their Agent before this Act, since there is no Non Obstante Clause of Usage & Custom contained in the Act, As to me I am out of the Case, for I shall not depreciate my Service for 200 Per An: when Mr Paris was to have had 300, and now Mr Montague 500, tho' perhaps not enough to engage that Gentleman to leave the Country Life he has (as I am told) held for some Years.[3]

The Point and the only Point I have therefore now to contend is that of the Agency on the Money granted to Virginia: other Agents in Right of their Office having claimed this, so did I, and Accordingly the Gentlemen who have the Remittance of all Moneys granted for American Services by Contract with the Treasury have given it up to the Agents in the Case of the £50000.

Whether this Matter will end with the Treasury here, or in

America, I cannot say, but as I have Reason to believe that this Money will become Subject to the Apportionment of the General Assembly, Governor Council & Assembly, considering that my Office of Agent was derived by the Authority of Govr. & Council, it becomes necessary for me to have a Resolution of your Board declaring my Right of Agency on this Money, for without such a Resolve and previous to the Assembly's Interfering with this Money, I shall be served by the Assembly as I was in the Case of my Account, which was rejected, because, *I was not appointed Agent by them*, had therefore no Claim on them for Payment.[4]

I must therefore be before hand with them, by the Sanction of the Govr. & Council to maintain my Right of Agency in this Case under their Resolve, Copy whereof please to transmit to me in order to prevent all Contests before the Treasury or elsewhere with the Gentleman who shall succeed me in Office if he should come to insist upon reaping the Fruits of my Labour & Expence, which I shall by no Means agree to, considering the Pains I have taken in these Negociations from one Ministry to another, in and out of Parliament, and with the Treasury, before I could bring about a Reference to Lord Loudon & Genl. Abercromby, before whom my Claim for Virginia now is, & with whom I am labouring my publick & private Influence for a large Proportion of this Money through their Approbation of the Services performed.[5]

I have wrote to Mr. Corbin whose Correspondence I was favoured with by Means of our Friend Mr. Dinwiddie on this Head;[6] tho this Letter is private, you may use the same as you shall see Occasion in or out of Council and to the Governor, if necessary, who if he had inclined might have diverted the Prejudice against me in the Case of the Merchant's Memorial he well knew how much I had laboured the Case with them.[7] I am afraid you will find that Sunshine of Favour with you in Virginia begets Clouds here, but that shall not concern me.

As I have a Prospect of being ere long in Parliament, the Disappointment of your Agency sits very light on me:[8] 'tis the Manner more than the Matter that I have Grounds to resent, however by the Govr. & Council doing me Justice in common with other Agents in the Agency of this Money I shall part on good Terms with the Publick, and Services shall not be wanting to my private Friends Complements to you Son & Family concludes me always Dr Sir &ca

LB, pp. 158–160. In a clerk's hand. Sent "By Mr Lucas."

1. In his letter to the Board of Trade of 14 Apr. 1759, Fauquier wrote that "the Agents Bill is pretty near the same as that which is at present in force for the Province of South Carolina [for which see JA to Corbin, 29 June 1759, n. 2, above], The Business and Instructions to the Agent being to be carried on by a Committee of 4 of the Council & 8 of the House of Burgesses according to Directions received from the general Assembly" (*Fauquier Papers*, 1:207–210 [quote on 209]).

2. See JA to Fauquier, 28 Dec. 1758, p. 277, n. 5.

3. Edward Montagu (ca. 1715–1798), the second son of James Montagu, of Lackham in Wiltshire and brother of Adm. John Montagu, was admitted to the Middle Temple on 3 May 1737 and to Gray's Inn on 4 May 1773. By 1773 he was a master in chancery, and in 1776 he was elected treasurer of Gray's Inn. Montagu was appointed agent for Virginia (especially for the House of Burgesses) by the agency act of Apr. 1759 at a salary of £500 sterling per year, and he acted as agent until about June 1770. In 1765 Montagu became British agent for the king of Poland.

4. At its meeting of 12 Dec. 1759, the Council upheld JA's right to his commission on this transaction (*EJC*, 6:151–152).

5. JA wrote to Loudoun on 16 July 1759 in an effort to have Virginia's portion of the funds released. He stated that it "is to me of very great importance to bring this matter to a conclusion with the Offices, before the Agency for Virginia [falls?] into other hands, which by Mr. Ludwells letter to Mr. Dinwiddie there is cause to suspect, may be the case" (Loudoun Papers 6123, Huntington Library, San Marino, Calif.).

6. See JA to Corbin, 29 June 1759, pp. 301–305.

7. See JA to Dinwiddie, 3 Nov. 1757, p. 212, n. 1.

8. JA was returned, apparently unopposed, for Clackmannanshire for the Twelfth Parliament, which convened on 3 Nov. 1761. He served in Parliament until 1768.

To Samuel Swann

Dr. Sir   July 20th 1759

Hearing of this Conveyance from Portsmouth I write the inclosed to the Committee,[1] and acknowledge your Favour of the 7th March, with a very singular Bill in Chancery, and the History explanatory thereof,[2] It is not to be wondered at that a Person whose Imagination carries him from the North west Passage to the Revelations in Pursuit of Futurity, should forget what he is about, so as to lose himself in this World. I shall, so far as I can do him Justice in his Proceedings with Regard to those for whom I am concerned, but it will take Time & Opportunitys I can only act one Part & for one Part as Agent for the Assem[b]ly; clogged occasionally by Smith heretofore Secretary to the North west Passage, now Agent to the Govr. & Council of No. Carolina. As the Case stands with regard to the Money, now depending at the Treasury, I am obliged much against my Inclination to go on smoothly with Smith, in order that no Advantage may be taken of our not Concurring together in getting the Money from the Treasury; I do not find that, after I had opened my Mind to him, that he presumes to have the Money issued to himself alone, the Truth is that as the whole of this Negociation has been carried on & conducted by me, while Agent, and Since Mr. Dobbs had finess'd me out of the Agency, And as Lord Loudon's Report of Approbation of the Claim will come into my hands, Mr. Smith must be under the Necessity of taking such Measures as I shall prescribe, at least I shall be able to prevent this Money becoming subject to the Governors Will and Pleasure, which his famous Message to the Assembly seems to point to, and it may not perhaps be long ere Mr. Smith become tired of his honorary Service of a very false Friend, having found, so I have Reason, so to call him.[3]

I do not doubt from the Reception that the Chief Justice gave my Recommendation of Mr Barguen, that he will take him into his Service,[4] I hope my Letters by Mr. Eyres,[5] who I believe set out with the Chief Justice, will come safe to hand. This Conveyance I have preferred to that by Mr Child with his Wife, by the New-York Packet, as Mrs. Child is almost ready to lye in, & his & her Motions become slow and uncertain;[6] I am soliciting very earnestly the Confirmation of Mr Jones, as Collector of Beaufort, The Commrs. of the Customs, on my Application have recommended him to the Treasury, and this I have seconded at the Treasury, but there is no Security till I get the Commission I shall do all I can for him,[7] As I cannot multiply my Letters by this Conveyance please to make Complements for me to my Friends. I have not forgot Mr Barkers being recommended to me as a proper Person for being Chief Baron,[8] but this depending on the Board of ——— Mr Rutherford's Case must be first determined, from thence I shall be better able to judge what Weight any Deviation from the Go————rs Plan of Proceedings may have, in the mean time I think it is adviseable for me to be quiet in Points of Favour. Complements to your Brother concludes me always most Sincerly &ca

LB, pp. 165–166. In a clerk's hand.

1. See following letter.

2. Letter and enclosure not found.

3. JA alludes here to a dispute between Governor Dobbs and the Council, on the one hand, and the lower house of the North Carolina Assembly, on the other, over the method of disbursing North Carolina's portion of the £50,000 parliamentary grant. See Introduction, pp. xxix–xxxi, above.

4. The chief justice was Charles Berry, for whom see JA to Swann, 5 Oct. 1758, pp. 269–270.

John Burgwin (1731–1803), a native of England who arrived in North Carolina about 1750 via South Carolina, was an attorney who served as clerk of the Bladen County Court 1756–1759, clerk of the Council 1760–1772, and later in the lower house of the assembly.

5. Not identified.

6. Thomas Child's second wife, whom he married in Mar. 1756, was Ann Faver, of Stafford, Staffordshire.

7. For the failure of Robert Jones's application for this post, see JA to Randolph [and Byrd], 28 July 1759, pp. 320–322, and JA to Jones, 3 Aug. 1759, pp. 323–324.

For JA's efforts (ultimately successful) to secure the North Carolina attorney generalship for Robert Jones, see JA to Swann, 5 Oct. 1758, and JA to Jones, 5 Oct. 1758, pp. 269–270 and p. 271.

8. Of the Exchequer. See JA to Swann, 1 June 1759, pp. 297–298, n. 5.

To the Committee of Correspondence of North Carolina

Gentlemen of the Committee   July 20th 1759.

With this, by Portsmouth, you have Copy of my Letter of June 1st,[1] by Mr. Eyres Passenger in a Ship that sailed about that time, since that the Agents for the several Colonies have been heard on their respective Claims before the Treasury, and first on their Claims on the 50000, and hereupon their Lor[d]ships were pleased to signify that the Claims on the 50000. were not to be carried further back than to the Commencement of the War, 2dly. they are not to come further than to the End of the Year 1757, as the Claim for Services for 1758 must come upon the 200000. lately granted, by this means the several Sums, as stated in the Claim transmitted to me by the Committee for Services in *1748* amounting to 6000, are totally laid aside, and the two Articles of 7000 & 4000 charged to the Account of 1758 are transferred over upon the 200000, and accordingly our Claims on the 50000, subject to those Rules, are now, by Order of the Treasury to the respective Agents, laid before Lord Loudon as the then Commander in Chief for his Approbation thereof.[2]

With regard to the Claims on the 200000, all the Agents for American Colonies, interested therein, being heard, much Squabling ensued thereon, after all, 'tis probable that the Lords of the Treasury will follow this Rule of Apportionment, vizt. to grant the several Proportions, according to the Number of Men actually clothed and paid according to Genl. Abercromby's Returns to their Lordships of the Numbers Clothing and Time of Service, Copy whereof he has favoured me with, and accordingly I lay the Same before you,[3] whereby you will observe what a small Figure North Carolina Troops make in the List, by Major Halket's Return, who acted as Brigade Major under Brigadier Forbes. On this Hearing before the Treasury, the Paymaster's[4] Demand for 500 advanced by Lord Loudon's Warrant, and the like Sum by Mr. Shirley's, and a further Sum not as yet ascertained by Brigadr. Forbes, was exhibited to the Treasury as payable out of the North Carolina Dividend, *I am of Opinion that when this Money* comes to be issued by the Treasury, it will be issued under this special Restriction, (viz) that the same shall be subject to the Application of the General Assembly, and this is what I have already, & shall continue to contend for and that Security be given accordingly by the Person or Persons who shall receive the same; This is all I can properly do in the present Situation of this Matter, for I cannot find out that any Notice has been taken, in the way of Office, of the Assembly's Address to the King concerning the Application of this Money[5] nor indeed have I any Reason to suspect that the Crown will at all interfere therein, unless a Contest shall arise in the Province upon the general Application, & this cannot properly arise, till the whole Proportion coming to your Province is finally adjusted & settled here by the Treasury, so as to come compleat under the Cognizance of the Genl. Assembly, so soon as this is done by the Treasury, I shall acquaint you thereof, and of every thing else that may concern the Province: as the long Adjournment of Offices draws near, it may be some time before I shall have Occasion to trouble you on Provincial publick Affairs, but I am on all Occasions with great Regard Gentlemen &ca.

LB, pp. 167–168. In a clerk's hand.

1. Printed on pp. 294–296.

2. On 16 June 1759, JA and James Wright laid before Loudoun the claims of Virginia and South Carolina "together with that of the Province of North Carolina, as the same came transmitted to Mr. Abercromby late Agent for that Province." Appended to their covering letter was a sheet titled "Remarks on the North Carolina Claim" stating that the aids appropriated in 1748 "it is apprehended, go beyond the View of Parliament" and that the 1758 appropriations "are posterior to Your Lordship's Command" and accordingly are omitted from the claim (Loudoun Papers 6119, Huntington Library, San Marino, Calif.).

3. See JA to Blair, 25 June 1759, p. 301, n. 5.

4. William Johnston.

5. This address has not been traced.

To John Blair

Sir   London 25 July 1759.

I have your Favour of the 30th. of May informing me that the House of Burgesses have got an Agent of their own Choosing, having refused the Governors Recommendation of me from a Prejudice to my Proceedings in the Case of the Pistole-Fee;[1] I made some Remarks on this Case in my Letter of the 6th Inst.[2] supposing the Act now passd to be of the like Nature with the Bill formerly rejected by the Council. Your telling me that now you have two Agents confirms my own Opinion, as well as that of others, that by this Act my Authority as Agent of Govern: is not suspended: To continue therefore Agent, under the Authority of the Govr. &. Council, is more adapted to my Inclination (however inferior my Emoluments) than becoming subservient to a heterogenous Committee.

As to any Motion being made in Council to lay me aside in Consequence of this Act, I cannot conceive on what Principles such a Measure can be attempted; have not the House of Burges[ses] got what they wanted, an Agent of their own Nomination, subservient to their own Orders, with a very liberal Establishment, thro' the Concurrence of the Governor and Council? What is it then they aim at more? Is it consistent with the Principles of Government in Virginia (with the Rules of Government here) in Matters of State or Concerns of the Kings Revenue, of which the Govr. & Council of Virginia, by Laws peculiar to the Province of Virginia, are Trustees, independent of the Assembly, and more so than in any other of His Majesty's Colonies? Under such Circumstances can it be supposed that the Govr. & Council, or the Administration here, shall subject their Negociations and Correspondence to an Agent constituted & circumscribed by a Committee of Assembly?

What then have I done amiss in my Conduct with Regard to the Govr. and Council to incurr their Displeasure so far as to be dismissed their Service? In their publick and private Capacity I have endeavoured with great Fidelity & Assiduity to serve them; I am now labouring with the Treasury to serve them; permit me to say that the most effectual Argument to render this new modelled Agency reconcilable at home appears to me to be, by Urging that the Agent for the Governor and Council is not suspended by this Act; the Assembly, by pressing Matters too far, may lose their Aim, & the Govr. & Council, by giving way to them, may expose themselves to Censure, I mean, such of them as are immediate Servants of the Crown.

Mr. Dinwiddie, as well as I are pleased that you are not one of the associated Committee, and had wished the same of Mr. Grymes;[3] The Act as it now stands, if agreeable to the former Bill rejected by the Council, is liable to many Improprieties, by no Means (as Mr. Fouquiere alledges) consonant to that of South Carolina.

For my own part, since the Act does not suspend me, I wish it may stand its Ground with Government here in Favr. of the Assembly. Mr. Montague, their Agent, tho' I have not the Pleasure of knowing him, as he has lived in the Country for Several Years, (by what I have heard) may probably be a Gentleman, with whom I may have no Objection to cooperate occasionally in the Service of Virginia: through him I shall have less Trouble, at the same time, the Precedent of an adequate Establishment from the King; but let this rest for some Time till the Storm is over, as to the Assembly's Agent; some Variation in my Situation may probably bring Matters about more to the Service of your Government, and make a suitable Provision from the Crown more attainable for myself, as Agent for Governor and Council. In or out of Parliament, I shall have no Objection to act as Agent for the Government of Virginia.

I have transmitted your Bill to Lord Loudon, at the same time told him, that I had a Demand on him at meeting for £1.15.8, and Overpaymt. made his Lordship by you; Your Bills to me are accepted; the Overpaymt. of 11sh. 10d. you shall have Credit for in the next half Year's Salary.

The last Letter from the Auditor Genl.,[4] Copy whereof he will send by this Opportunity, points out to you the Manner of applying for Relief to the Recer. Genl. on the Variation of Exchange, and, in this Case, Mr. Roberts and Mr. Grymes[5] shall have all the Assistance in my Power, both as Agent and as Depy. Auditor, but we must contrive it so, that the Quitrents answer for themselves, for I have fully experienced at the Treasury the Difficulty attending Applications for Refunding to the Tobacco Revenue. On this head I have lately repeated my Memorials, but have no Answer,[6] and such is the disagreeable Method of doing Business at that Board that no Solicitation can insure Success or Dispatch in Money Matters, and on this Account I gave you the Hint for Payment out of the 50000, as the last Resource.

The Claims for the Dividend on the £50000, still rest before Lord Loudon, on the Reference from the Treasury, as Per the inclosed Copy thereof.[7] With regard to mine for Virginia, No Difficulty can arise; but his Lordship being in Scotland, the Settlement of this Matter will probably cost me a Journey to His Lordship's House,[8] in order to adjust those Claims with him, indeed before he left Town, we had several Conferences with him, and from thence had Reason to expect his Report directly in our Favour. The Moneys heretofore granted by the King, and by the several American Governments to Virginia, have nothing to do in the Dividend: my Claim on the Parliamentary Grant stands entire, without any Deduction on that Account. So soon as we get Lord Loudon's Approbation of our Claims, we shall lose no time in Applying to the Treasury to have it issued accordingly, and all that rests with your

Government in this Matter is the Appropriation thereof by Act of Assembly, when your Proportion is finally ascertained.

In the Establishment of the Virginia Claim perhaps I may have done it to equal Advantage as if I had received particular Rules to go by from the Province, all that I have to insist on, is, that the Govr. & Council will not now put the Negative to my having the like Emoluments, in this Case, with others, I could have wished to have thrown the Receipt of this Money into the hands of Messrs. Hanburys, this I did accordingly make mention of to you in my Letter of 30th. March,[9] to which having no Reply, I was under the Necessity of going on with my Application to the Treasury in the ordinary Course of Business, with other Agents, who will receive their respective Dividends, giving proper Security, unless the King shall otherwise direct the Paymt. thereof, for by the Act of Appropriation, the Money is to be paid to such Persons, & in such Manner, as His Majesty shall direct, the Services being first approved of by the Commander in Chief. I am Sir &ca.

LB, pp. 169–172. In a clerk's hand except for one change of wording and perhaps two deletions by JA.

1. Blair's letter has not been found, but JA submitted an extract of it to the Board of Trade in Nov. 1759 (*JBT*, 11:66). Blair wrote: "*The Burgesses have at last prevailed for an Agent of their own Choosing*; and tho the Governor would have gladly had you of their Nomination, yet he told me, he found they were so prejudiced, it could not be brought about. *I find they cannot digest your Opposition* to them in the Affair of the Pistole-Fee. I argued you would serve them as effectually, when employed by them, but to no Purpose; the Answer I got, any body but You; So at present we *have two Agents*, but this last on Such a footing, that the Governor, I find, thinks he cannot conveniently correspond with him. They have appointed Some of each House to be a joint Committee of Correspondence; *and that all to him, should go from them*" (CO 5/1329, fol. 166).

2. Printed on pp. 308–310.

3. The Virginia Committee of Correspondence comprised Councillors William and Thomas Nelson, Philip Grymes, and Peter Randolph, and Burgesses John Robinson, Peyton Randolph, Charles Carter, Richard Bland, Landon Carter, Benjamin Waller, George Wythe, and Robert Carter Nicholas.

4. Auditor-General Cholmondeley's letter to Blair has not been found.

5. Virginia councillor Philip Grymes and John Roberts (d. 1772), an absentee official who had been private secretary to Henry Pelham, jointly held the office of receiver general of Virginia.

6. On 23 July 1759, JA addressed a representation to the Treasury renewing his

request for a repayment to the account of tobacco revenue of money diverted to the quitrent account (T 1/389, fol. 107).

7. This enclosure (not found) could have been either another statement of Virginia's claim on the £50,000 or perhaps a communication from the Treasury referring that claim to Loudoun.

8. Presumably Loudoun Castle, in Ayrshire, about 20 miles southwest of Glasgow.

9. Printed on pp. 285–286.

To Francis Fauquier

Sir   Craven Street 26th July 1759

By Mr. President Blairs to me of the 30th May[1] and by yours to Mr. Pownal,[2] I find you have assented to an Act relative to the Agency, which you have been made believe was agreeable to that for So. Carolina, which is not the Case: Mr. Blair at the same time informs me that you used your Endeavours with the Assembly to nominate me, but their Prejudice to the Affair of the Pistole Fee stood in my Way; I am much obliged to you for your Endeavours to serve me in this Respect, but I am much better satisfied to continue Agent under the Authority of the Governor & Council as before (for Mr. Blair tells me that now they have two Agents) than under that of a Committee of Assembly, and if the Act stands its Ground, which may be much questioned if it is according to the Bill heretofore rejected, I shall for my own part have no kind of Objection to cooperate where the Governor or Council shall think proper to direct my Concurrence with Mr. Montague as Agent for the Assembly, and in this light, I wish the Act may stand in favour of an Agent for the Assembly, and it appears to me to be the most likely Means to establish this Act to give it this Construction leaving the Duty of the Agent for the Governor & Council to such Matters of State, and of Revenue coming under the Cognizance of the Governor and Council alone.

I am greatly concerned however to find by Mr Blair's, that some Motion had been talked of in Consequence of this Nomination of an Agent for the Assembly for laying me totally aside as Agent for the Govr. & Council, it being in the present Instance my own Case, may take off the Force of my Arguments with you, but upon the

Face of the Proposition, the Assembly having, by the Concurrence of the Govr. & Council, obtained what they have long aimed at, an Agent of their own Nomination, acting under their authority, whereas the Agent appointed by the Govr. & Council did the whole Business of the Province under the Direction of the Govr. & Council, and accordingly I find from the Records in Office here, the Establishmt. of the Agent to have been in Virginia ever since 1680,[3] why then shall they, the Assembly aim at laying aside the Agent for Government, who receives neither Pay nor Authority from them? Or, why shall the Govr. & Council on the other hand, throw Matters merely relative to Government & the Kings Revenue into the hands of a Committee of Assembly, or one acting under their Direction: Nothing can be more repugnant to the System of Government at home, it is therefore extreamly prudent in you to consider the Impropriety of corresponding in matters of Government with an Agent under the Direction of a Committee of Assembly.

My Letters to Mr. Presidt. Blair will inform you more particularly of the several Matters now in hand concerning the Publick, I have therefore little more to trouble you with at present, but to beg your Protection against factious Measures, and to continue in the Service under the Authority of the Governor & Council as before this Act.

I hope at last to get the 50000 issued, the Case is, by Reference from the Treasury directing the Agents to get Lord Loudons Approbation of our several Claims, Copys of my Claim for Virginia and of all Papers relative thereto I have transmitted to the President, And in this Case, whatever turn the Agency may hereafter take, I expect, on the part of the Government of Virginia the Same Emoluments as other Agents have on this Money.

The News Papers sent you will shew you the Situation of Affairs abroad, Nothing but a Superiority of Military Skill on the Side of the K of Prussia & Prince Ferdinand, and the Bravery of their Troops, can surmount the Superiority of Numbers of their Enemy.[4] Complements to your Lady & Family concludes me always very sincerely Sir &ca

LB, pp. 173–174. In a clerk's hand.

1. See preceding letter, note 1.

2. JA probably meant Fauquier's letter of 14 Apr. 1759 to the Board of Trade, which Pownall would have dealt with (*Fauquier Papers*, 1:207–210).

3. It is not clear why JA used this date; there was an agent of some sort for Virginia during most years from 1624 until 1690 (except for the years 1676–1688), and a regular agent from 1691 onward (Lonn, *Colonial Agents*, 392–393).

4. King Frederick II, operating in eastern Germany, was considerably outnumbered by the Russians and Austrians, and the Russians were advancing into Brandenburg. Ferdinand, duke of Brunswick, commander in chief of allied forces in western Germany, had 43,000 British and Hanoverian troops to oppose 60,000 Frenchmen; he was defeated near Frankfurt in mid-Apr., and early in July the French seized Minden and threatened Hanover.

To Peter Randolph [and William Byrd]

Gentlemen.   Craven Street Lond. July 28th. 1759

After a very long Solicitation of the Treasury I have at length prevailed with their Lordships to refer your Memorial as Indian Commissrs. to the Auditor General of the Plantations, Copy of which Reference is inclosed;[1] having now brought it this Length, my Influence and good Offices shall not be wanting to procure a favourable Report and I am in hopes that the Objections taken to your Memorial, on the Part of the Lords for Trade may be set in such a Light as to obviate the same with the Treasury, and procure you Relief.[2]

I have occasionally, through your particular Correspondents, informed you where the difficulty in this Case lay, vizt, the Want of Journals as Documents to confirm the Allegations of the Petition, and in Fact having over & over made Enquiry at the Plantation Office, the Journals for April, May and June 1756 are not to be met with, yet Govr. Dinwiddie does insist they were transmitted with other Records,[3] but if the Journals did appear (properly authenticated) from Copys now before me I find they do not take up the whole Case: In order to obviate these Objections, I procured Govr. Dinwiddies Certificate of your Commissions, and Instructions on your Appointment together with Copy of the Treaty concluded by you with the Indians, all which, and thereto added Mr. Dinwiddies particular Recommendation of your Case, were given in to the

Treasury,[4] and ever since Novr. 1758 have I solicited the Consideration of the Case.

Altho' this Matter has cost me a great Deal of Trouble, & must still cost more, Nevertheless I shall go through with it, and in the End it will give me Pleasure to be of Service to You expecting no other Return for my Services here than Yours for me in my Concerns with your Government.

It is extreamly mortifying to me to find that the Ground is sliping from under me in the Council, while I am doing every thing in my Power to serve Particulars in their publick and private Capacity.

I hope it is not intended by the new projected System of the Agency to dismiss me your Service, & thereby supersede the ancient Authority of the Govr. & Council, of nominating an Agent or Solicitor, which, by looking into Office here for the Establishment of the Agent, I find to have been with the Govr. and Council & that without Interruption ever since 1680, what is it then I have done to disoblige the Lieutenant Govr. and Council through me to hurt Government? Now, as the Assembly have got their Agent, why may not the Govr. & Council retain theirs? To have two Agents argues no Sort of Impropriety being for different Purposes of Government, on different Establishments in point of Authority and Salary.

I have, on my own Part, no Sort of Objection, so far as concerns me personally to cooperate with Mr. Montague, (whom I have not the Pleasure to know, as he has lived for some Years past in the Country) as Agent for the Assembly, where the Business in hand may concern the Legislature, or otherwise, if particularly instructed by the Govr. & Council so to do, but I am persuaded that the Govr. & Council will see the Propriety of my Acting alone in Matters of State & Revenue, particularly cognizable in the first Instance by the Governor & Council alone; considering how jealous Publick Offices are of Assemblys taking the Lead in publick Affairs, it will be necessary for the Govr. and Council to maintain their Independency in such Matters, and more immediately So for such of the Council as are the immediate Servants of the Crown to keep up to the Spirit of their Authority.

I am vastly concerned that your Nomination of Mr Jones for Collector of Beaufort in No. Carolina has not stood its Ground at the Treasury:[5] On receiving your Letter inclosed to me by Mr

Jones, I went directly to the Customhouse and from thence immediately brought with me the Commissrs. Recommendation of him to the Treasury, I thereupon apply'd to the D. of New Castle, and to Mr. West seconded herein by Govr. Dinwiddie on Mr. Jones Application to him, and had conceived hopes of Success, but, to my very great Mortification, it has after all fallen into the hands of the Fellow in the World the least deserving of any Office under the Government, one McCulloch, who has for this 20 Years past, throu[g]h the most fallacious and secret Suggestions, imposed upon every Office in Government; and I am on the present Occasion inclined to believe that he has played the same Cards of Deceit by giving no favourable Impression of the Conduct of the Officers of the Customs in North Carolina, and from thence suggested to be for the Service of the Revenue to put the Collection into his hands for himsel[f], his Son or Nephew,[6] which of the three may best suit the End and Purposes of his remaining here in the Prosecution of his injurious Land Jobb. As my Information now Stands, he has Carretuck & Beaufort, are they not distant Collections, at such a Distance incompatible; If you think the Case deserves a Remonstrance for the Service of the Revenue under your Inspection, represent the Same & it shall be seconded at the Board of Customs I am &ca

P.S. I am in Advance in the different Offices for Fees on References & Reports, on the Memorial, you'll please therefore direct your Correspondent here to reimburse me, and for what I shall have further Occasion to advance for Fees in this Case.

LB, pp. 175–177. In a clerk's hand. The marginal address at the head of this letter names only Randolph and identifies him as surveyor general of the plantations, but the salutation, the first three paragraphs, and the postscript suggest that Byrd is also addressed.

1. The Treasury's referral of the memorial (for which see JA to Fauquier, 20 July 1758, n. 2, above) to Auditor-General Cholmondeley was evidently contained in a letter from Secretary of the Treasury Samuel Martin of 27 July 1759 (see T 1/401, fols. 203–204).

2. The Board did not actually object to the memorial, at least according to its journal. See JA to Fauquier, 20 July 1758, p. 263, n. 2.

3. No contemporary manuscript copies of the journals of the House of Burgesses

for the session that met from 25 Mar. to 5 May 1756 are to be found in the Public Record Office (Charles M. Andrews, ed. "List of Journals and Acts of the Councils and Assemblies of the Thirteen Original Colonies, and the Floridas, in America, Preserved in the Public Record Office, London," *Americal Historical Association, Annual Report for 1908* [Washington, D.C., 1909], 1:490–509). The journals are printed in *JHB, 1752–1758*, 335–397.

4. Dinwiddie's commission and instructions to Randolph and Byrd, both dated 23 Dec. 1755, are printed in Brock, *Dinwiddie Papers*, 2:298–299, 301–303. The text of the treaty was printed as *A Treaty Held with the Catawba and Cherokee Indians, at the Catawba-Town and Broad-River, in the Months of February and March 1756* (Williamsburg, 1756). Neither Dinwiddie's "Certificate" of the commission and instructions, nor his "particular Recommendation" of the case has been found.

5. Randolph had been surveyor general of the customs for the southern district since 1749 (*APC*, 4:798). He had evidently nominated Robert Jones to be collector at Beaufort (see following document).

6. The post went to Henry Eustace McCulloh, son of Henry McCulloh (for whom see JA to Swann, 6 Apr. 1770, p. 441, n. 1). The elder McCulloh's nephew was Alexander McCulloh (John Cannon, "Henry McCulloch and Henry McCulloh," *WMQ*, 3d ser., 15 [1958]: 71–73).

To Robert Jones

Dr. Sir   London 3d Augt. 1759

Notwithstanding the Prospect of Success in your Case, from the Recommendation of the Commissrs. of Customs to the Treasury, seconded by Mr. Dinwiddie & my Recommendation to the D. of Newcastle & Mr. West, I am after all disappointed, and what is the more mortifying, the Offices of Collector of Beaufort and Carretuck added to Beaufort are given to a fellow the least deserving of Favour from Governmt. Henry McCulloch, who has for many Years attended the Treasury under Promises, and in this Case has succeeded, the Office I am told is for his Son.[1]

I do assure you I am much concerned for your Disappointmt, and wish I could devise any Method to make Reprisals on McCulloch, who, I have some Suspicion, has insinuated, that such Offices are better in other hands, than such as derive their Recommendation from abroad; this is the Card he has play'd in his whole System of Deceit on the publick Offices, and I cannot help suspecting the same in this Case. I thought I had silenced this Impostor, when his extraordinary Commission was, through my Means, suspended;[2] but he has taken up other Ground, and thro' new Arts and underhand Deceit, he still continues his Negociations.

I am affraid least the temporary Execution of this Office may have put you to some Inconvenience as well as Expence, I hope this will come to hand soon enough to prevent more. I have acquainted the Surveyor Genl. the Turn that this Affair has taken, and submitted to his Consideration, how far these Offices at such a Distance are not incompatible. I hope he will insist on McCulloch's R[e]sidence at one or the other of the Ports.

Poor Rutherford, after fighting a hard Battle upon his Suspension I find is restored to his Office of Recr. Genl.[3] I hope the next Attempt in your Service will have better Success, beli[e]ve it cannot have more of my Inclination to serve you being on all Occasions Dr. Sir &ca.

PS. Capt. Dobbs[4] is just now arrived, but as yet Nothing transpires of his Fathers Proceedings; the Boards being under their long Adjournment, these Matters will rest till Octr. I have taken some Steps that may remove ill Impressions on the Proceedings of the Assembly, should he have attempted anything that way, thro' himself or Mr. Smith, who, I fancy, may not find his new Employmt. agree with the Mercantile Business except in the Case of the Parliamt. Money, not as yet adjusted by Lord Loudon, and in that too he may find himself mistaken.

LB, p. 178. In a clerk's hand.

1. See preceding document, n. 6.

2. See JA to Johnston, 7 Oct. 1751, pp. 16–18, and JA to Glen, 29 May 1752, pp. 36–37.

3. The Treasury ordered Rutherfurd reinstated as receiver general, but it was not until Apr. 1761 that the Privy Council restored him to the Council. The Privy Council's Plantation Committee "Thought it desirable for the service of the revenue that the holder of this office [receiver general] should be a member of the Council" (*APC*, 4:386).

4. Edward Brice Dobbs (1729–1803), son of Gov. Arthur Dobbs, accompanied his father to North Carolina in 1754 and served as a captain of the provincial militia during the French and Indian War. He was appointed to the Council in 1756.

To John Blair

Sir   London 3d Augt. 1759
   In my Letter of the 30th June[1] I informed the Council of my
being heard before the Board for Trade on Mr. Camm's Complaint. I did expect that this Case had rested on the Report of that
Board for Repealing the Act, but on a new Remonstrance presented by Mr. Camm to the King in Council, Copy whereof I
inclose herein, I was summoned to Appear & be heard by Council,
accordingly the Case came on that Day, and after the most learned
Arguments on both Sides for & against advising the King to declare
the Law ab initio void, the Point was determined in our Favour (to
wit) to go no further than the Repeal, as it stands on the Report of
the Board for Trade.[2] Never was a Case of so great Importance
argued in Council, the Kings Prerogative, the Validity of the Rules
of Government, under which his Representative is circumscribed
engaged the Attorney Genl.[3] on the side of the Clergy and
Merchants too, whose Petition to the King in Council was thrown
into the Case, And the Grand Point in Argument was whether this
Case, coming by way of Petition to the King in Council, in their
Legislative or Ministerial Capacity could authorize their Lordships
to determine in the first Instance what was, or was not, Law, We
argued that this could not be done otherwise than by a Judicial
Appeal to their Lordships, and that then & not till then their
Lordships sitting in Judgment as Judges, according to the Consti-
tution of Colony Government could in the Kings Name, as Judges
declare what was Law and, in Support of this Principle, urged the
Statu[t]e of the 17th of King Chas. 1st., whereby the Jurisdiction of
the Star Chamber & Council Board was taken away in Cases of
Property &ca.[4] tho' this Point had been taken up by me, before the
Board of Trade, it did not become me to take the Field agt. the
Attorney Genl. in so Capital a Case, whereon rested the Rights and
Libertys not only of the People of Virginia but of all His Majesty's
Subjects whether in the Colonies or otherwise, but the Order, as
you see it, was peremptor to be heard by Council, what I have done
therefore, I hope will be approved of and the Expences made
good; an Account whereof shall be transmitted, in the mean time,
as is usual in such Cases, I have advanced Money towards the
Solicitors Expences for Council. By this Argument the best De-

fence was made in behalf of the Legislature for the Principles of the Act which nevertheless is repealed.

I have now the Satisfaction to acquaint you that I have at length procured a Reference to the Auditor Genl. of my Memorial from time to time repeated to the Treasury for Aid out of the Quitrents, and on this Occasion the Council may be assured of all the Favour & Assistance depending on me.[5]

I have nothing more to Offer to the Consideration of the Council, but to desire to know their Pleasure in what Shape I am henceforth to conduct myself in their Service, there being in Fact two Agents, and if the Law lately pass'd shall stand it's Ground, acting under different Authoritys and Establishment that the Service may go on with Cordiality & Propriety in the Offices, it will, I conceive, become necessary for the Govr. and Council to prescribe my Duty to the Negociation of Matters of Government & the King's Revenue, pertinent to, and immediately cognizable in the first Instance by the Govr. & Council alone, And in Legislative Matters to cooperate occasionally with Mr Montague, where the Interposition of Governmt. may add Weight & Countenance to the Matter in Agitation, And for Mr. Montague's Conduct as well as mine in the Publick Offices and with the Administration, the sooner I have your Instructions to obviate any Difficulty that may arise herein, so much the better, in the mean time be pleased to lay this before the Board,[6] & believe me to be with great Regard to the Gentlemen of the Council & to you in Particular Sir &ca

LB, pp. 179–181. In a clerk's hand.

1. Printed on pp. 306–307.

2. On the date of this letter, JA had appeared before the Privy Council's Plantation Committee (PC 2/107, pp. 84–87). The committee took into consideration the Board of Trade's representation recommending disallowance of four Virginia acts (see JA to Blair, 30 June 1759, n. 5, above); a petition of the Anglican clergy of Virginia (see JA to Blair, 20 May 1759, nn. 1, 2, above); and a petition of London merchants trading with Virginia against the 1758 act (CO 5/1329, fol. 139). The committee recommended that the Board's representation be accepted, and on 10 Aug. the Privy Council disallowed the four acts (*APC*, 4:420–421).

The "new Remonstrance presented by Mr. Camm" may have been the petition of 3 Aug. 1759 from the clergy to the Privy Council signed by Camm requesting that the disallowance of the four Virginia acts be made retroactive to the dates of their passage (Fulham Papers, 13:278–281; erroneously docketed 3 Aug. 1760).

3. Charles Pratt (1714–1794) was attorney general from July 1757 to Jan. 1762. He was created Baron Camden in 1765 and Earl Camden in 1786.

4. JA probably alludes to 16 (not 17) Charles I, chap. 10: "An Act for the regulating of the Privy Council, and for taking away the court commonly called the Star-Chamber."

5. See following document, note 2.

6. On 12 Dec. 1759 Blair laid this letter before the Council, as well as JA's letters to him of 20 May, 25 June, 30 June, 25 July, and 3 Aug. 1759 (all above). Upon reading all these letters, "it was the Advice of the Council, that the President acquaint Mr. Abercrombie they are willing he should have the same Advantages with the other Agents, on remitting their Portion of the Parliamentary Grants—that they approve of his Conduct in supporting the Act of Assembly remonstrated against by Mr. Camm, and shall readily allow the extraordinary Expences he has incurred in that Service—that the President send him an exact Account of all the different Sums which have been raised here for the Defence of the Colony, and the public Service, that he may be enabled to ascertain their Claim on the £200,000—They further advised that a Memorial be drawn to the Lords of the Treasury, praying them to direct that the Sum which shall be apportioned to Virginia may be paid to Mr. Abercrombie, upon his giving Security to remit the same to such Person, and in such Manner as his Majesty shall be pleased to order—And that the President would signify their Pleasure that he ensure the same, and transmit it in a Man of War—and also acquaint him it is expected he will on all Occasions conform himself to the Directions he shall receive from this Board, and that, in any Emergency when he can't wait for their Instructions, he regulate his Conduct, and act according to his own Discretion" (*EJC*, 6:152–153).

To John Blair

Sir   Decr. 15th 1759

In my last Publick Letter of the 3d of Augt.[1] I informed you that I had at length obtained the Memorial of the Governor and Council for Aid out of the Quitrents to be referred to the Auditor General for his Opinion thereon: he has accordingly reported in favr. thereof, and by bringing the Deficiencies in the Tobacco Revenue down to the 25th of April last, the Sum of £2193.1.3 has been added to the Claim specified in the Memorial, so that the whole Sum so reported by him upon the Memorial is £5272.5.6. which is submitted to the Treasury to be paid out of the Quitrents and accordingly becomes the Subject of my Solicitation.[2]

The unaccountable Delay we have met with by Lord Loudon's

Absence, his Approbation to our Claims on the 50000. being necessary has hitherto prevented the Payments of the respective Proportions to the several Agents, but as we are now in daily Attendance upon him, we hope soon to put ane End to this tedious and troublesome Negociation. In the mean time I have got the King's Warrant for £20546.—.— being the Proportion due to Virginia out of the £200,000. but as the Warrt. following the Words of the Act of Parliament directs that this Money shall be issued to the Person or Persons, who is, are or shall be duly authorized for and on the behalf of the said Province, a Doubt arises amongst the several Agents, who have not special Instructions or Powers to receive Money, how far their general Powers of Agency do authorize them: a little Time will determine this Point.

If special Instructions shall become necessary, in such Case, for the Justification of the Govr. and Council, as well as for my own, and that no Umbrage may be given to the Assembly, I shall be glad that I am required to give proper Security to account for this Money to such Uses & Purposes of Government as the Legislature of Virginia Shall direct. In the Case of the 50,000. the Act of Parliament directs that the Money shall be paid to Such Person or Persons as His Majesty shall direct, whether or not in this Case Security will be required of the Agents I cannot tell, what is done by others shall be comply'd with by me, in the mean time I think myself much obliged to His Honour the Lieut Governor for being so explicit with me in declaring and adhering to my Right to whatever Emoluments may arise and become due to the Agents on the Money granted by Parliament to these Provinces.

In the Case of Virginia I hope no Pretensions shall defeat mine, and accordingly to obviate all Doubts thereon I have Mr. Secretary Pitts Testimony of my Services and Pretensions signified to the Treasury:[3] It was through his good Offices that I at length obtained the 50000, after being baffled by his Predecessor in Office in my Claim for Virginia and North Carolina upon the Money granted in 1755 to the Northern Colonies: for so long ago, and when standing alone in behalf of the Southern Colonies was this Parliamentary Aid taken up by me, surely then whatever may be the Profit arising therefrom, I may with great Justice claim the Merit thereof. It became necessary for me in the several Provincial Concerns under my Solicitation to take the Attorney Generals Opinion upon the

Agency Law lately passed Copy of which Opinion His Honour the Lieut Governor will lay before the Council; you will thereby see that the Authority of the Govr. and Council, acting in their State Capacity remains entire as before the Passing of the Act, and that I am well authorized to pursue their Service notwithstanding the said Act.[4] I shall therefore take no Part therein: but it cannot but appear very strange to the Council that no such Person as Mr. Montague is to be met with or heard of, tho' I have made all Possible Enquiry in and about the Temple for such a Person, yet I have been able to learn no further than that a Gentleman of that Name had Chambers in the Temple about 10 Years ago, & had retired to the Country from Business.[5]

If this Act takes place & Mr. Montague appears to act under it, I shall so far as shall be consistent with my Duty to the Govr. & Council for the general Service of the Province, give him all the Assistance in my Power. I have been called upon by the Merchants of Virginia and other Colonies to Countenance their Application to Parliament for a Bounty on Hemp and Flax and from the Reception We have hitherto met with there seems no great Difficulty, but as to the Quantum of Such Bounty to be given.[6]

I have not been able to get Mr. Sharps Bill on the Case of Mr. Camm, in this and some other Matters in behalf of your Government I Stand indebted to him. Wishing you & the Gentlemen of the Council the Complemts. of the Season. I remain with great Regard Gentlemen Your most obdt Servt

J. A.

LB, pp. 183, 183A, 184, 184A. In a clerk's hand. Sent "Per Mr Hyndmans Ship 28th Jany. 1760."

1. See preceding letter.

2. JA's account here is problematical. No report from Auditor-General Cholmondeley to the Treasury of about this date specifying a transfer of £5,272.5.6 from the quitrents to the two-shillings-per-hogshead tobacco revenue has been found. However, the auditor-general's report to the Treasury of 18 Feb.1760 was favorable for Virginia and recommended a transfer of £3,079.4.3, the amount specified in JA's memorial *before* the addition of £2,193.1.3 (T 1/400, fols. 230–233).

3. Not found.

4. The opinion of Attorney General Charles Pratt on the agency act was actually dated 24 Dec. 1759 (*Fauquier Papers*, 1:288–289). In his letter to Fauquier of 25 Jan.

1760, pp. 335–338, JA indicated that the queries put to Pratt had been "framd by Mr Sharpe," probably Joshua Sharpe. It seems likely that JA sought Pratt's opinion at about the same time that he presented a memorial to the Board of Trade, read on 21 Nov., in which he represented that the executive in Virginia was relatively independent of the assembly and had always appointed the agent for the colony, who was paid from the revenue of the two-shillings-per-hogshead export duty on tobacco; that a new agent had been appointed by an act assented to by the governor even though it had no suspending clause, a violation of his instructions; and that the assembly had rejected his bill of £196.7.0 for services rendered, including negotiations for Virginia's share of the money awarded by Parliament. The memorial requested, finally, that the Board of Trade should advise the king either to assume the direct appointment of an agent or to order the governor and Council to continue JA in his office, with an appropriate salary and expenses. The memorial and various papers attached are CO 5/1329, fols. 152–169 (see also *JBT*, 11:66–67).

In his opinion, Pratt held that the agency act "does not supersede the ancient Agent; For he being the King's proper Officer, paid out of his Revenue, and employed about his Affairs, under the Directions of the Governor and Council cannot be laid aside by Implication, and swallowed by another Officer, who as far as I see is the Servant of the Assembly in Opposition to the Crown"; that JA was empowered to transact business and entitled to the salary and perquisites of his office "'till he is removed"; and that "If the Governor lays aside this Agent and concurs with the Assembly, in Intrusting their Agent [with] all the Colony Business, He will in my Opinion behave improperly, and become liable to the Censure of the Crown."

5. It is true that little information can be found on Montagu's activities in the years between about 1742 and 1759, but he was hardly a nonentity, being a member of a rather distinguished family and apparently a competent lawyer.

6. No action in this regard was taken until 1764. See JA to Fauquier, 6 Feb. 1764, p. 420, n. 6.

To Francis Fauquier

Sir   Decr. 22d. 1759.

I have your Favr. of 29th Septr. relating to the Agency Law, which at length is come to the Office, from whence I have a Copy thereof and find no Variation therein from the Bill heretofore rejected but in the Name and Salary to the Agent thereby nominated.[1] The Presidents Letter to me of the 30th of May[2] confirmed me in my Opinion that I was not superseded by Virtue of this Act, for he expressly tells me that no Step had been taken in Council to lay me quite aside, for that now they had two Agents and my Salary as usual had been paid to him, however that I might act with the greater Propriety in the several Provincial Affairs under my Solicitation, it became necessary for me to take the Opinion of the Attorney Genl. Copy whereof I send you as the Same is entered in the Several Offices here,[3] and as the Act does not Affect the special Authority of the Govr. and Council, or that of the Agent acting under their immediate Authority, the Act now in Question shall stand or fall upon the Propriety or Impropriety thereof without any further Interposition on my part, and under this Explanation thereof I sincerly wish you may escape Censure, which I am afraid must have attended this Act, had an Opposition been taken to it on Argument before the Council in Consequence of the Attorney Generals Opinion thereon.[4] It seems strange that the House of Burgesses should have thrown the Affairs of the Province into the hands of a Person who has never appeared, I have made all the Enquiry possible after Mr. Montague, but no such Person is to be heard of in the Temple or elsewhere, about ten Years since there was in the Temple one of that Name, who about that time retired to the Country from Business, whether dead or alive, I have not been able to learn.

Under all these Difficulties that have been thrown in the way of my Service, I am very much obliged to you in particular for being so explicit in testifying your Opinion, and adhering thereto, on my Right in the Case of Virginia to whatever Emoluments may hereafter become due to the Agents on the Money granted by Parliament to the American Provinces. It had been cruelly hard and unjust to have found myself deprived, and more especially in the Case of the £50,000. of such Emoluments, since that Money was absolutely obtained through my Means in the first Instance taken up by me alone and solicited with different Administrations since 1756, and finally accomplished thro' Mr. Secretary Pitt's good Offices to me; And in Testimony thereof I have his Recommendation to the Treasury as the proper Person to receive it for the Use of the Province and I make no Doubt of having the Kings Warrant accordingly for the Proportion of the £50000 which by the Words of the Act of Parliamt. is to be paid to such Person, or Persons, and in such Manner as His Majesty shall direct, and had it not been for the unaccountable Delay given us on the part of Loudon, whose Approbation, of our Services in the Case of the 50,000 becomes necessary, the money had been long since issued to the Agents.

In the mean time the Provincial Proportions of the 200,000. are adjusted and accordingly I have in my hands the Kings Warrt. for £20,546, which is the Proportion given to Virginia but as the Warrt. to the Exchequer does direct that this Money shall be issued to Such Person or Persons, who is, are, or shall be, duly Authorized for, and on the Behalf of the said Provinces, a Doubt arises amongst several Agents who have not special Powers, how far their General Powers as Agents and not particularly named in the Warrant, will Authorize them to receive this Money;[5] a little time will determine this Point Should a Special Power be deem'd necessary it may be done by order of the Govr. & Council under the Provincial Seal, and in order to avoid all kind of Umbrage to the Assembly, for Justification of the Governor and Council and of my self, I desire that I may in the Power or Instruction given me to receive this 20,546 be required to give proper Security in the Exchequer for Accounting for this Money to such Uses & Purposes of Government as the Legislature in Virginia shall direct.

I have taken Notice to Genl. Abercromby that he had not acknowledged the Recet. of your Letters,[6] he says he did receive them but as he was immediately called home, he did not incline to open a Correspondence on Business which had given you an additional Trouble, hopes therefore, with his Complemts. to be forgiven.

The News Papers will shew you our Publick Affairs here & abraod, & with Compls. to your Lady and Family I always am Sir &ca

JA

LB, pp. 184A–187. In a clerk's hand. Sent "By Mr Hyndmans Ship 28th Jany. 1760." See JA to Fauquier, 25 January 1760, source note, p. 338.

1. Fauquier's letter has not been found, but an extract of it survives (T 1/389, fol. 29). Fauquier wrote that JA should get the entire commission for transacting the parliamentary grant. "I should think it highly unreasonable and not just" that an agent appointed after the transaction "should be entitled to any Profit accruing thereby, and I shall be explicit in expressing my Sentiments in this manner before the Council, for you may be assured that I never will give my Voice to do you the least injury, which I think the depriving you of any Emolument arising from this money would be. If there is any it should be yours."

2. See JA to Blair, 25 July 1759, pp. 314–317.

3. See preceding letter, note 4.

4. JA was not careful to avoid a suggestion of censure. In addition to this observation, he appended to his memorial an extract of a letter of 22 Mar. 1759 to Dinwiddie from Philip Ludwell (quoted in JA to Corbin, 29 June 1759, p. 305, n. 1).

5. In the margin at this point JA wrote: "See my letter to Mr Blair . . . of March 30d 1759."

6. Letters not found.

To Peter Randolph

Sir   London Jany 1st 1760

In my former Letter I informed you of the Reference of your Memorial to the Auditor General,[1] I am now to inform you that he made his Report to the Treasury, and recommends the Allowing £1000, Sterlg. for the personal Services of the Indian Commissioners,[2] In Consequence hereof you may be assured that I shall use my best Endeavours at the Treasury to have this Report carried into Execution, and in Case you shall fail at the Treasury, give me Leave to Suggest an Alternative out of the Money granted by Parliamt., under this Grant your services very naturally may come for Revision, and perhaps fore more than we could on the Strength of Precedents presume to Suggest to the Treasury, If you approve of this Alternative I shall contrive to give it this Turn at the Treasury, in case it is not likely to take Place upon the Audr General's Report to the Treasury I am &a

JA

LB, p. 187. In a clerk's hand. Sent "By the Same Ship" as the preceding letter.

1. JA to Randolph and [Byrd], 28 July 1759, pp. 320–322.

2. JA's account here is problematical, for no report by Auditor-General Cholmondeley of about this date has been found. However, in a report to the Treasury of 15 May 1760 Cholmondeley suggests that £1,000 might be a suitable compensation for Byrd and Randolph (T 1/400, fols. 203–204). On 31 July 1761 the Treasury issued a warrant authorizing the payment of £700 out of the Virginia quitrents to Randolph and Byrd (T 52/52, pp. 446–449).

To Richard Corbin

Dr Sir   Jany 1st. 1760

I am favoured with yours of the 27th of Septembr,[1] which came
to hand on the 20th Ulto. I thereby find that preceeding Letters
from and to you had been miscarried.

I am very sorry that your Health has prevented your Attendance
in Council for some Months, this in some Measure accounts for late
Proceedings, whereon I have heretofore recd. your Sentiments;
the Opinion now inclosed will shew you, how well grounded your
Sentiments are. I am much affraid that Mr Fauquier's good Nature
& Complacency to designing People with you has already made
very unfavourable Impression here. I dare not therefore, as
Matters stand at present ask Ld. H–l—xs Interposition in my
behalf, whatever weight I May have with His Lordship I cannot ask
his private Expedient in my Favour, when it is to be apprehended
his Lordship in his Publick Capacity may be obliged in Publick to
pass Censure on late Measures. However much I have been
unjustly reproached by some of the Council and injured by the
Assembly, I do not mean to inflame Matters, it is enough for me
that the Blow intended has missed, and whether the Agency Law
stands or falls, it does not much concern me as Agent for Matters
of State immediately under the Direction of the Govr. and Council,
and in Other Matters recommended to me by the Govr. and
Council. I am greatly obliged to you for doing me Justice in your
own Judgment. I ask no more of Others, I have not the Honour to
be known to Mr. Thos. Nelson,[2] if I was, he would be satisfied that
I never assumed to my Self, the Character of a Notable Agent,
living at this End of the Town, I aim at no more than Serving those
who Employ me to the Utmost of my Power, but I cannot alter the
Nature of Thing's, find Laws where they are not thereby to turn
Paper into Gold & Silver, nor can I make others be convinced to the
Possibility of so doing: No Man ever took more Pains to bring the
Merchants to adopt Mr. Nelsons Belief than I did, but after all I
find them Infidels and it is not in my Power to reclaim them, My
Friend Mr. Dinwiddie's Arguments have no better Success, What
we cannot then do by Conviction, may be done by Persuasion with
them to acquiesce under the necessary Expedient of Paper Money
at least while the War continues.[3]

Untill the Agency Act is determined I shall take no further Steps on Blackeston's Salary.[4]

Your Son needs no additional Recommendation to me, beyond his own merit: he promises well in Person and Capacity; Now he is in the Temple I shall have more frequent Opportunity's of seeing him, and I am sensible I cannot do a more obliging thing to you than to take Notice of him I am &ca

JA

LB, pp. 188–189. In a clerk's hand except for a few minor corrections in JA's hand. Sent "By Mr Hyndmans Ship 28th Jany. 1760."

1. Letter not found.

2. Thomas Nelson (1716–1787) served as secretary of the colony 1743–1776, in the House of Burgesses 1745–1749, and on the Council 1749–1775.

3. The instructions to Montagu "in Defence of the paper Currency" enclosed in a letter from the Virginia Committee of Correspondence to Montagu of 12 Dec. 1759 stated, "If our notable Agent at the other End of the town had known and stated these things [about Virginia currency legislation] to the Merchants, they would hardly have thought it necessary to present any Memorial about it" (*VMHB* 11 [1903–1904]: 3). The author of the instructions was Councillor William Nelson (1711–1772), not his brother, Thomas.

4. See JA to Blair, 8 Mar. 1758, p. 237, n. 1.

To Francis Fauquier (presumed not sent)

Sir   Jany 25th 1760

I have your favour of 29 of Septr[1] chiefly relating to the Agency, the Act has now made its appearance with no variation from that heretofore rejected by you, but, in the name and Salary to the Agent, Mr President Blairs Lre to me after passing the Act vizt 30th of May confirmd me in my opinion that I was not thereby Superseded and that whatever might have been the Intention of the Assembly, and perhaps of some of the Council giving way to the views of the House of Burgesses to Supersede me from their resentment to me on Account of my fidelity in the Service of the Governour and Council, (to whose Service alone my Duty then led me) that no Step had in consequence of the Act been taken in Council to lay me quite aside, for that now they had two Agents and my Salary as usual paid, had not this Explanation come in Justice to my own Reputation in Justice to the Governour and Council who in the Case of the Pistole Fee acted as the Immediate Servants of the Crown, (not in a Legislative Capacity) and having the Kings approbation to their Measures justifying my Conduct and con-demning at the same time that of the House of Burgesses and their agent under such Circumstances I should have thought myself obligd to have claimd the Kings Protection in behalf of the Govr and Councils Authority and my own Conduct upon an Argument before the Council, against the Act as the Attorney General (whose opinion it became necessary to take) points out in the answer to the 3d Quere.

The Act is now before Sir Mathew Lamb and must stand or fall by itself without any further Interposition on my part, for or against it.[2]

It is indeed strange that Mr Montague nominated in the Act if any such person there is has not appeard, I have made all the enquiry possible in the Temple and elsewhere all I can learn is that such a Person about 10 years since did live in the Temple, but then retird to the Country from Business.

I am very much obliged to you for your being so explicit in declaring your opinion on my Right in the Case of Virginia to whatever Emoluments may be allowed to the Agents on the Money from Parliament, It had indeed been cruely Injust to have been deprivd more especialy in the Case of the 500000[3] of such Emoluments Since that Grant was in the first Instance absolutely projected by me alone in 1755 and finaly conducted and Procurd by my Negociations alone with and through Mr Pitt, and lest any difficulty might arise at the Treasury notwithstanding the Remit-ters had renounced all claim upon this Money I thought it advisable to get Mr Pitts Certification to the Treasury of his Inclination that the Money should be Issued in my name, by the Kings Warrant for that purpose as the Act of Parlt directs & nothing hinders the Conclusion of this Affair but the Unaccount-able delay on Lord Loudons part in not giving his approbation to our several Claims, which he has had under his consideration for 6 Months and upwards.

In the mean time I had yesterday from the Treasury the Kings Warrant for our proportion of the 200000, which amounts to

20546, but as the Kings Warrant directs that this Money shall be Issued Unto Such person or Persons who is or are or shall be duly Authorisd and Impowered for and on the behalf of the Said Province a Doubt arises amongst the Several Agents who have not Special Powers how far their general Powers may carry them in this Case, how soon this point is settled amongst us we shall apply to the Excheqr for payment, which the Lords of the Treasury have Signifyd to the Excheqr their pleasure that the same shall be paid by Tallys bearing 4 per cent Interest for the ease of Government here til the Money arising by Taxes come into the Exchqr which of course will be about Tues Day next, you will please to observe the difficulty that I am under from the Words of the Warrant and unless your letter together with the opinion of the Attorney General shall particularly Establish my Authority to be sufficient at the Exchequer the Money on the Warrant now in my hands cannot be recoverd till a Special Power as to this Money comes over, It is otherwise by the Act of Parlt with regard to the 50,000 there the Act directs that the Money shall be issued to the Person or Persons whom the King shall Nominate by his Warrant to receive the same.

In whatever manner the Governour and Council shall think fit to Impower me to receive this proportion of the 200000 it will be proper on their part as well as mine to require me, to give proper Security here to the King for being answerable for the Money to such Uses and purposes as the Legislature of Virginia shall direct by Law or by the Resolutions of the General Assembly that is Gover, Council & Assembly, this I think absolutly necessary to take off any Objection on the part of the Assembly.

Inclosd you have the Attor Genals opinion on Query's framd by Mr Sharpe from the Agency Act[4] & I Hope the Act will be productive of no bad consequence to your Administration, I shall do every thing in my power consistent with Justice to Government and to my self to obviate Resentment on this side, but I sincerly wish for your own sake you had not assented to it.

I have taken notice to General Abercromby that he had not acknowledgd your letters, he says the reason and his only reason for not doing it was, that he was immediatly orderd home, & might have led you into a Correspondence with him which he had it not in his Power to go on with, and desires his Complts to you in this head.

The News papers herewith sent will let you know how publick Affairs stand here and in other parts of Europe & with Complts to your Lady & Family I am &ca

LB, pp. 182, 182C, 182D, 183. A marginal note at the head of this letter indicates that it was sent "per Mr Hyndmans Ship," but the entire letter is crossed through and was no doubt replaced by the letter to Fauquier of 22 December 1759, pp. 330–332.

1. Letter not found.

2. Matthew Lamb, counsel to the Board of Trade, submitted his opinion on the agency act to the Board on 15 May 1760 (*Fauquier Papers*, 1:379–380). For a summary, see Introduction, pp. xxxvi–xxxvii, above.

3. I.e., £50,000.

4. See JA to Blair, 15 Dec. 1759, pp. 329–330, n. 4.

To the Council of Virginia

Feby 15th 1760

Having presented the Warrant for 20546.0.0. for payment at the Excqr by way of Loan at 4 & $\frac{1}{2}$ Inte[re]st till paid as by the Warrant is directed out of the Supply for 1759 I was told that the Rules of the Excqr. require Special Powers in money matters & that such must be under the Seal a Resolve of Gover & C[ouncil] will do, but desire Security may be given in the Exqr by me to the King for the use of the Legislature of Virginia to acco[u]nt accordingly.[1]

The Proportion of 50,000 as aprovd of by Ld. Loudoun & for which my Memorl is now before the Treasury for payment by Mr Pitts Recomdation is 32814.19.0$\frac{1}{4}$[2] some difficulty may attend the Manner of Ld Loudouns Certificat which becomes the greater from the great Scarcity of Money to answer the Ex[i]gencys of Govert at home, but Hope to get over these difficultys I am not Sure but it may become necessary for me to apply for further Supplys this Session I shall act according as I find the Disposition of the Ministry for other Colonys I have but just time to send this by a Ship in the Downs, the 20546.0 may be payable in May I am Gentlemen Yrs &ca

LB, p. 190. The letter is addressed in the margin to the Council, but another marginal note indicates that the same letter was sent to Fauquier. It is not clear whether the note means that a copy was sent to Fauquier or that substantially the same letter, with appropriate changes in the salutation and the complimentary close, was sent to him. Further notes indicate that whatever was sent to Fauquier went to Mr. Hanbury's on 21 February 1760 and then went by Bristol soon after. And, finally, a note indicates that a duplicate of the attorney general's opinion was enclosed. It is likely that this opinion was the one that JA had already sent to Fauquier in his letter of 22 December 1759, above, but the note does not make it clear whether the duplicate of the opinion went with the letter to the Council only or with that to Fauquier as well.

1. Virginia's portion of the £200,000 parliamentary appropriation for services in 1758 was £20,546.

JA and James Wright had complained to the Treasury in representations read on 12 Feb. about the difficulties they had encountered in receiving payment of the £50,000 (T 29/33, p. 285).

2. In fact, Virginia's portion of the £50,000 grant, as determined by the Treasury on 4 Feb. 1760 (and agreed to by JA), was £32,268.19.0$\frac{1}{4}$ (T 29/33, p. 282; T 1/376, fols. 201–202). JA repeated his reference to the higher figure in his letter to Fauquier of 20 Mar. 1760, pp. 342–343, and to the Council of 20 Apr. 1760, pp. 348–350. However, the correct figure is reported in his letter to Fauquier of 10 May 1760, pp. 350–351.

Loudoun's "Certificat," read at the Treasury meeting on 4 Feb. 1760, may have been his signature on a document composed by JA: "Accot of Money raised by the Colony of Virginia for His Majestie's Service, as appears by the Letters that past between the King's Ministers, Commanders in Chief in America, and the Lieut. Governor of this Province." The document itemizes appropriations from 1754 to 1757 of £217,500 Virginia currency. At the foot of the table is a statement, dated 31 Jan. 1760 and signed by Loudoun, certifying that the amounts for 1754 and 1755 appear to have been raised by Virginia for the king's service, and that the amounts for 1756 and 1757 were raised "and applyed for His Majestie's Service with my Approbation during my Command" (T 1/402, fol. 99).

To the Committee of Correspondence of North Carolina

Gentlemen of the Committee   Londn. 21st Febry. 1760
    Herewith you have Copy of my Letter of July 20th. 1759.[1] I am now to acquaint you that after great Delay thro Ld. Loudoun's Absence from London, we have at last got his Lordships [Report] to the Treasury upon the respective Claims on the £50,000 granted by Parliament, Copy whereof is inclosed: from thence you will observe his Lordships Remarks on what is due by the Province to Govr. Shirly & to his Lordship for Money advanced on Account of the Province.[2]

The Claim thus formed and approved of by his Lordship comes far short of the original Claim by me given in to the Treasury, and as such referred to his Lordship, amounting to 56,020 Proclamation: Notwithstanding of such Reduction by his Lordships Report I am in hopes to bring up our Proportion according to the Claim heretofore exhibited by me, if so done, the Proportion due to No. Carolina will amount to £7789.1.1 Sterlg. from the £50,000 Sterlg. granted in 1757. With Regard to your Claim on the 200,000, whereupon I attended the Treasury before their long Adjournment, their Lordships have hereupon fixed the respective Claims of the Several Provinces: In my former Letters I observed how poor a Figure the Services of No. Carolina made in Genl. Abercromby's Report, from Major Halkets Return to him; the Lords of the Treasury have therefore appropriated no Share of the 200000. to North or South Carolina.

I cannot help thinking that No. Carolina is hardly dealt by in the Case of the 200,000, and so far I found myself obliged occasionally to observe thereupon that the Zeal of the Province for His Majesty's Service could not be properly exerted without the mutual Concurrence of all the Branches of the Legislature, and as the Govr. & Council had not thought proper to concur with the Assembly in such Measures as they thought might advance the Service, the necessary Supplies were thereby prevented: but after all, so far as the Service of 150 Men went, some Consideration became due: It is my Duty to do Justice to that Part of the Legislature whose Service I have undertaken: let others answer for themselves. So soon as the Treasury have discussed Lord Loudoun's Report, I shall do my utmost to comply with your Instructions, that this Money do not become liable to the Disposal of particular Persons here, or abroad, and by next Opportunity I hope I shall be able to acquaint you with the final Settlement of this Negociation, which from first to last has given me infinite Trouble, & more so of late, since the Contraversy about the Agency stands in the Way of my Service, but under all Difficulties you may rely on my best Endeavours to Serve the Province I am Gentlemen &ca

LB, pp. 191–192. In a clerk's hand except for two marginal rubrics and the routing memorandum in JA's hand. Sent "per Mr Carvers Ship from Portsmouth 10th April

1760." The bracketed word in the first paragraph was omitted and is supplied from JA's marginal note.

1. Printed on pp. 312–314.

2. Enclosure not found.

To Samuel Swann

Dear Sir   March 1st 1760

The inclosed for the Committee[1] will inform you of your Publick Affairs, what relates to the Dividend of the 50000, I hope to finish ere long, and notwithstanding the disagreeable Task of Sollicitations, acting under the Authority & Directions of the Assembly alone, I am resolved to persevere in their Service; while I continue to be listned to by the Administration at home, and when the Good of the Publick and the King's Service are concerned, I shall be heard by them as Agent for the Assembly; where the Authority of the Executive Part of Government is in the opposite Scale, more Address becomes necessary in my Conduct than otherwise, but as Mr. Rutherford has brought his Matters almost to an Issue, he will soon Leave this, by him you shall have my more intimate Sentiments on Provincial Affairs. Truth & Justice in his Case have prevailed over the most obstinate Opposition to both on the G————s[2] Part. But Rutherford is hereupon advised to shew no Resentment herafter.

All the Belligerent Parties in Europe are preparing for a most Vigorous Campaign, as the last, Such Preparations must rather forward whatever Tendency some of the Parties have shewn for Peace, and this is thought the Case of France, where Naval Expeditions conclude with Monsr. Thurots Death & Capture of his little Fleet, after having paid a Visit to Castle Dobbs in the North of Ireland.[3]

I shall not conclude without acquainting you that an Acquaintance is now brought about with your Son, with whose Conduct & Behaviour I am vastly taken, and you may be assured, when Vaccation brings him to Town, I shall have him with me so often as I can. I must do him and his Guardian Mr. Barclay Justice: Both of them are cautious of associating in London with those who take more Liberty in Diversions than becomes prudent for one of his

Years. I have not seen more Solidity and Attention in the Space of his years, and his Person promises well. My best Complements to your Brother concludes me Always very Sincerly your most obedt Servant

JA

LB, pp. 193–194. In a clerk's hand except for three marginal rubrics and the routing memorandum in JA's hand. Sent "per Mr Carvers Ship from Portsmouth."

1. Probably the preceding letter.

2. Governor's.

3. As part of an overall French plan to invade the British Isles, French privateer François Thurot (1727–1760) sailed from Dunkirk on 15 Oct. 1759 with six or seven ships and 1,200 men (under the command of Brigadier General Flobert) for a descent upon Ireland. Although the main French fleet was defeated by the British in the channel in Nov., Thurot and his squadron made their way to Sweden, Norway, and the Faeroe Islands before reaching the coast of Ireland in Jan. 1760. And although apprized of the fate of the main French fleet, Thurot was still intent on carrying out his mission. In Feb. the French troops landed and captured the town of Carrickfergus (two and a half miles from Castle Dobbs), but within a week the French, with few resources and little of the expected assistance from the Irish, set sail for France. Thurot's squadron was intercepted on 28 Feb. near the Isle of Man, and Thurot was killed in the ensuing action.

To Francis Fauquier

March 20th 1760

Herewith I have the honour to transmit to you a letter from the Treasury, which they inform me signefys to you that it is their pleasure to Issue the Proportions of the 50,000 to the respective Agents acting for these Provinces for the use of the said Provinces on their giving proper Security for the due payment thereof to such Person or Persons as shall be Impowerd to receive the same for the use of the said Province; at the same time desiring you to use your Endeavours that proper Powers may be transmitted to receive such Monies as Parlt may hereafter Grant[1] this agrees with what I have heretofore suggested to you and to the Council, and which becomes necessary, in the Case of the Proportion of the 200000 heretofore alloted for Virginia according to the Claim given in by me on the part of Virginia, and for which I have his

Majestys Warrant for payment of £20546: but my name not being expressd in Said Warrant, and my general Powers of Agency not coming up to the Rules of the Excqr in Money Matters, the warrant must remain with me til I have proper Powers from the Province for receiving the same as my letter of the 15th Feby signefyd to you and to the Council.[2]

In that letter I likewise acquainted you, that I should apply to the Administration for further Supplys and from the Treasury letter to you it would appear that the Ministry had in view a further Supply for Services performd by the several Colonies in 1759, and how to asertain those of Virginia I can form no other Judgment than from the Supplys for Military Servies that may be met with in the Journals and Provincial Acts transmitted to the Plantation Office.

As The Lords of the Treasury have not as yet finally asertaind the respective Sums payable to the Provinces in consequence of Lord Loudons approbation I cannot precisely tell you the Virginia proportion that I am to receive but as it stands on my Claim it ammounts to $32814.19.0\frac{1}{4}$ for Virginia, to North Carolina $7789.1.1\frac{3}{4}$ South Carolina 9941.19.10 which together make 50000.0.0.[3]

The utmost efforts are making for a Vigorouse Campain, at the same time their seems to be some tendency towards Negociation for Accommodation, on the part of some of the Powers at War, and chiefly on the part of France, with Compts to your Lady & Family I am with truth Sir

---

LB, pp. 195–196. At the foot of this letter JA wrote: "NB to the Admiralty by the Virginia Convoy inclosd in the letter was the Attory Generals opinion & Mr Pownalls Attestation of my Credentials. NB the receipt of the above Letter is acknowledged by Mr Fouquieres of 22d June." Sent "per the Convoy."

1. On 25 June 1760 Fauquier communicated to the Council a letter to this effect (not found) from Samuel Martin, secretary to the Treasury, dated 19 Mar. 1760 (*EJC*, 6:165).

2. Printed on p. 338.

3. The sum of these three amounts is £50,546. See JA to Virginia Council, 15 Feb. 1760, p. 339, n. 2.

On 25 June 1760 the Council considered this letter from JA and advised that a copy of its proceedings of 12 Dec. 1759, regarding a memorial to the Treasury (for which see JA to Fauquier, 1 June 1760, pp. 359–360, n. 2) and a full power of attorney for receiving Virginia's share of the two grants from Parliament should be sent to JA (*EJC*, 6:165–166).

To the Committee of Correspondence of North Carolina

London April 12th 1760

In my last of 21t Feby[1] I transmitted to you, our Claim as approvd of by Lord Loudoun, at the same time told you that I should use my endeavours to prevent the Money being issu'd to the disposal of particular Persons under particular Influence, as the whole of this Affair had been negociated by me I accordingly Petitiond the Treasury that the Money should be paid to me giving Security to apply the same to the Use of the Legislature, finding this was likely to have been Contested on the part of the Governor & the Council, an Expedient was proposd that the Money be issud to Mr Smith and to me in equal Proportions giving Separate Securitys to apply the same for the use of the Province[2] to which the Treasury have agreed and after the Holidays we do expect that the Money will be accordingly issud to us in equal proportions, and by this opportunity the Treasury acquaint Gover Dobbs with their Resolution and at the same time, recommend it to him to use his endeavours that proper Powers be transmitted to authorize the Receipt of such Money as the Parlt may hereafter grant[3] this becomes absoluty necessary for by the Rules of the Exqr particular powers are necessary to receive money at the Exqr and rather than obstruct the Service by any controversy with the Governor I shall for my own part make no objection to being joind with Mr Smith in special Powers in Money Matters as done here in the present Case of the money to be now Issued to us; I have no other Motive in Suggesting this Expedient to you, than in order to forward the Public Service, and prevent clamour by our obstructing the adjusting the Several Claims of the rest of the Colonies equally Interested in and to the Money granted by Parlt, however unsuccessful in the last Grant of 200000 I shall put in my claim to that just now granted[4] as was done last Session of Parlt by way of "Recompense for *Levying Pay* & *Cloathing* of Troops employd in the Kings Service" and least your Services shall not appear by the Acts &

Journals in the Plantation Office you will be pleasd to transmit to me particulars thereof (as was done heretofore) so soon as possible.

I shall lose no time to inform you when the Money now in agitation is paid that you may give directions as to the Remittance thereof or the application thereof as the General Assembly shall direct by Bills to be drawn for the same, which appears to me to be the most advantageous method for the Public Service however in whatever manner you shall direct payment of the Ballance of this money it shall be complyd with.

You will please to take notice of the Claim for 500 Ster for repaying Gover Shirley likewise 500 Ster to Lord Loudoun, these are the only Demands made by the Public here on this Money, the 500£ for repaying Brigadr Forbes I know nothing of, otherwise than as I find it in the last Agency Bill which was rejected by the Council[5] I shall expect your Answer on these points, and on all Such as may help me out in Your Service being with great regard and Sincerity Gentlemen

PS please to observe that the 200000, voted by Parlt the 1t Instant, is for Provincial Services for 1759, Your Instructions to me must therefore be particular as to such services.

LB, pp. 200–202. Sent "per Mr Carvers Ship from Portsmouth under Virginia Convoy."

1. Printed on pp. 339–340.

2. JA and Samuel Smith to Samuel Martin, secretary to the Treasury, 3 Mar. 1760 (T 1/401, fols. 142–143).

3. The Treasury's letter to Dobbs (not found) was probably similar to the letter its secretary, Samuel Martin, wrote Fauquier on 19 Mar. 1760. See preceding document.

4. On 31 Mar. 1760 a committee of the whole House of Commons resolved that a sum not exceeding £200,000 be granted "to enable his Majesty to give proper Compensation to the respective Provinces in *North America*, for the Expences incurred by them, in the Levying, Clothing and Pay, of the Troops raised by the same, according as the active Vigour and strenuous Efforts of the respective Provinces shall be thought by his Majesty to merit" (*JHC*, 28:847–848).

5. JA may be referring to the aid bill to which a rider concerning the agency was attached. See JA to Swann, 20 July 1759, p. 312, n. 3.

To Francis Fauquier

Sir   April 14th 1760

In my last[1] I informed you of my Intention to apply with the rest of the American Agents for a further Supply from Parliament, which being done, a Vote is accordingly passed for £200,000 to the several Provinces for *Levying Pay* and *Cloathing* of Troops in 1759.[2] Having no particular Instructions thereon I must have Recourse to the Acts & Journals in the Plantation Office for Vouchers to support our Claim to the due Proportion thereof from the Treasury, which being done, it will rest with you and the Council to send me proper Powers to receive this Money as well as that for which I have the King's Warrt: as heretofore told you.

This with many other Negociations of late give ample Proof that the Affairs of Virginia are altogether in my hands without the least Interposition, or so much as the Appearance of any other Person on the Part of the Province.

You may easily conceive how much you & the [Council] had been blamed by the Administration here, and how m[uch the] Province had been injured by throwing your Affairs, co[ncerned] as they are, with National Measures, and with the gen[eral] Preservation of His Majesty's Dominions into so precarious [a] Channel as that depending on the Operation of the Agency Law which is attended with so many apparent Objections, and rendered moreover precarious from the Uncertainty of a Gentleman in Mr. Montague's Situation in Life, taking upon him the Charge of such Business, many had been the Inconveniencies to the Publick, and great the Prejudice to your Administration had I not stood my Ground in the Management of your Publick Affairs, & therein Conducted myself with due Consistency to the King's Service, and to that of the Province as you will see by the Attorney General's Opinion,[3] by the Testimony of the Board of Trade[4] & by Mr. Secretary Pitts Letter[5] in my Favour Copy whereof I ommitted to send you in my last Letter, Standing on such Ground I hope the Assembly will not press the Operation of the Agency Law in any Respect to my Prejudice, whose Cause the Attorney General plainly points out to be the Case of Government, and must be treated accordingly. So soon as I have received the Proportion of the 50,000, I shall notify the same to you for your Instructions as to the Application thereof to the Use of the Legislature agreable to my Security given for so doing. I am &ca

J. A.

LB, pp. 203–203A. In a clerk's hand. A piece is torn from the outer edge of the leaf, and what is assumed to be the missing text is supplied in brackets.

1. JA to Fauquier, 20 Mar. 1760, pp. 342–343.

2. See preceding letter, note 3.

3. See JA to Blair, 15 Dec. 1759, pp. 329–330, n. 4.

4. See JA to Fauquier, 25 Jan. 1760, p. 338, n. 2.

5. Letter not found.

To John Blair

Sir   London 14th April 1760.

Neither Mr. Auditor General[1] nor myself having of late any Letter from you, I have by this only to point out to you the Strange Dilemma your Measures in relation to the Agency of your Affairs had brought the Province into, had I not adhered to the Management of your Publick Concerns, in Spite of the Opposition intended me by the Agency Law, which Law, it now seems clear, tho pass'd under the fallacious Pretence of a Consistency to other Agents Laws in other Colonies, will appear to stand on Principles calculated to give the Sanction of Law to Measures that have been already condemned in the Case of the Pistole Fee, wherein Mr. Attorney General Randolph's Agency was very severely censured, and tho the present Case of the Agency is in other hands, the Principles thereof are the same. You will see by the Opinion thereon,[2] that the Case becomes the Case of Government, and will be treated as such whenever the Agency Law comes in Question. I have hitherto taken no Other Step than what became absolutely necessary for me in Support of my Authority from the Govr. and Council to act as Agent for the King's Service, and for that of the Province: if this Step I have taken, has in any Degree affected that Part of the Govr. and Council's Conduct for Assenting to a Law whereby the Publick Affairs are thrown into a New & precarious Channel of Negociation, if on the other hand I have prevented much greater Inconveniency [   ]³ and a far more severe Censure & Blow to Govr. Fauquieres Administration (in other Cases, I am sorry to say, exceptionable at home)⁴ by being thereby enabled to act the proper Part for Governmt: and for the Service of the Province, which had I not done, Ministerial Measures for national Purposes and for the Good of the whole, must have stood still for Want of some Body to appear for Virginia. I leave it then to the Govr. and Council to judge, how much they are indebted to me on their own Account and that of the Publick for my Conduct in their Service. I hope I Shall meet with a Suitable Return I am always Dr Sir &Ca

JA

LB, pp. 203A–203B. In a clerk's hand.

1. Robert Cholmondeley.

2. See JA to Blair, 15 Dec. 1759, pp. 329–330, n. 4.

3. The copyist left a blank space at this point, perhaps indicating that he could not decipher a word in JA's letter.

4. For the British administration's displeasure with Fauquier, see Board of Trade to Fauquier, 13 June 1760, and enclosures, in *Fauquier Papers*, 1:375–380.

To the Council of Virginia

April 20th 1760

In my letter of 15th Feby¹ I acquainted you that on presenting the Kings Warrant at the Exchequer for payment of 20546, the proportion comming to Virginia of the 200000 Granted by Parlt for Services in 1758 I was told that a Special Power of Attorney or Authority under the Provincial Seal Was requird, and that such Power from the Governor and Council would be effectual.

Since that, the Lords of the Treasury have informed his Honour the Lieut Governor that they have agreed to Issue the respective Proportions of the 50000 to the Several Acting Agents for these Colonies on our giving Security for applying the Same to the Uses of such Colonies, we are accordingly giving Security in the Excheqr for double the Several Sums and after the Holidays when the Board meet, hope to have the Money issud Subject to the Order of the Governour the Council and Assembly, our Proportion is as given in to the Treasury is 32814.19 out of which are to be deducted the Usual Agency or Commission of 2 & $\frac{1}{2}$ Per cent, with Fees of Offices and Incidental Expences particulars whereof shall be duely transmitted when paid.[2]

I likewise told you that I should apply for a further Grant according as I should find the Kings Ministers disposd for American Operations I have now the Satisfaction to Inform you that the King having recommended a further Grant to the American Colonys, the Parlt on the 31th of last Month, Voted accordingly 200000 by way of *Recompensation for the Expences incurrd by the respective Provinces in the Levying Cloathing and Pay of the Troops raisd by the same*[3] to Ascertain such Services on the part of Virginia I must as heretofore done have recourse to the Journals and Acts of Supplys passd in 1759 to be met with in the Plantation Office Major Stobo now here will be able to Instruct as to the Number of Provincial Troops in your Service, I am doing all in my Power to Serve this Gentleman.[4]

My Negociations are full proof that the Affairs of your Colony are all together in my hands, and from the oppinion of the Attorney General heretofore sent you on the Agency Law,[5] it is probable I shall have no Manner of Assistance from the Assemblys Agent under that Act.

Mr Montague I have at length found to reside at Notton in Wilshire where he is marryd and there Practises the Law, and is now doing Duty as Captain in the Wilshire Militia, and must take the Field this Summer with the Imbodyd Militia Forces I have seen a friend of this Gentlemans who assures me that Mr Montague knows nothing directly or Indirectly of the Affairs of Virginia, has no acquaintance with any one person there except Mr Randolph the Attorney General, an Acquaintance contracted some years Since but not carryd on for some years past, In justice to this Gentleman, to the Kings Service, to the Service of your Province, and to my own Character I thought it incumbent on me to signefy to Mr Montague my Concern with the Affairs of Virginia and to write to him to know what Instructions he had from thence,[6] his

Answer confirms what his Friend told me, So that I stand alone in the Service of your Colony and as such I am receivd by the Lords for Trade and His Majestys Ministers as the Enclosd Documents thereof,[7] will shew you, all which became necessary for me to take to Authorize my appearance in behalf of the Province I am with great truth Gentlemen

LB, pp. 197–199. At the foot of this letter JA wrote: "NB to the Admiralty by Virginia Convoy."

1. Printed on pp. 338–339.

2. A royal warrant of 16 Apr. 1760 authorized the payment to JA of £32,268.19 for Virginia; to James Wright of £9,941.19.10 for South Carolina; and to JA and Samuel Smith of £3,894.10.7 *each* for North Carolina (T 52/50, pp. 467–468).

For the Treasury's letter to Fauquier, see JA to Fauquier, 20 Mar. 1760, pp. 342–343.

For the discrepancy in Virginia's proportion, see JA to Virginia Council, 15 Feb. 1760, pp. 338–339.

3. See JA to North Carolina Committee of Correspondence, 12 Apr. 1760, p. 345, n. 3.

4. Robert Stobo (1717–1770), of a Glasgow mercantile family, attended the university there and went to Virginia in the 1740s. He received a captain's commission in the Virginia Regiment from Dinwiddie in Mar. 1754 and arrived at George Washington's encampment at the Great Meadows soon thereafter. Following Washington's capitulation at Fort Necessity on 3 July 1754, Stobo and Capt. Jacob Van Braam were turned over to the French as hostages. Stobo remained a prisoner at Montreal and Quebec for nearly five years, escaping to Louisburg in May 1759. Stobo spent the last ten days of Mar. and the first three weeks or so of Apr. 1760 in London. From 1760 until his death he served as a captain in the 15th Regiment of Foot (Robert C. Alberts, *The Most Extraordinary Adventures of Major Robert Stobo* [Boston, 1965]).

5. See JA to Blair, 15 Dec. 1759, pp. 329–330, n. 4.

6. Letter not found.

7. Enclosures not found.

To Francis Fauquier

Sir   May 10th 1760

It is by Chance I hear of an Opportunity in the Downs to inform you that on the 8th Inst. the £50,000. so long depending was then issued to the Respective Agents, the Proportion for Virginia to me, amounting to £32268.19. as per Accot. inclosed, I know of no farther Charges on your Government except Mr. Sharps Bill,[1] which I reckon to be about £50, but I choose rather than keep the Account open for this Article, to ascertain the Ballance as it now stands, which Ballance, by the Bonds given by the Agents (Copy whereof I send you)[2] you will please to observe is to be paid to such Persons as the Governor Council and Assembly shall direct to receive the same, I am therefore to wait their Orders accordingly. Of all the Solicitations I ever was engaged in, this has proved the most tedious and troublesome, owing greatly to the Difficultys and Delay given us by a certain Noble Lord,[3] whose Approbation to our Claim became Necessary. Mr. Montague in Consequence of a Letter I had wrote him some time since, has been in Town and as he seems inclinable to act under the Agency Law I have thereupon informed him, that I shall very readily concurr with him for the Publick Service, reserving to myself the Liberty Nevertheless of acting alone where particular Instructions from the Govr. and Council shall require it. Be pleased to Communicate this with the inclosed to the Council. & beleve me to be very sincerly Sir Your most obdt Servt

JA

LB, p. 204. In a clerk's hand except for a marginal note in JA's hand at the head of the letter that reads: "Original per Bristol per Mr Hanburys care Duplicat per Passenger from London per Mr Wrights Convoy Triplicat to the Coffee House in July." Fauquier must have communicated this letter to the Council on 16 September 1760, although it is not cited by date (*EJC*, 6:169). It is probably one of the letters Fauquier mentioned in his address to the assembly on 6 October and sent to the House of Burgesses the same day (*JHB, 1758–1761*, 184–185).

1. This is probably a reference to Joshua Sharpe's bill for queries put to Attorney General Pratt concerning Virginia's agency act, for which see JA to Blair, 15 Dec. 1759, pp. 327–329.

2. JA must have sent copies of bonds given by himself as agent for Virginia, by James Wright as agent for South Carolina, and by JA and Samuel Smith as agents for North Carolina. No form of the bonds has been found.

3. The earl of Loudoun.

Enclosure: Account

James Abercromby Esqr. doth Charge himself with the Money recd. from the Excheqr. being the Proportion due to the Province of Virginia out of the 50,000 granted by Parliamt. in 1757 to Virginia No. & South Carolina Vizt.

1760

May 8th Reced. on Account of Virginia	£32268	19	—
Whereof He discharges himself as follows Vizt. Jany. 29th. To Lord Loudoun's Secry. &ca. on Receiving His Lordships Approbation on the Virginia Claim	1	14	6
May 6th Paid Mr. Tomkins & Messengers at the Treasury Fees on the Warrant &ca.[1]	21	—	—
Paid Mr. Jennins at the Audr. of the Excheqrs. Office Fees &ca[2]	39	15	—
Paid at the Pell Office Fees &:ca[3]	17	11	—
Paid Do at the Tellers Office[4]	80	2	6
Paid for the Sign Manual[5]	—	14	—
By Commission or Agency at the usual Rate of $2\frac{1}{2}$ Per Ct on the £32268.19.	806	14	—
By Mr. Abercromby's Salary from 25 April 1759 to Do. 1760, retained out of this Money, and to be allowed, and made good to this Money by the Govrs. Warrant on the Tobacco Duty at £200 Per Ann.[6]	200	—	—
By Money due to Mr. Abercromby from the Governmt. of Virginia for Fees at Offices paid by him & not repaid (the said Disbursements being made at sundry times from 1753 to 25 April 1760) by the Province[7]	88	19	—

By Expences of Travelling (Horse hire in-cluded) being 4 Days to Ld: Loudoun's House, in order to Settle Matters with his Lordship 5 5 —

Paid Mr. Francis for Bond of Security &ca.[8] 3 3 —

Paid Fees to Council &ca. in Mr Camms Case[9] 13 13 —

Discharge £1278 11 0

Ballance due to Virginia £30990 8 —

£32268 19 —

LB, p. 205B. In a clerk's hand.

1. Thomas Tompkins was underclerk at the Treasury 1742–1776. Probably he was the Treasury official who originated the warrant for payment of Virginia's share of the grant from Parliament.

2. Mr. Jennins probably was the official in the office of the auditor of the Exchequer who entered the Virginia warrant upon its arrival from the Treasury.

3. The warrant passed (though perhaps not directly) from the auditor of the Exchequer to the clerk of the pells (which were the parchment records of receipt and disbursement kept at the Exchequer).

4. The warrant was endorsed by the clerk of the pells and passed on to the teller, who made the payment directed by the warrant.

5. The Virginia warrant was drawn up in the form of a royal sign manual.

6. No record has been found of an agreement whereby JA was to withhold his salary and expenses from this grant. The warrant for his salary of £100 from 25 Apr. to 25 Oct. 1759 had been signed on 6 Nov. 1759, but probably the salary had not been paid because there was a large deficit in the two-shillings-per-hogshead account; JA no doubt assumed that payment of his salary for 25 Oct. 1759 to 25 Apr. 1760 (for which the warrant had been signed on 7 May 1760) would likewise be delayed.

7. The relation between this account and an earlier account for £196.7.0 submitted by JA is puzzling, since it appears that nothing had been paid on the earlier account (see JA's letter to Blair of 8 Mar. 1758, enclosure, p. 240, n. 1).

8. Mr. Francis has not been identified, but he may have been the Thomas Francis who was assistant solicitor to the Treasury 1750–1781 and seems also to have had a private practice.

9. After John Camm was dismissed from his appointment as professor of divinity at the College of William and Mary in 1757, he procured a mandamus (dated 4 Nov. 1758) directing the governor or the visitors of the college to reinstate him or show cause at the General Court. On 10 Oct. 1759 the General Court quashed the writ, and

Camm appealed to the Privy Council to reverse the judgment. Presumably the counsel to whom JA paid fees were Solicitor General Charles Yorke and Alexander Forrester (ca. 1711–1787); both barristers were counsel for the respondents when the Privy Council heard Camm's appeal in 1763.

To the Council of Virginia

[10 May 1760]

The Gentlemen of the Council are no Strangers to the very great trouble I have had during this long and vexatious Negociation, the usual Perquisite of Agency in Military Services is by no means adequate thereto, but to avoid all Contest I have confind my self to Rule and Practice of the like nature in Office here, particularly to the Rule in the Auditor of Imprests Office as admitted by the Treasury in the Money heretofore issud to Virginia 2 & $\frac{1}{2}$ per cent thereby allowd to Mr Hanbury for Negociating that money in which case I must observe their was no trouble on Solicitation, in this my Case greater difficultys perhaps than ever attended a money transaction at the Treasury not only in obtaining what had been refusd us in a former administration, but after it was got in adjusting the respective Proportions thereof, and in the manner of Settlement you must take notice that I have saved to the Province above 25 per Ct by giving their Proportion of Money Expended by them at its Legal Value and not at the Negociable Value that is, I have given their Claim at the rate of 100 Ster for 125 Currency Expended by them whereas according to the Merchantile valuation of Money the Province ought to have been allowd only 100 Ster for 145 or 150 expended and thus much Virginia has had the advantage of South Carolina by my managment of their Claim in 50,000 Currency a circumstance too meritorious to be overlooked by your Government.
May 10th 1760

LB, unpaginated, but follows presentation page. This may have been a draft of a portion of a longer letter of the same date, the fair copy of which, in a clerk's hand, is printed below.

To the Council of Virginia

Gentlemen   May 10th. 1760

By this Conveyance of a Ship in the Downs I have informed His Honr. the Lt. Govr.[1] of Paymt. to me of the Proportion to Virginia of the 50000, and transmitted an Account thereof, likewise Copy of the Condition of the Bond given to the Crown by the respective Agents for paying over the Ballance to such Persons as the Govrs. Council & Assemblies shall appoint to receive the Same, and thereupon I must have Orders accordingly.

The Gentlemen of the Council are no Strangers to thc very great Trouble I have had during this long Negociation, the usual Perquisite of Agency is by no means adequate thereto, but to avoid Contest I have confined my self to the common Rules and Practice of Business of the like Nature in Office here and more particularly to the Rules of the Exchequer in the Money heretofore issued for Virginia, but in that Case there was no Trouble of Solicitation, in this greater Difficulties first in obtaining and afterwards adjusting the Proportions perhaps than ever attended Negociation, owing to various Circumstances, which I need not now repeat. I cannot however omit the one, thrown in the Way by Mr. Montague on his Coming to Town a few days since to enquire into the State of the Agency Law of which I had some time before given him Notice, and the only Notice he has had thereof, this Matter was however very soon understood by Mr. Montague, and he has fully explained himselt thereon, and from what he has Since told me, I have good Ground to believe he has signified to his Correspondents in Virginia, that by Entering a Caveat, he had no other Intention than to have an Opportunity of enquiring into the Agency Law, and by no means to call in Question my Authority & Negociations in the Case of this Money heretofore solicited and finally settled by me, and like the Man of Honour and business does not contend for the Fruit of my Labour on the Moneys granted by Parlt in 1757 & 1759 being Solicited and adjusted by me, previous to his Appearing as an Agent, in which Capacity, altho he is altogether in the Dark, as he seems disposed to act under the Act of Assembly, I shall think it my Duty, while this Act continues, to concur with him for the Publick Service, reserving nevertheless to myself Liberty of Pursuing particular Instructions in Special Cases from the Governor and

Council. This Plan I have Reason to think will be agreable here, and I should think it lyable to no Objection with those in Virginia, who wish for Peace & Quietness in the Administration of Government and Success to their Measures at home[2] I am with very great Regard. Gentlemen &ca

JA.

LB, pp. 205–205A. In a clerk's hand except for several interlineations in JA's hand.

1. JA to Fauquier, 10 May 1760, pp. 350–351.

2. Montagu's letters to the Virginia Committee of Correspondence concerning the agency act and his relationship with JA have not been found, but the committee's minutes indicate that they were read on 7 Oct. and 3 Nov. 1760. On 5 Nov. 1760 the committee wrote to Montagu, "We think you judged very right in refusing to sign the Papers offer'd to you by Mr. Abercrombie, as you are by no Means to look on him as Agent for Virginia, but to consider yourself as such to all Intents & Purposes, & not to suffer any other Person to interfere with you in the Execution of your office. However, it is not our Intention to restrain you from joining Mr. Abercrombie, or any other Gent. in any Sollicitation that may probably be for the Benefit of this Colony" (*VMHB* 11 [1903–1904]: 10–11, 12).

To the Committee of Correspondence of North Carolina

Gentlemen of the Committee   May 10th. 1760.

I take the first Opportunity to inform you that on the 8th Inst. the £50000, so long depending was issued to the respective Agents, accordingly the Proportion to No. Carolina being £7789 is issued to Mr. Smith & to me, to each of us £3894.[1] by different Warrants and Securities, Copies of which Securities I inclose[2] and thereby you will see that the Ballance is to be paid to such Persons as the Govr. Council and Assembly shall direct to receive the Same.

As Mr. Smith has had no Share in this troublesome Negociation, he can with justice I conceive claim no Share of the Perquisites incident thereto, I have accordingly deducted the usual agency being $2\frac{1}{2}$ Per Ct. on the full Sum granted.

The Gentlemen of the Commee are fully sensible of the Difficulties that attended this Transaction: By being circumscribed in my Authority as Agent, I have been under the Necessity of making Use of private Connection and Interest for the Service of the Province in this as well as in other Cases, but in this Situation my

Duty as Agent for the Assembly becomes more laborious, I hope therefore no Objection will be taken to my having charged in my Account the usual Contingencies and Perquisites of Office.

I have heretofore informed the Committee of the Paymasters Demand for Paymt: of the £500 advanc'd by Genl. Shirleys Warrt: on Account of No. Carolina, also of £500 advanc'd by Ld. Loudouns Warrt. for the same Acct:, which said Sums, it seems, were to be repaid out of the Money granted by Parliamt., you will be pleas'd therefore in Concurrence with the Govr. & Council to instruct me on this head.

Altho' the Ministry thought fit to make no Allowance to either of the Carolinas out of the £200000. granted last Sessn. of Parliat., I shall nevertheless claim for No. Carolina a due Proportn. of the 200000 granted this prest. Session, and the Situation of the Colony in an Indian War may induce the Administn. to make an Allowance accordingly. I have no Information of the Share your Province takes in the Cherokee War, yet it is to be hoped that Govr. Dobbs has given full Information thereof to the proper Officers of State.[3] I am with great Regard Gentlemen &ca

JA

NB PS Please to observe that altho Mr Smyth has given me to understand that the Commission or Agency of this Money of right belongs to me as my Negociation previous to his being Agent Yet to avoid all Contest I submit myself herein to the directions of Govr Council and Assembly and for your further Information enclose you Mr Pitts letter to the Treasury in this case.[4] Please also to take Notice that this Negociation was carrying on and at a time when I had no Salary from the Province.

LB, p. 206. In a clerk's hand except for several emendations and the postscript in JA's hand.

1. In fact, one-half of £7,789 is £3,894.10.

2. Enclosures not found.

3. War with the Cherokee on the southern frontier broke out in 1759 and did not end until a peace treaty was finally ratified in Dec. 1761. See W. Stitt Robinson, *The Southern Colonial Frontier, 1607–1763* (Albuquerque, N.M., 1979), 217–222.

4. Letter not found.

Enclosure: Account

James Abercromby Esqr. doth Charge himself with the Money reced. from the Excheqr. being one half of the Proportion due to the Province of No. Carolina out of the £50000 granted by Parliament in 1757 to Virginia & the two Carolinas Vizt

	£	Sh	D
1760 May 8th. Reced. on Account of North Carolina	3894	—	—
Whereof He discharges himself as follows Vizt			
1760 Janry 28.			
Paid to Ld. Loudouns Secretary on receiving his Lordship's Approbation of the Claim	1	1	—
1760 May 6th Paid Mr. Tomkins at the Treasury Fees for Warrant & ca	12	12	—
Paid Fees to Mr. Jennins at the Audr. of the Excheqrs. Office	4	11	—
Paid Fees at the Tellers Office	9	12	2
Paid Fees at the Pell Office	2	8	—
Paid for the Sign Manual	—	14	—
Paid Mr Francis Solicitor to the Treasury for Bond	3	3	—
Paid Expences of Travelling to Lord Loudouns in order to settle the Points of the Claim (four days Horse hire included)	5	5	—
By Arrears of Sallary, allowed (by the Resolves of Assembly of the 20 & 23d Decr. 1758) to Mr Abercromby	332	9	7[1]
By two years Sallary retained, payable out of this Money, according to Resolve of the Assembly of 20 Decr. 1758 at £150 Per Ann: from March: 1st 1759 to Do. 1761	300	—	—

By Expences disbursed by me in the Service
of the Province from 25 of March 1757 to
April *1758* being 1 Year, during which time
I did in Fact act as Agent in Offices and in
Parliamt. particularly in the Salt Affair,
yet no Salary is allowed for said time   31 — —

By Contingent Expences during two Years
Service from March 1759 to 25 March 1761
being the usual Contingent Expences at £31
Per Ann: 62 — —

By Agency of $2\frac{1}{2}$ Per Cent on the full Sum
of £7789. Mr Smith having had no Share in
the Negociation and Solicitation of this
Affair the Agency of right belongs to me in
full   194 14 —

Tot: Discharge   £959   9   9[2]

Ballance due to No. Carolina is   2934   10   3

£3894 — —

LB, p. 207. In a clerk's hand except that in the last entry (£194.14) the second word and the last nine words are in JA's hand. At the foot of this account JA wrote: "NB original to Mr Swann by Convoy to So Carolina Duplicat per George Pollock by Sd Convoy via Virginia to Saml Jones Junr Triplicat by Ship Thomas Capt Scott NB Mr Wrights Convoy Saild about the 20th July Mr Pollock in Novr about 20th to Pheladelphia." (The phrase "by Ship Thomas Capt Scott" is in a clerk's hand.)

1. See JA to Swann, 13 Apr. 1758, p. 253, n. 2.

2. The assembly later attempted to recover from JA some of the funds he withheld. See *NCCR*, 7:622, 666, 670.

To Francis Fauquier

Sir   June 1t 1760

A few days ago I had Duplicate of your Letter of 14th Decr.[1] the original no doubt gone to France or otherwise lost, and with your letter I had the Memorial from you and the Council to the Treasury for paying to me the Virginia Proportion of the 50000 & the 200000£[2] the first being already paid as heretofore I informd you, I shall now apply for the Last, and the Security requir'd will no doubt be of the same nature as that before given, and Your Directions concerning the Disposition of the money must be accordingly transmitted to me, whether I am to be drawn upon by Bills or to remit the same in Specie, in whatever Manner it is to be done, by the Condition of my Bond to the Crown you will please to observe that the total concurrence of the Governor Council and Assembly is necessary in such directions to acquit me so as to get my Bond up and properly discharged.[3]

I find on enquiry at the Plantation Office that the Acts amongst others the Negro Act recommended to my attention are miscarryd,[4] Mr Presedent Blairs letter to me containing Instructions from the Council relative to my Conduct as Agent being likewise miscarryd,[5] and it is probable so has the Committee of Correspondence letter of Mr Montague,[6] however as to what relates to the Service of the Province, my letter to you of the 10th May will let you see that I had taken up the very system of Conduct with regard to the Agency and what is now pointed out to me by you and the Council and you may be assurd of my Concurrence accordingly with Mr Montague who I believe is now doing Regimental Duty at Winchester Incampment.[7]

It will however become necessary Since your former letters to me have misscarryd to transmit Copys of your Reasons for passing the Negro Act[8] and also for Mr President Blair to furnish me with Copys of his former letter containing the Councils Instructions to me for my future Conduct.

I shall not fail to communicate to your Brother from time to time what may personally concern you.[9]

The Armys of the contending Powers being in the Field some Capital blow is soon expected which may decide as to Peace or War, in the mean time the arrival of and the Negociations of the Spanish Ambassador, since his Arrival gives us hetherto no public notification of either[10] I am

LB, pp. 209–210. A marginal note at the head of this letter indicates that a duplicate was sent "by Mr Wrights Convoy." Fauquier communicated this letter to the Council on 16 September 1760 (*EJC*, 6:169–170). It is probably one of the letters Fauquier mentioned in his address to the assembly on 6 October 1760 and sent to the House of Burgeses the same day (*JHB, 1758–1761*, 184–185).

1. Letter not found.

2. The memorial has not been found, but it is assumed that it was drawn up about 12 Dec. 1759, when the Council considered a number of letters from JA. See JA to Blair, 3 Aug. 1759, p. 327, n. 6.

3. See JA to Fauquier, 3 July 1760, p. 363, n. 3.

4. JA must be referring to some or all of the acts passed in the assembly session of 1–21 Nov. 1759, presumably sent with Fauquier's letter of 17 Dec. 1759 to the Board of Trade (*Fauquier Papers*, 1:281–284). The Negro act was "An Act to oblige persons bringing slaves into this colony from Maryland, Carolina, and the West-Indies, for their own use to pay a duty" (Hening, *Statutes*, 7:338–340), which Fauquier certainly enclosed in his letter to the Board of 17 Dec.

5. This was probably a letter of about 12 Dec. 1759, for which see JA to Blair, 3 Aug. 1759, p. 327, n. 6.

6. This was probably the committee's letter to Montagu of 12 Dec. 1759 (*VMHB* 10 [1902–1903]: 342–353).

7. Salisbury Plain, near Winchester, about 65 miles southwest of London, was much used for military maneuvers.

8. See JA to Fauquier, 1 Oct. 1760, p. 367, n. 1.

9. William Fauquier (ca. 1708–1788) was elected a member of the Royal Society in 1746 and became a governor of the Foundling Hospital and a member of its general managing committee in the same year. He was made a director of the South Sea Company in 1757. William Fauquier was apparently a businessman of some kind, and in 1758 he was appointed secretary to the comptrollers of army accounts. He appears to have acted as a business agent for his brother Francis on many occasions.

10. The count de Fuentes, the new Spanish ambassador, arrived in London on 24 May 1760 and presented his letters of credence to the king on 27 May. It does not appear that he had undertaken any negotiations by the first of June, although he had paid several visits of courtesy to George, prince of Wales, and other members of the royal family.

To Samuel Swann

June 6th 1760

I have been alarmd with accounts of your late illness contradicted by later letters.

Copy of the Bond given by Mr Smyth and me herewith sent to the Committee will shew you that the joint order of Governour Council and the Assembly becomes necessary whether by Bills to be drawn on us for the Money or Remitting in Specie their Concurrence is necessary.

This Affair being negociated by me alone and as Mr Smyth has signefyd to me that the Perquisites of Agency of right belongd to me I have accordingly chargd it whatever Mr Dobbs may think of this the Justice and Equity of the Case is for me.

I am next to apply for the share in the 200000 Granted this present Session the Cabinet Council & not the Treasury determind against us in the last.

There is still much talk of Peace tho large Armys on both sides in the field Complts to your Brother concludes as always Sincerly

LB, p. 211. Sent "by Capt Malan & Governor Wright."

To Francis Fauquier

Sir   July 3d 1760

I am now to acquaint you & the Council that I have recd. Paymt. at the Exchequer of the Sum of £20546 Sterlg. being the Proportn. due to Virginia out of £200,000 granted last Session of Parliamt. and, for this purpose, I was obliged to obtain the King's special Sign Manual, as the Memorial of the Govr. & Council to the Lords of the Treasury in this Case,[1] not being authenticated under the Provincial Seal, was not held Sufficient Authority. The Ballance being as by the inclosed Account, £19,901.1.4, is subject, as the former Money, to the order of Govr. Council & Assembly.

In Mr. Montague's Absence, with his Regimt. at the Incampment at Winchester I have given in our Claim for a due Share of the £200000, granted this last Session in proportion to 1400 Men clothed and paid by the Province for last Year, which Number, including 400 Rangers by Major Stub's[2] Information I ventured to give in, the Publick Journals being taken by the Enemy or otherwise lost, from thence I could form no Document of the Number of Troops. If I am Short, as there is no Disposition of the Treasury to make Partition of this money, their long Adjournmt. taking Place, this Matter may lay over 'till towards the Meeting of Parliamt., so that you will have time to set me to Rights, and at the same time to transmit proper Powers to receive the Money, and as Mr Montague and I are now acting conjunctly, I submit it to you, that the Power under the Provincial Seal be accordingly directed to us jointly, being signed by the Govr. Presidt. of the Council and Speaker, which will at once obviate all Obstruction at the Treasury & Exchequer on the Rect. of the Money.[3]

The Board of Trade are now Adjourned for their long Vaccation: the Treasury do the same towards the End of the Month, from thence will ensue a Stagnation to all Bussiness for some time, except Military Operations. Last Mail brought us an Account of a severe Blow on the Confines of Silesia given by Genl. Laudoun with his Austrian Army to Genl. Fauquet & Prussians,[4] another such will probably enable the Austrians & Russians to give Laws of Peace to the K. of Prussia, who must at last give way to Superiority of Numbers, which all our Money cannot make up to him, with Regard therefore to Us, a General or Separate Peace must in all Probability be produced by the present Operations in Germany I am Sir &ca.

J. A

LB, p. 213. In a clerk's hand except for the routing memoranda in both JA's and the clerk's hands, which read: "Original by ships under Mr Wrights Convoy Dup: per N York Pacquet Triplicate per Randal [i.e., *Randolph*] Capt Walker NB Mr Wright said about the 20th July." Fauquier communicated this letter to the Council on 16 September 1760 (*EJC*, 6:169–170). It is probably one of the letters Fauquier mentioned in his address to the assembly of 6 October 1760 and sent to the House of Burgesses the same day (*JHB, 1758–1761*, 184–185).

1. See JA to Fauquier, 1 June 1760, pp. 360–361, n. 2.

2. Major Stub was probably Robert Stobo (for whom see JA to Virginia Council, 20 Apr. 1760, pp. 348–350).

3. Fauquier communicated this letter (and JA's letter of 1 June 1760) to the Council on 16 Sept. 1760. The Council advised that consideration of the letters should be deferred until the meeting of the assembly; Fauquier referred to JA's letters in his address to the assembly when it convened on 6 Oct. and transmitted them to the House of Burgesses. On 8 Oct. the House resolved that proper persons should be appointed to receive money granted to Virginia by Parliament; on 15 Oct. the House passed "An Act for appointing persons to receive the money granted, or to be granted, by the parliament of Great-Britain, to his majesty, for the use of this colony," which was accepted by the Council, and assented to by Fauquier on 20 Oct. The act authorized the governor, the president of the Council, and the Speaker of the House of Burgesses to draw bills of exchange on JA for the funds in his hands. The act went further, though, and "authorized, directed and empowered" Montagu to receive any other funds that may already have been or might be granted to Virginia by Parliament (*EJC*, 6:169–170; *JHB, 1758–1761*, 184, 187, 194, 196; Hening, *Statutes*, 7:372–375).

4. On 23 June 1760 the Austrian general baron von Laudon defeated the Prussians under baron de La Motte-Fouqué in an engagement at what was then Landeshut in Lower Silesia, and is now Kamienna Góra, in southwestern Poland.

Enclosure: Account

James Abercromby Esqr charges himself with the Receipt of £20546 Sterlg July 3d. 1760. the Proportion alloted to Virginia out of the £200000. Sterl. granted to the American Colonies in 1759 for their Respective Services

	£ Sh D	
1760 To Cash recd. at the Exchequer on July 3d. Account of Virginia		20546 — —
Discharges himself thereof as follows Vizt		
By the usual Commission thereon at $2\frac{1}{2}$ Per Ct	513.13.—	
By Fees pd. at the Treasury to Mr. Tomkins on the two Warrants from the King and the Treasury Warrants, and for Several Orders	35.14.—	
By paid the Messengers at the Treasury	2. 2.—	
By Fees paid to Mr Jennings & others in the Auditor of the Exchequer's Office	27.17.—	
By Fees paid at the Pell Office	11.11.—	
By Fees paid at the Tellers Office on Do	50.18.8	
By paid Mr Francis for Bond	3. 3.—	644 18 8
Ballance due to Virginia is		£19901 1 4
		£20546 — —

LB, p. 214. In a clerk's hand.

To Samuel Swann

July 5th 1760

Your favour by Mr Heron, gives full Account of Mr Dobbs Administration, which does not appear with unan[im]ity.[1] I do not wonder at your retiring from Public Affairs.[2] shall long to hear how the Charter Assembly proceed People here shew uneasiness at the fluctuating State of your Public Measures I am no stranger to Your Remark of Mr Dobbs deviation from Truth and Candour in more Instances that are of Public and Private Nature. I have reason to reproach Mr Dobbs for his Conduct to me, at the same time in all my Negociations I have avoided everything personal, how long it may be so I cannot tell. I never through voluntary resignation shall open a door for his Projects & while I continue in the Service, for my own and the Reputation of the Assembly shall not expose my[self] to Censure of a promoter of Fractiouse Measures Mr Dobbs has no cause to lay this to my charge or to the Assembly.

As to Peace or War Battles soon will determine My Best Wishes to you & Your Brother I am always Dr Sir

LB, p. 212. Sent "via Charlestown to Mr Thos Smyths Care per Convoy."

1. Swann's letter has not been found. For the political turmoil that racked North Carolina during this period, see Ekirch, *"Poor Carolina,"* chap. 5.

2. Swann continued as Speaker of the lower house of the North Carolina Assembly until 1761, and as a member until 1762. After his retirement from the assembly he continued to practice law for another decade.

To Francis Fauquier

Sir London Octr. 1st 1760

A few days ago I was favd. with yours of the 22d June inclosing Duplicate of that of the 14th Decemr., also a Copy of Reasons given by the Council for your Passing the Negro Act, together with Copy of Minutes of Council of 12th Decr. confirming my Authority as Agent, with a Power of Attorney to receive the Money granted by Parliamt., likewise Copy of your Letter to Mr Martin and One to the Lords of Trade, which I have delivered accordingly.[1]

Duplicates of the Acts of Assembly (the Originals whereof are lost) not being come to the Office, the Negro Duty Act,[2] & others passd at the same time, cannot be taken up, In the mean time I have considered the Reasons for giving your Assent to the Negro Duty Act, they appear to me very strong, And to which may be added, that in other Colonies, under like Instructions with yours, Dutys payable by the Importers of Negro's have been imposed by Provincial Acts without Blame, and whether imported by Land or by Water does not alter the Principles of the Case.

It gives me great Pleasure that the Plan agreed upon twixt Mr. Montague & myself for our Conduct in Negociating the Affairs of Virginia, as stated to you & to the Council by my Letters of the 10th of May last,[3] is approved of, and thereupon by next Ships I hope to receive Duplicates of the Presidents Letters, the Originals whereof have miscarried. Had the Power of Attorney now come, arrived (which probably wou'd have been the Case, had not the Ship been Lost or taken) before the Controversy took Place upon the Agency Law, I might, as you observe, have Shewn the Country could have got the Money from home by yours & the Councils Authority alone: As the Case now stands, Altho' by Mr. Secretary Pitts Interposition with the Treasury their Lordships determined the Matter in my Favour from my personal Services therein, yet they laid me as well as Others under an Obligation for the Disposal thereof as the Govr. Council & Assembly shall direct: Of all which Circumstances relative to this Money, my Letters to you and to the Council of the 10th. of May, inclosing the particular Accounts of the Money, two days after Receiving the Dividend, will inform you, Original of which Letters, that no time might be lost on my part, was transmitted by a Ship from Bristol, the first that offered for Virginia, Duplicate by a Ship from hence, Triplicate by Virginia Ships in July under Govr. Wright's Convoy.[4] By which said Ships my Letters of the 3d July (having that day received the Second Dividend) informed you and the Council of the Same, & inclosed my Accounts thereof.[5] Duplicates of said Letters Of 3d July were sent by the New York Pacquet, & Triplicates by the Randal, Capt. Walker,[6] & so it rests with the Legislature to order the Disposal of the Ballance of this Money, agreeable to the Security given by me to His Majty in the Exchequer, whether by Bills drawn on me or by remitting it in Specie I cannot take upon me to direct. It will no doubt occur to the People of Business in both Houses that by Bills of E[x]change Freight & Insurance will be saved, besides the high Price of Silver & Gold in time of War.

In whatever manner the Legislature, whether by Act of Assembly, or by a joint Resolution under the Seal of the Province, shall direct Payment of the Ballance, I am ready to Comply therewith. From the Nature of my Security, Copy thereof heretofore sent, you will observe that I cannot comply (however willing I am so to do) with your & the Councils Advice in paying Mr. Dinnwiddies Demand.[7]

Next Week, or the Week thereafter, the Treasury Board meets; I shall then renew my Solicitations for Aid out of the Quitrents. The Audr. Generals Report thereon is Strongly in our Favour.[8] I send you Copy of Mr Montagues Letter to me,[9] from the Camp, by which you will see his Disposition to Concur with me in the Publick Service of the Province, and believe me to be very Sincerly Sir & Ca

LB, pp. 214–216. In a clerk's hand. Sent "per Charming Jeany Capt Todd."

1. It is likely that JA mistook the date of Fauquier's letter or that Fauquier had misdated it, and that it was written about 25 June 1760, for on that day the Council agreed to send JA some of the items Fauquier enclosed (see JA to Fauquier, 20 Mar, 1760, pp. 343–344, n. 3). Of the other enclosures: 1) Fauquier's letter to JA of 14 Dec. 1759 has not been found; 2) the "Reasons given by the Council for your Passing the Negro Act" was a copy of the Council journal of 20 Nov. 1759 advising Fauquier that he could assent to the bill (for which see JA to Fauquier, 1 June 1760, p. 361, n. 4) "consistently with the Spirit of his Instructions" (*EJC*, 6:149–150); 3) Fauquier's letter to Secretary to the Treasury Samuel Martin of about 25 June 1760 (not found) presumably enclosed another copy of the Council's memorial of ca. 12 Dec. 1759 concerning the payment to JA of Virginia's portion of parliamentary grants (*EJC*, 6:165); and 4) Fauquier's letter to the Board of Trade of 2 June 1760 (*Fauquier Papers*, 1:371–373).

2. Fauquier explained his reasons for passing the act in a letter to the Board of Trade of 17 Dec. 1759 (*Fauquier Papers*, 1:282–284).

3. Printed on pp. 350–356.

4. Presumably this was the convoy in which James Wright, appointed lieutenant governor of South Carolina in the spring of 1760, had sailed to that colony.

5. JA to Fauquier, 3 July 1760, pp. 362–363.

6. The *Randolph*, Capt. Robert Walker.

7. The nature of this demand has not been ascertained.

8. In a letter to the Treasury of 18 Feb. 1760, Auditor-General Cholmondeley reported favorably on Virginia's request that the revenue of the two-shillings-per-

hogshead tobacco export tax be paid £3,079.4.3 from the quitrents (T 1/400, fols. 230–233). Despite this, however, the application was denied by the Treasury (see JA to Fauquier, 12 July 1761, pp. 392–393).

9. Letter not found.

To John Blair

London Octr 27th 1760

The Duplicates of such letters and Papers to me from you on the part of the Council as have miscarryd, not being come I have by this only to acknowledge Copy of the Minutes of Council so far back as Decr 12th transmitted to me in his Honour the Lt Governours letter of 22d June,[1] by those Minutes I find all my letters antecedent thereto were reced, My Several letters some that [are] relative to the Money reced from the Excqr Triplicates whereof went by the Randal Capt Walker[2] will shew the Council how far I am circumscribd by the Authority of Governor Council & Assembly in the application of the Ballance of such Money according to my Security given to the Crown copy whereof has been sent, It therefore now rests with the Legislature to Direct this Money accordingly Whether by Bills drawn on me, or by Remitting in Specie is at their Discretion, to the People of Business in both Houses of Assembly it will no doubt have occur'd, that the most advantagious method will be by Bills as thereby Freight Insurance and Price of Silver are saved.

The Event of the Kings death which happend on Saturday the 25th about 7 oclock in the morning[3] suspends for some time my Solicitation at the Treasury for aid to the Quitrents, and until Such time as the Wheels of Government are again set agoing in the ordinary course of Bussines I do not expect their Attention to Affairs of a privat Nature.

I have heretofore informd you of my giving in to the Treasury a Claim on the part of Virginia for a proportion of the 200000 Granted last Session of Parlt All the Journals and Acts of Assembly relative to Provincial Services being lost I could not particularize such Services so minutly as in former years, Neither was Mr Montague better Instructed, however in his absence with the Regiment, I could not omit giving in the Claim on behalf of

Virginia,[4] I do not expect that this Money granted last Session of Parlt will be soon disposd of for the Use of the Colonys, Other Services are become more Urgent, however it must at length be applyd for the Use of the several Colonies as the Cabinet Council shall direct for so the 200000 heretofore granted was directed.

I hope to have Mr Montagues Assistance so soon as his Military Service is over, hetherto he has no manner of Instructions from the Province. You may be assurd of my concurring with him in the Service of the Colony and in conforming my Self to the Particular directions from your Board, and regulate my Conduct to the best of my Judgment in Cases where your particular Instructions may be wanting I send you the enclosed Paper[5] whereby you will see more particularly the Steps taken by Government here in this great Event, and In hopes of receiving by next Ships your Directions on the part of the Council relating to the Money and other Public Affairs with Duplicates of all such letters and Papers as are lost I am always with great regard Sir Your Most Obedt svt

LB, pp. 217–219. Sent "to Mr Hanbury Copy to Capt Carlisle Sent Octr 30th to Coffee house." At the foot of this letter JA wrote: "NB to Mr Hindman by his Ship."

1. Letter not found. See preceding letter, note 1.

2. The *Randolph*, Capt. Robert Walker.

3. Upon the death of George II (1683–1760), his grandson succeeded to the throne as George III (1738–1820).

4. This claim has not been traced.

5. Not identified.

To the Committee of Correspondence of North Carolina

Gentlemen of the Committee of Assembly   Nov 1t 1760

Least Originals and Duplicates of my former Account of your Proportion of the Money granted by Parliament should not have come to hand I repeat an Account thereof by Mr Herons Ship from Portsmouth and thereupon Expect the orders of the Governor Council and Assembly according to the Bond or Security given by me to the King copy whereof I have heretofore transmited to you by two Several Conveyances.

The late Event of the Kings death tho it will occasion no variation of the General System yet has occasiond Some hurry in the Public Offices, in that American Affairs of a more privat nature are not likely now to find room.

As My Authority of Agent for the Assembly will expire by the 25 of next March, before then I shall expect your further Commands and shall on every Occasion very readily comply therewith[1] I am with great regard Gentlemen

P.S. I have according to my former Letter entd. a Claim in behalf of the Province to a Proportn. of the £200,000. granted last Session of Parliamt. to the American Colonies,[2] but from the extraordinary Demands of Money for Services thought more immediately necessary. I find that 'tis altogether hitherto uncertain when or in what manner such Money Shall be distributed.

LB, pp. 219–220. The postscript is in a clerk's hand. Between the complimentary close and the postscript JA wrote: "NB this the last letter to the Committee." Sent "per Capt Herons [s]hip to Portsmouth inclosd open to Mr Swann [i.e., enclosed in JA to Swann, 10 November 1760, below]."

1. In the margin opposite this paragraph JA wrote: "NB that is acting under the Resolves of the Assembly" (for which see JA to North Carolina Committee of Correspondence, 1 June 1759, p. 296, n. 1).

2. This claim has not been traced.

To Samuel Swann (presumed not sent)

Sir   London Novr 10th 1760
    To say anything to you on Public Affairs of the Province, now you are perhaps in a State of Retirement, may break in upon your System of life become I dare say more agreable, than long and fruitless endeavours to Correct abuses in Governors and Government, for my own part tho I am in the Service of the Assembly til 25 of March I am absolutely at a loss as to the Situation of their affairs, I hear of formal Complaints against the Governor, But as I am absolutely in the dark with regard to the Members of the Commee forgive me for directing My letter to the Commee

whoever they are to Your care, which you will please to forward, without taking Note that it came to you open.

LB, p. 221. This letter is crossed through and was evidently not sent.

To Samuel Swann

Sir   Novr 10th 1760

Not knowing who are Members of the Committee I give you the trouble of my letter to them herein inclosd,[1] I by Report hear of Complts in Form against Mr Dobbs, if of the same complexion with those transmitted to me by you under a reserve it may go hard with Mr D——s Administration; but is it not strange the Commee should have said nothing to me thereon if they are actualy Complaints so far advanced. The Kings death will stagnate business of this sort. No variation thereon will attend the general System of Affairs, the King of Prussias Victory over Daun is very momentuouse.[2] Complts to Mr John Swann I hope soon to see Your Son of whom I have good Accounts. I am very Sincerly Your Affectionat H Serv

JA

Saml Swann

LB, p. 222. In the margin at the foot of this letter JA wrote: "NB this is my la[s]t publick Letter of Correspondence." Sent "per Capt Herons Ship Portsmouth."

1. JA to North Carolina Committee of Correspondence, 1 Nov. 1760, pp. 369–370.

2. Count Leopold Joseph von Daun (1705–1766), the Austrian field marshal and commander in chief, was heavily defeated and seriously wounded at the battle of Torgau (on the river Elbe about 38 miles northeast of Leipzig), which began on 3 Nov. 1760.

To Francis Fauquier

London Decr 1t [1760]

I am favour with yours of 2d Septr.[1] by which I find other letters are a missing, I hinted in former letters by what means I became circumscribd in regard to the Public money chiefly owing to Lord Loudouns delay which gave time for the Contest about the different Agents, tho properly speaking the Authority quasi Agent was out of the Case yet it furnishd Mr Montague with the pretence of interfering by the Assemblys Authority but to this moment he has reced no Instructions of any kind so that he remains with his Regiment at Wells. By Copy of your letter to the Board of Trade[2] I find their Lordships on Sir Mathew Lambs Report do find the Agency Law defective and have thereupon proposd an Amendment[3] as no opposition is to be given to that Law it probably may be agreed to when properly amended, I wish however it may not occasionally prove a thorn in the side of the Governor & Council.

The Event of the Kings death and thereupon the various Negociations for supporting the Possessors of Offices in their own Offices will probably divert their Attention from those in Office in America, but whatever ill will might have been shewn to some of your Measures more particularly those relative to the Clergy Act, and on the back thereof the Repeal of some other Acts I have no reason to think the seeds of Discontent to Your Administration have taken deep root however to speak the language of a friend you cannot after such Alarm given to the Different Boards by former Steps be hereafter too much upon your guard against giving too great Way to the Assembly where your Instructions are at stake, I sincerly do not know that you have one Enemy here from public or private Motives, and you may rest satisfyd thereof so far as my Judgment may be depended on Nor do I think so much stress as to the Indignity you mention is to be laid on the manner in which the Kings Instruction in Mr Camms Case came to you,[4] there is nothing more Common in Cases before the King & Council, than for the Attorney to the Party to get the Instruction which is in Fact the final Judgment of the Council Board put into his hands on paying the Fees for the same, I have done it on several Occasions, Mr Camm has no reason to boast of this being given him in Contempt to you, the Partys concerned have always a right to Serve such Instructions on the Party, against whom Judgment goes, and such Instructions are not to be looked on as the Kings privat Rules of Governt but rather as Judicial Sentences, to which the Partys have right to make use of, this being the case you need not give yourself much trouble to sift into the matter [I have always found more affected Secrecy at the Plantation Office than in any other of the Public Offices, and the reason seems to be that they are only the Channel through which Matters of Government pass, and in few Instances can take upon them to act independently of Superior Offices, and in my privat opinion could not properly have calld upon the Council Office for the Instruction in Camms Case.][5]

You may be assurd that I shall continue to be attentive to what may concern you personally & consult from time to time with your Brother, when the exigency of the Case requires our so doing I am Sir

PS tell him to Send letters in small Packets to avoid Postage, that the next Parlt letters are to come free to me being a Member.[6]

LB, pp. 225–227. The postscript is evidently a memorandum of what JA wrote in the postscript of the receiver's copy. A marginal note indicates that the letter was to be sent by Capt. Carlisle "if not gone."

1. Letter not found.

2. Fauquier to the Board of Trade, 1 Sept. 1760 (*Fauquier Papers*, 1:403–406).

3. See JA to Fauquier, 25 Jan. 1760, p. 338, n. 2.

4. Fauquier, in his letter to the Board of 30 June 1760 (*Fauquier Papers*, 1:383–385), remonstrated at length about the manner in which he had received the Order in Council of 10 Aug. 1759 disallowing four acts (ibid., 232–233) and the additional instruction of 21 Sept. 1759 relative to the passing of laws (ibid., 249–250).

5. The passage in brackets here was crossed through in the letter book.

6. Although the Parliament of 1754 was not dissolved until 20 Mar. 1761, JA evidently was sure of being elected to the succeeding Parliament, and in fact he was elected member for Clackmannanshire in Scotland on 10 Apr. 1761, apparently unopposed.

To John Blair

Decr 20th 1760

I did not receive your favour of the 26 June[1] before yesterday, with 2d Bill for my Salary to 25 Octr 1759 the first Bill being already paid I have given Credit for it as half years Salary to 25th of Octr 1760 I cannot account for this letter being so long in faling into my hands as certainly it came by the same Ship that brought me the Lt Governors of the 22d of the same Month with the Minutes of Council of the 12 Decr 1759 whereby I find that my

Proceedings previous thereto are approvd of, It is some Satisfaction to me that my correspondence to Virginia has had better Success, than that to me from thence, and if that good luck has attended all my letters for these 10 Months last past you cannot be at a loss in any one circumstance of your Affairs under my direction, and the Case of the Public Money heretofore issud to me must be fully understood. The 200000 Granted last year is not as yet proportiond nor do I learn when it is to be done, it is some Months since I gave in a Claim on the part of Virginia, but for want of particulars in the Provincial Supplys I could not be explicit therein, By Yours I now find that such Supplys ammount to 50000 which will occasion an Additional Memorial to the Treasury. But I must observe to You, that the Application of Money granted by General Words for the use of the Colonys rests in the heart of the Kings Ministers in the Cabinet and not in the Treasury and so the Grant of 200000 in 1758 was proportiond and I never could find out upon what Principles we of Virginia had 20000 thereof and the Carolinas nothing tho their Services were at the same time with others asertaind in their respective Claims, what may be the Case of the 200000 hereafter to be issud by the Treasury I cant say at present. I have some reason to believe that it will not be discussd for some time By the Bills drawn for former Sums I observe the Province gains greatly Not only by Negociating Such Money by Bills, but from the Manner in which I settled their Dividend with other Provinces by Rating their Money at i[t]s Legal Value instead of its Merchantile in the course of Traffick, that is I gave to Virginia 100 Ster for 125 Disbursd by & in Virginia whereas I think the difference when I adjusted the Proportions was as 100 Ster is to 160 or more, on the present Establishment I observe Exchange at Fourty you gain 15 Per ct which advantage had probably been exhausted by Freight Insurance & great value of Specie at this time I am glad to find the Assembly do admit the justice of the Claim to Commissions on the Money the same Commissions have been alowd on former Grants of Money in Virginia.

You can have no Idea of the difficulty and Delays attending Solicitations at the Treasury Ministerial Affairs, Military Supplys for Services at home & Abroad together with Parliamentary Business do totaly engage the D of N———le and of late by the Kings death, the re:establishment of the Civil List and arrangment thereof through every appartment of the Kings Houshold and Officers of Government is thrown in to the channel of Business at the Treasury; from thence judge of the improbability rather the impossibility of gaining ground in the Minute Settlement of Virginia Affairs; You are sensible that in so far as it depended on my Services the Case of Aid to the Tobacco Revenue out of the Q Rents met with neither Difficulty or Delay, and I shall continue my endeavours therein at the Treasury being Sir very Sincerly

P[S] I approve of your denomination of Solicitor insted of Agent for Virginia[2] And I shall correspond through the Gover or the Council hereafter.

LB, pp. 231–232. "Jany 10th" and a couple of illegible words are crossed out before "Decr 20th 1760." See JA to Blair, 10 January 1761, pp. 377–378.

1. Letter not found.

2. This to distinguish JA from Edward Montagu, technically the agent of the colony, but principally of the House of Burgesses.

To Francis Fauquier

Decr 25th 1760

Within these few days Several Bills drawn by you, Mr Blair President, and Mr Robinson Speaker[1] to the account of the "£32268.19. allotted by his Majesty to Virginia out of the 50000 granted in 1757 to North South Carolina and Virginia" have been presented to me for Acceptance; whereupon a difficulty does arise for the Bills so drawn do not expressly set forth that the Persons who draw such Bills are Authorisd by the Legislature (viz) the Governor Council and Assembly to draw nor is the Value reced in Virginia said to be for the Use of the Province, and as the Rules prescribd by the Treasury and as my Security given to the Crown several Copys whereof were sent you do require that the Money shall be paid to Such persons as are or shall be authorisd by the Govr Council and Assembly to receive the same Such Authority then not appearing from the Tenor of the Bills nor from any letter of Advice from you, or from the Council or Assembly and neither Act of Assembly nor Journals appearing in the Plantation Office to signefy the Authority of the Legislature to you & those Gentlemen for drawing Such Bills; under this difficulty for my justification and that of my Securitys I must lay the Bills before the Treasury for their pleasure thereon, and unless their Lordships shall peremptorily *order me to suspend payment* I am resolvd to pay them, and to Trust to your being properly Authorisd and if not that you will procure the Authority of the Legislature to justify your drawing such Bills which you will please to transmit to me under the Provincial Seal that I may pass my Accounts at the Treasury, that my Security be dischargd. No Motive but that of discharging myself of this Money and at the same time the desire I have to keep Matters quiet and to avoid bringing you and those Gentlemen under any difficulty or reproach here or in Virginia for not keeping expressly up to the Terms prescribd for payment of this Money Such then being my Motives for departing from the express Condition of my Bond I do not doubt but that you will without loss of time take the proper Measures if not already done as to your Authority with the Council & Assembly to Indempnify me and my Securitys for paying your Bills, the Treasury being under Adjournment for 10 days I shall take the first opportunity on their meeting to lay the Bills before them, and in the mean time I have signefyd the same to the Merchants in whose hands such Bills are I am always Sir

LB, pp. 223–224. Sent "per Capt Carlisle to Mr Hyndman."

1. John Robinson (1705–1766) was treasurer of Virginia and Speaker of the House of Burgesses from 1738 until his death.

To Francis Fauquier

Jany 6th 1761

In my last[1] I acquainted you that the Bills drawn on me for the ballance of the Public Money, not being in proper Form, I did intend to take the opinion of the Treasury thereon, before acceptance and during the Adjournment of the Treasury having laid one of the Bills before some of the Gentlemen of Business at the Treasury & finding their opinion by no means clear, rather than have the Objection had by the Treasury so as to delay payment I have for the honour and credit of the Drawers with the Consent of my Securitys resolvd to accept them and many of them are accordingly accepted for payment By this means, I have laid myself under the difficulty of having my Security and Accounts lay over till I can make it appear that the Drawers of the Bills had the Authority of Gvr Council & Assembly so to do, and this you will be so good as to Certify to me under the Colony Seal by the first opportunity I am Sir Your Most Obedt

LB, p. 228. Sent "to [Harley?] per Bristol Copy per New York Packet."

1. See preceding letter.

To John Blair

Jany 6th 1761

By the demise of the late King the re:appointment of all Officers at home and Abroad becomes necessary I have thereupon notice given me from the Plantation Office in regard to the Governor & Council & Attorney General of Virginia, desiring to know whether I will Solicit the said Commissions and Warrants and undertake for the Payment of Fees thereof, both which I have taken upon me to do, You will therefore be pleased to acquaint the Gentlemen of the Council herewith that they may direct their Correspondents here to Indempnify me with regard to the Fees of the several Offices, and as for my trouble in the Solicitation it is at their Service Wishing You the Complts of the Season I am always

LB, p. 229. Sent "per Bristol Copy per N Y Packet."

To John Blair (presumed not sent)

London Jany 10th [1761]

I did not receive Your favour of 26 June[1] before yesterday with the 2 Bills for Salary to 25 of last Octr, first Bill whereof is already paid.

The Lt Governors letter of the 22d June long since reced with the Minutes of Council of 12 Decr 1759[2] enclosd therein refers me to A letter from You[3] on the part of the Council agreeing with their Minutes of Council of the 12th with regard to the Money heretofore issud from the Treasury I find by the Bills drawn upon me to the Account of the 50000 granted in 1757 to you are aprisd

LB, p. 230. This letter lacks the year in the dateline, ends abruptly, and is crossed through. It was evidently replaced by JA's letter to Blair finally dated 20 December 1760, above.

1. Letter not found.
2. See JA to Fauquier, 1 Oct. 1760, p. 367, n. 1.
3. Letter not found.

To Francis Fauquier

London Jany 14th 1761

This day I reced from Mr Ed Hunt[1] a Box containing two Acts of Assembly relative to the Public Money in my hands[2] a List of the Bills already drawn on me[3] and a letter of Nov 6th from you, the President and the Speaker,[4] By these Acts and letter of Advice the difficulty with regard to the Authority of the Drawers of the Bills suggested to you in my former letters is removed, and as I have before informd you that notwithstanding such difficulty I had accepted Bills so drawn on me, so I shall according to your new letter of Advice continue to accept and Pay your Bills to the Ammount of 5089.9.4 being the Ballance in my hands as by my Accounts heretofore by Several Opportunitys transmitted will appear.[5]

I observe you take no notice of my Accounts whereby the said Ballance is asertaind but from your former letters and by Mr Blairs of the 26 of last June[6] on the part of the Council reced but of late I have ground to believe that the Article of Commissions will not be calld in Question by the Assembly for in support of this charge I have the former Presidents of the 20000 Issud to Virginia, whereon the like Commission of 2 & $\frac{1}{2}$ was allowd by the Treasury to Messrs Hanburys the Persons who Negociated the same[7] and in that case they had no manner of trouble in the Solicitation no extraordinary trouble attending the formation of Claims and the Critical Adjustment of Provincial Proportions in all which I have done ample Justice to Virginia and perhaps more than Justice and amongst other Instances of my attention to the Interest of Virginia giving their Services the Legal in place of the Mercantile value of Money expended by them, whereby from the new Exchange upon their Bills I find they are gainers above 15 Per Ct, this Advantage of itself is more than enough to stiffle all opposition to the usual Comm[issi]ons on this Money and I am accordingly determind to adhere to it You will therefore in your Drafts on me take care not to exceed such Ballance asertaind by my Accounts Mr Montague now Authorisd to receive all Moneys henceforward[8] may do as he pleases I am glad to be so far relieved I shall by letter communicate to him the Purport of the Laws now transmitted to me, he is now and ever since his appointment has been I believe mostly in the Country and with the Regiment and in fact the whole of the Virginia Affairs have hetherto been negociated by me alone, it is now full time that the Provincial agent had his Share in the Service, in which he shall have a just and reasonable share of my Assistance as Solicitor, a Denomination usd formerly so now given me, for you & the Council in Government Matters.

LB, pp. 235–236. Sent "to Portsmouth to Capt Herron per Coledge to Virginia if not returnd from Portsmouth."

1. Probably Edward Hunt, a London merchant and owner of the ship *Mary*, which traded to Virginia.

2. The two acts Hunt delivered were probably "An Act for recruiting and further continuing the old regiment in the service of this colony, and for other purposes therein mentioned," and "An Act for appointing persons to receive the money granted, or to be granted, by the parliament of Great-Britain, to his majesty, for the use of this colony," both passed in Oct. 1760 (Hening, *Statutes*, 7:369–375). The former act authorized the governor, president of the Council, and Speaker to draw bills of exchange, jointly, on JA, to the amount of £20,000; the latter act authorized the same three persons to draw on JA for the balance of money remaining in his hands.

3. List not found.

4. This letter (not found) probably reported the passage of the two acts mentioned above.

5. See the accounts enclosed in JA's letters to Fauquier of 10 May and 3 July 1760, pp. 352–353 and p. 364.

6. Letter not found.

7. The "former Presidents" or precedent JA cites was the allowance of a commission of $2\frac{1}{2}$ percent to John Hanbury, Capel Hanbury (1707–1765), and Osgood Hanbury.

8. The latter of the two acts delivered to JA (cited in n. 2, above) authorized Edward Montagu to receive all sums of money granted by Parliament for the use of Virginia other than the money in JA's hands.

To Francis Fauquier

Jany 19th [1761]

Perhaps this may overtake Capt Cooledge at Portsmouth[1] to acknowledge yours by a Vessel to Whithaven,[2] as appears by the Post Mark on your letter of 23d Novr which incloses Duplicates of your lettres of 22d June and 31t Octr Originals of both probably lost or taken and the Address said therein to have been sent to Mr Montague I have heard nothing of nor from him who is with his Regt at Wells, from the hint given me of the Contents thereof I am preswaded it is by no means proper as you justly observe for you or for me in your behalf to take part therein.[3]

I did expect some animadversion on the 2 Articles you mention but I am glad that they are agreed to in General Assembly and lest your having signefyd this to me may not Satisfy the Treasury and as the Money is negociable by you the President and Speaker, it is necessary that you three do write me a letter declaring the Same and that you are accordingly to draw or have already drawn for the Ballance in my hands which joint letter with vouchers by the Bills when all paid will relieve my Bond; I am glad that the Correspondence on Government now rests alltogether between yourself and me, and as this letter will be soon followed by another by a Ship from hence I conclude, with remarking that your direction to the Agent for Virginia differs from that of the Presidents denomination as Solicitor for the Affairs of Virginia, Will it not be more consistent with the Attorney Genls oppinion,[4] which you had sent you upon my Office, at the same time prevent altercation at Offices between Mr Montague & me, acting under distinct appointments That my Denomination be Solicitor or Agent for the Kings Affairs so I find by some of the ancient Establishments Salarys paid to the Virginia Solicitor in England this I submit to your due consideration. In my former of 14th Jan[5] acknowledged the receipt of the two Acts of Assembly concerning the application of the Public Money in my hands, with letter of Advice of the Bills Drawn and a Particular List of Bills drawn for the Same and as one of these Acts authorisd Mr Montague to receive all Subsequent Money I thought proper to communicat the same to him directly at the Devizes where he is quarterd with his Regt[6] I am Sir

LB, pp. 237–238. The marginal routing memorandum reads: "to John Buchanan for C Cooledge at Ports[mou]th NB returnd to me & went from London by Mr Hyndmans Ship Copy by another also from London."

1. Portsmouth is the city, harbor, and naval base in Hampshire on the southern coast of England, 65 miles southwest of London.

2. Whitehaven, a market town and port, is in Cumbria on the northwestern coast of England, 38 miles southwest of Carlisle.

3. Fauquier's letters of 22 June, 31 Oct., and 23 Nov. 1760 have not been found (but for that of 22 June, see JA to Fauquier, 1 Oct. 1760, p. 367, n. 1). The address must have been the address and representation to the king stating the reasons for the assembly's passage of acts lately disallowed, which was signed by the president of the Council and the Speaker of the House of Burgesses and delivered to the committee of correspondence for transmittal to Montagu, who was to present it to the king (see *JHB, 1758–1761*, 188, 196; copies of the address and representation, referred by the Privy Council to the Board of Trade, are CO 5/1330, fols. 50–56). The address, dated 20 Oct. 1760, expresses apprehension of the king's displeasure, which had been indicated by his disallowance of several acts lately passed by the General Assembly; the members of the assembly presume to offer their reasons for passing those acts and hope to erase any impression that they had tried to encroach on the king's prerogative. The representation, also dated 20 Oct. 1760, offers a detailed review of Virginia laws regarding payment of levies and fees and distraining and sale of the property of delinquents, and particularly of the acts to enable inhabitants of the colony to discharge their debts in money. In summary, the representation begs the king to allow the governor's assent to necessary acts of less than two years' duration and to acts altering or repealing other acts that have not received the king's approval, that relate only to Virginia, and that do not affect the king's prerogative or the trade of Great Britain. For the outcome of the address and representation, see JA to Fauquier, 15 June [1761], p. 388.

4. See JA to Blair, 15 Dec. 1759, pp. 329–330, n. 4.

5. See preceding letter.

6. Devizes is a town in Wiltshire in the west of England, 16 miles east of Bath, and about 30 miles northeast of Wells. Perhaps JA meant to say that Montagu and his regiment were temporarily at Wells but were quartered for a longer period at Devizes.

To John Blair

privat   London Jany 22d 1761

For your privat Information and not in the way of Office or direction from the A: G:[1] I send you the Case as it stands at the Treasury, and judge from it whether or not the Receiver General in ballancing the Accounts with his late Majesty he may not venture to repay himself out of the Q Rents by replacing so much as he has Advancd or in Fact lost to the late King out of the Virginia Revenue, in Remitting the Q Rents to London, if this is done and Exception thereto taken at home the Labor in Soliciting the Kings Warrant ex post Facto cannot be greater than one now a priore, such are my privat notions with regard to that part of the Report relative to the Money advancd out of the Tobaco Duty for Remitting the Q Rents,[2] I am not clear however favourable though the whole the A Gs Report is, that the Lords of the Treasury will agree thereto, and indeed I am much affraid they will not carry their approbation so far, by Directing the whole Sums so deficient in the T Revenue to be made good now and Occasionally hereafter out of the Q R. this was considerd in making the Report and therefore laying the stress upon former Precedents which I very narrowly searchd for in order from such Precedents to recover what is passd, likewise in the Report any Position that certainly must have been rejected by pointing at a Permanent and arbitrary Drain from the Q R.

From a little Criticism that some of the Gentlemen of the Treasury passd on my Soliciting for Public & Privat Aid out of the Kings Revenue, I thought it might be more for the Service of the Indian Commissioners to throw the Solicitation of their particular Case upon their friends and Correspondents, who having the A Genals Report to Countenance & Support their Solicitation are at liberty to plead the Case without the Imputation Suggested to me of being both Judge & Jury in their Case,[3] it is from this Motive Thought adviseable that Messrs Hanbury & Lidderdale[4] should become the Solicitors at the Treasury for the Commissioners. I have been the more circumstantial in this Case that you & the R. G.[5] may judge if any & what use is to be made of my privat Sentiments with regard to that part of the Report relative to the Aid requir'd to make good former Deficiencys on the Remittance of the Q Rents, which from the difficulty arising at the Treasury to have such Deficiencys made good, must suggest to you the expediency of leting the Q Rents stand their own chance as to the Exchange by Remiting thereof to London Before I conclude I must inform you how very uneasy the Au General is on account of the long intermission of Letters Accounts and Supplys from you, the miscariage of the many Ships is urgd in your favour, but often the best Plea is our expectation from the next Ships now expected, I am Dr Sir

LB, pp. 233–234. At the foot of this letter JA wrote: "NB Origl & Duplicates by 2 Ships from London in June, or July."

1. Auditor-General Robert Cholmondeley.

2. For Cholmondeley's report, see JA to Fauquier, 1 Oct. 1760, pp. 367–368, n. 8.

3. For the memorial from Indian commissioners Byrd and Randolph, and for Cholmondeley's report on their claim, see JA to Fauquier, 20 July 1758, p. 263, n. 2, and JA to Randolph, 1 Jan. 1760, p. 333, n. 2.

4. London merchant John Lidderdale.

5. Receiver General Philip Grymes.

To Francis Fauquier

March 9th 1761

Since my last Jany 20th[1] Mr Montague having reced his Credentials, with the Representations from the Council and Assembly[2] is come to Town, and has taken the field of business, we have conferrd together and so far as his Negociations on the part of Assembly may effect you is well understood between us, at first he seemd desireous that I should attend the Plantation Board along with him when these Matters came under consideration, but I satisfyd him that my appearance might be deemed as on your part &, so rather hurt than promote Success, my judgment is founded on something that came out in general conversation on the Affairs of Virginia, suggesting as if the confidence between you and the Assembly had drawn you into too great a Subservience to their views on all occasions, and in this the Conduct of the Council was at the same time animadverted on, how far the Hints I have from time to time given you to be on your guard in this respect are consistent with your Letters from the Plantation Office I cannot say but I think it my Duty acting in your immediate Service to aprise you, how things appear to me. I could almost wish that you had some favorable opportunity given you to convince people here, that you, as well as the Council had resolution to give the negative to Measures however strongly urged upon you, where such measures have tendency to lessen your Authority, such an opportunity faling in your way might make amends for your former complacency which gave no favourable Impression of your Administration at first seting out, [In short from long experience in American Affairs I am convinc'd the way to Govern long is to adapt ones administration to the Ideas of Government at home rather than to those abroad and of all other American Governments that of Virginia is the best adapted to the Rules of Government here the Governor being to all Intents and Purposes Independant, and this has been often Made the Remark on your Administration,][3] Your Brother has communicated to me that part of your letter concerning Mr Row[4] I shall take an opportunity through my friend the Bishop of Bristol to Silence that turbulent Priest but I do not hear that he has in any shape busyd himself in any of [the] Offices about the Affairs of Virginia since his arrival.[5]

Mr Montague is now engaged in negociating at the Treasury the Distribution of the 200000 granted in 1759 I am laid under the [obligation] of being extreamly cautious in payment of the Bills on me for former grants, having met with more than one Instance of the Same Bills negociated through different channels I am much obligd to you & the other Gentlemen for giving me letter of Advice with particulars of the Bills drawn on me by this means I have been more readily enabled to discover the deception of the same Bills being negociated by different hands for acceptance.

Nothing very material from abroad since my former, our Administration at home has undergone some alteration by Mr Leggs Dismision suceeded by Ld Barrington[6] and probably more will now be replaced Mr C Townsend to the War Office[7] amongst others and Lord Halifax has now the best chance for going to Ireland,[8] many others having refusd that honour Complts to all with you I am Sir

PS   as the Parlt ends the 19 I thereupon proceed to Scotland for my Election for next Parlt.

LB, pp. 239–240. At the foot of this letter JA wrote: "NB to Mr Hanbury Origl & Duplicat to the Coffeehouse."

1. JA's last letter to Fauquier in the letter book is dated 19 Jan. [1761], pp. 380–381.

2. See ibid., note 3.

3. JA marked this bracketed passage with a marginal bracket and the word "out," suggesting that it was not included in the receiver's copy.

4. Fauquier's letter to his brother has not been found.

Mr. Row was the Rev. Jacob Rowe (born ca. 1730), who in 1758 became professor of morality, or master of the philosophy school, at the College of William and Mary. In Sept. 1758 Rowe was accused of making scandalous and malicious utterances about the House of Burgesses and was taken into custody, but was released upon making an apology and paying some fees. In Apr. and May 1760, Rowe was examined by the visitors of the college on charges of drunkenness, profanity, and insubordination; Fauquier, as rector, admonished him severely, and Rowe promised to mend his ways. In Aug. 1760 Rowe was accused of leading the boys of the college in a fight with the Williamsburg apprentices and of insulting the visitors of the college; he was dismissed from his appointment and ordered to remove himself and his effects by 29 Sept. (Fulham Papers, 13:284–287; *JHB, 1758–1761*, 16–18).

5. The bishop of Bristol was the Rt. Rev. Philip Yonge or Young (ca. 1711–1783), who had been a schoolmate of JA at the Westminster School in London; his father, Francis, and younger brother Henry, at various times in the service of South Carolina, were possibly other links with JA, who was attorney general of South Carolina 1730–1742. It is not clear how the bishop could provide an opportunity for silencing Rowe.

6. Henry Bilson-Legge (1708–1764) was dismissed from his office of Chancellor of the Exchequer in Mar. 1761. He was succeeded by William Wildman Barrington, Viscount Barrington.

7. Charles Townshend (1725–1767) was named secretary at war in Mar. 1761.

8. The earl of Halifax was named lord lieutenant of Ireland in Mar. 1761.

To Francis Fauquier

[June] 2d 1761

I am favour with yours of 24th May[1] and since my last the Negro Act is arrivd,[2] what judgment the Board may form thereon I cannot as yet inform you, in the mean time I have urgd your Reasons for assenting thereto, During my absence on my Election to Parliament Mr Montague attended the Board on the Several Matters recommended to him by the progress made in the Case of the Representation relative to the Kings Instructions to the Govor no great hopes hetherto of any explicit Relaxation of those Instructions,[3] he informs me that he usd his Endeavours to give a favourable turn to your particular Conduct as Governor, and there is no doubt of his good Inclinations to serve you But I need not repeat what I have heretofore more than once hinted to you that the Assembly & you must not on every Occasion be thought drawing together, the Kings Instructions being the Test of a Governors Conduct and this dayly becomes more and more the Language of Office here. The Idle Report of the Virginia Forces having laid down their Arms from some difference between you & Col Bird[4] came first from the City and was Trumpeted in this end of the Town by some of the Northern Partisans who from the beginning to the end of the American War have given the most unfavourable turn to Measures calculated for the Southward Parts of the Continent, this began in Shirleys Administration,[5] and much Pains and Labor came to my share before I could draw the attention of People of Rank to assist us to the Southward with Men and money but under Mr Pitts Administration we have had our share, your Brother and myself soon became able to falsefy Such Report, which I could not learn had ever made any impression.

With regard to New Comissions your Brother had yours and has transmitted it according[6] The Reappointment of the Gentlemen of the [Council] is containd in the New Comm[issi]on to Mr Amhurst,[7] and thereby Part tho a very small part of the Fees became saved: By the Demise of the King every Authority ceases, the Offices on renewal thereof therefore look upon themselves enti-[t]ld de novo to Fees accordingly, In order to Save Fees for the Reappointment of the Council I urgd their being Reappointed by the Govrs Commission, they admit an exemption of Fees in the Case where the Council are Nominated in a New Governors Commission, because their Authority never ceased but in the Case of the Kings death it is otherwise and accordingly Mr Sedgwick[8] makes his demand on such Gentlemen as have Correspondents [who] have here engagd themselves for their Fees it is not my Business to become forward in Advancing Money without particular Instructions so to do, what was necessary for me to do I did very early by Soliciting their Continuance as before the Kings death, and gave you Notice accordingly for their particular Information.

The Town and also the outworks being ours We every hour expect to hear of the Citadel of Bellisle being ours[9] also a glorious pledge upon the approaching Peace the first apparent Instance whereof is Mr Stanleys arrival at Paris and Monsrs Busseys At London[10] other Motives no doubt will forward this great Worke the King of Prussia able in Negociation as well as in Arms has unknown to all the Powers of Europe brought about an Offensive Treaty with the Turks, their vast Armaments as if against the little Island of Malta comes out now to be against Russia, perhaps end with the Empress Queen[11] My Complts to all of your Family

LB, pp. 241–243. Although the date of the letter is clearly written as "May 2d 1761," the account of Montagu and the address and representation from the General Assembly involve events that took place, or became known, after 8 May certainly, and perhaps after 20 May, while the comment on military and diplomatic events toward the end of the letter could not have been written before the very end of May. It is assumed, therefore, that the letter should have been dated 2 June. The words in brackets were presumably left out by accident. At the foot of this letter JA wrote: "Original per the Coffee house Ship June [1t?]."

1. No letter of 24 May from Fauquier to JA has been traced, and it seems that JA was mistaken in the date; he could hardly refer to a letter of 24 May 1761, and it is not likely that he refers to a letter of an earlier year.

2. JA's most recent letter to Fauquier in the letter book is that of 9 Mar. 1761, above. For the Negro Act, see JA to Fauquier, 1 June 1760, p. 361, n. 4.

3. On 8 May 1761 Montagu was heard by the Board of Trade in support of the address and representation of 20 Oct. 1760, for which see JA to Fauquier, 19 Jan. 1761, pp. 380–381 (*JBT*, 11:195).

4. No other mention of this report has been traced.

5. William Shirley (1694–1771), governor of Massachusetts 1741–1757, served also as commander in chief in North America for about a year, from the death of Braddock in July 1755 until Lord Loudoun assumed command in the middle of 1756.

6. Fauquier's commission was dated 13 Mar. 1761 (*Fauquier Papers*, 2:488–489). He presented it to the Council on 11 Sept. 1761 and took the usual oaths (*EJC*, 6:195–196).

7. In fact, the councillors were named in Amherst's new *instructions*, issued on 27 May 1761 (CO 5/1368, p. 79).

8. Perhaps Edward Sedgwick or Sedgewick, who was at this time solicitor and clerk of reports to the Board of Trade.

9. The British were besieging the town of Palais on the island of Belle-Île-en-Mer off the west coast of France. The French were driven from the town into the citadel on 13 May, but news of this retreat did not come to England until 28 May.

10. Hans Stanley (1720?–1780), sent to France to negotiate a peace, arrived in Paris in early June, while the French envoy, François de Bussy (1699–1780), arrived in London on 31 May.

11. A treaty of friendship and commerce between the Turks and Prussia was signed at Berlin on 12 Mar. Contemporary reports were that the Turks intended to capture Malta and had declared war against Russia. The "Empress Queen" was Maria Theresa (1717–1780) of Austria-Hungary, allied with the French and the Russians against Prussia and Britain.

To John Blair

[ca. 2 June 1761]

{On p. 243 of the letter book, after Abercromby's letter of 2 [June] 1761 to Governor Fauquier, and before the abstract of his letter of 15 June 1761 to Fauquier, is the note "Per Do to Mr Blair in answer to his of 28 Feby." Presumably the "Do" refers to a memorandum following the letter of 2 [June] to Fauquier, "Original Per the Coffee house Ship June [1t?]" or to a line, deleted and illegible, following that memorandum.}

To Edward Montagu

[8 June 1761]

To Mr Montague June 8th 1761

LB, unpaginated but follows presentation page.

To Francis Fauquier

[15 June 1761]

To Mr Fauquire June 15th All laws past[1] tell him of the Report of the Board of Trade being agt the Address from the Assembly for Relaxation of the Instruction[2] in answer to his letter 2d March.[3]

LB, p. 243.

1. It appears that JA refers to "An Act for granting the sum of twenty thousand pounds, for the further security and protection of this colony," passed in Mar. 1760; and to "An Act for recruiting and further continuing the old regiment in the service of this colony, and for other purposes therein mentioned," to "An Act for appointing persons to receive the money granted, or to be granted, by the parliament of Great-Britain, to his majesty, for the use of this colony," and to "An Act to explain and amend the act, intituled, An Act for appointing an agent" (Hening, *Statutes*, 7:369–377), all three passed in Oct. 1760. On 22 May 1761 the Board of Trade considered four acts passed in Virginia in Mar. and Oct. 1760 along with Sir Matthew Lamb's reports on them, and since there appeared to be no objection to the acts "they were ordered to lye by probationary, untill the further effect and operation of them should be known." The acts are identified by Lamb's letters (CO 5/1330, fols. 59–62) reporting on the acts, read at the Board meeting of 22 May 1761 (*JBT*, 11:198).

2. On 20 May 1761 the Board of Trade submitted a report (copy in CO 5/1368, fols. 89–92) to the Privy Council upon the address and representation of 20 Oct. 1760 from the General Assembly to the king (for which see JA to Fauquier, 19 Jan. 1761, p. 381, n. 3). The report disapproved of the proposal that the governor be allowed to assent to acts, without the suspending clause, altering or repealing laws that had been confirmed; it recommended that the governor be allowed to assent to acts authorizing the payment of clergymen's salaries in money in the counties of Frederick, Augusta, Hampshire, Princess Anne, and Norfolk, provided the clergy consented; and it disapproved in general of the proposal that the governor be allowed to assent to acts of less duration than two years and to acts altering or repealing other acts that had not received the king's approval. The tenor of the report was that the proposals of the General Assembly tended to subvert the prerogative of the Crown as well as the constitution of Virginia.

3. Letter not found.

To John Blair

June 29th [1761]

On perusal of the Lords Justices Order of 2d Augt 1750 upon the late Audr Generals Report on Mr Roberts's Representation for Regulating the Payment of Q Rents at 19 penny Weight I find the Receiver General is thereby authorizd to charge in the Quarterly Account the extra Expence of Remitting the Q Rents by Bills in the preceding Accounts and the Accounts for the Year 1745–1746–47 and 48 are therein particularly comprehended, and further, that the expence for Remitting by Bills is to be chargd by the Receiver

General upon the Quitrents till such time as the Regulation for payment of Q Rents at the rate of 19 penny Wt shall operate & take place as intended, which 19 penny Wt was thought sufficient to enable the Receivers to remitt at Par.[1]

Notwithstanding of the said Warrant authorizing the Expence of Remitting to be charged to the Quitrent Acount I take notice that in the State of the Deficiencys upon Rem[i]tting the QR as transmitted by you you State the Deficiencys for the [year] 1745 at 371.8.2 in *1747* to *77.16.6* as being paid out of the Tobacco Revenue, and also I believe that the late A. General by his Report to the Treasury on 22d April 1748 on Mr John Grymes's Memorl (Praying to be allowd the Expence of Remitting by Bills as the same is chargd in his Q Rent Accounts) takes occasion to press it with the then Lords of the Treasury, the making good from time to time the Deficiencys on Remitting the QR out of the Tabacco duty by way of Contingencys for the Service of Govert[2] However as the Case of the expence of Remitting the Q Rents was not finally determind till the order passd by the Lords Justices as aforesaid in Augt 1750 and thereby the Recr General was authorizd to charge for Remitting the Sum of 1029.18.6 in his former Accounts Including the Remittances for the Accounts for the years 1745 and 1747 how comes it that the Receiver General did not make good to the Tobacco Revenue such payments in those Years out of the Q Ren[ts] according to the Said order.

I shall be much obligd to you to let me know how far this order of the Lords Justices with regard to the charges for Remitting per Bills has been carryd into Execution previous to the order for payment of 19 penny Wt takeing place that I may be ready to answer at the Treasury should their Lordships take the case up with a greater retrospection of Accounts than before and in another light than in that wherein it is favourably set forth in the Recent Audr Generals Repor[t] thereon,[3] which from an Extract thereof hertofore sent you you may easily guess what share I had therein I am

LB, pp. 245–246. Sent "per Mr Atthaws inclosd with a few lines to the Lt Govr as it regards a Solicitation now with me from the Govr & Council."

1. An Order of the Lords Justices in Council of 2 Aug. 1750 (T 1/348, fols. 248–249) was issued in accordance with a report of 1 May 1750 from Auditor-General

Horatio Walpole on a memorial by John Roberts (1712–1772), receiver general of Virginia. Roberts held (and Walpole and the Privy Council agreed) that Virginia quitrents should henceforth be payable in silver at 19 pennyweight for 5 shillings sterling, or in tobacco at 3 farthings per pound, rather than the rates prevailing at the time: in silver at $17\frac{1}{2}$ pennyweight, or in tobacco at 1 penny per pound. The "extra Expence of Remitting the Q Rents by Bills" for 1745–1748 arose because of the much higher rate of exchange between Virginia currency and the pound sterling. Virginia's receiver general, Philip Grymes, explained in a petition to the Treasury of 20 Oct. 1747 (T 1/328, fols. 96–97) that for the years 1745 and 1746 he had deducted $12\frac{1}{2}$ percent from the quitrent revenues rather than the usual allowance of $5\frac{5}{8}$ percent to compensate for the exchange rate. When Auditor-General Walpole learned of the large allowance Grymes had taken without his prior approval (but with the consent of the governor and Council), he expressed his displeasure, hence Grymes's petition to explain his actions, acknowledge his error, ask that the allowance for those two years stand, and seek directions for his future conduct. The Treasury referred Grymes's petition to Walpole, who submitted a report on 22 Aug. 1748 (T 1/330, fols. 49–53). Walpole recommended allowing the $12\frac{1}{2}$ percent charge for those years but warned against authorizing the governor and Council "to bring any new Charge upon his Majesty's Revenue, for . . . such a power once fix'd there might perhaps prove hereafter of bad Consequence to the rights of the Crown."

2. Walpole's report of 22 Aug. 1748 (see note 1 above) recommended that if Virginians continued to pay their quitrents at $17\frac{1}{2}$ pennyweight rather than 19 pennyweight for 5 shillings sterling, "directions shou'd be given that, Upon the rise of Bills of Exchange above the Value of the Currency, the difference for Enabling the Receiver to remit the full Balance home . . . shou'd be charg'd in the Article of Contingency's" of the two-shillings-per-hogshead accounts.

3. See JA to Blair, 5 Mar. 1758, p. 232, n. 2, and JA to Fauquier, 1 Oct. 1760, pp. 367–368, n. 8.

To Francis Fauquier

[ca. 29 June 1761]

{On p. 246 of the letter book, after Abercromby's letter of 29 June [1761] to John Blair, is a note that that letter had been "inclosd with a few lines to the Lt Govr as it regards a Solicitation now with me from the Govr & Council." The lines to Fauquier probably concerned the application for aid from the quitrents to the tobacco revenue; in his letter of 12 July 1761 to Fauquier, Abercromby wrote that within the past few days he had learned that the Treasury had refused the application.}

To Francis Fauquier

Sir   July 12th 1761

I have your favour of May 8th[1] inclosing copy of your letter to Mr Pitt,[2] if the joint letter from you, the President and Speaker and the Bills for the Remaining sum still in my hands come safe from thence I shall be enabled to Exhibit my Accounts in the Excheqr in the mean time I think myself very much obligd to you for your particular Attention to what concerns me in this Matter, and in all others in the way of my Office.

In my last to you,[3] I informd you that altho the Address to the King relative to an alteration of Powers to Governors was Reported against by the Lords for Trade, and that no doubt remaind but that such Report will be confirmd by the King in Council that I was nevertheless well pleasd to find less fire in the Report than expected, and I hope you will by your Office Letters find the language of Office in this case free from any degree of Resentment.

Lord Sandys being gone to the Country his Board is now under their long adjournment[4] however the Office is open for all Dispatchs: directed to the Plantation Office. I had heard from your Brother the Generosity of the House of Burgesses to you, but I confess myself on your Account much better pleasd to hear from yourself that it was a Present in *the usual way* and within the rule of your Instructions tho exceeding the usual Sum, and I hope if anything appears of this present upon the Journals, that all insinuation of Novelty is avoided.[5]

I never had heard of the smallest degree of misunderstanding between you and Mr Dinwiddy;[6] The Offices of Treasuerers in the Colonys have all along been Matter of Contention between the Colonys and the Board of Trade In New Settled Colonys and particularly in Georgia & Nova Scotia the Crown have assumd the Nomination, in other Colonys Government here have been obligd to Temporize and acquiesse in the ancient Custom of the Colonys, such was the Case in South Carolina wherein I was concerned on the part of the Colony and carryd my part so far as that the Matter rests undetermind indeed the Treasurers Law in S Carolina had been confirmd and deemd Perpetual[7] in your Case it is temporary tho of long usage, any Alteration therein as you rightly observe must beget very great disturbances and confusion in the Province and if your Instructions are explicit in Case the Treasurers come up Arguments ab inconveniente[8] cannot be more properly urged than at present in time of War, and such arguments may probably satisfy their Lordships so far as to acquiesse under the present Establishment of the Office, and acquit you for not urging the Alteration proposd by the Instruction,[9] this is the language most likely to be attended to with Success here should the Matter come in question, how far you are calld upon to take this case up I cannot say, if not particularly enjoind so to do, I should be of opinion to steer clear of this rock of Discord at home and abroad.

I am sorry to find our Warlike measures have been censurd, but this Matter will be soon set to rights from your State of the case transmitted to Mr Pitt which I shall in justice to the Province more fully discuss with Mr Wood.[10]

Your Address of Condolence and Congratulation will take the proper channel of conveyance to the King through the Secretary of State and from thence to the Gazette which shall be transmitted to you.[11]

Your opinion of the application for Aid out of the Quitrents to the Tobacco Revenue being rejected is well founded, for I have within these few days got my answer on this head vizt that their Lordships have given a Negative thereto, neither the favourable Report from the Auditor General nor his Solicitation added to mine have been able to overcome the difficulty attending a repayment from the Quitrents.[12]

Within these few days his Majesty in full Council has declard his Intention of taking the 2d Princess of Mecklenburgh for his Queen her arrival here is fixed for the 20 of next Month Conducted by Lord Harcourt, the Coronation takes place on 22d of Septr,[13] as to Peace or the continuation of war we are still in the dark, and during the uncertainty, much blood will be spillt in Germany Superiority of numbers must be made up by Valour on our part my best Complts to all your Family from Sir

[PS] Mr Montague is in the Country [*illegible*][14] during the Vacation of the Offices.

LB, pp. 247–249. "Sent this to Mr Hyndman July 14th."

1. Letter not found.

2. Probably Fauquier's letter to William Pitt of 11 Apr. 1761 (*Fauquier Papers*, 2:506–507) concerning Virginia's raising of troops for the war.

3. JA to Fauquier, 15 June 1761, p. 388.

4. The Board of Trade, over which Samuel Sandys (1695–1770), Baron Sandys, presided, did not meet between 23 June and 25 Aug. 1761.

5. On 6 Apr. 1761 the House of Burgesses resolved that £1,000 of the public money should be paid to Fauquier, as an acknowledgment from the Houses of his prudent and zealous management of the public business. What Fauquier wrote to JA about this present is unknown, but the transaction was clearly contrary to Fauquier's instructions, which forbade a governor of Virginia or his deputy to consent to any law or act calling for a present to him from the assembly, and furthermore forbade the governor or his deputy to accept any present from the assembly or any other source. In spite of the instructions, the House had voted a present of £500 to Governor Gooch in 1728 and a present of the same amount to Governor Dinwiddie in 1752; £500 was evidently the "usual Sum" referred to. The approval of the resolution for the present to Fauquier is recorded in the House's journal for 6 Apr. 1761 (*JHB, 1758–1761*, 250), but the journal makes no further mention of the present, and the journal of the Council in assembly does not notice the present at all.

6. The context suggests that JA was responding to something Fauquier had written about Dinwiddie's connection with the Board of Trade's objection to the customary manner of appointing the treasurer in Virginia. Dinwiddie had appeared before the Board of Trade on 7 Mar. 1758, when he described the "improper practice" of uniting the offices of Speaker of the House of Burgesses and treasurer of the colony and recommended that "some directions" be given to Fauquier on this point before his departure from England (*JBT*, 10:386). Two days later Fauquier attended the Board, when "it was recommended to him to use the most prudent endeavours, and to take all such measures, as he should judge consistent with the good of his Majesty's service to put a stop to" the practice (*JBT*, 10:387).

7. The appointment of treasurers in South Carolina was regulated by an act of 1721, commonly called the Treasurer's Act (Thomas Cooper and David J. McCord, eds., *The Statutes at Large of South Carolina*, 10 vols. [Columbia, S.C., 1836–1841], 3:148–149), which provided that appointments were to be made by joint action of governor, Council, and Commons House. In actual practice the Commons continued to manipulate the appointments, but the law remained in force, theoretically, despite the opinion of the Board of Trade that it was an encroachment on the royal prerogative. See Greene, *Quest for Power*, 224–233.

8. Arguments *ab inconvenienti* are those founded upon the hardship of the case and the inconvenience or disastrous consequences to which a different course of reasoning would lead. The six words preceding the phrase are very hard to decipher, and may be wrong.

9. JA probably refers to the Board of Trade's letter to Fauquier of 20 Nov. 1759 regarding the separation of the offices of Speaker and treasurer (*Fauquier Papers*, 1:269); no additional instruction on the subject has been traced.

10. JA evidently refers to Fauquier's letter of 11 Apr. 1761 to Pitt (cited in n. 2, above). Mr. Wood was Robert Wood, undersecretary of state.

11. The address was that to George III from the governor, Council, and House of Burgesses of ca. 10 Apr. 1761, transmitted to the Board of Trade in Fauquier's letter of 12 May 1761 (*Fauquier Papers*, 2:524–527).

12. The Treasury read the auditor-general's report (for which see JA to Fauquier, 1 Oct. 1760, n. 8, above) and rejected Virginia's application on 8 June 1761. The Treasury minutes state simply that "My Lords do not think fitt to comply with the Petition of the Memorialists" and include the notation "Agreed to by the Duke of Newcastle" (T 29/34, p. 95).

13. Charlotte, the second princess of Mecklenburg, was about nine years younger than her one surviving sister. Simon Harcourt (1714–1777), Earl Harcourt, was appointed on 3 July 1761 ambassador extraordinary and minister plenipotentiary to Mecklenburg-Strelitz to demand the hand of Princess Charlotte in marriage for George III. The marriage took place on 8 Sept. and the coronation on 22 Sept. 1761.

14. About four words are illegible here.

To Francis Fauquier

London altho at Tullebody[1] July 23d 1761
Favourd with your 28 May[2] with notice that the Presd & Speaker demur in their approbation by letter of my accounts[3] vide this letter at large in Bundle[4] and therein what passd with Mr Wood as to the Number of Troops in 1760.

LB, p. 250.

1. Tullibody is a village in Clackmannanshire (JA's constituency) in Scotland, two or three miles northwest of Alloa; JA's family lived near the village.

2. Letter not found.

3. It is not clear which accounts JA refers to, but the records of the Virginia Committee of Correspondence indicate that the president of the Council (John Blair) and the Speaker (John Robinson) declined to approve JA's accounts because he set his commission at $2\frac{1}{2}$ percent, whereas they had resolved that he must reduce his commission to $1\frac{1}{2}$ percent. See the committee's proceedings in *VMHB* 9 (1903–1904): 22, 24.

4. Here and elsewhere JA refers to what seems to have been a file of copies of his letters to various correspondents that has not been discovered; some of these copies were evidently full copies of letters of which only an abstract appears in the letter book, while others seem to have been copies of letters that are apparently complete in the letter book.

To Francis Fauquier

Tullebody London Octr 13th 1761

Vide this letter in Bundle thereby agree to reduce my Commission to 2 per ct.[1]

LB, p. 250.

1. See preceding entry, note 2.

To Francis Fauquier

London Octr 13th/29th 1761

Herewith you have the general Account of the Virginia Cash issud to me,[1] with the Commission reducd to 2 per ct of which I acquainted you in my former letter[2] I have likewise acquainted Mr Montague of this who may signifie the same to his Committee[3] and thereupon I have nothing further to add than that as I have made the Rule of the Treasury in particular my guide I do therefore expect no further trouble on the part of the Assembly of Virginia on this head and accordingly I hope to have your the Presidents and Speakers joint letter declaring your approbation of my Account which tho not absolutely necessary in the way of Office I incline to have it if it can be had without any Demur. Tell of Mr Pitts Resignation and the consequence likely to arise.[4]

LB, p. 250. In the date, "13th" is written above "29th," perhaps to indicate the dates the letter was begun and finished. The last sentence is evidently a note for an addition to the letter. At the foot of this letter JA wrote: "Vide this letter more at large in Bundle Octr 13." Sent "To the Coffee house."

1. The enclosed account (not found), was evidently sent by Fauquier to the House of Burgesses on 14 Jan. 1762 (*JHB, 1761–1765*, 34).

2. See preceding entry.

3. The committee of correspondence in Virginia.

4. Pitt resigned as secretary of state for the Southern Department on 5 Oct. 1761 and was succeeded by Charles Wyndham, second earl of Egremont.

To Francis Fauquier

Decr 10th 1761

Duplicat of the above and of the Account[1] and tell him that I do not hear the least agitation of the Treasurers & Speakers Case from Mr Pownall, that the Journals are not come to the Office tho impatiently expected there[2] nothing material by way of news only that the Spanish Affair with us is not cleard up as yet[3] Complts of the Season to you from Sir Yours

LB, p. 250. Sent "per a ship at the Coffee hous."

1. See preceding entry.

2. JA must refer to the journals of the General Assembly's session of 6 Oct. 1760–10 Apr. 1761, sent with Fauquier's letter of 15 Sept. 1761 to the Board of Trade (*Fauquier Papers*, 2:572–574). The Board discovered, through unidentified letters from Fauquier, that the journals were sent by Captain Norton in HMS *Assistance*, which had arrived in England about 1 Dec., and the Board therefore ordered on 16 Dec. that Norton be asked to send the Virginia papers to the Board as soon as possible (*JBT*, 11:235).

3. Presumably this refers to the British request to Spain for information on the terms of the Franco-Spanish treaty concluded in Aug.–Sept. 1761 (the Family Compact) and the intentions of Spain toward Great Britain in the current war. According to the *Gentleman's Magazine* (31 [1761]: 599), on 1 Dec. the papers carried a letter from Madrid reporting a Spanish declaration to the British ambassador that expressed astonishment at Britain's rejection of French proposals of peace and threatened Spanish intervention in America.

To Francis Fauquier

Jany 22d 1762

Have only to add to my last,[1] the turn that our P: Affirs[2] have taken, by the Declaration of War agt Spain,[3] which you will receive by a Frigate Express to Va, the most vigorous Measures are taking by Unan[im]ity in Parlt and Cabinet for carrying on the War to a better Peace than while Spain acted the part of a Secret Enemy for that Tenderness on our part which has hetherto prevented our operations to the South is now removd.

Yesterday the Kings Message came to Our House for Money to North American Colonys[4] & no doubt will be granted tho the

Gentlemen of the Assembly have no longer thought proper to give any share in the Emoluments I shall use my Endeavours to serve the Province so far as lys in my Power I am Sir

JA

LB, p. 251. At the foot of this letter JA wrote: "NB To the Coffee house per Ship under Convoy & inclosd therein a News paper with the Declar of War against Spain."

1. Presumably the preceding entry.

2. JA probably means public affairs.

3. The king declared war against the king of Spain on 2 Jan. 1762. The text of the declaration is printed in *Gentleman's Magazine* 32 (1762): 16–17, and in *Fauquier Papers*, 2:649–651.

4. The king's message was read to the House of Commons on the afternoon of 22 Jan.: "His Majesty being sensible of the Zeal and Vigour with which His faithful Subjects in North America have exerted themselves, in Defence of His Majesty's just Rights and Possessions, recommends it to this House to take the same into Consideration; and to enable His Majesty to give them a proper Compensation for the Expences incurred by the respective Provinces, in the Levying, Clothing, and Pay of the Troops raised by the same, according as the active Vigour, and strenuous Efforts of the respective Provinces, shall justly appear to merit" (*JHC*, 29:113).

To Samuel Swann

March 20th & 28th [1762]

2 letters per Mr Heron.

LB, p. 251.

To Francis Fauquier

March 24th 1762

Send the Spanish Papers & Pamflet thereon[1] tell him the Public News between R & Prussia[2] and Parliamentary News, And that the D of Newcastle is so well disposd to oblige him that shall avail myself thereof to ask further Encouragment in the Way of Office.[3]

LB, p. 251. Sent "per Capt Heron to Portsmouth."

1. Presumably JA sent *Papers Relative to the Rupture with Spain, Laid before Both*

Houses of Parliament, on Friday the Twenty Ninth Day of January, 1762, by His Majesty's Command (London, 1762), a pamphlet of 71 pages, and John Wilkes's anonymous pamphlet of 52 pages, *Observations on the Papers Relative to the Rupture with Spain, Laid before Both Houses of Parliament, on Friday the 29th of January, 1762, by His Majesty's Command. In a Letter from a Member of Parliament to a Friend in the Country* (London, 1762).

2. Hostilities between the Russian and Prussian armies had ceased on 1 Feb. 1762; on 23 Feb. the czar declared to the ministers of his allies that he was determined to have peace; and on 16 March he concluded a suspension of hostilities with the king of Prussia.

3. Thomas Pelham-Holles (1693–1768), duke of Newcastle, was at this time First Lord of the Treasury, but a conflict with Lord Bute and the court forced Newcastle to resign the office in May 1762.

To Samuel Swann

[28 March 1762]

{See JA to Swann, 20 and 28 March [1762], above.}

To John Rutherfurd

[ca. 28 March 1762?]

Per Do from Portsmouth.

LB, p. 251. This memorandum immediately follows that for JA's two letters to Swann of 20 and 28 March [1762], above. The "Do" evidently refers to Capt. Heron.

To John Blair

Sir   April 26th 1762

I have your favour of 30 Decr 1761[1] a few days ago by the Diana inclosing a Bill for 100 Salary for $\frac{1}{2}$ year to 25 of Octr last which is since accepted by Mr Atthaws.[2] I have not been able to settle your Small Ballance with Lord Loudoun so much taken up since his return from Scotland and preparation for his Command in Portugal,[3] I am glad your Demand is so small on his Lordship considering the difficulty of adjusting Accounts with People of his

Rank so circumstancd, I shall however repeat my application. I have more than once made mention of your Views with regard to your Sons being joind with you in the Deputation as Auditor, I have heretofore told you, that on my having urgd this matter heretofore to the Audr General he had given me to understand that he had a friend of Mrs Cholmondelys[4] on his hands to be provided for, and should an opportunity come in his Way in America he should find himself in some measure obligd to avail himself thereof for her Friend, thus it rested at that time; on the revival of my Solicitation for your Son, the Proposal of adding 50£ per annum seems to have made greater Impression and he has promisd me to give you his thoughts thereon by this opportunity you may be assurd that I shall not lose sight of my object in doing what I can to Serve your Son in this case.[5] As the Lords Justices Order of 8th Augt 1750[6] Authorizing the Allowance for Remitting the Quitrents by Bills will be found amongst the late Recr Generals Papers, or amongst Mr Burwells to whose hands it came,[7] it may be had, and thereupon you will consider how far that order can now operate, this Point I have not touchd upon as yet with the Auditor General, but I shall take an opportunity to give him my thoughts thereon. I have heretofore wrote to the Lt Governor telling him that as I had restated my Accounts and reducd my Commission on the Public Money from 2 & $\frac{1}{2}$ to 2 per Ct[8] making the Establishd Rule of the Treasury at home in like cases my Rule for so doing in this, tho I thought myself well warranted from Messrs Hanburys Example to have stood to the first charge of 2 & $\frac{1}{2}$ yet for the sake of avoiding discord having reducd it to 2 per Ct I therefore desird a joint letter from him, as Lt Govr from you as President & from the Speaker approving of my Accounts, to this letter I have as yet no answer I wish it was come that I might exhibit my Accounts for passing in the proper Offices for my Quietus I am Sir Your

LB, pp. 252–253. Sent "per Capt Heron per Convoy."

1. Letter not found.

2. Edward Athawes was one of the foremost of the London merchants trading to Virginia.

3. After Spanish forces invaded Portugal in early May 1762, Count William von der Lippe-Bückeburgh arrived in early July to become commander in chief of the allied forces. Shortly thereafter Loudoun arrived with 6,000 troops to reinforce those

already in Portugal. By autumn the Spanish invasion had ground to a halt, and the Spanish commander withdrew his troops to Spain.

4. Auditor-General Robert Cholmondeley had married, in 1746, Mary Woffington (d. 1811), daughter of Arthur Woffington and sister of the celebrated actress Margaret Woffington.

5. See JA to Blair, 7 Mar. 1758, p. 236, n. 3.

6. Actually 2 Aug. 1750; see JA to Blair, 29 June [1761], pp. 389–390.

7. Lewis Burwell (1710–1756), president of the Council, served as acting governor 1750–1751.

8. JA to Fauquier, 13 Oct./29 Oct. 1761, p. 396.

To Francis Fauquier

June 1t 1762

Tell him the alteration in the Ministry[1] that nothing material had happend Since my last, except the difficulty attending the asertaining the Numbers of Provincials, which Mr Montague & I had difficulty to obviate but at last it seems to be understood that they were the same for last year as per former, tell him of Lord Ansons death to be succeeded per Lord Hali[f]ax[2] during the recess I shall go to the Country to recover health.

LB, p. 254. The letter as sent probably bore a date later than 1 June; see n. 2, below.

1. In the last week of May 1762 Bute succeeded Newcastle as First Lord of the Treasury; George Grenville (1712–1770) replaced Bute as secretary of state for the Northern Department; and Francis Dashwood (1708–1781), fifteenth baron le Despencer, became Chancellor of the Exchequer.

2. Anson died on 6 June, so that JA's letter was completed later than 1 June. Halifax was appointed First Lord of the Admiralty on 19 June 1762.

To Francis Fauquier

[24 July 1762]

Vide letters July 24th on the Indians also Letter August 15th on the Commission on the Money from Tullebody and 15 Septr Do from Tullebody all in Bundle 1762.[1]

LB, p. 254.

1. None of these letters has been found. The Indians mentioned in the letter of 24 July were several Cherokee who had embarked for England in May 1762 (see *Fauquier Papers*, 2:726–729; *EJC*, 6:213–218). Fauquier communicated the letters of 15 Aug. and 15 Sept. (along with JA's letter of 10 Nov. 1762, below) to the Council on 28 Apr. 1763. The three letters are abstracted indiscriminately in *EJC*, 6:252–253 (where the date of the Sept. letter is given as 13 Sept.): "His Honour was also pleas'd to communicate Letters from Mr. Abercrombie of the 15th of August, the 13th of Septemr. and the 10th of November last, signifying he should cooperate with Mr. Montague in supporting the Paper Currency Bill—his acquiescence under the one and a half per Cent, Commission, which he hopes he shall be allow'd intire and without throwing upon him the Fees of Office for passing his Accounts, which paid in the several Offices in order to his final discharge in the Exchequer amount to £140.—Also inclosing his Majesty's Warrant to the Receiver General dated June the 21st 1762 for allowing him £200, Sterling per Annum as an additional salary out of the Quit-Rents to commence from that Day."

To Francis Fauquier

[Tullibody, 15 August 1762]

{See preceding entry.}

To Francis Fauquier

[Tullibody, 15 September 1762]

{See JA to Fauquier, 24 July 1762, above.}

LB, p. 254. The date of this letter is given as 13 September in *EJC*, 6:252–253.

To Francis Fauquier

1762 Novr 10th

In my last[1] I acknowledged your[s] of the 25th of May[2] inclosing the Protest of Messrs Nelsons & L against the Act for Emitting more Paper Money,[3] the Business at the Plantation Office being resumd I have there perusd the Merchants Memorial against Paper Money,[4] in which there is nothing conceivd that has any direct Tendency to Impeach your Conduct, on the contrary they have urgd it as an Argument against the Assembly that altho the Kings Instruction had been laid before them by you that they had paid no regard thereto, there is no Argument made use of in the Memorial but what has been more than once agitated at the Board of Trade, in Parlt and with the Merchants themselves, the circumstances and Necessity which begat the use of Paper Credit being the same at Virginia and elsewhere as heretofore, it is in vain to contend for the abolishing thereof, which the Memorial seems to contend for, tho most of the Merchants have signd the Memorial probably in compliance with Mr Athaws who has always been a warm Advocate against Paper Money[5] nevertheless I find that Many of them do admit the Utility and necessity thereof, Should they persist so far as to bring the Matter to a hearing the Stress of the case will turn upon its being a Tender in Law, but this we shall be able to Support.

I shall in conjunction with Mr Montague give my attendance thereon In my former letter I acquainted you that in complyance with yours and the Councils Instructions to me for reducing my Commission to 1 & $\frac{1}{2}$ per Cent being what the Assembly had thought proper to allow to Mr Montague, that I had accordingly notwithstanding what you had wrote to me before that of the 2 & $\frac{1}{2}$ being agrced to acquiessd in taking 1 & $\frac{1}{2}$,[6] and being circumscribd in this case by the allowance to Mr Montague, I flatter myself that I shall be allowd the 1 & $\frac{1}{2}$ per Cent entire & without having thrust upon me the Fees of Office for Passing my Accounts and geting my Bonds up, which work a very considerable reduction on my Commissions, & shew manifest partiality the Fees of Office and incidental Necessary Expenses are expressly allowd to be deducted by me by the Tenor of my Bonds, to the Crown and no doubt on an application to the Treasury I should prevail in this Article however I shall not take any Steps that might occasion Contest unless your Interposition with the Assembly gets over this Article I shall therefore submit to the Justice of the Gover of Virginia on this point whereupon I have advisd with Mr [Farraine] DA of the Imprest[7] who informs me that the Fees in the several Offices[8]

I heartily congratulate you on the prospect of Peace abroad I wish I could do so on the appearance of Peace and Harmony at home, without the Reasonings publishd in News Papers on the various Motives for entering into Particulars of Resignations amongst the Servants of the Crown, whether, from a Dislike to Persons[9] or to Measures I can forsee very warm opposition is likely to arise, within & without Doors People will argue according to the Principles they adopt they who are Advocates for New Acquisitions of Sugar Colonys will Impeach the Surrender of Guardaloupe & St Lucia those for New acquisitions on the Continent in some Measure will likewise disagree, those for the Northern Colonys will prefer Canada entire as it is stipulated preferable to all other Acquisitions those to the Southward give the preference to the Acquisition of Louisiana which we are to have hence to the Missessippe from its Mouth to the Source thereof, but this in the opinion of others is not enough, Not a French Man say they should have been left on the Continent, I own for my own part that I have some Satisifaction that we are to attain on the Part of the Southward Colonys by Negociation what after the most pressing Solicitations by my own means and that of others from the beginning to the end of the War we never bring about by Operation (viz) to remove the French Men from between us and the Indians hence to the Missesipe.[10]

If the Peace when Notifyd to you in Form coincides with your Ideas you cannot make your first letter to Lord Egremont [more effectual] than by an early Congratulation thereon nor the Province a more acceptable turn than by an Address with regard to yourself the more early notice you take thereof so much the better; I shall take care to give your letter thereon proper Introduction to his Lordship in whose Department you still are[11] I am very Sincerly

PS   I took notice in my former letter that the King had been pleasd to add 200 per an out of his Q Rents to my Salary, the Warrant for this purpose comes to the Recr General by this opportunity[12] on passing my Accounts will come to 140 besides the Gratuitys usual in such cases But to remove all difficultys I shall take upon myself the Gratuitys by which means the money to be retaind in place of 200 as below stated for these Fees on passing my Accounts will be 140 and Commission at 1 & $\frac{1}{2}$ per Ct instead of 2 per Ct inde Ballance in favour of Virginia in place of 40.13.6 as per former Account will now be 304.14.5 Inde the Total diference favor Virginia is 444.14.5.

LB, pp. 254–256. There is what seems to be a later version of this letter (either a receiver's copy or a signed copy in JA's hand) now in the Henry E. Huntington Library, San Marino, Calif. (Brock Collection, Box 257, printed in *Fauquier Papers*, 2:822–825). Substantive differences between the two versions are accounted for in notes to the present letter.

1. Probably the preceding entry.

2. Letter not found. The Huntington version refers to Fauquier's letter of 21 May.

3. Councillors William and Thomas Nelson, Richard Corbin, and Philip Ludwell Lee protested against the proposed "Act for granting an aid to his Majesty and other purposes therein mentioned" at a session of the Council in assembly before the bill was read a third time (*Fauquier Papers*, 2:772–774). They feared "the Consequence of issuing more paper-money, and making it a legal tender."

4. JA no doubt refers to the resumption of business at the Board of Trade after its summer holiday, although the Board had met six times between 11 June and 11 Nov. and handled a few items of routine colonial business during those meetings. The date when the merchants' memorial was received at the Board is not recorded. It was the memorial of merchants of London trading to Virginia (CO 5/1330, fols. 129–130), in which they reviewed their objections to emissions of paper money by Virginia and the declaring of that money to be legal tender; complained of the lack of attention to their previous representations on that subject; and asked for a further royal instruction that would provide that no paper notes or bills of credit should be legal tender for payment of sterling debts, which should be payable only in sterling money. The memorial further asked the Board to defer approbation of any act to authorize emission of paper money until the property of the memorialists should be secured. The text of the protest by Corbin, the Nelsons, and Philip Ludwell Lee against paper money (see note 3, above) is appended to the memorial, following the names of the subscribers.

5. The first of the eighteen signatures on the memorial is that of Edward Athawes; he appeared before the Board on various occasions when paper money, settlement of debts, and other matters of colonial business were under consideration.

6. The letter to which JA refers has not been identified, but was probably either that of 15 Aug. or 13 Sept. 1762 to Fauquier (see JA to Fauquier, 24 July 1762, p. 402, n. 1).

The Council considered several of JA's letters and his account claiming a 2 percent commission on 7 May 1762, when it decided that he ought to be satisfied with $1\frac{1}{2}$ percent. Fauquier communicated this decision to JA in a letter (not found) of about 10 June 1762 (*EJC*, 6:219, 227).

7. The name within brackets here is illegible both in the letter book and in the Huntington version. Perhaps it was meant to be Farraine, for Thomas Farraine was a deputy auditor of the imprest in 1762. The name of the second deputy auditor at this period was John Lloyd.

8. At this point JA's sentence breaks off. In the Huntington version the text reads: "the Deputy Auditor of the Imprest whom I have consulted on this matter informs me will make the difference of 70£ upon each Account, so that on the two Accounts it will come to 140 exclusive of the Gratuitys Usual on such Occasions, however to obviate all difficultys I shall take the Gratuitys upon myself by which means the Money retaind for Passing the Accounts will amount to 140 instead of 200 in my former Accounts and thus Commission at 1 & $\frac{1}{2}$ instead of 2 per Cent inde Ballances to be drawn for use of Virginia in place of 40.13.6 as by my former Accounts will now be 304.14.5" (*Fauquier Papers*, 2:823). JA's figures here cannot be reconciled with his two statements of account to Virginia for the money from parliamentary grants, those of ca. 8 May and ca. 3 July 1760 enclosed in letters to Fauquier of 10 May and 3 July 1760, pp. 350–354 and pp. 362–364. Probably he refers here to balances shown in two statements of account that have disappeared.

9. Earl of Bute. See following note.

10. In the Huntington version this paragraph reads: "I heartily congratulate you on the approaching Peace, I wish I could do so, on Peace and Harmony at home, many of the Kings Servants, have of late resignd, whether from Motives of Personal dislike to Lord Bute, or to Measures not as yet known to the Publick, I do not presume to say, be that as it may, I can forsee warm Worke at St. Stephens's this Session; the Preliminarys are not as yet published by Authority, but in the meantime I have some satisfaction by knowing that the Mississippe from the source, to the mouth thereof becomes our Boundary with France, this much we have got by Negociation, what all our applications could not bring about by directing our operations that way."

The preliminary articles of peace between Great Britain and France were signed on 3 Nov. 1762, and on 8 Nov. Egremont informed the lord mayor of London of this event so that he could publish the news in the City as soon as possible. A copy of the draft treaty had been sent to England from France on 24 Sept., and rumors of its terms had been current since the latter part of Aug. (In Dec. 1762 Fox counted JA among those in favor of the preliminary articles.) Among the king's servants to whose resignation JA alludes were the duke of Devonshire, lord chamberlain; Lord George Cavendish, comptroller of the household; and the earl of Bessborough, postmaster general. In fact, Devonshire was abruptly dismissed because he disagreed with Bute's policies on terms of peace, and his brother Cavendish and brother-in-law Bessborough resigned in protest. The warm work at Saint Stephen's (a familiar term for the House of Commons) that JA foresaw was no doubt the consideration of the preliminary articles of peace at the session of Parliament that was to open on 25 Nov.

The French surrendered their West Indian islands of Guadeloupe on 1 and 2 May 1762, and Saint Lucia, one of the so-called Neutral Islands, on 26 Feb. 1762. Britain returned these islands, among other possessions, at the Peace of Paris.

For JA's "pressing Solicitations" throughout the war on the French threat, see Charles F. Mullett, "James Abercromby and French Encroachments in America," *Canadian Historical Review* 26 (1945): 48–59.

11. This paragraph does not appear in the Huntington version.

12. JA announced the addition to his salary in his letter to Fauquier of 1 July 1762 (not found), abstracted in *EJC*, 6:239–240. The warrant of 21 June 1762 for the additional salary was noted in the journal of the Council on 28 Apr. 1763 (*EJC*, 6:253).

To Francis Fauquier

Sir   Feby 4th 1763

This day the Lords for Trade gave judgment on the Merchants Petition against Paper Currency, the result whereof Mr Pownall conveys to you by this opportunety, Of a Ship detaind for two days on purpose to notify to you their Lordships Judgment,[1] I am sorry to find that a Measure wherein necessity requird your concurrence should have drawn so much censure upon you I do not know what the language of Office may be, in this case but I have reason to think that the tenderness of the Merchants both in their Memorial and in their manner of Supporting their Memorial which I have reason to think was upon a plan of opposition by no means pointed particularly at you but rather has not taken off the reprimand that attends your assent to the last Emission of Paper Money In short I can discover such a Spirit in Office for the Support of the orders of Government that no American Governor is safe without the most tenacious adherence to his Instructions, I have repeatedly told you my Sentiments from the Duty I owe to my conexion with you to be upon your guard in the point of Instructions, let me once more as a personal friend apprise you of the Danger that attends your giving way to Expediences beyond your Instructions[2] If the Safety of the Province in time of War, and the Kings Service recommended by a Secretary of State in such times of Danger cannot protect Governors from Censure be assured that on occasions less urgent a Disregard to The Kings Authority and Ministerial Ideas of Government will not rest on Censure alone and whatever Influence you have with particular persons in the Assembly I beg you will exert to bring about a Law home to the Spirit of the Instruction heretofore given to you & which it is thought In your Speech to the Assembly was recommended to them heretofore with too much tenderness and with an Insinuation *as if the* Laws as they now stand had not allready made sufficient Provision, the King and his Ministers whose Instructions are no doubt Laws to Governors did then think and do still think otherwise Your own Prudence will then dictate to you the Expedient and the only Expedient to set you in a more favourable Light, at the same time allow me to Suggest to you with the freedom of a Friend that from the Light in which your administration appears here in your situation I should think it adviseable if the Assembly are not siting on the arrival of these Dispatches to call them directly and with great earnestness lay them before them and press upon them an Act comming home to the very letter of the Instruction The rise of Exchange to a degree much beyond that when the Memorial was set on Foot has not only now engaged the Whole Body of London Merchants trading to Virginia, but likewise those of Liverpool and Glasgow to Exhibit Memorials to the like purpose as that of London at the same time the Lords of the Treasury having taken it up on the part of the Kings Revenue injurd not only in the first payment of Quitrents by the Tennant, but likewise on the Remittance of the Ballance by the operation of the Paper Money lately Emitted, which appears in so odious a light could the Lords for Trade upon Constitutional Power of Office have recommended an Instentaneous Repeal of the Act,[3] And I am fully convincd that the King if this Paper Money is not taken out by the Legislature of Virginia on the Footing proposed by the Kings Instruction, (which Instruction was grounded upon a Compromise between the Merchants and myself when a former Complaint was taken up on their part) finding themselves frustrated in this Expedient you may be assurd they will go to Parliament with the whole weight of Government against the Legislature of Virginia, and for this they have a direct Example in the Act of Parlt 1751 against the more Northern Charter Governts Colonys,[4] altho Virginia was then out of the Question yet in the first Formation of the Bill it stood for a general Extension of the Provision against Paper money to all the Colonys yet upon the argument by Council at the Bar of the House on the Part of S Carolina for which Province I was then concernd it was urgd that the Bill in Question ought not to have an Extension to other Colonys, Because there the Kings Instructions became Law to his Governors and moreover that some of the other Colonys particularly Virginia was not within the Mischief having no Paper Money.[5]

The Case being now alterd Instructions not complyd with and Paper Money Emitted contrary to the Instructions and to Parliamentary Principles there cannot arise a doubt at this time of Day upon the Extension of the Act of Parliament with the Penaltys annexd thereto against American Legislatures and Governors,[6] I hope then that the Assembly will give in to the sence of Government and of Parliament at all Events it will be expected that as Governor you act the consistent part as the Servant of the Crown and Government and which becomes my Duty in Office as well as yours in Government Matters and in which Light And in that alone can my Endeavours as Agent or Solicitor for the Kings Affairs and for Government be of use to you in Parlt or elsewhere and those of the Kings Council adhe[r]ing to the true Principles of Government justice to the Publick and to Individuals I most sincerely wish you Success in such Measures now recommended to you and I am

LB, pp. 257–259. After the complimentary close JA wrote: "here ended my letter to the Governor" and crossed through two paragraphs that may have been part of the letter as first written. Fauquier communicated this letter to the Council on 28 April 1763 (*EJC*, 6:252).

1. The Board of Trade took the memorial against paper money from the merchants of London into consideration on 1 Feb. 1763. At that time the Board also received similar memorials from the merchants of Glasgow and Liverpool (CO 5/1330, fols. 137a, 138–139) and heard from Montagu in favor of the laws for emitting paper bills of credit. (JA also attended, but the journal does not record that he was heard as well.) The following day the Board decided in favor of the merchants and announced its decision to the interested parties on 4 Feb. 1763. The Board's letter to Fauquier of 7 Feb. 1763 communicated this decision and censured Fauquier's conduct in the matter (*JBT*, 11:330–332, 333; *Fauquier Papers*, 2:909–911).

2. The Board's censure of Fauquier concerned his disregard of an additional instruction of 9 Feb. 1759 (for which see JA to Dinwiddie, 3 Nov. 1757, pp. 212–213, n. 1).

3. JA probably meant to continue with something such as "they would have done so," but the text between this and the next comma is incoherent, apparently because JA failed to delete some part of it.

4. JA initially wrote "Northern Colonys" and then interlineated "Charter Governts" between those words without striking out "Colonys."

5. For South Carolina's exemption from the provisions of the Currency Act of 1751, see JA to Glen, 7 Oct. 1751, p. 19, n. 5.

6. The Currency Act of 1751 held that any act contrary to it was ipso facto null and void, and that any governor who assented to such a contrary act was to be dismissed from his governorship and rendered incapable of holding any public office or place of trust.

To Francis Fauquier (not sent)

Feby 5th 1763

I cannot help acquainting you with an application some time since made to me by a Gentleman concernd in the Virgin[i]an Trade, in behalf of a friend of his, to this purpose That an Address is preparing to his Majesty from the Council to remove Mr Robert Burwell (who was lately appointed) from their Board, on account of his extreme weakness *and Incapacity to discharge the Duties of that Important Station, which Address will reach England by the Fall fleet in the mean time by a timely* application his Friend might have a better chance of succeeding, to this application I replyd that I was an absolute Stranger to Mr Burwells Capacity or Incapacity having no share in his nomination I should not Interest myself in degradation, nor could I conceive that the Council of Virginia would take so precipitate a Measure without very strong ground to stand upon, some time after I made further enquiry and found that Mr Burwell had realy signefyd to his Friends here that such Address was in Agitation and prepard his Friend Messrs Hanburys for it by whose recommendation and that of Mr Dinwiddie to Lord Granville I found this Gentleman was appointed to be of the Council, finding the case to be so I calld on your Brother for further Information, who assurd me that it was no measure of yours, at the same time I found that he thought you hurt thro the recommendation of this Gentleman to the Council; without your approbation or recommendation, had he been long enough acquainted with things of this Nature he had found that Promotions of a more Interesting Nature are dayly done by particular Interests at home for their Friends abroad and that it is adviseable for American Governors to acquiesse in Such Appointments where the King is taken to be the Judge of his Servants till their Misbehaviour coud Drop them whatever may be Merit or Demerit of Mr Burwell I shall be extreamly concernd that an Address of this kind came before the Board for Trade in the present Situation of Affairs, and much more so least your name appear as accessary thereto in any shape whatever but Since the arrival of the Fleet at Corke I have heard nothing of this Affair, should it come through my hands Duty will certainly Urge me to Present it at the same time had I any

Latitude given me I should be of opinion to Suspend it at least for some time.[1]

The Definitive Treaty is every hour Expected and with it I hope universal Peace at home and Abroad, the Storm of opposition which seemd to be gathering at the commencement of the Session Evaporated totally into Smoak by an opposition of two days to the Preliminarys of Peace agreed to 219 to 63, a Minority too impotent to keep up the Spirit of opposition or to gratify the Curiosity of the Publick[2] I most heartily wish you Success in the Measures now recommended to you and with Complts to your Lady & Family I am Sir

LB, pp. 260–261. JA wrote "not Sent" at the head of this letter but did not cross it through.

1. Robert Burwell (d. 1777) served as a burgess for Isle of Wight County 1752–1758. He was appointed to the Council by a royal warrant dated 19 Apr. 1762 (*Fauquier Papers*, 2:721), which was read by the Council at its meeting of 30 July 1762, at which time Burwell took the oaths and was admitted to the Council (*EJC*, 6:228–229).

JA was unaware that Fauquier did, in fact, oppose Burwell's appointment. In a letter to the Board of Trade of 31 July 1762 (*Fauquier Papers*, 2:781–784), which the Council had read and approved the previous day, Fauquier stated his understanding of the instruction that required him to recommend persons to fill vacancies in the Council, described the broad responsibilities of councillors, and wrote: "I must do Mr. Burwell the Justice to acknowledge that He is a Gentleman of a very fair Character, of a very good Family, and of a convenient Situation, and that there can be no Objection to him but what relates to his mental Qualifications, and an unwarrantable Impetuosity of Temper." The Board read Fauquier's letter on 2 Mar. 1763 (*JBT*, 11:339) and replied on 11 Mar. 1763 (*Fauquier Papers*, 2:929–930), disputing his interpretation of the instruction. The Board held that the governor was required only to transmit the names of persons qualified to be councillors, "but His Majesty reserves the Decision, and it never could have been designed by the Instruction to have conveyed to the Governor any implicit right of actually filling up Vacancies in the Council. . . . Mr. Burwell was recommended to His Majesty by this Board, upon the representation of many very respectable persons, and therefore We have judged it proper, and in some degree necessary, from the Sense now put upon the Instruction, to support the recommendation."

JA was correct in assuming that the Council planned to protest the appointment. At the meeting of 30 July 1762, after Fauquier laid his letter to the Board before the Council, Thomas Nelson "produced a Representation which he had prepar'd in the name of the Council, to his Majesty upon the same subject requesting that he would be graciously pleas'd to appoint some other more able and discreet person in the room of M'r Burwell and the same being read, the consideration thereof was postpon'd to October Court for a fuller Council" (*EJC*, 6:229). Nothing more is heard of the Council's representation.

In a letter to the Board of Trade of 28 May 1763 (*Fauquier Papers*, 2:956–957), Fauquier claimed that the Council had "prompted" him to write his letter of 31 July 1762 and that "The Affair gave some Discontent at first, on Account of the commonly received Opinion of Mr. Burwells Capacity; but all this is now quite subsided."

2. This debate took place on 9 and 10 Dec. 1762. In fact, the vote to present an address of thanks to the king for the preliminary articles, taken on 9 Dec. in the Commons, was 319 in favor to 65 opposed. The vote on the address itself, taken on 10 Dec., was 227 in favor to 63 opposed (*Parliamentary History*, 15:1272–1273).

To John Blair

Feby 28th 176[3]

The Auditor General did me the favor to give me your Bill for half years Salary to 25th Octr last drawn On Messrs Hanburys [*illegible*] by Corbin, which is paid,[1] I waited the arrival of the Fleet in hopes Messrs Cary & Co[2] might have reced Effects from Lewis Burwell wherewith to have Payd my Bill for the preceeding half years Salary which Bill now inclosd to you Protested, with Messrs Cary & Cos letter to me concerning their refusal of the Bill. I have desird Copy of the Order of the Lords Justices of the 8th Augt 1750[3] to be made out for You, and if ready shall be sent by this Conveyance.

I am now preparing a Memorial to the Treasury[4] praying them to procure his Majestys Order in Council for Paying the Quitrents ad Valorem, which when done the Audr General will no doubt transmit to you, as the order of Augt 1750 grants an allowance for the extraordinary charge on the Recers Accounts on Remitting the Q Rents no further than to the time that the New Regulation shall take place, will it not become necessary for the Recr General to apply to the Treasury for an Allowance of such charge in like manner as was done by his Predecessors on such Emergencys, without which the Accounts cannot pass.

In my privat opinion I am very clear that the formation of a New Rent Roll is a Worke of too extraordinary nature to be gone through in the ordinary course of office without an Additional compensation and you shall not want my recommendation thereof, at the same time I can forsee difficultys that may arise upon a Proposition to the Treasury for a Stipulated allowance before the Work is finishd, I could wish therefore that by next letter you will Suggest some Estimate of the Expence that may attend employing more Clerks for such a Voluminous Performance than become necessary in the ordinary course of your Duty besides the expence of Books Pen Ink and Paper, for which the Auditor General has occasionally had an allowance[5] How far the Treasury may be brought to make proper compensation or how far they shall look upon it as a matter of Duty incident to the Office of the Auditor General I can not take upon me to say, without Precedents are to be found and however much it is for the Devised Revenue in my privat opinion I do not think that the Audr General will take upon himself to allow any charge of this new nature in the Revenue Account without the previous approbation of the Treasury I shall therefore advise his application to the Treasury for an extraordinary allowance upon the principle of its being productive of great Service and advantage to the Revenue and beyond the ordinary Duty of Office Clerks.

PS   As I have fully explaind myself to the Governor heretofore on my Accounts I hope from thence to have a joint letter of approbation Mr Townsend appointed first Lord of Trade in Lord Sandys Room.[6]

LB, pp. 262–263. JA erroneously dated this letter 1762. The postscript must have been written on or after 2 March 1763, when Charles Townshend replaced Lord Sandys on the Board of Trade.

1. Blair's bill (not found) was probably for £149.9.1 $\frac{1}{2}$, which represented half of the £298.18.3 remitted to Auditor-General Cholmondeley from the revenue of the two-shillings-per-hogshead tobacco export tax for the period 25 Apr. 1762 to 25 Oct. 1762. Cholmondeley's income of £298.18.3 comprised £50 in salary and £248.18.3 as an allowance (5 percent) on the £4,978.5 collected in the period of the account (*Fauquier Papers*, 2:1062–1063).

2. Probably the mercantile firm of Robert Cary & Co., which in 1758 signed the protest against several Virginia acts (for which see JA to Dinwiddie, 3 Nov. 1757, pp. 211–212).

3. Actually, 2 Aug. 1750; see JA to Blair, 29 June [1761], pp. 389–390.

4. Not found.

5. Blair submitted a lengthy undated paper to the Treasury (with an appended testimonial in its favor by Fauquier dated 23 Sept. 1763) describing the colony's quitrent procedures and recommending measures to put them on a proper footing, along with an estimate of the expenses involved (T 1/423, fols. 72–76).

6. See source note, above. Samuel Sandys, Baron Sandys, was president of the Board of Trade from 21 Mar. 1761 to 2 Mar. 1763.

To John Blair

6th May 1763

I have yours 13 Feby[1] with 2d Bill for Salary to 25 Octr last the first Bill already paid by Mess Hanbury on whom I wish all my Bills on the Acct of the 2 Shills as well as the Q Rents other Bills are precarious have heretofore Remitted with the Protest Messrs Carys Bill for 100.

I have read your letter to the Audr General[2] my privat opinion is that your proposd allowance for the great work of a Compleat Rent Roll is reasonable, the Remittance to the Audr General came very opportunely Mr Corbins Accounts exceeding former Collect[i]ons very well taken, a Memorial on the Exchange chargd in his Account must be sent to the Treasury by him, shall Advise the Audr General to Suspend his Report on the last Accounts till the Exchange is allow'd by the Treasury. Comlts to Mr Corbin and assure him of my Services I am dr Sir Yours &c

LB, p. 266. At the foot of this letter JA wrote: "NB Sent to the Coffee house for the first Ship to Virginia."

1. Letter not found.

2. Letter not found.

To Francis Fauquier

May 9th 1763

I have your favour of 23d Feby concerning his Bills of Exchange drawn by Capt Longbottom Master of the Amitys Addition a

Transport wherein you desire my assistance by Soliciting the Navy Office for payment of the Bill for 901.1.0 indorsed to Mr Bowden should any difficulty arise thereon[1] on receipt of your Instructions I went to the Navy Office in order to prepare the Board for the reception of the Bill, and in a day or two after that calling on Mr Bowden I found the Bill was accepted, considering the delays frequently attending Money Matters at the Navy Office I had laid my Account with a Solicitation in an Office of more Authority for their Directions, but I am agreeably disapointed by the readiness of the Navy Office upon the Plan suggested to them by your letter for their Reimbursement.

I have heard nothing of the Bill for 194 on the Victualling Office nor do I know in whose hands it is, on application to me I shall in case of Difficulty give my Assistance with Mr Wallace the first Commissioner.[2]

Privat

The Parliament is within these few days Prorogud[3] we were beginning to become warm towards the close of the Session which occasiond some very late days introductory probably of many more on our next meeting The News papers will shew you the Variations that have happend amongst the Ministers on the close of the Session, there are many of opinion that the present Arrangement will still undergo variations before the next meeting of Parliament.

Lord Butes Resignation drew after it many alterations some for Honorary Promotion to the House of Peers others for Lucretive Employments as Commoners, Mr Charles Townsend in the Space of a Few Weeks was first Lord of Trade, first Lord of the Admiralty and is now become a privat Person by the Kings Special command no longer his Servant by Insisting on some personal Priviledges as first Lord of the Admiralty he brought this upon himself. Lord Shelburne is now head of the Plantation Office but its generally said (A)[4] the D of Bedford returns to France as Ambasador but while and has resignd the office of Privy Seal in consequence Lord Holland who aims at the Pay Office is not inclined to resign his Pay Office (A) thus from this short Sketch of the Ministerial Picture you see that it is not quite finished.[5] I do not find that the arrangment for our American Conquests is as yet finally settled, the Settlement of the Domestick Departments has no doubt retarded the Foreign arrangements which probably may be left to General Amhursts final Execution before he takes leave of America, your Brother was very well the day before yesterday and I am very Sincerly Sir

LB, pp. 264–265. The date was originally written as "April 27th 1763."

1. Fauquier's letter has not been found. William Longbottom, master of the transport *Amity's Addition*, was to carry the Spanish military and naval forces that had surrendered at Havana from that city to Cadiz. When his ship sprang a leak at sea, Longbottom put into Norfolk in Oct. 1762 for repairs. On 28 Mar. 1763 Fauquier informed the Council that he had endorsed Longbottom's bills on the navy office for £901.1.0 payable to himself and had advised the commissioners of the navy that he had done so; evidently the bills were for materials used to repair Longbottom's ship (*EJC*, 6:248–249). Perhaps Fauquier referred to bills because he had in mind the several copies of a bill of exchange that were normally sent. The Mr. Bowden to whom the bill was endorsed was a retired Virginia merchant living in London.

2. The bill for £194 on the victualing office was perhaps to pay Col. John Hunter's account for victualing Longbottom's transport for seventy days or, less probably, to pay Charles Steuart's account for supplying the Spaniards from the *Amity's Addition* from about the beginning of Dec. to about the middle of Feb., some seventy days (see the correspondence between Fauquier and Steuart from Nov. 1762 through Mar. 1763 in *Fauquier Papers*, 2, and the Council minutes of 28 Mar. 1763, when Fauquier produced Steuart's accounts and vouchers [*EJC*, 6:249]). It is assumed that the bill for £194 was a sterling bill, and the equivalent of about £290 in Virginia currency (since the exchange rate was something like £100 sterling for £150 currency). James Wallace was one of the seven commissioners of victualing as early as 1746.

3. The king prorogued the Parliament on 19 Apr. 1763.

4. The significance of this parenthetical letter (and the one several lines below) is not known.

5. Lord Bute resigned the office of prime minister on 8 Apr. 1763. Townshend was appointed to the Board of Trade on 2 Mar. 1763; in April he was invited to be First Lord of the Admiralty, but declined to accept the office unless his nominee, William Burrell, was also appointed to the Admiralty Board. Thereupon it was intimated that the king had no further need of Townshend's services, and on 23 Apr. 1763 Townshend was replaced at the Board of Trade by William Petty (1737–1805), second earl of Shelburne (in the Irish peerage). The duke of Bedford had come from Paris to London after Bute's resignation, refused to take office in the new government, and was replaced as Lord Privy Seal by the duke of Marlborough on 22 Apr. 1763; Bedford returned to France as ambassador "but while," or temporarily. Henry Fox, the paymaster general, was created Baron Holland of Foxley on 16 Apr. 1763 and managed to retain the post of paymaster after a long altercation with Bute and Shelburne.

To Francis Fauquier

May 26th 1763

Tell him the present state of Affairs and Send him pamphlet Consideration of the Dangerous Crisis of Affairs.[1]

LB, p. 266. The first digit of the day's date was apparently written first as "1" and then "2," while the second digit seems to have been written first as "8," then as "9," and finally as "6."

1. The pamphlet was no doubt *Considerations on the Present Dangerous Crisis*, attributed to Owen Ruffhead, of which three editions were published in London in 1763. The author offered a temperate criticism of Lord Bute's recent administration and a much ruder comment on Bute's opponents.

To Richard Corbin

May 26th 1763

Tell him how acceptable his diligence is, the Auditor Genals sence thereof by letter to Mr Blair assure him of my Services in office my connexions with Virginia and him in particular become more Interesting and more agreeable to me by his Majestys Favour, that the Instance of my Case has producd the same Establishment of Office as other Colonys where the King has Revenue Independt of the Assembly, credit thereby added to Government and thank him for my last Bills on Messrs Hanbury and hope he will continue to give me Bills on them tell him Wilkes Fermentation by the North Brittain[1] and to write occasionally to the Aud: General on Matters of the Revenue.

LB, p. 267.

1. On 23 Apr. John Wilkes (1727–1797), a member of Parliament, published the notorious forty-fifth issue of his radical journal, *The North Briton*, which had long printed attacks on the ministers of George III. No. 45 went so far as to criticize the king's speech from the throne closing the session of Parliament on 19 Apr., and it precipitated Wilkes's arrest and subsequent release, expulsion from Parliament, and flight to Paris. See George R. Rudé, *Wilkes and Liberty* (Oxford, Eng., 1962).

To Francis Fauquier

Septr 2d 1763

Acknowledge his of June 23d[1] with account of approbation of my conduct in the Paper Money case, Hint to him his being on the reserve as to persons with whom I am connected who are his Enemys assure him no motive or Engagments stand in the way of my intention and Inclination to serve him, tell him I am Satisfyd in the character of Agent for the Kings Affairs, otherwise might probably procure a Commission from the King, for the same with pleasure therein that the House of Burgesses have agreed to my Accounts in the manner he had recommended them.

LB, p. 267. Immediately after this abstract JA continued: "Sent from Scotland to Mr Parr for the Virginia Bag See Lre in Bundle."

1. Letter not found.

To Richard Corbin

Septr 2d 1763

Thank him for his standing order for payment of Q Rent Salary[1] vide letter Bundle.

LB, p. 267.

1. JA was to receive his salary of £200 per year from the quitrent revenues in quarterly payments of £50. See *Fauquier Papers*, 3:1215.

To John Blair

Jany 30th 1764

Acknowledge his of Novr 12 with Bill for 100 Salary Tobacco Duty to 25th Octr last past.[1]

LB, p. 267.

1. Blair's letter has not been found. It enclosed a warrant for £100 for a half-year's salary to JA as "Solicitor of the Virginia Affairs" from the revenues of the two-shillings-per-hogshead tobacco export tax (*Fauquier Papers*, 3:1217).

To Francis Fauquier

Feby 6th 1764

Tell him the Affairs now under the Deliberation of B for Trade[1] Taxation,[2] Paper Currency as to the Legality of the Tender,[3] Salt application suspended,[4] Beaver draw back taken off[5] Bounty on Hemp of 8 £ per Ton.[6]

LB, p. 267. At the foot of this memorandum JA wrote: "NB to the Coffee house per [*illegible*]."

1. Probably JA meant that the affairs being considered by the Board of Trade were the five specific matters that he lists here.

2. JA alludes to the Commons' consideration of the bill that received royal approval on 5 Apr., the Revenue Act of 1764 (also known as the Sugar Act; 4 George III, chap. 15). Despite his knowledge of the colonies, and despite the fact that Americans in London were brought in for advice, JA did not enter the Commons debate about Grenville's program. The Scots merchant Charles Stuart noted, "The colonies mustered their forces. New England was pretty strong; Virginia made no figure at all" (quoted in Sir Lewis Namier and John Brooke, *The House of Commons, 1754–1790*, 3 vols. [New York, 1964], 2:2).

3. On 10 Jan. 1764 the Board of Trade took into consideration the state of paper currency in the American colonies, not comprised in the Currency Act of 1751 that restrained such currency in New England, and on 19 Jan. it heard the arguments of several of the principal merchants trading to the colonies, and the respective agents, for and against extending the provisions of the 1751 act to the other American colonies. Two days later the Board again took up the problem, and then on the following day it read a petition and memorial of the merchants of Glasgow (CO 5/1330, fols. 287–289) praying that paper money in Virginia should not be made legal tender for debts either in sterling or in currency and proposing a settlement of the paper money problem. On 2 Feb. various current and former governors and other colonial officials attended the meeting of the Board, were heard on the subject of paper currency, and agreed that an act of Parliament to stop the emission of paper money as legal tender would be proper and expedient, although spokesmen for Pennsylvania seemed to wish that the act should be deferred until the next session of Parliament, so that the colonies might present their opinions. The next day the colonial agents expressed the same wish, but the Board urged the inconvenience of delay and asked whether the agents would oppose any bill in Parliament on the

subject; on 7 Feb. JA and several other colonial agents informed the Board that they could not agree to the plan for regulation of paper money in the colonies and were unanimously of the opinion that a certain amount of paper currency should be allowed in each colony as legal tender in all dealings within the colonies and that each colony should have time to report what that sum should be (*JBT*, 12:3, 4, 6, 15, 18). In the event, Parliament passed "An Act to prevent paper bills of credit" (4 George III, chap. 34), commonly known as the Currency Act of 1764.

4. On 24 Oct. 1763 the Board of Trade read a memorial (CO 5/1330, fols. 255–256) from Edward Montagu, agent for Virginia, and Charles Garth, agent for South Carolina, representing the need in those colonies for adequate supplies of the right kind of salt and expressing the hope that the Board would not object to their applying to Parliament for permission to import salt from any part of Europe into Virginia and South Carolina. On 26 Jan. 1764 the Board considered the proposal and pronounced its opinion that it could not recommend a measure that would check or even suppress the manufacture and produce of the mother country, unless it might be shown that the colonies could not be supplied with salt at reasonable rates from Great Britain. Evidently Montagu and Garth suspended their application for nearly two years; it was not until 26 Sept. 1765 that the Treasury referred to the Board of Trade an almost identical memorial from Montagu and Garth to the Treasury (CO 5/1331, fols. 37–39), laid before the Board on 10 Oct. 1765, at which time consideration of it was postponed indefinitely (*JBT*, 11:399; 12:9, 213).

5. On 26 Jan. the Board of Trade considered a memorial from makers of beaver hats addressed to the Treasury regarding duties on beaver skins, ordered various accounts of imports and exports, and invited the governor of the Hudson's Bay Company and the principal importers and exporters of beaver skins to attend a hearing. After further consideration of the subject on 30 Jan., the Board met on 1 Feb. to hold a formal hearing, at which it was generally agreed that it would be beneficial to remove the duty on the importation of beaver skins but lay a similar duty on exported skins (*JBT*, 12:10–11, 13, 14). The result of the business was "An Act for repealing the duties now payable upon beaver skins imported" (4 George III, chap. 9).

6. On 13 Dec. 1763 the Board of Trade read a memorial from merchants trading to the American colonies praying for a bounty on American hemp (evidently the memorial from London merchants that is CO 323/17, fols. 52–53). After consultations with the navy and the customs and a hearing attended by interested persons, the Board decided on 26 Jan. 1764 to tender a representation favoring bounties on hemp imported from the British colonies, and thereafter read a further memorial on hemp (probably CO 323/17, fols. 116–117) from London merchants to the Treasury (*JBT*, 11:420, 12:9–10). Subsequently, Parliament passed "An Act for granting a bounty upon the importation of hemp and rough and undressed flax from His Majesty's colonies in America" (4 George III, chap. 26), one provision of which was a premium of £8 sterling for each ton of hemp or rough or undressed flax imported between 24 June 1764 and 25 June 1771.

To Mr. Lampton

[12 March 1764]
Mr Lampton & Govr Wrights inclosd March 12th 1764.[1]

LB, p. 268. Sent "to the Coffee house."

1. Lampton has not been conclusively identified, nor have JA's letters to Lampton and Gov. James Wright been found. Lampton was perhaps Richard Lambton, a Charleston merchant who was in partnership with Joseph Wragg 1742–1750 (*Bio. Dir. S.C. House of Rep.*, 727).

To James Wright

[12 March 1764]
{See preceding entry.}

To Francis Fauquier

March 15th [1764]
Tell him the State of American Affairs before Parlt about the regulation of Dutys,[1] about the Resolution for Stamp Duty,[2] about Paper Money propose to him that the Assembly take out the Legality of Tender on Sterling Contracts, and thereby join Issue with the Merchants and Govert here, wherein I shall take part to accommodate Matters, tho neither he nor myself concernd directly.[3]

LB, p. 268. Sent "To the Coffee house."

1. This letter probably provided a report on the current state of matters discussed in JA's letter to Fauquier of 6 Feb. 1764, p. 419.

2. On 10 Mar. 1764 the committee of the whole House presented to the Commons several resolutions that concerned the expenses of defense and the British colonies and plantations in America, one of which read: "Resolved, That it is the Opinion of this Committee, That, towards further defraying the said Expences, it may be proper to charge certain Stamp Duties in the said Colonies and Plantations" (*JHC*, 29:935).

3. On the matter of paper money, see JA to Fauquier, 6 Feb. 1764, p. 420, n. 3.

To Francis Fauquier

March 29th 1764

Answer yours Decr 28th and Jany 2d about your Memorial sent your Brother with whom have conferrd, make no doubt of your Succeeding thereon for reimbursement your Charges on the Congress[1] acquaint him about the Business relative to American Taxation repeat my Notions of the Tender on Sterling Debts of Paper Money and offer my Assistance thereon.

LB, p. 268. Sent "to the Coffee house."

1. Fauquier's memorial and related correspondence have not been found. However, a letter to Fauquier of 26 Jan. 1765 from Thomas Whately, secretary to the Treasury (*Fauquier Papers*, 3:1226–1227), indicates that the Lords of the Treasury had read Fauquier's memorial, which prayed for restitution of £230 that he had lost because the president of the Council was entitled to half the profits of the government during Fauquier's absence of ten weeks at the Congress of Augusta. Whately's letter informed Fauquier that he should apply to the colony for relief.

To Francis Fauquier

May 2d [1764]

In my letter in April I acquainted you,[1] with what had passd between your Brother and Mr Grenville on the Subject of your Memorial and the difficultys started thereon by Mr Grenville, I have since that personally applyd to Mr Grenville who still persevers, in his opinion that your Claim however well grounded ought to be paid by the Province, tho the Service was extracolonial yet it was relative to the Safety and Security of the Province.[2] The Precedent of Mr Dinwiddie being allowd his Expences, when he met at the Congress at Philadelphia[3] was urged in support of your Claim But the answer thereto is that out of the Money which was remitted from hence by the Treasury to Mr Dinwiddy for the Military and all other Services relative to the defence of the Province the Share of the Expences at the Congress of Philadelphia was allowed on Account of that Money your case is a paralel Case, out [of] the Money granted by Parliament you ought therefore to be paid.

I have thereupon talked with Mr Montague on the case of the Money granted for Virginia Services in which you know I am not concernd in virtue of my office he tells me that he has just now reced from the Treasury between 9 & 1000 for Virginia at the Disposal of the Government of Virginia which he conceives to be appropriated in discharge of the Public Debts of the Province, altho the Administration the Treasury do admit your claim to be very well grounded nevertheless as The Grant of this and former Money for American Services to the Several Provinces is so expressed by the words of the Act of Parliament, that it must be applyd as directed by the Provincial Governments, and not as shall be directed by the Treasury in consequence of any Warrant from the King,[4] you can therefore have no particular Warrant from hence for payment out of this Money, But the circumstances of the Case being thus Represented to the Assembly your Service in executing the Kings orders being in the eye of Government at home deemd a Debt due by your Government for the relief whereof this Government has in a most ample Manner from time to time contributed it cannot be supposd they will hesitate one Moment in admitting your Claim upon the Money so granted by Parliament,[5] In this light the case appears to me and its my Duty to represent it to your Government so as to Prevent any Altercation or difference between the Administration at home and yours abroad about so trifling an Expence that has attended the Execution of his Majestys orders in a Matter so essentially necessary for the Protection of the Southern Colonys and for Virginia in particular, so far as you are personally concerned in this Matter it cannot be supposd that the Assembly will demurr in concurring with the opinion of the Treasury in doing strict Justice to one who has deservd so well of them by a harmonious Administration in times of trouble and danger and here the matter must rest till I shall have your Sentiments hereon I am on all occasions very Sincerly Sir Your

LB, pp. 268–270. Sent "to the Coffee house with another privat letter to the Lt Governor of the same date."

1. This was JA's letter to Fauquier of 29 Mar. 1764, above (see preceding entry); JA first wrote "of 29 of March" but replaced those words by "in April."

2. George Grenville had been First Lord of the Treasury and Chancellor of the Exchequer since 10 Apr. 1763.

3. This was the meeting, in Mar. 1757, of the governors of North Carolina, Virginia, Maryland, and Pennsylvania with the earl of Loudoun.

4. The money granted for Virginia services, discussed with Montagu, was presumably Virginia's share of the £133,333.6.8 voted by Parliament in "An Act for raising a certain sum of money . . . for the service of the year one thousand seven hundred and sixty-three" (3 George III, chap. 17). No act of Parliament has been found stating that money granted to the American provinces was to be applied as directed by the provincial governments.

5. It does not appear that Fauquier asked the General Assembly to pay his claim. It is possible that the claim may have been paid from the revenue of the two-shillings-per-hogshead tobacco export tax as an item of contingent charges.

To Francis Fauquier

[2 May 1764]

{See preceding entry, source note.}

To Richard Corbin

[3 May 1764]

Lre to Mr Corbin on Sons appointment for Yorke River.[1]

LB, p. 270. Sent "per Do Ship," i.e., by the same ship that took the preceding two letters to Fauquier. Date supplied from Corbin's acknowledgment (see note 1).

1. Gawin Corbin was appointed comptroller of customs of the York River district by a warrant of 31 Mar. 1764 (T 11/27, p. 457).

In his letter to JA of 17 Dec. 1764 (Corbin Letter Book, p. 160, Colonial Williamsburg Foundation), Corbin acknowledged receipt of this letter and thanked JA for his "Friendly Endeavours to Serve My Son." Corbin noted that the profits from the York River post were "Inconsiderable, and woud be Accepted by my Son, only as evidence of your Friendship & the hopes of a more Ample Compensation." He then asked JA to inquire about a possible vacancy in the Upper James River district.

To Francis Fauquier

Jany 30th 1765

Give him his answer on his Memorial for payment out of the Q rents that the Treasury have rejected it and refer him to the Province, tell him that Mr Montague & I have conferrd on the Clergy appeal,[1] and that he is to apply to Mr Jos Sharpe for his Brieff on a former occasion in this Cause.[2]

LB, p. 271.

1. The "Clergy appeal" grew out of the second Two Penny Act, which had been disallowed by the Order in Council of 10 Aug. 1759. Camm and other Virginia clergymen held that the act was void from the very beginning, while proponents of the act contended that it was void only from the time the disallowance of the act was proclaimed in Virginia. Camm's suit against Charles Hansford and William Moss, collectors of the levy for Yorkhampton Parish, was first brought up in the General Court in Oct. 1759, but the court delayed action until 10 Apr. 1764. At that time the court passed judgment against Camm by a vote of five to four. Camm appealed this decision to the Privy Council, presenting his petition for a hearing on 6 Feb. 1765. The respondents entered an appearance on 16 Feb., although the appeal was not heard until 27 Nov. 1766, when it was dismissed. See Joseph Henry Smith, *Appeals to the Privy Council from the American Plantations* (New York, 1950), 611–625.

2. The pronoun reference is ambiguous, but JA must mean that Edward Montagu, the agent, was to apply to Joshua Sharpe, the solicitor in Lincoln's Inn often associated with colonial cases, for a brief he had prepared for some earlier event in the controversy over the Two Penny Act, very probably the sitting of the Board of Trade on 27 June 1759, when JA, representing the colony, and John Camm and his solicitor Ferdinand John Paris, representing the Virginia clergy, appeared for a hearing on the address of the Virginia clergy complaining of the Two Penny Act (*JBT*, 11:46). Sharpe perhaps prepared the brief for whatever arguments JA presented.

To Edward Montagu

Sir   Feby 7th [1765]

I hope you will find what I told you upon the information of several Members of experience to be true, viz that the proper time for offering Your Petition is when the Question comes to be put in the House upon the Report of the Committee for leave to bring in the Bill.[1]

After what Mr Grenville said to me I could not move Your

Petition yesterday till he had opend the Matter and from what fell from him in the opening I am now extreamly glad for the sake of my Constituents the Governor and Council that I did not move the Petition, he gave us to understand that the Governours and others in the service of Government had signefyd their Sentiments on the propriety of the measure, whether Gover Fauquire and the Officers of Govert in Virginia are amongst the rest I know not but as they have not said one word to me on this Subject I think it prudent for me for my own sake as well as for theirs to take no step whereby through me they may suffer in the opinion of their Superiors, Your situation as well as mine in this important Question is very delicat, You have Instructions for your Conduct I have none and I should be extreamly glad that your Instructions do admit of the Petition conveying the Sence of the House of Burgesses only but of this you are the best judge but as I am all together in the Dark what may have passed in the Correspondence with the Administration here I shall by no means interfer with your Instructions in this case.

LB, p. 182A. A further line and a half after "case" are deleted and the letter breaks off abruptly. The reverse of the page is blank.

1. JA probably alludes to a petition against the proposed stamp bill that Montagu hoped to introduce into the House of Commons. It appears that four petitions against the bill were presented to the Commons on 15 Feb. 1765: one from Jamaica, one from Montagu on behalf of Virginia, one from Connecticut, and one from three South Carolinians then in London. Other petitions from the colonies so bluntly questioned the right of Parliament to levy taxes that no members could be found to submit them to the Commons, and it is supposed that this challenge to Parliament was the reason for the rejection of the three petitions from North America, that from Jamaica having been withdrawn by the member who presented it. See Peter D. G. Thomas, *British Politics and the Stamp Act Crisis* (New York, 1975), 85–96.

To Francis Fauquier

Feby 26th [1765]

Yours of the 20 & 26th of Decr[1] the L for Trade allow your Enacting the Bill relative to the Distemper,[2] as to Francis Kennedys Pardon you must circumstantially write to the Lords for Trade the King requires all circumstances in cases of Murder.[3]

The Petitions from Colonies against the Taxation of Stamps

universally rejected by Reason they call in Question the Right of Parlt.

You do well in tender points of Govert to leave me at large without Instructions to act as I find more for your Interest.

LB, p. 271. At the foot of this letter JA wrote: "NB to the Coffee house."

1. Letters not found.

2. In a letter to the Board of Trade of 24 Dec. 1764 (*Fauquier Papers*, 3:1201–1203), Fauquier enclosed a copy of a bill entitled "An Act for the preservation of the breed of cattle" (*Fauquier Papers*, 3:1203–1205), which had been passed by both the House of Burgesses and the Council but which Fauquier had not signed because it lacked a suspending clause. Fauquier explained that the bill had been passed because both houses believed "that the Cattle drove thro this Colony from North Carolina to the more northern Colonies spread Infection and Desolation wherever they pass'd." Fauquier sought permission to pass the bill without a suspending clause, concluding that the calamity "is greivous and calls for speedy Relief, unless the Distemper being among us should render the Case already desperate, and incurable." The Board of Trade gave Fauquier permission to pass the bill in a letter of 15 Feb. 1765 (*Fauquier Papers*, 3:1228), but the bill did not become law until 11 Apr. 1767 (Hening, *Statutes*, 8:245–250).

3. Francis Kennedy was convicted of the murder of John Owsley by a jury at a court of oyer and terminer, but the court believed that as the evidence showed "that the Affair was transacted in passion, the said Kennedy not having time for cool reflection, and no premeditated Malice between them," the jury should have returned a verdict of manslaughter. Following JA's suggestion, Fauquier asked for a royal pardon for Kennedy in a letter to the Board of Trade of 1 Aug. 1765, in which he enclosed the court's opinion (*Fauquier Papers*, 3:1266, 1270). Nothing more is known of the Kennedy case.

To John Blair

[26 February 1765]

{The letter book, p. 271, refers to letters "To Messrs Blair & Corbin at same time 26 Feby 1765."}

To Richard Corbin

[26 February 1765]

{See preceding entry.}

To Richard Corbin

May 26th 1765

In a former letter I informd you of the difficultys attending your Accounts, the greater on your part as neither the Auditor General nor Mr Roberts, however well inclind to interest themselfs in your behalf stand at present in a favorable Light at the Treasury, in this situation I told you that I should personally Interpose, and accordingl[y] after repeated Promisses to have your Accounts considered, I have at length so far prevaild and within this Week have twice attended the Board taking Mr Capel Hanbury with me in order to Support the grounds of my Argument in your Favour for having acted properly in the Execution of your Office. The Treasury having appeard to be satisfyd that the Remedy proposed hereafter for receiving of the Qt Rents Ad Valorem of Exchange is the only proper Remedy applicable to the situation of Virginia, it rested then to get over the grand objection as to allowing in your Accounts the loss to the Crown, hetherto by Remitting the Paper Money Payments in Bills of Exchange, the Treasury had adopted the Notion that as Recr you ought to have taken payment in Tobacco at $\frac{3}{4}$ according to the Kings warrant rather than Paper Currency. On this Point I desird their Lordships would be pleasd to take the opinion of Merchants this being Agreed to Mr Hanbury gave very full Evidence that it was impracticable to have reced the Quitrents in Specie of any kind, That by taking of Tobacco the Crown had become a much greater loser, and so clear was he in this point that no Merchant knowing the Tobacco Trade could be found to take a Contract with the Crown at $\frac{3}{4}$ That on the point of your Remittance that your Bills as chargd in your Accounts were actually on better Terms than Merchants Bills, upon the whole their Lordships now seem satisfyd in every Point alledged in your Memorial[1] and by me in Support thereof and of the Auditor Generals Report thereon,[2] and having brought it this length it rests now with the Treasury to Expedite the Kings Warrant the Solicitation whereof is left with the Auditor General, for after a very long Winters Campaign I am glad to get out of Town.

Our friend Mr D[3] is at Bath, and much recoverd and expected in Town, my Complits to your Son concludes me allways Dr Sir

PS   By the several letters reced of late from the Lt Governour I observe he directs to me as Solicitor and Agent for His Majestys Revenue of Virginia, having thus chang'd the Character I conclude that it is done in order to avoid my interfering with the Provincial Agent in Matters of the Legislature and to draw a Line between his Duty in Provincial concerns and mine concerning the Crown Revenues I much approve of His Distinction, for I should not incline to take part in every Provincial Negociation in the Character I now act in it would ill become me and those who preside in Virginia to take part in every Measure A Provincial agent may think incumbent on him to take I must however observe that while the Character of Solicitor and Agent for His Majestys Virginia Revenue opens a door for me to the Treasury, at the same time they may hereafter take upon themselves the Nomination of the Officer.

LB, pp. 274–275. Sent "to the Coffee house."

1. Corbin's memorial to the Treasury of 17 Dec. 1764 held that the low price of tobacco and the virtual disappearance of specie from the colony left paper money as the only available means of paying the quitrents, and that the high rate of exchange between the pound sterling and Virginia currency and the great quantity of paper money recently emitted by the colony had diminished the quitrent revenues (Corbin Letter Book, 159, Colonial Williamsburg Foundation).

Corbin had enclosed a copy of his memorial in his letter to JA of 17 Dec. 1764 (ibid., 160). He wrote: "I must intreat the favor of your Assistance to have this Revenue put upon Such a foundation as to do equal Justice to the King & his Tenants."

2. Cholmondeley's report on Corbin's memorial has not been found.

3. Robert Dinwiddie.

To Francis Fauquier

May 26th [1765]

The Session of Parlt being concluded I am glad to change London for Country Air Long Sederunts and late Nights by no means agree with Rheumatick Complaints, the Regency Bill now passd into a Law occasiond great Discord within Doors,[1] and the Silk Bill Rejected by the Lords causd Tumults without Doors amongst the Weavers & all the Vagabonds about London who associated and assembled with them,[2] the Discord within is ended by the Victory gaind by the Ministry over a certain Earl who has long been the Object of Resentment for Personal Influence, the Signal of Victory was declared the day before yesterday by taking the Privy Seal and the Character of Minister for Scotch Affairs from his Brother, giving the Seals to Lord F. C and retaining the Ministerial Power to the Secretary of State here a Measure long wishd for by every North Brittain who saw the Mischief produced by reviving a National Distinction that untill these few years was not thought on.[3] Lords Holland and Northumberland as grand Allys to the Favourite Earl are Displaced Mr C Townsend has the Pay Office and Lord Waymouth Lord Lt of Ireland[4] other Alterations may insue in the mean time Offical Business is resumd.

By a proper disposition of Military Force more than by the operation of the Civil Magistracy the Riot is quelled, the House of Peers taking Cognizance of the Dangerous Attack upon the D. of Bedford producd a Reprimand from the Bar of the House of Lords to the Justices of Peace of Westminister for Remissness & for some days past all is quiet, and all the Natural & Political bad Humours appear for the present to have subsided.

The Acts passd last Session of Parlt relative to the Plantations will be according to Custom transmitted to you, Some I am affraid will occasion Discord, I have nothing particularly Interesting to yourself to communicate to you only that I have heard the remissness of your Chancery Business animadverted on,[5] I observe in your late letters that you have alterd your Direction and do now direct to me Solictor and Agent for His Majestys Revenue in Virginia I conclude the alteration of Character is done in order to avoid interfering with the Provincial Agent in Legislative Matters here or in Virginia I approve of your Alteration, for in this Character it would ill become me and those who preside in Virginia to take part in many Measures which a Provincial Agent may think incumbent on him to take with or without particular Instructions.

LB, pp. 275–276. Sent "Coffee House per Ship."

1. The session of Parliament had ended on 25 May 1765. The regency bill was "An Act to provide for the administration of the government, in case the crown should descend to any of the children of his Majesty, being under the age of eighteen

years; and for the care and guardianship of their persons" (5 George III, chap. 27), which vested in the king the power to appoint as regent and guardian for his successor either his wife, Queen Charlotte; his mother, Augusta, Princess Dowager of Wales; or some other person of the royal family descended from George II and usually resident in Great Britain. The root of the discord over this bill was the question of whether the Princess Dowager of Wales was to be among those named as possible regents.

2. The silk bill was passed by the House of Commons on 6 May 1765 as "An Act for laying several additional duties upon the importation of wrought silks and velvets; for the encouragement of the silk manufactures of this kingdom; and for preventing unlawful combinations of workmen employed in the said manufactures"; the act imposed additional duties on imported silks and velvets and allowed a drawback on exported silks. On 13 May the House of Lords rejected the act, supposedly at the instigation of the duke of Bedford, and a mob of rioters gathered at the House of Lords, attacked Bedford himself, and besieged his house. Disturbances went on for several days until put down by the military.

3. The "certain Earl" was John Stuart, earl of Bute, who had not held office for a couple of years but had retained the king's confidence. George Grenville, First Lord of the Treasury and Chancellor of the Exchequer, in May 1765 persuaded the king to promise that Bute would never again have anything to do with the king's business and contrived to have James Stuart Mackenzie (1718?–1800), Bute's brother, dismissed from his office of Lord Privy Seal for Scotland, to which office Lord Frederick Campbell (1729–1816) was appointed on 24 May 1765.

4. Henry Fox, Baron Holland, was replaced as paymaster general by Charles Townshend, and Hugh Percy (1715–1786), earl of Northumberland, was replaced as lord lieutenant of Ireland by Thomas Thynne (1734–1796), Viscount Weymouth.

5. JA's mention of chancery business probably refers to delays in the equity side of the General Court's proceedings. See Frank L. Dewey, "New Light on the General Court of Colonial Virginia," *William and Mary Law Review* 21 (Fall 1979): 1–14.

To Francis Fauquier

Nov 29th [1766]

Governor Fauquier on coming to Town meet with nothing for your Information tell him the Fluctuation of Administration[1] & Parltary news.[2]

LB, p. 277. The year of this and the following three entries is written at the top of the letter-book page.

1. The fluctuation of administration must refer to the replacement, on or about

27 Nov. 1766, of George Edgcumbe (1721–1795), Baron Edgcumbe, as treasurer of the king's household, and a number of resulting resignations: William Henry Cavendish Bentinck (1738–1809), duke of Portland, resigned as lord chamberlain, and the earl of Hertford resigned as master of the horse to become lord chamberlain; William Ponsonby (1704–1793), earl of Bessborough, resigned as postmaster general; Sir Charles Saunders (1713?–1775) resigned as First Lord of the Admiralty; Augustus Keppel resigned as groom of the bedchamber; and Richard Lumley-Saunderson (ca. 1725–1782), earl of Scarborough, resigned as cofferer to the king's household.

2. Parliament met on 11 Nov. 1766 specifically (according to the king's address) to consider the high price and shortage of wheat, which had caused distress and rioting. On 26 Sept. two Orders in Council had been issued to place an embargo on wheat and flour and to prohibit the making of wines and spirits from wheat products. The embargo was viewed as a serious breach of the constitution, involving the dispensing power, or the doctrine that the king enjoyed the power of dispensing with the law, and on 24 Nov. an indemnity bill was introduced in the House of Commons that called forth a long debate in both houses.

To James Wright

Nov 29th [1766]

Governor Wright Do in answer to his,[1] mention Widow Swintons Dower and desire he will sound her on the Quantum thereof.[2]

LB, p. 277.

1. Letter not found.

2. The widow Swinton may have been Hannah (White) Swinton, widow of William Swinton (d.1742?). Swinton, a native of Scotland, had come to South Carolina about 1729 and undoubtedly knew JA, his fellow Scot, there. He served in the Commons House of Assembly 1735–1736 (*Bio. Dir. S.C. House of Rep.*, 664–665).

To G[eorge] Seaman

Nov 29th [1766]

G Seaman In answer to his abo[u]t Widow Swintons Dower,[1] agree to Deposit the 3d of Purchase Money & pay the Interest thereof by way of Indemnification.

LB, p. 277.

1. George Seaman (1705–1769), a native of Scotland, immigrated to South

Carolina in the 1730s and settled in Charleston, where he became a wealthy merchant. JA undoubtedly had known him during his South Carolina years (*Bio. Dir. S.C. House of Rep.*, 606–607).

His letter to JA has not been found.

To Mr. Lampton

Nov. 29th [1766]

Mr Lampton to the same purpose and about the Land at Dorchester to sell if he can for what he can get.[1]

NB all the above to Seaman & Lampton and Fauquiere are Copys thereof in Bundle 1765.

LB, p. 277.

1. JA evidently had asked Lampton (Richard Lambton?) to dispose of some land in Dorchester, S.C.

To Francis Fauquier

3 March [1767]

To Governor Fauquere 3d March, Tell him the loss of the Question on the Land Tax,[1] The Arguments thereon on all occasions urgd ag't the Ministry for giving up the Cyder[2] and American Tax[3] whereby a Suplemental Tax laid on the Country[4] that Mr T——n——d has warmly declard his opinion that America should and ought to be taxed for its own Expences, for the first time others of the administration have concurd with him, and though Ld Chatham from thence was thought after all that has passd was imagind to give in to the System of Taxation of America,[5] the Ideas of the Ministry seem to turn towards a *Duty* but could not with certainty give my opinion thereon as the Measure was not ripe in Theory or Practice.[6] Tell him had a visit from his Son in return to one by me to Mrs Focquere future occurances shall be transmitted by me if not Instructive alwa[ys] amusing to those abroad I am sorry to hear of his delicacy in the Fall to Shift climat the only remedy I am &ca

LB, p. 277.

1. The budget presented to the House of Commons by Charles Townshend, Chancellor of the Exchequer, included the usual land tax of 4*s*. in the pound. On 27 Feb. 1767 Townshend's opponents combined to pass a resolution whereby the land tax was reduced to 3*s*. in the pound and a deficiency of about £500,000 in the government's revenue was created.

2. The reference was to arguments for and against legislation laying a duty on cider and perry. The act 3 George III, chap. 12, which laid a duty on cider and perry of £2 for every ton imported and of 4*s*. for every hogshead made in Great Britain, excited objections and was repealed by 6 George III, chap. 14, which made changes in the administration of the tax but laid a new duty on cider and perry of £3 for every ton imported and of 6*s*. for every hogshead made in Great Britain and sold at retail, or of 16*s*.8*d*. for every hogshead made in Great Britain and consigned to a factor or agent for sale.

3. It is not clear whether JA meant a specific measure of taxation, such as the Stamp Act, or rather the general idea of imposing some tax or taxes in America.

4. Probably the meaning is that giving up a tax or taxes in America would entail heavier taxes in Great Britain.

5. For Townshend and American taxation, see Peter D. G. Thomas, *The Townshend Duties Crisis: The Second Phase of the American Revolution, 1767–1773* (Oxford, 1987).

6. The reference was probably to ministerial plans for colonial import duties, the general trend of which was public knowledge by the middle of Feb. 1767.

To John Blair

[3 March 1767?]

To Mr Blair acknowledging his Bill Salary 25th Octr 1766 tell him the State of his Rent Roll application, and give him advise not to give Judgment on any point that relates to the Diminution of the Revenue till calld upon.

LB, p. 277. In the margin at the head of this memorandum JA wrote: "Do 3d [*illegible*]," presumably referring to the date of the preceding letter.

To Francis Fauquier

[31 March 1767]

March 31t Governor Fauquier of Ludwells death[1] & the East India Affairs[2] mention the nomination of Councillors being in the Secretary of States at present.[3]

LB, p. 277.

1. Philip Ludwell had gone to England about the middle of 1760 and died there on 25 Mar. 1767.

2. When the Chatham administration took office in the middle of 1766, it was evident that the East India Company was becoming a government rather than simply a trading company, and that fact, along with the company's potential for giving financial aid to the country, led to an examination of the company's affairs in Parliament. JA probably wrote about the motions in the House of Commons, in the first half of Mar. 1767, regarding the printing of East India Company papers presented in that session: the Commons ordered that the papers be printed, but a few days later voted to rescind the order upon the petition of the company and subsequently approved a motion that the printing of any of the company's papers except charters and decrees would be prejudicial to its affairs. For a review of the East India business, see Lucy S. Sutherland, *The East India Company in Eighteenth-Century Politics* (Oxford, 1952).

3. This was evidently not true in practice. On 6 Jan. 1767 the Board of Trade submitted six representations to the king, recommending persons to fill vacancies in various councils in America, and ordered the drafting of a letter to councillors then resident in Great Britain to warn them that the Board would recommend persons to the king to replace them if they did not immediately signify their intention of returning to their respective colonies. On 26 Feb. the Board sent another represen tation to the king recommending a person for appointment to the Council in the Bahama Islands. On 16 Apr. the Board sent to the king three representations to recommend persons for appointment to the councils of New York, East Florida, and Virginia. George William Fairfax was recommended to take the place on the Virginia Council left vacant by the death of Philip Ludwell (*JBT*, 12:354, 370–371, 382).

To John Blair

Sir London April 4th 1770

I have reced yours Decr 20th[1] inclosing Bill for 25th October Salary at the same time rejoice to learn that you are in health. I have since had frequent opportunitys of seeing the Audr Genal and have not faild to throw out my good Wishes for your and your Sons Interest, in the Office. I still persevere to urge his Succession to you, and hereupon I must entreat you not to think of attempting any present in the way of Office without his being previously apprisd of it by yourself and taking his advice thereon, I hint this to you from what you seem inclind to have attempted by an Application to the Treasury for some Consideration for your Services out of the Quitrents, any application of that Sort must necessarily come by reference to him and without his approbation thereof you may miscarry therein at the same time disoblige I can on this head therefore give you no Encouragment to attempt any Application with any degree of Success, the only point wherein I may be able to Serve you effectually is by your Sons Succession, and while I have Weight with the Audr General is the proper time of geting this Matter done, and for this purpose I should think the most effectual Means is by your Resignation in his favour for should a Vacancy take place I cannot answer for the Success of your Son in such Case its therefore for you to consider seriously of a Resignation in his favour while I am on the Spot and let me know your Mind herein without delay & I shall use my endeavours to bring it about, your letter to me on this head will be authority enough with the Auditor General, & believe me that the continuation of my Services to Mr Cholmondely tho with some trouble and no profit to my self is in great measure to get your Son provided for, and this I hope will influence you to facilitate the Same by a Resignation in his favour[2] I am Sir Yours

PS   I find Mr Cholmondely totally averse to Dispose of the Deputation in a Pecuniary Way so that its in vain to try it on that bottom any longer.

LB, p. 278.

1. Letter not found.

2. Blair did not resign, but his son still succeeded him. See JA to Blair, 7 Mar. 1758, p. 236, n. 3.

To John Blair, Jr.

April 4th [1770]

I have by this Opportunity wrote your Father very pressingly to Resign the Office in your favour as the most effectual way for my Suceeding in my endeavours that you suceed,[1] I cannot take upon me to say that if a Vacancy should happen by your Fathers death what may be the consequence, you are no Stranger to the Situation of Mr Cholmondelys privat Affairs great oeconomy becomes necessary in his Domestick life I know his Wants and its not for your Interest to conceal them, It may even become necessary for me to urge with him your acceptance of the Office on terms some what more advantageous to him than your Fathers, but as I write my own Sentiments only, not his I do not Conclude that this may be requird of you or any other Sucessor at the same time, if I find it necessary I should be glad to know your Mind as to an abatement of half per Cent, I very well know that there are about him some persons who would gladly acept of his Deputation for Virginia upon the Terms of receiving only 2 per Cent in stead of 2 & $\frac{1}{2}$. I am aware of an Objection that may arise to you on this point (viz) that by your Fathers Resignation he may expect to Share with you the profits of Office, but at any rate my views being to Secure to you the Office, I do not so much enter into the Family Terms of the Transaction as otherwise I might do, but I should blame my self if through my delicacy in not mentioning to you my Plan without reserve how to Serve you, my endeavours so to serve you shall miscarry You will therefore lose no time to let me know, whether you will give in to any abatement and what Abatement of the thing becomes necessary for me to avail myself of Such Expedient. How far it becomes necessary for you or not to open this to your Father you are judge I have said nothing further to him than to urge his Resignation for Your sake; Mr C——————— I know owes your Father money and I cannot say that such Debt can facilitate your sucess by way of paying for the Deputation for he is absolutly averse to treat upon that footing of a Sale I have tryd him often in this po[i]nt but to no purpose, the correspondence on this head I hope is understood as from me alone for what I send is the project of my own Imagination thereby to serve you who am Sir Yours

LB, p. 279.

1. See preceding letter.

To Samuel Swann

Dr Sir London April 4th 1770

I have still and ever shall retain the long friendship that has subsisted & for that reason the moment I heard of the unfortunate turn to Mr Rutherfords affairs it came into my Mind that you was his Security to the Crown as Recr in the dark how his Crown Revenue Accounts or his privat Concerns may turn out I cannot lose one Moment to assure you on your particular Account and on his that I shall be ready to assist you with the Auditor General in what may become the business of that Office,[1] you will therefore lay your Commands on me directed to Mr Russells Downing Street Westminister Pray remember me to you Son and believe me Dr Sir Your Most Obedt Sert

LB, p. 280.

1. John Rutherfurd was ill in the late autumn of 1769 and the winter of 1769–1770 and could not properly attend to the North Carolina quitrents. At its meeting of 18 Dec. 1769, the colony's Council concluded "that the state of the Receiver Generals Account now produced is too imperfect to be transmitted home (which may be occasioned by his ill state of health) His Excellency [Governor Tryon] therefore Orders that the Receiver General lay before him at the next Court of Claims a full and perfect Account of his Colection of His Majestys Revenue, with copies of the same attested and fairly transcribed in order to be transmitted home, and to produce the proper vouchers relative thereto" (*NCCR*, 8:164).

To Samuel Swann (not sent)

Dr Sir   [6 April 1770]

Soon after I had wrote My letter to you Mr MCulloh Son to our old acquaintance calld upon me and gave me to understand that he was Agent for No C[1] and by Special Power from the Committee and the Treasurer came to call upon me for my Accounts of the share of the N C money granted by Parlt & issued to my hands by the Treasury, after some days spent in perusing my Papers and Accounts I have furnishd him with a Compleat Account and accordingly Ballanced by the Vouchers, from Bills paid, and gave by him a letter explanatory thereof I was in hopes to have got from him a final discharge, but I find by him that he must transmit them over and be further instructed in Some points relative to the Deductions by letters from you I find that these Accounts tho not agreed to by the Council for particular Reasons had passd the Assembly with some few minute objections on some points and particularly as to the charge of 31£ by way of Extraordinarys for Coach hire Postage of Letters Christmas gifts to Office keepers and

the Foregoers and Porters at Doors and many other such small
Expences of this Nature which for some years I used to charge
more minutely in Articles but of late years during my Agency I
reducd into one gross Sum and as such were allways allowd in my
Accounts and as they stand Deducted in my Accounts transmitted
heretofore and now copy thereof deliverd to Mr MCulloch, the
other Article animadverted I find by Your letter is the Commission
of $2\frac{1}{2}$ per Cent for the whole Sum lest Mr Smith should have
chargd the half to the Province this $2\frac{1}{2}$ is the same as was chargd on
the Virginia Money and allowed to me without dispute, and its well
known to you and the then Members of Assembly the immense
trouble I had during that Affair through Govr Dobbs's Litigation
with the Assembly in Carolina not only as to the person but in the
manner of Solicitation, but likewise of the application of that
Money and had I not stood in the field alone for Virginia North
and also for some time for So Carolina the proportion for No:
Carolina had miscarryd and so Sencible was Mr Secretary Pitt of
my Services in the respect that he took my Cause up and accordingly recommended me to the Treasury as doing me Justice in that
Solicitation which you may well remember was actually carryd by
me during two years from March 1757 to March 1759 when I had
no Salary for the Agency but was expird March 1757 during which
time while my Frends were contending for the act being renewed
and in my favour against Mr Dobbs's friend Mr Smith I was
contending the Cause of North Carolina against his privat Agent
here Mr Smith, surely these freinds cannot be forgot so as to
contend with me the Commission of $2\frac{1}{2}$ per cent of the whole for
to no part does Mr Smith pretend, all controversy on that head
ceased on Mr Secretary Pitts letter in my favour to the Treasury
and by the Condition of the Bond which allows me Reasonable
Deductions for expences & in the remittance I have and shall abide
by the $2\frac{1}{2}$ as allowed in the very same case by Virginia, and was my
Accounts to come to Litigation and thereby opend again, I should
certainly charge Salary for these two years while I was carrying on
the Service of the province and amongst other things the Solicitation & application of this very Money the now Committee of
Assembly in their further Intructions to Mr McCulloh their agent
will no doubt look back to these Matters and do me Justice and I
hope they will not lay me under necessity for so paltry a Sum not

in the whole Commission 200 for business in which they did not think proper to give me the Allowance of Salary while I was as their agent never dismissed by them tho the Act ende[d] Publick Faith of being allowed the Salary nor did the Provincial Disputes about the renewal of the Agency Act abate my Zeal in their Service and the Success thereof shewd my diligence application & propriety of Conduct, for the honour of the Province then for their Internal peace I hope they will [not] take any Step whereby a Litigation between Governor and assembly about application or Negociation of Publick Money may come in question it was my study all along then to avoid such Contest and great trouble I had therein during the whole of that Money business it becomes the Business of those who now take the lead in the Assembly to avoid it now on their part; Party Disputes that then distracted public Concerns I Hope are forgot I have not the honour of knowing Govr Tryon[2] but his Conduct the steadiness of his Administration, shews him in another light than his Predecessor, and suceeding Agents may probably have less trouble than I had in the Service of the Province & more especially while Mr Dobbs Govern'd, but these concerns are now over to you as well as to myself but privat friendship still remains and during the many years concern I had with your Province nothing I regretted so much as never having at my Power to have given you more essential Testimony of what was due to you, from Government I did on various Occasions attempte it but without Sucess, I know not now that Mr Jones is dead if any other of my friends of the Assembly of those days are alive if Mr Barkcr is be so good as remember me to him.[3]

I find his name in Many of my letters as also Mr Hanburys my former personal Acquaintance, should they come in your way be so good as remind them of our former correspondence this with my best wishes to yourself and Son concludes me

PS   I think it may become necessary for my Justification in My Accounts if they do undergo any further examination to revive the memory of those who may now remember those transactions from the hints now given you be so good as to do it.

LB, pp. 280–282. The entire letter is crossed through. A marginal note at the head of this letter reads: "NB this not sent but vide the letter next to this which was," a reference to JA's letter to Swann of 9 April 1770, below. Date supplied from letter of 9 April.

1. Henry Eustace McCulloh (ca. 1737–ca. 1810) has been described as "shrewd, unscrupulous, and salacious." He had been born in London, taken to North Carolina as an infant, educated in the law at the Middle Temple, and called to the bar. McCulloh then returned to North Carolina in 1761, staying six years during which he served as a councillor, customs collector, and agent for his father's vast empire. McCulloh returned to London in 1767 and was appointed agent in 1768. He held the post until 1773. With the outbreak of the Revolution, McCulloh became a loyalist and lost his North Carolina lands through confiscation (Michael G. Kammen, *A Rope of Sand: The Colonial Agents, British Politics, and the American Revolution* [Ithaca, N.Y., 1968], 135–137, 325).

2. William Tryon (1729–1788) was lieutenant governor 1764–1765 and governor 1765–1771 of North Carolina.

3. Thomas Barker (1713–1787), probably a native of Massachusetts, moved to Edenton, N.C., in 1732 to study law with his uncle, William Little, who was chief justice of the colony. Barker served in the lower house of the North Carolina legislature 1734–1745 and 1754–1762.

To [Joseph Montfort]

Sir[1]   London April 8th 1770

In consequence of your Power to Mr McCulloh I have deliverd to him my Accounts of the Money granted by Parlt, which was issud to me by the Treasury at the same time a letter explanatory of the Deductions made, together with extract from the Bond given by me to the Crown, whereby I am authorized to deduct for all reasonable Charges incident thereto, likewise copy of Secretary Pitts letter to the Treasury in testimony of my Services relative to this Parliamentary grant, which Accounts letters and papers no doubt will be transmitted by him.[2] I am much concernd that any of your Bills should have been protested, I assure you I am totally ignorant thereof.

In consequence of your letter to me of 12 March 1764[3] telling me of your Powers[4] to negociate this Money on the 23d May thereafter I transmitted for the 3d time copy of my accounts shewing the ballance former Copys went to Mr Swann and the Committee, Dupplicat by Mr Polluck, Triplicat by Capt Scott in the Ship Thomas, and a 4th Copy by Mr Hunter, My Accounts thus transmitted any over drafft on me had been prevented, I therefore conclude that such protest is not with me,[5] by Mr Swanns letter 25 of May 1762[6] I find that my Accounts had been reced and passed the Assembly subject to a few objections on some trifling Articles viz the charge of Extra disbursments in my Agency Accounts for 3 years of 93£ these extra charges having been for several years charged and allowed in my Accounts in a gross Sum, in place of particulars for Coach hire Postages Christmas gifts and other Articles of Offices I saw no reason to leave them out in my last Account especially when the Service requird more extraordinary disbursments than usual and as to the Commission of $2\frac{1}{2}$ per Cent Mr Swann observes that the objection thereto did not arise upon the quantum but as lest Mr Smith should perhaps charge one half thereof.[7]

In this situation my services went still on for 2 years without any allowance from the Province disregarding party quarells about the renewal of the agency Law while my personal Influence had weight to serve the Province I did not so much mind the form of my Authority for acting and indeed personal influence and conexions added greatly to the Success of my Services so that my case is singular with regard to this Money Negociation for North Carolina, from Virginia where I had a Salary and a reputable one Commission was allowed for this Special Service, from North Carolina where I had no Salary the trouble infinitly greater from Provincial Contests Commission liable to be questiond by new people unacquainted with the Nature of the Service and the difficultys in my way I must therefore in justice to the Province and to myself beg you will take a review of the Journals and my Correspondence with the Committee if necessary in instructing the agent on these Articles of Deductions in order to avoid giving me any further trouble on this account, the Sum is too trifling to appear before any Board here at the same time its a matter of Reputation that will call upon me to support these articles of Deductions more especially that of Commission as being within the Condition of my Securety to the Crown,[8] I shall be glad you do me the favour to acknowlege this letter by directing for me at Mr Russells Downing Street Westr I am Sir

LB, pp. 286A–287. At the foot of this letter JA wrote: "Sent to Mr Bridgen to be forwarded." A draft of this letter, unaccountably dated 9 April 1770, is on pp.

285–286 of the letter book. Substantive differences between the two versions are accounted for in notes to the present letter.

1. Joseph Montfort, or Montford (1724–1776), a native of England, went to North Carolina about 1750. He was treasurer of the northern counties from 1764 until the Revolution and served in the lower house of the North Carolina legislature in 1762 and 1764–1774.

2. None of the documents has been found.

3. Letter not found.

4. The "draft" of 9 Apr. includes the phrase "from the G. Assembly."

5. The "draft" of 9 Apr. reads: "I must therefore conclude that this Bill of 300 never came to me for acceptance."

6. Letter not found.

7. The "draft" of 9 Apr. reads: "but as to Mr. Smyths perhaps laying Claim to one half thereof." The "draft" also includes the following conclusion to this paragraph: "but Mr Smyth sencible that the whole of this Service was performd by me alone laid no such claim, Mr Secretary Pitts letter to the Treasury on this very question removed all doubt on this point, and had I charged by way of a Quantum thereof I should have been justifyd in deducting 5 per Cent if not more, however I made my allowance from Virginia in the same case of this Parliamentary grant of 50000 my Rule for charging to N. Carolina it has been allowed in one case and I have no doubt will be so in the like case of No Carolina this indeed its a matter cognizable by the Exchequer here in consequence of my Bond to the King to account only for the ballance all reasonable charges being deducted, you will therefore be pleased to take notice of this Matter and explain it so as to avoid Contest in Offices at home, which can redound neither to the honour nor Interest of the Province for so trifling an article which has allready been allowed in the Similar Case, but I must carry this Matter nearer home to North Carolina and should my Commission on Account of this Money be opend I shall think myself at full liberty to charge the Province for two years Salary viz from March 1757 to Do 1759 during all which time I was actually engaged in Soliciting this Parliamentary Supply the Act whereby I had been appointed Agent expird March 1757 and thereupon a Contest arose in the Province about the renewal thereof Bill after Bill presented for my continuance and project after project carrying on the Revenue for the appropr[i]ation of this Money before I had got it, the Governors agent by the Governors orders counteracting the Assembly."

8. The "draft" of 9 Apr. includes the following passage in place of this paragraph to this point: "in this situation did my Services for two years continue for two years without any allowance of Salary and controverted as my former Nomination was my Services ended with Success to all which my personal Influence made use of for the good of the Province carryd weight and added no small Share to my Success disregarding Party quarrells I did not Mind the form of my authority while my so that my case is singular with regard to North Carolina with a Salary and a very Reputable

one from Virginia I had an Allowance of $2\frac{1}{2}$ Commission without a Salary from No Carolina & the business infinitly more bothersome My commission may perhaps be questioned by those unacquainted with the Nature of my Services and the difficultys I had to encounter I must therefore on this head beg you will do me the Justice to take a Review from the Journal of the assembly and the Correspondence should these Articles of Deduction occasion any Dispute at home, which I sincerly hope will not happen between me and the New agent I have been too long in the Field of Bussiness and now taking leave of it to be engaged in any Office controversy upon so trifling Articles and was not my reputation at Stake to do myself Justice I should take the Revenue of the 2 years previous and every Emolument arising from the Revenue."

To Samuel Swann

April 9th 1770

I had just finishd my letter of the 6th[1] when Mr MCulloh Agent for the Province calld upon me to account for the money which I reced from the Treasury for N C: accordingly I gave him the accounts ballancd by the Sums paid by Bills drawn on me which with the Deductions as transmitted by various opportunetys in my Accounts to the Province compleat the whole he objected to give me a discharge saying they must be Remitted for further Instructions upon the articles deducted by me (viz) the article of Extra charges in my Agency Accounts of Coach hire Postages Christmas Gifts at Publick Offices and various other minute Disbursments which in my first Accounts while agent I charged particularly but of late years I have charged in gross and have accordingly allways been allowed at 31.0.0 per an and therefore in my last Accounts they are so charged and as to the article of $2\frac{1}{2}$ Com its the very same as charged and allowed on the same money had for Virginia and by my Bond to the King for the payment of this Money I am authorized to deduct out of it all reasonable charges & expenses and whatever the Province may think of the like reasonable[ne]ss of the $2\frac{1}{2}$ Com Virginia has thought it reasonable and I have no doubt that the Treasury to whom I am accountable in this Article will likewise think it so by your letters to me you inform me that my Accounts had passed the Assembly with some few objections but you are [not] particular in any except that for charging the Commission of the full Sum lest that Mr. Smyth should charge the Province for the half thereof but as Mr S: never intended so doing and from Mr Secretary Pitts letter to the Treasury giving me the Sole claim to the Money Affairs I accordingly think myself fully Authorized to charge the full and should it be brought before the Treasury I doubt not will be allowed as reasonable however I shall be very Sorry that the agent should force me to make my appeal to that Board or anywhere else and for that reason I hope the Committee will do me justice by their Instructions to him on this head and if they dont think proper to take my Accounts as they now stand I shall think myself at full Liberty to correct a mistake therein for just now on examination of my Correspondence with you and the Committee I have found out that I have charged in my Accounts the extra charges on my Negociations for the year only whereas I should have charged both Salary and extra expences for two Years viz from March 25th 1757 to Do March 1759 in which two years I was acting in the Service on from the expiration of the Agency Law untill the Assembly by their Resolves of the 20th of Decr 1759[2] of their own authority renewed my Salary finding the repeated Negatives given by Gover Dobbs and by the Council to the agency Bill presented to them for my reappointment, during the whole of the Provincial Contest concerning this Money which commenced by the Govr and Council claiming not only the Solicitation but the application of the Money by Mr Smyth, I did everything in my Power to keep peace here and to avoid Contest which at all times ought to be avoided about the power of intermedling or applying the Public Money in the Plantations with much trouble to myself in opposition to Governor Dobbs I did avoid it and at the same time carryd on the service with Success, I hope therefore that the now Assembly will upon these principles support me and avoid Contest between the different Branches of the Legislature which by calling in question my Services may bring on. You and the Committee are fully acquainted with the nature of this Affair and I hope the present Committee of Assembly will make themselves likewise master so as to avoid dispute either at the Treasury or elsewhere for so paultry a Sum under 200£ for the recompence for such Services You may communicate these remarks to whom it may become necessary to have for information I am Sir yr

J. A

PS   it may become necessary to lay this letter before the Speaker[3] or Committee of Correspondence if so you have my Authority for so doing ——— in my name.

LB, pp. 283–284.

1. Printed on pp. 438–440 (but evidently not sent).

2. See JA to North Carolina Committee of Correspondence, 1 Nov. 1760, pp. 369–370.

3. The Speaker of North Carolina's lower house was Richard Caswell, Jr. (1729–1789). He served in the lower house 1754–1776, as Speaker 1770–1771, as a delegate to the First and Second Continental Congresses, and as governor of North Carolina 1776–1780.

To Richard Corbin

Jany 1t 1773

On my return to Town, an Interview with Mr Williams was my first business, your Principals are now Mr Williams Uncle to Lady North and Mr North Son to Lord North,[1] various Solicitations on the part of Virginia were made to Mr Williams the Acting Recr Genal, none more urgent than by Mr Lee whom I take to be the Husband of Miss Ludwell,[2] whether in his own or in the behalf of another I did not enquire, it was Satisfaction enough for me to find that you had prevaild and on the same Terms with Mr W as with Mr Roberts. It had been suggested to him that as the Revenue had increasd and continues to increase, that his Terms might have been enlargd, however he is by no means disposd to a vary from the Deputtys Establishment under Mr Roberts at the same time a reconsideration of Mr Hanburys allowance by way of prompt Payments in London seems to be in speculation, but this like many other Revenue Reformations at home I presume will come to nothing in the end; in short the Improvement of the Kings american Revenue requires, more Solid Measures than cramping the Incouragment given to Revenue officers. Nothing in agitation in Parlt this Session more Interesting to the Nation than a Reformation in the East Indies, Public and Privat abuses have too long existed in that part of the world and some thing must and without doubt will be done by way of correction in Power of Government as well as of Revenue.[3] I rejoice that Affairs in Virginia go on without discord or Noise at home at least I have heard of none; Mr Walpoles Grant after a good deal of Discord I understand rests at present on the Mode of Government Expedient for that Projected Colony,[4] I could have wishd Govert had attended seriously to regulate the Frontiers of old rather than make New Settlements our Frontiers with the Indians now seem more exposd to the irregularitys of our own subjects than of Foreign Enemys I might have shard in this adventure but have declind looking upon it Injuriouse to the King, his Govert and to Virginia more particularly and if any Measure can be more absurd in the face of recent Experience from Charter and privat Governments in the East and West Indies that of Mr Walpole and his Associates taking upon themselves the Govert of this new Colony rather than continuing as at present under the protection of that of Virginia the Example of the late Earl Granville in the neighbouring Colony might have taught them better these are my present Notions what are yours of this Request I remain allways very Sincerly Dr Sir Yours &c

PS   I beg my best Complts to the Messrs Nelsons and other frends of the Council.

LB, pp. 288–289.

1. George James Williams (1719–1805) and Francis North (1761–1817), afterwards fourth earl of Guilford, were joint receivers general of Virginia from 1772 to the end of royal government in 1776. North was a son of Frederick North (1732–1792), second earl of Guilford.

The elder North's wife was Anne (Speke) North (d. 1797), whom he had married in 1756.

2. William Lee (1739–1795), son of Col. Thomas Lee (1690–1750) and brother of Arthur Lee, Thomas Ludwell Lee, Philip Ludwell Lee, Richard Henry Lee, and Francis Lightfoot Lee, married Hannah Philippa Ludwell, daughter of Philip Ludwell, of Green Spring, in London in 1769.

3. For the financial crisis that had overtaken the East India Company and the resulting legislation by which the government exercised greater control (including the Tea Act of 1773), see Benjamin Woods Labaree, *The Boston Tea Party* (New York, 1964), chap. 4.

4. In 1769–1770 the Walpole Associates, headed by London merchant banker Thomas Walpole (1727–1803), petitioned the Crown for the purchase first of 2,400,000 acres of land on Virginia's frontier, and then for an enlarged tract of more than 20 million acres. Opposition by Virginians and the earl of Hillsborough, and finally the American Revolution, brought about the failure of the effort. See Thomas Perkins Abernethy, *Western Lands and the American Revolution* (New York, 1937), and Jack M. Sosin, *Whitehall and the Wilderness: The Middle West in British Colonial Policy, 1760–1775* (Lincoln, Nebr., 1961).

Dr. Parker to James Abercromby

[6 February 1773]

Dr. Parker[1] presents his Complimts to Mr Abercromby & desires the Favr of his Company at dinner tomorrow at three o'Clock.

Saty Feb. 6.

LB, pp. 397A–397B. This small sheet was inserted in the letter book. On the verso is the address to "Mr Abercromby Downing Stret," and the endorsement, in JA's hand, "Kings Warrant on Tobacco Revenue 1755 pro 20,000£ to repay Pay office." The year is inferred from those in which 6 February fell on a Saturday and in which JA is known to have lived in Downing Street.

1. Perhaps William Parker, D.D. (1714–1802), rector of Saint James, Westminster, from 1763, chaplain to George II, George III, and the bishop of London, and an eminent pulpit orator; or conceivably Sir Harry Parker, D.D. (d. 1782).

To John Blair, Jr.

Sir   Feby 13th 1773

A few days since I have yours Decr 10th[1] inclosing Mr Corbins Bill Salary to 25th last past on Messrs Carys & Co by them accepted and have according to your desire indorsd as by your sd letter Decr 11th £58.0.4 on Mr Cholmondelys Bond to your Father as part payment I should be sorry any Misunderstanding should have arisen between Mr Corbin and Hanburys, but from repeated Interviews I have latly had with Mr Williams Recr General and Mr Hanbury; I can see that Matters will be cleard up upon the Receipt of Mr Corbins Deputation with the several letters attending it; Mr Corbins letter to Mr Williams of Decr —[2] gives Mr Williams much

Satisfaction, and convinces him that he is by no means deceivd by the Character given Mr Corbin by his friends here.

As I have nothing of Moment to Communicate to you of Public or privat Importance, my best respects must attend Mrs Blair[3] must conclude that I am on all Occasions Sir your

JA.

PS   desire my best respects and Condolance to Mr Nelson on his Brothers death.[4] My letters directed for me in London allways find me but in Downing Street is my new residence.

LB, p. 289.

1. Letter not found.

2. Letter not found.

3. Jean (Balfour) Blair (d. 1792).

4. Councillor William Nelson (1711–1772) had died on 17 Nov. 1772. JA's condolences went to Nelson's brother, Thomas (1716–1787), also a councillor and the secretary of the colony.

To Richard Corbin (not sent)

Feby 13th 1773

Yours to Mr Williams of Decr very satisfactory,[1] agrees with my Acct of the Office for 10 years past; your recommendation of Mr Norton occasiond some speculation of the difference between you & Mr Hanbury,[2] but from the part taken by Mr H since the Deputation had no doubt of a thorough good understanding taking place again as I do not know the particulars between you & Mr Hanbury[2] nor I apprehend does Mr Williams know, but so far as Mr W is concernd any variation of conexions appears to him rather disagreeable.

I have long enough been conected with the Revenue Officers of Virginia to know that the middle Men between the Treasury and Rec General must occasionally be in disagreeable circumstances, arising in some measure from the irregular Calls for Money from such persons for the Kings Service the ease of the Treasury and of the Revenue Officers fixd payments would be lost, at present & for some time past the Audr General and Mr Hanbury have been teazed for payments and in some degree threatend for neglect of Duty they on their part complain alledging more Regular and greater payments than heretofore; Mr Hanbury is willing to Agree with the Treasury for 2 payments on the year Day and hour fixed upon taking his chance of Bill payments in London and no doubt ought to have good Terms, for few Merchants would be disposd to take up such ground with the Treasury from some Memorandum Issud 1758, 5 per Ct allowd to Cary & Co for prompt payment, but those Matters do not concern me but on the Principles of Friendship I should hold it clear that the Rec General should hold to the present Mode [*illegible*] the Treasury and Mr Hanbury or any other Person make these new bargains, not consistent for the Treasury nor the Recr General to become the Merchant by Payments over Remittances per Bills or Goods or Tobacco; desire my Respects to Mr Wm Nelson new President[3] offer my Service to him & Mrs Corbin[4] as their Humble Svt

JA

LB, pp. 289, 292. The entire letter is crossed through. At the head of this letter JA wrote: "NB Not sent vide Feby 22d," and at the foot of this letter JA wrote: "not sent vide Feby 23d 1773," both evidently references to the next, undated, item in the letter book, which is also crossed through. This letter and the one following were evidently replaced by JA's letter to Corbin of 1 March 1773, below.

1. Letter not found.

2. Corbin had for many years relied on the services of the Hanburys to make payments into the Treasury, for which services Hanbury received 6 percent of the amounts paid. Corbin came to believe this too generous an arrangement and proposed to put the business into the hands of John Norton (1719–1777), of the firm of John Norton & Sons, who was a London merchant who dealt extensively with Virginia planters and merchants. The new arrangement does not seem to have been put into effect. See Frances Norton Mason, ed., *John Norton & Sons: Merchants of London and Virginia* (Richmond, 1937), 302, 313, 315.

3. In fact, it was Thomas Nelson who became president of the Council upon the death of his brother, William.

4. Corbin had married Elizabeth Tayloe (1721–1784), daughter of John Tayloe, in 1737.

To Richard Corbin (*not sent*)

Dr Sir   [22 or 23 February 1773]

In my last of Jany 1t[1] I hinted that Mr Hanburys allowance as I was told of 6 per Ct for prompt payment of the Q R Money was under speculation tho this matter comes not properly within my Line, as it concernd your office I paid some attention to it, through the intercourse between Mr Williams and me brought about by a particular friend of Ld North, it might occasionaly be productive of your Service.

I am not acquainted with the Nature of your agreement with Mr Hanbury as your Security and Correspondt in Office, but from the state of Remittances on your part by the Account thereof transmitted to Mr W—— I plainly see that the Ultimate Ballance of the Revenue due by the Recr is very inconsiderable but it would require more particular Investigation of the particular times and quantums of Money payments made the Treasury by Mr Hanbury to ascertain the justice of his Claim of 6 per Ct by way of Prompt Payments, and without prompt payments are bona fide made by Mr Hanbury I shall not be surprisd that Mr Williams as the Principal in Office (under favor of the premier of the Treasury)[2] whose Son a child is joind in Commission with Mr W——[3] do avail himself of this Gratuity of office from the Treasury under colour of Prompt payment; you will pardon me from Interfering with this Matter relative to your Office which indeed does not properly belong to me, at the same time as the Difference between you and Mr Hanbury has brought about the discussion of New matter which in the end may concern your situation with Mr Williams as well as with your own Security Mr Hanbury I could not help under confidence giving you a friendly notice recommended probably you and Mr Hanbury may come to a better understanding on the receipt of your Deputation, which Mr W——s apprehends may be the case I am nevertheless inclind to think that this gratuity to Mr Hanbury for prompt payment to the Treasury will take some new turn in Office, But to convince Mr Williams that his allowance of 500 per an from you as Deputy was on your part fully adequate to the Income of the Office I take the trouble to give him the Income of the Virginia Revenue, then from the Accounts for 10 years past from thence as a Medium you have scarce 200 per an for the Execution of Office and this I found came confirmd by your own Account thereof by your last letter to Mr Williams which is very candid and full and gives him all satisfaction, whatever measure may take place from this Matter now in speculation.

I can by no means agree to the Idea of payment of the Virginia Qt Rt Revenue by a Banker, this may be done with practicability where Military or other regular Establishments are paid in America by Contractors or Pay Masters there in either case the London Banker may possibly become the Instrument of Negociating Payments, or he may likewise become so for the Income of Landed Estates in England and the Land Stewart may settle their Lords Accounts annually But neither of these cases will apply to Virginia, where no regular Military Payments of Troops or Contractors from England exist & where the Recr General here as Principal in Office must have his Deputy in Virginia for Executing his Office in Virginia, the Deputy must accordingly find Security in England and who in England will become and Stand Security without some intermediate profit whether in the Banking or Merchantile Line of Business But the Merchant correspondent in this case seems to be the Most natural Intercourse for negociation on such Terms as the Partys shall mutually agree; At present the case seems to be the Recr General 500 per an, the Deputy not above 200 per an including the $\frac{1}{2}$ per Ct for Negociating Bills on London Mr Hanbury your Correspondent and Security 6 per Ct for Negociating Bills in London the difference of Negociation of Bill of Exchange C[urren]t in London must naturaly Strike one, without allowing for his advance of Money which begets 5 per Ct, on this being the case comes the question whether Mr Williams or Mr Hanbury shall partake of Treasury favour But as I have allready observd these matters concern me not once more tho let me entreat you to hold this as friendly communication only from one attentive to your Interest, Mr Cholmondely has letters from you stating to him the Revenue account as you have to Mr Williams his residence being for the most part in the Country its but occasionally I have seen him of late, he is much your friend and it grieves him, that difference should have arisen between you and Mr Hanbury but in this and in all my Money transactions and conexions the partys are to judge for themselves. In point of Office you did it right to lay before him the Revenue Account as it stood with Mr Hanbury and you My best Complts to Mr Secretary Nelson now Presidt on the death of our friend the late Presidt I shall on all occasions be glad to receive and to execute his Commands in the Line of Duty or otherwise I have not been honrd with any from Lord Dunmore since his arrival[4] and I shall not become troublesome to his Lordship by a farther repetition of the tender of my Services till calld upon in the way of Duty, for nothing more disagreeable to me than becoming the Monger of News or Reports in general as fertile and as fluctuating in their Nature as the Factions Temper and Disposition of Self Interested or Disapointed Retailers thereof can contrive to propagate.

LB, pp. 292–295. The entire letter is crossed through, and at the foot of this letter JA wrote: "Not Sent." For dating, see preceding letter, source note. This letter and the one preceding were evidently replaced by JA's letter to Corbin of 1 March 1773, below.

1. Printed on pp. 446–447.

2. Lord North was First Lord of the Treasury from Feb. 1770 to Mar. 1782.

3. See JA to Corbin, 1 Jan. 1773, p. 447, n. 1.

4. John Murray (1730–1809), fourth earl of Dunmore, was royal governor of Virginia from 1771 until the Revolution.

To [Thomas] Nelson[1]

Feby 24th [1773]

The accounts I have reced of our good friend your Brothers death calls upon [me] to lament his loss to his friends and the public, his Commands I allways reced with great pleasure, be assurd that I shall yours with equal pleasure whether of public or private concern of the first I have nothing at present to trouble you this therefore goes by way of preliminary to our further occasional Correspondence in the mean time I am Sir

JA

LB, p. 296.

1. JA confused the Nelson brothers, as he had done in earlier letters; he inadvertently addressed this letter to William Nelson, president of the Council.

To Richard Corbin

Sir   March 1t 1773

In my Letter of January[1] I informd you that the Treasury had taken Notice of 6 per Ct being allowd Mr Hanbury for what Quitrent Money was Occasionally paid by him in to the Treasury by way of prompt payment; your letter to Mr Williams containing a full and very candid state of the Office likewise takes notice of this 6 per Ct and by the Account of Money Matters between you & Mr Hanbury transmitted with your letter it appears that the Ultimate ballance due by you to the King is a mere trifle, and that your Remittances from time to time to Mr Hanbury had been so far sent him in Cash as to invalidate his Claim of 6 per Ct for payment on demand the result of which I have reason to apprehend will be that Mr Williams the Principal in Office whose conection with Lord North his Son of 12 years old being joint Patentee will draw after it every advantage of Office in the Line of the Treasury to convey in Mr Williams favour, and in this light I see the 6 per Ct will come to him and that you will have Instructions from him to transmit to him a particular List or Docket of the Bills remitted by you to your Correspondent for discharge of the annual Ballances due to the King, the Money arising from such Bills to be paid to Mr Williams and by him to the Treasury, so your Correspondent by this means having nothing to do with prompt payment to the Treasury the full Execution of the Offices resting between your principal and you the Deputy to be alone ameanable to the Treasury; should the office go in this channel, it may become a doubt whether Hanbury will continue your Security and Correspondent or Mr Norton whom you have recommended to Mr Williams, which ever of them I should think these Men have like Commision on the Bills remitted by you should be allowed out of the 6 per Ct and you thereby acquitted of paying any commission to your Correspondent.

Mr Williams has endeed suggested to me that Mr Norton was disposd to do the business gratis, however every Man deserves his pay pro tanto,[2] he must become your Security and Correspondent consequently has reason to expect some degree of Profit as a Merchant by Protested Bills for such no doubt there will be besides he must become liable for the punctual payment of the annual

Establishment to the respective Offices according to the Kings Warrants and for the 500 per An payable by you to your Principal; The Idea of laying aside a Merchantile correspondence and carrying on the Kings Business between your Principal and you by means of a Banker Mr Williams is satisfyd cannot take place with respect to Virginia where no Military Payments nor Govert Contracts are made chusing to remit Money per Bills alltogether, this is an affair out of my Line, but from Mr Williamss acquaintance with me formd at the desire of a very particular friend of Lord Norths I can not help attending to the Event of this Matter with a view to serve you therein, and from these confidential hints you will be able to take such Measures as may best answer your purpose by a good understanding with your principal, I gave Mr Williams the proceeds of the Fee of 5 per Ct and also $\frac{1}{2}$ pro Negociating Bills on London from the original Accounts in the Aud Generals Office for 10 years past in order to convince him that the 500 per An was on your part fully adequate to the profits of the Office and I find this [*illegible*] agrees with the state of the Office transmitted by you to him through Mr Norton whom I do not know personally but by Character I find him a very good Man I am allways

PS   I expect Mr Cholmondely in Town soon, and on his arrival, as he is well disposd to Serve you I shall bring about an Interview with Mr Williams not being personally acquainted. I hear not a word of Virginia Public Concerns I opend a Correspondence with Ld Dunmore in a privat Line but as he has not followd it I shall not trouble his Lord[ship] hereafter unless [*illegible*] public [*illegible*] call on me.

LB, pp. 295–297. At the foot of this letter JA wrote: "NB Sent by Ship from Coffee house March 3d."

1. Printed on pp. 446–447.

2. Translation: to a certain extent.

Index

(Boldface numbers refer to footnotes containing biographical information)

The Letter Book of James Abercromby, Colonial Agent: 1751–1773 was set in Caslon type by the William Byrd Press, of Richmond, Virginia, and printed on 70-lb. Glatfelter Offset B–31, an acid-free permanent/durable paper, by the Delmar Company, of Charlotte, North Carolina.